ENVIRONMENTAL LAW AND POLICY: NATURE, LAW, AND SOCIETY

3d Edition

Teacher's Manual

Zygmunt J.B. Plater
Boston College Law School

Robert H. Abrams
Florida A&M University College of Law

William Goldfarb
Department of Environmental Sciences
Cook College, Rutgers University

Robert L. Graham
Jenner & Block, Chicago

Lisa Heinzerling
Georgetown University Law Center

David A. Wirth
Boston College Law School

ASPEN
PUBLISHERS
1185 Avenue of the Americas, New York, NY 10036
www.aspenpublishers.com

ISBN 0-7355-4144-2

Note: This manual is made available as a courtesy to law teachers. Portions of the materials contained in this manual are designed to be photocopied by teachers as handouts for student use in the course. Permission is granted to reproduce any material from this manual for classroom use in course offerings which have adopted the coursebook. Permission to photoduplicate copyrighted material included in this manual, for classroom use only, has been granted by any individual authors and copyright holders.

If any commentaries, data, or analytical materials in the manual or its updates are quoted or cited for publication, an attribution to this manual along with references to the relevant page numbers would be appropriate.

Copies of this manual are available on computer diskette. Each summer an Update for Professors is prepared by the authors and made available on request. The manual and updates are also available in down-loadable form on a password-protected Coursebook Teachers' Website –

http://www.bc.edu/schools/law/library/coursebook/envtlaw/teachers

As noted in the book, a separate Coursebook Users' Website is maintained for students, and includes materials posted selectively from the Coursebook Teachers' Website.

Teachers may register for a complimentary diskette copy of the manual, for a website access password, and for the annual summer Updates, by e-mail at legaledu@aspenpublishers.com, by calling the Aspen Publishers sales assistant at 800-950-5259, or by writing:

Permissions
Aspen Publishers
1185 Avenue of the Americas
New York, NY 10036

1 2 3 4 5

CONTENTS

A continually growing collection of background and supplementary materials is made available to teachers who adopt the coursebook, including simulation exercises, important new judicial decisions posted in edited form shortly after they are handed down, many with Commentary & Questions, plus public law materials and short articles of interest. Those of general interest are also posted on the student Coursebook Users' Website.

Most of these background and supplementary materials are not reproduced in this Manual, but instead are posted, arranged according their linkage to coursebook chapters, in a folder on the Teachers' Website, which you may wish to bookmark:

http://www.bc.edu/schools/law/library/coursebook/envtlaw/teachers

Several dozen chapter-by-chapter entries were posted at the time of publication of the coursebook. Further materials are posted opportunistically through the academic year, and more systematically each summer in concert with publication of the annual Updates for Professors that are sent to teachers who have registered with Aspen Publishers.

To receive a User Name and Password for the Teachers' Website and for the free annual summer updates contact the Aspen Publishers sales assistant by calling 800-950-5259, or by e-mail at legaledu@aspenpublishers.com.

Teachers who do not have ready access to the Internet should contact the authors to arrange availability of background and supplementary materials.

A partial index to background and supplementary materials as of June 2004 appears in Part III. This index and a table of cases contained in these supplementary materials are updated and maintained on the Website.

PART I
DESIGNING THE COURSE

INTRODUCTION

The governing reality facing all teachers of environmental law today is that there is too much to cover in the time allotted to the course. Environmental law is a monumentally sprawling body of doctrine and policy.

So this is a cafeteria-style book, large and comprehensive, from which you can shape your course to suit your own needs. It is extremely unlikely that anyone would have the temerity to plan to march his-her students through all 26 chapters in the coursebook.

The job of this manual is to help you design and teach your course – helping you choose from the cafeteria menu of the book's 26 chapters to tailor your syllabus from an array of possibilities according to your individual goals and interests and the amount of class time available – and providing further information and teaching suggestions on each chapter to make your class preparations more efficient.

As noted in the introductory sections of the coursebook (and we suggest that teachers, at least, will find it useful to read both the Preface and Introduction), the book tries to cope with the depth and breadth of the field by following an organizational outline modeled on the structure of the American legal system itself, drawing materials from all areas of environmental law and practice.

This manual, of course, can serve only as a starting point for what each teacher wants to make of the course. Environmental law inevitably provokes flights of imagination and a diversity of teaching approaches. We aim, however, to provide a foundation from which each teacher's individual course can build and evolve.

Each teacher will use the coursebook (which we usually refer to as "NLS" - Nature, Law & Society) in her-his own way. Some will use it with an overall economic perspective (some following the book's approach to economics and some "teaching against the book"). Some will use it for a structure-of-government inquiry, or take the opportunity to bring in particular ecological or other science-policy themes. Some will focus on technical litigation and "lawyering" issues and statutory analysis, or the strategic role of citizens, or environmental justice, or undertake a general inquiry into the sociology, jurisprudence, and evolution of law. We believe NLS offers a structure serving many approaches, including each of the forgoing options.

The book is designed to support the basic environmental course in the law school curriculum and make it more enjoyable, and also to build a springboard for other, more advanced, environmental elective courses.

The materials that follow in this **Part I** are designed to present the teacher with suggestions for designing the course; Part III has more advice on syllabus & prospectus.

Part II's Chapter-by-Chapter coverage sets out suggestions for day-by-day classes, including themes, leading questions, background ideas, and answers to the questions posed in the text. This material is keyed to specific page numbers in the text. Throughout the chapter-by-chapter section of the manual, referenced coursebook pages can be found quickly by noting the page numbers set out in **bold** type in the paragraph leads:

as in, **Page 352-354. The *New York* case.** This case reflects New York's challenges to the Low-Level Radioactive Waste Policy Act....

Each chapter section begins with suggestions for page assignments, starting with introductory and "core assignment" pages in each, with brief descriptions, with further page blocks in the chapter that can be added to the core assignment, likewise accompanied by brief descriptions. Your own choices as to pace and depth of coverage – and the specific time constraints of your course – will shape your decisions on which page blocks to incorporate and which to skip. We continue to be interested in hearing your comments and suggestions on different chapters, and about your experiences with the course.

Part III presents Supplementary Materials intended to help in designing the syllabus, paper assignments, and exams – as well as a 2d→3d Edition Chapter Concordance and Transition Guide and a chapter-by-chapter cumulation of background information items for teachers and extended update Handouts that can be given to students.

ELECTRONIC ACCESS: This Manual and annual Updates and Supplementary Materials are available on-line through the password-protected Teachers' Website –

http://www.bc.edu/schools/law/library/coursebook/envtlaw/teachers

All materials on the Website are posted in readily-downloadable PDF format, and can be cut-and-pasted to serve teachers who want to customize their teaching notes in electronic form.

PRACTICAL COURSE DESIGN ISSUES

How many class hours–credit hours? The most critical practical constraint on the design of the course is time. If the teacher has the option of adjusting the time and credit allocations for the course, this coursebook offers a range of choices. The book can be taught and taught well in a three- or four- semester-hour, fifteen-week format, or longer, but the syllabus in each case will be quite different. Some of us have tried both modes and prefer the four-credit-hour class; some have taught NLS as a five-hour course, or stretch it over two semesters as a six-hour course. In a regular semester curriculum we prefer the four-hour mode, taught in two or three classes per week; if you plan to integrate problem-solving exercises and simulations into the course, you may then want to conceptualize the weekly schedule as two "hour-and-a-half" traditional classes, with the remaining one-hour class used opportunely for simulations as well.

Problem-solving exercises and simulations: Problem-solving exercises and simulations are a dynamic way to translate this field (or any field of study) into active comprehension by our students. The coursebook materials were designed to facilitate a number of such exercises, and teachers have reported effective class sessions casting students into role-playing or advocacy-drafting exercises. For a comprehensive compilation of regulatory exercises and simulations that can be integrated into your course design, we suggest you consider Professors Jerry Anderson and Dennis Hirsch's ENVIRONMENTAL PRACTICE: PROBLEMS AND EXERCISES FOR SKILLS DEV'T, (2d edition, Carolina Press 2003). Their book contains problems and exercises under each of the major federal environmental regulatory systems, using CFR and other regulatory materials. The book casts students into various roles as government attorneys, corporate counsel, and public interest advocates, in the four principal areas of environmental practice — compliance counseling, administrative enforcement, environmental litigation, and the environmental aspects of business transactions.

Syllabus: Some professors prepare the course syllabus with all of the day-by-day reading assignments stipulated in advance. Others prepare the syllabus as a series of "block assignments" to be moved through at the pace the class arrives at through actual experience. The latter form obviously has advantages for teachers presenting a course with a new book, and is the form two of the authors follow. We provide some model **Draft Syllabi** in Part III of this manual.

Course requirements — an exam: All offerings of this course that we know of have required a final exam, even if there is a required term paper. An exam, even if it is a fairly short exercise, keeps the students engaged with the entire field throughout the semester, and makes them pull it all together at the end. Exams can be short and generic, not focusing on a particular area that might unduly favor students who have written papers on that point. Without an exam, students tend to put all their effort and attention into their papers, to the detriment of the class as a whole. Some model exams are provided on the Teachers' Website in the Supplementary Materials.

Course requirements — a research paper: There are strong arguments for the proposition that a paper assignment should also be a part of the course if at all possible. Environmental law has become so broad that a single course risks becoming a fast-moving blur. In a course of this scope, there is a danger that a final exam can too easily become an unsatisfying exercise in broad-brush generalities. For this reason, offerings of NLS have frequently required at least one research paper to give each student an experience of depth as well as breadth in the field. A paper helps students dig deeply into one piece of the terrain, and often deepens insights generally. The paper should be held to a manageable legal research format length. A 10 or 12-page legal memo can be a rigorous, challenging assignment, and the need to condense a complete analysis to this format improves quality substantially. For the teacher, moreover, large course enrollments for environmental classes these days make tight page restrictions a necessity. See the sample paper prospectus in Part III.

For the students, finding and defining a paper topic is a basic critical task. Putting a collection of environmental and industry newsletters, etc. on reserve at the library is one way to direct this effort. A session where the teacher lays out possible topics is another useful idea. See the compilation of some past course paper topics are provided on the Teachers' Website in the Supplementary Materials. If certain areas of the coursebook are skipped in the class syllabus, some students may wish to look in those unassigned chapters for paper topics. Many of the comments and questions in the coursebook are designed to suggest interesting topics for term papers.

A basic decision is whether the teacher wants fact/policy type papers, or more specifically "legal" research-and-analysis papers on technical issues arising in environmental law. Most teachers using NLS to date, given its legal process structure, have opted for the latter type of assignment. There are plenty of other forums for students to develop policy and fact analyses, but for many of them this is the only place to do a piece of work delving into the craft of environmental lawyering. As noted in the model paper prospectus in Part III, the most satisfying approach has been for students to identify (with the teacher's help) interesting legal questions arising in some environmental controversy, and to develop that legal analysis as the focus of the paper. Students too often choose topics based on fact/policy appeal, only to discover later that the legal issues therein are diffuse or not very interesting. This pitfall should be explained early in the term to avoid pre-deadline traumas. Having a paper topic sign-up preemption list at the Law Library reserve desk, for instance, is a good way to force students to define a workable topic early on and to get their research going.

Students should be reminded that it is the legal analysis, not a paper's political point of view, that counts. Too often some students think they must prepare rousing advocacy pieces that end up being superficial fluff, and must be reminded that a good legal analysis must carefully anticipate the opposing parties' toughest predictable counter-arguments.

Many students ask what further readings will help them get oriented in the field. For them and for your own illumination we suggest the following overviews and anthologies:

- Bob Percival and Dorothy Alevizatos' LAW AND THE ENVIRONMENT, A MULTIDISCIPLINARY READER (Temple University Press, 1997)
- Richard Lazarus' A Different Kind of Republican Moment in Environmental Law, 97 Minn. L.R. 999 (2003)
- Fischman, Lipeles, & Squillace, AN ENVIRONMENTAL LAW ANTHOLOGY (Anderson)
- Richard Revesz's FOUNDATIONS OF ENVIRONMENTAL LAW AND POLICY (Foundation)

AN OVERVIEW OF CHAPTERS

Chapters that most of us co-authors consider "core" chapters are marked with ** *double asterisks.*

	CHAP.	NUMBER of HOURS?	(APROX. NO. OF CLASS SESSIONS, EXCLUSIVE OF SIMULATIONS & EXERCISES)
I: ENVTL. LEGAL PROC.	1	1	Introduction to environmental analysis & basic themes
	2	1-2	History, and crosscutting themes: economics, risk, and politics
	3**	1-4	The common law in environmental law
	4**	1-3	Toxic torts, with a transition to public law
II: THE DIFFERENT SOVEREIGNTIES	5	½-1	The development & structure of environmental public law [and an intro to federal-state tensions]
	6	½-1	State-federal environmental regulatory issues
	7**	1-2	The administrative law of environmental law
	8	1	The effect of int'l envt'l law on domestic law
III: STATUTORY APPROACHES	9**	1-2	Disclosure strategies: NEPA
	10	½-1	Corporate disclosure: required production of information: EPCRA & TRIs
	11**	½-1	Regulatory standard-setting based on harm: the CAA; Envt'l justice
	12**	½-1	Regulatory standard-setting based on technology: the CWA
	13	1	Regulatory standards based on cost-benefit analysis
	14	1-2	Market-enlisting strategies: trading, and market incentives
	15	1	Regulatory standard-setting based on technology-forcing — auto emissions regulations
	16	1	Stark prohibition statutes: endangered species
	17	1	Market-access controls: ToSCA and FIFRA
	18	1-2	Life-cycle waste control strategies: RCRA
	19**	1-2	Remedial strategies: CERCLA
IV: COMPLIANCE, ENFORCEMENT, ADR	20	1-2	Environmental criminal prosecution
	21**	1-2	Regulatory enforcement approaches; citizen enforcement; corporate compliance mechanisms; ADR
V: PUBLIC/PRIVATE RTS. & RESP.	22**	1-2	The public trust doctrine, and other rights & duties
	23	1-3	Public rights and private property
	24	1	Public resource management
	25	1-2	Land use-based environmental protection, siting
VI: GLOBALIZATION	26	1-2	International and comparative environmental law

Some possible chapter clusters: 4-5-17-18-19 — cross-analysis of 11 & 12— 22-16-24 — 5-7-21... and consider the addition of practical exercises and simulations to complement chapter clusters. See Part III Syllabi.

THEMES AND SEQUENCING

The nine chapters that we think probably should probably be basic core chapters for any course are marked by asterisks on the preceding chart. For a three-hour course, another half-dozen chapters, well-chosen, can be added without straining the semester; a four-hour course can add a few more. (The amount of simulation exercises you add to the course, if you do so, will substantially affect the number of chapters you assign.) In general the standard sequence of chapters presented here builds from basics into the complexities of command and control regulatory systems. Because the book is designed to facilitate a menu-choosing approach, however, a good many other sequences are possible. to serve teachers' particular approaches and inclinations.

Ultimately most courses end up as a blend of themes and approaches. Some teachers, for example, choose to put their primary emphasis on toxic substances — common law, regulatory, and policy issues — and design their chapter sequences to emphasize that theme. Inevitably, however, they also find it necessary to include coverage of property rights, public trust, administrative law, and other issues playing active roles in the daily environmental news.

Some of the alternative sequences to the coursebook's lineup might include:

- A toxics focus: Chapters 1-4 (with Harr's A CIVIL ACTION and associated materials), then 5, 13, 17, 18, 19, 21....
- A concentrated entry into pollution regulatory regimes:
- Chapters 1, 2, 3, 5, 7, 11-15, 17–19, then a selection from the NEPA and resource management chapters, 9, 16, 24, and the broader doctrinal chapters 22–23 etc.
- On a smaller scale, component units can be organized focusing on a particular area of regulation — air pollution, for instance: perhaps Chapters 3, 5, 11, 13-15 — then building the rest of the syllabus on that specialty.
- An active unit on ADR (21) to study the availability and existence of relatively non-adversarial alternative legal processes, right after 3 & 4 (which focus on litigation), with a unit on hazardous waste siting from 25 including the environmental justice simulation located in the Part III Supplementary Materials for Chapter 25; (or after 7, 18-19 (which focus on administrative process).
- An environmental justice theme, beginning with the Kepone setting, 2, and the ADR/ environmental justice simulation on hazardous waste siting using parts of 21 & 25, including the EJ negotiation exercise in the Part III Supplementary Materials for Chapter 25, then tracing these issues through cases in which disproportionate impacts on communities of color and low income can be noted: *Boomer* (3), *Woburn* (4), *Overton Park* (7), EPCRA (10), *Film Recovery* (20), *Poletown* (23), reference to *Bhopal* (26, and in Chap. 26 Supp. Materials), etc.
- A continuing interplay between domestic and global perspectives, building from 1-2, to 8 and 26, then pulling the international themes into the study of NEPA and the pollution regulation regimes.

and so on....

Some overview notes:

- The first chapter sets out a broad reconnaissance of the field, with case studies and materials presenting many analytical themes and strategies that shape modern environmental law; the second chapter observes the ongoing evolution of environmental law, from the "first generation" of the 1970s to the second, third, or fourth generation of present practice, with a straightforward message about the need to take express account of the role of national political considerations.

- From the start, statutory and regulatory materials are integrated with the common law foundation of environmental law, leading to coverage of the full range of public law approaches to regulatory standard-setting and implementation systems.
- The early chapters introduce the trend beyond command-and-control toward market-enlisting approaches for achieving environmental quality noted in Chapter 14.
- The toxic torts chapter (Chapter 4) provides a fascinating integration of tort and public law materials centered upon the intriguing Woburn toxics case – chronicled in Jonathan Harr's bestseller A CIVIL ACTION, a book many of your students may have read or seen in the 1998 motion picture starring John Travolta – and this can lead into a toxics focus in later chapters: 5, 13, 17, 18, 19, 21....
- Chapters 20 and 21 focus on enforcement – the growing credibility of criminal enforcement, and evolving approaches to civil enforcement, both governmental and private, including industrial self-enforcement.
- The book contains a variety of materials on "brownfields" and "brownfielding," the redevelopment of contaminated sites, an active and intriguing area of modern environmental practice.
- The last chapter, on "Global Environmental Law," contains not only a basic survey of international environmental law, including a post-Rio view of sustainable development, but also a section on comparative environmental law, illustrating the analytical skills required in moving between different legal cultures, domestically as well as internationally. Simulated exercises with notes on teaching them are in the Website's Part II for Chapter 26.

PAGE BLOCK ASSIGNMENTS

Exercising restraint on the volume of pages we assign is extremely difficult, but highly appreciated by our students! To figure out what page blocks to assign within each chapter, you can look at the Draft Cumulative Syllabi in the Part III Supplementary Materials. You can also review the chapter page blocks noted at the start of each chapter's coverage in the Part II Chapter-by-Chapter section of this manual, deciding which you wish to focus on to initiate discussions and which are not really necessary for the approach you wish to take to the chapter. Surveying the various page blocks, teachers can decide to assign all, or only core assignments, or to adopt "skim" assignments for selected portions.

MISCELLANEOUS

For exercises and simulations to complement your coursebook chapter assignments, consider **Anderson and Hirsch's, ENVIRONMENTAL PRACTICE: PROBLEMS AND EXERCISES FOR SKILLS DEVELOPMENT**, (2d edition, Carolina Press 2003). Further simulations and case study problem sets are available from (1) the archives of the

University of Maryland's Environmental Program, contact Professor Rena Steinzor, rstein@law.umaryland.edu (2) Harvard's Kennedy School (http://www.xanedu.com) or (http://www.ksgcase.harvard.edu), and (3) many more from the Stanford Law School's Environmental and Natural Resources Law & Policy Program, on-line. The Stanford program maintains an on-line portfolio of situational case studies and simulations which present narratives of real-life events and ask students to identify and analyze the relevant legal, social, business, ethical, and scientific issues involved. The case materials are intended as complements to the casebook-based curriculum, adding interactive skills training in factual investigation, legal research, counseling, persuasive oral communication, and recognition and resolution of ethical dilemmas, to name a few. The full text of the case studies and simulations, plus teaching notes, can be downloaded free-of-charge from Stanford University Law School's case studies web site at (http://casestudies.stanford.edu).

For a quick guide to problem-oriented definitions of environmental regulatory concepts, we suggest you tell your students about Professor Steven Ferrey's ENVIRONMENTAL LAW EXAMPLES AND EXPLANATIONS (Aspen, 1997).

For staying current with the environmental law field generally (if indeed that is possible), we recommend regular reading of one of the loose-leaf services noted in the book's Introduction (i.e. the Environmental Law Reporter or BNA's Environment Reporter, GREENWIRE, or similar on-line briefing services. Having the Law Library route a weekly highlight summary to you, like ELR's "Update," is likewise a useful coping device. A list of relevant Websites potentially useful for both teachers and students is included in Part III's Supplementary Materials.

The Supreme Court of the United States and the environment: Previously not a pretty picture. Now? The environmental profile of the Supreme Court is always a looming backdrop to our courses. Until *Laidlaw* and *Tahoe-Sierra* the environmental profile of the Court has been generally depressing. Since those recent cases we may cross our fingers. For an orientation on the Supreme Court's environmental stances, note:

- Prof. Richard Lazarus's "Thirty Years of Environmental Protection Law in the Supreme Court, 19 PACE ENVTL. L. REV. 619 (2002)(noting the prior history, then the shift in *Laidlaw*; the article accurately anticipates the *Tahoe-Sierra* decision).
- Prof. Dan Farber: Dan Farber traces environmental law's modern roots to two federal statutory enactments: the National Environmental Policy Act (NEPA), 42 U.S.C. § 4321 (1994) (passed in 1969) and the Clean Air Act (CAA), 42 U.S.C. § 7401 (1994) (passed in 1970). In the next 25 years "the Supreme Court decided roughly two or three environmental law cases per year - or somewhere between fifty and one hundred cases altogether." Professor Farber discerns five extremely passive strategies taken by the Court to "minimize its own influence on the development of environmental law and policy," to wit:
    - Hearing a lot of cases with unique or atypical facts, so the holdings will be irrelevant or difficult to apply in more typical cases.
    - Refusing to hear cases in some vital areas of environmental law.
    - Shunting as many issues as possible away from the judiciary entirely.
    - Adopting a strong policy of deferring to administrative agencies on environmental issues.

- When a decision on the legal merits cannot be avoided, basing it on an extremely narrow, technical ground having little general significance.
- Farber, Is the Supreme Court Irrelevant? Reflections on the Judicial Role in Environmental Law, 81 MINN. L.REV. 547 at 549 (1997).

- Prof. Bill Rodgers: As to NEPA, Rodgers says the Court's record is particularly grim:

> Environmentalists are clear losers under this small body of Supreme Court case law - no wins, no favorable dicta, not even a favorable statement of the facts. Six of the eight decisions on the merits contradict the environmental position in large measure.... Environmentalists lose to intuitive notions of fairness when the legislative history is on their side, lose to the legislative history when the plain meaning is on their side, lose to the plain meaning if intuitive fairness is tempted to run their way, and lose to economic efficiency if the purpose of the law holds out encouragement....
>
> The popular account, which is close enough to the truth to bear repeating, is that the Supreme Court is to NEPA as Joseph Hazelwood is to the wreck of the Exxon Valdez. Twelve times the Court has taken NEPA cases and twelve times has decided in favor of the government. The decisions, collectively, are known as the NEPA "Dirty Dozen," although a closer count shows not twelve but twenty-two NEPA issues that have been subject to judicial pruning in these cases. Without belaboring the factors that have brought the Court to this posture, a 12-0 (or 22-0) pattern of judicial decision is worthy of notice by anybody in the business of prediction. The Court, at various times, has protected the discretion of the agencies in deciding whether to prepare an EIS, and when, and what goes into it. The Court has opted for a narrower standard of judicial review (the arbitrary and capricious rather than the reasonableness test) in adjudging whether an agency should supplement an EIS. The Court has read broadly the extent to which other laws may work exceptions to the NEPA duties. And it has read narrowly the obligations of the agencies to discuss the psychological effects of their actions, "worst case" outcomes, and ways to mitigate environmentally damaging activities. The Court has thoroughly repudiated any concept of substantive NEPA, and in the process has confined the Act solely to concerns about how decisions are made, not the environmental damage that is done. William Rodgers, ENVTL. LAW TREATISE at 183, 195 (1999).

Modern environmental law is built of a bewildering horde of statutes, and statutory and regulatory acronyms. Many teachers have their students buy one of the annually-updated compendia of major environmental statutes. You may also want to draw your students' attention to the **Statutory Capsule Appendix**, at the back of the coursebook, beginning at Reference Page 48, providing brief functional descriptions of the state and federal statutes most active in environmental practice, and an inventory with citations of the most important international Conventions and Treaties — supplementing the annotated **Glossary of Acronyms and Abbreviations,** at the back of the book, beginning at Reference Page 5, both of which they may wish to tab.

To make sure that you are kept current with annual updates for the coursebook, please be sure that your name, address, phone number, and e-mail address are registered on Aspen Publishers' list of professors who have adopted the book.

Upon request Aspen Publishers will provide teachers adopting the coursebook with three-ring binder versions of the book cleanly spine-cut in loose-leaf format, which some teachers prefer for organizing notes and text.

Unlike all of the generations that came before us, we cannot take the functioning of nature for granted. We continue to depend on the daily miracles of photosynthesis and the water cycle as utterly as did our remotest ancestor. The difference is that nature now depends upon us as inevitably as we depend upon nature. Human actions now plot the course of life on this planet.

Diana Muir, REFLECTIONS IN BULLOUGH'S POND: ECONOMY AND ECOSYSTEM IN NEW ENGLAND 258 (2000)

Education is not the filling of a pail, but the lighting of a fire. – Yeats

PART II
CHAPTER-BY-CHAPTER TEACHING NOTES

The chapter-by-chapter format used here in Part II of the manual has three categories of material for each chapter:

- ***Page Block Charts*** — setting out page blocks of readings in the coursebook, to facilitate syllabus design.
- ***Overall Teaching Themes & Course Design Considerations*** — setting out different approaches, and thematic leading questions.
- ***Teaching Items, Answers to Questions Asked in the Book, and Notes*** — presenting a sequential commentary on materials and questions in the text, with a variety of short pieces of information relevant to the coverage of the chapter.

A number of useful charts and items are printed in Part II's chapter-by-chapter sections. A number of other resource items are collected in the Part III Supplementary Materials on the Teachers' Website. They include background items for teachers, handouts available to students on the general coursebook website, including edits of recent important cases and formatted commentary & questions, and other materials that may be useful to you. You may wish to review the Index to Part III's Supplementary Materials in the Teachers' Website Table of Contents.

Nature, to be commanded, must be obeyed.
— *Francis Bacon, Novum Organum*

To secure our common future, we need a new international vision based on cooperation and a new environmental ethic based on the realization that the issues with which we wrestle are globally interconnected. This is not only a moral ethic but also a practical one — the only way we can pursue our own self interests on a small and closely knit planet. — *Gro Harlem Brundtland*

I was always taught as I was growing up that democracy is not something you believe in, not something you hang your hat on. Democracy is something you do.
— *Abbie Hoffman, closing argument to jury, in Commonwealth v. Hoffman, et al., Amherst, Mass 1988*

Chapter 1.
BASIC THEMES IN THE LEGAL PROCESS OF ENVIRONMENTAL LAW

Chapter contents:

— and check the Teachers' Manual Website for SUPPLEMENTARY MATERIALS:
http://www.bc.edu/schools/law/library/coursebook/envtlaw/teachers

The list of Supplementary Materials in Part III of this manual, and on the Teachers' Website, indicates materials posted on the Teachers' Website that are relevant to this and other chapters.

OVERALL TEACHING THEMES & COURSE DESIGN CONSIDERATIONS

Many of us try to make the teaching theme of the first class "An Introduction to Virtually Everything in the Course," and that's not a bad idea. The first chapter's material seeks to provide a basis for introducing ecology, economics, and environmental policy, and how they relate to environmental law. No matter what material you choose to focus upon for this first class, you will be able to raise in broad terms the congeries of issues that will inhabit the rest of the course, because everything is connected to everything else.

In our experience students are not likely to have done any reading even if it was assigned, so you might as well do a presentation that assumes no preparation.

For some of us the highway salting is a vivid prosaic example that has much to teach. (Glance ahead to Chapter 2's pages 80-85 for more implications from salting.) You can use it to show how a quite clearly irrational outcome in public economic terms (with rational alternatives readily at hand) has been virtually unassailable. Environmental analysis focuses on identifying externalities, and trying to determine ways to mitigate, minimize, or eliminate dysfunctional external costs. The salt example's legal and political discussions show that our governance system has no automatic mechanisms for achieving the consideration of better alternatives, even in the face of major net social costs.

Garrett Hardin's Tragedy of the Commons is always a useful exemplar, though many students may have worked through it in other settings. (The tragedy metaphor's analysis is somewhat re-defined in Chapter 2's pages 60-62 and 78.)

You might want to consider starting the course with a presentation of facts and themes drawn from the book OUR STOLEN FUTURE: A SCIENTIFIC DETECTIVE STORY, an extremely instructive, incisive scientific and policy analysis of a universal problem of environmental exposure, the plenary presence (and potential consequences) of chlorinated hydrocarbon chemical residues in land, sea, air, and our bodies. The book, by Theo Colborn, Dianne Dumanoski & John Peterson Myers (Penguin, 1996), has been translated into a dozen languages, and is the transmillenium's SILENT SPRING. It provides powerful and useful metaphors, graphics, and attention-grabbing linkages to sperm counts and birth defects — carrying students from the local to the global and back in terms of theories of governance as well as issues of science, public health, sustainability, and law.

Or you may want to present a current events issue raising complex issues of law and policy, like a factory-closing putatively prompted by environmental regulations, an international environmental problem, or an environmental justice dilemma. (Environmental justice, [EJ] issues are noted on page 16 and developed further on pages 63-64, and in Chapter 11 as well as other chapters.)

This first class can be used to raise a catalog of analytical themes that can continue to be invoked throughout the course —

- Uncertainty, scientific complexity, and risk
- Human nature, the externalization of social costs, and environmental law's attempts to "internalize" costs
- Biodiversity: ecological biodiversity, and also an evolving diversity of laws and legal approaches
- The strategic roles of both common law and public law
- The goals of environmental law and democratic governance
- Risk, and cost-benefit analyses
- Industrial moves toward accommodation and compliance in the marketplace, and, on the other hand, anti-regulationism, "Wise Users," and the dramatic milestone political history of industrial efforts in the 104th Congress
- Sustainable development and intergenerational equity
- Environmental justice
- The race to the bottom: state and federal jurisdictions
- The role of citizens in the environmental law system, and "multi-centric pluralism"
- The ambivalent systemic roles of "outrage"
- The strategic role of the media
- Remedy and enforcement choices
- The "three economies" — our schematic construct of economic and political relationships between the marketplace, the systems of the natural world, and human society's overall needs and values
- the "polluter-pays" principle, and alternatives
- The variety of available public law options, and administrative process technicalities
- International convergences
- Intergenerational equity, the public trust doctrine, and cultural values beyond market values

The second day can move on to a class which students can be expected to have prepared in both technical and policy terms in assignments from Chapter 2, which uses the classic Allied Chemical Kepone pollution case, analyzing basic tensions between industrial production and the civic values of ecological and environmental protection, and legal remedies, then moving to a survey of the contemporary technicalities of industrial pollution cases, the multi-layered complexity of modern environmental regulation, and the strategic systemic role of citizen enforcement and industry accommodations to modern environmental regulation.

TEACHING NOTES, COMMENTS, & ALL QUESTIONS ANSWERED

For many teachers the question is how much to try to fit into the first class meeting, given that inevitably some students haven't yet bought books or have not confirmed registration, and first-day class preparation is always spotty. Our feeling is that a class session is too precious to waste, so that one should get right to it.

The question remains how much to try to accomplish on the first day. If you are not able to do as much as you wish on the first day, remember there are dozens of further sessions remaining. We count our efforts successful when the first day introduces the students to the scientific and policy complexities of the field, and gives them an idea of how law has been and may be applied so as to implement environmental analyses.

Pages 3–8. Introduction to the broad scope of environmental issues. *Why are all these issues called "environmental"?* This point is fairly self-evident, and doesn't require a lot of class time. The common theme is that "environmental" cases involve recognition of less direct, longer-term, less-tangible, or non-monetary values and harms, which are nevertheless very real. The teacher may want to add some particular current global, national, and local issues as examples to the list on pages 3–4, looking especially for instances where the "environmental" label is intuitive but not definitionally obvious, *e.g.* lead paint, or Cuna Indians in Panama being disrupted by the Pan-American highway.

Pages 8–13. Ecology. Aldo Leopold, in the first excerpt from Sand County Almanac, sets out some ecology fundamentals. Ditto Rachel Carson's discussion of bacteria (pages 10-11) (from her SILENT SPRING, publication of which is regarded by some observers as the most important single event in the history of American environmentalism), which can show students how some very miniscule things can have global implications. The point is to demonstrate some lessons of ecology: that existing systems including human systems evolved over millennia into a dynamic equilibrium of unseen processes, all interconnected, deserving understanding before we casually disrupt them. Leopold adds the pyramid, and Sancton (page 21) carries the reader to global consequences.

Garrett Hardin once ruefully noted that ecologists, who are trying to preserve the life systems of an entire planet, are among its least-honored and lowest-paid professionals, while economists, who merely fiddle with units of intangible wealth, are not. (The words for ecology and economics are both based on the Greek root "oikos" which means "home," as in our planetary home.) Hardin, "Sweet-Singing Economists," Chapter 9 in EXPLORING NEW ETHICS FOR SURVIVAL (1972).

Carson, an immensely respected scientist, had sufficient credibility to awaken the media and politicians to the systemic dangers she described. The chemical industry's earnest attempts to discredit her failed, and her ecological message moved far beyond the agricultural chemical field.

Rachel Carson's ideas about various technologies' interconnected residual consequences provided a fundamental framing-concept for many if not most subsequent development of environmental policy in this country and abroad. Even those who earnestly oppose her conclusions must deal with her paradigm of a world that can no longer be intellectually conceived as an array of isolated autonomous actors. A latter-day exploration of Carson's writings is Peter Manus's "Natural Resource Damages from

Rachel Carson's Perspective: a Rite of Spring in American Environmentalism," 37 WM. & MARY L. REV. 381 (1996), which might be interesting reading as you prepare classes for the year.

Pages 11-14, C&Q #1. Leopold, ecology, and the romantic misnomer of "natural equilibrium," & #2.. The broad reverberations of Rachel Carson's microcosm. These introductory comments are straightforward and the questions are rhetorical.

Pages 14-16. Talbot Page's concept of "false positives" and "false negatives" provides a basic vocabulary for risk analyses in many sectors of the field. Page differentiates what he calls environmental risk from classical pollution. Page's thesis is that environmental risks ought to be managed with great care, preferring to manage with an eye toward avoiding false negatives. That is, Page believes with environmental risks the cost of managing them inadequately if they prove to be real risks, is so high that we ought to pursue a course of extreme care. For Page, the opposite is true in managing classical pollution. For classical pollution, occasional under-regulation is not problematic because the consequences all are, almost invariably, short-term problems that can be you remedied later. At this point you might just introduce the concept, noting the difference in most people's internal reaction to the risk of false positives between, say, criminal conviction determinations in a capital criminal case, and FDA regulatory decisions whether to release a heart disease drug onto the market.

Page 16, C&Q #1. "Classical pollution" and "environmental risk." Page's hallmarks of environmental risks. Students also should be introduced to the zero-infinity risk. These concepts are revisited in Chapters 2, 4, and elsewhere.

Page 16, C&Q #2. Environmental risk and environmental justice. *Is environmental injustice a form of racism?* At this point most students know little about environmental justice issues. Rather than seeking an answer now, the pedagogic function of the question is to alert the students to the fact that "pragmatic" siting decisions and risk management decisions that adversely affected disadvantaged groups have a disproportionate impact on those groups and may, in some cases, have a racist component.

Page 16, C&Q #3. Species eradication as a catastrophic ecological cost. *How should risks of species extinction be managed?* Students are likewise not ready to answer this question at this point. What is more important is that they begin to think about species eradication as requiring a policy determination about its acceptability. Once that is done, then the question of managing those risks becomes salient. Techniques for their management, or at least the principal technique that is currently in force is discussed in Chapter 16.

Page 17 C&Q #4. External cost transfers and political power. This textual note tries to alert the students to the frequent occurrence of situations presenting environmental risk, and noting that in many instances those situations present a decision maker that does not bear the risks being created by the activity. You might ask the students whether that is analogous to having the ability to externalize the costs of pollution in more conventional settings.

Pages 17, C&Q #5. Burdens of proof and liability rules in environmental risk

management decisionmaking. This is another textual note. It tries to foreshadow the use of burdens of proof and persuasion in toxic tort cases, a subject that will be studied in Chapter 4. Page's thesis clearly is relevant to those issues and this note attempts to get the students to be looking for that as they read the toxic tort materials.

Page 17, C&Q #6. This textual note first distinguishes between a risk assessment and risk management. It then tries to raise doubts in the students mind about whether there is a real distinction between the two. Perhaps more importantly, the note begins to raise a cautionary flag in regard to unquestioned reliance on quantitative risk assessment analysis. When uncertainty of measurement is piled on top of uncertainty of measurement, the results that are generated become very unreliable. Shere goes so far as to call them meaningless. That may be harsh, but judgment has to enter in as a complement to what the numbers say.

Page 18, C&Q #7. This note chronicles in very truncated form, the events of the *Reserve Mining*. That case appeared as a principal case in the first edition and is set out as Chapter 2 Supplementary Material on the Teachers' Website. That landmark case was one of the first earnest efforts on the part of a court to come to grips with the uncertainties of toxic pollution.

Pages 18-20. G. Tyler Miller's ecology texts are standards in the field. The concept of eco-systems is a basic analytical tool that can be extended beyond biological systems, as noted.

Page 20, C&Q #1. Text is rhetorical.

Page 20, C&Q 32. ***Can the ecosystems metaphor be applied to human systems?*** Yes, we think so. Think what happens to a community when there is sudden change in health or economics, or to a nation's textile industry when a new technology or labor practice is thrust into the market.

Page 21, C&Qs #1 & #2. Sancton's overview and these notes survey the all-too-depressing global condition that your students are inheriting, and remind us that interconnections of systems are the fabric of reality. We choose to emphasize that syncretic knowledge and creativity can and always have made a difference, and in a modern society attorneys have special capabilities and responsibilities in making incremental improvements in the human and planetary condition.

Pages 23–27. Environmental ethics. Law and ethics; this material also sets up the following questions on the Public Trust Doctrine.

Should law always be congruent with morality? (Can the law be immoral, or morality illegal?) Does ethical change cause legal change or does the law lead to changes in morality? A superb bibliography on environmental ethics is D. E. Davis, ECOPHILOSOPHY: A FIELD GUIDE TO LITERATURE (R&E Miles Press, San Pedro, 1989). A further collection of environmental essays is Donald Scherer, ed., UPSTREAM/DOWNSTREAM: ISSUES IN ENVIRONMENTAL ETHICS (1990).

Environmental law as morality: The coursebook's introductory chapter raises some basic issues of environmentalism as an ethical and moral construct. We should note that some religious organizations, perhaps awakened by the apocalyptic anti-environmental tone of the first session of the 104th Congress, have begun to take an active interest in preserving and strengthening environmental protection laws as part of their mission. The NRPE (Natl Religious Partnership for the Environment) has been formed by the Evangelical Environmental Network, the U.S. Catholic Conference, the National Council of Churches, and the Coalition on the Environment and Jewish Life. The Union of Concerned Scientists is its scientific advisory body, and can be contacted at 2 Brattle Sq. Cambridge, MA 02238. Besides political defense of environmental legislation, the coalition is working on environmental justice issues with the Louisiana Interfaith Stewardship Initiative in Louisiana's "Cancer Alley," and with the Black Churches Environmental Justice Regional Training program, Shreveport, LA. And see Barlow, "Why the Christian Right Must Protect the Environment: Theocentricity in the Political Workplace," 23 BCEnvtlAffLR 781 (1996); DeCosse, "Beyond Law and Economics: Theological Ethics and the Regulatory Takings Debate," 23 BCEnvtlAffLR 829 (1996).

Environmental Justice: If you want to set up environmental justice as a continuing theme in your course, you can do so on the first day, and continue on the second day with the Kepone narrative. Several excellent new EJ resources are available, coming from a collaboration between the ABA and EPA. You can connect with the resources by contacting <environmental-justice-epa@epa.gov> or <nicholas@targ.com>. The EPA's Environmental Justice Bibliography Database (EJBib), http://cfpub.epa.gov/ejbib/, is available: a fully-indexed bibliography of published materials relating to environmental justice, as well as such related topics as risk assessment and social justice. Intended as a research tool, the database is a project of the U.S. Environmental Protection Agency's Office of Environmental Justice. One aim of the bibliography is to identify significant references to environmental justice in a wide range of literature. The database represents an ongoing effort that already contains more than 2600 records documenting the environmental justice dialogue. Currently, materials included in EJBib come from various Internet databases of legal, medical, engineering, urban planning, and science periodical articles and books, as well as materials in non-print formats, such as documentary videos, interactive programs on CD-ROM, and other electronic media. To access, go to http://cfpub.epa.gov/ejbib/.

Also, an Environmental Justice Assessment Tool is now available. This new tool replaces the EnviroJustice Mapper with new features and new technology. It is the result of a n Agency-wide work group and provides information relevant to any area in the Continental U.S. The framework for this Tool is based on the assessment methodology in the EJ Toolkit. Factors relevant to environmental justice are described in the EJ Toolkit in the discussion of Environmental Justice Indicators, and they generally fall into four categories, i.e., environmental, health, social, and economic. The conditions these indicators seek to illuminate include, but are not limited to: adverse health or environmental impacts, aggregate or cumulative impacts, unique exposure pathways, vulnerable or susceptible populations, or lack of capacity to participate in decision making process. As these data become available, they may be incorporated into the Tool. Once fully developed, the Tool will provide the information necessary to conduct a robust preliminary analysis of any area of concern, with the goal of taking action (whether programmatic or regulatory in nature) to address any environmental justice concern that may arise from the analysis. Use of buffers is incorporated into the Tool; population estimation is accomplished through the area-weighted methodology. The smallest unit of geographic resolution is the census block. This Tool is meant to serve as a module to be incorporated on the front end (e.g., screening) of all appropriate Agency assessments, and is currently accessible at http://www.epa.gov/enviro/ej.

The ethics of wilderness. Some of your students may be nature-absolutists. The following excerpt from an article by Margaret Talbot reviewing Bill McKibben's Maybe One: A Personal and Environmental Argument for Single-Child Families (1998) may provide relevant grist for that mill:

Bill McKibben's first book, *The End of Nature* (1989), was the first general interest work to explain the threat of global climate change, and it did so with clarity and conviction. Still,...*The End of Nature* was marred by its embrace of the sort of eco-dualism in which the human and the natural are seen as utterly separate and inevitably at odds. Nature is dead and man is the perpetrator, for any and all manipulation of the natural world is a violation of its essence. (Never mind that conservation itself is a manipulation of nature.) Thus, in a trenchant essay called "The Trouble with Wilderness," the historian William Cronon has written rather witheringly that the McKibbenish perspective is possible –

> only if we accept the wilderness premise that nature, to be natural, must also be pristine – remote from humanity and untouched by our common past. In fact, everything we know about environmental history suggests that people have been manipulating the natural world on various scales for as long as we have a record of their passing. Moreover, we also have unassailable evidence that many of the environmental changes we now face also occurred quite apart from human intervention at one time or another in the earth's past. The point is not that our current problems are trivial, or that our devastating effects on the earth's ecosystems should be accepted as inevitable or "natural." It is rather that we seem unlikely to make progress in solving these problems if we hold up to ourselves as the mirror of nature a wilderness we ourselves cannot inhabit. To do so is merely to take a logical extreme the paradox that was built into wilderness from the beginning: if nature dies because we enter it, then the only way to save nature is to kill ourselves.

These are serious objections. The point is not only that an overly pious view of nature can actually inspire a debilitating fatalism about the prospects for preserving it. Cronon's criticism suggests a more far-reaching problem: the sort of thinking in which a theological awe of nature is supposed to furnish a basis for human ethics. Such thinking is now widespread; but humanist philosophers have been warning against this fallacy at least since Mill, and with good reason. For there is nothing moral in nature – nothing, that is, that we have not ascribed to it.

> There is beauty in nature, beauty unbounded, but there is no justice and there is no mercy. "Either it is right that we should kill because Nature kills," Mill wrote in his great essay on Nature, "torture because Nature tortures; ruin and devastate because Nature does the like; or we ought not to consider at all what Nature does, but what it is good to do." The urge to restore Nature, to undo the damage that humans have done to the environment, is itself an impulse of culture. It is a supremely civilized — which is to say, a supremely unnatural — urge. Margaret Talbot, The Perfectionist, The New Republic, July 20, 1998 at 32.

Page 26, C&Q #1. The public trust doctrine. The PTD, and its resurrection in the late 1960s, may be environmental law's most innovative contribution to legal doctrine. You can introduce it to your students now so that they can see its resonance in most of the chapters that follow, using our rubric of "three PTD settings," and examples drawn from Chapter 22, at pages 1066-68 (we especially like the Methusaleh Tree).

You can ask students *"How is any of this philosophical public trust abstraction relevant to practical environmental law?"* The answer starts with the three different areas in which the trust functions — against derogation, diversion, and alienation — noted on page 1068, in each area of which it adds elements of protection that are often intuitively compelling but often not justified by usual legal principles, as in the examples on pages 1066-68. A society needs some principle that integrates its long term future needs into current enforceable law, and the public trust's legacy principle can do that. It serves to bring many considerations of the natural and civic-societal economies into practical application against the limited calculus of the marketplace. When the public trust exists in a particular setting, it potentially limits private property rights, a point that tends to focus students' attention.

Page 27, C&Q #2. Beyond strict human utility. The public trust doctrine is a way to conceptualize values and reasons for protecting particular resources even if the marketplace accords no economic value to them. What, for instance, does it matter if a human decision to use a pesticide, or spread road salt, or drain a swamp, results in the extermination of an endangered plant or animal? What is the societal importance of an ancient tree? a fossil bed (pages 1091-99)? You get fairly soon to some kind of idea of societal legacy, with the implication that intergenerational resources should not be cavalierly dissipated.

Endangered species provide a nice way to get to the ethical questions: do we protect endangered species because they may ultimately be discovered to be the source of a precious medicine that cures cancer? (One Senator perked up at a committee hearing in 1980 when the witness noted that toxins found in an endangered whelk shellfish in the Florida Keys had shown promise as a cure for genital herpes.) Or is there an argument beyond human utility? These issues are discussed in the text. Of course, direct human considerations must weigh in. The Endangered Species Act specifically does not protect disease bacilli. And if human needs are compelling, and no alternative is reasonably available (which is rare), human needs should probably prevail. Should trees, etc. have legal standing, or legal rights? What if my grass doesn't want to be mowed, according to my neighborhood deist?

"Beyond utilitarianism." Note, however, that all ethics are human-based utilitarian in the sense that they are crafted to satisfy human philosophers' desires to enjoy a moral order that comports with their idea of what is true, fitting, and just in human terms.

Pages 27-31. Garrett Hardin's "Tragedy of the Commons." Depending on the prior training of your students, Hardin's Tragedy may prove very familiar, but it remains an important background concept to put all students on the same plane in discussing the need for law and the use of legal controls to supplement (or replace) self-interested private decision making.

Hardin makes several points that recur throughout the course: (1) he asserts the key principle of environmental resources as limited, finite commodities that are subject to overuse and destruction; (2) he posits the basis for the social contract by which members of society can be thought to have assented to limitations on their freedom of action, even when there is no overt manifestation of express consent (here, for example, think of the flood plain zoning takings cases noted in Chapter 23, or the *Lucas* case forbidding construction on South Carolina's barrier islands); (3) he makes the point that even inaction is action — to refuse to act is to permit continuation of an on-rolling status quo;

and (4) in portions of the article that were not reproduced, he raises the problem of population ("Freedom to breed is intolerable") as a key contributing global threat to environmental quality.

Atlantic coastal fisheries, the commons, and privatization. A useful recent example of the problem of managing common resources comes from the Atlantic coastal groundfish (flounder, cod, halibut, etc.) industry.[1] In 1976 the Magnuson Act drove most foreign trawlers from the newly-declared 200-mile U.S. territorial waters economic zone. This attracted a hundred or more new boats into the groundfish fishery, resulting in a doubling of the domestic U.S. catch in four years time.

As Peter Passell noted in the NY Times, however:

> The bonanza proved short-lived. Landings of diverse species of groundfish have fallen by two-thirds since the 1980 peak, and the harvest is still on the decline. A fishery that by federal estimate could sustain 360 million pound catch is now producing less than 200 million....
>
> Lee Anderson, an economist of the University of Delaware and a member of the Middle Atlantic Council [one of seven regional councils that regulates ocean fishing] thinks the way to get individual fisherman to guard the natural resources to give them a direct stake in its future productivity.

In the 1990s the Middle Atlantic Council experimented with a regulatory system that in effect "privatized" the taking of certain shellfish species. All owners of existing commercial boats in the particular shellfishing fleet were assigned permanent vested quotas in proportion to their past commercial catch.

> These quotas can be bought and sold, giving owners the assurance of amassing sufficient rights to keep the boats working full-time or to bow out of the business with a fat severance bonus. Economic logic suggests that most boat owners will eventually take the money and run. To keep the catch at sustainable levels last year, individual boats were only allowed to harvest a total of 144 hours. Thus just 15 or 20 vessels could have done the work of an entire 140 boat fleet. Passell, "More Fishing, Fewer Fish," New York Times, Wednesday, July 10, 1991.

The theoretical application of the tragedy of the commons to this story, and of the privatization remedy to similar resource management settings is worth discussing. The existing resource management structure for ground-fisheries are set out in a 1993 case, Conservation Law Fdn. v. Franklin, 989 F.2d 54 (1st Cir. 1993).

Page 31, C&Q #1. Common resources, environmental damage, and the "rational maximizer." This note brings the economic concepts of the rational maximizer and the individual actor's inherent drive for social cost externalization into the commons mix, and sets out a basic principle of environmental law — that if the full social costs of individuals' actions are re-internalized back to them through damages actions or regulation, they will tend from the outset to make decisions that are more socially optimal overall.

Page 31, C&Q #2. Extrapolating to global scale. *Does Hardin's analysis apply beyond the cowpasture?* The tragedy of the commons extrapolates well to a larger scale, as the note implies, taking stratospheric ozone depletion and global warming due to the emission of greenhouse gases as prime examples. Other examples are the eradication of valuable

---

[1] *See also* the text on fisheries in the article "Facing a Time of Counter-Revolution: The Kepone Incident and a Review of First Principles," 29 U. Richmond L.R. 657 (1995).

species by over hunting or over fishing. Here the marketplace sends precisely the wrong signal, raising prices as the supply becomes more scarce. See also pages 60-62, and 80-85.

Pages 32-33, C&Q #3 & #4. John Locke and a political philosophy of the tragedy of the commons; The pessimism and optimism of the commons. Self-explanatory.

Pages 33, C&Q #5. The commons and positive outcomes. Questions are rhetorically answered in the note.

Pages 33, C&Q #6. Measuring sustainability. *How to define the point where externalized harms hurt the carrying capacity of the ecosystem? Is absolute purity necessary? What constitutes tolerable depreciation?*

Defining carrying capacity in real life is an arcane art. We sometimes use the idea of carrying capacity of a commons to raise the issues of uncertainty in standard-setting for ecological sustainability that are more usually more obvious in the hazardous pollutant exposure context.

You want students to focus on the point that in some parts of the spectrum of pollution of the environment, the social costs of allowing pollution are acceptable. Student-regulators are often quick to say that the carrying capacity has been reached and any further pollution must cease. They should consider the cost of pollution prevention as a check on their regulatory zeal. The various standard-setting processes studied in Part 3 all have to wrestle with these subjective balances.

Page 34, C&Q #7. Law as mutual coercion. *What kinds of intervention are likely to be effective and appropriate to protect a commons?* This question is broad, and is addressed at some length in the salt analysis text, pages 35-41.

Page 34, C&Q #8. The Coase theorem Self-explanatory.

Page 34, C&Q #9. The view from "free market" advocates. This note introduces the "Wise Use" movement through its principal spokesman, Ron Arnold, setting out for students a decidedly different view of the world, and only in terms of the concept of commons.

Where is the commons in this rhetorical text? Our point is that the marketplace-oriented private property privateers visualize the physical, ecological environment as a relatively infinite, inexhaustible, and resilient resource base for human exploitation, rather than as an intricately inter-relating, long term context in which human society will attempt to flourish along with other natural systems. The different viewpoints have different political consequences, but the debate will ultimately play out in physical as well as rhetorical terms and we'll see which is right. Science increasingly tends to show the reality of the environmentalists' concept of life in a commons.

More on managing commons. In his book, Living Within Limits: Ecology, Economics and Population Taboos (Oxford University Press, 1993), Garrett Hardin moved further towards defining the role of law in preserving the earth's ecosystems from human destruction. Hardin suggests using legislation to develop a reward and punishment system to promote negative population growth and limit immigration and the trend toward multiculturalism – not uncontroversial goals. Unlimited population growth is viewed by Hardin as an impending disaster for the human race, and only through firm governmental control on personal freedom can humanity be protected from humans.

In a related book, The Wealth of Nature: Environmental History and the Ecological Imagination (Oxford University Press, 1993), Donald Worster embraces the concepts of communal property ownership and rural society without reliance on capitalism as the means to stop over consumption and unlimited economic growth. Worster argues that "all consumption beyond a level of modest sufficiency is pathological," and calls for a new social order. "A stable, enduring rural society in equilibrium with the processes of nature, does not allow much freedom or self-assertiveness to the individual." He argues for a "revised Constitution" based on the overweening principle that "all the lands of these United States belong in a final sense to all the people."

Both books acknowledge the horrors and failures of most previous common-ownership social experiments, that produced corruption, human rights violations, poverty and ecological destruction. How would such ruralist/communitarian systems be governed? Can citizens trust leaders, much less themselves, to be altruistic philosopher-kings?

For another perspective on the management of common resources, see Governing the Commons (Cambridge: Cambridge University Press, 1990) by Elinor Ostrom. Ostrom studies the creation of cooperative organizations instituted and maintained by the users themselves with the purpose of managing common pool resources (CPRs). Her book analyzes examples of successes and failures of CPR management throughout the world and offers a framework for future commons management systems. According to her analysis of successful systems, the requirements are: clearly defined boundaries (both individual and physical), congruence between operational rules and local conditions, individuals having a voice in modifying rules, monitors responsible to users, graduated sanctions, low-cost conflict resolution mechanisms, rights to organize recognized by external governments, and "nesting" of the community in a broader institutional setting. Unfortunately most of these criteria require a relatively small scale.

Pages 35-41. The highway salting example. This example illustrates the "environmental approach" to environmental problems — an overview analysis of costs-benefits-alternatives, using long-term as well as short-term economic, ecological, and social values; various legal avenues available for forcing a fuller accounting.

Page 38, C&Q #1. Evaluating the benefits, costs, and alternatives to salting. *Is salt an environmental problem?* We obviously think it is a pretty good example of interconnected economic and ecological considerations, human behavior, and the problems of addressing them rationally. The fact that, overall, the choice of salt instead of CMA is, well, stupid, why does our governance system roll on doing the dysfunctional diseconomic option?

Page 38, C&Q #2. Costs, economic and natural. In order to chart out the full range of costs and benefits that derive from the salt-based model of highway maintenance, it is useful to do a schematic drawing of the setting, indicating the range of salt pollution sources and effects — a highway, with drainage into wetlands and groundwater, bridges, utility lines underground, cars, people, fish, endangered plants, etc.

Compare a fundamental overall *societal* calculus of the problem with the narrower calculus of those *individuals* who actually make the operative decisions whether to dump salt instead of alternatives like CMA.

COMPREHENSIVE ENVIRONMENTAL ANALYSIS OF BOTH INTERNALIZED AND EXTERNALIZED COSTS/BENEFITS/ALTERNATIVES

	COSTS OF PROPOSAL	BENEFITS	ALTERNATIVES
above the line: [the line separates costs felt by the decisionmaker from those that are externalized to the public.]	$200m cost of the proposed action, as proposed	$200+ ?, in terms of doing the job of making highways relatively ice/snow free	[$300+?] unknown cost of selective sand-scrape-salt, CMA, or other alts.; not likely to be wildly greater than salting model cost
below the line: social costs and benefits, not internalized to the decisionmaker.	$150 water supply, health effects	$ __? "safety" (?)	**[costs and benefits:]** $ __? "safety"? more accidents than 100% salt model, fewer fatalities; less pollution
	$500 highway struct. damage	$ __? time savings	
	$50 vegetation		$ __? cost in time
	$2000 vehicle damage caused by salt	$ __? faster quality of life	$ __? social benefits of added employment
	$10 damage to underground utilities $ __? costs at salt production site (local pollution effects, etc.)	$ __? greater certainty of winter highway usability	$__? values of natural resources not polluted
	$ __? loss of wildlife, including endangered species utility values		$ __? lesser health costs, other costs
	$ __? *ethical* costs: to nature and to humans affected by salt in their systems And so on...	$ __? more work opportunities for auto and roadworkers, etc.	$ __? benefits of slower-paced lifestyles (?), etc.
	TOTAL: **$2,910,000,000 plus,** Not including HEALTH, or ENVIRONMENTAL costs	ca. $700M - $1b?	cost/benefit of various alts.? $300-$500m / $700m - $2b?

An analysis of how environmental problems occur will be focused in most instances on the mental calculus of the human decisionmakers who make the critical action-decisions. What considerations enter into the rational calculations of the person who decides on the particular course of action, heavy road salting, that presents environmental problems?

The chart of costs-benefits-alternatives has been consistently and fundamentally useful to the way we teach the course: an overview analysis of how decisions are actually made, reflecting a rational cost-internalization/externalization process. It is drawn from the perspective of the decision-maker who makes each decision that imposes environmental consequences, and it identifies and distinguishes between "**above the line**" and "**below the line**" values. "Above the line" indicates the costs, benefits and alternatives that the decision-maker will normally consider. "Below the line" identifies the far wider range of values that are generally ignored, but which environmental analysts would insist are relevant to making a rational decision.

The chart from the EPA report, on page 39 of the coursebook, will get you started (costs are in millions of 1976 dollars). Other possible categories can be added.

Starting in 1960, Frost Belt road commissions began to turn to salt, which now is the overwhelmingly dominant model. Take the perspective of the official who makes the decision whether to apply salt.

The major point is that the official decision-makers in most environmental cases (and elsewhere as well) will fail to confront many or most of their decisions' real costs. (The system is better at pulling in benefits, tangible and intangible.) Without an accounting of the full costs and benefits, in the context of real alternatives, decisions are not particularly likely to be rational in the long run. Like all of us, decision makers tend to "look out for Number 1."

This material introduces the basic idea of "internalized" and "externalized" costs and benefits, a simple economic construct developed further in Chapter 2. The point is that environmental law is a method for "presenting the bill" to actors, in direct and indirect ways, so that they will have to take account of – internalize – environmental costs that they would otherwise ignore; their decisions will to that extent be compelled to be more rational – ecologically and economically.

Alternatives, and their relative efficiencies and political contexts, are critically important to most environmental analyses. In the salt case, CMA – discussed at pages 40-41 – is an important available alternative, and its short term costs contrast dramatically with its overall massive societal net benefits. Significantly, CMA remains a rarely used option except on the most vulnerable structures like bridges, and in Oregon.

As with all these notes, teachers working through the above-the-line/below-the-line accounting exercise will undoubtedly find new twists and turns to build into it.

Some students will ask why the cost figure for highway and bridge repair is not "above the line," i.e., surmising that the highway official will be hit with and take account of those costs. The answer is that reconstruction costs are not typically paid out of the highway commission's funds, but rather from state and federal appropriations and the Highway Trust Fund, hence are not tangible costs to the decision-maker. This raises also the question of the role played by subsidies in the market calculus. Within large sectors of the private marketplace, as well as in governmental agencies, direct and indirect public subsidies hide real costs and promote otherwise dis-economic behaviors. As to public agencies, we remember a revealing moment in Michigan highway-building when state officials could have avoided having to build a $500 million skyway bridge for the north-south flow of I-75 by spending a mere $100K on new signs redirecting the highway route along an already-constructed 6-lane alternate loop (with no net extra distance traveled, and possible economic benefits to the sagging economy of Saginaw). Guess which option they chose? As to how subsidies are factored into private corporate calculuses, hiding the real costs of industrial activity, consider where nuclear power would be without the Price-Anderson Act capping liability, or the example of the timber industry's clear-cutting in the federal forests noted in Chapter 16.

Salt is perhaps an unusual example where we have some specific figures from the EPA study that show the very large scale of externalized costs. In many environmental cases the accounting is not so available, though the decisional phenomenon is the same.

It should also be remembered that environmental analysis tries to incorporate costs and benefits that are intangible as well as tangible. This produces problems:

To move into more indistinct ecological values you can ask students, *"What if the salt is likely to destroy a particular endangered species in a marsh near salted highways?"* and *" Does it matter whether the species is a beautiful egret, or a slimy slug?"* (see notes for page 22, C&Q#2) That should be good for a bit of discussion on ecology and ethics. It also offers a link to the Public Trust Doctrine materials at the end of this chapter, as well as a chance to explore the sometimes-hidden but important utilitarian function of environmental issues: an endangered species' endangerment (as with the spotted owl controversy in Chapter 16) may be a sensitive barometer of potential costs to humans. And the endangered spotted owl can show that "good ecology is good economics." It reveals that the grossly subsidized timber cutting in the last of the federal old-growth forests threatens a dis-economic loss to humans as well as extinction for the owl, and the alternatives that will save the owl will also save public funds and the public values of our national resources legacy. The Public Trust Doctrine can give these values a voice.

The discussion of legal remedies (which links nicely with Hardin's Tragedy of the Commons cow pasture model) should also include a realistic discussion of the politics involved: Locally, note the different motivations of the road commissioner. (The salt sample ZP spreads on a desk top to start the class was collected from a road in March, with no snow on the road; a snowfall was predicted and the Road Commission wanted to dump as much of their salt stocks so that there would be no leftover that would diminish the next year's budget allocations.) And note the ties between the commercial marketplace and state and federal agencies, set out in the text at pages 41 and 80-82. Oregon has apparently made a statewide regulatory decision to halt highway salting, primarily focusing on the perceived direct threat to salmon stocks.

• **Looking ahead: Woburn toxics as a case study.** For those who will devote course time to toxics regulation and toxic torts, you may want to give notice at this early moment of future class discussions incorporating Jonathan Harr's gripping book about the Woburn toxics case, A CIVIL ACTION (used as a backdrop in Chapter 4, which integrates its story). Students are riveted by the book, and may have seen the motion picture starring John Travolta in the role of plaintiffs' attorney Jan Schlichtmann (see page 201). You may wish to suggest that students start reading the book early in the course. The book not only shows the obstacles and erratic course of such plaintiff litigation, and the whims and vagaries of the judicial process, but also raises larger questions about whom the legal system can rely upon to implement effective rational accountings for social externalities, in a society where knowledge and resources are not evenly available. The book is not an unambiguous paean to citizen plaintiffs.

You can end the first class with a reminder to students to delve into the full complexity of analysis of each case; that's what they'll have to do in practice. Reality exists in the interplay of facts, with their ecological chains of causation; ethical and personal values, tangible and intangible; psychology and politics; and an array of legal remedies, not always orthodox. Environmental law forces us to confront the Spaceship Earth realities — everything is connected to everything else, everything has consequences, what each person does matters, and the law plays its part.

[We try to sandwich the practical course details — on research sources, exams, papers, etc. — into the last ten minutes of the first class hour.]

Chapter 2.
CROSS-CUTTING THEMES IN ENVIRONMENTAL LAW

Chapter contents:

– and check the Teachers' Manual Website for SUPPLEMENTARY MATERIALS:

http://www.bc.edu/schools/law/library/coursebook/envtlaw/teachers

The list of Supplementary Materials in Part III of this manual, and on the Teachers' Website, indicates materials posted on the Teachers' Website that are relevant to this and other chapters.

OVERALL TEACHING THEMES & COURSE DESIGN CONSIDERATIONS

Chapter 2 can be a one-day flying tour of the behaviors and legal structures of the field, or split into two days, with the latter session choosing a recent regulatory controversy to develop an example for the discussion of science, politics, economics, and tactics of modern environmental law. The chapter starts with an overtly political history of environmentalism, then keys upon the classic Allied Chemical Kepone pollution case, analyzing basic tensions between industrial production and the civic values of ecological and environmental protection, and legal remedies, before moving to a survey of the contemporary technicalities of industrial pollution cases, the multi-layered complexity of modern environmental regulation, the economics battlefield, the strategic systemic role of citizen enforcement, and the interplay between industry and Capitol politics in modern environmental regulation.

TEACHING NOTES, COMMENTS, & ALL QUESTIONS ANSWERED

The chapter begins with an experiment on our part, the summary history of environmental regulation, page 42-47, which inevitably forces students to address the politics so prevalent in the field. The history reveals (1) the long tradition of ignoring environmental consequences as individuals and corporations strive to maximize their economic positions, (2) the sudden recognition in the 1960s of the problem of systemic disruptions of the natural and human environment, (3) the two major eras of environmental law-making – the Nixon-Carter years, and the Bush, Senior years – and the three epochs in which industry (mostly industry of the old economy) was able to mount sustained assaults against environmental protection laws – Reagan, the Gingrich 104th Congress, and the Bush, Junior, Administration's dramatic broad-swath initiatives undercutting the corpus of environmental law built up over the prior 30 years. Understanding the changing political backdrop over the years does much to clarify details in the regulatory systems studied throughout the book, and prepares students for the real-life process of environmental regulation in which they will play a professional part.

Pages 48–65.
KEPONE, A MILESTONE INDUSTRIAL POLLUTION CASE FROM THE 1970s

We think you can travel far within the Kepone case, which played a significant role as a societal wake-up call and catalyst to legal action, as well as an illuminating case study of how things happened then and now.

The material starts with the narrative description of the poisoning of the James River and Chesapeake Bay with Kepone by Allied Chemical and the LSP company formed by two Allied executives to continue Kepone production. The Kepone story is self-explanatory, even if the underlying profit motive driven conduct seems so outrageous given its human health and other environmental consequences. This is a core assignment not only because it gives a vivid example of how costs are externalized by releasing wastes into the commons, but also because the book will later return to the Kepone case on a number of occasions, and will also use the Kepone case as a referent for purposes of contrast and comparison.

As noted in the coursebook text, Allied Chemical settled all civil litigation except *Pruitt*, at page 160-62, so that *Pruitt* and the Tax Court decision, 63 TCM 2672 (1992), noted on page 48 at footnote 11, are our only caselaw windows into the Kepone controversy.[1] The Tax Court opinion rambles, but offers further illumination into the general Kepone story, the personal politics of the case, as well as the specific tax issue. Allied had claimed the converted $8 million fine/public interest fund as a deduction, which was disallowed by the IRS.

Page 57, C&Q #1. Why did the Kepone disaster happen? A systems breakdown? Some of your students will have immediately cast Allied in the role of devil. Others may from the beginning adopt the theme of this note , that corporations "working for their shareholders," routinely made such seemingly callous decisions. Although there is no easy answer to the lack of intervention to stop the grossly inadequate Kepone handling practices, one avenue of inquiry is into societal norms and social ethics. In an earlier era, much of what was done in the case might not have seemed so odious and unconscionable. The tougher question is whether Allied behaved worse than the "average" industrial manufacturing concern in the era of the 1970s. We don't know how to judge that.

Who could be expected to keep a close eye on Kepone production? The point is that there is no automatic review-and-control forum within government or industry, nor an automatic incentive to assure societal safety, unless there is clear risk of liability. Government is not automatic, and requires a huge expenditure of effort and resources.

Page 58, C&Q #2. Attempts to reform corporate power. Corporations are part of the unwritten Constitution that governs modern society. Environmentalism and other

[1] On Jan. 23, 1995, in an unreported opinion, a panel of the Third Circuit unanimously affirmed the Tax Court decision in *Allied-Signal*.

public interest initiatives utilize a society-wide civic lens. Corporations and commercial law focus on individual economic actors and their bottom line. Given this inherent contradiction, and the huge political mass of the corporate world, it is inevitable that a number of civic movements will continue to try to reform the economy's corporate structure. Even trivial reforms are difficult, even post-Enron. Stay tuned.

Page 58, C&Q #3. Allied's tolling agreement with LSP. Self-explanatory. You may ask whether the tolling agreement meant that Allied could properly be held liable for all the Kepone and THEIC pollution. See the criminal liability discussion at pages 979-81.

Page 58, C&Q #4. A state tendency toward laxity? This is a good place to raise the race-to-the-bottom concept that underlies the federal pollution statutes. See pages 296-98, 460-61. We and most practicing environmental attorneys have little doubt that the arguments for devolution of authority to the states are motivated by a realistic conviction that federal standards will be weakened if states are again given primacy in pollution control.

Page 59, C&Q #5. Legal repercussions of the Kepone incident. The legal repercussions of the Kepone disaster occurred at each level of government, but because of Allied's policy of settling each personal injury tort claim with a gag clause we have very little information on civil damage recoveries, except for the indirect damages decision in *Pruitt* at page 160. Note the Gilbert et al. v. Allied Personal Injury Complaint excerpt, page 61. (The full text of the *Gilbert* complaint, one of the personal injury civil complaints in the Kepone case, is set out in Part III's Supplementary Materials on the Teachers' Website, along with the state government's civil complaint.)

(The "gag orders" that accompany toxic tort settlements are rather commonplace in modern practice. The most obvious interest of the defendants is to suppress information and prevent other plaintiffs and would-be plaintiffs from learning of the potential value of their cases. This reduces their respective bargaining power and incentives to sue. Still, that does not address the question of whether, from a larger social perspective, the suppression of this information is in the public interest. See Twomey, Beaking the Silence: Examining the Enforceability of Private Settlements which Conceal Environmental Hazards, 4 NE Envtl Law Forum 109 (1997).)

On the public law of the incident, note the criminal liability role played by the 1899 Refuse Act in the Kepone case. See pages 979-84. This invites a question, raised again at the start of Chapter 20, about the legal process issues of resurrecting an obsolete [?] statute to address problems far from the original intentions of the legislators. Also invites a discussion about the primitive state of federal and state pollution statutes at the start of the 1970s, and the interstate competitive "race-to-the-bottom," noted above and picked up again in Chapters 5 & 6.

What about natural resources damages? As noted, the realm of natural resources damages was untouched in the Kepone case, although the state of Virginia apparently characterized some of its cleanup expenses as natural resources damages. By looking ahead to Chapter 3's materials on the Exxon Valdez spill at pages 185-89 you can catalog the range of probable damages to the ecology. Note also the public trust damage recovery material at pages 1099.

To what extent did Allied have to account for the totality of the costs? This is a good opportunity to survey what private and public legal remedies can and cannot bring into an accounting for injurious actions. Natural resources damages again are a significant point, but the economic costs to the community, and the long term residual health effects to the population, are unlikely to be measurable, and will not generally enter into any accounting. The marketplace accounting thus will never capture the entire consequences of an action, positive or negative.

Page 60, C&Q #6. To what extent was Kepone a tragedy of the commons? Allied was not suffering the direct consequences of its own actions, as it would in the pasture-herding model Hardin presents. We nevertheless can discuss environmental commons in Allied's natural tendency to maximize cost externalization into non-owned, non-market resource systems, the air and water.

Page 62, C&Q #7. Kepone and the role of lawyers. *Could the attorneys for Allied have raised the hazards issues?* Of course, but students will quickly see the human realities conjoining to deter professionals from playing a societal watchdog role, at least until the point where death or immediate grave injury was clearly likely. This can lead to some very useful ethics discussions.

Page 63, C&Q #8. Kepone and environmental justice. The Kepone case also opens up issues of environmental justice that can be revisited in a number of cases throughout the course, an integrated theme rather than a separate area with its own chapter. According to an official of the town of Hopewell interviewed by phone, the houses in the Arlington subdivision, in the lower left corner of the map on page 52, south of Cattail Creek, are predominantly occupied by families of color and low income, as a thoughtful analysis of the map would predict. In his speech at the 1994 AALS Conference session on Environmental Law, Professor Richard Lazarus advised –

> If you, like so many of us now, are pretty tired of having the same old organizing themes – the uncertainty and scientific complexity associated with pollution regulation, or the tensions between moral outrage and cooler-headed analysis, or the subtle administrative law distinctions between hard looks and soft glances – try environmental justice for a change. [And] don't just think about allocational efficiencies, but about distributional implications as well. Lazarus, Environmental Justice and the Teaching of Environmental Law, in Symposium, Essays on Environmental Justice, 96 W. Va L. Rev. 1025, 1035 (1994).

The theme of sensitivity to impacts upon low income and minority communities can be woven into your coverage of a great deal of the material in the coursebook. Page references incorporating environmental justice considerations: 16, 63-64, 124, 245, 302, 374, 529, 604-611, 728, 733, 1230-1231.

Page 64, C&Q #9. A first-generation regulatory setting. Beyond the story of how Allied found itself in the Kepone predicament lies the ineffective legal-regulatory context at the federal-state-local level that this note addresses. This offers you the chance not only to review history and introduce the race-to-the-bottom, but also to note the practical demands of any regulatory setting.

Pages 65–77. BEYOND KEPONE: TRACKING SEVERAL DECADES OF ENVIRONMENTAL LAW DEVELOPMENT

This is your transition section, carrying students from the fairly simple pollution paradigm represented by the Kepone narrative to modern pollution control law.

One way to do this initially is to have the students plot out on the map on page 52 all the linkages that could be made on the Kepone facts, if they were to occur today, with the parade of statutes on pages 67-70. You can refer students to the Statutory Capsule Summaries at the back of the book, Ref. pages 50-60, or can label each statute by the regulatory "handle" that would link it to the facts on the map. You should also indicate the voluminous extent of these statutory systems, indicating that there are many professional lifetimes lurking in this array of laws. The array of statutes shows students how multi-layered and complex the job of complying with environmental laws can be (and remind them that all the statutes are backed up by a ream of regs. Students often recoil, wondering how they as well can process such a volume of law. Part of what we answer is that they wil learn to analyze these laws in terms of their design. The "taxonomy" approach used in this book gives students familiarity with a number of archetypes, providing a basis for extrapolation into other regulatory areas.

You can use the CWA to illustrate this: review with them briefly how in the years since Kepone effluent standards are defined by the statute and by EPA (available technology standards backed up by harm-based WQSs as studied in Chapter 11), how the standards are applied (by state agencies certified under the federal NPDES), how they are enforced, and so on, as well as their relationship to potential common law actions. In preparing this, you may wish to review the "conceptual building blocks of regulation," at pages 302-305.

Page 71. A biodiversity of public law statutes. Self-explanatory. The note is intended to prompt students to think of environmental regulatory systems as a large and diverse mass that deserves subtle analysis. There is not one "average" statute.

You may wish to note for students the chart on page 301 – FIGURE 5–1, SOME MAJOR FEDERAL ENVIRONEMNTAL STATUTES AND THE AGENCIES THAT HAVE MAJOR RESPONSIBILITY FOR THEM – showing which federal agencies have jurisdiction over which statutory programs.

Page 72, C&Q #2. Getting a handle on statutes: a statutory "taxonomy." One fundamental aspect of this book, and one of the ways we try to teach our students the subtle analyses required in environmental regulatory practice, is the concept of identifying a "taxonomy" approach to different statutes, looking for different forms in which the laws are structured as to standard-setting and implementation.

For a quick primer on this approach, look at the catalogue of chapter taxonomies on pages 469-70.

Page 72, C&Q #3. The standard default regulatory design – the comprehensive "prescriptive-federal-standards" model ("command-and-control). We do not like the phrase "command-and-control," thinking it a Trojan horse carrying strong pejorative connotations into the discussion. But the phrase is hard to budge.

The model of pollution control that has brought us from the dire conditions of the 1960s to a much cleaner state has been the large prescriptive-federal-standards regulatory system of the CAA, CWA, and others. You might note that 30-year progress, and then introduce the current arguments that these systems have outlived their usefulness, and should make way for less intrusive, "more efficient" systems.

Page 73, C&Q #4. Citizen enforcement. The question of *who* can enforce — federal or state agency, or citizens — is a recurring focus of environmental law, and *how* that prosecutorial enforcement will be done, and how it will be judicially executed. The critical role played by citizen suits in the development of modern environmental statutory systems is a major point . You can ask your students, *"How much enforcement would be likely in the different areas of environmental regulation if there are no active citizen efforts, or the threat of citizen enforcement?"* The answer varies from case to case, of course, but it is our strong impression that the threat or actuality of citizen suits has been critically important throughout the evolution of today's environmental statutes, with the possible exception of the toxics statutes where congressional pressure has typically been strong enough to induce agency enforcement rigor. It is the clarity of statutory violations that makes most citizen enforcement actions possible. Agency discretion or subjectivity in determining the terms of compliance undercut citizen enforceability. It makes a systemic difference whether there exists the potential for multiple enforcers, or on the other hand the restricted "bi-polar" model limited to regulatees and official regulator agencies.

Page 74, C&Q #5. The biodiversity of law: the common law's continuing roles. This too is one of this coursebook's premises: that the common law continues to have an active, dynamic role in handling environmental conflicts.

Page 74, C&Q #6. Generational differences: new expectations, new remedies, new science. Self-explanatory.

Page 75, C&Q # 7. New kinds of concerns. This note is a caveat that the traditional pollution scenario misses a major new reality — that environmental problems today are likely to be systemic and often transboundary in scope. Here too we urge consideration of the eye-opening book OUR STOLEN FUTURE: A SCIENTIFIC DETECTIVE STORY, by Theo Colborn, Dianne Dumanoski & John Peterson Myers (Penguin, 1996).

Page 75, C&Q #8. International convergences. This note is a reminder of how environmental law increasingly deals with international interconnections. If you wish to integrate this perspective as a continuing theme in your course, you should look ahead into Chapters 8 and 26 at this point.

Page 77, C&Q #9. The legal skill of comparative law. This rhetorical note raises an issue we have never seen discussed in a coursebook before, but which all of us who have worked in the field instinctively recognize: comparative law skills and training address the need to be able to "read" and adjust to conditions and conventions that differ from community to community and legal culture to legal culture. We encourage you to discuss this skill with your students, perhaps revisiting it at various points in the course and at the start of the last chapter.

Pages 77-85. POLITICS AND TACTICS

This material attempts to acknowledge forthrightly the central political tensions shaping the development of environmental law. As always, environmental law gets to the heart of almost everything, including democratic theory, and offers a window on the future. The debates about deregulation and devolution offer an opportunity to raise questions about private property rights, the legitimacy of state and federal regulatory government under different conceptions of the social contract, and the pragmatics of contemporary politics and political discourse.

The tactical importance of citizen action in creating and enforcing the structure of modern environmental law is a continuing theme. Professor May's article, noted on page 85, acknowledges the significant changes in context and format from the early years of environmental law, but indicates that the empirical record continues to show that citizen litigation is a critical factor in a major portion of modern environmental law enforcement.

Pages 85-88. ECONOMICS

The classic false tradeoff argument (which to some degree at various times we all probably buy into), holds that environmental protection and economic productivity are counterpoised — so that to have one you must trade off the other. This section of the materials tries to frame a basic premise of modern resource economics: a society's economic health is not to be measured in a vacuum, in a collection of fractionalized corporate balance sheets or otherwise. "The Three Economies," built on Professor Sax's perceptive article, asserts that economic analysis is naïve unless it considers the surrounding supporting economies in which the standard daily cash register economy exists.

Pages 88-96. ARGUMENTS FOR REFORMATION

To understand what they will read in the newspapers and hear on the airwaves about this field they are studying, it is necessary for your students to be aware of the contending agendas of the blocs that wrestle over environmental protection law. Anti-regulationists have shown such substantial strength in Congress and many statehouses that we believe an environmental law course must take direct account of such initiatives. Your students will see references to them in research they do on contemporary command-and-control statutory and resource policy issues (not to mention on the Rush Limbaugh Show).

Page 94, Hold it right there. Haven't we done enough already? The Teachers' Website has a memo and text on the controversy engendered by Bjorn Lomborg's THE SKEPTICAL ENVIRONMENTALIST.

Anti-Regulatory Initiatives. Regulation and effective citizen litigation have been targeted by draft legislation at the state and local level as well as federal. If regulation is substantially weakened by reform initiatives, we will be left with societal strategies relying upon the dubious efficiency and consistency of bureaucratic agencies, and-or the self-restraint of the market forces that threaten environmental quality — not a cheering prospect — or upon a reawakened common law.

Environmental law — reflecting the ecology truism that "everything is connected to everything else" — turns out to be intimately connected to democracy and political theory generally. If a basic principle of human society is the survival and long-term flourishing of the society and its physical context, can we ignore the negative "externalities" so widely generated by human production decisions? what is the true definition of "conservatism"? do individual entrepreneurial rights exist in a vacuum or in a context of civic responsibilities? does a legal system require principles like the public trust doctrine that acknowledge and value future needs and legacy values? ....

The political issues represented by anti-regulation debates in Washington can be developed in a number of chapters. Analyzing the real-life contending forces and political-economic context of environmental law cases and legislative initiatives is fundamentally necessary to informed understanding.

Will Enron save environmental law from the anti-regulationists' attacks? Robert Kuttner writes:

> The entire system of self-regulation has collapsed. Free markets, it turns out, don't prevent brokers from peddling junk to unsuspecting investors while they enrich themselves, or auditors from conspiring with executives to cook company books. Market discipline doesn't stop insiders from selling shares they are promoting to the public even as the company is rotting from within, or senior company officials from looting the pensions of workers, or CEOs from scheming to pump up stock so they can cash in options. Only regulation can change these perverse incentives..... As even Bush tacitly admits, the remedy for the self-dealing, the accounting frauds, and the other conflicts of interest that are now placing the entire economy in jeopardy is government regulation—something the Republicans have vilified since Ronald Reagan. Kuttner, Boston Globe, July 10, 2002 AT A19.

If you survey the array of theoretical critiques and efforts to revise environmental law at this point (or you might do this survey after teaching one or more of the pollution statutes) you should note that the Latin/ Ackerman-Stewart debate on softening regulatory controls appears below at pages 318-321.

Pages 96-102. A SUMMARY SURVEY OF THEMES

Here is the cumulative introductory round-up. You can tell students to treat this catalogue of concepts as a checklist to be internalized for the continuation of their studies in the field, each representing a potential node of analysis or pitched battles.

Acknowledging the Bush II Environmental Agenda. As noted earlier in this chapter the Bush II Administration brought an unprecedentedly broad-spectrum anti-environmental agenda to Washington. To catalogue an accurate picture of many of these initiatives – which are so voluminous, intricate, and low-profile as to shield themselves from public awareness, while causing the media to glaze over or throw up their hands.

See the Bush II Administration Supplementary Materials for Chapter 2 on the Teachers' Website.

You also might review:

Michael Blumm, The Bush Administration's Sweetheart Settlement Policy: A Trojan Horse Strategy for Advancing Commodity Production on Public Lands, 34 ELR 10397 (2004).

Pat Parenteau, The Bush Environmental Agenda: Whatever Industry Wants, 14 Duke Envtl L. & Pol'y Forum No. 2 (2004).

Richard Lazarus, A Different Kind of Republican Moment in Environmental Law, 97 Minn. L.Rev. 999 (2003).

Carter, Leahy, and Snape, Cutting Science, Ecology, and Transparency Out of National Forest Management: How the Bush Administration Uses the Judicial System to Weaken Environmental Laws, 33 ELR 10959, 10960-10961 (2003).

Carl Pope & Paul Rauber, STRATEGIC IGNORANCE: WHY THE BUSH ADMINISTRATION IS RECKLESSLY DESTROYING A CENTURY OF ENVIRONMENTAL PROGRESS (2004).

Chapter 3.
THE COMMON LAW IN MODERN ENVIRONMENTAL LAW: NONSTATUTORY CAUSES OF ACTION

Chapter contents:

—and check the Teachers' Manual Website for SUPPLEMENTARY MATERIALS:

http://www.bc.edu/schools/law/library/coursebook/envtlaw/teachers

The list of Supplementary Materials in Part III of this manual, and on the Teachers' Website, indicates materials posted on the Teachers' Website that are relevant to this and other chapters.

OVERALL TEACHING THEMES & COURSE DESIGN CONSIDERATIONS

This chapter is designed to explore the foundation of modern environmental law in the common law system, including an extended inquiry into theories of liability, defenses, and remedies that will be relevant throughout the course in public law as well as private law settings.

- Litigating a pollution case as a common law private nuisance – the ease and accessibility of common law tort litigation in the environmental setting, as a means of "presenting the bill" for otherwise externalized pollution costs.
- The special relevance and doctrinal twists underlying environmental litigation under common law theories: parsing the elements of different causes of action, different theories of culpability, the range of narrow and broad affirmative defenses, crafting new remedies and new forms of old remedies, including natural resources remedies.
- The importance of private litigation in building the structure of modern environmental law, including private lawsuits forcing polluters to face their externalized costs.

TEACHING OPTIONS (DAYS OF COVERAGE) Almost 100 pages in length, this chapter on common law Torts can be taught in a variety of ways, depending on the overall course design. The principal options are for two, or three, or four class hours of coverage, depending on the overall course design. A single hour is an option, but requires very hard choices that depend on what students can confidently be presumed to have learned in Torts.

Absolute minimum coverage recommendation: Pages 106-124 (or 103-124[1]), note 2 at 166-167 and 172-174

In terms of importance, there are few cases more helpful to understanding the issues of common law remedies for environmental torts than *Boomer* and *Wilsonville*. *Boomer* demonstrates the classic cost internalization effect of private tort remedies in a challenging remedial context in which *stare decisis* (which would ordinarily have produced an injunction shutting down a major new facility), is rejected in favor of the payment of permanent damages. Students may need guidance to discover the nuanced result: a *de facto* act of private condemnation of an easement allowing defendant to dictate the use of plaintiffs' property as a disposal site for dust and vibration. *Wilsonville* offers a very sharp contrast, in which another new facility, which has an arguably flawed siting record, is enjoined based on very speculative risk calculations, a result that is almost certainly orders of magnitude more dangerous than improving the existing site. Together these cases provide a vital prism for examining the institutional competence of common law courts as environmental decisionmakers.

Two class hour suggested coverage:
Hour 1 -- 103-128, 137-145
Hour 2 – 146-160, 163-185

Three or four class hour suggested coverage
Hour 1 -- 103-137
Hour 2 – 137-163
Hour 3 – 163-194
Hour 4 – 194-199 and space out the readings for hours 1- 3 a bit more

A final option that is NOT recommended, is to skip this Chapter in reliance on the fact that the students have had it in their Torts course. There are two principal objections to that approach. First is the risk that (1) the students will either not remember the material, (2) they will have glossed over key items for environmental setting, such as intentional torts, or (3) they will have very different levels of command over the concepts. Second, and more important, the fundamental *Boomer/Wilsonville* legal process, institutional analysis of cost internalization, and risk management competence of courts in relation to other decisionmakers will be lost.

TEACHING NOTES, COMMENTS, & ALL QUESTIONS ANSWERED

Chapter 3 begins in earnest the consideration of how citizens can affect and influence environmental outcomes. Tort causes of action have a degree of deterrent effect, and the possibility of injunctions, restoration remedies, natural resource damages, and punitive damages raises a host of possibilities beyond that. Chapter 3 also ventilates critical questions about the relationship between the law as a medium for adjusting private disputes and the law as a means of adjusting group interests.

Chapter 3 is a fundamental chapter in the structure of the coursebook. Most of the

[1] Adding Pages 103-106 (materials about Tort law generally) is recommended. It does not greatly lengthen the reading and it ensures that all students have a shared working model of Tort law in this context.

book's authors teach the chapter as an introduction to the way environmental and economic analyses can underlie the simplest environmental cases, as well as doctrinal analyses of legal technicalities — thoughtful choices of causes of action, theories of liability, defenses and remedies. It has been our experience that most law students are in need of this functional integrative study of legal doctrines which they have seen at various points in their legal education, but have not internalized in coherent fashion.

In this chapter and Chapter 4 on toxic torts, the political and legislative initiatives against government regulation are echoed in marketplace attempts to constrict common law as well. Federal and state bills capping punitive damages, restricting class actions, and shielding polluters from tort liability in a variety of settings, all represent a continuation of market force reactions against various external accountings.

The continued importance of the common law. Students sometimes wonder why we spend time on the common law. The common law is of course a basic foundation upon which all regulatory systems have been built. The common law also is playing a role in current national policy debates. Common law is being pushed as a broadly preferable legal alternative to regulation by some modern anti-regulation laissez-faire proponents. Thus you can tell students that you are studying the environmental uses of common law not only on their own terms, but also in the context of ongoing political wars. An interesting book representing such anti-regulatory political initiatives is Roger Meiners and Andrew Morriss' Common Law and the Environment—Rethinking the Statutory Basis for Modern Environmental Law (2000), a compilation of articles that generally advocate deregulation and reliance on common law to protect the public interest. This book was supported in part by PERC, the Bozeman research center which receives funding from oil-industry foundations that has produced much of the anti-regulatory literature in the environmental area.

If you are expanding the coverage of your course beyond the traditional industrial pollution paradigm, note that the common law as a substitute for regulation is even less likely to have effective application in regulating problems within the service economy noted in Jim Salzman's article,2 much less to the issues of ambient multiple chemical exposures raised by Colborn, Dumanoski, and Meyer in OUR STOLEN FUTURE.

PAGES 103-107 -- THE "LCD" MODEL OF TORTS

This material is new in the third edition and attempts to review and reformulate the students' prior knowledge of Tort law into a more structured syntax for analysis and comparison of the several torts most germane to providing remedies for environmental injuries. This material is intended to be self-explanatory to the students. The overarching organizational precept is the term "Liability." That concept is meant to convey more than just a modern cause of action or a set of elements derived from traditional forms of action inherited from the English writ system. Instead, it is meant to have explanatory power by isolating a combination of elements each of which helps demonstrate why Tort law shifts the loss from where it has fallen on Plaintiff back to a defendant, assuming that Plaintiff can also prove causation ("C") and ("D") a combination of loss-related elements that justify injunctive or other relief besides damages. Usually L is determined as a combination of qualitative aspects of

1. Salzman, *Beyond the Smokestack: Environmental Protection in the Service Economy,* 47 UCLA L.REV. 411 (1999).

Defendant's conduct (mental state and degree of care exercises) and the nature of the particular interest of Plaintiff being invaded (which indicates, to a degree, societal expectations about the degree of protection against invasion that is being provided). The goal of this approach is to highlight why, as a matter of social policy, the losses are being shifted. Once that is done, the approach also has the advantage of showing the extent to which causation and remedial issues tend to be similar across all torts.

Pages 107-115 -- *Boomer*

N.B. The text makes the assumption that its users will be reading most of the materials in the Chapter, including the *Boomer*-specific material on remedies that appears in C&Q #2 on pages 166-67 and on permanent damages on pages 172-174. That placement choice by the authors, which tends to defer discussion of those issues to the remedies segment of the Chapter, is not the only workable choice. At least one of authors, tends to front-load that discussion with the discussion of what it takes to bring a nuisance action to highlight the legal process aspects of *Boomer* and the comparison with *Wilsonville*. These Teacher's Manual notes, however, assume that many of the remedial and legal process aspects of *Boomer* will be covered later.

Pages 107-115. The classic *Boomer* case. Many students will have encountered *Boomer* before, but it offers a particularly useful opportunity to walk students through the actual litigation of a pollution tort case, (which probably represents most of the "environmental" actions brought each year in the U.S.). It might be realistic to invite the class to imagine Oscar Boomer coming into a plaintiffs attorney's office, and beginning to set out the case. Oscar Boomer clearly is angry (angry plaintiffs, with sufficient wrath to carry them through months and years of litigation, are typically a requirement of our profession.) You can role-play the interview with Mr. Boomer, who undoubtedly has very crude initial characterizations of the harm, and the remedy he wants. ("Have them pay me my losses, and shut the plant down.")

Sketching the layout of the *Boomer* case on the blackboard may be useful, with a cement plant, and eight plaintiff households downwind. (You might note the relevant information that would be supplied by a "wind rosette" on the schematic overview, indicating the prevailing wind blowing from the plant and toward the plaintiffs' homes.) Such commonsense graphic features emphasize to students the practical necessity of understanding the physical setting, so as to be able to analyze and set out the elements of potential causes of action that later may be litigated.

During the course of the interview with Oscar Boomer, the plaintiff's attorney would have to be wondering how easy it would be to prove substantial damages caused by the cement plant. On the board you can show that the cement dust is undoubtedly not just coming down on Boomer and his neighbors, but extends far downwind with increasing diffusion and diminished impact. It might be useful to note that although there are undoubtedly natural resources damages arising from the cement dust pollution, no one in this case pays any attention to them. An obvious question is whether Boomer and his family suffered any health injuries. The fact that we hear nothing about them indicates strongly that there were no health claims to be litigated. The primary injuries that Boomer could prove were damages to property - corrosion of gutters and house paint, destruction of garden crops, and corrosion of vehicles stored on Mr. Boomer's premises, as well as decline in the value of his real estate. If there were physical health injuries, the mood of the case would change, even for Judge Bergan, we suppose. Note that courts typically allow health damages as part of the recovery in private insurance suits, implicitly extending the tort to a personal injury theory.

Part of the context of this case can be set out with a quick shorthand summary of the cement plant management's calculus of costs and benefits. In reviewing the *Boomer* case, how much of the externalized cost ultimately gets accounted for in this ad hoc common law litigation fashion? It is clear that the cement company is externalizing substantial costs to the neighbors, and to the environment. Clearly the alternatives of locating in an even less sparsely populated area, or installing better pollution control devices, were not justified in the corporate managers' calculus of costs. Their cost for air pollution control was basically the purchase of a smokestack. Even after paying permanent damages to the Boomer plaintiffs, massive amounts of dust emitted into the atmosphere will end up being deposited on lands not belonging to Atlantic Cement Company, leaving the degree of cost internalization far from complete.

An interesting point should be made here, despite the reference to the facility having "state-of-the-art" technology in place, it appears that factual conclusion may have been untrue. There *did* exist, contrary to the court's conclusion/supposition, a form of "baghouse" fiberglass-curtain dust collection technology that could have substantially abated the problem. The courts' technological information in these cases is only as good as the attorneys' research and presentation on these points and it might not be surprising that the local attorney representing the plaintiffs here did not have access to information that would have informed him of that fact, or of the resources to controvert whatever testimony defendant may have put in on the subject.

Another part of the *Boomer* context is seen by considering the legal system more broadly. Boomer's attorney obviously had no effective possibility of going to the official state pollution control commission nearby in Albany. Thus the common law offered a far more accessible and responsive forum. The text then examines the special characteristics of the "intentional" theories of tort culpability.

Page 111, C&Q #1: *Boomer* as an environmental case. *Did Mr. Boomer regard himself as an environmentalist?* The point is that the case has important environmental accounting consequences, and lessons to teach in the application of common law, even though this was just a normal lawsuit arising in the law of neighbors.

Page 111, C&Q #2: Nuisance basics in *Boomer*. The text stresses the intentional tort of nuisance, not nuisance based on negligence. As the Restatement 2d of Torts makes clear, not only are both possible, nuisance in a strict liability context also is contemplated. This Teacher's Manual discussion will give a bit more play to the concept of negligence based nuisance because it helps explain language that appears in some older cases and the surrounding commentary on the subject.

Restatement 2d Torts § 822. General Rule

One is subject to liability for a private nuisance if, but only if, his conduct is a legal cause of an invasion of another's interest in the private use and enjoyment of land, and the invasion is either (a) intentional and unreasonable, or (b) unintentional and otherwise actionable under the rules controlling liability for negligent or reckless conduct, or for abnormally dangerous conditions or activities.

An intentional tort does not even require that "substantial certainty" of subsequent nuisance injury be foreseen from the beginning, but only that at some point it becomes obvious that subsequent acts would be substantially certain to create harms, and Boomer's complaints to the company pretty clearly fulfilled this requirement. Because the Atlantic Cement Co. continued to produce pollution after it had received petitions and complaints from the neighbors, it is clear that the company acted with "civil intention" as to the subsequent pollution. The trial court had no trouble in finding Boomer and his neighbors were suffering an unreasonable burden, so the intentional tort elements were extraordinarily easy to show in the *Boomer* case.

This section of the restatement 2d sets out a notable example of how parsing the different elements of tort causes of action can produce very significant changes in the character of environmental litigation. The section draws upon the distinction made in the old *Ducktown Copper* (206 U.S. 230 (1907) case. The point is that when a case is brought as intentional tort rather than negligent tort, concern for the comparative utility of defendant's conduct in relation to the harm it causes is transferred from an element (negligence) of the cause of action (whereby plaintiffs can be completely dismissed unless they can prove a greater utility), to a post-liability question, merely determining whether the further remedy of injunctive relief will be added to the payment of damages. As the note mentions, most contemporary nuisance cases are litigated as intentional torts.

Shifting the question of "unreasonableness" from a question weighing defendant's actions in a context that weighs defendant's production in the public welfare, to *plaintiff's* individual unreasonable burden, the law-of-the-jungle battle that takes place in negligence-based cases is finessed. Historically, courts had to be educated in the difference between negligence and intentional liability. (The third basis for nuisance liability, strict liability, is not applicable here. Cement dust is obviously not an abnormally dangerous instrumentality. So Boomer draws only on the first two potential basis of culpability - negligence and intentional tort liability.) By avoiding questions of the *defendant's* unreasonableness, intentional tort changes the question dramatically, focusing on the plaintiff's injury. Although a few courts and commentators have said that the unreasonableness of plaintiff's burden should be weighed in light of the utility of defendant's conduct (thus bringing in many of the balance of utilities considerations from negligence jurisprudence — see Padilla v. Lawrence, 685 P.2d 964, NM App. 1984, completely excluding liability, on a balance), the *Ducktown* court and the majority trend that follows it accepts that every person, including the poorest who typically would suffer most in such a balance of utilities context, has a right to a relatively unpolluted use and enjoyment of their land. Although one cannot insist on absolute purity of one's environment, it appears that the question to the jury is whether a plaintiff has suffered more than the average American in general should bear. Accordingly, intentional tort makes the imposition of injuries on the neighbors subject to straight-forward liability.

The payment of intentional tort damages makes compensation a straight-forward cost of doing business. In terms of both law and economics that is a dramatic shift.

Page 112, C&Q #3: *Boomer* and the cement company's "cost externalization." This textual note explores cost externalization. Together with the next note, students should grasp that not all externalized costs are internalized by tort actions.

Page 112, C&Q #4: The "cost internalizing" effect of the *Boomer* lawsuit. *How much gets internalized here?* Note here that the named plaintiffs get only the market damages they can prove (plus a small bonus noted in the permanent damages section at page 172) for property losses, with no recovery for health consequences, and no such recoveries by other plaintiffs, with no prayer of course for any natural resources damage recovery for injury to the environment.

Why not? Other plaintiffs within a close range to the plant can probably use threats of similar lawsuits to obtain small settlements for their respective property damage. Even that compensation to other landowners will taper off as the provable amount of injury decreases with diffusion and distance. As a result, much real diffuse property damage and health effects that are not substantial enough to produce injury (as opposed to annoyance) will go externalized and uncompensated. In Boomer, perhaps as an indication of the less acute knowledge of the issues at the time, little mention was made of health and none of natural resources damages.

Does the difficulty lie in shortcomings in environmental cost-accounting? Perhaps that is part of the shortfall. Today perhaps there would be more scientific data available via consultants, and more vigilant health-oriented trial preparation, but still only a small chance of natural resource claims under common law or statute.

Do we have the time or luxury to try to account for all externalized costs? This question raises the triage question. As a society we have been choosing not to ignore totally environmental impacts to health, property, and nature, but still are undecided when and to what extent. The cost of information is great, so that the process of trying to achieve full cost-internalization would be a quixotic venture, but a prioritized targeting of sources of injurious pollution to be regulated or adjudicated makes sense. The process of inducing cost-internalization proceeds in both public and private law, although in somewhat opportunistic non-rationalized fashion.

Pages 113-114, C&Q #5: Tactics, politics, and the urge to litigate. *If the cement dust pollution was so obvious, why didn't Boomer go to the state air pollution agency in Albany?* This question introduces the realpolitik options available. Politically the state agency would in all likelihood not be eager to crack down hard on the plant, for reasons of time, place, and context that you might examine.

What practical advantages lie within the common law option? This invites a comparison between public and private law. In terms of initiative, the private plaintiffs are certain to get at least a hearing; relying on administrative process invites inertia and lessens the degree of control of the proceedings that can be exercised by the affected citizens. In terms of remedy, damages go to plaintiffs, civil fines don't; injunctions are more likely in common law actions. In terms of the law, common law causes of action are far easier to prove than violations of public law regulations; agencies could use public nuisance if they wished, in order to avoid the technical burdens, but usually don't.

Are the regulatory systems likely to provide the Boomers with a sympathetic forum? This question and the following questions in this note are rhetorical, again emphasizing the tactical and contextual differences, with an emphasis on the practical advantages of common law to most ordinary citizens.

Page 114, C&Q #6: Environmental tort remedies. More on the practical advantages of common law. Was the common law's balance satisfactory? Here we lead into the shortcomings of the court's consideration of private and public harms in the balance of the injunction remedy.

Pages 114-115 C&Q #7: A word about public nuisance. This note briefly traces the roots of public nuisance. The note alerts students to be aware that public nuisance has a different history and traditional legal function than that of private nuisance.

PAGES 115-124 -- *Wilsonville* and Risk Management

This chapter uses the *Wilsonville* case as an example of risk management in the environmental tort context. In *Wilsonville,* students see the risk management decisionmaking made by a number of different institutional actors. The decision makers include the project proponent, federal and state agencies, and courts reviewing the decision (at the behest of the local, affected citizens and public officials). This case is a very good introduction to risk management and the various ways in which the legal system "produces" risk management via authorities it grants to private parties, governmental officials, and courts.

Wilsonville presents a dramatic illustration of the competing perspectives that come into play in siting a hazardous waste disposal facility. The private parties originally selected a rural location adjacent to a small town in southwestern Illinois, not far from the city of St. Louis. The site was given approval by the relevant state agency, with some oversight by the federal EPA. This is one of the first facilities that was permitted under the newly enacted RCRA legislation. As it turns out, the site was flawed in regard to its subsurface geology and, possibly, as to other factors as well. The operations began at the site and, if nothing more, the trucks rambling through town and spilling small amounts of their contents constituted a nuisance. The town went to court and sought an injunction. The township, eventually, was joined by the Illinois attorney general in seeking an injunction against the maintenance of a nuisance and removal of materials that had already been discarded at the site. The case features excerpts that describe the testimony that led the court to its decision finding both the nuisance and the problem of sufficient magnitude that injunctive of relief was required. The concurrence of Justice Ryan is very interesting in that he focuses on the uncertainties involved and small chance of a very large hazard. He turns the case into a judicial opinion responding to a zero-infinity problem, finding it to be susceptible of the judicial resolution.

Page 122, C&Q #1: *Wilsonville* as compared to *Boomer*. Focusing first on similarities helps students see the cases as parallel situations, i.e., logical private decisions made in regard to the siting of necessary industrial facilities. Comparing beyond that begins to uncover differences, not all of which point toward a more plaintiff-friendly result for the *Wilsonville* case. For example, the real world tactile harms (dust, vibration, noise, etching, etc.) in *Boomer* are considerably more extensive than the extant harms (a small amount of in-transit spillage) in *Wilsonville*. Other differences may do more to help explain the differences in result. The key element, if the proofs are viewed uncritically, is the potential for harm in *Wilsonville*. Perhaps more important is the public perception of the potential harm and the public outrage caused by the waste site and the deceitful way in which it was promoted by SCA. For the judge, the fact that the public authorities, including the state attorney general have joined with the citizenry (who also are the electorate to whom he is accountable) may make it an easier matter to credit the testimony of the plaintiffs side of the case. What seems oddly lacking in *Wilsonville* is a careful balance of the equities in deciding on an injunction as was done in *Boomer*. See, Part D, §1 at page 163 of the text.

Pages 122-123, C&Q #2: Private parties as risk promoters. *What factors motivated SCA's decision to select the Wilsonville site as a repository for wastes generated primarily in the nearby St. Louis metropolitan area? Are those factors the same ones that ought to be considered by the IEPA and USEPA (or the courts) in their roles as risk managers?*

SCA was plainly influenced by the economic factors such as the lower land costs and the relative proximity of the site to St. Louis, where many of the materials involved were being generated. This note alerts the students to the fact that many siting decisions, particularly in the past, were made exclusively by the interested party who was building the facility. The subsequent rhetorical question regarding the role of the agencies points out that their concerns in risk management are quite different than the concerns that drive the siting decision for a private party. Students should see, however, that a rural locale is appropriate for SCA Services as a matter of risk management as well as economics.

Page 123, C&Q #3: Local politics, community involvement, and environmental risk management. *Was this an optimum result from a public policy standpoint?*

Probably not. The next rhetorical question points out that moving the material from the present site was probably riskier than leaving it there.

Should the courts have given more credence to USEPA's suggestion that exhumation and removal would pose a greater risk of explosion, among other things, than "containing" the site (e.g., laying a cement cap over the site to prevent further infiltration, building an underground slurry wall around the site, and installing leachate monitoring systems and "pump and treat" technology in case leaching of toxics into the groundwater did occur)?

As the tenor of the question implies, exhumation is a very risky choice, almost certainly more risky than improving the present site's monitoring and leachate controls.

Should the courts have considered the comparative economic costs of both alternatives?

In fact, it took one year and cost five million dollars--in 1981 dollars--to perform the court-ordered remediation. At this juncture the students will have a hard time deciding if that is expensive or not, but it is worth trying to get them to decide what the costs of the alternatives are, including the supposed nightmare of having toxins leach from the site and migrate through the mineshafts and then find their way into water supplies in sufficient concentrations to matter, and then someone has to ingest it and have a toxic reaction. What may happen is that the students will begin to see that the zero side (unlikeliness) of the zero-infinity problem renders the possibility of harm quite remote. Moreover, in comparison many Superfund sites and other types of toxic exposure, the infinity side of this problem (the harm that might occur as a result of a release) is not large. Recall that the aquifer that might become contaminated has only one active well serving livestock, a future dwelling that plans to use well water, and any release that could, via a tortuous path, reach the Mississippi River, would be so greatly diluted as to be unlikely to cause harm. Bringing down the likelihood of migration even more is the fact that there is still time to install monitoring at the site before release. Even a post-release cleanup or containment effort (e.g., pump and treat or slurry wall) would not cost much, especially in comparison to the multi-million dollar known cost of relocating the waste and creating risks at the new site.

What about the risks of transporting the wastes offsite and depositing them in another landfill that might pose even greater risks than the Wilsonville site?

The Resource Conservation and Recovery Act (RCRA), set the standards for other dumps, but RCRA was the same law that set the standards that SCA met at Wilsonville. Thus, it would seem that other sites would not be materially safer, and exhumation and transport was demonstrably risky.

To what extent are common law courts capable of determining the overall public interest in the context of lawsuits between specific litigants?

If it is riskier to move the material than to leave it in place, isn't the better course of action to leave it in place? Moreover, as this latter question asks, when the experts are saying that leaving it in place is the better course of action, on what basis is a court justified in overruling that expert opinion. That might be a policy choice about how to respond to outrage, but if that is so, then the courts seem to be the wrong branch of government to make hazardous waste policy. That seems to be a legislative function and the legislature delegated the details to the agency, not the court. This argument is worth exploring as a foreshadowing of the Huber excerpt that appears in Chapter 4 at page 271.

Wilsonville presents a marked contrast to *Boomer*. The Illinois Supreme Court is willing to take on the public health concerns and make (usurp?) the risk management decision. It is worth comparing the two cases to see whether the comparative judicial activism of the Illinois court is justified. Students at this juncture may still side with the result reached by the Illinois court, but those taking a more dispassionate view of the facts of *Wilsonville* may be less inclined to agree that the Illinois Supreme Court is correct.

Pages 123-124, C&Q #4: Administrative agencies as risk managers. *What, then, explains the lackluster performance of the state and federal agencies in the Wilsonville case? What explains the willingness of those public agencies to support, through the grant of so many permits and other favorable actions, a project that they later came to view as fundamentally flawed, sufficiently so that the State of Illinois filed suit against SCA on their behalf?*

The answer to this question is, necessarily somewhat speculative. The best guess is that the agency was just becoming familiar with the nuances of RCRA and its administration. Moreover, once the site was approved, the agency very likely relied on that decision in making its subsequent decisions to permit the deposit of material at the facility. It is probable that the action of the Illinois Attorney General was, at least in part, politically motivated.

Page 124, C&Q #5: Risk, scientific uncertainty, and expert testimony. *In the Wilsonville case, why were plaintiffs' experts believed rather than defendants' experts? Whose witnesses were better prepared to testify regarding the actual possibilities of release of materials from the Wilsonville site? In the ordinary case where individual citizens sue a large corporate defendant, whom would you expect to present the better qualified and prepared expert witnesses? Did the joinder of the Illinois Attorney General on the plaintiffs' side in this case alter the usual imbalance of resources?*

It is difficult to be sure why plaintiffs' experts fared better in the litigation than did the defendant's, but some speculations are possible. First, the trial court was located in the vicinity of the site, and the fact finding (whether by judge and/or jury) is going to be done by persons who empathize with the citizens of Wilsonville. This case gets tried in Macoupin County. It is a bit of an overstatement, but the entire county has an interest in what they perceive as ridding the county of an environmental threat foisted on them by apparently deceitful representations made by SCA to the Wilsonville community. It also appears that the plaintiffs' experts did more to give site-specific testimony than did the experts presented by the defense. In some additional historical research we have done about the case, it does appear that the decision of the Illinois Attorney General to become an advocate on the plaintiffs' side of the case was important to securing and paying for the testimony of the experts.

Page 124, C&Q #6: *Wilsonville* as environmental injustice. *Apart from the previously identified economic motivation facing SCA Services, are there other factors that might have influenced a decision to site a hazardous waste landfill at this clearly inadequate location?*

Our research seems to indicate that *Wilsonville* was not an environmental justice case, at least not in regard to having a discernible racial component. What is true is that Wilsonville was a poor community having little political clout and lower land prices. This made it a target of opportunity in the siting process conducted by the private entrepreneur.

It is premature for the students to be able to answer a question regarding whether a disposal facility siting statute might have prevented a bad siting decision in the *Wilsonville* case. The cross reference is intended to alert students to the fact that there are such commissions. What becomes interesting later in the year is to use *Wilsonville* as a hypothetical for testing the various statutes that are described in Chapter 25.

PAGES 125-128: *Schenectady Chemical Company*

Pages 125-128. Public nuisance. Public nuisance provides some special advantages to environmental plaintiffs, and offers extraordinary evolutionary possibilities for the incorporation of evolving public rights and private responsibilities.

First, the *Schenectady Chemical* case provides an interesting tactical example, where the government of New York found it more expedient to proceed for a remedy under public nuisance than under its own statutory laws. That deserves comment. To prove the statutory case, a series of administrative procedures and extensive testing would be required, with statutorily-defined negotiations over an extended period of time. Under public nuisance the state could move straightforwardly for essentially the same remedy - defendant's payment for clean-up (under a common law restoration damages remedy, noted later at page 190). There is virtually no question that defendant's activity constituted a public nuisance as well as a private nuisance.

Predecessor liability and public nuisance? For a court that was willing to allow public nuisance theories to be argued by a plaintiff to address the environmental contamination of its property by a prior owner of the same parcel, see Westwood Pharmaceuticals v. Nat. Fuel Gas Dist., 737 F.Supp. 1272, order affirmed 964 F.2d 85 (2d Cir. 1992).

Page 127, C&Q #1: Why public nuisance? The greater efficiency of public nuisance is undoubtedly the major answer. *What did the defendant know was "substantially certain" to occur, in order to allege and find civil intent?* The *Schenectady Chemical* court scarcely discusses the civil intent culpability element; apparently it was enough for the court that the company dumped on the Loeffel site with knowledge of the contractor's sloppy methods and the danger of toxic contamination in the event of improper disposal. The court may further have drawn upon the "continuing" nature of the contamination: once the toxics started to leak, the defendant was apparently apprised of the fact, and failed to stop the continuing leakage.

Is the balancing of equities in a remediation case the same as in Boomer? Remediation is quite a different matter, compared to injunctions requested merely to stop injurious conduct. As to the balance underlying equitable remedies, it seems realistic to say that in public nuisance, public values obviously must be considered in the balance as to whether an injunction will issue (thereby diverging from Judge Bergan's assertion in *Boomer* that a court cannot consider broad public questions in a private nuisance setting). Beyond that, there appears to be a practical presumption, at least where the public nuisance plaintiff is a *governmental* unit, for the award of injunctive relief.

As to the balance of equities in public nuisance, it should be noted that *damages* as well as injunctive orders are available. This part of public nuisance law is little developed. Where a government plaintiff is suing for damages, there should theoretically be no balancing of equities at all, either in the elements of an intentional public nuisance tort, or as to the amount of damages.

What about private plaintiffs in public nuisance? When they recover public nuisance damages, what would be the measure of damages, and what becomes of the compensation fund? This question has scarcely been considered in the case law, but is a fascinating point.

If private plaintiffs can recover a large fund on behalf of the public, are they then free to go and spend it as they will, or must they set up a compensation/restoration funding mechanism? We believe that public nuisance damages, though theoretically a legal remedy, nevertheless sound in equity under the "common fund" reasoning encountered in public interest fee-shifting and similar doctrines. This makes it likely that the funds are held not for personal use and benefit, but for purposes for which the common fund exists.

Page 127, C&Q #2: Vicarious liability. *Did Schenectady Chemical create the nuisance, or was it created by Loeffel, the independent contractor?* This raises the vicarious liability–independent contractor issue. One answer is that this liability is based on an implicit finding of strict liability for the disposal, overriding the independent contractor bar. In that regard, it also can be described as a non-delegable duty. The *Schenectady Chemical* case indicates how courts are not hesitant to extend liability retroactively, despite the old doctrines that insulated corporations through independent contractors. The opinion, at page 126, showed that there were several theories under negligence, intentional nuisance, and strict liability, by which the court would ignore the traditional buffer against liability of an independent intermediary.

Page 127, C&Q #3. Aquifers attract toxics. Self-explanatory.

Page 128, C&Q #4: Public nuisance actions for contamination of public drinking water supplies. The widespread public resource nature of the harm and availability of a public entity plaintiff (the water service provider that serves the public) render this setting a suitable one for public nuisance treatment.

PAGES 128-134: *Spur Industries*

Pages 128-134. The *Spur* case. *Spur,* although sounding in public nuisance, is brought by a private party as plaintiff. The private plaintiff, however, is not a completely sympathetic character. (Beyond whatever else may be charged against Del Webb in relation to the facts of the case, along with Dan Topping, Webb owned the New York Yankees baseball team. If that is not character assassination enough, Webb and Topping sold the team to George Steinbrenner.) Here, Del Webb Development Co. clearly used the public nuisance action to avoid a problem of incompatible adjoining land uses that it had helped to create. As the court's opinion indicated, Webb decided consciously to move out into this agricultural area to commence building, and later to move south toward the Spur operation, contemplating this lawsuit would improve its original investment position.

Spur can be used to show the requirement of special injury standing that is the traditional rule for private plaintiffs attempting to bring public nuisance actions. Of greater interest is the nature of the public nuisance in *Spur.* Flies and smells clearly offended public sensitivities, although there appears to have been no evidence of health consequences or injury to property. A generation ago, would such conditions out in the middle of the desert have been considered sufficient basis for a public nuisance action? Evolving public sensitivities seem to carry the potential for expanded public nuisance liability. (See C&Q #3, page 132.)

Although the expanding judicial recognition of non-traditional public nuisance conditions raises some interesting questions about judges acting as legislative policy-makers (See C&Q #6, page 133), it is clear that the phenomenon of expanded public nuisance coverage is going to continue. In the Alaska oil spill case, Alaska based its lawsuit in part on public nuisance. C&Q #4 on page 132 raises a number of credible novel applications of the doctrine. Further, since public nuisance straightforwardly concerns itself with "public senses" including aesthetic sensibilities, it is likely to take the lead in aesthetic tort situations. In 1975, for instance, an investment group was on the verge of building a hundred-foot long nightclub in the shape of a Spanish galleon ship-in-a-bottle (really) on a ridge adjoining the Great Smoky Mountains National Park, a project whose financing collapsed only when law students threatened a public nuisance action based on injury to the visual prospects within the wilderness areas of the Park. Would this suit have succeeded? One of us thought it might.

Page 131, C&Q #1: The twist in *Spur*. *Is Spur a case of comparative fault?* Spur's liability is based on civil intent, and it is altogether likely that Spur saw what was happening to his newly imported neighbors who lived in Sun City. What is likewise apparent, it that Del Webb's initiative in the siting of Sun City so near to the lands of Spur weighed in the court's strange remedy. *Next time?* Webb will let a suffering resident bring the suit next time, thereby not being a party to the case and most likely sidestepping the requirement of paying for the injunction. *If Webb lacked funds to pay?* The court might have hesitated in shutting down Spur, instead leaving Webb to buy off homeowners. *Judicial land-use Solomonizing?* This contextual balancing certainly looks like it. For some old public nuisance environmental cases, see *American Smelting,* 158 Fed. 225 (1907) *U.S. v. Luce,* 141 Fed. 385 (1905).

Pages 131-132, C&Q #2: The "right-to-farm" debate. The thrust of right-to-farm legislation is to change the common law and immunize farms from nuisance liability. In a sense, this is a legitimate political expression of the public will through its elected representatives regarding community norms - what is considered "unreasonable interference" - i.e., farming activity in what is still a farm dominated area is not an interference with community expectations as to what constitutes quiet enjoyment of a parcel. In that way, as an expression of community will, it is not a case in which one neighbor, the farmer, places a servitude of smell on its neighbor; the property law of the state now says that the neighbor did not have a "right" to be free of such a smell in such a location in the first place. The problematic cases that raise serious takings claims, if there are any, ought to be ones that involve a major diminution in value, where the adversely affected neighbor has suffered a loss of most or all economic value. See generally, Chapter 23. In these settings that will not be the case - what will be taken is, at most, the very high value use of the would-be-residential parcel for use as a residence. The parcel can still be farmed, or used in other ways that are consistent with the region. Moreover, to the extent that some right-to-farm statutes are drawn with reference to regional character, which changes over time, as the city and suburbs "encroach" on the farming sector, the character of the area will be changed and the protection of the legislation may be withdrawn. In those cases also, the growth of the urban and suburban areas create an economic climate in which continued farming, while possible, is likely to give way to the economic incentives generated by the prospect of development for higher valued uses. What is probably in order, if protecting farming is to be assured, is a combination of right to farm and zoning.

Page 132, C&Q #3: The tactical advantages of public nuisance. *What tactical advantages did Webb get from using public nuisance?* Our answers follow the question in the text.

Would Boomer have gained from filing in public nuisance? Most certainly, not only in broadening the range and avoiding estoppels, but also in forcing the judge to realize that the public interest in favor of an injunction would legitimately have to be weighed in the remedy balancing. As noted previously, if Del Webb is not a party to the case, the remedy that requires the cost of Spur's relocation be paid by Del Webb is unlikely to be advanced.

Pages 132-133, C&Q #4: A widening role for environmental public nuisance? *How far can the tort be extended?* Our answer is that all the settings hypothesized might be appropriate for the evolving public nuisance doctrine, which can respond to novel recognitions of public harms – not only to health and property, but also to aesthetics and the senses.

Page 133, C&Q #5: Public nuisance/private plaintiffs. (Public nuisance standing) *Isn't is paradoxical that in order to represent public values in public nuisance actions, private plaintiffs have to prove their interests are substantially different from the public's?* Yes. The anachronism derives from the criminal law/prosecution-as-official-function history of the tort. There is only a secondary level at which the test serves as a litmus for interest sufficient to ensure that the private person suing in public nuisance is an adequate litigant. A third reason for having a limitation is the need to limit the class of potential public nuisance plaintiffs so that the defendant, who manages to prevail in defending a public nuisance claim, cannot be harassed by a series of parallel lawsuits.

Pages 133-134, C&Q #6: Judicial zoning under public nuisance? *"Judicial zoning"?* Yes. *Would the court have enjoined Webb's southward march if a timely action had been brought by Spur?* It sounds as if that might indeed have occurred, but what cause of action? Perhaps merely a declaratory judgment that Webb and Webb's grantees would have no bootstrapped claims against Spur's flies and smells. That judgment, recorded on Webb's title, would probably have allayed the threat.

The judges' role in dictating land uses? Problematic, but inevitable and therefore an invitation to serious efforts at rural land use planning.

Pages 134-137. Borland, Trespass, and Other torts. The trespass materials (focusing on "*trespass quaere clausum fregit,*" physical trespass that "breaks into the plaintiff's close') offer interesting examples of advantages of this cause of action, in terms of longer statutes of limitations, longer periods of damage recovery, etc. In some cases quite conservative courts have seemed to be readier to grant an injunction in trespass cases than in nuisance cases, focusing on the defendant's physical invasion of plaintiff's premises, on the rationale that "a man's home is his castle," and in other cases, that "it is by protecting the little person in his domain that each American is given the opportunity to compete, and to follow the American dream." Some such psychological advantages may also attach to the trespass action.

Page 136, C&Q #1: Trespass and tactics. Comments are self-explanatory

Page 136, C&Q #2: How far can trespass go? It has been applied to light photons and invisible fluoride ions. Electromagnetic waves and ugly views would be pushing it.

Pages 136-137, C&Q #3: Defenses to trespass and nuisance. *The "no-market value loss" defense.* We believe that trespass liability attaches not just for the use values foregone, but also to address the "violation" of plaintiff's space represented by unauthorized entry into the plaintiff's close (quaere clausum fregit). This correlates well with the overall view of environmental torts taken at the beginning of the chapter - there is a reason for the L (liability), here, protecting the well-settled long honored right of exclusive possession.

PAGES 137-141: The Role of Negligence

Pages 137-141. Negligent nuisance and negligence. This material is a follow-on to the effort to review and describe tort law as it relates to environmental settings. As such, it explores the concepts of duty and breach and particularly the role of foreseeability in negligence cases. This is important because the use of negligence in environmental tort settings has the tactical advantage of putting defendant's conduct on trial, not just its results. Thus, when the conduct seems to be substandard, but the injuries caused are a bit surprising, the *Palsgraf* debate springs back into relevance.

Page 139, C&Q #1: Standards of care. This material is all textual and emphasizes the means by which the standard of care may be erected in a negligence proceeding. It emphasizes the extent to which regulatory standards can be imported as the standard, and the failure of defendant to comply with the standard can serve as proof of negligence.

Page 140, C&Q #2: Custom, regulatory compliance, and state of the art as satisfaction of the standard of care. The idea of this note is to walk the students through the various means by which a defendant might attempt to rebut the thrust of the negligence claim that asserts the defendant's conduct is substandard. In essence, the defendant, in each instance, attempts to prove conformity with an independently set standard, whether it is custom, industry practice, regulatory compliance, or state of the art. The obvious point of the note is that those standards are not, necessarily, relevant standards for determining whether defendant's conduct was negligent (exposed plaintiff to an unreasonable risk of harm) under the circumstances. As the proof moves along the continuum from custom to state-of-the-art, however, the likelihood that it falls short of what is reasonable under the circumstances diminishes.

Pages 140-141, C&Q #3: Deterrence, the role of benefit-cost analysis in determining negligence, and cost internalization. *Does the threat of negligence verdict deter polluters?* The note tries to sketch the standard economists answer of both "Yes," and "No," the former when the costs of avoidance of pollution are less than the expected costs of accidents (pollution) and the latter when the expected costs of pollution control exceed the expected costs of damage actions. The note next moves onto the question of whether "optimal" results (least total social cost) that the theorists claim will be realized in negligence actions, even if it occurs, is the right target as a social result. Attitudes regarding either culpability or cost internalization that tend toward the view that plaintiff has a right to be free of pollution and that all costs should be borne by the polluter also tend toward the conclusion that negligence is not the right rule because it systematically undercompensates victims and under-internalizes costs.

Page 141, C&Q #4: Less obvious tactical advantages of negligence claims. The note points out that negligence may result in a verdict payable from insurance when no recovery might be had on other theories due to insolvency of the defendant and also as a means of coming within a limited waiver of sovereign immunity.

PAGES 141-145: Strict Liability. Different definitions of strict liability as a basis for loss-shifting. The coursebook notes that torts are generally subject to three different theories that consider the qualitative nature of defendant's conduct as part of the basis for loss-shifting - negligence, intentional action [under the civil intent definition], or strict liability. It should be noted that in some states the definition of strict liability has actually gone far beyond the Restatement of Torts version, allowing a form of strict liability without regard to whether there is "abnormally dangerous activity." In Maryland, for instance, the tort law seems to be interpreted that

> Maryland has long adhered to the rule that proof of nuisance focuses not on the possible negligence of the defendant, but on whether there has been unreasonable interference with the plaintiff's use and enjoyment of his or her property.... We have held that where a trade or business as carried on interferes with the reasonable and comfortable enjoyment by another of his property, a wrong is done to a neighboring owner for which an action lies.... Virtually any disturbance of the enjoyment of the property may amount to a nuisance so long as the interference is substantial and unreasonable and such as would be offensive or inconvenient to the normal person. Washington Sanitary Comm'n v. CAE-link Corp, 622 A.2d 745 at IA (Ct.App. MD, 1993).

Such phrasing of the rules, in this case for private nuisance, inevitably undercuts any express consideration of the defendant's intentional or negligent conduct, converting the entire question to the *unreasonable effect* upon plaintiff irrespective of defendant, and making payment of damages to cover plaintiff's injuries a straightforward cost of doing business. In a sense the nuisance calculus begins to look more like strict liability and a rote effort to internalize all costs that exceed threshold annoyance that all citizens are expected to tolerate in a complex industrialized society. In practice we suspect the word "unreasonable" nevertheless is applied so as to incorporate some consideration of defendant's actions, as well as effects upon plaintiffs. The continuing confusion about defining the different bases of responsibility and the extent to which they require culpability in nuisance cases shows little sign of abating.

The instinct for many environmental plaintiffs' attorneys is to go straight for a strict liability basis for actions in the nature of nuisance. This section is intended to note the availability of strict liability, but also its parallelism with intentional nuisance. In many cases the two will be substantially equivalent because fault is not at issue in intentional tort, properly viewed. If at any point in the liability horizon the defendant should be substantially certain that harm of a certain character will occur to a certain class of plaintiffs from its actions, why bother showing that its actions are "abnormally dangerous'? These issues are discussed further in the answers to questions immediately following. Strict liability does avoid certain defenses, like independent contractor cut-offs, and is more familiar to judges. Likewise the inherently dangerous character of defendant's conduct may make a trier of fact more comfortable in shifting the loss back to the person who put the course of events in motion even though that person acted with care.

Pages 144-145, C&Q #1: Why strict liability? And C&Q #2: "Abnormally dangerous." These two questions focus on the fact that in *Branch*, as in many other environmental toxic cases, the courts will turn to strict liability out of a sense that there should be no-fault liability. It is not obvious that storage of waste water as in *Branch* is an "unnatural" use of the land as in *Rylands*, nor that it creates the abnormal danger to human life of direct dramatic injury that characterizes the traditional strict liability realm. Nor is it a situation where danger can not be avoided through the exercise of due care (as with explosives or poisons threatening the safety of the populace). In *Branch*, as in many toxic pollution cases, the injury is incremental and mitigatable by the plaintiffs when they recognize by smell or taste that there is a problem with their water. The judge in *Branch* looks at two bases for awarding strict liability: First, a parade of cases where courts had similarly used strict liability in pollution. Second, a reference to public policy and the court's underlying motivation that it felt that these are the kinds of costs that defendants should bear as a normal cost of doing business. The cases cited are not all obvious cases for the application of strict liability, though some of them, involving mine-blasting and sudden direct poisoning of water supplies, are. What they may represent is the fact that in American jurisprudence, other courts were motivated to do what the judge talks about second in *Branch*, extending automatic liability as a cost of doing business. But if that is the case, in many if not all cases of non-accidental contamination, intentional tort would be a fully equivalent basis for liability. Instead strict liability is used to avoid the perceived shortcomings of normal negligence and intentional tort doctrine. Where spills are sudden and accidental, intentional tort may not be so available because not substantially foreseeable, and so strict liability will continue to be a strategic avenue to recovery.

Page 145, C&Q #3: Foreseeability. The key to making Western Petroleum's activity liable in intentional tort is the foreseeable substantial certainty of the injury to the plaintiffs. *What is Davis's argument?* It is that by now such underground transport is completely foreseeable. Footnote 18 (original footnote 6) as noted in the comment would allow the court to find civil intent from what the petroleum company either should have known in the beginning or subsequently should have known upon the repeated complaints conveyed by the plaintiffs.

Might Branch just as well have been litigated under intentional nuisance? We think so, not seeing any marked doctrinal advantages here for strict liability.

Page 145, C&Q #4: Strict liability for what harms? *Why does the Branch opinion go into negligence and willfulness evidence?* As the text notes, it is not necessary to the strict liability action, but is very helpful to the punitive damages count, at page 175.

Strict liability for what harms? This material is intended to emphasize the role of Restatement §519(2), that liability in strict liability is supposed to be "limited to the kind of harm, the risk of which makes the activity abnormally dangerous." Instead courts tend to find an activity abnormally dangerous, and then not parse the different kinds of injuries arising consequentially from that activity to determine whether they should be compensated under strict liability. In the cases noted in the comment, or considering the economic injuries caused downstream by Allied Chemical's Kepone pollution (noted in *Pruitt* at page 160), injuries for which recovery is sought seem quite different from harms which would be the ones that serve to make the pollution subject to strict liability.

On the other hand, the Restatement does not make it clear that "danger" must be a serious danger to human life and property, although that is probably what was intended. Therefore it could be argued that when strict liability is applied to contamination of ground water or for other injuries in the environment, even where there is no likelihood of severe human injury, the words of the Restatement may be evolving to incorporate environmental ecosystemic harms. Courts may be recognizing that dangers that extend over time - as well as sharp, immediate, drastic injuries - deserve recognition.

Intentional tort, however, may still may offer advantages in some settings: in workers' comp occupational injuries, for instance, strict liability and negligence are overridden by statute, but intentional tort theories may not be.

Page 145, C&Q #5: Environmental applications of other tort theories. Reminding students of the potential utility of other tort causes of action, you might refer again to the Allied Chemical Kepone disaster, in which Allied's products liability failure to warn proved to be the most effective threat inducing Allied to settle with victims.

For additional material on how plaintiffs sometimes seek remedies based on traditional torts in order to avoid difficult causation see Christopher McAuliffe, Resurrecting an Old Cause of Action for a New Wrong: Battery as a Toxic Tort, 20 B.C. ENVTL. AFF. L. REV. 265(1993). For other possibilities under battery theories, see Field v. Philadelphia. Electric, 565 A.2d at 1173 (radioactive gases) the *Firestone* case, 661 F.Supp. at 193 (which, however, thought intentional tort would not lie because malice had not been shown) National Steel, 607 F.Supp. 1430 (1985, battery on workers and neighbors) and Mink v. Univ. of Chicago, 460 F.Supp. 713 (1978, DES tests).

Defenses

Pages 146-152: Defenses. The first defense level is the defendant's denial or rebuttal of the plaintiffs' factual allegations. In environmental cases, the most obvious factual denial typically is of *causation*. Where there are multiple potential causative defendants, and uncertain epidemiological proof that the plaintiff's injuries were caused by defendant's actions, the factual rebuttal is often determinative. These questions are considered first in

Part C of this Chapter that begins at page 152, and again in Chapter 4 when the question is that of causation in toxic tort cases. In many "conventional" environmental torts cases, often it is enough to note that (as in the *Boomer* case, for example) there is apparently no question that it was the Atlantic Cement Co. that caused Boomer's injuries, and that they were substantial.

The affirmative defenses, however, offer defendant an extensive opportunity to make further arguments, and the *Schenectady Chemical* case offers a laundry list. In teaching the case and its subsequent materials, it may be useful to go paragraph by paragraph, characterizing and analyzing each defense quickly, asking, "does this defense implicate larger societal balances that should play a part in an environmental accounting?" Several defenses arguably raise larger issues. The statute of limitations and vested prescriptive rights arguments deal with society's attempts to obtain closure, so that private decisions and economic enterprises do not have continuing disruptive possibilities of uncertain future liability. Coming-to-the-nuisance would be another form of this kind of certainty-estoppel defense. Its modern eclipse indicates that, at least in modern America, the status quo is not guaranteed a right in effect, to, control the development and use of neighboring property.

Another argument raising public policy issues is the allegation of preemption by statute of common law actions, a defense that typically is expressly denied by the terms of state pollution statutes, as noted in *Schenectady Chemical*. It echoes, however, in the permit defense and merits a bit of discussion. For example, you might ask the students why the Atlantic Cement Company's valid State of New York official air pollution permit should not be the grant of a "right" to pollute up to that level. It can be argued that the common law and police power regulations operate in two different theatres. In most cases the common law adjudicates the conditions of the neighborhood, while the public permit applies a minimum average "slowest-boat" state-wide standard. What if, however, the state permit was based on a review of local conditions? At that point the students can wrestle with the difference between what the state is purporting to guard against, and what the neighbors are suffering and wish to bring to a common law court. Another way to ventilate this issue is to ask whether the existence of a valid permit, although not a defense against damages for harm to individuals, is nevertheless an expression of the state's authority that the activity ought to be allowed to operate on those terms, and therefore, be a good defense against an injunction. Although a somewhat closer question, this latter claim is still deficient if the balance of equities, that includes public interest considerations that might be linked to proven adverse health effects, tilts in favor of an injunction. The permit is, in that light, a prospective, provisional judgment by the state that the level of harm is likely to be acceptable.

The prior discussion leads nicely into the primary jurisdiction defense (C&Q #3). If the students decide that just holding (and complying with) a valid state pollution permit is not enough to stop a private tort action, why not nevertheless transfer the controversy to an official agency for full official proceedings before the tort action is heard? This discussion allows a balancing of the arguments for uniformity, expertise, and division of labor in favor of the agency, against realistic arguments of administrative torpor, the availability of damages and injunctions in common law systems to those suffering substantial injury as a result of defendant's activities, etc.

Page 147, C&Q #1: Evaluating *Schenectady Chemical's* defenses. *Which of Schenectady's defenses deserve legitimate attention?* Probably the most challenging defense here is a possible time-bar argument: You can ask your students, *"Is this a permanent nuisance, so the statute has run, or is it a continuing nuisance?"* The *Schenectady* court quickly implies that this is a continuing nuisance, and goes onward.

Most courts treat this issue peremptorily as did *Schenectady Chemical*. The California Supreme Court, however, in Mangini v. Aerojet General Corp, 51 Cal. Rptr. 2d 272 (1996) appears recognize the *Potomac Electric* permanent nuisance/statute of limitations defense, described at C&Q #5, page 150. The permanent nuisance defense is a two-prong approach. Initially, plaintiffs suing under continuing nuisance must prove that (1) the problem is abatable and (2) the abatement can be done cost effectively - proof that the *Mangini* plaintiffs could not make in this case of massive TCE contamination. If plaintiffs fail on either of those proofs, the nuisance is deemed a "permanent nuisance" because it is either physically or economically cannot be abated, At that point, once the label permanent nuisance attaches, the statute of limitations can become a complete defense in tort, which was the case in *Mangini.* According to defense counsel for Aerojet, once the permanent nuisance is declared and once tort actions become time barred, the only remedies that remain available are under environmental compensation laws, such as CERCLA. The authors find this a most bizarre position - that the difficulty or expense of abatement can combine with the passage of a short limitations period combine to immunize a nuisance against any tort remedy that would otherwise be open to for neighbors. The rulings in the *Mangini* decision are even harder to fathom. First, the California Supreme Court affirms a JNOV overturning a $13M jury verdict. Second, the trial court - apparently in the alternative - found the claims for permanent nuisance either time-barred or inadequately proved (implying the plaintiff had the burden of proof on permanence). Third, the trial court apparently placed the burden of proof on the reasonableness of the cost of abatability on plaintiff, a view which was upheld by the Court of Appeals and the California Supreme Court. Finally, Aerojet was largely responsible for many of the delays that went into determining what cleanup was possible, but the plaintiffs were being charged with that time against their statute of limitations (Justice Mosk, outvoted 6-1 made this point in dissent). Finally, perhaps the strangest part of the *Mangini* court's ruling is its holding that the plaintiffs had not provided sufficient evidence that the hazardous waste contamination was reasonably abatable. That the contamination is abatable seems almost irrefutable, given that Aerojet had entered into a consent decree with EPA under CERCLA to remediate the site.

Page 148, C&Q #2: The permit defense. *Why shouldn't permit compliance always be a good defense?* The most obvious answer is that permits are usually set based on generic statewide or industry-wide factors, and do not purport to address the particular conditions of the neighborhood, which has been the particular focus of the common law since King Edward II. To override the local protections of the common law with a set of politically-derived administrative standards and procedures can leave local property owners bereft of protection.

That of course was the intention of the industry lobbyists who successfully passed the Alaska bill noted in the text, hoping to preempt environmental tort law. HB 178, signed by Gov. Wally Hickel on April 29, 1994, effectively repeals the common law in some environmental cases:

> ALASKA STATUTES §09.45.230. Actions based on private nuisance....
>
> (b) A person may not maintain an action under this section based upon an air emission or water or solid waste discharge, other than the

> placement of nuclear waste, where the emission or discharge was expressly authorized by and is not in violation of a term or condition of
>
> (1) a statute or regulation
>
> (2) a license, permit, or order that is...issued after public hearing by the state or federal government....
>
> (e) Notwithstanding other provisions of law...a person may not bring a civil action to enjoin or abate a private nuisance or to recover damages for a private nuisance unless the action is authorized by this section.

A precipitating cause of the amendment may have been a local community's efforts to resist massive air and water pollution discharges from a large foreign-owned paper pulp mill closely linked to a leading member of the state Senate. Your students may recognize the dramatic shift in the climate for Alaskan industry accomplished by this provision.

The common law is traditionally aimed at particular localized conditions; police power regulatory permits are typically set with reference to generalized state-wide minimum standards in a hurly-burly administrative process, and do not purport to be affirmative authorizations of a right to pollute to such levels.

Are there cracks in this statutory barricade? What is required to show "expressly authorized?" Does this amendment apply only to private nuisance actions, leaving the field open for inventive trespass and public nuisance actions?

As to the constitutional question - the fascinating issue of whether it violates private property due process rights to strip a landowner of her traditional tort protections - the amendment provided a fascinating fallback cover:

> (f) A person who is shielded under (b) of this section from a nuisance action shall indemnify, defend, and hold the state harmless from a claim or court for inverse condemnation, including damages, costs, and attorney fees, for which the state may become liable because of the air emission or wastewater or solid waste discharge for which the person is shielded by (b) of this section. The state shall immediately tender the defense of the inverse condemnation claim or court action to the person. The provisions of (b) of this section do not apply to shield the person, if the person fails to accept or refuses the tender of the defense. A person who prevails in the defense of the claim action for inverse condemnation described under this subsection shall be awarded attorney fees and costs.

You can ask your students, *"Is it unconstitutional to remove common law protections from local property owners?"* A remarkable article analyzing this question, concluding that rescissions of common law do violate substantive due process *(!)* is Jan Hasselman's "Alaska's Nuisance Statute Revisited: Federal Substantive Due Process Limits to Common Law Abrogation," 24 B.C. Envtl Aff. L.Rev. 346 (1997). A Fourth Circuit panel has explicitly held, however, that nothing in the due process clauses of federal or state constitutions prevents prospective abolition of common law causes of action. Dinh v. Rust International Corp. 974 F.2d 500 (4th Cir. 1992).

The Alaska amendment can be the basis for an interesting class discussion about statutory interpretation, the interaction between common law, statutes, and property rights, and politics. Alaska may be a special case, where industry has an almost unfettered control over the legislative process. Alaska has been called "the world's northernmost banana republic." See also J. Frohnmeyer, Extreme Conditions: Big Oil and the Transformation of Alaska (1993). Students can be invited to see how this proposed amendment fails to accomplish what its lobbyist sponsors thought they were doing, by focusing its terms upon private nuisance.

Page 148, C&Q #3: Primary jurisdiction. *Why do plaintiffs bemoan a primary jurisdiction finding?* It typically spells interminable delay before they can get back to court, in which time the record has been muddied by time and administrative process, with no hope for a damage recovery action until long afterwards. It is ironic and instructive to see corporate executives so eager to flee to the arms of the bureaucratic agencies they love to execrate, finding them preferable to the effectiveness of common law courts.

Page 149, C&Q #4: Is the utility of a facility a defense to liability? This note is largely textual. It attempts to stress the importance of separating the issue of liability from that of remedy. The utility of defendant's entity, in a balance of equities, will be a factor that weighs against an injunction, but it should not absolve the defendant from liability.

Pages 149-150, C&Q #5: Statutory preemption of common law? Statutory preemptions can be explicit or implicit.

What would be the consequence of putting the phrase "exclusive remedy" into a statute? It pretty clearly means that the lobbyists have successfully eliminated the potentially more-effective common law remedies otherwise available. (But see Jan Hasselman, Alaska's Nuisance Statute Revisited: Federal Substantive Due Process Limits to Common Law Abrogation, 24 B.C. Envtl Aff. L.Rev. 346 (1997).) The *Silkwood* excerpt shows how courts frequently construe a statutory preemption narrowly, limiting the nuclear safety preemptive override primarily to state statutes, not the continuation of traditional remedial state common law.

What about injunctions? The Supreme Court opinion in *Silkwood* doesn't think about this, but it seems to us that injunctive relief is far more similar to state statutory regulation than to compensatory or punitive damages, and to the extent that it tries to prescribe safety procedures, it would probably be preempted. The Supreme Court has not yet picked up on this idea, despite having had it presented as an option in International Paper Co. v. Ouelette, 479 U.S. 481 (1987). In that case, noted in the text at page 667, the Supreme Court allowed an interstate common law nuisance claim to go forward. (Recall that Illinois v. City of Milwaukee II, 451 U.S. 304 (1981), had previously found federal common law of interstate nuisance "displaced" by the Clean Water. Act.) The United States intervened in the case and argued in its brief that the permit granted under the CWA should prevent an injunction to a New York entity whose pollution damaged Vermont riparians. Instead, the Court ruled that the case could go forward, but it must proceed under New York nuisance law as a federally required choice of law principle, rather than Vermont nuisance law without regard to Vermont choice of law principles that otherwise would apply to the case. The rationale for the Court's ruling was that such regulated facilities should be able to look to the law of a single state, the source state, to determine their obligations in regard to the pollution caused by their operations.

A 1993 Maryland case raised the interesting question whether a sewage disposal plant that created noxious odors in a neighborhood could claim preemptive override against common law because it was specifically ordered to be constructed at that place by a series of federal court orders. The state court found that the federal authorities had directly mandated that the plant be built, but not how it should be built, so there remained open an area of conduct subject to nuisance liability. The court so held even though there was no evidence of negligence in construction of the plant, basing the defendant's liability upon the mere fact that it had caused unreasonable burden to the neighbors. (Washington Sanitary Commission v. CAE-link Corp, 622 A.2d 745 at I(B) (Ct. App. MD, 1993).

Page 150, C&Q #6: Statutes of limitation, other time bars, and prescriptive nuisances. *Do you see that "continuing nuisance" and "permanent nuisance" are not easily distinguishable?* The discussion comparing a "continuing nuisance" with a "permanent" nuisance should show that it is not at all clear how to distinguish them. A case like Boomer v. Atlantic Cement provides an example. The company's air pollution, if it had begun enough years prior to Boomer's suit so that the statute of limitations had run, could easily be said to meet the tests associated with permanent nuisances. No doubt the plant was intended to perform as it did from the very beginning, hence, if New York subscribed the to "permanent nuisance" doctrine, the statute would have run on the "permanent" nuisance. In our view, there is no legitimate basis for the "permanent nuisance" doctrine. Properly conceived, every day that a plant causes its neighbors to endure an unreasonable interference with quiet enjoyment is a violation of their rights and, therefore, is a continuing nuisance. That allows plaintiffs to litigate and recover for at least the past period of time that lies within the statute. To recognize the doctrine of "permanent" nuisance changes the ordinary statute of limitations into the virtual equivalent of a prescriptive easement having a far shorter than usual prescriptive period. That, obviously, is within the legislature's power, but it would be a most unusual thing for a court to convert an ordinary statute of limitations enacted as such into a legislated law of prescription without any hint that such was the legislature's intent. More pragmatically, contemporary courts are becoming more leery of finding "permanent" nuisances because of the increased modern emphasis on protection against environmental pollution, backed by many regulatory statutes at federal, state, and local levels.

Pages 160-161, C&Q #7: Coming to the nuisance. *Would a coming-to-the-nuisance defense have worked in Boomer?* Not likely. Boomer had been there first. Other questions here are self explanatory. It may be a good thing to emphasize the analytical flaws in the coming to the nuisance defense that are set forth in the text.

Page 151, C&Q #8: Releases from liability. The text is largely self-explanatory. The effect of the releases is a matter of state law and the students should be cautioned to check, for although the text states the majority position (release that is silent as to effect on claims against non-settlers, does not release the non-settlers), not all states have expressly adopted this position. The text also points out the important fact that settling tortfeasors are usually entitled to contribution protection. The reason for this is the goal of encouraging settlement, which is squarely behind the rule of non-contribution of settling tortfeasors.

Pages 151-152, C&Q #9: The best defense is a good offense? "SLAPPs." Students love the discussion of SLAPP suits as defensive techniques. There has been much discussion in the press recently about SLAPPs. An example in one of the author's experience regarded a canoe livery on the Delaware River. It was putting in flotillas of canoeists who did not know how to steer, supplied with kegs of beer. Raucous and disruptive behavior followed them downstream. The local government drafted an ordinance that required liveries to ensure that canoeists could steer, and prohibited alcohol beverages in canoes. Local landowners filed a public nuisance suit (which included claims of regular invasion of their property for urinary purposes). The canoe livery filed SLAPP suits: The local board members were sued for a million dollars each for "violating...civil rights by a confiscatory regulatory taking," and the public nuisance plaintiffs were sued for defamation for a million dollars. Both the ordinance and the public nuisance suit were quickly dropped in fear of the totally frivolous but nevertheless frightening SLAPP suit.

Students may wish to talk about SLAPP-backs: counter-claims or Rule 11 motions against SLAPP suits. To date there have been very few such retaliatory counter-claims against SLAPP suits, because SLAPP targets are chosen for their general lack of resources and knowledge of the legal system. This issue bears watching, and a search in Infotrack® should reveal several recent articles on point.

On June 17, 1996, the governor of Alaska vetoed H.B. 158 – a *pro*-SLAPP suit measure *(!)* passed by the Alaska Legislature which, on its face, was intended to reduce the number of "frivolous" lawsuits being brought by creative plaintiffs' attorneys. The effect of H.B. 158 would have been to encourage SLAPP suits, allowing for SLAPP claims even where citizens plaintiffs were successful on the merits! Although the Alaska bill was ultimately vetoed – due in large part to active opposition by environmental and civil rights organizations – it provides a striking example of the potential impact of tort reform on environmental legislation.

Page 152, C&Q #10: The strategies of environmental defendants. The material on defense strategies is self-explanatory.

Pages 152-163: Causation in Conventional Environmental Tort Suits

Page 153, C&Q #1: No causation-in-fact if it would have happened anyway. *Is the failure to fence a cause-in-fact?* This classic tort hypothetical is usually answered in the negative, sometimes using confusing language that would deem the reckless driving a "supervening cause" of the injury. Its point, of course, is to alert the students to the usual plaintiff's burden on the issue and the fact that defendant can seek exculpation on the basis of showing that its act is not the cause-in-fact. This issue takes on great prominence in toxic torts and, in that context, becomes the subject of special rules that take into account the difficulty of proving causation-in-fact in moving from toxic exposures to the subsequent onset of disease after the passage of a substantial period of time. Chapter 4 works with that problem at length. *What is the proper analysis when the acts of separate defendants, each of which is capable of doing all of the harm, join to cause injury to plaintiff? Can each defendant then deny that he or she was the cause-in-fact of the injury because the injury would have happened anyway?* This classic tort hypothetical is usually answered by holding both defendants' acts to be cause-in-fact of the injury, sometimes using the (confusing?) language that labels both acts "independent sufficient causes" of the injury. As the text hints, the defendants are then held jointly and severally liable, and if either pays a disproportionate share of the damage, a claim for contribution will lie against the other.

Pages 153-154, C&Q #2: Proving too much with "but for." This textual material is meant to sound two cautionary notes: (1) the scope of tort duties is relational or situational, and (2) remoteness of effects is a basis for limiting tort recoveries.

Section 2. Joint & Several Liability and Velsicol Chemical Corp. v. Rowe This material provides a refresher on joint and several liability, highlighting the role it plays in tort cases. The case involves recovery against Velsicol for all damages by a downwind victim of several upwind polluters. The key elements of joint and several liability, indivisibility of injury and that the defendant was a substantial factor in causing that injury are laid out quite plainly by the excerpt. The court also traces the reasons prompting the introduction of joint and several liability as it explains why it is no longer willing to honor its own earlier precedents rejecting the application of joint and several liability.

Page 157, C&Q #1: Problems of joint liability. *In Rowe, and the Landers and Michie cases Rowe discusses, is it clear that the plaintiffs have suffered a single harm from the air or water pollution?*

The plaintiffs have suffered a single type of harm in each of the three instances, but no single defendant is the cause-in-fact of the entire extent of the harm suffered. In fact, if each factory's dust and emissions were differentiable, it would be clear that Rowe had suffered several distinct, concurrent invasions.

What justifies "extending" the liability of each potential defendant? Is the extension effectively offset by the availability of an action for contribution?

The justification lies in the fact that plaintiff is an innocent tort victim and all of the defendants are wrongdoers vis-à-vis plaintiff. They are also in a better position (see Summers v. Tice) to ascertain who was responsible for what portion of the harm, if apportionment is to be made.

Page 158, C&Q #2: The "single bullet" problem. *What if it had been a "single bullet" injury, however?* The note answers this question by pointing to the convergence of several theories and doctrines, e.g., strict products/ultra-hazardous activities theories of cost and risk internalization, concert of action principles, etc. *A further extension is the "Blue Bus" theory: if plaintiff was injured by a fast-moving hit and run bus on a dark and lonely road one night, can you use the fact that 70 percent of the buses on that route belong to the Blue Bus Company to assess full (or 70 percent) liability against that defendant?* This is perhaps a bit tedious by now, asking yet again whether attributable/relative risk should be used by the legal system. In this setting, where the probabilities would serve as a basis for cost allocation among defendants in a non-pro rata contribution suit, it seems as enticing as it is going to get. Absent other, better evidence, what else is there?

Pages 158-159, C&Q #3: The power of joint and several liability. *What makes the availability of joint and several liability so important to plaintiffs?* The principal thrust of joint and several liability is to allow a plaintiff who can make out a case against any one of a group of joint tortfeasors to be assured of full relief even when the case or the collectibility of others in the group is uncertain. This goes a long way towards ensuring that plaintiffs are compensated, even in cases where the precise cause-in-fact contribution of various defendants may be hard to prove. This tactical advantage can be used to encourage settlements by one or more defendants that would be combined with contribution protection, thereby ensuring that each defendant caps its exposure at the amount of the settlement. This strategy is explored more fully in relation to the use of such tactis by EPA and private parties in the Superfund setting explored in Chapter 19.

Page 159, C&Q #4: Contribution and indemnity. *This use of FRCP 14 and the liberal joinder rules encourages efficiency by joining more of the issues in a single lawsuit, but it does not alter the plaintiff's option to enforce the ensuing judgment in toto against a single defendant. When is that option important?* When one or more of the defendants is uncollectible, joint and several liability shifts the risk/loss of uncollectibility from the plaintiff to the jointly and severally liable defendants. As previously noted, the plaintiff also is freed from proving allocation. *What avenues might a polluter in Rowe consider in trying to pay less than a pro rata amount?* They might compare their operating characteristics to that of the other defendants, items such as design capacity, pollution control devices in place, record regarding the types and amounts of fuel, or other indicia of the volume of emissions.

Pages 159-160, C&Q #5: Predecessor landowners' liability. *Can the prior owner of a contaminated parcel of land be held liable for common law damages when the toxics are subsequently discovered?* Yes, and, more relevantly to this part of the book, there is often joint and several liability with the current owner of the parcel under CERCLA and some state tort laws and mini-CERCLAs. This is a note without a home in this edition, so it seems a bit out of place. It might better be placed on page 198 after C&Q #4.

Proximate Causation

As noted before, this volume treats proximate causation as an inquiry unto itself. Some commentators treat proximate cause as an umbrella concept that includes cause-in-fact inquiries as well. Under the present terminological structure, the proximate cause inquiry functions as a limit on recoveries for environmental damages that are causally linked to tortious acts of defendant, but are considered too remote to be compensable as a matter of sound loss-shifting policy.

Pages 160-162, Pruitt v. Allied Chemical Corp.

This section uses a Kepone follow-up case to survey a basic issue: *How far down a chain of foreseeable economic causation can awards be made?* Judge Mehrige is unwilling to stay with the old rule of no such recovery, but is left with no logical reason not to award all economic losses directly provable to have occurred foreseeably.

The far-flung interconnectedness of environmental causation is the backdrop of this section. Whereas environmental analysis can trace the effects of an action along extended chains of real causation, courts typically have limited liability through theories of foreseeability and proximate cause, motivated by ideas of justiciability and pragmatic principles of toleration of certain remote injuries as *damnum absque injuria.*

In the Kepone case it is clear the chain of consequences traveled far and severely, spreading out from the Allied and LSP plants and extending throughout the Chesapeake Bay region. Kepone illustrates pollution's negative multiplier effects.

The question posed in *Pruitt* is whether the Court will hold the line of liability at physical damages and direct economic injuries, or will extend liability further to encompass real injuries suffered by real plaintiffs farther down the chain of indirect economic causation. In many environmental cases like Kepone or the Alaska oil spill, direct physical injuries to private property are limited. (What do "direct" and "indirect" economic injury mean?) Absent injury to a plaintiff's physical property, courts have generally held that economic damages are "indirect," sort of by analogy to the physical injury emotional distress rule, noted later in Chapter 4.

But the rule against indirect economic recoveries is starting to erode, as noted in Judge Merhige's opinion. It is clear that indirect injuries were completely foreseeable when the executives of Allied and LSP dumped poisons surreptitiously into the upstream water courses. By what principle is liability held not to travel as far as the foreseeability? In these cases, moreover, it is clear that defendants can be held to have "civil intent" sufficient to base intentional torts, rather than just negligence actions. Yet the traditional rule would refuse compensation for injuries suffered, even if there is proved to have been an intentional tort, i.e., that defendant knew to a "substantial certainty" that persons in the situation of plaintiffs would be injured.

Judge Merhige tries to be Solomonic, and flounders. By allowing one stage of indirect recovery he breaches the traditional rule, but with no standard for restricting further recoveries except that he says so. Where do you draw the line, if you allow indirect economic recoveries? It is clear, as the Judge notes, that recoveries beyond the first level (commercial fishermen and marina and tackle shops) would not constitute "double recovery" at each subsequent stage, because the plaintiffs in each of the various classes (which you can chart out on the board in a schematic sketch of the Bay, category by alphabet category) are claiming *net*, not gross losses, and although these are cumulative they are not redundant. But could the liability, once the traditional wall has been breached, extend to a restaurant in Washington, DC, which specializes in Chesapeake seafood and has suffered a loss? That loss too was probably clearly foreseeable, but we sympathize with the Judge in this case, noting that there has to be an articulatable proximate cause boundary for liability, beyond mere de minimis limits. Or is there? Some students will say that a company that acts wrongfully in such a case should be liable for all foreseeable injuries that derive therefrom.

In a number of jurisdictions, the ban on indirect economic damages is falling, at least as a matter of state law, especially where plaintiff had no reasonable possibility to mitigate the losses. In Massachusetts one such case used public nuisance theories to breach the doctrine. Stop n Shop v. Fisher, 444 N.E.2d 368 (Mass. 1983).

Page 162, C&Q #1: The rationale for barring indirect damages. *Is there any compelling reason for the rule barring indirect economic harm recoveries?* The rule barring indirect economic recoveries seems backed by historical happenstance grounded in the remedies provided under the formulary writ system that was inherited from the English. Modern courts have largely dispensed with this limitation and regularly combine tort recoveries for both bodily injury, property damage, and economic loss. The "indirect" nature of the losses also parallels some limitations on tort and contract damages that are deemed "special" or "consequential."

Page 162, C&Q #2: Of double-counting and foreseeable losses. *What is the double-counting danger?* The judge rightly notes that the proposed recoveries of lost profits in the chain of causation are not double recoveries. *Is it correct to limit recovery for allowed* *claims to replacement value of the investment?* Allowing arguments about speculative lost benefits-of-bargains strikes us as problematic. The sale, however, should not totally disqualify the claim. There is no reason to treat the transferee of a going concern worse than would have been the treatment given the transferor had the transfer not occurred. *Is it fair that the judge drew the compensation line at the water's edge?* It would seem that economic injuries are potentially as accurately provable as direct physical injuries, so that the procrustean line-drawing here is merely prudential, not institutionally necessary. The court's holding is best viewed as a step in a probable evolutionary progression that will ultimately dilute the traditional immunity from indirect economic claims. *How complete an accounting did Allied face for total harms caused?* You can note the fact that no natural resources damages have been assessed and never will be. We presume there were major occupational injury recoveries within the employee force, but recovery beyond that was far from comprehensive. Allied and LSP's criminal liability remains to be examined (in Chapter 20), but the criminal penalties did not by any means make a comprehensive accounting, either. See pages 979-982.

Pages 162-163, C&Q #3: Proximate cause as loss-shifting policy. This note tries to offer an array of reasons for limiting extended recovery, specifically, transaction costs, conservation of authority, and deliberate cost externalization to protect against the wealth and welfare distribution effects of making products "too" expensive. These are not irrational or illegitimate concerns, but they evince no obvious standard for their appropriate effectuation. Once that is accepted, then there is no plainly better mechanism than the tort law doctrine of proximate cause that tries, case-by-case, to apply community norms to define by an iterative inductive process, just how much of the more remote costs of environmental tort injuries are to be internalized.

Pages 163-194. Remedies. These text blocks cover a variety of different remedies, from normal compensatory damage remedies, to equitable remedies, questions of punitive damages, indirect economic injuries, and natural resources remedies. If this entire block has been assigned, it is feasible to treat them all or most of them in one comprehensive, hypothetical setting. If not, the following suggestions can be separated out for each respective page block assignment.

One approach is to draw on the blackboard one major environmental problem where liability for wrongdoing has been ascertained and the only further question is the structured array of remedies that may be applied. The Exxon-Valdez Alaska oil spill, for instance, offers a nice opportunity to go through almost all issues (with the exception of permanent damages).

Presuming that liability in negligence, public nuisance, and perhaps strict liability have been established, the students should be invited to see that the presumptive automatic remedy is compensatory damages, and this can be addressed first: What is the easiest category of injuries for which compensatory damages can be claimed? Discrete provable injuries to personal health or to property are obviously the easiest to obtain, but in many environmental cases like the Alaska oil spill these damages will not amount to a great deal. The actual physical damage of owned property is relatively small, and causation of health effects may be quite hard to demonstrate and quantify. As in *Boomer*, however, any such injuries that can be quantified will be paid by defendant.

(It is useful to note also that in big environmental cases like the Alaska oil spill, there are public plaintiffs as well as private: the State of Alaska filed a common law damage action, as well as did 180 private individuals and groups affected by the oil spill. In some instances, as for the claim for mental health injuries resulting from the oil spill, individual claims would be hard to prove and the state included such claims as part of its overall theory of the case. The state, in its capacity as parens patriae, settled its claims against the Alaska Pipeline Consortium and Exxon. It is not at all clear, however, to what extent that estopped future private mental health claims.)

The largest claim by far in the Exxon-Valdez case resembles the James Bay fishery and related claims in the Kepone case (*Pruitt* page 160). The entire fishing season was wiped out in the Gulf of Alaska, both by contamination of fish, by consumer aversion to Alaska fish products, and by a state ban on any sale of fish showing any detectable residue, a ban designed to assure consumers that the state would hold its fish harvest to the highest levels of cleanliness to protect its long-term market. As noted in the questions following *Pruitt*, there is a long-standing judicial reluctance to award "indirect economic damages," especially in maritime admiralty cases under the *Robbins Drydock* rule, and the "physical injury" rule applied in many inland tort jurisdictions. In part this is to avoid the dangers of "speculative" quantification, but the reality is that it would be easy for a jury to determine the approximate amounts of lost net revenues for all of those involved in the fisheries and tourist industries. In *Pruitt*, Judge Merhige represented a growing trend, led by environmental cases, to recognize that some indirect economic recoveries should be allowed. Once that dike is broken, how far do consequential recoveries go? Foreseeability extends throughout the chain of causation beyond fishermen, to include processors, canners, distributors, wholesalers, retailers, and restaurants, and perhaps costs to consumers beyond that. Economists like to talk about the positive mutipliers in bringing a company like Allied Chemical or the Alaska Pipeline to a locality. These economic injuries illustrate that the multiplier effect works negatively as well, but courts are understandably leery about going much further than Judge Merhige did in the Kepone case.

Awarding damages solely for loss to economic interests amounts to a failure to account for natural resources damages, a point that students often raise in discussion. Note how a number of the measures of natural resources damages noted in the text represent a form of indirect economic damage assessment for injuries caused to *human* interests, not measures of the wildlife and natural resources losses themselves.

Beyond human-based natural resources damage claims, where can we go? This is where students may come up with the idea of "restoration costs," basing an economic recovery on actions that could be taken to hasten recovery of the damaged resources. Because of difficulties in measuring natural resources injuries in monetary terms, this category of damage may exist camouflaged within punitive damage assessments, or help persuade courts to issue equitable remedies.

The Restatement of Torts 2d §929 states:

> §929. Harm to land from past invasions
>
> (1) If one is entitled to a judgment for harm to land resulting from a past invasion and not amounting to a total destruction of value, the damages include compensation for
>
> (a) the difference between the value of the land before the harm and the value after the harm, *or at his election in an appropriate case, the cost of restoration* that has been or may be reasonably incurred....

The Comments add: "(b)... If, however, the cost of replacing the land in its original condition is disproportionate to the diminution in value of the land caused by the trespass, unless there is a reason personal to the owner for restoring the original condition, damages are measured only by [market value diminution].... On the other hand, [where special uses are particular to the owner, examples are given of recovery beyond net diminution].... Likewise, if the defendant is a willful trespasser, the owner is entitled to recover from him the value of any profits made by the [tort]."

Cleanup costs are typically an available measure of damages. Note the difference between the public and the private plaintiff. The public plaintiff who has spent large amounts of money for cleanup efforts is presumptively justified in spending all of that money. The defendant is not likely to be successful in arguing that a particular cleanup action was not necessary or disproportionate in the circumstances. These latter arguments, however, do occur when private actors clean up. What about the commercial fishermen in Alaska who themselves took on cleanup activities? As to their own equipment, cleanup costs obviously would be part of the damage to private property assessed above. But when they go and clean up public resources like beaches and shorebird rookeries, as some commercial fishermen did, they must be able to show that they were operating, not as hyper-fastidious volunteers, but pursuant to state-sponsored guidelines and plans for cleaning the contaminated area. This private restitution argument is difficult, and still proceeding through the courts.

EQUITABLE REMEDIES... Damages, however, are arguably an insufficient remedy. In a case like the Alaska oil spill, for reasons noted above it can be argued that injury to unique resources cannot be completely compensated. At this point it should be noted that, under the *Boomer* and *Ducktown* rules, plaintiffs can obtain injunctive remedies by showing that the array of interests in favor of the injunction outweigh the array of interests militating against the award of an injunction. Part of the inquiry is a consideration of the various equitable orders that might be available.

As to *Boomer*, it is useful to remind students that Judge Bergan was quite clearly wrong: public values *can* be weighed in the decision as to whether to issue an injunction, since even in purely private actions "equity must do equity" to the public interest as well as between the parties. If the plaintiffs had filed in public nuisance rather than private nuisance, that point would be inescapable. As it was, a more even-handed balance is discussed in C&Q #2, page 166.

The variety of equitable orders available in a case like the Alaska spill deserves some categorization: some will be retrospective, like orders for creation of hatchery programs, cleaning contaminated resources, and the like. Others can be prospective. Where a defendant's course of conduct has been shown to lead to dangerous conditions that in fact produced a calamity, plaintiffs can get more "bang for their buck" by asking the court to add prospective injunctions assuring that such wrongful conduct will not continue, through prohibitory orders and even the imposition of environmental court-appointed monitors, or corporate receivers. These alternatives have begun to receive attention in the literature as well as in court. These latter should be good for a discussion of the evolving role and relevance of equitable remedies.

As to restoration, as noted earlier with reference to pages 168-171, 190-192, one canon of equity jurisprudence is that "equity will not order a vain thing," so that if a court is convinced that restoration is impossible (or problematic in contributing to negative impacts on the resource), then such orders should not issue .

Ultimately, surveying the array of damage and equitable remedies, one can ask whether there is any possibility of fully remedying the effects of many large environmental calamities. When it costs thousands of dollars per animal's life saved, and solvents used to clean beaches kill more micro-organisms than the oil does, and attempts to accelerate the natural rate of restoration are more or less quixotic, then the arguments for future preventive remedies grows apace.

Pages 165-166, C&Q #1: A range of equitable remedies. A range of equitable remedies appears in the excerpt.

Pages 166-167, C&Q #2: The balance of equities. *Would you be surprised...if courts facing a strict injunction rule in the event that there is a nuisance tend to reach no-liability holdings?* That's what often happened between the early 1900s and 1960 in many states including New York.

What items were allowed into the remedy balancing considerations in Boomer? Judge Bergan clearly did not want to consider public harms in the private litigation balance. The plaintiff could have noted to the judge (1) that an equity court is supposed to do public equity in issuing its remedies, not just equity between the parties; (2) that the judge was quite happily balancing public interests in favor of the defendant, not just private corporate interests; and (3) a reminder to the judge that if this were brought as a public nuisance action, the public balance would have been straightforwardly incumbent upon the court, so there's nothing inherently improper in this kind of public balancing.

Would the Boomer case have been different if the plant had made and broken specific assurances to the plaintiffs? Yes, clearly, as in *Staso*.

Pages 167-168, C&Q #3: Constraints on equitable remedies. The "anticipatory nuisance" defense (or "prospective nuisance" defense as it was called in *Wilsonville*, page 115, deserves some exploration. Environmental cases are often in the position of establishing liability for newly-discovered problems, making wait-and-see a frequent and frustrating response to an injunction request.

Page 168, C&Q #4: Other equitable actions. *Does equity embody a free-floating cause of action, so that an equitable remedy can issue wherever a wrong is shown to exist?* Not according to normal theories of legal process. But there are situations, especially in environmental law, where matters cry out for an injunction, and the public trust doctrine, an equitable cause of action, comes to provide the necessary doctrine. See the *Florissant Fossil Beds* injunction below at page 1091-1093.

Pages 168-171, C&Q #5: Restoration remedies. This analysis of restoration and remediation orders is important. The notes are generally self-explanatory.

When should restoration be ordered? As the *Escamilla* case (discussed at pages 169-171) indicates, there will have to be a lot more academic consideration of this issue before the balance gets clearer. The *Weissmann* tests, footnote 32, page 170, are also somewhat helpful.

Page 171, C&Q #6: Restoration and other injunctive relief as legalized extortion. The note explores a theoretically possible means of guarding against the possibility that plaintiffs will use the threat of restoration or an injunction to "extort" greater damages from the defendant. The cited article suggests that an "inalienable" injunction or restoration remedy prevents the plaintiffs from severing the award from the benefited parcel, and offers an alternative of higher compensation, but not extortionate compensation, as a safeguard against undercompensation that might result from compensatory damages alone.

Pages 171-172 -- Compensatory Damages. *Does compensation based on imputed lost rental value adequately capture the sum total of values harmed?* Of course not. Environmental law is constantly trying to integrate more of the reality of losses into the calculus.

Hedonic/quality of life damages. The interesting concept of "hedonic" damages noted in the coursebook text at 172 and 188 is sometimes cast in terms of "quality of life." The latter phrasing, for instance, was used in the *Ayres* case, in the coursebook at 215. "Quality of life" damages as used there and in most cases, however, are really compensations for *past* "loss of enjoyment" of property, and quite different from the concept meant by "hedonic" damages - the *future* qualities of living that are foregone because of the wrongful act.

Pages 172. Permanent damages. This short section is self-explanatory. Permanent damages are not yet a frequent remedy, it appears. The calculation of proposed permanent damages in the original *Boomer* trial court decision is not sensible, measuring the property value at time of trial against value at the time the pollution started, as if economic conditions had stood still in the interim.

The proper measure is to compare values as of the same moment, with and without pollution. The most interesting question raised is that of the value of "involuntary sales" to private pollution defendants - should they have to pay a premium beyond what the government would have to pay for actual loss of market value?

Page 173, C&Q #1: The measure of permanent damages. *Do permanent damages provide the equivalent benefit of an injunction?* No, because damages only comprise compensable items, whereas an injunction shutting down a polluter would convey many other benefits as free-riders that would not have been adducable as damage claims.

According to Judge Herzberg's original formula, what would the amount of permanent damages be if the land had appreciated back to the original value before pollution? Apparently zero, which reveals the mistake of comparing value at different dates, rather than at one time with and without the pollution.

Can the court assess an extra amount to account for plaintiff's unwillingness to sell? Instinctively we feel that some premium for involuntary "sales" of easements should be paid by private interests like Atlantic Cement, but not by public condemnors (the risk of eminent domain is part of the social contract). The right to exclude other private interests from your real property is a substantial part of the fee simple bundle of rights. This involuntariness appears to have been integrated into the judge's decision on remand, as cryptically noted by the judge and analyzed in the cited Hiley article.

How are courts to avoid extortionate evaluations of permanent damages, as well as the opposite tendency to give only market value loss? The premium for suffering an involuntary loss of rights to prevent pollution goes beyond mere market value loss, but should have no relationship to how desperate a defendant is to buy off the potential injunction. Defining the proposition as the cited Hiley article attempts to do, and giving the question to a well-briefed jury, is probably the way to go.

Page 173, C&Q #2: Do permanent damages create private expropriation? *Private expropriation*? As noted, forced private sales occur in other contexts, such as easements of necessity for land-locked parcels. There, however, the impetus that creates the public policy based exception to the ordinary rules of land owner choice in matters of sale of easements is not the result of a freely chosen course of action engaged in by the easement purchaser. At times, easement-by-necessity suits are brought by the land-locked owner as declaratory judgment actions. Consider how such an action by Atlantic Cement would appear, especially if it brought that action prior to constructing the plant, i.e., at the time before its unilateral action created the necessity. That suit would very much resemble private condemnation, with Atlantic Cement as plaintiff seeking to force the sale to it of an easement from an unwilling seller.

Pages 173-174, C&Q #3: The decision to award permanent damages, and C&Q #4: The future of permanent damages. Rhetorical open ended discussion points. Part of the evaluation of the desirability of permanent damages depends upon the standards and accuracy of compensation calculations. If permanent damages can be fairly and accurately assessed, they can provide Solomonic answers to some pollution problems where complete victory for either side would not be in the public interest. As the Boomer quantification shows, however, courts as institutions do not now know exactly what is required of the permanent damages balance.

As a litigant, how valuable is the permanent damages sense of closure? For defendants, you can ask students *"What do you do as soon as you get a decision granting a no-injunction permanent damages award?"* You record it! It's security against future actions from these properties, whether plaintiffs stay or go. For plaintiffs permanent damages are likely to feel less satisfying than the cleanup many will have hoped for; if the plant shuts down prematurely, however, the permanent damages fund is a windfall that does not have to be returned.

Is there something distasteful about permanent damages? Do they imply that pollution is acceptable as long as money changes hands? Not necessarily, we guess, although the tendency will be to undervalue all the private and public concerns that motivate injunction actions and will not be served by monetary reimbursements. The balance should feel more appropriate if it integrates a wider range of public costs and values in the decision whether to issue injunctions or merely permanent damage awards.

Pages 174-185 -- Punitive Damages.

Punitive damages offer an available further remedy in many cases. In the Alaska oil spill case, one could ask students what evidence would be most likely to impel a grant of punitive damages, focusing on punishment for complacency, sloppiness in operations, and total failure to prepare for spill response demonstrated in that case, or to offer strong deterrents to future delinquencies by the defendants and others. The punitive damages materials are designed to show that punitive damages can play a role in environmental accounting but are volatile and crude. To some extent, punitive damages can capture otherwise intangible injuries, like natural resources injuries. (This again raises the question whether a successful plaintiff has any obligation to spend those recoveries to remedy the injuries). Punitive damages can be designed, as in the Ford Pinto litigation, to recapture the profit made by the wrongdoing.

The comments and questions are designed to show first, that the mere fact that a tort is "intentional" should not be enough to awarded punitive damage, and further that there is little basis for predicting the proper occasions and amount of punitive damages to be awarded. The emergent constitutional due process standard set out in *Haslip* and other cases appearing in C&Q # 6, page 182-184, is as clear as the courts get in describing the award of punitive damages, and the reasoning in remittitur decisions is rarely clearly explained to provide guidance. Insofar as punitive damages are part of cost internalization, in other words, they are a rough and ready unpredictable component.

This material will be somewhat familiar to the class. Students tend to leap to the presumption that Western Petroleum deserves punitive damages, but it seems to us that this depends on the proof in the case. If the proof were to show that Western really didn't know that its wastes were polluting groundwater (and its experts were still contesting that at trial), and reasonably did not know exactly where the boundary line was, all you are left with is continued activity after notice. The latter sounds like civil intention as in *Boomer;* could Boomer have gone for punitive damages? It is clear to us that civil intent is not enough for punitive damages, contrary to the *McElwain* court's ill-reasoned take on the matter (pages 178-179).

The *Fischer* case, page 175, is dissected in the notes. Problems of manageability of mass torts (although *Fischer* is an individual action) are the focus of our interest here.

Pages 178-179, C&Q #1: Do all intentional torts deserve punitive damages? Punitive damages and civil intent. *Do all intentional torts deserve punitive damages?* No, that's the flaw in the *McElwain* reasoning, playing on the word "intentional" to equal malice, by no means an equivalent. As noted above, arguing that civil intent equals malice proves too much, to the potential detriment of the logic of both areas of doctrine. QQQ to RHA: Students will be pulled by strong desire to equate intentional with malice (partly because they will be invoking partly-remembered doctrines and definitions from their tort and criminal law classes). It might be good idea to give reminder to instructor to go over the definition of "intentional" in this context to show exactly how "intentional" differs from "malice" as legal construct in environmental law setting.

Page 179, C&Q #2: The availability and measure of punitives. *What is the proper measure of punitive damages? What checks are imposed? Are juries free to vent their spleen? (or respond to bloody-shirt-waving attorneys?)* The danger is that there are no clearly-delineated guidelines. The Supreme Court's endorsement of Alabama's standards for remittitur review in *Haslip,* at page 182-184, offer useful bases for discussion of the questions posed, including a hint at a camouflaged recapture of wrongful profits.

Pages 179-180, C&Q #3: Proving punitives. *What kind of proof is likely to incite a jury to award punitives?* The examples given are intended to illustrate incendiary material. Ask students whether they think such cold marketplace reasoning is an aberration; and should it be? In the Ford Pinto cases (referred to ghoulishly by some of Ford's corporate counsel as "shake-and-bakes"), a leaked company memo revealed that by not putting in a firewall over the gas tank, there would be a net savings of $x million after paying personal injury claims. The jury awarded that amount as punitive damages.

The point of this comment is that the asbestos company allowed new workers to come in without warnings and subject themselves to fatal asbestos exposures. That is reprehensible.

How about other cases, however, where a company makes a judgment that a product could be made safer, but at great cost in dollars and performance detriment (a car built like an ergonomic tank), and makes a reasonable compromise? Admitting that Ford's compromise was skewed, the phenomenon nevertheless sometimes militates in favor of less safety and more utility. How safe is safe? Punitive damages loom behind the incorrect guesses of the industrial defendant, and that is not necessarily fair.

Page 180, C&Q #4: Punitive problems in mass cases. Problems of multiple punitive damage recoveries. *Does this produce a race to court to get first crack at huge punitive recoveries?* It clearly can, or there can be an opportunistic multiduplicaton of punishments. The Ford Pinto cases were adverted to in the prior note. The first Pinto jury to find liability used the savings figure from the memo to assess punitive damages. Fine. And the next did the same. Serves Ford right. Then the next.... At some point logic says that the punitive point has been made.

Should there be a national clearinghouse? A national clearinghouse for punitive awards in mass torts theoretically makes logical sense - acting as a common fund so late-suing plaintiffs will not find the defendants' bank busted - but is a logistical and jurisprudential nightmare.

Pages 180-182, C&Q #5: The Exxon-sponsored attack on the concept of punitive damages. The Exxon-funded article by Viscusi claiming that punitive damages fail to achieve appropriate results in the settings of corporate environmental and safety awards is deeply flawed, yet interesting. The flaws are presented well by the Luban article. The main points of both appear in the Comment. The Viscusi position is novel insofar as few have argued that punitives are simply a bad idea, rather than attacking the various difficulties in their administration.

Pages 182-184, C&Q #6: Constitutional checks on the award of punitive damages. The Supreme Court and punitives. Self-explanatory text describing the Supreme Court's steps to-date in regulating the proliferation of number and amounts, and the potential for multi-layered duplications of punitive damage awards.

In *BMW of North America, Inc. v. Gore*, 116 S.Ct. 1589 (U.S. 1996), mentioned in the note, an automobile purchaser brought an action based on a failure to disclose that the automobile had been repainted after being damaged prior to delivery. The Alabama trial Court entered judgment on jury verdict awarding buyer compensatory damages of $4,000 and punitive damages of $4,000,000. The Alabama Supreme Court reduced the award to $2,000,000. The Supreme Court, in an opinion by Justice Stevens, held that the due process clause prohibits an Alabama court from considering lawful conduct by the distributor outside of the state in making an award of punitive damages. The court reversed the judgment, holding that "The Due Process Clause of the Fourteenth Amendment prohibits a State from imposing a 'grossly excessive' punishment on a tortfeasor," and applying the same factors described in *TXO* and *Haslip*. This trend of trying to link punitives more tightly to the harms suffered in the case at bar in the relevant jurisdiction continued in the *State Farm* case that is considered in the Comment. Not all Justices seem as concerned on this front. Justice Scalia, joined by Justice Thomas filed a dissenting opinion arguing that the BMW opinion represented merely "the latest manifestation of this Court's recent and increasingly insistent 'concern' about punitive damages that 'run wild'." Justice Scalia went on to argue that "Since the Constitution does not make that concern any of our business, the Court's activities in this area are an unjustified incursion into the province of state governments."

Page 184, C&Q #7: Remittitur. This ancient writ has ultramodern significance in clarifying when and how punitives awards are to be second-guessed by judges as a matter of due process.

Page 184, C&Q #8: Punitive damages and insurance. Usually, the insurance contracts by their express terms exclude coverage for punitive damages. In some states, even in the absence of such contractual exclusions, coverage for punitive damages is deemed to violate public policy. An interesting idea that is sometimes considered in lieu of punitive damages is uninsurable tort fines.

Pages 184-185, C&Q #9: Creative accounting in damage remedies: ill-gotten gains and punitive damages. Disgorgement of ill-gotten gains. As both a statutory and a common law matter, making disgorgement of "ill-gotten gains" a measure of damages or fines opens up an intuitively appropriate but devilishly difficult remedy process. This can occur as an element in punitive awards, and otherwise. But how does one measure how much of a gain is ill-gotten in whole or part?

Legislation on punitives. Note the House and Senate bills. The standards for award of punitive damages in one such bill can be useful in class discussion:

> 104 H.R. 956, §201(e) – In determining the amount of punitive damages, the trier of fact shall consider all relevant, admissible evidence, including –
>
> (1) the severity of the harm caused by the conduct of the defendant, (2) the duration of the conduct or any concealment of it... (3) the profitability of the specific conduct... (4) the number of products sold, the frequency of services provided, or the type of activities conducted by the defendant... (5) awards of punitive damages to persons similarly situated to the claimant, (6) possibility of prospective awards of compensatory damages to persons similarly situated to the claimant, (7) any criminal penalties imposed on the defendant as a result of the conduct complained of by the claimant, (8) the amount of any civil and administrative fines and penalties assessed against the defendant as a result of the conduct complained of by the claimant, and (9) whether the foregoing considerations have been a factor in any prior proceeding involving the defendant....

Texas Gov. George Bush signed bill S.B. 25 in April 1996 capping punitive damages claims. The bill lowered the cap on punitive damages to two times economic damages plus no more than $750,000 in non-economic damages, or $200,000 whichever is greater. Ten of 12 jurors must vote in order for such damages to be awarded. In addition, the bill requires a plaintiff to prove fraud or malice and changes the burden of proof from a preponderance of the evidence to clear and convincing evidence. The bill's practical effect will be interesting to follow.

In addition to private parties, who may seek punitive damages? A California Court of Appeals held that a city may seek punitive damages against companies that recklessly dispose of toxic wastes. Sanger v. Occidental Chemical Corp., Calif. Ct.App, 1st App. Dist., No. A057295 (July 1992).

An asbestos case in Maryland consolidated 8,500 plaintiffs and used a punitive damages multiplier whereby defendants paid plaintiffs from 35 cents to $2.50 in punitive for each dollar in compensatory damages. Each defendant was assigned a specific multiplier value by the jury, based on the length of time the particular defendant knew of the asbestos danger and continued to expose plaintiffs to it. ABATE v. AC&S, Inc., Md. Cir. Ct. Balt. No. 89236704, (Aug. 10, 1992).

Pages 185-194 -- Natural Resource Remedies and Damages.

This area has been called "a sleeping giant" and will be increasingly active in environmental law. It is developing in both common law (this chapter's focus) and statutory realms (for instance in the CERCLA natural resource remedies). This section of the book opens up many of the issues, using the Exxon Valdez spill as a didactic example and as a jumping board for discussion of recoveries for natural resources losses. Inevitably such recoveries will be split between human-based accountings and some attempts to recover beyond human-based injuries. For your own background information on the Alaska oil spill, the Picou collected readings may be interesting. J. S. Picou et al., The Exxon Valdez Disaster: Readings on a Modern Social Problem (1997). You also can get much information from the Exxon Valdez Oil Spill Trustee Council, 800-283-7745, <http.//www.oilspill.state.ak.us>.

The Complaint excerpts show how Alaska was trying to recover money for NRD. It does not discuss how that money would be spent. Both questions are important.

It might be useful to note the continuing debate in the aftermath of the Alaska oil spill. Observers wonder whether it has been worth $88,000 per otter's life saved, and whether it wouldn't be more economically realistic to take the $10 million spent on saving oiled marine life and use it for alternative, more cost-effective purposes. Then there is the problem that many remediation costs turn out to have been spent for technologies that did more harm than good, killing off all biological life on the beaches that were being cleaned. There is, however, distressing scientific evidence that the ecological pyramids of Prince William Sound - previously quite a pristine and extremely fertile marine environment - are suffering serious dislocation due to hydrocarbon pollution effects: part of the data shows not just a drop-off in some species' populations but a disturbing increase in genetic aberrations within species ranging from protozoans to higher life forms. This debate will continue.

Pages 188-189, C&Q #1: Non-marketplace human-based remedies. This note introduces the tension: under marketplace pressures, the Reagan Interior Department's NRD regulations focused the valuation of NRD on marketplace economics. If a school of fish had a market value, that would provide a basis for the regulatory NRD value. If not, valuation would potentially be diluted or inconsequential. The court struck the market bias down, and new regulations from Interior and NOAA have been far more attentive to ecosystemic and non-market values.

Page189, C&Q #2: Natural resources' own intrinsic value? *How can you measure the intrinsic values of lost natural resources, and who is to bring such actions?* These questions are answered rhetorically through the note. The practical answers for resolving the definitional miscommunication between the Three Economies here may follow from a normative societal decision to seek restoration, remediation , or mitigation, and a quantification and specification of how to do that, which is the focus of the next note. A superb bibliography on environmental ethics is D.E. Davis, Ecophilosophy: A Field Guide to Literature (R&E Miles Press, San Pedro, 1989).

Pages 189-190, C&Q #3: Natural capital. Natural capital and ecosystem services are two concepts that are being advanced to measure more fully the value of natural systems and, correlatively, the cost of injury to them. There are sharp attacks on these concepts that come from both sides of the intellectual spectrum, but in the end, the ideas lie near the heart of rational decisionmaking - actions ought to be undertaken with a full accounting of their costs and benefits, including lost opportunity costs and damage to systems that help sustain the systems that are critical to our collective well-being. An extensive symposium volume on the natural capital represented by ecosystem services supplied to the marketplace economy by Mother Nature is published in 20 Stanford Envtl Law J. 309 (Number 2, 2001), with Jim Salzman setting a new record as co-author of four of the seven articles therein appearing.

Pages 190-192, C&Q #4: Ecological restoration remedies. *What does Alaska's complaint mean when it demands restoration?* As one of us who helped draft the complaint can testify, nobody had a clear idea of what that might mean.

This note is a small essay on the elements of designing and deciding upon restoration responses to a catastrophe like the oil spill. The questions are answered rhetorically. Cost is part of the balance, and brings in issues of degrees of fault and culpability as well as feasibility, issues which deserve clearer definition, especially when one notes that the principles developing here can apply to a wide range of other settings, large and small, involving Exxon or next-door neighbors.

Page 192, C&Q #5: Must restoration awards be used to restore? *Must restoration awards be used to restore?* Marketplace politics tend to try to grab NRD recoveries and divert them to human political advantage, as the Alaska proposals demonstrate. Is expenditure on scientific baseline studies of the ecosystem *after* the incident an appropriate use of the money? Half the Exxon Valdez fund is going to scientific research projects of various sorts.

Pages 192-193, C&Q #6: NRD precedents from the Alaska oil spill. The Exxon Valdez Trustees Council will establish important precedents on NRD generally. *Are they trustees under the public trust doctrine as well as creatures of particular statutes?* It is bemusing that the legal status of the Trustees Council is unclear. The Council itself is made up of government staffers who tend to think only in terms of statutes and regulations, but if they went to court asserting public trusteeship beyond their statutory directions, it seems to us they could assert broad public trust powers. The question then is whether they could be constrained by traditional judicial trust oversight principles.

If you are interested in using the Exxon-Valdez oil spill as an example of punitive and natural resource damages, Deborah S. Bardwick wrote a useful article, entitled The American Tort System's Response to Environmental Disaster: The Exxon-Valdez Oil Spill as a Case Study, 19 Stan. Envtl. L.J. 259 (2000). Her note examines three strategies for recovery pursued in the litigation following the spill—recovery by the state and federal government of damages under the public trust doctrine, private individual plaintiffs' claims, and Alaska Natives' maritime public nuisance claims for loss of their subsistence lifestyle—and discusses the role played by traditional tort and statutory law.

Page 193, C&Q #7: Mitigation and substituted resources. Is mitigation a satisfactory NRD remedy? etc. Pragmatically, the example of forest purchase around Prince William

Sound shows a real effect in maintaining the ecosystem which had been injured, against predictable imminent harm from a totally different yet more redressable cause. You can ask *"Is there any reason why the NRD money has to be directed to the specific kind of damage that generated the money?"* (we think not, but are not sure how far afield mitigation should be allowed to go) and *"Does it seem inappropriate that the forestry purchase is being done because everyone concedes that the river watersheds would be destroyed by logging because the timber operators would not effectively be forced to comply with federal and state laws?"* (this may be unseemly, but realistically if you want to protect the Gulf of Alaska it is more effective to buy out the loggers than to try to make them obey the laws).

MORE NOTES ON THE AFTERMATH OF THE EXXON VALDEZ OIL SPILL. The causation of the Exxon Valdez oil spill has been laid at the door of governmental and corporate complacency and cupidity. "Industry tends to measure success as operating the biggest vessel with the thinnest hull and the smallest crew at the highest speed with the quickest port turnaround consistent with meeting the minimum government requirements." Spill: Report of the State of Alaska Oil Spill Commission, Jan. 1990.

A summary of legal actions. A brief catalogue of the various legal actions arising from the Alaska oil spill and their varied outcomes or present circumstances is printed in the Appendix of this Manual. The Exxon Valdez oil spill produced more than a hundred private lawsuits, most seeking recovery for indirect, nonphysical economic injuries as in *Pruitt*, coursebook at 160, and private and public lawsuits seeking to recover for ecological and other non-economic injuries.

The review includes discussion of how civil damages earmarked for restoration are being spent. Several proposals for land acquisition using money from the restoration fund created by the settlement have been vetoed by Governor Hickel, and the federal and state Trustees Council has moved tentatively on budgeting restoration expenditures. Much of the money spent to date has been for research, scientific study, repayment to government agencies, and administrative costs. This has alarmed environmental and Native American groups that believe land acquisition should be the top priority.

Innovative damage claims. If you want to discuss issues of indirect economic damages and Native American claims, there are additional course materials: Innovative damage claims in the Exxon oil spill available for photocopying in Part III for this chapter, with excerpts from the trial court rulings limiting indirect economic claims of fishermen and claims made by various Native American communities.

Natural resource consequences of the Alaska oil spill. The long term status of Prince William Sound's ecosystem is still unknown. While much of the visible oil has dissipated, testing for hydrocarbons within the cells and tissues of various organisms is continuing, and shows continued contamination within the food chain and metabolism of different species in the ecosystem. The effect of the pollution on the genetics and reproduction capacities is not yet known, though some genetic anomalies have been found.

The Exxon Valdez Trustee Council's report, "Five Years Later: The 1994 Status Report on the Exxon Valdez Oil Spill" (1994), indicates serious losses and gradual recovery of population numbers for major species in Prince William Sound. The report has been criticized for failing to consider ecosystem-wide effects of the spill, focusing on major photogenic species, and doing numbers counts that fail to incorporate indications of genetic damage within the ecosystem and its populations.

Insurance issues: insurers'' responsibility for *voluntary* cleanups? Exxon's insurers have maintained that claims related to Exxon's cleanup of Prince William Sound were not covered by their policies. They allege that the payments were voluntary measures taken by Exxon to promote their public image. As a result of these claims both Exxon and their insurers have filed lawsuits in Houston and New York.

In a similar case, Washington state's highest court, in a unanimous opinion, held that an insurance company must pay for the insured company's cleanup of a hazardous site even though the government did not order the company to take such action and no lawsuit was filed. Weyerhaeuser Co. v. Aetna Casualty and Surety Co., 1994 WL 195382 (Wash. 1994). The court found that such actions were not gratuitously voluntary because the cleanup was an attempt to comply with state statutes, and such cooperation should be encouraged.

What if the policy includes specific language that prohibits voluntary payments? In Augat v. Liberty Mutual, 571 N.E.2d 357 (Mass. 1991), the court found that an insurance company did not have to reimburse cleanup costs where the policyholder voluntarily commenced cleanup because of threats by the state, because the policy explicitly prohibited voluntary payments without consultation with the insurance company.

The *Weyerhaeuser* opinion points out that allowing insurers to refuse to reimburse for cleanups unless government has ordered them causes problems. Failure to begin cleanup at the earliest moment may result in much greater costs. Also if the policyholder waits and lets the government clean up they may be faced with treble damages of two or three times the cost of cleanup. As a result, if a policyholder refuses to cooperate with government officials and later is forced to pay greater damages because of this, there may be a failure-to-mitigate-damages problem.

On the other hand, insurers may rightfully fear gratuitous giveaways by insureds who undertake cleanup liability too generously, for PR purposes or the like, as Exxon's insurers argue.

An answer may be that representatives of the insurers be invited into cleanup negotiations between government and the insured, and be part of any cleanup agreements made in lieu of enforcement proceedings.

Page 194, C&Q #8: Prospects. The text merely states the obvious, natural resource damage is a concept that has a current place in the law and, despite difficulty in computation and administration, will continue to receive attention

Pages 194-199 -- Other Nonstatutory Causes of Action

This text is a legal process reminder. The strip-mining/ deed interpretation example is intended to force students' attention away from exclusive nonstatutory focus on torts. The note thereafter raises an array of other possibilities. (Note also the corporate law tactics that might be effective in certain settings, presented in Chapter 21 at page 1049-1062. On the Teachers' Website, moreover, is a short set of materials on the junk bond Pacific Lumber takeover that destroyed thousands of acres of sustainable redwood stocks— inquiring whether corporate law might have provided collateral protective remedies.)

The strip-mine deed issue provides a vivid example of how legal words may change in context over time. The broad form deed clearly was executed by parties who did not expect that a future form of mining as drastic as strip-mining would arise, effectively obliterating the surface estate retained by the Appalachian landowners. In 1987, the Supreme Court of Kentucky decided, in Akers v. Baldwin, that strip-miners had to pay for surface damage unless the deed had specifically contemplated strip-mining. 736 S.W.2d 294. This is a major change.

Page 197, C&Q #1: Interpretation of strip-mine broad form deeds. The broad form deed could be considered as a property instrument or as a contract. *Should courts consider that grantors typically signed with an X?* As a property instrument, the court typically construes a deed against the "dominant" grantor. In this case, however, the deed for most Appalachian coal land was typically prepared by the *grantee;* the large land speculation companies, who purchased mineral rights through a corps of itinerant purchasing agents, prepared these broad form deeds in pre-printed form books, buying substantial rights from completely illiterate hardscrabble farmers. And the argument that the price, averaging three dollars per acre, exceeded the full-fee simple value is not sufficient to prove that the coal companies have the right to destroy the surface estate: Presumably many of the surface owners would have refused to sell had they been asked to sell the entire fee simple even if offered a premium. Now their successors are discovering that the "subordinate" mineral rights can completely destroy the surface estate.

In contract law there would be other possibilities, if the judge could be persuaded to consider this case under currently evolving contract doctrine. Changed circumstances may in dramatic cases be held to result in subsequent unconscionability of the contract. The strip-mine setting, with its dramatic changes in technology and disruptive effects, would seem to be an example of such "undue hardship" upon one of the parties, and therefore make the broad form's enforcement unconscionable in so far as it can be characterized in contract terms.

Page 197, C&Q #2: The broad reach of private land controls. Private land-use controls exemplify the strength and the particularity of private environmental controls as opposed to public ones. This may be an appropriate point to raise the question of "élitism." In many environmental settings it is clear that the sensitivities of an "élite" may provide for long-term preservation of resources that otherwise would be destroyed. The Elgin Marbles from the Parthenon would quite clearly have been destroyed in the internecine Greek warfare, so that their removal and preservation in London by an artistic aristocrat was the only reason we still have those world treasures. This is a question of "environmentalism versus democracy" which occasionally recurs in environmental law. Compare Sax's Mountains Without Handrails, with Tucker's Environmentalism and the Leisure Class.

Page 197, C&Q #3: Prescriptive easements. *How do private plaintiffs overcome claims of prescriptive rights to pollute?* Using an analogy to adverse possession, where public rights cannot be estopped by the adverse possession statutes of limitations, courts have argued that public nuisance trumps a private claim of prescriptive easement to pollute. Furthermore, any change in the quality and quantity of a pollution load over time presumptively is not protected by the easement and can be the subject of litigation.

Pages 197-198, C&Q #4: Equitable restrictions. Equitable restrictions — negative reciprocal covenants created and running at equity. Self-explanatory.

Page 198, C&Q #5: Toxic breach of implied warranty of title. Although students will be astonished, the overwhelming majority of courts that have considered this question have apparently held that the presence of toxics on the land does not make the title sufficiently "unmarketable" to allow a purchaser to rescind a sales agreement. It thus appears that purchasers can be forced to go through with the closing and take the conveyance, or lose their deposits.

Page 198, C&Q #6: Breach of warranty – products liability. Self-explanatory.

Pages 198-199, C&Q #7: Environmental breach of federal contract. There is a clear potential for the Federal False Claims Act to be the basis of private *qui tam* actions for substantial bounties in many cases of environmental violations committed by federal contractors. See the interesting article by Morenberg, Environmental Fraud by Government Contractors: A New Application of the False Claims Act, 22 B.C. Envtl. Aff. L. Rev. 623 (1996).

Page 199, C&Q #8. Other Horizons. Hortatory.

Chapter 4.
THE SPECIAL CHALLENGES OF TOXIC TORT LITIGATION

Chapter contents:

—and check the Teachers' Manual Website for SUPPLEMENTARY MATERIALS:

http://www.bc.edu/schools/law/library/coursebook/envtlaw/teachers

The list of Supplementary Materials in Part III of this manual, and on the Teachers' Website, indicates materials posted on the Teachers' Website that are relevant to this and other chapters.

OVERALL TEACHING THEMES & COURSE DESIGN CONSIDERATIONS

This is a long and challenging chapter. It demands two class periods at least. Depending on depth of coverage, it can easily consume three. Teachers wanting to stress toxic torts should spend a fourth hour with the material, but that comes at the expense of other subject matters that will have to be cut short or omitted in trade.

The material has a number of different modes, more than most of the chapters. First, it tells a story, the Woburn story, that is the central plot line of the book/movie *A Civil Action*. The material touches on the Woburn story first in an excerpt from plaintiffs' attorney Schlichtmann's own writings about the case. The *Anderson* case comes next. Toward the end of the chapter a review of toxic tort litigation includes several notes that address issues that were of importance to Woburn and as to which the Woburn litigation took some action. The chapter ends with a part that introduces public law remedies and traces how they were applied to Woburn. Due to the centrality of the Woburn story as an organizing point, the Teacher's Manual for this Chapter reprints in a separate §3 (after the page-by-page entries), a wealth of material that one of the author's has collected in relation to that case over the years since the second edition appeared. Importantly, these materials support a simulation exercise for those wishing to make this a focus of the course. A small amount of that material has made its way into the text of the principal volume, but not all.

In addition to telling the Woburn story, a second mode that figures prominently in this chapter is doctrinal development. The chapter presents several lines of cases that discuss the elements required to state a claim in a toxic tort case and explores what elements of damage the law allows. The focus on case law and doctrine continues as the materials address the extremely difficult topic of proof of causation. *Donaldson v. Central Illinois Public Service Company*, a recent case decided by the Supreme Court of Illinois in 2002, replaces *Chevron Chemical Company v. Ferebee* as the starting point for an exploration of exposure and causation.

The chapter's third mode is more abstract and is captured in the title of Part C, "Law and Science." That portion of the chapter, somewhat more abstractly considers how courts deal with highly technical subjects. The subjects that are of importance at trial, are fully understood only by experts, who offer their expertise to the fact finder through testimony. This portion of the chapter includes excerpts from the already legendary *Daubert* case. Thereafter, Part D of the chapter presents a pragmatic side that describes how toxic tort cases litigate. The materials canvas issues that seldom arise with comparable complexity in other litigation contexts. Not surprisingly, courts have worked out some special responses. Finally, Part E addresses how toxic tort litigation is linked to broader questions of public law and regulation.

The variety of approaches that are represented in the materials allows you, as the teacher, to take one of several approaches to the material. The most conventional approach is to stress the cases and the doctrinal side of the material. This has several advantages – first, the students will be familiar with that way of proceeding, having done doctrinal analysis in many of their prior classes. Second, the cases in this chapter are interesting ones that the students will enjoy reading, and there are enough cases (as opposed to text and textual notes in the C&Q) to cover many of the main topics in this chapter.

An alternate approach is to stress the law/science/uncertainty themes. Using that approach tends to turn this chapter's discussions into a laboratory for measuring the extent to which tort litigation is a viable vehicle for internalizing costs associated with the risk-producing activities inherent in the production and use of toxic materials. It tends to highlight the theoretical side of the cases – why should the traditional burden of proof on cause-in-fact be satisfied by proof that is less than "more likely than not?" How should scientific advancement be honored by the courts as an evidentiary matter without opening the process to manipulation by facile quacks and glib charlatans? What is a fair balance between plaintiffs who can show tortious carcinogenic exposure for which defendants are responsible and recoveries that force defendant to pay many times over for damages that are not definitely attributable to it?

Without regard to the manner chosen for teaching this material, it is advisable to keep the students on a relatively short leash. Speaking from personal experience, more than any other area in the materials, I (RHA) have had to re-teach these materials on an extra day because the first day got the students so hopelessly confused. To avoid that fate, when questions are answered incorrectly, I think it may be risky to let the error go for long, potentially solidifying the erroneous belief and misleading other students, as well.

TEACHING NOTES, COMMENTS, & ALL QUESTIONS ANSWERED

Pages 200-201. Introduction. The introduction begins to get the students thinking in terms of exposure and effect and that the law needs to embody a risk management orientation as well as a self-absorbed attention to doctrinal detail.

Pages 201-205. Schlichtmann excerpt. Describes how the Woburn plaintiffs found that they had been injured and how they began to turn their injuries into a cause of action that could be litigated under the governing law in Massachusetts.

Page 205, C&Q #1: Woburn background notes. This note adds a few historical details about the site and the fact that its transformation into a high visibility case was a fortuity, not a predictable or likely outcome.

Pages 206-207, C&Q #2: Causes of action. This note links the case to its legal roots in tort and is very important. It also shows that fact finders, including judges, may harbor wildly incorrect views about scientific matters.

Shouldn't any dumper know, however, that it is extremely likely that toxics dumped on the ground will enter the groundwater, and travel along with the groundwater, thence to some public well?

Even on a foreseeability-based theory such as negligence, the sophisticated user of toxics ought to know (or reasonably should know) of the migratory characteristic of the relevant chemicals with which it works in the event of a release.

Pages 207-210. *Anderson v. W. R. Grace* case. This decision discusses the plaintiffs' emotional distress claims and the Massachusetts state law physical injury requirement that must be satisfied before recovery for emotional distress can be obtained. The case is very doctrinaire insofar as it has very highly articulated and nuanced ways in which the requirement can be met if either the emotional distress causes, or is caused by, bodily injury. A second facet of the opinion deals with potential recovery for the emotional distress associated with witnessing the death of a family member, and addresses issues of legitimacy and genuineness which complicate the law's response. Finally, the opinion rejects claims for increased risk of future illness. It is plain that the court is struggling with ripeness/accrual issues as to this claim, but there is even more to its reticence. In one passage the court finds the proof lacking on the magnitude of the increased risk, a point that is amplified and explored better in some of the other excerpted cases. The court also finds recovery to have an arbitrary lack of relationship to whatever the future may bring for the victims. If a present award was granted it holds the potential for both over- and under-recovery by those who avoid illness and those who contract cancer respectively.

Page 210-211, C&Q #1: Physical harm/emotional distress. *What is the relevance of physical harm in a claim for emotional distress? Is it possible that an individual could be greatly distressed without suffering any injury whatever?*

The requirement is used as a proxy for genuineness of the claim, which can easily be faked. As the note itself points out, the physical harm requirement functions imperfectly as a proxy for genuineness.

Are the physical damage requirement and the required causal link between physical injury and emotional distress intended to substitute for a policy debate about whether the defendant's conduct should, as a matter of law and policy, result in liability for this type of injury?

The authors feel that the answer to this question is, "Yes." That does not make the line more or less arbitrary than other proximate cause lines that courts draw in the sand (cf., *Pruitt*) or at the side of the tracks (cf., *Palsgraf*) and so on.

Even if you are hostile to attempts to limit emotional distress claims for those personally victimized by contamination, is the argument for prudential limitations stronger in the case of those who suffer by witnessing the suffering of others? Is it simply too expensive to compensate these non-economic losses and still maintain affordable prices for goods that produce hazardous materials as by-products of their manufacture?

This question is one of several forays into the "price of 'progress'" that we pay as members of a technologically sophisticated society. It may intrigue students in this context more than it did in the far blander explanation that nuisance is actionable only if the interference with quiet enjoyment is "unreasonable," or that products might become unaffordably expensive if unlimited liability follows all ill-effects, however remote and better borne by the victim.

Page 211, C&Q #2: A Civil Action. The cited materials are potential references for students seeking more information on the Woburn case. A voluminous and excellent civil procedure-oriented sourcebook is Lewis Grossman &Robert Vaughn's A Documentary

Companion to *A Civil Action* , with notes, comments, and questions (Foundation, Summer 1999).

Simulations: Consider doing a FRCP 16 Pre-Trial Conference on the Woburn toxics case, or on other cases offering simulation opportunities: Several of our classes have explored the Woburn toxic contamination case study with an in-class simulation based on the Rule 16 Pre-Trial Conference format, based on the materials in Chapter Four and A CIVIL ACTION , the best-selling book by Jonathan Harr (and the movie with John Travolta, available in video cassette). A memo on doing Rule 16 Simulations is on the Teachers' Website for Chapter 4 Supplementary Materials.

Pages 211-215, C&Q #3-8. These materials recommence the telling of the Woburn story in a quasi-Q&A format.

Pages 215-218. *Ayers v Township of Jackson* case. At some level, this case was a governmental nightmare come true. The local town dump is successfully sued for leaching toxic materials into groundwater. The case presents a host of potentially expensive theories of recovery for damages, some of which involve compensation for intangibles and, accordingly, the chance that outrage factors will incite a jury to give high awards where there is no "objective" guide for determining the amount that ought to be recovered. The opinion does a careful job of respecting the limitation on the waiver of sovereign immunity in New Jersey that is designed to protect the fisc against recovery for intangibles, while at the same time allowing other items of damage that are unconventional, such as the lost quality of life compensation, and the medical monitoring award.

Page 218, C&Q #1: The medical surveillance remedy and latency compensation. *Would the Anderson court have allowed medical surveillance, although it foreclosed recovery for risk?*

Possibly, at any rate, it should. A very strong argument can be made that medical surveillance is like present compensation for future medical specials in conventional tort litigation. For example, the cost (and pain and suffering) of a later operation to revise a scar is a frequent part of the compensation awarded in cut or burn cases. Medically indicated surveillance is analogous, it is presently predictable appropriate medical treatment made necessary (caused) by defendant's tortious conduct.

Are there persuasive rebuttals to these assertions of over- and under-compensation? Is there a further argument that compensation for enhanced risk systematically under compensates those victims who actually contract the feared disease?

This introduces, in the main, the question asked in C&Q #3 below, adding the illustration of the prudent insurer as further proof that exposure is a present injury, or at least a present loss of the value attached to being in better health by contemporary society when it uses markets to monetize such things. The expected additional health care costs (represented by the increased premiums) prove that a monetizeable event has already taken place. The way to avoid under-compensation is to allow suit for the disease. A set-off for the earlier increased risk recovery can be included to avoid even the appearance of double compensation.

To what extent is it necessary to know whether subsequent lawsuits (when diseases actually appear) will be barred by the statute of limitations or by doctrines of res judicata?

If subsequent suits are not available (as with statutes of repose, or impossibly difficult proof problems due to loss of witnesses, etc.) then, in justice, the law ought to be more open to allowing some form of present recovery. Depending on the ripeness rules and the accrual of tort cause of action rules, it is very unlikely that res judicata will apply to a later bodily injury claim when the former litigation sought only compensation for increased risk and there was no reason that the plaintiff should have realized the disease was already at work.

Page 218, C&Q #2: The medical monitoring remedy since *Ayers*. This note adds the four-part test for medical monitoring erected by the 3rd Circuit in the *Paoli* litigation.

Pages 218-219, C&Q #3: Damages for increased risk of future illness. *Can exposed persons sue against identifiable sources of the contamination prior to the onset of disease, not for the disease but for the increased risk?*

As the note itself answers, probably not, citing the overcompensation argument adverted to above in the description of the case. Literally that is a sufficient response, and it is an accurate description of what the *Anderson* opinion and most courts trot out when responding to that claim. That is a convenient response, but it may not be among the best answers. A somewhat more helpful analysis of the injury makes it quite clear that all identifiably exposed individuals have suffered present damage — they are like shopworn goods, or circulated collectibles, less valuable than the new, pristine mint condition ones. If you have the least doubt about the fact that "value" has been taken by the defendant's action, ask yourself would I be better or worse off to be free of the exposure. So far as we know, toxic exposures are not like a mild case of the measles, leaving immunity in their wake. Similarly, would you voluntarily take a TCE bath, or drink a TCE soda without compulsion or compensation? And, of course, your life expectancy, post-exposure, is statistically just a little bit shorter, maybe not by a quantifiable amount, but there can be no doubt of the direction. Thus, the decision to refuse to compensate is not properly grounded on fear that compensation is being paid to non-victims. The fear is that the compensation is too great in most cases: too great in relation to the loss, and too great in the cost it imposes on consumers of goods and services linked to the toxic materials involved.

Page 219, C&Q #4: Hedonic "quality of life" damages. *What items of damage seem to have been included in the Ayers "quality of life" recovery?* Loss of amenity value.

Is there any recognition of the stigma of living in a contaminated community? No, the realtors testified about the difference in price based on other attributes.

Is there any argument that separates toxic tort cases from ordinary tort cases when it comes to compensation for subjective intangibles? Quoth the text, "The mass exposure aspect of toxic tort cases implies that defendant's financial exposure may be great." You might add that outrage factors combine with the mass tort aspect of the cases to make that potential quite great.

Under what circumstances will that justify modification of the ordinary substantive rules? This policy question can have only a policy answer, but it is clear that courts as policy makers are hesitant to move too far too fast in embracing broad liability for intangibles in toxic tort cases.

Pages 219-221, C&Q #5: Stigma and the new tort of "toxiprox." *What is the legal theory supporting recovery in these cases?*

Plaintiffs have suffered demonstrable, provable economic loss as a result of defendant's nearby activities. The loss can be easily proved, but it is far less clear what legal right has been invaded unless nuisance is to take on an expanded meaning having an element that includes freedom from (possibly irrational) fear of the migration of toxic contamination. It is not hard to see the plight of the plaintiffs. As between them and the defendants, they did nothing; the defendant's conduct in creating the condition has caused them a loss. If a cause of action is to be found, however, it will need to go beyond conventional notions of actionable damages in tort. The three capsule descriptions and the *Scribner* case are evidence that courts are, at times, willing to grant damage remedies for injuries based on proximity to risks, whether toxics or EMF. An alternative approach, funded compensation, was tried briefly under the New Jersey statute until an administrative interpretation eliminated compensation for parcels that were not themselves contaminated.

Pages 221-222, C&Q #6: Statutes of limitation – "I wasted time, and now doth time waste me." This brief essay explains how toxic tort cases, with the long period between exposure and onset of appreciable symptoms of disease, are reconciled with statutes of limitations in ways that permit victims to recover despite the fact that defendant's tortious conduct happened many years ago, many years more than the nominal number that appears in the relevant tort statute of limitations. The first doctrine delays accrual of the cause of action until all of the elements of the tort are complete, with injury being the long delayed element in these cases. The discovery rule adds a second prong, that the plaintiff ought to have notice of the tort and who has committed it. This means not only awaiting the onset of disease to start the S/L, but also giving the plaintiff a reasonable time in which to figure out why he/she is afflicted with cancer. Cutting the other way are statutes of repose that immunize defendants after some longer statutory period without regard to accrual or discovery.

Pages 222-223, C&Q #7: Sovereign immunity. *In an era where government is acknowledged to have many similarities to other corporate entities, why, for example, should a pedestrian negligently run down by a government-owned vehicle find her suit barred by governmental immunity when no such bar would encumber a suit against a private company? In the Ayers* *case, for example, why should Jackson Township be any less responsible for harms caused by its dump operations than a private landfill operator?*

The rhetorical question suggests that there is no reason to cut government any special slack when it does things that are not governmental, or regulatory in character. A slightly more charitable position is that immunity in these additional non-governmental cases preserves the solvency and ability to function of governments in their other core areas by not having their limited fiscal resources drawn off to pay tort victims. Do not let the students overlook the fact that this area is now dominated by statutory interpretation. The norm is immunity, and it is abrogated by statutes that are to be read narrowly.

Pages 223-224, C&Q #8: "Cancerphobia." This note makes an important technical distinction between cancerphobia, a distinct medical condition, and fear of contracting cancer, a form of more "conventional" emotional distress claim that is explored by the next comment. The key point is that the disease of cancerphobia, should be treated similarly to other forms of mental disease in the tort system.

Page 224, C&Q #9: Fear of cancer. *When courts raise the threshold barriers to tort recovery in mass toxic tort cases, are they making a social policy judgment that, for reasons of social utility, the damages for non-physical injuries must remain where they lie? Is that policy judgment analytically different from the judicial role in enforcing the ordinary private nuisance requirement that the interference with plaintiff's quiet enjoyment be "unreasonable"?*

This returns to a theme raised by the post-*Anderson* C&Qs as well. In this case, however, the analogy to requiring that the interference be unreasonable is not apposite. Even though large numbers of persons may be exposed, there is a basis for saying the injury is more than a mere annoyance. If that is so, the choice not to compensate is based more on the ground that it is not good policy for every toxic chemical spill to escalate into a "you lose your company" scenario.

Pages 224-225, C&Q #10: Fear of cancer and risk together in California. The *Potter* case is a very significant precedent and one in which a leading jurisdiction places significant (i.e., almost impossibly high) obstacles in the path of recovery for toxic exposure induced fear. The "more likely than not" aspect of *Potter* should be revisited after *Landrigan* (page 238). The *Potter* opinion is very forthright about saying it imposes the limitation as a check on recovery because of a floodgates problem that arises from the ease of fraud, the widespread nature of the potential claims, their extent, etc. As an interesting contrast, the *Potter* court is quick to cast off the more likely than not limit when the moral character of defendant's conduct is shown to be bad (e.g., fraud, malice, oppression).

Pages 225-226, C&Q #11: Supreme Court allows fear of cancer emotional distress actions under FELA and applies joint and several liability. This case, because it arises under the FELA, places the United States Supreme Court in the somewhat unfamiliar setting of highest court in a judicial system passing on a matter of that sovereign's tort law. Remaining true to the principle that FELA cases are to be liberal in granting recovery, the Court has no trouble in following familiar (Restatement (3d) of Torts) guidance to allow compensation for emotional distress (fear of cancer) consequent to tortiously caused bodily injury (asbestosis). Likewise, the Court rejected the railroad's attempt to avoid joint and several liability, noting that most moves away from joint and several liability and toward apportionment in the area of jointly caused tortious injury have been legislative, not judicial.

Page 226, C&Q #12: Distinguishing "community fears" from "rational fears." *Is there any compelling reason why this externality should be treated differently than most?*

The question is a bit ambiguous, because it is far from clear how most externalities are treated — some are internalized by tort law, others are not. Putting that ambiguity aside (the intent was to suggest that tort law does internalize externalities), there are other parts of tort law where recovery depends on truth value, such as defamation. There, if a statement is true and harmful, plaintiff loses; here, the threat to plaintiff's land must be true and harmful to support recovery on Churchill's thesis. There also are areas of tort where improper perceptions can form the basis for recovery, such as assault. The area is a perplexing one, but one in which policy concerns, such as those implicit in Churchill's position have limited compensation (but see, C&Q #5 pages 219-221).

Pages 227–228: Introduction to Complex Causation. This introduction continues the Woburn story before laying out the legal context under discussion: what the plaintiff must do to carry the burden of proof (persuasion) on the issue of causation-in-fact in a toxic tort case. It is worthwhile to hammer in the three points in the last paragraph of this material.

Pages 228-235: *Donaldson v. Central Illinois Public Service Company.* This case replaces *Ferebee v. Chevron*, a products liability case involving proof of causation of cancer following exposure to defendant's insecticide Paraquat. This is a better case for students to grasp the various types of expert testimony required to link disease back to exposure because it isolates the testimony of each of plaintiff's experts and shows how that testimony aided plaintiffs in establishing causation. As explored in C&Q #2, pages 236-237, *Ferebee's* views on proof of causation may no longer satisfy courts in a number of jurisdictions.

Pages 235-236, C&Q #1: Plaintiff's theories and the relevance of defendant's efforts at concealment. Concealment of the contamination from the public was done in contrast to alerting its own contractors to take precautions to limit exposure. That is relevant to demonstrate that reasonable steps could have been taken to better limit the public's risk of exposure. At least one of the authors is very puzzled about why the total disregard of public safety did not overcome defendant's motion for summary judgment in relation to punitive damages. Defendant's own contractors recommended evacuation of nearby houses, and those same employees were warned to take various precautions. That alone ought to be enough to make a triable issue of willful and wanton disregard for the safety of others. The nearby members of the public were likely to suffer an even greater exposure than were the workers, such as the drivers, who were on site only for short periods. The best line of counter argument for CIPS would be that the cleanup was done consistent with IEPA requirements, and that unrebuttably negatives willful disregard for the safety of others. In that setting, however, the pattern of data concealment and misinformation of IEPA would again (in this author's view) create a triable issue on disregard for safety.

Pages 236-237, C&Q #2: Linking exposure to disease and reaching novel conclusions. *In Donaldson, what is the most convincing evidence and testimony linking coal tar exposure to* *neuroblastomas? Could the jury have found for plaintiffs without the testimony of the epidemiologist?*

No, and as the materials cited in the rest of this C&Q #point out, that is increasingly the case. Epidemiological testimony will be required to quantify the portion of the risk to plaintiff for which defendant is responsible. In this case, it seems fair to say that Dr. Kramer, plaintiff's epidemiologist, was the star witness in this case. Critically, Kramer testified that there was a "greater than 50 percent probability" that exposure to defendant's coal tar caused plaintiffs' neuroblastomas. She also developed the extremely probative evidence that there was only a 1 in 10,000 chance that the confluence of the neuroblastomas was a random event. Winters, the exposure expert, testified in a clearly supporting role. Strauss, the toxicologist, though she offered an opinion that defendant's toxin was the cause of plaintiffs illnesses, testified as much to the possibility and plausibility of plaintiffs' theory of causation as she did to causation itself.

Returning to the Ferebee facts, how would the Donaldson court characterize the testimony on causation of two treating lung specialists based on very small samples and their own personal knowledge and experience – as novel conclusions, or as flawed and unacceptable methodology?

The note tries to give a flavor of the *Ferebee* testimony of the two treating doctors, both of whom are highly credentialed, but neither of whom is able to ground his testimony with formal epidemiological methodology. It is highly unlikely, under either the *Frye* "general acceptance test that Illinois purports to follow, or *Daubert* (see generally text, pages 248-260) that either Crystal or Yusef's testimony on causation would have been allowed. Although it is premature to deem it a legal requirement, toxic tort cases will not be won without strong epidemiological testimony offered by plaintiff's experts.

Page 237, C&Q #3: Litigation involving rare cancers and litigation involving more common cancers. *In light of the importance of epidemiological evidence to proving linkage of exposure and disease, which cases are likely to be easier to litigate, cases involving relatively rare cancers, such as Donaldson, or cases involving more prevalent and, therefore, more frequently studied cancers?*

A seeming anomaly of *Donaldson* is that the rare cancer cases frequently will be easier to win than the common cancer cases. If, as in Donaldson, the plaintiff in a rare cancer case can develop the extraordinary evidence that the result is not a random event (Dr. Kramer), and there is evidence on exposure (Dr. Winters) and that the defendant is responsible for exposure to carcinogens having the potential to cause the rare cancer (Dr. Strauss), the plaintiff's case is extremely strong. One key here, however, was that there had to be a cluster of rare cancers, one cancer always can be deemed a random event. Contrastingly, with more common and well studied cancers, more correlations of prior history and exposure are available and offer confounding variables that weaken plaintiff's case. If a cancer is more common, finding a small number of cases in a given locale is that much more likely to be a random event.

Pages 237-238: #4: Legal theories in toxic tort cases involving occupational exposures. This note is intended to clarify, in advance of reading an occupational exposure case, the posture ordinarily seen in such cases, i.e., plaintiff employee suing a party other than the employer for creating the exposure to the toxin. The most common of these scenarios is that found in the asbestos cases, where the victim sues the asbestos companies on a defective products theory (or sometimes failure to warn theory) because of the systematic suppression by the asbestos industry of information related to the known health dangers posed by exposure to asbestos.

Pages 238-241: *Landrigan v Celotex Corporation.* This case involves an effort to recover for death due to colon cancer, allegedly caused by asbestos exposure attributable to defendant. Plaintiff relied on expert testimony to establish a causal link between the exposure and the disease. The court examines the epidemiological evidence used to attribute the likelihood of the disease to the relevant exposure. Thereafter, the court rejects defendants proposal that the attributable risk must exceed 50% (or a relative risk of 2.0 or greater) for liability to attach. The case also previews some of the *Daubert* issues in its instructions to the lower court on remand regarding how it is to scrutinize the testimony of the experts.

Pages 241-242, C&Q #1: Epidemiology, relative risk, and attributable risk. This note makes explicit what the opinion did not regarding the terminology and means of calculating attributable and relative risk.

A reminder to your students, correlations alone are not all the proof that is needed to establish "but for" causation. Finding that plaintiffs' medical expert failed to testify that "but for" the plaintiffs' exposure to trichloroethylene in their drinking water plaintiffs would not have contracted cancer, a federal judge in Arizona dismissed personal injury claims against defendant Hughes Aircraft. Yslava v. Hughes Aircraft Co., D. Ariz., No. CIV-91-525-TUC-ROS. The court acknowledged that although cancer may be caused by a confluence of factors, and isolating a single cause may be beyond the limitations of science, the judge said Arizona law requires an expert to testify that but for exposure to a single agent, the plaintiffs would not be ill.

Page 242, C&Q #2: Legal causation and statistical proof: comparing apples and pears.

What makes a relative risk value of 2.0 appear to be particularly important in the legal arena? The note provides its own answer: "A relative risk value in excess of 2.0 makes it appear more likely than not that the risk factor is the operative cause of the injury. This linguistic formulation tracks the standard that the plaintiff must meet to carry the burden of proof on the issue of causation-in-fact. That is, the plaintiff has the burden of persuading the trier of fact that defendant's action is more likely than not the cause of plaintiff's injury. Using the term attributable risk makes this linguistically even clearer, when the risk attributable to defendant is more than half (>50%) of the total risk it is easy to conclude that the defendant's act is more likely than not the cause of the plaintiff's injury."

Why shouldn't the failure to establish a relative risk value in excess of 2.0 be fatal to a plaintiff's case? The court treats relative risk as a single factor, based on the epidemiological evidence, in deciding the overall issue of causation. It is highly probative, but not conclusive in either direction.

Pages 242-243, C&Q #3: Legal causation and statistical significance: comparing apples and pear melba. *What does the distinction between legal significance and statistical significance mean for toxic tort cases?* The note explains that, given the difference in terminology, statistical significance is not the relevant measure for probity of legal proof.

Page 243, C&Q #4: The plaintiff's dilemma. *Under the Landrigan standard for proving causation, how often can plaintiffs win exposure-induced cancer cases where the epidemiological studies do not evidence a relative risk value in excess of 2.0? What will be the usual impact on available proof of the long latency periods between exposure and the onset of disease?*

As a speculative matter, the note takes the position that plaintiff will not often have other lines of proof that link the defendant's toxin to the plaintiff's injury in an individualized way. That is probably too harsh a suggestion. Plaintiffs will frequently have evidence of freedom from alternate exposures, such as being a non-smoker of cigarettes, or family health histories that show low incidence of relevant cancers, etc. Thus, a less than 2.0 relative risk will not scuttle too many cases after *Landrigan*.

Pages 243-244, C&Q #5: The pitfalls of probabilistic proof. *Is such a result absurd? Do the hypotheticals make it clear why the Landrigan court is chary of making a relative risk of 2.0 a litmus for recovery?*

The underlying question is one that the students invariably find exciting to discuss, whether probability alone is enough to carry the burden of proof on cause-in-fact. The literature usually suggests that it is not, and the over- under-compensation results argue for finding a different approach. Still, the fact remains that the risk proof is going to be just about the only highly probative information in these cases and to require more is often tantamount to non-suiting the plaintiff. In the unusual case where the relative risk exceeds 2.0, it seems odd to prevent recovery.

Should plaintiffs be relieved of their usual burden of proof because of these proof problems? Yes, at least that is what the court did in *Allen*, a very interesting (but incredibly difficult) case that was excerpted in the first edition. The court there transmuted the problem of cause-in-fact into one of proximate cause, asking whether the plaintiff had done enough to establish an exclusive causal relationship to merit protection in the legal system.

Pages 244-246: Introduction to Law and Science. This text probes the difficulties that the legal system encounters when cases require sophisticated scientific evidence and concepts be a part of the proceedings. The text tries to offer insights regarding the sources of tension between the two disciplines. The last half of the material begins the study of the *Daubert* case by placing it in historical context.

Pages 246-247: Introduction to excerpt from Peter Sandman's *Risk Communication: Facing Public Outrage.* This is vital material for the students. It presents them with their first introduction to the concept of risk and into the dichotomy in points of view between expert risk managers and the public, in terms of how risks are to be evaluated. The concept of risk perception is a critical one and students will frequently be required to discern whether the so-called "outrage factors" are influencing legal policy making.

Page 248, C&Q #1: Reactions to outrage. This note is textual and simply recounts some sources and points of view regarding the appropriate role of outrage as an element of risk assessment and risk management.

Page 248, C&Q #2: How EPA considers risk in environmental protection. This textual note comments on the current practices at the EPA. The note begins a very important linkage, linking levels of risk to regulatory action. This is not-too-subtle policy making, but it is not always seen as such. As a pedagogical matter, I (RHA) have had mixed results when I try to get the students to offer opinions regarding risk levels as action thresholds. Sometimes, it has sparked lively exchanges regarding what is the appropriate level, or why EPA of all institutions, is deciding how safe is safe. Other times, this material does not seem to stir up the students.

Page 248, C&Q #3: The law and outrage. *Should legal institutions take outrage into account? Is a court better equipped to do so than a politically responsible actor, such as a legislator or an executive branch administrative official?*

The question is asked more by way of introduction to the materials that follow than in hopes of having the student provide any answers at this time. The question foreshadows the fact that different parties and institutions have a role in risk management and the policy-making implicit in that risk management.

Pages 248-254: Introduction to and excerpt from *Daubert*. The *Daubert* case. This is the most celebrated case in the law and science area. In it, the Supreme Court establishes the ground rules *for the federal courts* regarding the basis for deciding whether to allow experts to testify on particular subjects and theories. It involves the interpretation of Federal Evidence Rules which is why states are not required to follow it for cases litigated in state courts, although several states have done so. The underlying case is a birth defects class action suit against the manufacturer of Bendectin. In the trial court, defendant won dismissal on a summary judgment motion, a ruling affirmed by the 9th Circuit. The record reflected a sharp division of the two sides' experts regarding the extent of the evidence linking Bendectin to birth defects and the proper interpretation to be given to many of the studies. The plaintiffs' experts were seeking to propound a somewhat novel set of ideas. In rejecting their appeal, the 9th Circuit cited *Frye* as the basis for rejecting the proffered evidence of plaintiffs' experts. The Supreme Court reverses, saying that *Frye* and its "generally accepted principles" position is no longer the rule in the federal courts. The Supreme Court reversed the ruling finding the lower courts' reliance on *Frye* was error and replaced the *Frye* standard with a far more intricate one that still guards the integrity of the scientific evidence allowed into the federal courts.

Page 254, C&Q #1: What did *Daubert* decide? *Apart from holding that Frye is not controlling in the wake of Evidence Rule 702, can you isolate the meaning of Daubert?*

The note answers its own question in language that captures the muddy essence of *Daubert*: the scientific evidence must be reliable and reliability is judged by reverence to several non-exclusive factors.

Pages 254-255, C&Q #2: Is *Daubert* a plaintiff's victory? *On remand, what outcome would you predict?* The open-ended question provides an entree to tell the subsequent history.

Even if the remand does not result in admission of the proffered testimony in Daubert, isn't it fairly clear that toxic tort plaintiffs, in general, are far better off having the Frye "generally accepted" test declared dead and buried, at least in litigation conducted in federal court? Yes, they are better off. The hint is intended to remind the students that in toxic tort cases (where there are usually several outrage factors, sympathetic plaintiffs with wrecked lives, and deep-pocket, risk-creating defendants), avoiding summary judgment is a critical victory in terms of leverage for settlement. If the plaintiff's experts can satisfy the

Daubert standard, there is almost sure to be a "genuine issue of material fact" sufficient to result in denial of summary judgment.

Pages 255-256, C&Q #3: The use of *Frye* in *Donaldson*. This long passage quoted from *Donaldson* may, or may not, be consistent with the usual understanding of *Frye*. Students are cautioned by the note that, whatever may be its true adherence to *Frye*, it is now the law of Illinois as announced by its highest court. To this reader, the *Donaldson* interpretation of *Frye* seems to have been influenced by the Supreme Court's explanation of its reasons for adopting the view that it did in *Daubert*. Thus, in answering the questions posed at the end of the Comment, it seems that this formulation is very similar to *Daubert* and not more restrictive.

Page 256, C&Q #4: *Daubert* and bad expert testimony. *Will Daubert change the result in cases where the testimony of plaintiffs' experts is unconvincing?* As the note explains, they probably will continue to lose because *Daubert's* barriers are not at all low.

Pages 256-257, C&Q #5: Expansion of *Daubert* by the Supreme Court. This Comment begins by using the *G.E. v. Joiner* quotation to clarify that there are two separate questions involved when a plaintiff's expert testimony comes under attack: (1) the *Daubert* question of admissibility at all of the testimony and (2) the ability of that testimony to ward off summary judgment. If the first question is answered against the plaintiff, i.e., if the expert cannot testify at all, then there is very likely to be no "genuine issue of material fact" on the summary judgment issue, and the plaintiff's claim will be dismissed. Likewise important, the excerpt also makes clear that the generous standard that favors the non-movant in avoiding summary judgment (taking their evidence as true, etc.) is inapposite to the threshold *Daubert* question. The Comment tries to make a further point about what appears to be the lack of familiarity of the majority with the normal forms of proof (extrapolation from animal studies at high doses relative to weight to humans at low doses relative to weight are routinely part of the basis for a finding of causation in toxic tort cases. If, instead, Chief Justice Rehnquist is commenting on the absence of other proof in support of the alleged PCB-small cell carcinoma correlation as a basis for upholding, on appellate judicial review a trial court's grant of summary judgment, the comments seem somewhat more in order.

The remainder of the Comment notes the growth of *Daubert*, including its application to other forms of expert witnesses in *Kumho Tire* and the lack of consistent application of *Daubert* in the lower courts. Perhaps consistency will grow over time, but a multi-factor approach seems destined to result in varied application of a standard. The Kesan article is critical of *Daubert* as a grudging and overly conservative approach. Despite Kesan's apparent disappointment, the results do not seem to be radically different than before. In difficult cases (conflicting methodologically credible but not fully accepted expert testimony) courts are feeling their way and the decisions have yet to converge on the same answer for similar types of evidence.

Pages 258-259, C&Q #6: Distinguishing innovative explanations of causation from junk science. *Is Huber correct in asserting that the legal system functions best when it follows scientific discovery rather than getting out ahead of it?* Yes. Even so, the new test of *Daubert* can hardly be considered a threat to get the legal system ahead of science.

Page 259, C&Q #7: The complex but necessary interplay between science and the

courts. This note is a counter point to Huber's position. It stresses the differences in purpose of the two systems, in which the need for the legal system to decide cases on the best evidence available bears a symbiotic relationship to science, sometimes helping to spur discovery, not replacing the methods by which discoveries are validated.

Pages 259-260, C&Q #8: Administrative agencies and "good science." The *Marita* case poses an unsavory example of bad science having the final say in decision-making. The overlay of its administrative law context and deferential review of in-house scientists adds a level of complexity to discussions about how expert testimony should be made a part of legal decisions.

Pages 260-263: Introduction to Part D - Litigating Toxic Tort Cases. This textual material highlights a number of the special problems encountered when litigating toxic tort cases. These include the multi-party structure of mass torts and/or modern defective products that are fungible and unidentifiable after their manufacture. The law has responded to the changing complexity of the economy and the transactions that result in injuries with a variety of allowances, including: new joinder devices (especially class actions), modifications to the substantive rules (such as allowing new items of damage), relaxing the burden for proof of causation, and imposition of joint and several liability (or *Sindell*-market-share-liability), etc. The text centers on the new procedural devices and the new problems they engender.

Page 263, C&Q #1: The multiplier effect of multiparty litigation. *To a defendant, what is the impact of procedural devices that result in the joinder of multiple similar claims into a single lawsuit?* The class action posture raises the stakes (even beyond the threat of *Parklane* non-mutual offensive use of collateral estoppel). The attorneys for the class have an interest in being sure that the full class is compensated, and the more members of the class, the greater the threat to defendant and the greater the leverage of plaintiffs in seeking settlements.

Is there anything unfair in this? The note rather glibly points the finger back at the defendant and answers the claim of unfairness by noting that it was the defendant who chose the risk laden conduct. Often, the unfairness that defendants claim, when pressed, is founded on the premise that the relevant comparison is with litigation in which each plaintiff must stand alone, i.e., the old status quo.

Can an individual plaintiff with a marginal case, by turning to a multiparty device, "extort" a handsome settlement of the case? This is defendants' best argument. Individual cases have nuisance value and may be settled, but the cost of even mounting a credible threat in areas of complex litigation deters most nuisance suits. The multiplier effect brings those cases into existence, if there is a class attorney willing to run the risk of vast amounts of work for no recovery. Thus, "extortion" is now possible, but in light of the chance of non-suit if defendant defends, these cases remain unattractive for plaintiffs. Keep in mind that defendants are now more likely to defend because the cost of defending is less than the cost of a "nuisance" settlement with the class. In that light, it seems that most bad cases will continue to go unbrought, even as class actions.

Page 264, C&Q #2: The benefits of using multiparty devices. This note points out benefits of class litigation including efficiency and equity in the distribution of proceeds when there is not enough to compensate all plaintiffs seriatim.

Pages 264-265, C&Q #3: Settlements and mass class actions. *Shults* is an interesting case. The interests of class members in toxic tort litigation are not always identical and, in regard to settlements, the class counsel's interest is not always identical to that of class members. For example, class counsel and class members play a zero sum game in relation to the distribution of lump sum damage awards. The judicial role in overseeing the fairness of settlements forces judges into a very unfamiliar role. The case law that is mentioned in the comment grows out of attempts to settle asbestos litigation, and the judicial antipathy to the so-called settlement class action in that context is directly linked to the conflicts of interest that can be found between different claimants (different as to resulting injury and whether the injury is presently manifested) and the conflict that likewise exists between settlement class counsel and those members of the settlement class who might be better off with the ability to seek individualized relief, and those members of the settlement class who are not in a good position to evaluate what would be in their best interest (for example, plaintiffs who do not yet have any of the diseases).

Pages 265-267: Introduction to the relationships between toxic tort and public law. These materials are the final installment of the Woburn story. The focus here is transitional to the study of what will come later in the book, public laws designed to prevent environmental harms or provide systematic remedies, enforceable by public authorities as well as affected individuals.

Pages 267-268, C&Q #1: Did public law contribute to the private law civil action and vice versa? *Looking at this chronology, one can ask, "to what degree, if any, did the parallel processes facilitate one another?" Were they at all coordinated, or were they moving on two quite separate tracks?* Yes, some of the governmental efforts aided plaintiffs, but not as much as might be expected because the plaintiffs were, in effect, ahead of the government in time, i.e., they needed to be able to prove their case sooner than the government had completed its work up on many of the most difficult to prove issues.

Did the private litigation aid the government's efforts?

Absolutely. The key witness in the criminal case was discovered by the private plaintiffs. The publicity on the private side was a factor in getting the agencies the needed funding to do more thorough investigations. The end result of the cleanup may have been affected by the publicity as well, with the government holding out for a more costly and thorough cleanup and defendants deciding to put an end to their public humiliation by agreeing.

Pages 268-269, C&Q #2: Comparative advantages of public law. This long textual note is worth the student's time. It begins the process of contrasting the comparatively narrow remedial policies and goals of tort law with the broader public welfare pursued by public law. It also begins the process of educating students to the concept of judicial deference to agency expertise.

Pages 269-270, C&Q #3: Comparative advantages of private law. *Do the two realms (public and private law) conflict with one another?*

This note extols the role of private law and points out ways in which it complements public law. It also stresses the role that individuals play in environmental cases in private law actions, roles that can bring public law enforcement in its wake.

Pages 270-271, C&Q #4: The "tort reform" efficiency debate. *Does the Woburn toxics case throw any light on arguments reflected in the Huber essay that follows (starting on page 271 of the text) that complex cases involving scientific subtleties and public risk should in the future be handled by government agencies under public laws rather than by private litigation in courts?*

If Huber is read to say those kinds of cases have no role to play in shaping long-term public policy and should not be allowed to go forward because the experts know best, then it seems clear that Huber has failed to recognize the push-pull relationship of the private suits and public agency vigilance.

What is the verdict on tort reform to be drawn from Woburn's Civil Action? The answer, of course, depends on what sort of tort reform is under consideration. Punitive damage caps are one thing, removing toxic tort jurisdiction and short statutes of repose are another. It is easy to be drawn into extreme positions. Some tort cases lead to ludicrous results that do undermine confidence in the ability of the legal system to maintain its legitimacy — cases must consistently have sensible results if respect for law is to be maintained. The civil justice side of this legal system is heavily dependent on voluntary compliance with its dictates, so maintaining confidence is not an idle goal. As a counterweight to calls for cutting back on tort recoveries, however, is the cynical observation that those making the calls for these changes are those that will be pocketing the money that is "saved." The net effect of tort reform, in virtually all cases, is a loss of autonomy of individuals in regard to risk promoting behavior. Every additional hurdle to recovery means that an additional area of privately chosen risk creation is unreviewable at the behest of the citizenry or the eventual victims. Protection against private overreaching becomes a function of the ability of over-worked over-matched regulators to joust with the politically powerful risk creators. Without tort reform there are at least some additional avenues to ventilate the nature of the risk creating activities.

Pages 271-276: Introduction to Risk Management Concerns and Excerpt from Peter Huber's *Safety and the Second Best: the Hazards of Public Risk Management in the Courts.*

The Huber article on safety and the second best is a fascinating excerpt of a very well written longer article. Huber advances the proposition that what he calls public risk is unfairly perceived by the general public as too dangerous. In fact, in Huber's view, public risk and accepting public risk is often the most risk reducing behavior available. As a second matter, Huber argues that risk managers, professionally trained, are in the best position to recognize the advantages posed by embracing enterprises that create public risks while retiring other forms of risk in greater amounts. Accordingly, Huber criticizes commentators who support stringent judicial review of technical decisions favoring public risk over other forms of risk taking. Beyond that, Huber criticizes courts when they substitute their judgment for that of the expert administrative agencies to which Congress has entrusted the risk management decision. It is very helpful to remind the students of other past readings that may help them think about the Huber article, specifically the Talbot Page excerpt that appeared at page 14 of the text, and the Peter Sandmen excerpt that appeared at page 246 of the text.

Page 276, C&Q #1: The benefits of public risk. *Does this mean that Page is wrong when he argues that environmental risk situations display the potential for catastrophic costs weighed against relatively modest benefits? How might Huber champion nuclear power in preference to* *fossil fuel generation of electricity? (Even putting all the factors on the table, is it certain that nuclear power generation is a bad choice?)*

It is hard to reconcile the Huber position and Talbot Page position (text, page 14) when you get down to specifics. Giving Huber credit for the risk reduction of public risk by displacing or retiring other forms of risk, is good benefit cost accounting. Still, that doesn't answer the policy question about Page's preference for what might be called institutionalized caution. As to nuclear power, as the note suggests, it is almost certain that Huber and Page would have different views about the desirability of increasing reliance on nuclear power.

Are courts in a position to measure the trade-offs? Courts would not be in a good position to measure tradeoffs between nuclear power plants and wood stoves. They do not have the same sort of technical fact finding capabilities to evaluate whole programs as do administrative agencies that have both a staff and the expertise to engage in such judgments.

Is one subject that Huber should address (but doesn't) the problems of risk assessment in high uncertainty (sometimes zero-infinity) situations? How do you suppose that Huber would analyze a technology that provided many calculable benefits but also posed a slight chance of destroying a significant part of the world? Should Huber also take public outrage seriously? Would Huber agree with the decision in Wilsonville? It is hard to determine what Huber would do with zero-infinity problems. What is clear is that he would not take the outrage factors involved in the zero-infinity problem very seriously. What is more difficult to be sure of is how Huber would review the uncertainties involved in a typical zero-infinity problem, that is, both uncertainties in measurement of the harm and uncertainties surrounding its likelihood of happening. If he took a conservative view of those things, then the resulting risk posed by zero-infinity problem rank very high and probably outweighs embracing the public risk.

Pages 276-277, C&Q #2: The opportunity costs of proactive regulation. *Is this an effective argument? Are these costs commensurable?*

The note raises the point of opportunity costs in the risk management setting. Regulation extracts a toll in terms of the cost it entails. Money spent on the regulatory process itself could be spent on other things that produce benefits. In fact, for any given number of dollars spent, particularly when money is spent in programs that benefit the poor (such as WIC, or pre-natal care, or vaccinations, etc.) a reduction in mortality can be achieved with lesser costs than through costly toxics regulation. This note asks students to come to grips with that fact.

Pages 277-278, C&Q #3: Stephen Breyer and other risk reformers. This is a long, and somewhat rambling note, that tries to assess whether risk ranking or special risk assessment panels can and/or should be used to make policy decisions. On one side, Justice Breyer is certainly correct in pointing out some cases of overzealous regulation and the need for clear-headed review of that process and its occasional tunnel vision. His call for greater reliance on expert judgment and for the creation of a special risk tribunal, however, may not be the best choice for solving the problem he noted. The material in the note sketches out some of the positions that arise in this area of debate. At the end, the note offers a short excerpt from Professor Hornstein in which he attacks the idea of using risk or risk ranking as the central factor in policy making. This critique parallels the critique of using efficiency as the central decisional criteria in environmental regulation.

Page 278, C&Q #4: Attacking Huber's assessment of institutional competence. This note offers two short excerpts from an article by Professors Gillette and Krier that directly attack Huber on the role of the courts in risk management. Gillette and Krier find that the courts are competent bodies to review administrative waste management decisions. This is very sophisticated material, and it is difficult for students to evaluate at this point in their study. They may do better having it recalled to them after they have been through the middle chapters of the book in which they see agencies implementing a variety of statutes.

Page 279, C&Q # 6: "Hormesis" - the benefits of toxins? Just as novel expansions of scientific theory have been brought to bear in favor of plaintiffs in toxic tort cases, hormesis awaits data and substantiation. If its claim for beneficial effects of low level toxic exposures to some toxics can be substantiated by empirical evidence and shown to exist in the absence of harmful effects from those same exposures, toxic tort litigation will account for that fact. The particular importance of hormesis at a more theoretical level is that, if verified, it stands as a counterpoint to usual assumption that all carcinogens should be treated as if there is no safe threshold of exposure.

Page 280, C&Q #7: Competing proposals for setting environmental priorities. This Comment should be juxtaposed with Comment 5, on risk ranking. While "worst first" is a sensible consideration in policy making, this Comment suggests that it is not the only plausible means for setting priorities. The commentaries cited all argue in one way or another that risk ranking is not a sufficient decisional criterion upon which to base all policy making.

§3. A Special Compendium of Woburn Materials

Lessons from the Woburn Toxics case and A CIVIL ACTION. This section presents further materials for integrating Chapter Four and the Woburn toxics case, including a FRCP Rule 16 pre-trial conference simulation on the Woburn facts.

Other tie-ins of the Woburn case narrative to further course coverage can be made in consideration of public law issues, administrative and criminal law liability.

We remind teachers of the excellent Summer 1999 sourcebook by Lewis Grossman and Robert Vaughn, A DOCUMENTARY COMPANION TO *A CIVIL ACTION*, WITH NOTES, COMMENTS, AND QUESTIONS (Foundation, 1999). This book has an extensive chronology of the case, organized according to its procedural history, with edited reproductions of virtually all the significant documents involved in the Woburn toxics civil litigation. The appearance of the Grossman & Vaughn book as a Civil Procedure curricular resource is a reminder that in the near future many of our students in Environmental Law will have been exposed to A Civil Action in their first-year Torts and Civil Procedure courses. You should ask students what their various prior exposures to the case may be. What then is the function of further coverage of the case study in Environmental Law, beyond providing a good vehicle for review of some first-year doctrinal points? Our answer is that in most cases the Environmental Law analysis of the case study is likely to be deeper, broader, and more interesting, expanding the students' consideration to the intermingled roles of private and public law, second-guessing the parties' litigation strategies including missed potential claims for multiple causes of action, innovative remedies, further tactical defenses, questions of societal policy in confronting chemical contamination, the public and private economics of the case, and so on. Beyond advantages in technical sophistication, students in the upper level course may also be readier to comprehend issues raised by the case in the realms of legal politics, ethics, the psychology of courtroom dynamics, other realities of litigative combat, and so on.

Page 265-267, Note the Woburn toxics Time-Line: a chronology of the parallel public/private law processes in the Woburn case.

More Background Facts on A CIVIL ACTION– a variety of potentially relevant notes on the Case, the Book, and the Movie[1]

History of Woburn. Woburn has historically been a heavily industrialized area. In 1853, Woburn Chemical Works was built in North Woburn. Throughout the 1850s, Woburn led the nation is the manufacture of shoes and boots, and by 1899 was the leading producer of pesticides using the arsenic process.

The EPA role. EPA has been involved at the Grace site since before the plaintiffs began their lawsuit. In 1982 Grace admitted to using TCE and began doing voluntary groundwater investigatory work. Then, in 1983, EPA issued an Administrative Order to Grace to look for buried drums, excavate them, and install groundwater monitoring wells. By 1984, Grace had completed the testing, inventory, and some of the drum removal as required by the 1983 Administrative Order. In the end, EPA settled for cleanup costs of $69.4 million with each company paying their own share. Ultimately the cost of the government ordered clean-up remedy undertaken by the defendants and other corporations will total far more than the $69.4 million.

EPA refused to testify during the course of the trial, according to EPA attorney Gretchen Muench, not because it didn't have relevant material, but because of an administrative policy against testifying in ongoing civil litigation.

The "Aberjona River." The Aberjona is not a surging river as depicted in the motion picture, *A Civil Action.* The movie scenes of the Woburn site were actually shot on the upper Charles River. Woburn's Aberjona is more like a meandering creek, only about eight feet wide, rarely as much as two feet deep, wending slowly through Woburn. The reason why this difference between actual and portrayed scale is significant for legal analysis is that it relates to the trial judge's ruling on "extraordinary" causation (coursebook at 289-90). The fact that ground water readily traverses below watercourses is easier to understand when the true size of the river is recognized. The watercourse in fact does not strike an observer's eye as a major physical barrier between the Riley property and Wells G & H. as it appeared in the movie.

The judge's ruling was briefly noted in the movie that the liability of the Beatrice Tannery, both parcels of which now appear to have been contaminated for years before and during the '60's, could only be based on proved dumping *after* August 27, 1968. Where did this date come from? The movie and the book do not indicate, but it came from a complex ruling under the Restatement of Torts §435(2), noted in the casebook at

1. Some of these notes derive from the first-named author's work on the case, some from personal interviews with parties and attorneys on both sides, some from a discussion panel at the Appleseed Foundation, Boston, January 14, 1999.

page 212-213. The judge took a provision intended to codify *Palsgraf* – where, if in hindsight it appeared to be *statistically extraordinary* that causation happened, then a judge can forgive defendants' actions – and the judge said it was highly extraordinary to him that solvents could flow in the groundwater from west to east under the Aberjona River to the wells. In hydrological terms, however, this flow of solvents in groundwater was not only *not* extraordinary statistically, but in fact geophysically inevitable, given the laws of science and the presence of wells. Nevertheless, because the court thus narrowed the liability window, the case against Beatrice was made substantially more difficult than the case against Grace. The jury members said the special interrogatories based on this ruling caused them a great deal of confusion and indecision. Understandably, neither the movie nor the book explore this strategic legal ruling, although the John Travolta character protests, "where do these dates come from?!"

Special jury questions in the Woburn toxics case. The judge's evidentiary ruling that Woburn defendant Beatrice Foods could be held liable only for toxins that flowed into the public well after the engineer's notice they received in 1968 required an impossible degree of chronological certainty from the jury, and the case against Beatrice eventually collapsed. An examination of the complexity and precision that the special jury questions entailed illustrates the difficulty of arriving at an affirmative answer. Here is that special interrogatory to the jury as to defendant Beatrice Foods, as contained in the Lewis Grossman and Robert Vaughn book, A DOCUMENTARY COMPANION TO A CIVIL ACTION, 635 [see also defendant Grace interrogatories at pages 652-653]:

> 1. Have the plaintiffs established by a preponderance of the evidence that any of the following chemicals were disposed of at the Beatrice site after August 27, 1968 <u>and</u> substantially contributed to the contamination of Wells G and H by these chemicals prior to May 22, 1979?
>
> | | | |
> |---|---|---|
> | a.) Trichloroethylene | Yes_____ | No__X__ |
> | b.) Tetrachloroethylene | Yes_____ | No__X__ |
> | c.) 1,2 Transdichloroethylene | Yes_____ | No__X__ |
> | d.) 1,1,1 Trichoroethane | Yes_____ | No__X__ |

The relevant geographic sites. The W.R. Grace plant is located a half mile from the public wells G&H, as the map of the site indicates. The Beatrice lowland parcel, about 15 acres, is only 800′ from the wells on the other side of the Aberjona Stream. The small Unifirst company, as noted in the text, is located 4/10 of a mile to the north of the wells. The Beatrice Tannery lies south and uphill of the lowland parcel (now "Wildwood Conservation land," a home for indigent wildlife according to the testimony in the movie). For purposes of understanding the law suit, it is probably useful to distinguish *three* relevant sites: Grace's Cryovac, and Beatrice-Riley's two parcels, the lowland parcel and the Tannery parcel itself.

The initial identification of potential defendants. The nearness of the W.R. Grace Cryovac Plant and Beatrice Foods Tannery to the Woburn wells, as the movie portrayed it, was discovered by Jan Schlichtmann, the plaintiff's attorney as he was stopped by a policeman on a bridge over the rushing river. In fact, the Environmental Protection Agency had identified these two companies, and three smaller firms, in 1979 as possible sources of the wellwater contamination that EPA had been studying for a year before Schlichtmann came into the case.

Plaintiffs were barred from testing on the tannery site. One of the most significant mistakes in the movie, which is virtually overlooked in the book as well, is that when Schlichtmann went onto Beatrice-Riley property with a warrant, he was emphatically NOT allowed by the judge to go onto the Tannery plant property itself, but was allowed only to test in the 15-acre lowland parcel lying some 1000′ from the Tannery itself. In the movie, the Travolta character says "I have a court order which gives me the right to inspect every inch of the Tannery as well," but this was inexplicably never allowed by the judge. The judge appears to have accepted the argument from the Tannery's counsel that since the Tannery has been subsequently re-sold by Beatrice Foods back to Mr. Riley and his employees, the court would no longer allow inspection at that site. Subsequently it appeared that the contaminants did exist on that site, according to the two reports that had not been revealed during discovery.

Distinguishing defendants. In the movie, William Cheeseman is portrayed somewhat as a fool, and W.R. Grace is considered substantially parallel to the Beatrice Tannery. In fact, there are substantial distinctions between the role of the two companies' different lands in the case. According to the EPA's Gretchen Muensch, the Beatrice lowlands parcel was the most highly contaminated site in the area, and the Grace site much less so. The Grace management and attorneys appear to have been surprised to find that their employees had been dumping materials in back of the Grace plant, and when they learned this were quite forthcoming with both the EPA and with the public announcements of the dumping practices that they had been able to discover. The Beatrice and Riley Tannery parties took a very different approach to disclosure of information, which is to some degree reflected in the movie and at greater length in the book.

Punitives? The plaintiffs' case was described as seeking punitive damages as well as compensatory damages. In Massachusetts there are very few grounds on which punitive damages can be awarded under state law. Accordingly there is an Erie question about whether a federal court in Massachusetts can consider a punitive damages claim.

Rule 11 hearing 1. There were two Rule 11 hearings — one at the beginning of the case filed by Mr. Cheeseman, and one more interesting ruling at the end of the case, touched upon briefly in the book but totally excluded from the movie, where the Tannery's defense attorneys were found to have concealed requested information during the discovery portion of the trial. On a complex uncertain balance the judge failed to order a re-trial. The first Rule 11 motion on the merits was unlikely to be successful, because although Schlichtmann had very little direct evidence that he himself had been able to accumulate, the EPA's study identifying probable sources of pollution were probably enough to survive a Rule 11 motion, at that time at least, in any court in the country.

Interviewing without counsel. When Al Love crossed the street and began to talk to Anne Anderson about the dumping behind Grace, it was probably unethical for Schlichtmann to speak with him off the record without Grace's counsel present. Love was still an employee of Grace and therefore should have been represented by Grace's counsel at any formal or informal discussions about what he did or did not know.

Grace's forthrightness. When Al Love began to talk about the dumping, Grace apparently did not attempt to silence him, as implied in the movie. Attorney Cheeseman, and Attorney Mark Stoler, corporate counsel for Grace, were embarrassed, and apparently responded with complete disclosure of whatever their employees subsequently told the EPA and the public.

The civil procedure bifurcation tactic. A critical question in the movie is how Jerome Facher will be able to keep the grief-stricken and emotionally powerful parents of the leukemic children off the stand. The character, after deposition, says that the parents' story must be kept from the jury at all costs. Later, the Duvall character says to Schlichtmann, "do you really think I'm going to let that happen?" (that is, letting the parents take the stand). And Schlichtmann replied, "I don't see how you can prevent it." The ultimate answer, briefly described in the movie, was "Bifurcation." Under F.R.C.P. 42B, as noted in the case book at page 212, a judge may split a trial into separate trials in the interest of efficiency. According to the leading article on the case, however, it appears that the judge, who picked up on this suggestion most emphatically, did something quite unusual in splitting the case multiply *within the liability case itself.* The first trial was bifurcated to be just on whether the solvents reached the wells, and the second on whether the solvents moved from the wells to the plaintiffs' homes, again, without allowing any of the victims to take the stand. Only the third trial would have reached the question of the medical causation of the plaintiffs' harms. Obviously, as the movie makes clear, the finances of a plaintiff's case are sufficiently complex that splitting a liability trial into three successive trials increases the opportunity cost such that substantial numbers of plaintiffs never can undertake such a chain of proof.

Settlement Offers — The "$20 million settlement offer." In the movie there is a scene in the courtroom corridor pre-verdict where Attorney Jerry Facher proffers Schlichtmann a $20 bill, and asks whether the plaintiffs would accept that bill as a settlement if there were six zeros after the 20, i.e. $20 million. If true, this interchange would raise serious ethical implications in Schlichtmann's not having transmitted the offer to his clients, an unethical practice implied in the opening scene of the movie. Attorneys Facher and Schlichtmann both, however, have affirmed to us that this interchange was complete fiction. Facher says he would never leave a twenty dollar bill near Schlichtmann, is proud that he has never paid anyone $1 million to settle a case, and never would. Nevertheless, earlier in the case, during a pre-trial conference, Facher says he twice hinted that he might be willing to settle for a little less than $1 million. A third potential settlement opportunity was during the preparation for trial, as the trial got closer, some of the Beatrice principals urged Facher to consider settlement discussions, and that "$1 million a family might do it" (there were 8 families in the lawsuit). Schlichtmann may have talked with Beatrice attorney Neil Jacobs, an associate of Facher's, saying that the plaintiffs might take $16 million, but the discussion never went anywhere.

The truth behind the corridor movie scene is important because many law school classes may build an ethical discussion on Schlichtmann's depicted failure to take the $20 million dollar settlement offer to the plaintiff families. In addition to demurrers from Facher and Schlichtmann, co-counsel Kevin Conway has told us that the firm always took real settlement offer to the families, who were the decisionmakers, eight families, totaling thirty-five people. Conway said that their firm preferred settlement offers to be written down so that agreements could be enforced. The concern was to protect the families from invalid offers that would be withdrawn when the families began to seriously consider them. Facher referred to these types of offers as "lawyer's code." Thus, there may indeed be an argument that not all implied, tentative settlement offers were transmitted to the plaintiffs.

The Four Seasons Hotel settlement conference. As to the settlement conference scene at the grand Four Seasons Hotel where Schlichtmann fell flat proposing a $400 million settlement, Grace attorney Michael Keating has said that the Four Seasons meeting was forced by the judge, who didn't want this case to go to trial and urged the parties to have a settlement conference. The defendants thought that it would probably be at one of the large firm's conference rooms, and were quite surprised to find that plaintiffs had scheduled it for the Four Seasons. The settlement scene has been called quite accurate, except as to the amount. Mr. Keating remembered that he had added the account up to the approximately $400 million that Schlichtmann was demanding. He said that the Grace attorneys were ready to talk at around $20 million, which was where Schlichtmann began, but the figure rapidly went out of sight, and they left the conference about as quickly as the movie depicts.

The movie depicts the Schlichtmann's partners as having been flabbergasted by the hug settlement numbers being proposed by plaintiffs' lead counsel. Plaintiffs' co-counsel Kevin Conway contradicts, saying that the amount was a carefully structured settlement, adding up to $175 million over a period of thirty years, that had been tried out successfully on several mock juries. Conway said that the plaintiffs' attorneys were willing to advise their clients to settle for far less than that $175 million structured settlement, but that Schlichtmann wanted to open the discussion with the defendants thinking in big money terms to loosen them up. Conway had warned Schlichtmann that if this were the way the conference opened, the defendants would just walk out. In the event, Conway was right. All the defendants walked out. Conway said, however, that given the plaintiffs' readiness to deal, the parties were really much closer than the defendants realized at the time. Jerry Facher says that he was not in the same Zen trance as Duvall appeared to be at the Four Seasons negotiation. He did keep the pen as shown in the movie, although it subsequently turned out not to work very well.

An arsenic issue. As EPA was finalizing its cleanup plan in 1989, high levels of arsenic and chromium were discovered in the Aberjona River. EPA did not expect this discovery, and owing to the late timing chose to break this problem off into a second phase study while it finalized the major solvent remediation plan. (There had been much resistance to EPA's initial cleanup plan from both industry and citizens, so having just overcome opposition to the original plan, EPA wanted to get the solvent plan underway.) EPA did not find substantial arsenic and chromium contaminants except in the river sediments. Research has shown that the concentrations of arsenic contamination increase as you go north from Wells G & H, with the highest concentrations *north* of Route 128, thus suggesting that the arsenic contamination is not coming from any of the sites currently being remediated.

The arsenic is apparently percolating up into the surface waters from the groundwater. Arsenic's full effects are not completely understood, but recent evidence shows that arsenic is carcinogenic at very low levels. Sediment cores from this area show that there are two historical peaks of arsenic concentration: 1916 and the 1960s. The 1916 peak corresponded to the height of pesticide manufacturing. Arsenic levels again peaked in the 1960s as a result of construction in the watershed. Scientists believed that the disturbance of surface areas mobilized the arsenic in the sediments, thus resulting in increased levels. These levels have decreased since the peak in the 1960s, but have not returned to zero. The arsenic contamination is important to the story of Woburn because it has long existed in the Aberjona river. Since 60% of the water in Wells G & H comes from the river, and arsenic is believed to be carcinogenic, this is another possible cause of the leukemia in Woburn.

Citizen resistance to cleanup plans. The City of Woburn and its citizens have been attempting to stall the cleanup of the contaminated sites. This stalling has not occurred because the people like living next to contaminated land, but rather because they fear that once the land is cleaned up, Wells G & H will start pumping again and they will be forced to drink that water. For example, the City refused to allow Unifirst to use city water for its pump-and-treat remediation system. This fear, however, may not be unfounded, since Massachusetts still lists the aquifer where Wells G & H sit as a drinking water source that it will use again in the future. This means that the CERCLA cleanup is theoretically geared toward bring the water quality of the aquifer back to safe drinking water levels — a Cadillac cleanup, despite the locality's nationally-known contamination and heavily industrialized history. Would a reclassification of this area be both a more practicable and politically realistic alternative?

The 1985 pump test. In 1985, Chuck Myette performed a thirty-day pump test for USGS and EPA. In setting up this test, his team identified fifteen or twenty possible sources of contamination, but none of them satisfied all of his team's criteria. The closest source was the tannery, across the Aberjona River. Unifirst was upgradient, but the chemical profile was not an exact match. Grace was a half-mile away in a low permeability glacial till, which was not a part of the sand and gravel aquifer.

EPA's goal in conducting this pump test was to limit the area looked at for liability. At the time of the test, EPA believed three companies would be involved in the remediation and had already ordered limited remedial investigations on the property and sent site inspectors. These three properties were: Beatrice, Unifirst, and Grace. The test also identified two other possible contributing sources, New England Plastics and Olympia.

Grace versus Beatrice as contamination sources. In the case, as reflected in the movie, Grace was hit with an $8 million settlement payout, and Beatrice walked away paying plaintiffs nothing. The consensus among scientists, however, seems to be that Beatrice's properties are likely to have been the primary source of local contamination that reached the wells. The tannery's lowland 15-acre parcel was one of the most heavily-contaminated sites in Massachusetts. The tannery itself had long had disposal lagoons out back, and had contamination showing up in its own on-site wells. Out of approximately fifteen sources of contamination for Wells G & H, Grace is likely to have been an extremely minor source of contamination, or not a contributor at all. The computer simulations tracing whether Grace's discharges could have migrated through the bedrock and consolidated substrates to reach the wells are based on models in which the worst case discharge conditions would have had to exist every day for twenty-four hours a day. This worst case scenario, with major contamination migration toward the wells from Grace's direction, would occur only when Wells G & H pumped full force at the same time, but in reality this only occurred 23% of the time. According to this worst case computer scenario model, after 20 years of continuous pumping in worst case conditions, DCE (the fastest moving of the Grace contaminants) would probably still be thirty feet away from the wells, unless there were rock fractures in the substrate undiscovered to date.

On the other hand, even if contaminants migrated from the Grace property to Wells G &

H, they could not have been the sole cause of contamination; the contamination at the Grace site was not high enough to cause the contamination that existed in the wells. Therefore, even in this situation there would have to be a second far larger source of contamination, and given the hundred-fold greater contamination on the Beatrice property, that is likely to be where the bulk of contamination came from.

The reason that Grace, the minor player, got hit with liability, while the major actors Beatrice and Riley did not, may be, as the Robert Duvall character says, because plaintiffs could find no one from the tannery who would confess in time for the trial, while at Grace they found Al Love. Another scarifying possibility is the casual report by one juror[2] that the jury was deadlocked with a critical bloc opposed finding both liable, so they 'picked Grace because we knew water runs downhill and so probably Grace was more liable.'

Causation. A Massachusetts Department of Public Health study in 1997 concluded that leukemia was more likely in children whose mothers consumed water from Wells G & H during pregnancy. Mothers were most likely to consume water from Wells G & H during periods of worst case pumping conditions. Worst-case pumping conditions occurred when both Wells G & H pumped at the same time, which was usually sometime in August as these wells only pumped when there was a shortage of water from the other sources. Of the seven children who developed leukemia, six had final trimesters that fell within periods of worst-case pumping conditions, thus suggesting that there is a correlation between the water and the leukemia. EPA attorneys report, as to the question of leukemia causation from the wellwater, statistics now show that childhood leukemia in the Woburn area dropped dramatically after the closure of Wells G and H, and that the Beatrice site was by far the most contaminated site in the area. The problem, however, is that no one has been able to determine whether VOCs, arsenic, chromium, or lead most probably caused the leukemia. Therefore, even if the trial were held today, Schlichtmann would still have great difficulty in proving what in the water, discharged by whom, probably caused the leukemia.

Although the Woburn Health Study done by the Harvard School of Public Health reported many occurrences of serious illnesses other than leukemia, cancer was as usual the dramatic bellwether chosen to carry the plaintiffs' attack. In cases of complex causation (see pages following 227) it may sometimes be possible to prove causation of the less-dramatic illnesses more readily than proving the cause of cancers. Not here, however, where many potential causes may have led to the various non-cancer illnesses. If the case could not be won based on the dramatic incidence of cancer, it probably would not be successful as to other claimed harms.

Defendant's attorney Keating, however, has argued that it was a good thing that the jury did not get the question of causation of cancer, because this is a highly scientific issue, which should probably be referred to a scientific court. The jury, facing the emotional injury done to the plaintiffs, would not discern the nuances of causation. They would find causation merely because the solvents were there in the drinking water.

The Unifirst site. While doing remediation work at the Unifirst site, the engineers made

2. The statement, ignoring all the scientific evidence, is viewable on the video of the 1998 Woburn symposium, on the Berkman Center website — **www.acivilaction.org.**

an interesting discovery. Behind the Unifirst building they uncovered an area of stained soil. Further research showed that the former owners had used this area as a disposal site. Photographs, taken during the 1960s show the stained area as well. The chemical composition of the stain is not currently known, but this suggests that more contamination might have come from the Unifirst site than previously believed.

Justice, and the jury? As to the question of jury justice, Facher says that he believes that the function of the trial is to find facts and reach a conclusion in a fair way, and that is a function well fulfilled by the jury, which of course had decided in favor of his client. Mr. Keating, whose defendant lost, says no one in the jury had special education and they should have had some special training in order to understand how to resolve a case of this complexity. Mr. Conway says that simple people using common sense were far more preferable than a panel of geologists or medical specialists in resolving real life cases like this. Conway also notes that according to later interviews, the jury was deadlocked 4-2 against both defendants. The judge sent them back and after only a short time, in order to reach a decision, the jury found for the plaintiffs on the Grace case and against on the Tannery case, but that the latter appeared to be a pressured retraction to cut a deal on a compromise verdict.

Individual characterizations. In our judgment, the movie gave realistic portrayals of Attorneys Facher, Schlichtmann, Conway, and Crowley, while the book was far more accurate in reflecting Attorney Cheeseman's professional abilities and ethical integrity. As Bill Cheeseman says, however, "the moviemakers had a hero-figure, and a villain-figure or two, so I guess they needed a clown,... and so that was me."

As to Judge Skinner, the defense attorneys have consistently argued that his portrayal in the movie was most unfair, that Judge Skinner was known for his decorum, courtesy, and thoroughness, leaning over backwards to help Schlichtmann and the plaintiffs. Any judge of a long trial sometimes loses his temper. The judge, however, was hampered by the fact that he could not talk to Jonathan Harr, the book's author, nor to the screenwriters of the movie, so that the movie inclines against him. The judge, according to the defendants, made a number of rulings in favor of the plaintiffs that he did not have to. The first Rule 11 motion — overruled; summary judgment — overruled; motion for directed verdict — overruled; the emotional distress physical cell nexus objection (coursebook at page 210) — overruled; objections against expert testimony which the defense attorneys thought was inadmissible — overruled. Mr. Conway counters that the judge undermined the plaintiffs' case badly, allowing the defense to depose experts endlessly which ran up the costs, as the movie showed. More than $600,000 was paid by plaintiffs for geologists' testimony, more than $900,000 for medical experts. Much of this was to pay fees through endless depositions, whereas the plaintiffs had done their depositions of experts within only two days time, approximately 15 minutes a piece. The plaintiffs had wanted to have the lawsuit focused on only one family as a flagship plaintiff, thereafter simplifying the trial by collateral estoppel. The judge would not allow it, forcing the full-dress trial, only later to bifurcate it. The second Rule 11 motion was inexplicable according to Conway and eliminated an important, justiciable case that should have been allowed to proceed on the merits. The judge's rulings, if not his physical appearance, seem to us as observers to have been well captured by the movie; Prof. Marilyn Berger, however, who is one of few who has interviewed the judge at length since the trial, strongly empathizes with the judge and supports his handling of the case.

Most importantly, however, the movie does not show how indefatigably hardworking and involved the families from Woburn were in the building and carrying-on of the case. *Anderson et al.* was one of those cases where attorneys and clients form a team for neighborhood fact-finding, media coverage, money-raising, and maintenance of morale, and to the extent that the movie does not reflect that it shortchanges a significant community reality.

Costs. The plaintiffs attorneys poured approximately $2.4 million into the preparation of the case, of which $587 thousand alone was for drilling test wells and testing groundwater. Schlichtmann's flair for spending money in preparing the case was certainly exuberant, as the book and movie show, but the major portion of the expenses in hindsight were not frivolities. Perhaps one concludes that the plaintiffs needed to find an attorney like Schlichtmann, who was willing to fly high with a very shaky case, risking his own money, house, and car (and ultimately losing them) to present the citizens' case. As a comparison, attorneys for defendants Grace and Beatrice spent approximately $7 million each, a total of almost $15 million, to prepare and present the corporations' defense.

Denouement. In the dramatic denouement of the story, the plaintiffs' attorneys bring the financial settlement back to the plaintiffs' families, about $350,000 per family after expenses, and Mr. Aufiero asks, "and they'll also clean the place up, right?" and the answer given is no. The plaintiffs in fact appear to have cared more about apologies and restoration than about cash damages, but the EPA was at that time in the process of cleaning up the site so that the dramatic scene's premise was incorrect.

At the end of the movie, the Schlichtmann character played by Travolta is seen passing the appeal and boxes of exhibits on to someone, with the implication that it might be the EPA. This was not the case. As noted in the casebook, at pages 213-215, his case actually went up to the First Circuit twice, and on *cert* petition to the Supreme Court of the United States, on the question of the Tannery defendant's failure to disclose test reports showing the Tannery with solvents on the property justified a re-trial.

The EPA settlement negotiations were complex; the CERCLA settlement agreement was at least an inch thick. The lead EPA attorney was distressed that the first day of conferences were spent trying to determine whose name would be first on the EPA petition in the case, which would mean that party would be the leading name in the style of the case. Everyone tried to avoid it. So finally, she announced that the leading name would be the last person to sign off on the agreement, which triggered a rush to sign on and the deal was closed.

Simulation: Consider a FRCP 16 Pre-Trial Conference on the Woburn toxics case.

Several of our classes have done an in-class simulation on the Woburn toxic contamination case study based on the Rule 16 Pre-Trial Conference format, based on the materials in Chapter Four and A CIVIL ACTION, the best-selling book by Jonathan Harr and the movie with John Travolta, available in video. The pre-trial conference can be held after completion of Chapter Four discussions in class, or as a relatively cold-turkey exercise after a single class session, setting up the simulation to be done thereafter on the fly. Giving pages 931-939 as a skimming assignment (on how EPA implements CERCLA), provides a useful public law element to be included in the pre-trial conference.

In such Rule 16 simulations, which one of the authors has used extensively in complex Property Law classroom simulations, the teacher dons the role of a federal magistrate judge preparing the case in a pre-trial conference (an initial conference, not necessarily the only pre-trial conference that would be held in such a complex toxic tort case) prior to trial in federal court. The purpose is to show students how the full factual sprawl of a case gets laid on the table, and legal arguments are sounded on the facts from every involved party perspective. It is an opportunity for students to see in practice what we tell them from day one of their legal educations, that they must think like lawyers, anticipating all relevant arguments and counter-arguments. (In fact, when we as attorneys are presented with complex factual and legal problems, don't we do exactly that, scoping it out analytically by running an imaginary Rule 16 conference in our heads?) The tone in an initial pre-trial conference can be quite informal, with questions left open at every turn as you march the parties through their theories and proof of the prima facie case and defenses thereto. You can say, "Judge So-and-So has low tolerance for trivialities – what factual stipulations can you make here to avoid wasting the court's time, and what issues and parties can you settle out of this so as not to try the Judge's patience?" If, for instance, a critical piece of information would be necessary for one party's argument but has not yet been developed in discovery [i.e. the student attorney doesn't know the answer], the magistrate teacher can say, "Alright, you'd need that to proceed on that matter at trial, so be sure you have it in admissible shape when we hold our next pre-trial conference, or drop it," and move on.

An alternative model is to split the pre-trial conference into multiple smaller sections, with each student given a role, which better encourages every student to prepare and participate actively. The downside is that the professor cannot play the role of presiding magistrate in several sections simultaneously. One solution is to have the professor take on simulations sequentially, a less taxing approach is to have several students selected and briefed to perform the role of magistrate in sections doing the simulation concurrently with the teacher.

On the following pages is the assignment for an experimental Woburn toxics Rule 16 simulation. Following the assignment is a brief set of teaching suggestions.

PRE-TRIAL CONFERENCE UNDER F.R.C.P. 16 — WOBURN TOXICS CONTROVERSY

Students will represent the following parties/interests (according to first letter of surname):

A-B	Juvenile leukemia victims and their families
C-D	Persons with non-leukemic illnesses (assume a substantially equivalent complaint filed, and a motion for joinder under consideration)
E-G	Town of Woburn
H-J	US EPA (here on a hypothetical motion by plaintiffs seeking to join EPA as a necessary party)
K-M	W.R. Grace Corp., owner of Grace/Cryovac
N-P	Beatrice Foods, owner for ten year interim in the 1970s-80s of the Riley Tannery and the adjacent 15-acre wetland parcel
Q-R	John J. Riley, past and present owner of Riley Tannery, though Beatrice is probably liable for all Riley's actions under purchase & resale indemnity agreements
S	Unifirst Corp., a uniform dry-cleaning company which uses large amounts of the solvents found in the wellwater
T-V	Salem Street Minor Commercial Businesses (Aberjona Auto Parts, Whitney Barrel Co., Murphy Waste Oil Co.) none of which has yet been proved to have dumped solvents
W-Z	Anyone else who could possibly be a party to the action (e.g. Massachusetts Dept. of Envtl Protection, sportsmen, environmental citizens organizations, etc. — choose a party, and come prepared to define your role)

Please prepare for a pre-trial conference on the facts of this case which you know from Jonathan Harr's A Civil Action and Chapter Four's text materials. Members of the class will sit in designated seating blocs according to client represented, and proceed through a concise pre-trial conference under the direction of the magistrate judge preparing litigation for the federal district court judge who has been assigned this case for trial.

•FEDERAL RULES OF CIVIL PROCEDURE

RULE 16. PRETRIAL CONFERENCES; SCHEDULING; MANAGEMENT

(a) Pretrial Conferences; Objectives. In any action, the court may in its discretion direct the attorneys for the parties and any unrepresented parties to appear before it for a conference or conferences before trial for such purposes as

(1) **expediting the disposition of the action;**

(2) establishing early and continuing control so that the case will not be protracted because of lack of management;

(3) discouraging wasteful pretrial activities;

(4) **improving the quality of the trial through more thorough preparation;** and

(5) **facilitating the settlement of the case.**

(b) Scheduling and Planning. Except in categories of actions exempted by district court rule as inappropriate, the district judge, or a magistrate judge when authorized by district court rule, shall, after receiving the report from the parties under Rule 26(f) or after consulting with the attorneys for the parties and any unrepresented parties by a scheduling conference, telephone, mail, or other suitable means, enter a scheduling order that limits the time

(1) to join other parties and to amend the pleadings;

(2) to file motions; and

(3) to complete discovery.

The scheduling order may also include

(4) modifications of the times for disclosures under Rules 26(a) and 26(e)(1) and of the extent of discovery to be permitted;

(5) the date or dates for conferences before trial, a final pretrial conference, and trial; and

(6) any other matters appropriate in the circumstances of the case.

The order shall issue as soon as practicable but in any event within 90 days after the appearance of a defendant and within 120 days after the complaint has been served on a defendant. A schedule shall not be modified except upon a showing of good cause and by leave of the district judge or, when authorized by local rule, by a magistrate judge.

(c) Subjects for Consideration at Pretrial Conferences. At any conference under this rule consideration may be given, and the court may take appropriate action, with respect to

(1) **the formulation and simplification of the issues, including the elimination of frivolous claims or defenses;**

(2) the necessity or desirability of amendments to the pleadings;

(3) the possibility of obtaining admissions of fact and of documents which will avoid unnecessary proof, stipulations regarding the authenticity of documents, and advance rulings from the court on the admissibility of evidence;

(4) the avoidance of unnecessary proof and of cumulative evidence, and limitations or restrictions on the use of testimony under Rule 702 of the Federal Rules of Evidence;

(5) the appropriateness and timing of summary adjudication under Rule 56;

(6) the control and scheduling of discovery, including orders affecting disclosures and discovery pursuant to Rule 26 and Rules 27 through 37;

(7) the identification of witnesses and documents, the need and schedule for filing and exchanging pretrial briefs, and the date or dates for further conferences and for trial;

(8) the advisability of referring matters to a magistrate judge or master;

(9) settlement and the use of special procedures to assist in resolving the dispute when authorized by statute or local rule;

(10) the form and substance of the pretrial order;

(11) the disposition of pending motions;

(12) the need for adopting special procedures for managing potentially difficult or protracted actions that may involve complex issues, multiple parties, difficult legal questions, or unusual proof problems;

(13) an order for a separate trial pursuant to Rule 42(b) with respect to a claim,

counterclaim, cross-claim, or third-party claim, or with respect to any particular issue in the case;

(14) an order directing a party or parties to present evidence early in the trial with respect to a manageable issue that could, on the evidence, be the basis for a judgment as a matter of law under Rule 50(a) or a judgment on partial findings under Rule 52(c);

(15) an order establishing a reasonable limit on the time allowed for presenting evidence; and

(16) such other matters as may facilitate the just, speedy, and inexpensive disposition of the action.

At least one of the attorneys for each party participating in any conference before trial shall have authority to enter into stipulations and to make admissions regarding all matters that the participants may reasonably anticipate may be discussed. If appropriate, the court may require that a party or its representatives be present or reasonably available by telephone in order to consider possible settlement of the dispute.

(d) Final Pretrial Conference. Any final pretrial conference shall be held as close to the time of trial as reasonable under the circumstances. The participants at any such conference shall formulate a plan for trial, including a program for facilitating the admission of evidence. The conference shall be attended by at least one of the attorneys who will conduct the trial for each of the parties and by any unrepresented parties.

(e) Pretrial Orders. After any conference held pursuant to this rule, an order shall be entered reciting the action taken. This order shall control the subsequent course of the action unless modified by a subsequent order. The order following a final pretrial conference shall be modified only to prevent manifest injustice.

(f) Sanctions. If a party or party's attorney fails to obey a scheduling or pretrial order, or if no appearance is made on behalf of a party at a scheduling or pretrial conference, or if a party or party's attorney is substantially unprepared to participate in the conference, or if a party or party's attorney fails to participate in good faith, the judge, upon motion or the judge's own initiative, may make such orders with regard thereto as are just, and among others any of the orders provided in Rule 37(b)(2)(B), (C), (D). In lieu of or in addition to any other sanction, the judge shall require the party or the attorney representing the party or both to pay the reasonable expenses incurred because of any noncompliance with this rule, including attorney's fees, unless the judge finds that the noncompliance was substantially justified or that other circumstances make an award of expenses unjust.

HISTORY: (Amended Aug. 1, 1983; Aug. 1, 1987; Dec. 1, 1993.)

TEACHING SUGGESTIONS FOR THE WOBURN TOXICS RULE 16 SIMULATION.

Here are some suggestions on conducting a Rule 16 pre-trial conference on the Woburn case. (In the materials earlier in this chapter section you can review some background facts on the Woburn case not reflected in the book or movie that you may want to inject during the discussion, or you may choose to share those new background facts with students beforehand.)

Start out by identifying the date - defining the time as prior to trial in the case being simulated. You might want to wear a robe, supporting your role acting as the magistrate judge in this pre-trial conference. Speaking in role, you can explain to the students the function of a "magistrate judge" (née federal magistrate) as facilitator here of the case's preparation for trial.

It makes sense to start by saying you've just been given this file and had only a brief opportunity to look over it. You'd like the student attorneys first to identify themselves, and then subsequently lay out all the various facts that will be on the table at trial so that you can see the shape of the case, so as to help get it ready for trial. ("Judge [Skinner] is a stickler who will hold it against you attorneys if you present a messy, ill-considered case that he thinks wastes his time on any unnecessary points.")

You may first ask, "Do you attorneys here representing each party all have authority to stipulate and settle as required under FRCP 16(c)?" (As facts subsequently come up in the discussion, you then can ask whether all parties can stipulate to that, or will it be contested.)

"Whom do you represent, and why is each of the defendants here?" This gives you a chance to have each party, probably starting with the plaintiffs, identify themselves and give you some very basic facts. ("Just the basic facts now. I don't want to hear your legal arguments until later when we've gotten all the basic facts out on the table....") As these basic facts are alleged, ask what facts can be stipulated by all parties, to get the factual layout underway. Ask if anyone has prepared a map or chart that can be used as common ground. (A good lesson: a party's map or chart can strategically shape such discussions. For this Woburn case you can refer participants to the site map on page 202 and use that, or bring in a site map blown up from the relevant websites.)

This stage of the proceeding may give defendants as well as plaintiffs an opportunity to do some tactical thinking. Some defendants, for example, may take this opportunity to try to duck and run. (Not Grace, Beatrice, and Unifirst. They were identified as probable sources of contamination in the initial EPA site analysis, though all will deny discharging.) EPA will probably take this opportunity to say they have no reason to be here as a party defendant. In fact, of course, EPA was never close to being named a defendant, and can say they have no statutory or common law liability to plaintiffs; they are doing their job. This interchange, however, can serve to incorporate consideration of what EPA does under CERCLA into the simulation, and remind all of the concurrent role of public law. EPA is likely to be dismissed forthwith on motion to the trial judge, but not before playing a useful pedagogical role here. The Town of Woburn was originally a defendant, but in actuality persuaded the plaintiffs to drop them in return for forthright assistance. They might be asked whether they wish to be *included as plaintiffs* under amended pleadings! This could set up new causes of action (public nuisance, public trust, parens patriae) and remedies. The minor businesses along Salem Street will not confess to dumping, and the proof will probably not be worth its cost to plaintiffs, given those defendants' limited funds. Unifirst early-on announced that its insurance company was ready to settle for $1 million, and in fact the Woburn plaintiffs quickly took that settlement offer in order to fund the further litigation against Grace and Beatrice.

(There is a question in these Rule 16 simulations whether you allow students to bring in new facts, invented or researched, not known to the other participants. It is best to hold the simulation to the case as presented in assigned materials, and not to allow the invention of facts or production of newly researched information by student attorneys. Imbued with the desire to win they may cook up some very inventive factual allegations not present in the case as presented in assigned materials. The easiest way to bring the pre-trial conference back to the given facts is to ask what that fact would prove if shown, why it had not been previously "noticed" by the student to the court and other counsel, and an admonition that it had better be solidly established in admissible form, with prior notice to court and counsel, before the trial or the next pre-trial conference. Then go forward on the premise that it is not part of the evidence.)

(As to various procedural motions here, hypothetical and actual – an initial Rule 11 motion to dismiss, motions to limit discovery, to bifurcate or "polyfurcate" the trial, to join parties plaintiff and defendant, etc. – you can encourage them to be made, take note of them, have the parties sound them out, but hold them for the trial judge. You do not have to make evidentiary rulings at this stage, though you may express your opinion about what the trial judge will make of them.)

After stipulable facts are set out, you should be able to say, "So this is a case where illnesses or injuries happened to plaintiffs.... So what happened? What kind of relief do the plaintiffs want?" – Sound out each possible kind of damages, and prompt if necessary for possible claims for equitable relief, including medical monitoring, neighborhood remediation which would cost a huge amount, etc. Note that here you can allow the student attorneys to go far beyond the Civil Action record in which private damages (including wrongful death, emotional distress, punitive damages, etc.) were the only type of remedy actively pursued. As the *Escamilla* case (at page 169-71, 270; opinion on the Teachers' Website) shows, private plaintiffs can also successfully win restoration-based injunctions or damages even where the EPA and state have ordered and are implementing Superfund remediation.

"So what causes of action are being advanced here?" Note here too that you can allow student attorneys to go far beyond the Civil Action record, where the private action for negligent (or strict liability) personal injury was practically-speaking the only cause of action considered by the court. Public nuisance is an obviously useful possibility, in addition to private nuisance.

For each cause of action you can ask, "What are the essential elements of that one?" In each case it will appear that *causation* is going to be a major issue, which can then be subjected to collective scrutiny:

"What will have to be shown to prove causation?" Here the defendants will set up a sequence of hurdles of logical proof required, starting with denial of the start of a chain of causation ("We never used or discharged that in the first place"). Then to "If we discharged, it never got to Wells G&H." If it got to Wells G&H, "it did not get there before the wells were closed," or "It didn't get there at a time when it could have affected these plaintiffs," or "It never got to these plaintiffs." If students are sharp they will get to the strategic "liability time-window" issue under Restatement of Torts 2d §435(2), at 212-

213, successfully argued capitalizing on the judge's surprise that groundwater could flow transversely under a stream. You can play dumb on this.

Behind the exposure issue lies the epidemiological causation question: "How do you prove that the exposure of these plaintiffs to these amounts of chemicals in these time frames caused these particular injuries?" This gets you into wonderful probability questions and a *Daubert*-style discussion of admissibility of expert testimony based on statistical analysis, novel medical testing (T-cell counts), etc. (You can decide whether to proceed under a modern *Daubert* rule, or under the old common law *Frye* Rule on expert witness testimony. See pages 249-256.)

Causation is likely to be the main contested issue, but there are others – sovereign immunity for the Town of Woburn, availability of emotional distress damages, the polyfurcation motion, availability of punitive damages, etc.

"Any affirmative defenses here?" (No, not much.) ... "Any counter-claims?" (Ditto.)

The goal of your shepherding the group through the conference is to reach the point where you can say, "OK, I now see the shape and elements of this case. Some of what we have discussed here should probably be dropped; other things you see you had better pin down because it's not enough now to take to trial; on some of this maybe some of you should be thinking settlement because the handwriting is on the wall...." and leave them with a notice of a further [hypothetical] pre-trial conference, or a time set for transmittal of the full case for trial.

In demeanor you can be quite peremptory, saying things like "Clarify that for me, because if you cannot present it clearly to me, you sure won't do well with it at trial"; "I've heard enough on that to see what you're saying, and I strongly doubt that it will fly," or "That sounds so flimsy that unless you have more than that you better not try it on Judge Skinner, or he's likely to hammer you," or "OK, I see what you're arguing, and we cannot determine it here; it'll have to be determined at trial," and move on. The job of the Rule 16 simulation is to sound out with your students the full scope of the elements of the case as it would have to proceed at trial, so that students get an anticipatory sense of complex countervailing details, logic, tactics, and strategy. It's a good lesson for professional life.

(Input from others trying this simulation setting will be gratefully received.)

Some Websites on the Woburn toxics case/A CIVIL ACTION. Here is a list of websites that approach the Woburn toxics case and A CIVIL ACTION from different viewpoints:

- **www.lessons.cali.org/web/civ20**
- **www.civilactive.com** – Environmental Media Service's take on the case, book, and movie
- **www.civilaction.org** – the Chemical Manufacturers Assoc.'s take on the case, book, and movie
- **www.acivilaction.org**– the Harvard Berkman Center Website, with extensive multi-format materials and interviews on the case, book, and movie
- **www. civilaction.com** – The Moviemakers' Website
- **www.civil-action.com** – W.R. Grace's Website
- **www.library.brandeis.edu/NSF/civil_action/index.html** – the Brandeis University Library has compiled and posted a valuable collection of

Woburn toxics study materials

www.geology.ohio-state.edu/courtroom/defendants.html — Ohio State University's Geology Department Website on the book and movie

www.bomis.com/cgi-bin/ring.cgi?page=5&ring=acivilaction&t=2648, — Bill Cheeseman's website (he represented Grace) gives a good sense of the man — go to "About the Author" — and also has links to skeptics

www2.shore.net/~dkennedy/woburn_trial.html — Reporter Dan Kennedy's topic-by-topic summary of the Woburn case

www.usfca.edu/pj/articles/Civil_Action-Asimow.htm — A law professor's critique of the movie

www.usfca.edu/pj/articles/Civil_Action-Hoffman.htm — A law student's critique of the movie

www.abcnews.go.com/sections/us/DailyNews/tomsriver990203.html — An update on the subsequent litigation and negotiation career of plaintiffs' attorney Jan Schlichtmann.

Woburn toxics civil action: Web simulation and video companion available. A Woburn web simulation and a video are available. The web simulation is entitled WOBURN: A GAME OF DISCOVERY and was created by Owen Fiss and Charles Berger as an interactive litigation simulation that involves the Federal Rules of Civil Procedure in the context of the Woburn lawsuit. The simulation can be accessed at http://lessons.cali.org/web/civ20. Or contact John Mayer for more information at jmayer@cali.org.

Marilyn Berger and Henry Wigglesworth have produced a video companion to A CIVIL ACTION, entitled LESSONS FROM WOBURN: THE UNTOLD STORIES. This video includes a unique interview with US District Court Judge Skinner, presenting a very sympathetic view of his role in the Woburn toxics case, unlike Jonathan Harr's book A CIVIL ACTION. Also interviewed are plaintiffs Anne Anderson and Donna Robbins, Jonathan Harr, attorneys for the defendant William Cheeseman and Michael Keating, attorneys for the plaintiffs Charles Nesson and Jan Schlichtmann, and others. The video runs half an hour and includes footage of the original courtroom, archival newspapers, photographs, and the City of Woburn. To obtain a copy of the video, contact Steve Errick, Publisher, Foundation Press via fax (212) 760-8705 or email, steve.errick@westgroup.com.

Chapter 5.
THE DEVELOPMENT AND STRUCTURE OF ENVIRONMENTAL PUBLIC LAW

***Suggested time budget*: one class session**

Chapter contents:

— and check the Teachers' Manual Website for SUPPLEMENTARY MATERIALS:

http://www.bc.edu/schools/law/library/coursebook/envtlaw/teachers

The list of Supplementary Materials in Part III of this manual, and on the Teachers' Website, indicates materials posted on the Teachers' Website that are relevant to this and other chapters.

OVERALL TEACHING THEMES & COURSE DESIGN CONSIDERATIONS

This is a transitional and introductory chapter, which can either be read by itself in a single assignment, or in conjunction with Chapter 14, on market-enlisting statutory strategies, in one or two assignments. Whichever approach is chosen, Chapter 5 should be supplemented by the Alaska Department of Environmental Conservation v. EPA ("ADEC") case excerpts, which can be found on the coursebook website. This critically important United States Supreme Court decision, which was handed down only weeks after this chapter was printed, has become an instant "classic case" on environmental cooperative federalism. It raises major questions in legal areas such as constitutional law, evidence, administrative law, civil procedure, and statutory interpretation, as well as environmental law. *ADEC* should be required reading for all students of environmental law. In the context of Chapter 5 as it stands, *ADEC* should be discussed along with the *Save The Valley* case, beginning on Page 306, and Professor Steinzor's case study of the Bethlehem Steel facility permit in Maryland, which begins on Page 312. It will be fruitful to compare and contrast the policies and administrative reactions of the States of Indiana, Maryland, and Alaska in these three case studies.

This chapter provides a bridge between the previous two chapters dealing with environmental private law (common law) and the subsequent analysis of sovereignties in environmental public law (Part Two) and the statutory taxonomy of Part Three. This chapter might also provide a bridge to Chapter 14.

The chapter examines the evolution and structure of modern environmental public law, with an emphasis on environmental cooperative federalism. It addresses questions such as, "Can we trust the states to regulate pollution adequately?" and "Who are the actors in, and what are the necessary elements of, an effective environmental regulatory system?"

TEACHING NOTES, COMMENTS, & ALL QUESTIONS ANSWERED

Pages 285-286. The Laitos excerpt describes succinctly the earliest American pollution control legislation, and its exclusive concern with smoke, and opacity in particular. That concern survives in some modern local ordinances law in the form of reliance on the ofttimes quite-arbitrary Ringleman Chart (a hand-held visual comparison chart with numbered circles of increasing degrees of opacity, that can vary wildly in results with time of day and angle of view) as the measure of statutory compliance or violation.

Page 286, C&Q #1. Why this system failed. This note is didactic in form and self-explanatory. Interesting discussions can follow from students' opinions about whether the three points remain accurate in describing why pollution control often fails, and the extent to which the modern economic and political influence of mega-firms threatens even federal regulation and enforcement.

Page 286, C&Q #2. Scaling upward—first, a shift from municipal to state level. This note is also informational and self-explanatory. It may be useful to remind students about the limited federal role in all areas of environmental regulation during this era. The sewage treatment grants came at what was probably the high point of federal activism.

Pages 287-288. The 1949 Michigan water pollution statute offers a glimpse at a classic "review and permit" statute, and sets up the *Utilex* case study to follow. By "review and permit" we mean a process whereby the administrative agency acts as a gatekeeper through the issuance (or denial, or conditioning) of permits. The agency reviews data submitted by the polluter seeking a permit and acts in accordance with legislative direction (often vague) set forth in the statute. Depending on how methodical you wish to be, you can use even these few excerpted quotations from the statute itself to tease out almost all of its provisions. The excerpts provide, respectively, the policy, the authority and duty to set standards (and the breadth of discretion that the agency will enjoy in that regard), and the permit requirement that forces the applicant to come forward and initiate the review process. The third provision also establishes a time line for agency action, a feature that can be manipulated to affect substantive results.

Page 291, C&Q #1. The administrative explanation. This note is a textual addendum to the bare bones list of "enforcement" activities that adds details learned from interviews that followed the search of the DNR files. Despite its anecdotal nature, the division of enforcement roles between the DNR and the attorney general's office is a common one, and it frequently has the effect of lessening enforcement. Students are alerted to the pragmatic side of budgetary and staffing constraints that agencies face in administering regulatory regimes that may, on their face, seem workable. This note also raises the question of the relationship between administrative effort and the use of the courts, noting the usual disjunction between the agency and its lawyers or those who prosecute violations of administrative permit systems. Chapter 21 considers enforcement in greater detail. In a subsequent unrelated study of Michigan's environmental enforcement done by one of the authors, an interview with the AG's office noted a good deal of frustration with the unsound evidence provided by the DNR's field people, including chain of custody problems with samples, mislabeled samples, and complaints about the performance of DNR personnel as witnesses in cases that did go to trial.

As a wry note you can ask students *"What was the most rapid agency reaction in this story?"* It appears to be the Spring, 1971 closing of agency files to the public, when the agency realized the critical case histories the ELS students were finding.

Pages 291-292, C&Q #2. The post—1949 mandatory permit system. *Why did the legislature decide to require a mandatory new and enlarged source permit system in 1949?*

The note highlights three separate issues in the development of pollution control regulation, the "Why now?" question, the "What evils are to be addressed?" question, and the "Who is going to be regulated?" question. The note suggests in an oblique way that the public had become concerned with the deterioration in environmental quality and that those concerns went beyond public health alone. A more cynical view is that industry itself was becoming concerned because the impurities in source water were damaging their own operations, or because they anticipated that public concern would lead to regulation and so this weak legislation would serve as a preemptive sop.

Why was the 1949 permit process only applied to new and increased sources? We suspect that this classic example of the regulatory impulse to grandfather existing uses was both practical and political: existing sources are harder to change than future uses, it is more disruptive to the status quo to try to do so, and it can awaken a firestorm of political trouble. A slightly more cynical view suggests that the current users of the resource for waterborne waste disposal wanted to use regulation to prevent new entry on an equal (i.e., free) basis. A more charitable view is that the regulation's inclusion of modified sources was thought to be adequate to catch current users soon enough and bring them into the regulatory regime because few businesses could afford to remain stagnant. The grandfathering, however, created a perverse incentive to maintain the dirtiest, grandfathered, uncontrolled emissions sources.

Page 292, C&Q #3. The standards to be applied by the WRC. *What standards must be applied under the 1949 Act?* §323.6 said "public and ecosystem health and welfare" whatever that might be interpreted to mean. This note urges the students to consider what the agency will do in translating the vague legislative "do good" standard into action. The legislative language calls for harm-based standards without going far enough to identify what harms it has in mind, nor the basis for translating prevention of those harms into actual regulation of dischargers. This vague statute will provide a helpful comparison to the harm-based ambient standards of the Clean Air Act as studied in Chapter 11. The subtheme of the question addresses the imbalance of technical resources between the polluters and the agency staffs of that era.

Are these standards likely to be effective? Hardly, absent unusual administrators in a supportive political context. The lack of efficacy of the system is made patent in the case study that follows.

Page 292, C&Q #4-5. Improving the system—standard setting. Improving the system —changing the bipolar paradigm. These notes are explanatory in nature, and are primarily intended to foreshadow the organizational way in which subsequent chapters will address issues raised by the mid-century statutes' failings.

How could the regulatory process be changed to incorporate a broader multi-polar conception of the public interest? Citizen suit enforcement, FOIA, and other regulatory diversifications are part of the answer, considered further in Chapters 7 and 21.

Pages 292-293, C&Q #6. Improving the system—intra-agency changes. This note about agency personnel is descriptive of the changes that began to take place. That idea can be revisited in conjunction with NEPA, which forced a massive infusion of ecologically trained individuals into the agency ranks.

Pages 294-295, C&Q #1. The eruption of environmentalism. This note is didactic and self-explanatory.

Pages 295-296, C&Q #2. The federalism of environmental law. Ditto

Pages 296-297, C&Q #3. The race of laxity as a justification for federal regulation. Ditto

Pages 297-298, C&Q #4. Federal law, the race of laxity, and modern devolutionism. Professor John Dwyer, in his article entitled The Practice of Federalism Under the Clean Air Act, 54 Maryland Law Review 1183 (1995), isolates the reason why the existence or non-existence of the race to the bottom attracts significant attention; i.e., it involves whether there is a need to replace unduly weak state regulation. If there really is a race, then federal law can justifiably be intrusive in its effort to stop the states from competing in the race. In the modern climate of ideologically driven preferences for and against devolution to the states on the part of many in Congress and their supporters, this debate, therefore, matters. For teaching the material, therefore, it is important to try to disassociate the ideology from the policy, that is, try to get the students interested in what evidence would support the claim that there is such a race, and what evidence would show its absence. Dwyer's article does not address that topic, but it gives a thorough history of how legislative and administrative events unfolded in the Clean Air Act as it affected the distribution of power between the feds and the states.

This note tries to capture Revesz' conclusions in his own words, including his own words of caution. The footnote, tries to show how the academic work can then be used by parties having an ideological or economic interest in a particular real world result. Quite frankly, we (the authors) do not think that Revesz' position is likely to lead to sound environmental outcomes. Our experience is that the students also find it hard to believe that eliminating federal floors will lead to improved environmental quality. If you want to discuss this material, it may be helpful to separate "efficiency" from "distributional consequences." Revesz has raised a legitimate debate regarding efficiency as a technical question of economic theory, i.e., "What course of regulation maximizes total social welfare?" Perhaps total welfare will be increased through devolution, but it seems likely that the increase in "efficiency" of regulation will be more than counterbalanced on the policy scale by undesirable distributional consequences, such as increased pollution burdens borne by persons living near facilities that are no longer subject to the overarching federal standards of the NAAQS and other facets of the CAA. Without regard to the merit of Revesz' theoretical position, as the footnote tries to imply, there are behavioral indications that his prediction that devolution will lead to increased efficiency that improves environmental quality, is doubtful. A significant number of relevant and interested firms (i.e., those most affected by the federal floor) seem to think that removing the floor will reduce their costs. Presumably, the reduced costs will come in the form of lowered performance standards that are less expensive to meet, meaning that more of the cost of their pollution is externalized. It is rather difficult to believe their support of H.R. 961 is bottomed on a belief that they will enjoy great savings when regulation is somehow made more efficient (without a decline in air quality) through the mere fact that the federal government has released the states from the strictures of the Clean Air Act.

Pages 298-299, C&Q #5. Responding to Revesz. This note tries first to isolate the economics debate between Revesz and Engel. If students are finding the debate too theoretical, refer them to the Tragedy of the Commons reference as an example of what Engel says happens when the states decide on a level for their standards. They consider what others are likely to do as it affects them, and will decide to grab the economic benefits of low standards knowing that they cannot insist on the environmental benefits of high standards due to the common pool nature of interstate airsheds and watersheds. Her empirical study is quite interesting and bears reading by those interested in the problem. In our experience, stringency of state environmental regulation is a point that firms use in their negotiations with states and localities over facility siting decisions.

"Why do states assist polluters in the effort to remove the federal agency and its more stringent demands from the case?" The question is answered by the remainder of the paragraph, but each of the factors implies slightly different institutional motivations are at work: pride and independence; expertise in what really matters locally; interest in promoting economic development.

Page 299, C&Q #6. Inverting the race of laxity. *Is it possible that states can invert the race of laxity into a race for enhanced environmental quality?* The simple answer is, "Yes, it is possible." A different answer is that not many states seem to be doing it. Students may cite California as doing more, with it toxics initiative and ZEV cars. California is exceptional. In part, it has the market power to force other states to follow its lead, or at least pay no penalty in the race of laxity. California is so big economically that all firms have to reckon with it. As for ZEVs, California's urban automobile pollution is so bad that it requires more stringent regulation.

Pages 299-300, C&Q #7. Other issues, other scenarios. In his article, The New Contractarian Paradigm in Environmental Regulation, 2000 U. ILL. L. REV. 35 (2000), David Dana argues that a number of recent federal and state regulatory initiatives (HCPs, Project XL, Brownfields, SEPs) reflect a new contractarian paradigm in environmental regulation, the defining characteristics of which are that (1) regulatory requirements are the result of formal negotiation and assent; (2) the requirements are site-specific; and (3) the default for the requirements is existing or threatened command-and-control regulation. Dana also explores the possible implications of the shift to contractual regulation for judicial review of agency action: notably, courts understandably might analyze contractual regulation from the prism of "private" contract law instead of "public" administrative law, and that change in analytic prism might result in judicial interpretations of regulations that more consistently favor the interests of regulated entities.

Pages 300-302, C&Q #8. The actors in the environmental political drama. This note is didactic and self-explanatory.

Page 305, C&Q. Ditto

Pages 309-310, C&Q #1. Findings under §342 (C)(3)... Ditto. Aspects of this note are further discussed in subsequent notes.

Page 310, C&Q #2. The dynamic tension of cooperative federalism; C&Q #3. The environmentalist citizen suit as a goad to administrative agency action. Ditto

Pages 311 and 312, C&Q #4. The pitfalls of federal oversight. This note is didactic and self-explanatory. EPA is statutorily authorized to treat some aspects of a state's water pollution control program (e.g., sewage sludge management and wetlands protection) as separate for oversight purposes.

Page 312, C&Q #5. "Overfiling" (and "underfiling"). "Overfiling" and "underfiling" are discussed in Chapter 21. One consequence of the fragmentation of environmental law is that each environmental regulatory statute contains a unique set of enforcement devices. Overfiling appears to be legally authorized under some environmental regulatory statutes but not others. Underfiling is probably acceptable under most statutes because, under the "federal floor" concept, states may be stricter than the federal government but not less strict. The enforcement equation is further complicated by the option for citizens to sue to compel compliance with federal environmental laws. (Environmental citizen suits are also discussed in Chapter 21.) For example, a citizen cannot sue where a federal or state agency is "diligently" prosecuting an enforcement action in court. Some federal environmental regulatory statutes include administrative enforcement actions under this bar to citizen suits. But "diligent" prosecution is open to judicial interpretation.

This would be an excellent juncture at which to discuss the central legal and policy disagreement between the majority and dissenting opinions in the *ADEC* case (see course website): Should state agency performance following delegation of primacy by EPA be reviewed in state or federal courts? This central issue entails subsidiary questions of constitutional law, civil procedure, evidence, statutory interpretation, and administrative law. Instructors may wish to assign papers or oral reports based on *ADEC*. Alternatively, classroom moot court arguments might be organized around this theme.

Page 312, C&Q #5. "Overfiling" (and underfiling"). This note is didactic and introductory.

Pages 314-316, C&Q #1. Environmental permitting as "Let's Make a Two-Way Deal." The best way to combine compliance with legal requirements and regulatory creativity and flexibility in the permitting process is make the process as transparent as possible, perhaps even enlisting the aid of knowledgeable and responsible public interest groups. Many of these organizations have access to personnel with expertise in environmental science and economics, who are alert to pollution prevention and control options that might generate "win-win" solutions for regulators and regulated industry alike. It might also be possible to negotiate disputes during the permit process through Alternative Dispute Resolution ("ADR")(see Chapter 21).

Page 316, C&Q #2. Environmental federalism in the permit setting. This note is didactic and self-explanatory.

Pages 316-317, C&Q #3. Improving environmental permitting. This note is didactic and self-explanatory. Questions are rhetorical and are answered within the note.

Pages 317-318, C&Q #4. Racing-to-the-bottom via lax enforcement. This note is didactic and self-explanatory.

Pages 320-321, C&Q #1. The pollution prevention strategy. Ditto.

Page 322, C&Q #2. Pollution prevention as one of many regulatory approaches. Ditto.

Page 322, C&Q #3. Beware the ghost of *Utilex*. Ditto.

Chapter 14 to follow? Instructors may wish to follow the Latin/Ackerman-Stewart debate bridge to assign Chapter 14 ("Market-Enlisting Statutory Strategies: Pollution Trading and Other Economic Incentives") either along with this chapter, in a single assignment, or as a separate subsequent assignment.

Chapter 6.
POWER RELATIONSHIPS BETWEEN FEDERAL AND STATE GOVERNMENTS IN ENVIRONMENTAL REGULATION

Chapter contents:

—and check the Teachers' Manual Website for SUPPLEMENTARY MATERIALS:
http://www.bc.edu/schools/law/library/coursebook/envtlaw/teachers

The list of Supplementary Materials in Part III of this manual, and on the Teachers' Website, indicates materials posted on the Teachers' Website that are relevant to this and other chapters.

OVERALL TEACHING THEMES & COURSE DESIGN CONSIDERATIONS

This chapter presents a foray into constitutional law, looking at how the Constitution divides authority between the national and state governments. As such, it is ancillary to the main thrust of the book, and can be given less emphasis than the chapters that surround it.

There are a few things students must know from this chapter, but it is likely that they already know them, or will surely be required to study them elsewhere. Those fundamentals have to do with federal supremacy and how that translates into a pattern of concurrent federal and state regulation, with only occasional instances of federal preemption. Likewise, the resurrection of the Tenth and Eleventh Amendments by the Rehnquist Court creates the opposite paradigm, broad areas of concurrent regulation with occasional instances where regulatory authority belongs to the states alone. Also, there are some forms of federal regulation of the states themselves that are not allowed.

As might be expected, because these matters are parts of federal constitutional law, there is a richness of doctrine in the case law that can be studied in great depth. To do so in this course is a quick path to the loss of several class periods, and discipline is required to resist the temptation to overdo the analysis.

For environmental law purposes, some understanding of federalism is absolutely fundamental. Federal supremacy and the role that it plays in cooperative federalism is the single most vital topic. Congress can insist on having its regulatory choices enforced, at least when it acts within the sphere of its powers and does not invade sacrosanct areas of state sovereignty, or subject states to jurisdiction of the federal courts in litigation initiated by private parties. Strategically, however, the differences between federal and state administration and regulation lead to polluters and other regulated entities having strong preferences for being in one system or the other, or being subject to only one set of regulation rather than being regulated by both the feds and the states. Those desires lead to the use of preemption, dormant commerce clause, and the 10th and 11th Amendments as a means to limit regulation to that of one or the other sovereign.

TEACHING NOTES, COMMENTS, & ALL QUESTIONS ANSWERED

Pages 324-327. Federalism. This material tries to pin down why it matters where the respective spheres of sovereignty of the states and federal governments begin and end. It tries to make students aware of the possibility that the division of power does have real world consequences for environmental regulation.

Page 328. Preemption doctrine. This textual material tries to explain the basics of federal preemption of state law.

Pages 329-330. These materials cover the case of *Ass'n of Int'l Automobile Mfrs. v. Mass. Dept. of Environmental Protection,* in which the court held that a Massachusetts program regulating automobile emissions was expressly preempted by the Clean Air Act.

Page 330, C&Q #1. California as super-sovereign? *Does California's "super-sovereign" status create room for special deals between California and the automobile companies? Is that what happened in this case?* Yes, California's special status under the Clean Air Act potentially creates room for special deals between California and the auto companies, and yes, such a phenomenon arguably happened in this case.

Page 330, C&Q #2. Win some, lose some. This note makes clear that the Northeastern states have not been entirely thwarted in their efforts to regulate automobile emissions.

Page 330-31, C&Q #3. Civil rights for car companies? This note describes the perhaps surprising holding of a U.S. Magistrate that Massachusetts had violated the constitutional rights of the automobile manufacturers through air pollution regulation, and thus should pay attorneys' fees to the companies as the prevailing parties in the litigation.

Page 331, C&Q #4. California's own preemption problems. This note describes California's unsuccessful effort to allow car companies more flexibility in addressing air emissions by giving them the option of adding more fuel-efficient technologies to their fleets.

Pages 331-32, C&Q #5. The *Engine Manufacturers* case. This note describes the *Engine Manufacturers* case, pending in the U.S. Supreme Court's 2003-04 Term.

Pages 332-33, C&Q #6. Is a state's purpose relevant? As the note makes plain, earlier suggestions by the Supreme Court that a state's purpose might save its regulation from preemption have been seriously eroded in subsequent cases.

Pages. 333-334, C&Q #7. Federal preemption of tort remedies. This note discusses federal preemption of state tort remedies.

Page 334, C&Q #8. Do savings clauses save anything anymore? The simple answer is: not as much as they once did. This note describes recent cases in which the Supreme Court has limited the effect of savings clauses aimed at saving state law provisions from federal preemption.

Pages 335, C&Q #9. Other environmental preemptions. This note describes other environmentally relevant areas in which preemption cases have arisen.

Pages 336-337. Interference-with-federal-programs preemption. This is, perhaps, the most subtle of the preemption problems. Ecology's black letter about everything being connected to everything else, when applied to concurrent state and federal regulation affecting regional resources, sets the stage for these cases. *Granite Rock* is a paradigmatic example. The feds own and regulate the forest as part of an overall plan for the National Forest System, and in relation to a more particularized plan for this forest under NFMA. California, concurrently, regulates all activities having sufficient environmental consequences in the coastal zone, which includes this forest. Because the federal permit is derived from a program, there is an implicit claim that the federal program will be deranged if the state acts in a way that amounts to a de facto veto of the federal permit. The Court squirms out of that box because of the procedural posture of the case, the state had not yet denied its needed permission for the mining , nor were the conditions that the state might require of the miner yet specified and/or known to be too onerous to permit profitable mining. Thus, the majority could get away with saying there is no frustration of federal purpose shown by requiring Granite Rock to seek a state permit for its activities. On the state's side is the traditional claim of its police power. For a Court that prides itself on protecting state sovereignty, undercutting state authority of so traditional a nature should not come easily.

Page 337-38, C&Q #1. The case for finding preemption. *What can the CCC now impose by way of conditions that would not be in conflict with the Forest Service plan?* Any requirements that are part of what California considers to be its environmental law probably pass muster.

Would erosion and dust emission control requirements that forced Granite Rock to keep excavated overburden covered during mining operations, or a strict post-mining reclamation requirement, be allowed? Yes. Especially if California regulates other mining operations in similar fashion Granite Rock could not be heard to complaint that they were being singled out for different treatment, thereby proving that California was simply trying to override the USFS decision to allow mining.

Does it matter how much compliance with such requirements would cost? What if, for example, the increased cost made the proposed mining project more expensive than other feasible alternative sites? If the court reviewing such a case had already found that imposing the requirements was not policy preempted, then it would seem to follow that the burden of the regulation would not alter its admissibility, unless it is an apparent sham, designed to do indirectly (prohibit mining) that which California could not do directly. As a matter of proper alignment of federal and state authority, there is no reason that as a miner on federal land in California, Granite Rock should be subject to less regulation than other miners in California.

Page 338, C&Q #2. Local expertise and pluralism. *Do concurrent regulatory authorities make sense?*

Perhaps. Both sovereigns can pursue their respective polices at the same time, neither overtly forces the other to the sidelines in areas that are normally within their regulatory competence. *Perhaps CCC has better local knowledge and environmental expertise than the federal district ranger? Or does concurrency reflect a salutary measure of respect for states' sovereignty?* In theory, the federal District Ranger should be fully apprised in regard to local conditions and, therefore, there is no basis for claiming that the states are the only ones with the needed expertise. The states are, however, the only ones politically answerable to the local constituency alone.

Page 338-39, C&Q #3. State regulation of the federal public lands. *Are these criticisms (of the fine distinction in the case) well taken?* The distinction is indeed a fine one, but it is not clear that the court could have found a far more convincing rubric for deciding the case in either direction.

Is it really within the power of the Court rather than Congress to unravel the complexities of concurrency? Yea, at a very pragmatic *real politic* level, courts have to decide cases, including ones of this sort. Congress, by ordinary legislation, can change the result if it wants to preempt, or if it wants concurrency.

Page 339, C&Q #4. Is preemption analysis better applied on a local or a national level? *Is preemption analysis better applied on a local or a national level?*

Professor Freyfogle makes an interesting plea for localization of planning and federal non-interference with that level of regulation.

Pages 339, C&Q #5. State regulation of federal facilities. *To what extent can states and local governments apply their environmental regulations to federal facilities in their territory?*

The answer is given in the note that the federal government is usually immune to state regulation unless it either voluntarily complies or Congress legislates that federal enclaves are subject to that regulation. Interestingly, Congress had to legislate that federal facilities had to obey the CAA.

Pages 339-40, C&Q #6. Requirements for federal-state coordination. Federal state coordination procedures. This note includes references to both OMB directives and a Executive Orders that try to get federal project agencies to coordinate their projects with state policies and desires.

Page 340, C&Q #7. Preemption of local municipal laws, etc. This textual note merely alerts students to the fact that local laws bear a roughly analogous position in relation to state laws as do state laws to federal laws.

Pages 340-341. Dormant commerce clause. This text introduces the concept of dormant commerce clause jurisprudence and tries to explain why the courts take a leading role in protecting federal (congressional) prerogatives, even when there is not a case for preemption. Congress acts in reserve to allow states to regulate when it deems state regulation acceptable after initial judicial invalidation.

Pages 342-345. Philadelphia v. New Jersey. This is the leading case in the area of bans on the interstate movement of wastes, and it is also the leading modern case on the dormant commerce clause jurisprudence more generally. New Jersey tried to limit out-of-state trash being deposited in NJ landfills. The embargo was discrimination against interstate commerce and was tested by the prevailing standard of "virtual per se invalidity." The attraction of a waste embargo in the NIMBY world of that era is obvious. Times have changed and the wheel has turned to where areas try to keep their trash home to fuel trash-to-energy facilities. The same dormant commerce clause doctrine invalidates flow control, as it is called.

Pages 345, C&Q #1. States try other tacks. Differential tipping fees and other regulatory expedients played a prominent place in the effort to avoid the *Philadelphia* precedent. The Supreme Court, and the lower federal courts have erected a steady stream of precedents prohibiting such schemes. Only the market participant doctrine has had any success, as described in the *Swin* case that appears at page 349.

Page 346. C&Q #2. Criticism of the nondiscrimination principle. This note provides a rare dissenting view of the Supreme Court's nondiscrimination principle under the commerce clause.

Page 346. C&Q #3. Preemptions of invalidity and congressional authorization of discrimination. This textual note explains the difference between preemption jurisprudence and dormant commerce clause jurisprudence in methodological terms that help students apply the contrasting rules to cases. The note also mentions congressional authorization - an important idea. One area where congressional authorization has been sought is for flow control legislation.

Page 346 C&Q #4. Evenhanded legislation and legislative purpose. This note explains the *Pike* balancing test for facially neutral legislation.

Pages 347, C&Q #5. The dormant Commerce Clause's balance of burdens. This note explains further the *Pike* test and shows its application by the Supreme Court to uphold a Minnesota paperboard use requirement against a dormant commerce clause challenge in *Cloverleaf*. The *Proctor & Gamble* case is an interesting one that sheds light on how burdens are weighed. The note also poses a series of rather self-explanatory questions, taking the *Association of International Automobile Manufacturers Case* as the launching-off point.

Page 348, C&Q #6. "A barrier is a barrier is a barrier," or is it sometimes a quarantine? *Does it make any difference for dormant commerce clause purposes whether Philadelphia v. New Jersey is an import ban (blocking the import of waste), or an export ban (blocking the export of landfill space)?* No, except for "valid" quarantine laws - an apparently shrinking category of laws, given the *Carbone* case discussed in this note.

Pages 348-349, C&Q #7. Insisting on cleaner, leaner garbage. *Can Pike or Taylor, as exceptions to the pattern of invalidation of commerce-restricting state laws, be adapted to aid states in their "garbage wars" effort to enforce differential tipping fees or otherwise disfavor out-of-state waste?* Not likely.

Suppose a state, by statute, requires predisposal treatment of waste as a precondition to disposal or as a basis for obtaining a lower tipping fee. Pretreatment could include mandatory recycling (to reduce volume), or segregation of waste streams to eliminate the presence of small volume hazardous materials such as household batteries and non-commercial volumes of paints and solvents. Are such laws evenhanded? Do they remain evenhanded if the state also makes pre-

treatment mandatory within its borders? Pre-treatment requirements have also been struck down despite their apparent evenhandedness. The grounds for such invalidation are a bit more complicated and include trenching on the principle that states are not allowed to engage in extra-territorial regulation as is explained in the note. The attraction of pre-requisites was the idea that they could be evenhanded, and thereby get into the *Pike* wing of the analysis. As seen in *Meyer*, even that lesser scrutiny can be sufficient to strike down garbage import bans.

Page 349. The market participant doctrine and the *Swin* case. In Reeves v. Stake, a state-owned cement plant was allowed to favor in-state purchasers in time of shortage on the ground that South Dakota was acting as a market participant and not a market regulator in choosing to prefer SD buyers of cement over their Wyoming competitors in time of shortage. The theory was that a state can spend its money on its citizens and need not subsidize non-taxpayers with its largess. Unlike regulation that does not involve state expenditures, running a state business in a non-business-like fashion is not a violation of the dormant commerce clause. In *Swin*, a state-owned (actually a county-owned) facility discriminated against haulers of out-of-state garbage and was upheld on the market participant basis.

Page 349, C&Q #1. The dissent in *Swin*. This note provides an excerpt from Chief Judge Gibbons' dissent in *Swin*.

Page 350, C&Q #2. When economic unreality resembles indirect taxation. *Is the market participant doctrine bottomed on the expectation that governmental entities will act in an economically rational fashion?* The *Swin* dissent (C&Q #1) attacks the market participant doctrine as a whole. Gibbons is, no doubt, correct that no for-profit business would prosper long in a competitive environment if it did not choose to make rational business decisions. The underpinnings of the market participant doctrine, however, do not dispute that point. What is at issue is the authority of the state to utilize its financial resources (as opposed to its legislative power) to subsidize its citizens. The Court, in embracing the market participant doctrine allows states the privilege of using their financial resources, and things like cement plants that can be bought with them, in ways that favor their citizens alone. The relevant constitutional protection for those who want the benefits of state citizenship, is the ability to become citizens, which is protected by a number of constitutional doctrines, sometimes lumped together in a "right to travel."

Pages 350-351, C&Q #3. Flow control that keeps garbage at home. *Do the very different results in Swin and Carbone potentially put brakes on the large trend toward privatization of governmental services?* Yes, in our view. In *Swin*, the preference passed muster because the government was operating the landfill. In *Carbone*, where the government sought to use the services of a private operator, the market participant argument was not available to avoid the commerce clause problem.

Pages 351-352. Limits on federal power imposed by the 10th Amendment as it limits the scope of the national commerce power. The text of the 10th Amendment appears here as does a brief textual description of its traditional interpretation as a sort of restatement of the basic precept of federalism, retaining for the states and people all that was not given to the federal government in its list of enumerated powers.

Pages 352-354. The *New York* case. This case involved New York's several challenges to the Low Level Radioactive Waste Policy Amendments Act of 1985, under which Congress tried to force the states to become participants in a series of regional systems for handling low-level radioactive materials. Most of what Congress did to cajole, bribe and pressure the states into joining up was upheld, however, a bare command to the states that they actually do something was held, because of the 10th Amendment, to be beyond Congress' power. That is a remarkable holding and trying to fathom its basis and limitations is an important effort.

Page 354, C&Q #1. The lines of dissent. This note mentions that the dissent did not find in the precedents cited by the majority to be as much limitation on Congress as did the majority. That position is interesting insofar as it seems to create the impression that even the dissenter's find that the 10th Amendment has independent content, rather than being a "mere truism."

Pages 354-355, C&Q #2. The new "truism." *Has the old "truism" taken on a new meaning?* As suggested in regard to C&Q #1, there is a new belief that the 10th amendment adds its own limitations of federal competence to those of the enumerated powers limitation.

To what extent is that view established as a general principle in the opinion and then applied to strike down the take title provision? Unequivocally. The entire Court agrees that the commerce power reaches the subjects as to which Congress was regulating.

Page 355, C&Q #3. Incentives and the dormant Commerce Clause. Not surprisingly, granting exceptions to dormant commerce clause limitations was held to be an incentive that Congress could validly use to entice the states to behave in the ways that Congress desires.

Pages 355-356, C&Q #4. Commanding state execution of federal law. *Can Congress require the states, or state officials, to take action in furtherance of federal law?* Answering this question requires great subtlety. There is a contemporary trend and a small number of cases that are beginning to refuse "to allow the states to be conscripted into the federal bureaucratic army." But there are some troubling consequences to a total denial of federal power to make state officials act. What can remedy state racial discrimination in districting for elections save a federal court order to the responsible officials to redraw the districts? The list of examples of that sort, and the Court's decision in *Reno v. Condon,* should make it plain that it would be hasty to read *New York,* or *Printz* too broadly.

Can ECPRKA's planning requirement be differentiated from requirements struck down in Printz? There is no ready basis for differentiation, although in FERC v. Mississippi, 456 U.S. 742 (1982), states were required by federal legislation to conduct certain administrative procedures in the public utilities regulation field. The requirement survived a Tenth Amendment challenge. It may be that the Court will keep both *Printz* and *FERC v. Mississippi* alive and chart a course between them.

Page 356, C&Q #5. Curbing congressionally mandated environmental remedial programs. *To what extent do New York v. United States and Printz limit the ability of Congress to require the states to take action to abate environmental hazards?* The note describes he *ACORN* decision that holds the federal government cannot require the states to retrofit schools to assure lead-free drinking fountains.

Page 357, C&Q #6. The Unfunded Mandates Reform Act. This is a note describing the Unfunded Mandates Reform Act of 1995. Possible answers to the question in the note are given within the note.

Page 357, C&Q #7. Cirucmventing *Printz* and the Unfunded Mandates Reform Act for federal environmental statutes? *If Printz or the Unfunded Mandates Act limit Congress' ability to order the states to take action, can Congress validly accomplish the same ends by offering the states a choice: saying they theoretically can choose not to do what the federal statute requests, but if so they will lose federal funding for various programs?* Thus far there are only hints that courts might find Congress' limited in its ability to withhold federal benefits. Consider this as an analogy to the market participant doctrine of the dormant commerce clause - if the feds fund it, they can choose how, and on which states, the money is spent.

Pages 358-359. The commerce power and the *Lopez* case. The commerce power is the interstate and international commerce power and, as such, was never intended to grant the federal government a local police power to regulate purely intrastate conduct having no discernible effects on interstate or international commerce. That distinction implies a limit on federal authority, that, until the 1930s, led to invalidation of federal laws on the grounds that they were not within the authority of Congress under Article I, §8, clause 3. In the 1930s, all that changed, when the Court acceded to the idea that even local transactions could have effects on the national economy. Thereafter ,Congress was free to regulate many intrastate transactions. In *Lopez,* a federal law that operated locally, the Gun Free School Zones Act, was invalidated as applied to a conviction for possessing a gun near a school. *Lopez* marks the return of an enforceable "interstateness" limit to the commerce clause. For environmental law, this may matter. Much federal environmental law acts on quintessentially local events, though in aggregate those events may affect the larger environment. Also, the entities engaged in the activities that lead to the environmental effects, are themselves often doing so as part of interstate commerce. After *Lopez,* there is a degree of uncertainty about a small number of applications of federal environmental regulation on the ground that they exceed federal power.

Pages 359-360, C&Q #1. *Lopez* and environmental law. *Does Lopez raise any serious doubt as to the constitutionality of those environmental laws?* Generally no, *Lopez* does not threaten invalidation of very many federal regulatory provisions in the environmental field. Air and water move across state lines, the industries that produce chemicals, etc. are obviously engaged in interstate commerce, and so on.

Page 360, C&Q #2. The legal process question in *Lopez*. *Which branch of government ought to decide whether federal legislation affects commerce?* This question is included for those who would like to teach constitutional law but have not been assigned to teach that course. Student familiarity with *Marbury,* the institutional relationships of the coordinate branches, etc., vary greatly. The more general question that lurks here is that of judicial deference to legislative "fact-finding." When will courts accept the view of the legislature, and when not?

Pages 360-361, C&Q #3. Violence against women. This note discusses the Supreme Court's decision in *United States v. Morrison,* striking down a provision of the Violence Against Women Act.

Pages 361-362, C&Q #4. Legislative record review. This note discusses scholarly criticism of *Morrison* and other recent commerce clause cases.

Page 362, C&Q #5. Which environmental activities are "economic activities"? *Which environmental activities are "economic activities?"* This note poses several questions all getting at the issue of determining which environmental activities are "economic activities" within the meaning of the commerce clause. As the note observes, these questions are asked, but not answered, in the *SWANCC* case that follows the note.

Pages 362-365. *SWANCC.* These pages provide an excerpt from the U.S. Supreme Court's decision in *Solid Waste Agency of Northern Cook County ("SWANCC") v. U.S. Army Corps of Engineers*, in which the Court held that the Clean Water Act's definition of "navigable waters" did not include isolated, intrastate wetlands deemed regulable by the federal government only on the ground that they provided habitat for migratory birds. The excerpt provided here is the Court's (nondispositive) discussion of the commerce clause issues raised by the case.

Page 365, C&Q #1. *SWANCC* and the CWA. This note describes the Court's statutory holding in *SWANCC*, discussed in more detail in Chapter 12.

Page 365, C&Q #2. The commerce Clause as a principle of statutory interpretation. This note remarks on the role of the commerce clause (or other constitutional provisions) in statutory interpretation.

Pages 365-366, C&Q #3. Aggregating effects from commercial activities. This note provides Professor Jonathan Adler's view that wetlands regulation does not involve economic activity and thus cannot be aggregated to produce a substantial effect on interstate commerce.

Page 366, C&Q #4. The viability of state regulation. *While the Supreme Court's decision in SWANCC does not prevent states from protecting isolated waters through administrative or legislative action, will the states do so?* The note provides reason for some pessimism in this regard.

Page 366, C&Q #5. The federal government's reaction to *SWANCC.* This note describes efforts by the Corps and EPA to deal with the aftermath of *SWANCC.*

Page 367, C&Q #6. The court's struggles with *SWANCC.* This note describes the court's struggles in determining the scope of *SWANCC.*

Pages 367-368, C&Q #7. What's next? Superfund? This note describes a Superfund case in which a commerce clause challenge was raised, at first accepted and then rejected by the courts.

Pages 368-369, C&Q #8. The Commerce Clause and endangered species. This note describes the various positions courts have taken in commerce clause challenges under the Endangered Species Act.

Pages 369-371. *Seminole* and the Eleventh Amendment. This material is very complicated. The crux of the doctrine is that states (including state agencies and political subdivisions) enjoy some degree of freedom from the jurisdiction of the federal courts, even when the case involved is adjudicating a state's liability for violation of federal law. The problem, however, is a real one for environmental law in cases where the state is being regulated as a polluter and is made liable to suit *by private parties* in federal court. Citizen suit provisions in environmental statutes do this frequently in the event that the state is the operator of a regulated entity.

Pages 371-372, C&Q #1. A short, simplified view of Eleventh Amendment jurisprudence for those who really want to know. For the brave (by the foolish who attempted to cover so much in so little space), this note tries to trace 11th Amendment jurisprudence from Chisholm v. Georgia to the present in one page.

Page 372, C&Q #2. *Seminole's* holding in its Eleventh Amendment context. This note is critical of the *Seminole* majority on a number of grounds, the most profound of which is that after *Seminole* the power relation between the states and Congress can only be changed by the Court or constitutional amendment. Before, Congress, the electorally responsible branch, was in a position to continually adjust the burdens of federal law on the states.

Page 372, C&Q #3. *Seminole's* holding in its environmental law context. This note tries to make it abundantly clear that the Court did not disable remedies against states under federal law when the federal government was the plaintiff.

Pages 372-373, C&Q #4. Getting around *Seminole* by going to state court: not anymore! This note observes that the Supreme Court has now held that the Eleventh Amendment bars suits against states even in their own courts.

Page 373, C&Q #5. Getting around *Seminole* in federal court: not anymore! This textual note is another deep dip into the 11th Amendment doctrine tank. A number of topics are covered in this note. The idea of constructive waiver is laid to rest after a quarter of a century of strutting and fretting its hour upon the stage. The fretting had the upper hand. Voluntary waiver is possible, although not altogether likely. Not many states respond to private environmental enforcement suits under federal statutes with a "Sue me, it hurts so good" kind of attitude. In the end, the principal protection against *Seminole* affecting environmental regulation of the state entities is the willingness of the federal government to condition benefits on good behavior, and enforcing defalcations by bringing suits in which the United States, rather than interested citizens, is enforcing the law.

Page 373, C&Q #6. State waivers of their own immunity. This note describes the possibility of getting around the Eleventh Amendment through states' waivers of their own immunity.

Page 374, C&Q #7. Changes in the federal-state power structure, changes for environmental law. This note discusses the potential implications of the Court's recent Eleventh Amendment jurisprudence for environmental law.

Pages 374-375, C&Q #8. Implications for environmental justice. This note discusses the potential implications of the Court's recent Eleventh Amendment jurisprudence for environmental justice.

Page 375, C&Q #9. Analogues to federalism in the European Union: subsidiarity. This note provides a comparison of federalism in the United States to subsidiarity in the European Union, with a couple of open-ended questions at the end designed to help students bring together the conceptual, policy-related lessons of the chapter.

Chapter 7.
THE ADMINISTRATIVE LAW OF ENVIRONMENTAL LAW

Chapter contents:

– and check the Teachers' Manual Website for SUPPLEMENTARY MATERIALS:

http://www.bc.edu/schools/law/library/coursebook/envtlaw/teachers

The list of Supplementary Materials in Part III of this manual, and on the Teachers' Website, indicates materials posted on the Teachers' Website that are relevant to this and other chapters.

OVERALL TEACHING THEMES & COURSE DESIGN CONSIDERATIONS

Understanding the details of administrative law is a fundamental requirement of legal literacy for modern attorneys. Some of the mechanics of regulatory agency practice are set out in Chapter 5. Here the focus is on administrative law doctrine, mostly studying what happens when agencies are in court. At the outset is a brief nutshell which past users have found useful for orienting students who have not had a course in Admin. Law. Then we introduce two very different settings in which agencies come to court: (1) where courts exercise *review* of agency decisions, and (2) judicial *adjudications* where courts hear complaints against agencies for themselves violating a provision of law. The two can get jumbled. Administrative process can be constitutionally and doctrinally byzantine. As the *Overton Park* case demonstrates, environmental law can present an entire range of structural and technical administrative law issues. An initial organizing theme in *Overton Park*, as in any administrative case is "What is really going on here, what is the agency doing, why, and how?" – looking at the agency's statutory authority and administrative program, procedural steps, and also at the underlying policies, tactics, and political settings. The second focus is analysis of the technical details of how those agency decisions are challenged in court. Behind the technical issues of judicial review lie systemic questions of the role of citizens intervening in the system – pluralistic citizen involvement in the administrative agency and judicial processes. A concurrent, contrasting, basic theme is *deference*. Given the opposing needs for government to be both effective and responsive to individuals and civic needs, what is the proper balance of deference to be accorded to agencies in the modern state? This raises questions of agency discretion, and separation of powers issues centering around the scope of judicial deference to agency fact-finding decisions, agency interpretations of law, and agency actions formulating and implementing official policy in the different programs and settings.

This chapter typically comprises one to three class hours. For a one-day format, you can just use *Overton Park* as a quick survey of administrative law issues. For a two/three-day format, delve into citizen enforcement as a legal process strategy.

Obviously you will need to address in some form the political turmoil brought to the governing process by anti-regulationism and other current political storms. The summary history of environmental politics in Chapter 2 offers a backdrop to the issues raised in this chapter, and the dramatic environmental agenda of the Bush II Administration offers a catalogue of relevant examples reflecting powerful initiatives by industry to limit the regulatory effectiveness of citizens and agencies.

TEACHING NOTES, COMMENTS, & ALL QUESTIONS ANSWERED

We don't know if you will want to use this chart of "The Three, or Four, or Five, or Six Branches of Government…" but some of our students said it had helped them visualize what was going on in the cases and their governmental contexts, so here it is.

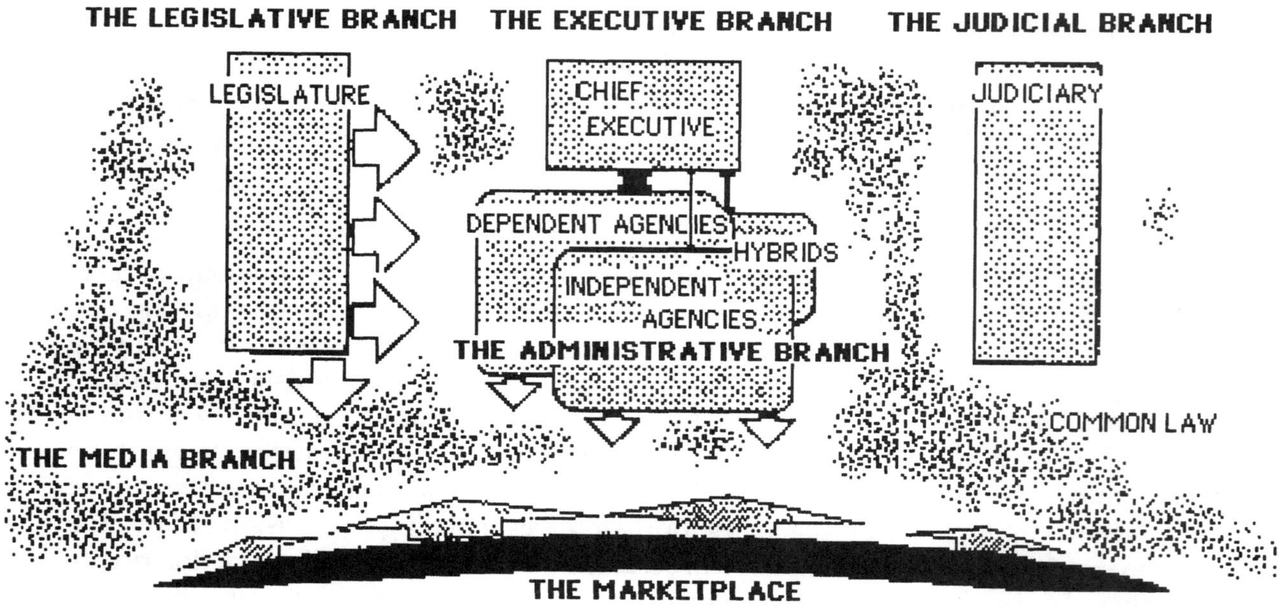

THE THREE (or Four, Five, or Six) BRANCHES OF GOVERNMENT IN THE UNITED STATES

This chart shows the legislative, executive, and judicial branches of government as they exist at the federal level and in each of the 50 states. The official active functions of daily government are the passing of statutes by the legislature, usually with approval of the chief executive. Statutes are directed to the administrative agencies, to the society at large, and in some cases to the chief executive. Pursuant to their statutorily-delegated powers, administrative agencies legislate (by issuing regulations), and adjudicate (by making formal or informal decisions applying statutes or regulations to particular factual cases). Judicial review of agency decisions takes place in the court system, as well as original adjudication under statutes, regulations, and the common law. A fundamental point of this chart's version of 8th grade civics is to emphasize that most of the work of government is done by the administrative agencies, which are not necessarily under the direct political power of the chief executive. Independent agencies are responsible to the legislature. Even in Cabinet-level (dependent) agencies, the chief executive controls only the top echelon of political appointees. Agency personnel with civil service status constitute the vast majority of government workers, and this civil service exists and rolls on day-by-day relatively insulated from changes at the top. The Media and the Marketplace are two other unofficial but strategic instruments of social and political governance.

Pages 376–378. Introduction and historical overview. The brief overview of the evolution of administrative government in the U.S. over the past 200 years is intended to remind students of the interplay between the private economic marketplace and government, and the relatively recent but highly significant function of citizen involvement in efforts to cope with complex problems of modern society.

Pages 378–388. A "nutshell" on administrative law. This is a short background primer, setting out technical details and issues to be picked up in subsequent discussions. We have been told that the historical overview and the nutshell have proved useful to students in the past who had not yet taken Administrative Law.

Page 384: Examples of what agencies do, and how their actions are challenged; current administrative process issues. This section offers a brief glimpse into what agencies do and some of the ways they get hauled into court. The excerpt from the CWA rulemaking sets up the NPDES placer mining effluent limits challenged by Alaska miners here and later in Chapter 12 at page 636. The political science of this can be discussed: how an agency sets limits, and how an industry fights back (more at page 636). The endangered species case excerpt is the quite different setting where the agency is not being brought into court for *review* of its regulatory decisions but as a violator itself of federal law. (We think students and judges should note the very different positions that agencies, and deference, should be accorded in these two settings.)

To offer further introductory glimpses, teachers might note other basic kinds of agency action that may come to court: Agency "adjudicative" decisions, where agencies apply their own determinations of facts to their own interpretations of operative legal provisions; *Overton Park*'s §4(f) determination by DoT is a prime ready example that can be contrasted with the Alaska placer rulemaking. Both agency actions are challenged, one by citizens, one by industry. You should note that both are "informal" in the degree of agency process they received. Agency "adjudications" are not necessarily made with trial-type procedures. (Indeed the classic 1947 Attorney-General's Manual on the APA notes that the vast majority of agency actions are informal adjudications.) And rulemaking just as well as adjudications can be done with full trial-type process if an agency wishes to do so, or is compelled to do so by a statute or court.

Further, you might want to note to students the significance of low profile administrative actions. Students have a general awareness of major regulations' importance, and of major agency determinations made under statutes and regulations like *Overton Park*'s findings of "no feasible and prudent alternative," but they do not generally have a sense of how much low-profile "play" there exists within agency practice. It is useful to give them a feeling for the tactical importance of internal procedures and definitions.

Prosecutorial discretion is a case in point. Here is an example of a Reagan-era internal procedural change that obviously had important consequences:

> **U.S. Army Corps of Engineers, Regulatory Guidance Letter No. 82-12...**
>
> (1) On 22 July 1982, changes made in 33 CFR 326 (Enforcement) became effective immediately [by sub-informal rule published in the Federal Register of that date, at page 31794]. Violations of the Clean Water Act, the Rivers and Harbors Act, or the Ocean Dumping Act that would have been

> sent to the U.S. Attorney for judicial enforcement [in certain described cases] *are now to be processed as after-the-fact permit applications....*

The direct and implicit consequences of this little procedural change are obvious. Students should get a sense that each day agencies make thousands of such low profile decisions that in the aggregate shape the bulk of what government does or does not accomplish. Only a tiny portion of government actions ever reach the public eye; much less being subjected to challenge by environmental lawyers.

The dramatic shifts in environmental administrative process that accompanied the Bush II Administration's coming into office likewise show the remarkable range of options for governmental action. Unlike prior anti-regulatory initiatives, the Bush II group's efforts did not focus on statutory changes but rather on pervasive sophisticated administrative alterations, many not even requiring notice-and-comment rulemaking. As an example, the Bush environmental record reveals widespread use of governmental acquiescences to court challenges against prior-existing regulations, the elimination or bowdlerizing of proposed rules through arcane new OMB/OIRA procedures, and substantial selective constraints on the availability of regulatory information. Perhaps the most dramatic examples of nullification-by-acquiescence occur in the natural resources field. Encouraged by the Bush victory in the 2000 election, a number of industry groups challenged regulations passed in prior administrations, like the snowmobile ban in Yellowstone National Park, endangered species listings of coho salmon and owls in timber country, and the Clinton Roadless Area Review rule that halted mineral and timber leasing and roadbuilding in a number of national forests. In some cases the Administration has responded by negotiating administrative or court-approved settlements that substantially concede the invalidity of the challenged regulations. In others the Administration has refused to defend the challenged regulations in court, and declined to appeal if the district court strikes them down or to defend on appeal if the court upholds the rule. Then, if adverse rulings were successfully established in one circuit, the Administration adopted them as applicable across the board. In the *Kootenai* case[1] an action filed by Boise Cascade and other timber interests against the Roadless Rule on grounds that its promulgation violated NEPA, the federal government declined to argue in defense of what officially was its own rule, and only the intervention of citizens defending the Roadless Rule prevented the regulation's collusive nullification by industry-White House cooperation.

A collection of useful anecdotal material on the Bush II environmental administrative actions is in the coursebook website's Chapter 2 Supplementary Materials.

Pages 388-398. *Overton Park* core assignment, and follow-up. The *Overton Park* case is a superb vehicle for raising and analyzing a remarkable number of technical issues and administrative law themes. Initially note the agency program (federally-aided Interstate highway building) and the institutional politics that underlay the decision to go through the park. The National Defense Interstate Highway System is a multi-billion dollar state and federal public works program with its own special constituencies and momentum. The operative decision to go through the park was a foregone conclusion; the agencies'

---

[1] United Kootenai Tribes v. Veneman, 313 F.3d 1094 (9th Cir. 2002), discussed in Parenteau, "Whatever Industry Wants... The Bush Environmental Record," 14 Duke Envtl. L. & Policy F. No. 2 (2004) and in the coursebook website materials for Chapter 2 (Bush II Environmental Record).

timing of the highway segmentation was clearly intended to circumvent §4(f). See page 395 at footnote 21.

In our "taxonomic" terms, §4(f) is, fittingly, a substantive roadblock-type statute: a specific prohibition clause (Secretary *"shall not approve* any [highway] project which requires the use of [parkland]") it is coupled with an exception clause written in very strict terms ("unless (1) there is no feasible and prudent alternative...*and* (2) ...all possible planning to minimize harm") - with the Secretary's determination subject to judicial scrutiny. (This resembles the Endangered Species Act §7 after the 1978 amendments - Chapter 16, pages 800-801.) Turning to the citizens" challenge, note the odyssey of this little group that began with a local community pro-park demonstration by the citizens of this mixed low-income neighborhood - there were baby strollers covered with signs, angry complaints about government high-handedness, bitter letters to the local newspapers.

The C&Q text, pages 394-395, describes the various threshold requirements - *reviewability* (an interesting example of an attempt to avoid review is the DoT's claim of unreviewable discretion at page 390-91, but such claims can often be overcome by reminding a court that APA §706 provides for review of "abuse of discretion" which presumes reviewability of discretionary actions), *standing* (no issue in *Overton,* but an opportunity to survey the evolution and current problems in standing, pages 402-410, and *ripeness and exhaustion,* page 395. (Note that the administrative law defense of primary jurisdiction is not relevant here because plaintiffs are not making common law claims - cf. page 148).

The Court chooses the most deferential level of standard of review of the Secretary's factual decision - arbitrary and capricious - but still holds against the agency and remands the decision. *"Why didn't the Court accept the Secretary's decision?"* Clearly the majority could have deferred to the official decision, but its serious attention to the §4(f) mandate meant that the obvious sketchiness of the evidence of §4(f) compliance could not be overlooked. (Would the Court overlook it today?) "Why didn't the Court follow Justice Black's lead and hold that a violation of the act had occurred?" This question is easier to answer. The Court obviously felt, given the delicacy of reviewing the decision of a separate branch under the lowest level of scrutiny, it was far more appropriate to remand for further procedures. The result might be the same anyway - the agency would effectively have to remake its §4(f) decision if it wished to proceed.

The classic tension between efficiency and due process in administrative law is a fundamental theme here. Judicial deference to agency interpretations of law used to be generally far less than to decisions of fact — see pages 396-97, but there has been a judicial move to extend deference under the *Chevron* rationale, see statutory interpretation material at pages 428-34. In discussing the degree to which courts will review and second-guess agency decisions (e.g. because many environmental cases desperately seek to strengthen judicial oversight of allegedly compromised agencies) it is worth noting that rigorous review can lead to paralysis of effective administrative action. (AFL-CIO v. OSHA, at 1026, is a simple example). *Corrosion Proof Fittings,* page 679, according to some observers, was another case where the EPA's serious efforts to regulate asbestos under ToSCA were unjustifiably nit-picked into oblivion. Judicial obsession with obtaining the fullest possible record led to stalemate.

> The predictable result of stringent "hard look" judicial review of complex rule making is ossification.... [The *Corrosion Proof Fittings* opinion was] so

> lacking in deference to the agency's exercise of expertise and policy judgment, and so full of attempts to impose on the agency the court's own views of the proper role of regulation in society, that it is virtually indistinguishable from the documents that [the anti-regulation pre-1992] OMB prepares in connection with its oversight of EPA rule making. McGarity, Some Thoughts on "Deossifying" the Rule making Process, 41 Duke L.J. 1385, 1419, 1423 (1992).

Obviously you cannot understand how many of these administrative law rulings are made unless you analyze whose politics are served by various decisions. In *Overton Park* and *Chevron* the agency was following marketplace politics, and the citizens were trying to defend the civic and natural economies. The Court chose to lower its deference in order to invalidate the agency decision in *Overton,* but upheld it in *Chevron*. In *AFL-CIO v. OSHA* and *Corrosion Proof Fittings* the agency was trying to resist the political pressures of the marketplace economy, and the court lowered its deference to override the agency's attempt. How can a suitable deference prescription be formulated, given the varying consequences of too much deference, and too little? "Deference should be given when it serves my policy preferences" - would seem a bit too self-serving as a judge's guiding principle. Dan Farber suggests:

> ...we might do better to vary the level of review [of rulemaking] depending on whether the agency is taking a dynamic or static approach to regulation.... We might lower the level of review when the agency can demonstrate that (1) its action will not cause irreparable injury; (2) it has taken steps to generate additional relevant information; and (3) it has a process in place that will in fact result in a reappraisal of current policy as the new information is developed.

To this a jaundiced environmentalist might add: "(4) evidence that the agency's position is designed to serve the civic-societal function rather than bow to the politics of the marketplace economy having been captured by its regulated interests." Professor Farber's attempt to define a principled line between judicial takeover and deferential abdication is worth further attention.

Page 394, C&Q #1. Threshold administrative law issues in citizen suits. The development of liberalized standing is noted at page 402 and following, tracking efforts to restrict standing and the reassertion of citizen standing in *Laidlaw*. The ripeness issue is frustrating in *Overton Park*'s construction chronology - where the state and federal agencies clearly were trying to foreclose all practical alternatives before requesting money for the park route. Citizens would have found it very difficult to bring a lawsuit prior to the actual decision to release funds for construction through the park. Prior to that point judicial process would probably have been unavailing.

After you have worked through Overton Park's administrative law twists and turns, you may wish to give your students the **Administrative Law Diagnostic Checklist for use after *Overton Park*** that is posted on the Teachers' Website in the Chapter 7 supplementary materials. You are invited to improve this draft, which was intended to be a Checklist that students could apply to any and all administrative cases they are called upon to analyze.

Page 395, C&Q #2. Administrative law tactics. *So why didn't the DoT win when the Court held that the deferential arbitrary & capricious test applied?* As noted, the Court's insistence on a record that supported the Secretary's decision was lethal to the agency's position even under the low arbitrary and capricious standard of review.

Page 396, C&Q #3. Interpreting statutory language. At this point, the teacher may want to mention the *Chevron* questions of deference to agency interpretations of statute.

Will courts sometimes defer less to agencies that demonstrate resistance to their civic mandates? Yes. sometimes. That was the amazing element in *Overton Park*. Courts clearly do take some account of agencies" posture toward legislation. Agency animosity to a statute can then be part of the court's decision to defer less to agency interpretations that undercut agency duties. This probably occurred in *Overton Park*.

Legislative history is always good for a critical comment. Justice Scalia treats most legislative history as a charade, and tends to ignore it. The plain meaning rule has its pitfalls, but there is a useful discussion on pages 429 note 69 and 432-33.

Pages 396, C&Q #4. The arbitrary and capricious test: *Could the Court have found the DoT decision arbitrary?* The Supreme Court could probably have found the *Overton Park* agency decision "arbitrary" - because as noted on 396-97 the word "arbitrary" has a broad range of meanings. The inclination to be delicate with a co-equal branch of government, however, led in *Overton Park* to a holding that not enough information had yet been supplied to explain the agency position.

Note the Court's call for the district court, on remand, to hold a "plenary review," page 393. It is not clear what this means. It sounds like "de novo" review, but evidently isn't. The best guess is that plenary review meant that, given the thin quality of the record, the district court on remand should review the entire scope of the administrative decision - including questions of law and discretion as well as questions of fact. But these are within the scope of any judicial review of agency action anyway so "plenary" may just have been an extra exhortation to the lower court to review the agency record vigorously.

An interesting case from Alaska's St. Matthew's Island in the 1980s shows how even courts operating under post-*Chevron* deference standards can sometimes find agency action substantively arbitrary and capricious. In National Audubon v. Hodel, environmental groups and a fishermen's association brought actions challenging the Reagan-era Secretary of the Interior's land exchange agreement whereby he transferred to three Alaska native corporations a wilderness area within Alaska Maritime National Wildlife Refuge in exchange for various already-protected areas in two other national wildlife refuges. Judge Fitzgerald held that the Secretary had broad discretion in determining the public interest, but his "Public Interest Determination" for the exchange suffered from serious errors of judgment and misapplication of law leading to a clear error of judgment, and therefore the land exchange was invalid.

> My review of the underlying record has convinced me that the Secretary, by failing to consider the protections otherwise provided by law and by failing to consider relevant facts appearing of record [of disruptions to a pristine island lasting up to 100 years which the Secretary characterized as "temporary"], seriously misconstrued the benefits to conservation system units and general wildlife conservation and management objectives

> advanced by this exchange.... Finally, the Secretary's determination under ANCSA §22(g) that a support base located within the Alaska Maritime NWR would be compatible with the environmental protection purposes of this refuge is contrary to the underlying record. The Secretary's Public Interest Determination thus constitutes a clear error of judgment. I conclude that the St. Matthew Island land exchange is invalid. National Audubon v. Hodel, 606 F.Supp. 825 (D. Alaska, 1984).

Page 397, C&Q #5. "Feasible and prudent" and the public trust: *What would the public trust doctrine mean here? Would costs be ignored?* On the merits of §4(f)'s feasible and prudent test, discussion can emphasize that there really is no indication how costs should be weighed. Public trust law, which arguably establishes a presumption against exploitation of protected resources, seems to be an applicable analogy requiring at least the showing of a thoughtfully articulated balance.

What would that balance be? Probably a requirement for weighing the nonmarket importance of legacy resources, and explicit consideration of the no-action alternative. In NEPA cases, the do-nothing, no-build alternative is traditionally one of the alternatives which must be considered by an agency in an EIS.

Page 397, C&Q #6. Subsequent History of the Overton Park story: self explanatory.

Page 398, C&Q #7. Trade offs: As a matter of policy analysis, the *Overton Park* case offers an opportunity to discuss proposed mitigation. Environmental law tends to try to protect resources where they exist, on the presumption that they are likely to be more in balance with their context and their maintenance of quality more certain, whereas mitigation measures are often quite iffy. In this case, moreover, the remaining bifurcated park would have been greatly disrupted, and the low income neighborhood needed as much park as possible where it was, not off in the inaccessible northern suburbs.

Page 398-402. Administrative process and citizen participation: a structural commentary. Some students will resist thinking about the political contexts of environmental administrative cases. You can tell them that the exercise is fundamentally utilitarian. Attorneys in practice in Washington and most state capitals, especially the super-lawyers that some of them wish to join, automatically process the political context of a situation before they begin to think of it in legal doctrine terms. "Agency capture," for example, is not a rhetorical screed but a commonly acknowledged phenomenon in practice and in the academic literature.

Doing a "quick-read" on the administrative agency and its political inclinations thus is a relevant part of competent administrative law analysis.

Pages 402-410. Standing and the institutionalization of citizen enforcement. Starting with the GrandDaddy of environmental standing cases, Scenic Hudson, we present an oscillating line of cases testing citizen standing in challenges to federal agency actions. Environmental advocates have a love-hate relationship with administrative agencies. When an agency takes account of environmental values, citizens often act as supportive backings to the agency program, supplementing agency enforcement with a citizen enforcement suits, etc. However, where agencies are relatively inert out of political caution, or are overtly tied to vested development interests, as in the "capture" phenomenon noted at pages 401, citizens are often at loggerheads with governmental agencies, treating them as major parts of the problem. Courts traditionally have deferred to administrative agencies in a wide range of areas regardless of the agencies" political position. This section reviews the basis on which citizen environmentalists established what is still at least a firm foothold in the process of second-guessing agency actions in court.

The 1990s decisions from the Supreme Court tightening requirements for judicial review standing invite development of the theme of citizen enforcement of statutes and the national policy consequences of restricting citizen enforcement. Professor Dan Tarlock has dourly written that the goal sought by 1990s Supreme Court majorities appeared to be to return –

> back to the 19th Century, [with] the elimination of the public action [and] rapid resource exploitation [as] the paramount goal.... The Supreme Court's decision in *Lujan v. Defenders*...comes close to making the assertion of citizen standing a common law crime.... Tarlock, "Environmental Law, But Not Environmental Protection," in L.J. MacDonnell and S.F. Bates, Natural Resources Policy and Law 162, at 183 (1993).

Section 318 of the Dep't. of Interior and Forest Service Appropriations Act, on page 417 provides a good foil, along with the *Lujan v. Defenders* decision from the Supreme Court, on page 410, contrasted with *Laidlaw* on page 411..

In the commentary and questions on Lujan II, a number of technical standing issues are set out. Students may not automatically realize the dramatic importance of these technicalities, and may have to be reminded of the functional role played by plaintiffs in federal environmental law. As so often is the case, the technicalities in environmental law reflect swirling currents of public policy battles.

Students interested in citizen enforcement, clinical work, and studying the technical demands of active involvement in the administrative process, should be apprised of a very useful treatise: Michael Axline, *Environmental Citizen Suits* (Butterworth, 1992).

Page 414, C&Q #1. *Laidlaw*, a home run for citizen standing? We think, as the note text implies, that Laidlaw signals a substantially enhanced openness to citizen standing, but the awkward terms that have developed to define standing (like "injury" without regard to how it serves the purported purposes of standing review) remain. Much of the variation in these rulings on standing are less a question of evolving judicial principle than ends-oriented organic decisionmaking. Doesn't it appear in many cases that a Justice's position on standing depends on whose team is at bat?

Page 414, C&Q #2. How much harm is necessary for standing? a $5 bounty? The definition of what is a sufficient standing stake continues to evolve. *Laidlaw* accepts direct allegations of potential use. As we read the *Lujan II* decision, a $5 bounty would indeed create Article III standing, a fact that calls the whole test into question. We prefer Cass Sunstein's critical analysis and suggestions for broadened standing made in the Michigan article cited in the note.

Shouldn't the potential for expert witness and attorney's fees then be enough to satisfy Justice Scalia's standing standard? A rhetorical question. We think so, which forces one to confront the lack of logic in making the constitutional test turn on material stakes.

What's the CPSC's standing interest? Sunstein has also told us he shares our quandary about what the legal basis for agency standing is, given the logic of *Lujan II*. Take, for instance, an independent agency like the NRC or the CPSC: if Congress can grant such an agency authority to sue to enforce relevant statutes and that is sufficient to create Article III standing for such agencies under *Lujan*, why cannot Congress grant the same standing to citizens? We believe both grants should be valid, and the distinction seems to be merely political.

Page 415, C&Q #3. Redressability: Over dissents by JJ. Scalia and Thomas, *Laidlaw* adopted a less stringent redressability definition in allowing plaintiffs to proceed even though they were not eligible for either injunctive or personal damages relief. This is a major shift from the redressability jurisprudence in *Lujan II* in which Justice Scalia implied that it would be ineffective in redressability terms if a court could do no more than to tell agencies that they are violating the law, if it didn't have the power to force agency compliance, which strikes us as bemusing to say the least.

Is Lujan's requirement of a finding of redressability an invitation to political science predictions? Yes, and that's not a good idea.

Page 415, C&Q #4. Standing and the "diligent prosecution" jurisdictional defense. The CWA forecloses citizen enforcement actions if an agency is diligently prosecuting, but the Laidlaw Court did not hesitate to scrutinize the political realities of South Carolina's enforcement.

Page 415, C&Q #5. Self-explanatory.

Page 416, C&Q #6. Is citizen standing a mistake? prosecutorial discretion? This note raises some basic questions about the course of environmental law which, as the histories in Chapter 2 and this chapter note, was shaped by persistent citizen activism. *What happens to agency discretion if citizens can make the decision of what and when to enforce?* You can juxtapose this question with Justice Scalia's law review dictum on page 408 arguing against citizen standing on the ground that a number of regulatory programs "ought to get lost...in [the] vast hallways" of the bureaucracy. The question is a litmus of what you think about pluralistic democracy, "the Establishment," and what statutes mean. We think that Congress's explicit decision to grant citizen enforcement standing necessarily changes the traditional role of prosecutorial discretion. It echoes the shift from the old bi-polar system of governance (see pages 43, 377-78) to the multi-centered pluralistic model of government that broke upon the world in the 1960s.

Page 417. RESISTANCE TO CITIZEN ENFORCEMENT

The old bi-polar Establishment is well-represented in the Pacific Northwest forestry battles that provide the backdrop for the appropriation bill provision noted on page 417, clearly trying to return the question of whether and how the national forests would be clearcut to the traditional "legitimate" established players: the industry and the federal agencies that service them. Period. No citizens. Have your students figure out the logic and premises of this remarkable rider:

Page 417, C&Q #1. The spotted owl appropriations rider. *What's going on here?* The issues raised by §318 of the 1990 Interior-Agriculture Appropriation Act are explained at some length in the first note. This timber rider is a vividly instructive vignette revealing the importance of citizen enforcement, and agency-industry cooperation. Sardonic public interest observers would say the rider's purpose is to eliminate citizens from the process and get back to the bipolar business of capture. All the questions in this note are rhetorically posed and answered, except the last paragraph's.

Page 418, C&Q #2. Can Congress foreclose judicial review? The question that is not answered, and perhaps cannot be, is the question *Is there any limit to legislation's ability to foreclose judicial review?* Can Congress completely remove judicial jurisdiction for enforcement of a statute? Most federal environmental public law, of course, is a pure creation of the Congress, yet there are substantial arguments that due process is violated when something which seriously affects people and resources outside the government is declared to be law, but is unenforceable in the judicial branch. If Article III legislation excludes application of the law of the land to certain specific fact situations under the law of the land, are fundamental rights eroded, or is it merely that the law of the land itself is thereby narrowed?

Page 419-28. CITIZENS' ATTEMPTS TO EXPAND AGENCY PROCEDURES

Vermont Yankee is a classic case and yet another chapter in the battle between the politics of the old marketplace economy and the citizen advocates of civic-societal considerations, in this case threats of long term radiological hazards.

This section picks up on the earlier discussion of environmental citizens' attempts to improve agency process by intervening in ongoing agency decisionmaking. In *Vermont Yankee* the focus is on the extent to which citizen interveners can attempt to obtain extended procedures in an agency proceeding that offered them less than formal trial-type process - in particular their desires for discovery and cross examination.

Initially it is useful to quiz your students on the administrative tactics being employed by the Nuclear Regulatory Commission in *Vermont Yankee*. The agency clearly wished to avoid having to deal with the questions posed by nuclear waste disposal in each and every plant-licensing adjudication, and accordingly tried to shift the issue into rule making to be incorporated thereafter in each future licensing case (page 420, and described in C&Q #1).

Vermont Yankee is an extraordinary opinion in the strength of its procedure-chilling rhetoric, in the fact that it was a seven-zero vote, and in its milepost position beginning a trend of constraining the federal courts' prior tendency to give citizen interveners increased procedural protections. The rhetoric and the unanimous vote may be explained by the Supreme Court's resentment of the D.C. Circuit Court's virtual monopoly on administrative law jurisprudence. The court also seems to feel that too much required procedure could bring governmental decision-making to a halt. The Court's decision may also reflect skepticism about the pluralistic model that had informed prior court opinions - a model tending toward insuring that parties obtain the process necessary in the circumstances in order to have meritorious consideration of their cases.

You should remind your students about Matthews v. Eldridge, 424 U.S. 319 (1976)(see page 382, note 8, weighing how much process was due in cutting off SSI benefits) an extremely useful non-environmental case that they can use in many future settings to set out the articulated tests for requiring further procedural due process. *Matthews* announced a nifty three-part test: In determining whether agency procedures are sufficient, the court must weigh –

> three distinct factors: *First*, the private interest that will be effected by the official action, *Second*, the risk of an erroneous deprivation of such interest through the procedures used, and the probable value if any of additional or substitute procedural safeguards and [*Third*], the Government's [procedural] interests, including the function involved and the burdens that the additional or substitute procedural requirement would entail. 424 U.S. at 335.

In cutting the procedures that federal courts could require of agencies back to the bare minimum provided by the APA, Justice Rehnquist used (out of context) language from *Wong Yang Sung* which had actually emphasized that the APA was creating a *minimum* floor of procedural requirements for agency action. In citing that case as a reason to make the APA a *maximum ceiling* on required procedures, the Court ignored the fact that in *Wong Yang Sung*, where no procedures were required by statute, the Supreme Court had in fact gone on to require a full trial-type hearing.

Vermont Yankee may also serve as a basis for considering a renaissance of statism - deference to whatever the executive agencies have disposed - on the part of the Court.

Page 422, C&Q #1. Tactics*: What was the NRC trying to do?* The agency was trying to shift the whole radioactive disposal dilemma into informal rulemaking to avoid the tough question in general and in every licensing case that would come up.

After Vermont Yankee, will citizen interveners wither away? The result of *Vermont Yankee* was nevertheless a remand to the agency to build a sufficient record to justify the decision reached, and what should be emphasized to the students is that even though the citizens had no right to increased procedures, the needs of the judicial review process under Article III provided leverage for a remand that in fact resulted in further extended agency procedures. Airing (and attempting to meet citizen quibbles about the decisional record continues to be a practical leverage pressure for citizen requests for participation.

Page 423, C&Q #2. The Vermont Yankee holding? This note answers the questions posed about Rehnquist's terms, and emphasizes the actual remand. The Supreme Court later upheld the final rule in *Baltimore Gas and Electric*, but in reality the rule had gone through extensive revision and further factual analysis. It appears to have become a better rule because of the remand.

Page 423, C&Q #3. The substantive question in *Vermont Yankee*? *Might cross-examination have revealed on the thin facts?* It later appeared that the conclusory Pittman Report upon which the safety of the nation for 25,000 years depended had essentially been prepared in little more than a week by Dr. Pittman and his secretary, and that would have made for cross-exam drama. This note serves the prior point if cross examination had been available, the incredibly thin evidence supporting the NRC's critical decision would have become blatantly evident. As it was, it required back door whistle-blowing from within the NRC to reveal the facts of the matter.

Page 423, C&Q #4. Remand and back: the rest of the *Vermont Yankee* case's story.

Page 424, C&Q #5. The "hard look" doctrine: *Does Vermont Yankee do anything to dampen courts' scrutiny of agencies' "hard looks"?* The tone of the opinion clearly was intended to chill courts from imposing procedural constraints on agency process. Analytically, however, the holding of Vermont Yankee seems to support the requirement that courts be shown a sufficient record of agency decisions to support their deference to the agency ultimate decision. In terms of rhetoric, the tone of *Vermont Yankee* clearly was intended to dampen judicial imposition of further procedures on agency decisions, at least where rule making is concerned (as opposed to agency adjudications, which are not subject to Vermont Yankee's argument of APA prescription, because the APA spells out no adjudication procedures except as to formal adjudications).

Page 424, C&Q #6. Rulemaking / adjudication: Note again that *Vermont Yankee* does not apply to adjudication, because although Rehnquist could say that the APA set out a clear prescription for less-than-formal rule making, the APA does not provide anything of the sort for informal adjudication. Presumptively, courts are free to require additional procedures in all "adjudicatory" proceedings, under Matthews v. Eldridge or otherwise as necessary.

The other question noted in this comment, the question of when rule making, as opposed to adjudication, must be followed, remains an unclear area after New York v. Thomas. *Would further application of this New York v. Thomas holding overrule Overton Park?* The rule set out in that case conflicts with cases like *Overton Park*, if you apply Judge Scalia's novel, mechanistic, definition of what a rule is. (The Secretary's finding in *Overton Park* clearly had "future effect" and so could be held to required rule making procedures under Scalia's reading.) A few subsequent cases have ordered mandatory rule making, thereby undercutting agency orders, but this issue remains fundamentally unresolved.

Page 425, C&Q #7. Citizens interventions in agency proceedings: these are on a different basis from judicial standing which is shaped by Article III. Intervention in agency proceedings gives the intervener a place at the table, but there is little academic analysis of intervention by public interest citizens in less-than-formal agency proceedings where most of the government's work gets done. APA §555(b) offers intriguing possibilities. Under §555(b), *Who is an interested party, and when would "the orderly course of business" limit citizen participation?* We think "interest" should be measured functionally, in terms of whether the individual is sufficiently invested in a matter to commit to preparation of views, no more. Agencies, however, like the NRC when it was authorizing shipment of nuclear materials to India in *Edlow*, often desire to limit citizen involvement, and interpret intervention requirements as paralleling the Supreme Court's Article III tests.

Page 426, C&Q #8. Standing in courts and agencies. More on standing basis in agencies as different from courts.

Page 426, C&Q #9. The role of agencies when citizens intervene. The quoted Burger opinion in *Office of Communication of the United Church of Christ* is a remarkable recognition of the need for agencies to accommodate citizen interveners on a different basis from the normal agency proceeding where controversy is between two competitive vested interests. In the OCUCC case, Burger emphasizes that citizens are allies of the public process rather than of private interests. As in *Scenic Hudson*, pages 403-404, it is not appropriate for an administrative law judge in citizen intervention cases merely to sit back "like an umpire blandly calling balls and strikes."

Page 426, C&Q #10. Citizens access to information. Self-explanatory. Information disclosure under FOIA can play a critical role in the practicalities of enforcement of regulatory programs.

Pages 427, C&Q #11. Official public participation policies. As noted, with Ms. Whitman's departure the EPA's newly-adopted public participation policy entered an administrative limbo.

Page 427, C&Q #12. "Internalizing costs" through public law? *Do public agencies face the same call to internalize social costs?* If human nature is the source of the externalizing tendency, human administrators are not immune. If fact the narrowed official perspective has been an evident point since the highway salting materials ion Chapter 1. Public officials get caught up in the thinking of the marketplace economy, losing sight of civic-societal optimalities. Statutes like NEPA and the ESA's §7 are designed to try to force some modicum of internalization of social costs, but often are resisted by agencies as much or more than by private actors.

A quick note on other relevant administrative process hurdles. Chapter 20 goes more deeply into the difficulties of financing citizen enforcement. A number of environmental advocacy groups - a notable example is the New Jersey Student Public Interest Research Group - have managed to earn substantial fees enforcing major pollution statutes.

The federal Equal Access to Justice Act, 28 USCA §2412, deserves mention:

> ...Unless expressly prohibited by statute, a court may award reasonable fees and expenses of attorneys [defined to include reasonable expenses of expert witnesses, studies, analyses, engineering reports, or tests necessary for the preparation of the case, §2412d(C)2(A)] to the prevailing party in any civil action brought by or against the United States....The court shall include...fees and other expenses...unless the court finds that during such adversary proceeding the position of the US was substantially justified, or that special circumstances make an award unjust.

This sounds very much like a presumption in favor of fee-shifting for prevailing parties. Note that it can also be the basis of suits by prevailing *federal* parties as well!

The future development of fee shifting under non-statutory theories of equity in the state courts remains incipient.

Pages 428-434. STATUTORY INTERPRETATION: HOW? BY WHOM? — agencies or courts — *Chevron.* *Chevron* is the leading case for the proposition that courts should defer broadly to agency interpretations of law, slightly modified by the 2001 *Mead* decision. The contrary position is that, in many cases, courts will find that statutory language is sufficiently clear that the court can determine on its own whether the agency interpretation of law is correct. That in fact was what was done in the leading case, Hearst v. NLRB, 322 U.S. 111 (1944).

In determining what courts actually do, faced with agency interpretations of statutes, consider the following from Professor Colin Diver's post-Chevron article "Statutory Interpretation in the Administrative State," 133 U. Penn. L. Rev. 549, 562 (1985):

> The prevailing judicial orthodoxy... consists of three tenets:
>
> 1. Only if the statute's "plain" meaning (as illuminated by judicial examination of its text and history) fails to solve the riddle is an inquiry into deference appropriate
> 2. The decision to grant deference depends on various attributes of the agency legal authority and functions and of the administrative interpretation at issue and
> 3. The consequence of granting deference is to convert the court's task from determining whether the contested interpretation is correct to determining whether it is "reasonable."

We take this to recognize the reality that judges tend to believe that courts are always competent to interpret statutes and will do so looking at the traditional sources of judicial interpretation of statutes. Only where a matter does not appear to have statutory law on point is the *Chevron* "gap filling" appropriate.

On the other hand, *Chevron* is typically quoted by the present Supreme Court and other courts less sophisticated in administrative law as a wide ranging justification for deference to agencies' statutory interpretations.

Page 429, C&Q #1. The strategics of definition: Bubbling: *Do you see how a bubble might result in cleaner air?* In policy terms, allowing an air pollution "bubble" basis for emissions measurement, averaging over and entire industrial site, means that a company does not have to meet the highest and best current technology standards. Nevertheless bubbling allows industries to retrofit their existing plants at less than maximum cost.

If an industry knows it will be held to highest standards what might result? The alternative may well be to encourage industries to run their existing dirty plants into the ground, while building their new plants overseas.

This is a good place to remind students of the minuet of deference being danced by the judges and the agencies. Ultimately the courts have arrogated to themselves the power to define how much they will intrude on agencies' findings of fact and law. The degree of deference/scrutiny they choose to apply will often be outcome-determinative. Courts must respect the separation of powers. "But deference does not mean abdication," as Justice Marshall said in *Belle Terre*, 416 U.S. 1 at 13.

Pages 430-31, C&Q #2. Deference to agency interpretations of law: *Does Chevron set out a general principle of deference to agency interpretations of law, or just where there is a need for "gap-filling"?* This picks up on the prior commentary on *Chevron*. We suspect that the Court's unanimous vote was in part attributable to the supposition that it applied only to a narrow class of situations (as in the regulatory takings *Lucas* case). Its rhetoric was cast however to spill over into a deference principle of broader application. Many courts now apply it (in the 2-step process noted) as a rule of plenary deference in all reviews of agency interpretations of law, and some even apply it as a rule of deference on agency fact findings.

The last question, *whether courts, in deciding how much to defer to an agency, can take into consideration the agency's political stance toward the provision?* seems to us an eminently realistic proposition. If we were arguing for non-deference to an agency's diluted interpretation of a provision that the agency had unsuccessfully argued against in published congressional hearings, there is no way we would not introduce those hearings into the record. Everyone knows what is going on when the Corps of Engineers interprets NEPA not to apply to ongoing projects, and so on, and we think most sophisticated judges integrate the political alignment of an agency on a matter as part of their considerations.

Page 431, C&Q #3. Judicial deference on agency interpretations of law after *Chevron*, and *Mead*: Descriptive notes. *Mead* seems to leave undisturbed the premise of deference to expert agency law-interpreting *regulations*, but not for informal adjudications?

Page 432, C&Q #4. The "plain meaning" finesse. A mini-essay on "plain meaning": The excerpt from the Hercules v. EPA case indicates how courts may defer far less on questions of law than they do on questions of agency fact finding. The Court not only looked at the statute's "plain" language, but also reviewed the legislative history and the policy intentions of the statute itself.

Page 433, C&Q #5. Differential deference? Relativity: The 2004 *ADEC* case (see Supplementary Materials for Chapter 6 on the Website) raises the question whether agency "guidance" documents, which have not been issued in notice-and-comment rulemaking nor as part of formal agency adjudications can nevertheless claim deference from a court. The ADEC majority seems to say there is a relativity — sort of a persuasive authority but not compelling a binding deference, if that ever is true.

Page 434, C&Q #6. Organic decisionmaking? This note repeats the idea that administrative process and its judicial review are sufficiently slippery that judges can choose to frame cases in ways that are outcome-determinative, even where *Chevron* had seemed to set out such a ringing presumption for deference.

Page 434, C&Q #7. Administrative law as a crap game? Ditto. Yes, but it's a game our students and we have to play.

Chapter 8.
INTERNATIONAL AGREEMENTS AS DOMESTIC ENVIRONMENTAL LAW

Suggested time budget: 1–2 class sessions

Chapter contents:

Taught as a one-day unit:

435-440 The treaty power
440-443 Missouri v Holland
443-448 The Whaling Convention
448-454 Japan Whaling v American Cetacean Society

Taught as a two-day unit:

Day 1*:*
435-440 The treaty power
440-443 Missouri v. Holland
443-448 The Whaling Convention
448-454 Japan Whaling v. American Cetacean Society

Day 2*:*
454-458 International trade agreements
458-460 George E. Warren Corp. v. EPA
460-462 NAFTA side agreement
462-467 Migratory birds factual record

—and check the Teachers' Manual Website for SUPPLEMENTARY MATERIALS:
http://www.bc.edu/schools/law/library/coursebook/envtlaw/teachers

The list of Supplementary Materials in Part III of this manual, and on the Teachers' Website, indicates materials posted on the Teachers' Website that are relevant to this and other chapters.

OVERALL TEACHING THEMES & COURSE DESIGN CONSIDERATIONS

This chapter, which is new to the third edition, presents international agreements as a source of domestic environmental law. The choice of this subject matter reflects the increasingly inescapable role of international agreements as the legal authority for regulatory actions of the federal government, in many cases supplementing or replacing a domestic statutory framework in that role. At the same time, this material is new or unfamiliar to many environmental teachers and lawyers, who have concentrated on domestic law. Accordingly, every effort has been made to present the material in this chapter in a stepwise manner that is relatively straightforward to teach and that tracks the other themes and approaches of the coursebook. Because of the need to lay the basic structural foundation before moving into the more challenging analytical applications, two class sessions should be allocated for this material. If only one is available, it is advisable to truncate the material with the Japan Whaling case and omit the remainder, rather than to attempt a survey of the entirety of this complex chapter in an hour.

The material is arranged in a manner that moves to increasing analytical complexity throughout the chapter, which in effect is a capsule course on the law of foreign relations as applied to the environment. Missouri v. Holland and the factual record of the Commission for Environmental Cooperation are separated by more than 80 years, but the subject matter and analytical challenges are remarkably similar. The material in this chapter has been expressly selected to emphasize questions of domestic law; chapter 26 addresses treaties in their role as international compacts. However, the unusual nature of international agreements is reflected in domestic legal doctrines, including most notably Missouri v. Holland.

The architecture of the chapter begins with a concrete problem, protection of migratory birds whose range spans the United States and Canada, with Missouri v. Holland serving as a template for the domestic legal effect on our federal structure more generally. The analysis then moves on to a multilateral agreement -- the International Convention for the Regulation of Whaling -- as a more complex example. Issues of implementation are addressed in the Japan Whaling case, which also serves as a vehicle for addressing the very large category of "executive agreements," which are concluded without Senate advice and consent to ratification. These two cases taken together nicely illustrate the tension between external obligations on the United States on the one hand and the structure of our country as a federal state characterized by separation of powers on the other.

Because of the somewhat different analytical treatment required, a separate section has been devoted to the "hot topic" of the potential or actual conflict between international trade agreements and domestic environmental regulation. Mechanisms for supposedly offsetting the adverse effects of trade agreements, as exemplified by the environmental side agreement to NAFTA, round out the chapter, bringing the subject matter full circle by again using migratory birds as an example.

TEACHING NOTES, COMMENTS, & ALL QUESTIONS ANSWERED

Pages 435-440. Instead of beginning with a doctrinal exposition of the treaty power, you as the teacher might prefer to begin the first class session with the substantive problem of migratory birds that range over the territories of more than one country, perhaps the simplest example of a shared natural resource. If one state (the standard term in international law, referring not to a subnational unit of the United States, but to a country or a nation) within the birds' range chooses to allow destruction of the animals and their habitat, then the other suffers the loss of the resource. A negotiated solution in the form of a treaty -- an international contract between states as represented by their governments -- is a vehicle for articulating and reconciling both parties' needs in a cooperative mode intended to conserve the resource. The text of the treaty memorializes the deal and serves as a reference point to measure future implementation and compliance.

Having drawn that out, you as the teacher might ask what sort of obligations the parties would want to include in a hypothetical treaty. This is a good occasion for class discussion, and students will typically include measures that would ordinarily be found in a domestic statute, such as restrictions on hunting and habitat degradation. The parties may well want to include other provisions designed to assure themselves of the other's compliance, such as reporting requirements. Focusing on the former -- domestic measures to implement the agreement -- you can then ask the class how those requirements come to be incorporated into domestic law.

The answer is that the President, after having negotiated and signed the treaty (his sole prerogative under Article II § 2 of the Constitution), submits the agreement to the Senate for its advice and consent by a two-thirds majority. If, and only if, the Senate gives its advice and consent may the President ratify the agreement, perfecting the obligations in it. You might note that, contrary to popular wisdom, the Senate does not ratify treaties; this is an exclusive (and probably unreviewable) prerogative of the President, who may choose to withhold ratification even if the Senate has given its advice and consent. You might observe as well that signature ad referendum under such circumstances is only a preliminary indication of an intent to be bound.

You might take a few minutes to discuss why the Framers set the system up this way. Previous unsatisfactory experience with Congressional involvement in foreign relations under the Articles of Confederation led the Framers to conclude that a strong President should have the exclusive prerogative to negotiate international agreements. Note that this system turns the ordinary process of lawmaking on its head, with the President crafting the law in the first instance. The Framers, however, recognized that the President could not make law for the Nation without checks and balances, and consequently assigned the Senate the advice-and-consent function to assure a measure of accountability. The supermajority (two-thirds) requirement is intended to ensure a high level of consensus -- particularly, at least before the Senate was directly elected, among the quasi-sovereign states comprising the United States. From a doctrinal perspective, Senate advice and consent plus Presidential ratification places an Article II § treaty on the same legal footing as a federal statute.

Pages 440-441. Missouri v. Holland explores the question of the extent to which treaties negotiated, concluded and ratified by the President after Senate advice and consent can -- operating through the Supremacy Clause -- displace inconsistent state law. (Technically speaking, the instrument under review in the case was implementing legislation adopted after simple majority vote in both Chambers of the Congress, a detail that may tend to confuse discussion of this case, but which assumes larger significance in the last section of this chapter.) Regulation of hunting of wildlife and the use of land have been generally understood to be reserved to the states. This is demonstrated concretely by the carryover paragraph from page 440 to 441, describing cases that held a virtually identical federal statute not supported by a treaty to be unconstitutional. (These holdings reflect an early twentieth century notion of the limits of the commerce clause that might not be relevant today, but the principle of the case is unaffected.) Justice Holmes states that, even if those cases were correctly decided, the treaty and the implementing statute are constitutional and supersede inconsistent state law because that result is necessary to implement the treaty with Canada. Doctrinally speaking, the exercise of Congressional power is "necessary and proper" for implementing the treaty.

Pages 441-442, C&Q #1 & 2. Migratory birds and states' rights; Avoiding a "flap" with Canada — are wild geese a matter of national security? Students naturally have a tendency to assume that any judicial holding is inevitable and self-evident. You might explore the costs of the doctrine of Missouri v. Holland (which, incidentally, has an analogue in most other federal states such as Canada and Australia, see C&Q #4 below). Isn't Justice Holmes saying that merely by finding a willing foreign power, the President and the Senate have a blank check to intrude on states' rights? Doesn't that invite abuse in the form of Presidential collusion with foreign powers to accomplish what he could not if acting alone? What are the limits, if any, to the doctrine of Missouri v. Holland?

- Treaties are subordinate to, and must be consistent with, the structural requirements of the Constitution. So, for example, a treaty might be invalid if the President were to ratify it before the Senate gave its advice and consent.
- So, too, a treaty might be invalid if it attempts to accomplish a goal that does not fall within the power of either the federal government or the states under the Constitution -- e.g., requiring cruel and unusual punishment, or regulating speech in a manner prohibited by the First Amendment. Justice Holmes distinguishes the migratory bird treaty (first full paragraph page 441) by noting that the power to protect birds has to reside somewhere in our federal structure, and that the treaty consequently represents a modest rearrangement of our internal federal structure to meet external (i.e., foreign relations) demands.
- The opinion also seems to support some limits on the subject matter of treaties. E.g., page 441, last paragraph of the opinion: protection of migratory birds can be accomplished "*only* by national action in concert with that of another power..." (emphasis supplied). This suggests some level of judicial scrutiny into the question whether the subject matter of a treaty is an appropriate one for an international compact -- i.e., whether cooperation with a foreign power is necessary or desirable. You might explore with the students the extent to which this is a meaningful limitation. Arguably courts don't have the expertise to apply this test as a judicially manageable standard, and doing so would risk intruding into the Executive's conduct of foreign relations.
- There are also political checks in the form of the supermajority requirement for Senate advice and consent. Even after the direct election of Senators, state governments with legitimate concerns about a treaty are likely to be able to inject them into debates on the resolution of advice and consent, and need only convince a third of Senators to accomplish the goal of rejecting the agreement. If the issue comes up, you might note as well that the Senate can give its advice and consent with conditions or "reservations," which like the treaty then operate as federal law.

Justice Holmes clearly has in mind the broader implications of the situation for the treaty power. If the case had come out the other way each of the 50 states might, for example, rely on state law to prohibit the destruction of chemical weapons within their borders even if the federal government had taken on such an obligation -- clearly a situation that cuts closer to the quick of national security than migratory birds (however important one may consider them in their own right). Another example from recent experience would be if each state were to decide for itself whether to implement a multilateral anti-terrorism convention

The structural posture of the case is also worth noting. Missouri brought suit only after the convention with Canada had been ratified and entered into force as a matter of international law. If the holding of Missouri v. Holland had been otherwise -- i.e., that the treaty lacked domestic legal authority -- the agreement would still be binding on the United States as international law. This attribute is common to almost all cases challenging the domestic legal authority for an international agreement, and strongly encourages deference to the political branches. Otherwise, the Court would run the risk of issuing an order that compels the United States to violate international law.

Page 442, C&Q #3. The long-range impact of migratory birds. The doctrine of Missouri v. Holland operates in much the same way as an expansive interpretation of the Commerce Clause in expanding the powers of the federal government vis-à-vis the states. For pretty much the same reasons as in domestic policy (see Chapter 6), Missouri v. Holland is wise policy to the extent that one considers uniform federal standards implemented evenhandedly to be a good idea. As on the domestic level, the price may be the suppression of experimentation at the state level through federal preemption. Justice Holmes's opinion says that the latter, at least so far as state policy may stray from the international legal obligations of the United States as articulated in a treaty, is too high a risk to accept.

If you as the teacher are interested in exploring this point further, you might draw the class's attention to Article I § 10 of the Constitution, the "Compact Clause," which specifies that "[n]o State shall enter into any Treaty, Alliance, or Confederation..." Quite obviously, the purpose of this provision is prevent the states (of the U.S.) from disrupting a uniform federal foreign policy. Yet some states have entered into what look to be international agreements on such issues as acid rain and global warming with their counterparts, such as Canadian provinces. Is it always the case that such efforts have a corrosive as opposed to constructive effect on foreign policy? While there is little law on this question, the Executive Branch (in the form of the State Department) has tended to look the other way so long as what is involved is coordinated trans-border actions that are otherwise within the powers of the states of the United States -- i.e., consist of the kinds of things that the states could otherwise undertake on their own in our federal system and that therefore do not disrupt a uniform federal foreign policy.

Pages 442-443, C&Q #4. Comparative law: the Canadian take on the Migratory Bird Convention. While the Canadian example stands for the weak proposition that all federal states have to at least be aware of the domestic implementation issue, it does not necessarily mean that the doctrine of Missouri v. Holland is essential. The most likely alternative would be for the federal government to engage in a negotiation with its constituent subnational units - states of provinces. Justice Holmes dismisses this result as unacceptable (last paragraph of the opinion). Note that, in doing so, he declines to limit the reach of the doctrine by reference to subject matter (migratory birds, according to the last paragraph on page 441, are "a national interest of very nearly the first magnitude"). Some other federal states, such as Canada, tend to rely on cooperation between the federal government and their constituent subnational units to a greater extent than does the United States. Another possibility, entirely consistent with Missouri v. Holland, might be for the President or the Senate to refrain as a prudential matter from ratifying (in the case of the President) or giving advice and consent (in the case of the Senate) until a supermajority of state legislatures had acquiesced.

Page 443, C&Q #5. Missouri triumphant? Even if the statute at issue in *SWANCC* did not provide the necessary jurisdictional basis, the Court might have looked to the migratory bird convention with Canada and its implementing legislation, the Migratory Bird Treaty Act, as a basis for federal authority. The question whether those authorities provided the necessary federal powers would then become a question of statutory and treaty interpretation Perhaps the Court impliedly concluded that the treaty and the MBTA did not govern the situation, suggesting at most a reluctance to rely on the preemptive effect of the treaty power; the Court's action did not in any sense overrule Missouri v. Holland.

Page 443, C&Q #6. One amendment to the Convention lays an egg, another takes flight. This question is designed to serve as a transition into the next section dealing with multilateral agreements. As noted in the text, under international law an amendment to a treaty is itself a new agreement, requiring in our system a renewed cycle of negotiation, signature, Senate advice and consent, and ratification. The reason for the international rule is to preserve a basic feature of treaty law, namely that states cannot be bound by an international agreement without their consent. On the other hand, from the point of view of environmental efficacy, the rule seems needlessly cumbersome. That may not be so apparent in a setting of a bilateral agreement where one can understand the requirement for the consent of both parties; any other rule would in effect give one party the unilateral right to amend the agreement. But in the case of a multilateral agreement, such as the Whaling Convention discussed in the next section, the international rule runs the risk of creating classes of parties -- some states party only to the parent agreement, some to the parent agreement and only the first amendment, some party to the parent agreement and the first two amendments, etc. This encourages fragmentation as opposed to the uniformity one expects from multilateral agreements, which are the closest analogue in international practice to legislative instruments.

Pages 443-447. This section introduces multilateral agreements, which as a matter of both international and domestic law are very similar to bilateral agreements. One twist you might note as the teacher is the frequent inclusion in multilateral agreements of provisions establishing rules for "entry into force." These are typically phrased as a condition precedent in the form of a certain number of ratifications. Consequently, even though the United States may have proceeded through its domestic process all the way to the point of ratification, the agreement does not establish binding rules of international law until the threshold for entry into force has been met. The analogue in a bilateral treaty is that the agreement does not bind the United States until the treaty partner has also perfected its obligations. You might ask the class what the consequences are of setting the threshold for entry into force at a high as opposed to low number of ratifications. The former tends to encourage a level playing field from a competitiveness point of view, in that states taking on economically burdensome obligations are not disadvantaged by comparison with laggards, holdouts, and free riders. A low number might be appropriate for an agreement intended quickly to establish minimum international standards of behavior.

Page 447-448, C&Qs 1&2. #1 Consensus as gridlock: should multilateral agreements find an alternative way? #2 The whaling Convention as paper tiger. The "opt-out" provisions of the Whaling Convention represent an attempt to streamline international decision making to encourage faster, more effective, internationally uniform action without going through the cumbersome amendment process (page 443, C&Q #6). For reasons similar to those motivating the rule governing amendments -- namely, that a state ought not to be bound without its consent -- the natural tendency of an international organization such as the International Whaling Commission is to operate by unanimity or "consensus." If states could not opt out of the IWC's catch limitation, there is a risk that they might be bound without their consent through a majority voting process. That in turn could discourage states from becoming party to the Whaling Convention in the first place, or withdrawing from it ("denouncing" it) after the IWC takes a decision that they perceive as contrary to their national interest. The opt-out formula is an attempt to balance these two competing concerns. Students who advocate binding majority voting regimes in response to these questions are typically reasoning by reference to the decision making procedures of national legislatures. The IWC would then begin to look like something approaching world government. The difficulty they (and we) have is getting states irrevocably to accept such procedures -- not an easy task.

Page 448, C&Q #3. Problems of enforcement. States may be reluctant to challenge each other's actions because of other bilateral dynamics, because they are concerned about making bad law, or because they worry about being held to similar standards themselves. An alternative is to put the power to initiate a dispute settlement process into the hands of individuals or citizens' organizations, the international analogue of a citizen suit (Chapter 21). A concrete example of such a mechanism is contained in the environmental side agreement to NAFTA and discussed in some detail beginning on page 461. Note that citizen enforcement actions on the international level can only be created by international agreements, as individuals and environmental organizations -- like corporations -- are not "subjects" of international law, which governs the relations among states.

Pages 448-452. The Pelly and Packwood amendments interpreted in *Japan Whaling* are an attempt to invigorate the enforcement of the Whaling Convention even when states opt out, as Japan did in this example. Note that Japan, having opted out of the IWC's quotas, is not in violation of international law, but may still be subject to sanctions under the stricter "diminish[ing] the effectiveness" test of the two statutory mandates. The Executive Branch response was to negotiate a phaseout in the Japanese take of sperm whales on a more protracted schedule than provided by the IWC. The plaintiff conservation organization claims that this is a violation of the statutory mandates, which it interprets as nondiscretionary. The Government says that its action is consistent with the legislative directives, by accomplishing results that are consistent with the statutory intent in a cooperative setting that might not be achieved through unilateral sanctions or punishments.

You as the teacher might observe explicitly that the only reason this dispute arises is that the agreement with Japan was done as an "executive agreement" without Senate advice and consent to ratification. (If you want to be scrupulous about terminology, you can distinguish between Article II § 2 "treaties" concluded with Senate advice and consent and "executive agreements" done without Congressional participation, with the term "international agreements" including them both.) The closest domestic analogue would probably be an executive order or Presidential proclamation. It is also probably worth noting that there would have been no dispute if the agreement had been submitted to the Senate for its advice and consent, in which case it would have the same legal effect as a statutory carve-out from the legislative scheme specifically for Japan. In the absence of Senate advice and consent, the agreement must be consistent with the statutory mandates; otherwise it is invalid.

The key to the case is the last paragraph in the majority opinion on page 452, beginning "We conclude..." Justice White says in effect that where possible an executive agreement should be harmonized with statutes. This has the arguably desirable effect of relieving the Court from having to order the Executive Branch to do exactly what it had promised Japan in a legally binding agreement that it would not do -- which quite likely would be a violation of the U.S.'s international legal obligations. On the other hand, the result suggests a malleable approach to the situation that could seriously disrupt domestic statutory mandates if carried too far.

Pages 452-453, C&Q #1. Unilateral action versus multilateralism These questions have no correct answer, but are designed to get students thinking about the relative merits of different modes of approaching international environmental policy.

Page 453, C&Q #2. Executive branch scare tactics. These questions highlight the potential for abuse if the approach of the majority in *Japan Whaling* is taken too far. The plaintiff in the case might well say that the deal with Japan was done as an executive agreement precisely to avoid Congressional scrutiny and that Justice White's analytical approach tends to encourage circumventing the Senate in the future. If the Secretary of Commerce were ordered by the Court to certify Japan, that state would no doubt protest the action as a violation of international law, which in turn could disrupt bilateral relations with the country.

Page 453-454, C&Q #3. Lessons for Congress. Congress could try to be more specific as to the contours of the statutory mandate, but it would be difficult to see how that would overcome Justice White's approach of harmonizing the statute and the executive agreement. Congress could disapprove the agreement, explicitly prohibit departures from the statutory standard by executive agreement, or establish standards for future executive agreements. Any or all of these, however, could raise questions as to Congress's Constitutional authority to intrude into the President's conduct of foreign relations. (Note by the way that *Japan Whaling* clearly stands for the proposition that the President's authority to conclude executive agreements consistent with statutory mandates can be implied and need not be explicitly granted by legislation.) As implied by the question, Congress could also exercise its oversight functions, for example by holding hearings, to pressure the President in a non-legally binding mode. Once the agreement is concluded, however, it is difficult to see how that would be very effective. The *Japan Whaling* case is a good example of a phenomenon widely noted by scholars of foreign relations law: that the President almost always wins.

Pages 454-459. The essential points to note in this introductory exposition are that

- International trade agreements are a hybrid of the model just examined -- executive agreements authorized by simple majority vote of both Chambers of the Congress. While trade agreements could probably be done as Article II § 2 treaties, the Congressional-Executive approach tends to track the distribution of powers in the Constitution, which allocates the exclusive power to regulate international trade to the Congress (Article I § 8) and the sole authority to negotiate international agreements to the President (Article II § 2). The distinctive feature of trade agreements is the adoption of implementing legislation on a no-amendment, up-or-down "fast track."

- The clash between trade and environment, probably familiar to at least some students, arises structurally from the fact that trade agreements contain "negative" obligations that tie the hands of governments in an effort to prevent them from disrupting a free international market, while our environmental laws contain "positive" obligations that authorize or require government affirmatively to intervene in the market to offset externalities such as pollution.

The *Warren* case illustrates the potentially disruptive effect of the negative disciplines found in international trade agreements when overlaid on domestic environmental regulations. At issue in the *Warren* case was a regulation, which could be and was amended by the Executive (EPA in this case) without further Congressional input in response to an adverse WTO ruling. The WTO Appellate Body's report is not binding as a matter of domestic law. Hence, this case has a posture similar to *Japan Whaling* in juxtaposing a binding domestic statutory mandate against an international directive that has no domestic legal effect.

The Ginsburg opinion relies heavily on *Chevron*, arguably inappropriately as there is little or no uncertainty in the statutory mandate. Additionally, in the penultimate paragraph on page 459 ("In the particular circumstances of this case..."), the opinion takes an approach reminiscent of *Japan Whaling*, counseling reconciling international directives with domestic statutory mandates. Carried to its extreme, this approach suggests that EPA's regulations are, in the words of one staffer, "like pawns on a chessboard, just waiting to be picked off in the WTO one by one."

Page 459, C&Q #1. Judicial review in a foreign policy setting. As a formal analytical matter, the court treated the WTO Appellate Body report as helpful although not binding in interpreting the statutory mandate. Whether this approach is good or bad can be a subject of legitimate disagreement, but students should be aware that due to the negative character of WTO obligations, the Ginsburg approach will *always* result in a weakening of the rigor of environmental regulation. In other words, the trade regime is asymmetric in allowing challenges to environmental regulations as too stringent, but not too lax; there are no minimum environmental obligations in these agreements, only tests to weed out excessively demanding requirements. The reliance on *Chevron* is arguably inappropriate, for the reasons noted above. There are strict standards for applying *Chevron* deference, and foreign affairs considerations are not among them.

Pages 459-460, C&Q #2. The WTO and the rule of law. The considerations in the note all suggest that the need for deference to the Executive in the *Warren* case might be less urgent than suggested in the opinion.

Pages 460, C&Q #3. Trade-based measures to protect the environment. The Pelly Amendment authorizes restrictions or bans on importation of fish products from states that "diminish[] the effectiveness" of the Whaling Convention. The state on which such sanctions are imposed could plausibly argue discrimination against it by comparison with other states in violation of the most favored nation discipline. It could also argue a violation of the national treatment obligation to the extent that the same product is produced domestically, as well as a violation of the prohibition on quantitative restrictions.

GATT Article XX in effect authorizes states under certain limited circumstances to take actions that otherwise would be inconsistent with that agreement. The respondent state -- the United States in this example -- could argue under GATT Article XX that the Pelly restrictions are "necessary to protect human, animal or plant life or heath" and "relat[e] to the conservation of exhaustible natural resources." By comparison with unilateral measures imposed by only one state, multilaterally-agreed measures that have been approved by a large number of states are less likely to appear to be motivated by protectionism and consequently are more likely to be "necessary" and "related to...conservation" as required by the exceptions in GATT Article XX

Pages 460-465. The Article 14/15 citizen submission process under the NAFTA environmental side agreement is something of an international analogy to citizen enforcement actions under federal environmental statutes (Chapter 21). In the text of the factual record, note how the Secretariat is almost compelled to engage in some speculation to make any sense of its task.

Page 465, C&Q #1. "Factual records " on "failures to enforce": law, fact, or paper tigers? There is little in the way of a detailed negotiating history on the NAAEC, but the choice of a "factual" record as the concluding phase of the Article 14/15 process is not likely to be an oversight. Governments are very sensitive about international processes that might potentially result in criticism of them, and "factual" is likely to have chosen for its limiting effects. While the NAAEC anticipates inquiries into enforcement discretion in a way that domestic courts rarely undertake, the process has no domestic legal consequences. That said, the content of the MBTA factual record leaves little to the imagination as to the nature of U.S. non-enforcement.

Pages 465-466, C&Q #2. Assuring the effectiveness of the NAAEC. Again, governments typically want more rather than less control over processes that might produce embarrassing results. The CEC is not a court, and consequently there is no prohibition on lobbying the three environmental ministers in a political mode, or on the citizen submitter's efforts to influence them. Among the approaches that might be considered for influencing the EPA Administrator in his/her role as a voting member of the Council are direct meetings with EPA officials; Congressional hearings; letters from members of Congress or state governors or legislators; and appeals to the court of opinion in the form of press releases, news stories, and op-eds. Similar actions could be undertaken in the other NAFTA countries. This note also highlights the difficult position of the CEC Secretariat, which has to walk a fine line between maintaining its independence, meeting the needs of the NAFTA party governments, and maintaining the confidence of the environmental communities in the three NAFTA countries in the integrity and objectivity of the process.

Page 466, C&Q #3. Safe harbors for delinquent governments. This question highlights what may be the greatest utility of the citizen submission: smoking out data on enforcement or the lack thereof. In the MBTA case, the U.S. raised as a "defense" that it had never enforced the MBTA as to logging operations and that therefore there was no need for a factual record to investigate an issue as to which there was no dispute! One other issue that emerged in the MBTA case was that EPA represents the U.S. in the CEC Council, but the allegations were all directed at the Department of the Interior, which used the division of jurisdiction as something of a shield. This suggests the need, at least in proceedings in which the United States is the respondent, to identify the underlying agency whose actions are challenged, and to target it as well as EPA so as to avoid the adverse consequences of this phenomenon.

Pages 466-467, C&Q #4. What's it good for anyway? For the reasons discussed in the earlier notes, a CEC factual record is unlikely to be of much use in a domestic court proceeding, in which the exercise of enforcement discretion is very difficult to challenge. The factual record may, however, be of use with the political branches and in mobilizing public concern, as discussed in the answer to C&Q #2 above.

Pages 467, C&Q #5. Do NAAEC factual records return home to roost as supplements to domestic law? This note underscores the somewhat paradoxical situation in which those NAFTA governments that demonstrate the greatest responsiveness to the "mobilization of shame" approach are those that are likely to attract the largest number of submissions precisely for that reason.

Chapter 9.
FEDERAL AGENCY DISCLOSURE: NEPA'S STOP-AND-THINK LOGIC, AND THE POWER OF INFORMATION

Chapter contents:

Suggested time budget: 2 or 3 class sessions

Day 1

471-478 Introduction and the statute
478-507 The *Chicod Creek* case study

Day 2

507-522 NEPA implementation issues
523-527 NEPA's international implications

or **Day 3** NEPA case study or simulation presented by instructor

—and check the Teachers' Manual Website for SUPPLEMENTARY MATERIALS:

http://www.bc.edu/schools/law/library/coursebook/envtlaw/teachers

The list of Supplementary Materials in Part III of this manual, and on the Teachers' Website, indicates materials posted on the Teachers' Website that are relevant to this and other chapters.

NOTE: STATUTORY TAXONOMY. If you have not already done so, you should remind students to look at the shorthand design summary – at pages 469-470 – of the regulatory systems incorporated in Part III's chapters, and at the statutory capsules printed in the Reference section at the back of the book, Ref. pages 49-61. You yourself may be interested in an orphan chapter, old Chapter 11, dropped in this Third Edition but available on the Teachers' Website, called "Process-Driven Standard-Setting." The chapter studied several statutes that do not have substantive congressional guidance for standard-setting, and instead leave regulatory standards up to a negotiation process between designated stakeholders. The historic preservation and rangeland management statutes are prime examples.

OVERALL TEACHING THEMES & COURSE DESIGN CONSIDERATIONS

This chapter should be allotted 2-3 class sessions in light of NEPA's conceptual and practical importance. The chapter has several different themes:

One is the importance of bringing critically relevant information to light - to the public and to the public consciousness of agency officials - in circumstances where the players otherwise would prefer to keep inauspicious facts out of sight. This strategy echoes the difference between the calculus of the marketplace (which includes agencies along with industrial actors) and civic-societal interests. The forced-disclosure approach to government agency decision making has great utility. The information disclosed commonly addresses externalized costs being passed on to the natural and civic spheres by agency and industry marketplace initiatives. Note the fundamental rationality of NEPA's broad blanket requirement that agencies look before they leap.

The second theme is the pragmatic litigative importance of NEPA's mandatory requirement of an EIS. Because of that (accidental) procedural requirement, substantial citizen litigation was possible at a societally critical moment in time, and NEPA cases helped build credibility and momentum for the development of the entire field. NEPA was thus an "empowerment" instrument, and a milestone in the integration of active citizen pluralism into the legal system. The evolution of NEPA is illuminating: the judicial shaping - and erosion - of an accidentally-legislated statutory requirement; and the role of citizen litigation - including acknowledgment of the long-running campaign by marketplace players (and judges who embody those marketplace politics) to circumvent citizen enforcement of the EIS requirement in court, which has always been NEPA's only credible compliance forum. From industry's perspective, consider the sad plaint of Don Hodel, in the epigraphs on page 527.

A corollary theme thus is that the meaning and effectiveness of NEPA are attributable to a fortuitous series of decisions in the federal courts. The Chicod Creek case in the first section is a prime example of this phenomenon of judges and citizen litigants making something effective out of nothing intended.

NEPA imposes frequently unwelcome transparency requirements on federal agencies, which they may attempt to evade through noncompliance or minimal compliance. Two NEPA paradoxes can be discerned: (1) NEPA requires that federal agencies disclose, fully and in good faith, the environmental impacts of, and alternatives to, proposals that they may, for political purposes, be eager to effectuate, and are thus tempted to take refuge in nondisclosure or distorted disclosure of potentially embarrassing environmental information; and (2) Because of this bureaucratic temptation to minimize or distort disclosure of environmental information, citizen plaintiffs must often develop independent access to the very information that they want an agency to disclose, so as to convince a federal judge to order the agency to formally disclose it through compliance with NEPA.

Because of federal agency ambivalence (if not outright antipathy) towards NEPA, strategic agency behavior aimed at minimizing NEPA compliance is central to an analysis of the "common law of NEPA." Several of the authors teach NEPA by highlighting the opportunities available to federal agencies to circumvent full disclosure of environmental information: E.g., (1) issuing environmental assessments and Findings of No Significant Impact instead of full-scale Environmental Impact Statements; (2) segmenting large projects into smaller units in order to conceal long-term, cumulative environmental impacts; and (3) delaying formal proposals, and consequent NEPA compliance, until the underlying projects have become virtually inevitable.

TEACHING NOTES, COMMENTS, & ALL QUESTIONS ANSWERED

The CEQ regulations, codified at 40 CFR §1501 et seq., are a remarkably useful tool for studying NEPA. For reference, we encourage you to get a current version of the CEQ NEPA regulations. The regulations include a brief but useful index and are written from the point of view that NEPA is intended to be functional, and seek to encourage good faith advance planning and disclosure. Current administration policies and Supreme Court interpretations of NEPA often can be contrasted to the terms of the regulations.

The comparison emphasizes the practical and political consequences that lie behind questions of statutory interpretation and judicial deference to recalcitrant agencies' procedures. For this chapter, in particular, the teacher will also want to check the index of one of the recent loose-leaf services to see interesting new twists that are arising in NEPA litigation.

Given the international significance of NEPA's environmental impact statement requirement, and its basic functional logic, it continues to be important that NEPA not be regarded as a frivolous piece of window dressing, although there are those who treat it as such.

Pages 471-474. NEPA, its conceptual context, and its legislative happenstance. To begin with, doesn't it seem completely obvious that governmental decision-making should consider its consequences, both negative and positive, and its alternatives, before acting? The core of NEPA – §102(2)(c)'s EIS requirement – requires government agencies to look far, wide, and deep before they take major actions that might affect the environment.

But the reality, of course, is that NEPA was able to come into existence only by happenstance, was bitterly resisted by the agencies to which it was applied, and has suffered a protracted war of attrition with the latter-day federal judiciary, so that many people now consider the NEPA process a quixotic attempt to hold back an inevitable tide.

The point is to remind students that our society has delegated many functions, major and minor, to agency establishments – whether it is nuclear power development, an interstate highway system, swine flu vaccinations program – all of which require a national level of effort and some centralized direction. In other cases the endeavors delegated to agencies are far smaller. The wetlands draining program of the Soil Conservation Service in Chicod Creek obviously did not require federal coordination. Private entities could have gotten together and arranged for the alterations if they made economic sense. The Chicod Creek channelization, unlike the foregoing national-level public programs, is an example of a governmental program that is quite clearly a subsidy, stepping in to do a job that the private marketplace would find too marginal, even disregarding the environmental costs.

As discussed in Chapter 7, however, each of these programs and projects can become its own little empire, intimately linking the federal agency with corollary state agencies and private industries, so that they become worlds unto themselves.

By the nature of things, these programs do not involve an overview accounting process. Those who raise negative questions about the projects and programs are deeply resented and shunted aside. Without the accident of NEPA, what would be the chance of getting the federal agency, or the state drainage authorities, to pay attention to economic and environmental values? The power of a highway-building or swamp-busting lobby is sufficiently large and focused that members of the public had no practicable means in most cases to raise a question.

NEPA changed all that, although it was close to accidental in its creation, and could well have been diluted and ignored from the start.

A remarkable range of federal agency projects have attracted citizen scrutiny and NEPA litigation. (Most students do not have a real grasp of how broadly federal agency initiatives are woven into the marketplace and landscape of the U.S.)

Page 475, C&Q #1. NEPA as paper tiger. There must be dozens, or hundreds, of agency projects and proposals for legislation that legally require EISs, but don't get them because no one sues. If every EIS-eligible project or program was hauled into court under NEPA, we suspect the system would break down of cumulative resentment and weight. As it is, NEPA is a broadly available cause of action for those who know and care enough to sue. Within the bureaucracy, the hope is that NEPA and the internal planning and review process it attempts to promote have some residual intra-agency effects even if litigation is not filed to force compliance.

Pages 475-476, C&Q #2. NEPA as international milestone and model for other jurisdictions. These comments are self-explanatory. See Section C. below.

Pages 476-477, C&Q #3. NEPA as accidental legislation. Largely self-explanatory.

What would have been the effect of the Aspinall Amendment? Pretty clearly it was understood by the House that passed it as an amendment serving marketplace interests by eliminating any legal effect from the bill, making it into a totally empty election-year exercise in symbolic reassurance to accommodate the media's sudden active interest in environmental problems.

What does the title of NEPA tell you? The National Environmental Policy Act echoes the non-mandatory intention.

Why didn't the marketplace forces so dominant in Congress recognize NEPA's mandatory potential? It slipped by, with some sloppy legal advisors thinking that its litigatability had been undercut by amendments to certain litigation-oriented phrases as noted in this Comment. (We suggest a brief discussion of the ethics of filing lawsuits under a statute the attorney knows to have been unintended by the legislators who passed it.)

Can the courts give the statute an effect that the legislators tried to eliminate?

What does the law say?

What does the accidental nature of NEPA's passage as an enforceable statute – an eminently sensible requirement that gets put on the books only because it slips through the marketplace bloc's filter – say about the legislative process? It is a far from perfect system, and deserves improvement. But once passed, the statute became consolidated as semi-holy writ in the case law, and that is how the game is played.

Pages 477-478, C&Q ##4-6. NEPA's de facto statutory strategy. The political science of NEPA. The role of citizens. Self-explanatory.

Pages 479-480, 483-486, 498. The Chicod Creek case — Part I. You may want to start this NEPA case study by asking why the creek was not already channelized if agriculture had been in the area for more than a century? The Weyerhaeuser Corporation, for one, had plenty of assets to drain their wetlands. if that were cost-justified, but apparently it was not without federal grants. The subsidy provisions of PL566 created this project, and like other public works programs the SCS because a formidable political establishment. According to the confidential interview noted in the text, the North Carolina wildlife and environmental protection agencies were afraid to raise questions within the government against the powerful SCS pork-barrel, and had given up hope of preventing such channelizations until the young Yalies of NRDC volunteered to take the case (at which point the state wildlife officials supplied substantial discreet help behind the scenes).

The subsidy point can be made vivid by asking what the purpose of this project was. If students say "agriculture," note that they have missed the point, because agricultural improvement only gets fifty percent federal subsidy under PL566. By calling this "flood control," however, the SCS and its local boosters are able to raise the federal ante to seventy-five percent, and of course much of the remaining twenty-five percent can be paid in in-kind donations of high- appraised easements. (Such high valuations, of course, raise the total budget of the project but are paid off in private dollars leveraged by four-fold federal subsidy.)

The legal elements of the first *Chicod Creek* opinion. The legal elements of this opinion are tracked in the questions that follow. The discussion can be used as an opportunity to review with the students the various steps of administrative law judicial review, reviewability, standing, cause of action, ripeness, etc. And these are largely covered in the notes that follow. But an important theme to add is to make the students recognize that this is a judge who had no great sophistication in administrative law, and virtually no understanding of environmental law, and yet receiving this new statute into his court for the first time, Judge Larkins asserts a straightforward set of judicial requirements that make the statute an effective limitation on the pork barrel process that previously would have brooked no scrutiny. In this light, note especially the judge's ruling on retroactivity, which presumed that the statute was supposed to do something, and thus had a prospective role to play, and Judge Larkins's reluctance to defer to the agency's finding of no significant impact (FONSI). A rural judge might well have been expected to defer to the expert opinion of fact and law of the federal agency. It was judges throughout the United States, interpreting and applying the statute so as to require functional compliance by federal agencies, that made the NEPA EIS requirement a meaningful federal law, when otherwise it could easily have been a symbolic gesture honored in the breach.

Page 481, C&Q #1. The factual setting. This is a description of the physical background of the case. Can you figure out what is going on here? You can adduce a physical description of the projects; the physical and ecological disruption of channelization is great, and the benefits in many but not all cases are insufficient to justify the projects.

Does the fact that the private market does not build these projects on its town show they are not cost-effective? Resource economists say that logical conclusion is probably accurate, emphasizing the narrowed political and economic logic that drives these projects.

Pages 481-483, C&Q #2. The political setting. The agency's internal motivations and the external subsidy combine into a powerful marketplace enterprise difficult to counter with rational economics or information. The citizen plaintiffs were clearly going up against a tough establishment.

Page 483, C&Q #3. Judicial attitudes towards NEPA challenges. *How do you interpret Judge Larkins at this stage?* He seems like a traditional jurist, reviewing an accepted practice being carried out by an official agency program backed by a local constituency, and probably has little skepticism about such projects and little familiarity or empathy for the iconoclast tree-huggers who have come down to represent the local rod-and-gun group that wants to stop the channelization. He is, however, a judge who is attentive to the laws, even if he is not familiar with them. The verb tense he uses implies to us his sense that the project will ultimately get past the legal hurdles.

Page 483, C&Q #4. Financial commitments and delay costs. As far as we were able to discover, the expenditures being claimed were largely paper commitments and in-kind transfers. The primary actual expenditure had been the SCS's administrative expenses. These financial claims introduce the arguments of "sunk costs," the tactics of getting so much money spent and physical work done that by the time the enterprise gets to court it is too late to go back. This tactic appears in Chapter 7's *Overton Park* case, and in many other settings, including Chapter 16's endangered species cases.

What relevance do these claimed expenses have for the judge, given the EIS's small estimated cost? The judge could have been swayed by the big project numbers and the small cost of the EIS to diminish the latter, or to characterize the compliance as unburdensome. He apparently chose the latter, although he set a huge bond.

Page 487, C&Q #1. Standing and ripeness. The NRDC had signed on local hunters and fishermen to assure that they had plaintiffs who had sustained an injury in fact for Article III purposes. As to the further administrative law standing test requiring that plaintiffs be "within the zone of interests" of a statute, the courts apparently presumed that anyone would be within the extremely broad scope of NEPA's zone of interests.

Page 487, C&Q #2. A cause of action? Our point is that the judge could have said "Where's the cause of action in NEPA?" and it's not there. American courts under the APA's §§702, 706, however, are able to craft causes of action for declaratory and injunctive relief. Even if a federal regulatory statute does not create a specific cause of action, if the defendant alleged to be violating the statute is a federal agency, and a citizen has standing because of injury in fact, then at least as to the federal defendants the Administrative Procedures Act provides a cause of action. The cause of action in NEPA apparently arises under the Administrative Procedures Act §706 (see Chap. 7).

> The reviewing court shall decide all relevant questions of law...and... (1) compel agency action unlawfully withheld or unreasonably delayed, and (2) hold unlawful and set aside agency action, findings, and conclusions found to be – (a) arbitrary, capricious, and abuse of discretion, or otherwise not in accordance with law....

Plaintiffs must show they are injured by agency violations of law, and here Judge Larkins thought the violation was pretty clear.

Page 487, C&Q #3 Laches. *Would the judge have decided differently if the construction contracts had been let?* The sunk costs question again, and the more that irretrievable expenditures are made, the more a court pays attention. Note that laches is an equitable doctrine. The public interest nature of the litigation is clearly relevant to the equitable balance of laches.

RETROACTIVITY & RETROACTIVITY REDUX: Retroactivity is explained in the court's opinion, and normally is no problem. In some cases, however, retroactivity still can be a problem. In Oregon Natural Resource Council v. Bureau of Reclamation, 49 F.3d 1441 (9th Cir. 1994), the Court of Appeals held that the Bureau did not have to comply with NEPA's procedural requirements in lowering water levels and applying aquatic herbicides, even though its continuing effects may have significant environmental effects, because these activities were ongoing on Jan. 1, 1970 and therefore did not constitute a "major federal action" subject to NEPA. The court also held that the listing of the shortnose suckers as endangered species in 1988 did not convert the bureau's ongoing activity of annual herbicide spraying into major federal action because only changes in the program itself constitute "major federal actions." In addition, the Bureau's attempt to salvage fish stranded in drained irrigation canals by transporting them to hatcheries was determined by the court to be an activity categorically excluded from NEPA requirements. Since the Bureau was required by the Fish and Wildlife Service to undertake the salvage operation as part of the Bureau's compliance with the ESA the court concluded that agency action mandated by statute does not trigger NEPA coverage, and the Bureau was exempt from NEPA requirements.

Pages 487-488, C&Q #4. The bureaucratic temptation to minimize. (This point, however, may be best saved until after the second *Chicod Creek* opinion, when the Soil Conservation Service had actually issued an EIS and the question is whether it is adequate.) Agencies throughout the U.S. understandably sought to minimize the reporting of negative aspects of their projects. Considering the Palmetto Bend environmental impact statement, do your students see that early on a deferential court could easily have said this statement was sufficient to comply with NEPA? It is a statement (three sentences) and contains many details. However because the courts acted on the presumption that NEPA required more than such obviously self-serving superficialities, the EIS requirement subsequently became meaningfully enforceable.

Pages 488-489, C&Q #5. The classic Calvert Cliffs case. The text is self-explanatory. CCCC is a significant historical and legal process marker that many teachers asked us to emphasize.

Pages 489-492, C&Q ##6-8. What is a "major federal action"? The "small handle" problem. "Significantly affecting the human environment." These three notes raise the question of when NEPA's EIS requirement is triggered, and can be well handled together.

If Chicod Creek were only 4 miles long...? The CEQ regs are helpful here in emphasizing the essentially subjective and relativistic balance that lies behind the threshold finding. See the §1508.27 reg on pages 491-492. (The item not noted is "likelihood to attract public controversy and litigation," which some officials tell us is often a de facto test.)

Should you take account of cumulative impacts? Section 7 of §1508.27 on page 491 says yes.

You can focus on the small handle problem case presented in Comment 7. The wharves that would have to be built along the Tennessee and Tombigbee waterways to serve the foreign wood chip clear-cut operations would actually be quite small wharves, arguably having virtually no effect on the riverine environment. But those several small wharves are the key to whether or not the southeastern mountains will be clear-cut in the way that Japanese corporations have clear-cut the forests of Malaysia and Indonesia. Without the wharves, which give access to the highly subsidized barge transit system, the clear-cutting will not take place.

There clearly is an interpretation that must be made here. The building of each wharf, which is the only action which requires a federal permit, is quite trivial. The unavoidable logical consequence of this small federal permit, however, is that it will determine whether or not that widespread environmental depredation will occur.

Look at the statutory language: "major federal actions significantly affecting the environment." It would appear that the word "significantly" refers to major federal actions, rather than setting an EIS requirement for any federal action significantly affecting the environment. But the CEQ regulations, §1508.18 on pages 489-490, define "major" as reinforcing "significantly," rather than vice versa. The CEQ regulations' definition of "significantly" is far more helpful, apparently focusing straightforwardly on the consequences of the action without regard to whether the federal component is "major." This interpretation comports with common sense, and with the constructive purpose which Congress supposedly held for NEPA, if it held any functional intent for NEPA at all. There is some question whether CEQ regulations are binding or merely persuasive on other agencies. The 1970 Nixon Executive Order 11514 authorized CEQ to issue guidelines, which were quite clearly not binding. Jimmy Carter's Executive Order 11991 (1977, which has not been rescinded) changed the word "guidelines" to "regulations," and added that "the heads of federal agencies shall...comply with the regulations issued by the Council except where such compliance would be inconsistent with statutory requirements." §3(g). (This still leaves open the question, however, whether the mandates of presidential executive orders extends to actions of independent agencies, like the NRC, TVA, ICC, etc.)

The statutory language, moreover, seems to require that there be a threshold finding of "major" federal action in order to trigger the EIS requirement. Nevertheless there are other good arguments that all of the effects of a federal action are relevant to defining whether it is major or not. It appears clear that, for instance, if an EIS is required it must discuss all of the consequences that are likely to follow from the federal action, whether they are private or public. See National Forest Preservation Group v. Volpe, 352 F.Supp. 123, 359 F.Supp. 136 (D. MT 1972, 1973) (where the EIS studies alternatives it must study alternative courses of action, even if they are not within the authority of the federal agency). If the EIS itself is required to cover all consequences, private and public, there appears to be little logical reason for restricting the threshold trigger of the EIS to the impact of the federal act standing alone.

Pages 492-494, C&Q #9. FONSIs and mitigation. In this comment, the students should realize that an agency inclines toward making a "negative declaration" FONSI so as to avoid the fairly elaborate EIS procedures required by the CEQ guidelines and the heightened judicial review that EISs receive. An environmental assessment (EA), that is all a FONSI requires, is almost universally a superficial, self-congratulatory agency document that doesn't serve to illuminate the environmental aspects of a project, nor is useful as a basis of judicial challenge. So citizen plaintiffs try to push agencies to issue an EIS. Judge Larkins baldly asserts that it is the court that must construe the statutory standards and apply them to the particular facts of the project, a conclusion that doesn't at all follow from normal administrative practice, where an agency's determination of the facts is generally compelling upon the court, and a mixed question of fact and law likewise receives great deference.

It may well be suggested that Larkins, like most federal judges reviewing agency FONSIs in the early years, instinctively recognized that these project agencies opposed NEPA and were seeking to wriggle out of its requirements. In those circumstances, which of course the courts did not expressly acknowledge, the traditional judicial deference to agency decisions pretty much evaporated. However, the United States Supreme Court has recently articulated that the "arbitrary and capricious" standard of review must be applied to agencies' threshold decisions regarding the environmental significance of proposed actions.

Also raised is the question whether the agency can find an insignificant impact based on alleged net impact, offsetting the project's purported benefits and mitigation measures against the gross negative disruptions the project would cause. This is exactly what the Soil Conservation Service was trying to do, and Larkins ignored it. In general, this process of rhetorical netting by agencies to avoid EIS compliance has recently been successful.

Page 494, C&Q #10. Formal compliance vs. "Functional equivalence." This process of exempting an agency decision from NEPA is potentially troubling. What are the consequences of these judge-made doctrine? There is, as noted in the second paragraph, a danger that procedures that are not as rigorous as NEPA's will be allowed to satisfy the NEPA statutory requirement. The fact that the doctrine has been largely restricted to the EPA is a small comfort.

Does "functional equivalence" address the element of public involvement? The likelihood is that it will not, and that is something courts could and should consider. We invite the student to see that where the court focuses on functional equivalence in terms of agency review of a question, the public involvement provided for in the CEQ regulations is largely ignored. EPA has been able to presume that whatever it does under specific statutory criteria is likely to be environmentally well-considered and exempt from EIS mandate. *Were the SCS's procedures the functional equivalent of NEPA in the Chicod Creek case?* The last sentence reflects that the Soil Conservation Service could easily argue that its own internal procedures for channelization projects were the functional equivalents of NEPA, and that would obviously be a miscarriage of statutory compliance.

Pages 494-495, C&Q #11. Conflicting statutory mandates. Self-explanatory.

Page 495, C&Q #12. Emergency exemptions from NEPA. *How are emergency exemptions from NEPA defined and applied?* This topic has few cases and less reasoning applied to it, but it obviously has great practical and philosophical importance. We are skeptical of CEQ or courts implying such overrides absent showings of extraordinary countervailing necessity. In addition, it is doubtful whether the CEQ possesses the authority to promulgate a regulation specifying an emergency exemption process.

Pages 495-496, C&Q #13. NEPA and national security. Self-explanatory. This topic could easily absorb several days of discussion. The *Catholic Action* case, noted in the commentary, is a fascinating example of how courts tend to abdicate judicial review when faced with a national security argument from the agency. Read carefully, however, *Catholic Action* nevertheless seems to require that the Navy go through the EIS process, even if it does not have to release the EIS publicly. In the circumstances, does that mean that the public has no right to require that an EIS be drafted and reviewed by the judiciary? The potential for *in camera* review would seem to be the answer: citizens could require that the Navy show evidence that it has produced an EIS, and allow the judge to review it in camera to determine its adequacy. The United States Department of Defense has vigorously sought an exemption to NEPA for all military training activities.

Pages 496-498, C&Q #14. The "human environment"? It is rather surprising that the phrase human environment has been regularly interpreted to mean just natural environment. In *PANE*, it would seem that the Three Mile Island trauma raised a real question of a federal decision's effect on the "human environment." By restricting the §102 definition to physical natural environment, however, Justice Rehnquist was able to cast the citizens' EIS claim into an attenuated proximate cause setting. It is hard to avoid the conclusion that Rehnquist is once again cutting away at NEPA when he has the opportunity.

Page 498, C&Q #15. The injunction. In Boston v. Volpe, 464 F.2d 254 (1st Cir. 1972) the court made an important point: if NEPA is supposed to be effective, it is not enough just to require the formality of EIS preparation, while cynically allowing the project to roll on toward its preordained end irrespective of the NEPA process.

> The concept of (NEPA] was that responsible officials would think about environment before a significant project was launched; that what would be assessed would be a proposed action, not a fait accompli. 464 F.2d at 257.

Does failure to consider environmental consequences in agency decisionmaking constitute irreparable harm? If NEPA's procedures are meant to have a meaningful effect on agency behavior, it would appear that failure to implement them justifies equitable relief. But courts have held that equities may be balanced in determining whether an injunction should be granted in NEPA cases.

Page 498, C&Q #16. A bond requirement? *Why not require a full and sufficient bond here?* The point is, of course, that if a court issues a bond that would cover all of a defendant's potential losses if it turns out the preliminary injunction is improvidently granted, citizen plaintiffs would never be able to proceed. Yet FRCP 65 seems to require an injunction bond.

Page 499, C&Q: The bond. *Does Judge Haynesworth's opinion reflect the reality of defendant's economic loss? What would be the consequence of requiring full bonds from public interest plaintiffs?* The defendants' potential losses were obviously far greater than $5000. The Haynsworth opinion gives a hint that the court has discretion to shape the bond to the circumstances, and that private attorneys-general should not be burdened inappropriately with a bond requirement as if they were commercial litigants. The Calderon article in footnote 14 offers a useful survey of the law and policy of the bond requirement in public interest litigation.

Pages 499-501, Chicod Creek - Part II. This is the case after the Soil Conservation Service produced an EIS. The environmentalists of course then challenged its adequacy.

Note the quotation from William O. Douglas that begins the opinion. It is clear that Judge Larkins has been captured by the logic or poetry of the NRDC brief.

You may ask the students if they have ever read an EIS. (It might be useful to put one on reserve for them to read.) The prose and format of an EIS are calculated, as noted earlier, to gloss over the negatives and emphasize the positives. But Larkins does not buy it.

What really aroused Larkins' skepticism about the EIS? Our own guess is that it probably was kudzu! For anyone who has lived in the South, Japanese kudzu is a plague, spreading at a remarkable rate across the ground, covering and killing all the native vegetation beneath it (with the exception of evergreens, which can survive by getting some photosynthesis in the winter months, when kudzu leaves drop). This kudzu is not a trivial plant. Road crews sowed it throughout the South because it was so cheap and quickly covered raw excavation with a green mat for the summer tourist season. Environmentalists unsuccessfully tried to block the kudzu program by emphasizing that it was a classical environmental problem: it was low in its initial costs to road crews, but its costs to nature and the costs to remove it are extraordinary. A friend of one of the authors measured one kudzu vine advancing at an average of twenty-two inches a day! To eliminate it one must cut it back three years in a row to the bare roots, a difficult proposition, or inject poisons into the root, or tether a herd of goats throughout the area. Once a Southerner like Larkins has seen what kudzu can do, traveling over hills and valleys destroying native vegetation, the SCS's casual mention that kudzu would be used to cover the excavated banks must have been a red flag.

But also look at the language the judge uses elsewhere. Although he never says, "This EIS is a pack of lies," his frequent use of the word "misrepresents" says the same thing.

In this judicial review of an EIS, in other words, it is clear that the NRDC attorneys were able to show enough problematic points to the judge that he refused to defer to the agency's decision that this document adequately complied with NEPA's requirements.

Pages 502-503, C&Q #1. Agencies and EISs—a shotgun marriage? *What was the nature and tone of the Chicod Creek EIS?* Clearly it was, as so many are, one-sidedly self-justifying. The comment here should be self-explanatory, except for the last paragraph repeating our hunch that many judges adjust their degree of deference according to the posture of the agency toward the particular statute. Where an agency obviously is inimical to the statutory purpose, often having lobbied against the bill in the Legislative process, courts must often realize that there is less reason to defer to the fox in the henhouse.

Page 503, C&Q #2. Judicial psychology. What happened to old judge Larkins? It is quite clear that he saw enough evidence of misrepresentation and self-justification to blow his stack. It may have been the fishing and sedimentation mischaracterizations, but anyone who has seen Carolinians trying to do battle with creeping Kudzu must imagine that his mention of that noxious weed indicates another item that raised his skepticism.

How do environmental plaintiffs get around the inclination to defer? Here it seems a combination of showing potential harms to the societal and natural economies that the established players are ignoring, and showing the defendants' lack of credibility.

Pages 503-504, C&Q #3. The EIS: what must it contain? EIS requirements. This section contains a number of particular issues about how an EIS must be prepared in order to pass judicial muster. The background question is, "Toward what audience is an EIS directed?" According to the apparent terms of NEPA, the audience for EISs is supposed to be the President and Congress, neither of which ever respond to EISs' revelations, and the agencies themselves, which are supposed to integrate the lessons of the EIS process into their ongoing decisionmaking, however unlikely that may be. In truth it seems that EISs are prepared as a political discipline, by which citizens have a handle to ask about the technical particulars of projects and a legal opportunity to hold up projects in court by putting the merits of an EIS before a judge for scrutiny. These latter functions are what give NEPA its effect, not the purported formal functions noted above. This strategic indirection should not surprise us in a statute that owes so much to happenstance.

It's notable that the five different divisions required of an EIS by terms of §102(2)c overlap extraordinarily - when reduced to their basic meaning, an EIS apparently is supposed to analyze impacts and alternatives.

Pages 504-505. C&Q #4. Alternatives. These have played an important role in the rationality of overall environmental analysis. Judge Clarence Thomas's opinion in the Burlington case, page 505, is therefore quite disturbing.

Page 505, C&Q #5. Interagency consultation. Theoretically, under the CEQ guidelines, the lead agency must solicit and receive comments from other federal agencies impacted by a project. Often these received comments are very deferential to the lead agency. No agency wants to be negative and confrontational to a sister agency, with a few dramatic exceptions in exceptional cases.

Pages 505-506, C&Q #6. Treatment of responsible opposing views. Self-explanatory.

Pages 506-506, C&Q #7. Epilogue to *Chicod* Creek. *Was this a civic success story, or a win for tree-hugging elitism?* It appears in the *Chicod Creek* setting at least that the state of North Carolina and the local population in the Chicod Creek area are quite happy with the ultimate resolution of the case.

Section 2. Recurrent Issues in Implementing NEPA

Segmentation. Segmentation is an issue that recurs. An interesting case on point is Village of Los Ranchos de Albuquerque v. Barnhart, 906 F.2d 1477 (10th Cir. 1990) where, after the Federal Highway Administration had financed a draft environmental impact statement on a bridge for a federal highway, and had paid for initial design work, the state decided the bridge was sufficiently problematic in environmental terms that it would reorganize the project so as to make it a completely state-financed construction venture. The new plan cut off the federal highway funding at the bridge's western approach. The court posed a series of tests - whether the bridge segment had independent utility, whether the stopping point for the federal highway segment was "logical" even though it might not be the "most logical" stopping point, whether the designation for full state funding foreclosed opportunities to consider alternatives, and whether there would be irretrievable commitment of funds for closely-related projects. 906 F.2d at 1483, citing Piedmont Heights Civic Club v. Moreland, 637 F.2d 430, 439 (5th Cir. 1987) It would seem a more realistic question was whether the bridge had been and continued to be substantially part of the overall undertaking which was concededly federal in character. Everyone knew what was going on, but the court permitted segmentation, deferring to the agency's decision using the four tests.

NEPA and Scientific Uncertainty. Self-explanatory. Questions raised are unanswerable and might be presented for class discussion.

Who really prepares the EIS? It is probably too much to hope that EISs would be prepared- by some objective entity within the federal agencies. Typically EISs are resented technicalities. They tend to be drafted by those who know the project best, and those typically are the entities involved in pushing the project forward. EISs recently have been increasingly farmed out to private consulting groups which specialize in preparing EISs for federal agency officials. Imagine the pressure on private consulting groups to write EIS's that fulfill the institutional desires of their employers. In the Chicod Creek case, the EIS appears to have been drafted in the first instance by the local promoters of the project working with the local SCS agent.

Enforceable agency promises? Fundamentally the answer is that a judge will not deem NEPA substantive, unless the agency decision appears to be arbitrary and capricious in the circumstances. But what about the case where an agency has promised something in an EIS which allowed a court to certify the EIS as adequate, and then the agency reneges? This happened in the Ogunquit Village case, cited on page 510, where the Corps had promised to rebuild a natural sand beach with transported natural sand, but when the navigation project was finished announced that it would not do what it had promised unless Congress gave it an additional multi-million-dollar grant. An EIS is not an enforceable contract: And apparently courts do not consider it contempt when an agency has affirmed the adequacy of an EIS because of contained promises and then reneges. But if a project can be caught in mid-process, a citizen suit seeking a supplemental environmental impact statement (SEIS) has the potential to force the agency to face up to its change of plans: a project which does not include the promised mitigation is a significantly changed or a new project, and accordingly requires an SEIS.

It should be noted again that under Executive Order 11991, the CEQ regulations have been given some enhanced standing vis-à-vis other agencies, at least as to dependent agencies directly under presidential control.

NEPA's substantive effect and judicial review. It is now obvious that NEPA is procedural, not substantive, in the eyes of the courts, and the question continues to be the degree to which the courts will defer to what often are self-serving agency interpretations and applications of the constraints on their actions represented by the EIS process.

Circulation and public comment. Self-explanatory. The questions raised are rhetorical. Note the conflict between the *minimum* timing required by the CEQ regulations (90 days minimum between a draft EIS and the operative agency decision, 30 days between the final EIS and the decision) and the theoretical goal of NEPA, which is that the EIS process will continue throughout the project's development so as to affect and improve the decision itself.

Scoping and timing. The *SIPI* case, at pages 572-573, can be used to, show an ascending line of investment in the federal breeder reactor research program. The point is obviously that the agency will wish to postpone as long as possible – up to the point of actually beginning to build a breeder reactor – the preparing of an actual EIS, so as to have as many millions of dollars in sunk costs so that there will be no turning back. Rational managers, or interested citizens, should want to have an EIS begun as early as possible in the process so as to avoid investment that is not rational, and to minimize impacts where possible. The four tests of the SIPI case appear to make sense in determining when an EIS should be issued where there is an ongoing program committing resources over time.

The programmatic impact statement concept is a highly useful one, but the *Kleppe* case, 513-515, is often read to destroy the *SIPI* programmatic principal. *Kleppe* is noted fairly extensively in the questions that follow it. It was quite clear to everyone that there was an ongoing plan in the latter years of the Ford administration to lease major areas in the northern Great Plains region to mining interests. But because the Department never announced it as an identified program, the court did not require it to do a regional EIS as part of the "tier" approach noted an page 516. The agency, of course, only wanted to do its very general, overall nationwide "coal programmatic EIS," and then a specific local EIS for whatever lease sales it undertook, when it undertook them. But the nature of the northern Great Plains region, your students should recognize, is an immensely fragile environment with major questions of water supply, transport, with limited ecological recovery and resiliency qualities. A coherent overall regional EIS would thus have been more useful, but the Supreme Court again used the technicality that the agency had not admitted it was undertaking a regional program to eliminate the duty to prepare a regional programmatic EIS.

Pages 515-516, C&Q #1.Programmatic impact statements. Self-explanatory.

Page 516, C&Q #2. Tiering of EISs. Self-explanatory. Was the court suggesting that the NGPRP was the functional equivalent of a regional EIS? Probably not consciously, but the implication is possible and subject to all the flaws of that reasoning noted at page 494.

Page 516, C&Q #3. To plan or not got plan. *Does Kleppe create a disincentive to agency planning by exempting such informal agency programs from NEPA compliance?* It does seem that *Kleppe* invites agencies to avoid EISs by avoiding comprehensive planning. Doesn't this contradict the logic of NEPA that emphasizes forethought? Yes.

Page 517, C&Q #4. Proposals. Should CEQ or the Court have the last word on interpreting NEPA? CEQ is designated the lead agency by Congress, but of course the Court can if it wishes always have the last word. The CEQ regulations, §1608.23, read that

> A 'Proposal' exists at that stage in the development of an action when an agency subject to the act has a goal and is actively preparing to make a decision on one or more alternative means of accomplishing that goal, and the effects can be meaningfully evaluated.... A proposal may exist in fact as well as by agency declaration that one exists.

The reality of the *Kleppe* decision is that the Administration pretty clearly had a "goal" of expanding mineral leasing in the U.S. public lands so as to increase energy independence. The question remains whether the goal was specifically enough directed to the northern Great Plains to require the regional EIS.

Do you agree with Justice Powell for the majority or Justice Marshall's dissent? The majority seems to adopt the position that the "arbitrary and capricious" standard is the standard of review that federal courts should apply to a wide range of NEPA decisions, including FONSIs. Justice Marshall's opinion, though directed to judicial review of agency determinations of law, reflects a more searching standard of review that is echoed in circuits like the Ninth Circuit, where the court is asking whether the agency decision is "reasonable." *Kleppe* certainly represents the Supreme Court's ongoing efforts to erode the enforceable statutory terms of NEPA.

Is Kleppe inconsistent with the desire for early-stage environmental analysis? As to the question of when in a process of agency planning an EIS must be prepared, §1508.23 says that "preparation of an environmental impact statement on a proposal should be timed (§1502. 5) so that the final statement may be completed in time for the statement to be included in any recommendation or report an the proposal." This sounds earlier in the game than *Kleppe's* minimum required compliance.

If you wanted to get a breeder reactor program rolling without having to go through an early NEPA disclosure, how would you do it? The danger, of course, is that an agency, naturally seeking to avoid public review of its decision, will postpone the "official action decision" until late in the process. A key definition is what kind of proposal triggers §102: is the proposal a proposal for action which is being bruited within the agency, or can the word "proposal" be narrowed to mean a formal proposal when it is presented by the agency to some outside decisional body, like Congress for funding, or when it is announced as official agency policy? The CEQ regulations seem to imply a functional decision-affecting EIS process, while the agencies' course of implementation and the Supreme Court's interpretations seem to favor the latter.

How successful would the environmentalists' claims of "arbitrariness" be in response? Not very, given the current mood of deference to agency momentum and expertise.

Pages 517-518, C&Q #5. The "irreversible and irretrievable commitment of resources" test. Self-explanatory. The questions raised are immediately discussed.

Page 519, C&Q #6. Cumulative impacts and NEPA. *Does it make sense to postpone consideration of cumulative impacts until projects are officially proposed? How useful is fragmented, individualized consideration?* Both of these interpretations seem to is to be further narrowings of NEPA's function by formalizing the requirements in narrowest terms with no integration of the foresight-planning logic inherent in the statute.

CEQ Regulation §1508.27(7) defines "significantly" as including -

> whether the action is related to other actions with individually insignificant but cumulatively significant impacts. Significance exists if it is reasonable to anticipate a cumulatively significant impact on the environment. Significance cannot be avoided by terming an action temporary or by breaking it down into small component parts.

Section 1508.7 notes that cumulative impact "is the impact on the environment which results form the incremental impact of the action when added to other past, present, and reasonably foreseeable future actions regardless of what agency or person undertakes such other actions." See also §1508.25(a) and (c).

Page 519, C&Q #7. Hard cases make bad law. Rhetorical. The Sierra Club was trying to define a strong argument for tiering.

Page 519, C&Q #8. NEPA as post hoc rationalization. *Is Justice Marshall correct in saying that NEPA lawsuits usually come too late to be effective*? Yes, unfortunately. The scoping process in §1501.7 of the CEQ regulations should answer justice Marshall's worries about the timing of NEPA challenges. Unfortunately, agencies have not been eager to go into a scoping exercise unless litigation is inevitable and opposition might be mollified by an appropriate scoping process.

Pages 519-520, C&Q #9. NEPA in the Supreme Court. Self-explanatory. The questions raised are rhetorical.

Page 520, C&Q #10. Where is NEPA's overview? Ollie Houck's comment is a wry, realistic summary of the combined result of agency recalcitrance and the Supreme Court's minimization of the statutory mandate.

Do you think that agencies avoid NEPA as part of planning so as to avoid early disclosure? Information is power, not to be shared unnecessarily or too early. Transparency brings in the public and tends to get in the way of daily internal and marketplace political accommodations. The job in this section, we suppose, is to be sufficiently realistic about the recent anti-NEPA efforts at the highest level of the government, while noting the ultimately rational and inevitably necessary character of the NEPA inquiry if the resources and development efforts of the nation are to be rational in overall terms in the long term.

Pages 520-521, C&Q #11. Has NEPA been worth the effort? Self-explanatory.

Page 522, C&Q #12. NEPA in the twenty-first century. Self-explanatory. The questions raised are rhetorical.

PAGES 523-527. NEPA's International Implications.

Page 526, C&Q #1. The President and NEPA. This note is purely informational. You might reinforce the point that, while the precise reach of the D.C. Circuit's reasoning is not clear, the case does not control all international agreements. The reliance on *Franklin* tends to confine the analysis to those situations in which the President has an expressly-identified statutory role.

Page 526, C&Q #2. NEPA abroad. The NEPA-abroad problem involves at least three structural attributes not found domestically, especially when the action challenged is in a foreign state (as opposed to an area beyond national jurisdiction such as the high seas or Antarctica): (1) it could constrain the exercise of foreign policy—including in particular the Executive's capacity to make commitments to foreign powers — by tying the Executive's hands with domestic statutory requirements; (2) it could create foreign policy difficulties with foreign states that consider an assessment of impacts within their jurisdictions a unjustified intrusion into their domestic affairs; and (3) it could raise separation of powers concerns related to the apparent judicial management of, or intrusion into, foreign policy. The principled response is that (1) NEPA is an internal rule of decision for the U.S. government only, and as such can never result in an intrusion into a foreign country's exclusive jurisdiction to govern within its territory (sovereignty); and (2) NEPA, at least as interpreted by the courts, is a procedural requirement that does not compel a particular substantive result. Note that, to the extent there is such a thing in this area, the Antarctica case described in the note is an easy one because there is no foreign sovereign to object - Antarctica, like the high seas, lies beyond any state's jurisdiction.

Page 526, C&Q #3. NEPA and foreign policy. As noted in C&Q #2 above, NEPA articulates primarily procedural requirements, in contrast to the substantive mandate at issue in the *Warren* case. Consequently, in the Mexican trucking case it is possible at least in principle to give effect to both NAFTA and NEPA simultaneously without as a matter of principle doing a disservice to either. One might well ask, however, what the point is if the international legal obligation under NAFTA admits of little or no discretion. The answer is that NEPA might nonetheless provide an entry point for public participation and an opportunity to ameliorate environmental impacts.

Pages 526, C&Q #4. Comparative law: EIA. Public participation is a difficult question in countries that are not democracies, or even in some that are but that nonetheless do not have a tradition of free expression. The U.S. system of judicial review has left many foreign countries with the impression that the sole purpose of NEPA is delay through appeals to judicial authorities. In at least one view, the U.S. system of judicial review assures strict implementation of the statute, which otherwise might be a dead letter (this is the response to the Will quote). In the absence of a requirement to consider alternatives, environmental impact assessment (EIA) basically boils down to a process for identifying mitigating measures — the decision to proceed with the project as identified in the proposal having been impliedly made before the assessment is undertaken.

Chapter 10.
CORPORATE DISCLOSURE: SHAPING PRIVATE RESPONSE BY REQUIRED PRODUCTION OF INFORMATION

Chapter contents:

– and check the Teachers' Manual Website for SUPPLEMENTARY MATERIALS:

http://www.bc.edu/schools/law/library/coursebook/envtlaw/teachers

The list of Supplementary Materials in Part III of this manual, and on the Teachers' Website, indicates materials posted on the Teachers' Website that are relevant to this and other chapters.

OVERALL TEACHING THEMES & COURSE DESIGN CONSIDERATIONS

This chapter introduces right-to-know statutes as a type of disclosure statute, and EPCRA and Proposition 65 as specific - and quite successful - examples of the right-to-know statutory strategy. The chapter introduces students to the advantages and disadvantages of right-to-know approaches, and concludes with a section on First Amendment challenges to such initiatives.

At 22 pages long, the chapter can easily be taught in one day. The material is highly teachable, and it generates excellent student discussion. For the teacher pressed for time, the materials on the First Amendment might be sacrificed, and the right-to-know materials paired with, for example, some portion of Chapter 9's NEPA materials.

TEACHING NOTES, COMMENTS, & ALL QUESTIONS ANSWERED

Pages 529-531. EPCRA. These materials introduce the reader to the federal Emergency Planning and Community Right-to-Know Act (EPCRA), which requires certain companies to report certain releases of toxic chemicals.

Page 531, C&Q #1. Evaluating EPCRA. This note discusses positive and negative aspects of EPCRA.

Page 532, C&Q #2. Should "materials accounting" data be reported? As the note indicates, this is an open question. A comparative analysis of the Massachusetts and New Jersey experiences might provide empirical data for resolving this dilemma. Unfortunately, no such study has come to our attention.

Page 532, C&Q #3. Does the TRI convey misleading data? This is a question the answer to which involves one's evaluation of the public's ability to perceive risk accurately and make informed decisions regarding risk management. There is no doubt that public responses to potential environmental risk may be manipulated. Buth both sides play at that game. In a democracy, it is axiomatic that the general public should possess more reliable information rather than less. (At least in this case, we presume that EPA's judgment about chemical toxicity is generally reliable.) Moreover, the "let the experts make the decisions" approach is itself subject to abuse, and there is no evidence that it produces a cleaner or healthier environment than public information and public participation. EPCRA's strategy of requiring EPA to list toxic chemicals, based on its expert scientific judgment, and then disclosing that information to the primary decision-maker in a democratic society - the people - appears to be a workable combination of both approaches.

Page 532, C&Q #4. TRI and performance benchmarking. This note is informational and self-explanatory.

Page 533, C&Q #5. Is green golden? This note is informational and self-explanatory. At several points in this book, we note the "green consumerism" is a powerful incentive to voluntary compliance.

Page 533, C&Q #6. International right-to know. *What does harmonizing up mean in any event?* Harmonization — meaning, in this context, to make domestic regulations compatible or identical — is but one of a number of theories of international cooperation that states might pursue. In the example in the note, the principal motivation for harmonization is trade, where the benefits are clear: after harmonization, products from one country will of necessity meet the domestic standards of the treaty partner, thereby removing those standards as a potential barrier to trade. However, as demonstrated in the note, the easiest way to do this is to accept the lowest standard as a least-common-denominator solution, which almost always implies less rigor from an environmental point of view.

While harmonization is perhaps a useful sentiment, what problems might you expect to encounter in implementing it in practice? For example, how would the governments of Canada and the U.S. encourage Mexico to "harmonize up"? Because harmonization almost by definition implies engaging with a state's domestic regulatory process, municipal law can be an impediment to effective harmonization. If the United States were to harmonize pesticide residue limitations or "tolerances" with Canada and Mexico, it could not alter those regulations without notice and comment -- that is, without complying with its own domestic regulatory requirements. The same may be true in other states -- again, with the result that the least-common-denominator solution is the most attractive. When one adds in pressure from domestic constituencies such as industry, the difficulties are augmented further. The most desirable posture in such a setting is for governments to engage with the effort prepared to tighten their own standards if necessary. That level of political will, however, may be difficult to mobilize, particularly when the impetus is coming from abroad. On the theory that "sunshine is the best disinfectant," harmonization conducted in a transparent setting, in which those such as environmental activists are in a position to demand more effective regulation, is a desirable and perhaps necessary condition precedent to "harmonizing up."

How does one compare regulations in situations in which the metrics are incommensurable? If standards are "incommensurable," the regulatory approach of different states may be so divergent that it may be difficult to determine which is the more stringent. For example, in negotiations on protecting the stratospheric ozone layer (Chapter 15, pages 759-760, C&Q #3), the U.S., Canada, and the Nordic countries had regulated particular uses, while the EU controlled production capacity. Neither approach was compatible with the other, and efforts by the each of the negotiating blocs to encourage the adoption of its own approach as the international standard initially produced deadlock. Another example would be air pollution regulations that measure only short-term spikes in pollution as compared with those that use time-averaged exposures. In principle, the most desirable approach in such situations would be to renegotiate from scratch, but that may be difficult due to impediments in the form of domestic regulatory structures.

As an environmental advocate, how might you use the EU's standards as a basis to encourage the U.S. to "harmonize up"? In situations such as the TRI example described in the text of the note, several states with higher standards may be in a position to "gang up" on a state with lower standards, encouraging it to raise its domestic standards. Note that in situations like this the rigidity of the domestic legal and political situation may have an "upward pull," as the states with the higher standards have little flexibility to modify their own requirements and consequently have only positive incentives to encourage upward harmonization. In situations such as the EU's directive on industrial manufacturing plants, other states such as the United States can look to foreign practice as a helpful example in establishing its own regulations. In such situations, the foreign jurisdiction's actions are something of a precedent (in the non-technical sense) that environmental advocates can exploit to encourage progress at home.

Pages 533-534, C&Q #7. Information disclosure and national security. This note is informational and self-explanatory.

Pages 534-535. These pages introduce California's "Proposition 65" as another example of a successful right-to-know statute.

Pages 535-537. These pages include an excerpt from a California court's opinion in *Nicolle-Wagner v. Deukmejian,* which upheld a California agency's decision to exclude naturally occurring carcinogens and reproductive toxins from the scope of the statute.

Page 538, C&Q #1. Too little information? This note raises the argument that Proposition 65 provides too little information insofar as it does not provide information on naturally occurring carcinogens.

Page 538, C&Q #2. Too much information? This note raises the opposite argument, that Proposition 65 provides too much information because people may overreact to the information the statute requires.

Pages 538-539, C&Q #3. "Clear and reasonable" warnings. This note discusses some of the challenges in providing "clear and reasonable" warnings under Proposition 65.

Page 539, C&Q #4. Results. This note is informational and self-explanatory.

Page 539, C&Q #5. EPCRA and Proposition 65: a one-two punch. This note is informational and self-explanatory.

Pages 539-540, C&Q #6. The interstate effects of state product regulation. This note is informational and self-explanatory.

Page 541, C&Q #7. Are mandatory disclosure laws "self-executing"? This note is informational and self-explanatory, with open-ended questions about students' responses to disclosures about environmental risks in the last part of the note.

Pages 542-548. These pages include excerpts from International Dairy Foods Association v. Amestoy, in which dairy interests successfully challenged, on First Amendment grounds, a Vermont statute requiring disclosure of use of bovine growth hormone in producing dairy items. The court thought the only justification for the law was the satisfaction of "consumer curiosity," and concluded that this was not adequate to justify compelling speech with which the dairy interests disagreed. Judge Leval, in dissent, thought other justifications for the law existed, and also believed that to strike down the law on First Amendment grounds would, ironically, produce less rather than more information in the name of this information-loving constitutional provision.

Page 548, C&Q #1. Agribusiness on the offensive: Watch your mouth: dis a cabbage, go to jail. *Given the robust free speech protection applied even in commercial settings like Amestoy, aren't statutes repressing individual citizens' comments about industrial foods facially unconstitutional?* Even under the First Amendment, one is not allowed to utter plain falsehoods that injure others; this is the lesson of traditional libel and defamation laws. But many of the food disparagement laws go beyond this traditional setting, and seem constitutionally vulnerable on this ground.

Page 549, C&Q #2. Mercury and the First Amendment. This note is informational and self-explanatory.

Page 549, C&Q #3. Nike's speech. This note is informational and self-explanatory.

Pages 549-550, C&Q #4. Citizen information initiatives in the securities marketplace? *If markets run on information, and citizens wants to bring relevant public interest information into the marketplace of ideas, to what extent do they have to fear SLAPP suits filed under tort theories of libel, defamation, and "interference with business advantage"?* Obviously, citizens faced with even poorly grounded lawsuits might curtail their information-disclosing behavior when threatened with such lawsuits, and in that event both markets and the marketplace of ideas likely will suffer.

Chapter 11.
HARM-BASED AMBIENT STANDARDS: THE CLEAN AIR ACT

Chapter contents:

—and check the Teachers' Manual Website for SUPPLEMENTARY MATERIALS:

http://www.bc.edu/schools/law/library/coursebook/envtlaw/teachers

The list of Supplementary Materials in Part III of this manual, and on the Teachers' Website, indicates materials posted on the Teachers' Website that are relevant to this and other chapters.

OVERALL TEACHING THEMES & COURSE DESIGN CONSIDERATIONS

This chapter begins in earnest the study of the regulatory statutes that now comprise so much of modern environmental law. The chapter requires at least two full class sessions for its proper treatment. Covering the material highlighted above in bold could fill two ample class sessions. The chapter's length and importance merits a third day if your choice is to teach a course that stresses the major regulatory statutes. If you supplement this material with excerpts from the statute even more time can be spent on this material. The Chapter covers both the workings of harm-based ambient standards as a response to the problem of the commons and traces how the Clean Air Act implements the portion of its regulatory program that relies on harm-based ambient standards.

To assist students, the chapter begins with a long textual description of how the CAA has transformed itself over time from its original passage in 1970 through the 1990 amendments. As part of that discussion, the text tries to explore how the several pieces of the CAA fit together. One point worth stressing in the coverage of this material is that the Clean Air Act is made up of several separate parts. The parts form an integrated whole, but it is sometimes hard to see exactly how the parts are meshed together. Students seem to need guidance about the nuances of how both non-attainment and PSD regulation "fit." Another problem arises in explaining how the separate auto emissions regulation dovetails with the stationary source regulation.

Harm-based concepts, in many ways, are the starting point for all environmental regulation. As prior materials should have made a clear, the policy decision regarding what goals are to be accomplished precedes the regulatory decision that implements it. The policy decision, frequently, is set in relation to public health concerns. Public health concerns are quintessentially harm-based concerns. In relation to the ambient air that we all breathe, it is easy to conceptualize the nexus between ambient quality and harm to health. Likewise, it is easy to correlate (at a general level) reductions in emissions and improvements in ambient receiving body quality. For that reason, this part of the CAA "makes sense." The crafting of a regulatory system to achieve the improvement or protection of ambient quality is, of course, devilishly difficult when you get to the details of real world implementation that can be accomplished without major social dislocations.

TEACHING NOTES, COMMENTS, & ALL QUESTIONS ANSWERED

Pages 552-557. Textual presentation that lays out the parts of the CAA and how they have developed (and been adjusted) over time.

Pages 557-558. Textual discussion trying to explain how harm-based ambient standards are responsive to the commons problem in regard to large receiving body media, such as air and water. The choice of harms that result as a function of different degrees of degradation of water quality is deliberate. It is the first of many efforts to urge the students to think about the regulatory devices as being independent of their context, or, perhaps more aptly, as potentially being transferable to other contexts.

Page 558, C&Q #1. Air, water, and what else? Would *harm-based ambient standards be a valuable regulatory technique in fields other than air and water pollution?* Yes, as to noise pollution of the commons. As the note points out, there are a wealth of harm-based regulations, but relatively few operate in ambient quality settings other than air and water.

Page 558, C&Q #2. The federal-state partnership under the CAA stationary source program. This note gives the students a tiny glimpse of the statutory language. It is an unusually clear and pithy sample. You might want to mention that in those regards it is atypical. The textual note accompanying §107 explains why harm-based ambient standards and cooperative federalism are such a comfortable combination.

Pages 558-559, C&Q #3. State primacy. *Why should "primary responsibility" for air quality be lodged with the states?* Traditionally, the state police power was the rubric under which health, safety, and welfare, was addressed. There is no corresponding national power. States had traditionally been the "front line": regulators in this sphere.

Does the national interest in the solution of the problem of air pollution end with the attainment of acceptable ambient quality The national interest has to include problems of interstate equity as well as attainment by the states acting as if they existed in a vacuum. As the note points out in answering the question it asked, Congress explicitly addressed interstate equity concerns. Materials toward the end of the chapter offer some evidence that the statute has not been entirely successful in controlling transboundary pollution.

Despite the statutory language regarding state primacy, who is really in control, the states or the federal government? The note answers that the federal government, via supremacy, is in control of the goals and can ensure that they are accomplished. When that fact is kept in clear view, state primacy is less than full sovereignty.

Page 559, C&Q #4. Preventing significant deterioration. This note about the PSD program is informational and self-explanatory.

Page 559, C&Q #5. This note is informational and self-explanatory.

Pages 559-560, C&Q #6. Federalism and PSD. *Should the federal sites of importance, the Yosemites and Grand Canyons, be insulated against loss of amenity values that is at times obtained at the expense of economic development in the host state?* The question (and the note) invite students to begin to think about the proper roles of the states and federal government in regulating air quality. There is no one correct answer to this question.

Page 560, C&Q #7. Ambient air quality standards and the race of laxity. *Do harm-based ambient standards eliminate the race of laxity among the states?*

Uniform national standards put a cap on the race but they do not prevent it entirely. Adding PSD, which limits the amount of pollution that can be added in clean air areas further shortens the race (as does NSPS). There remain a number of race courses, such as lax enforcement, creative manipulation of offsets, and other ways in which the states can still compete to attract polluting entities to locate within their borders by manipulating environmental regulation.

Pages 560-561. Text introducing criteria pollutants.

Pages 561-562. NRDC v. Train. This is a seminal case from early in the history of the CAA in which the 2nd Circuit ruled that EPA was not free to refuse to list lead as a criteria pollutant on the ground that the Administrator has discretion in those decisions, growing out of the statutory phrase, "plans to issue air quality criteria." That ruling eventually triggered the addition of lead as a criteria pollutant.

Page 562, C&Q #1. The criteria pollutants. In light of the generic statutory definition and the mandatory nature of EPA's obligation to add new criteria pollutants, does the brevity of the list surprise you? Many other pollutants of concern are picked up by §112 NESHAPs. Still, there is room for additional thought. On the one hand, it is surprising that there are so few criteria pollutants because there are many harmful compounds that are emitted by large numbers of "diverse mobile or stationary sources" in significant quantities. On the other hand, if there were many, many more pollutants listed as criteria pollutants, the SIP process would grind to a snail's pace and, potentially, burden the CAA so much as to scuttle it altogether. It is also the case that techniques that are effective to limit emissions of the current short list of criteria pollutants, when employed, have the tendency to limit other emissions as well.

What do you suppose happened to the other pollutants mentioned by Senator Muskie, such as fluorides and odors? They were never listed as criteria pollutants.

Pages 562, C&Q #2. Does overregulation lead to underregulation? *Might [the small number of criteria pollutants] reflect factors [other than the regulation of hazardous air pollutants under section 112]? Might a busy (or cost-sensitive) agency be reluctant to start this ball rolling in the first place?*

These questions aim to introduce students to the possibility that "overregulation leads to underregulation" - the notion that very strict standards, or "overregulation" in the view of some (such as the cost-blind standards of the NAAQS program) might in fact lead to underregulation, which might include the regulation of very few substances. An agency might well be hesitant to regulate when it knows that when it does, it must regulate to the hilt.

Might EPA's position make good sense, but still be a violation of the statutory command? Plainly, as more experienced observers of how statutes operate, we the teachers are familiar with statutes that impose less than perfect, even silly, burdens on the agency or the regulated entities. Students may be less aware.

Pages 563-564, C&Q #3. EPA's better way to control lead emissions. *In light of what you already know about the NAAQS program – that it sets national, harm-based standards for air quality to be achieved by each of the individual states – is this program a sensible way of addressing the problems posed by greenhouse gases?* One could want very badly for EPA to regulate greenhouse gases and still believe that the NAAQS program is not well-suited to the task. Not only does it do nothing about the global problem of climate change, but its harm-based focus may outstrip our scientific ability to figure out exactly how large out greenhouse emissions can be without threatening public health and welfare. Moreover, the state-based implementation of the NAAQS program seems a bad fit for global pollutants.

Pages 564-567. These pages introduce the problem of setting the standards for criteria air pollutants, and provide an excerpt from the D.C. Circuit's decision in *American Trucking Ass'n v. EPA*, famously (albeit briefly) striking down EPA's interpretation of the Clean Air Act on nondelegation grounds.

Page 567, C&Q #1. CAA unconstitutional? *What could EPA do in the wake of Judge Williams's opinion other than seeking en banc rehearing or seeking Supreme Court review?* (They did both, as the note says.)

If this opinion had remained good law, could EPA ever have implemented its health-safety mission without violating the nondelegation principle, if Congress is unable or unwilling in most complex regulatory settings to set out safety standards in explicit terms? It should be obvious that EPA would have had a tough time implementing its mission if this decision had remained on the books. As discussed in notes 3 & 4, below, even the D.C. Circuit's proposed solutions - cost-benefit analysis and QALYs - don't seem satisfactorily to deal with the court's concerns about open-endedness.

Pages 567-568, C&Q #2. Who is in charge? *Is there a sense in which Judge Williams is being disingenuous when he, an unelected, generalist judge, trots out antidelegation — essentially a separation of powers type argument — to block the primary agency's action and replace it with inaction?* The question invites students to think critically about who is being the activist here - EPA, or the court.

Does it seem a bit odd that the nondelegation principle here applied had never before succeeded as a ground for attacking EPA's setting of an NAAQS, and that the J. W. Hampton case relied upon as authority was decided more than seven decades before? Yes, to many people this seemed more than a bit odd. In response to the opinion, Professor Sunstein memorably pointed out that the nondelegation doctrine had had "one good year" - 1935!

Is the underlying thrust of this line of attack a means by which the judiciary could force Congress or EPA to engage in systematic implementation of risk ranking and management by relative risk principles? It does seem that the court is pressing toward this kind of result, but getting there by means of the nondelegation doctrine seems challenging at best.

Page 568, C&Q #3. Would cost-benefit analysis take care of the problem? *Would cost-benefit analysis indeed give EPA less discretion in setting the standards?* As Professor Sunstein's analysis suggests, even cost-benefit analysis leaves open an exceedingly wide range of possible outcomes. It is hard to see how this decision-making framework meaningfully addresses the "stopping point" problem the court sees.

Page 568, C&Q #4. Are QALYs the answer? *Does the opinion adequately defend QALYs against the charge of discrimination?* It seems that the opinion might try to avoid the problem of discrimination by creating a different problem of arbitrariness: note 13 of the opinion suggests that the agency could assume that a person disabled by illness in fact lost a full measure of health, rather than a partial measure, from the air pollution of concern. But it is not clear what the basis for this assumption would be.

May EPA, under the CAA, use QALYs in setting the NAAQS? The note suggests the answer may be no; EPA has traditionally asserted an obligation to address harms to all groups under the Clean Air Act, even the ill and elderly.

Pages 568-572. These pages present excerpts from the Supreme Court's decision in American Trucking, upholding the Clean Air Act against the nondelegation challenge and finding that the statute prohibits the consideration of costs in setting the NAAQS.

Page 572, C&Q #1. An anticlimactic ruling? The note is informational and self-explanatory.

Page 572, C&Q #2. Unresolved questions after *American Trucking*. *Are [the lower court decisions allowing agencies to consider costs unless Congress says otherwise] all "good law"?* The answer must depend on the specific statutory context. Certainly, the Supreme Court's decision suggests that an interpretive "default principle" presuming that costs are relevant unless Congress says otherwise is not appropriate. But it may be that specific statutes allow the consideration of costs, even if that consideration is not explicitly authorized, because their language, history, and/or structure suggests that this is warranted.

Page 572, C&Q #3. Justice Breyer's concurrence on risk regulation. *What does Justice Breyer's concurrence mean? Should it really be a dissent on the statutory issue – that is, is Breyer suggesting that EPA actually may look at costs in setting the NAAQSs? If he's not saying that, what is he saying?* It is a little hard to discern Justice Breyer's meaning, and even harder to figure out why he did not dissent on the statutory issue if what he really means is that EPA may sometimes consider costs.

Page 572, C&Q #4. *American Trucking* on remand to the D.C. Circuit. This note is informational and self-explanatory.

Page 573, C&Q #5. The next stop for industry. This note is informational and self-explanatory.

Pages 573-574, C&Q #6. Setting the NAAQSs under conditions of uncertainty. This note about the role of scientific uncertainty in setting the NAAQSs is informational and self-explanatory.

Page 574, C&Q #7. Protecting vulnerable subpopulations form subclinical effects. This note is informational and self-explanatory.

Page 574, C&Q #8. How much harm is too much? This note is informational and self-explanatory.

Pages 574-575, C&Q #9. Risk-risk tradeoffs. *Even if EPA may not consider economic costs and technological feasibility in setting the NAAQS, may it consider potential adverse health and welfare effects arising from the standards themselves?* As the note states, the answer is "yes," according to the D.C. Circuit.

Has Justice Breyer rejected the argument [that EPA must consider the adverse health and welfare effects arising from the costs of the NAAQSs? Again, Justice Breyer's concurrence is frustratingly vague. He certainly does seem to think it would be a good idea for EPA to consider such health and welfare effects, but it is not clear that he would hold that such consideration was statutorily required, or even permitted.

Pages 575-577, C&Q #10. The §112 experience. This long note discusses EPA's experiences regulating hazardous air pollutants under §112 of the CAA. It includes a brief excerpt from the first "Vinyl Chloride" case in the D.C. Circuit.

Does [EPA's proposal to exempt de minimis risks from §112] bring §112 closer to the harm-based approach rejected by Congress in the 1990 Amendments? Is EPA's new approach authorized by §112(d)? Yes, such a proposal would bring §112 closer to a harm-based approach, and it does not seem to be authorized by this explicitly technology-based provision. N.B., however: in its final rule for stationary combustion sources (the proposed rule is cited in the note), EPA dropped the risk-based approach. 69 Fed. Reg. 10512 (3-5-04). A month later, the agency proposed delisting several categories of stationary combustion sources based on the low levels of risk the agency thought they posed - a move that is expressly contemplated by the statute. 69 Fed. Reg. 18327 (4-7-04).

Page 577, C&Q #11. Mercury MACT or mercury trading? This note is informational and self-explanatory.

Pages 577-581. These pages introduce students to the SIP process, and to the *Union Electric* case. In *Union Electric,* the State of Missouri approved a SIP that placed onerous (at least in the firm's eyes) restrictions on the sulfur dioxide emissions of one of Union's power plants. Union, perhaps strategically, perhaps because they did not care to understand the CAA, chose to obtain a variance that, in essence, delayed compliance but acceded to the permit terms being applied at a later date. Missouri made the restrictions on Union part of their SIP, and EPA approved the SIP. EPA's role, as the case makes plain, is to check if the SIP will attain the NAAQS, not whether Union is being put too hard a task.

Pages 581-582, C&Q #1. EPA review of SIPs that do consider economic and technologic feasibility. *EPA cannot disapprove a SIP that does not take economic and technologic feasibility into account (for that reason). Can EPA disapprove of a SIP that does take feasibility into account?* This answer, too, is that EPA can approve SIPs without regard to cost and feasibility as long as EPA believes the SIPs will work and does not violate other federal requirements (such as tall stack limitation, etc.). The note raises the further question about timetables for attainment. When *Union Electric* was decided by the Supreme Court, the CAA was still relatively young and there was greater tolerance of some slippage in time. In the wake of the 1990 amendments, the suggestion in the text that EPA won't rock the boat over a little delay may still be true, but the level of tolerance is probably lower.

Page 582, C&Q #2. States as pollution allocation brokers. *What happens when states take advantage of their ability to consider economic and technologic feasibility in SIP formulation?* A lot of lobbying by those firms hoping to get the "breaks."

Is there anything wrong with this? No, that is part of the proper federalism allocation of duties in this arrangement, the states still control local decisions. If there is a downside it has to do with poor choices by the states that result in inefficient allocations.

How cogent are these criticisms if EPA still insists on NAAQS attainment? Does EPA's watchdog role become more difficult when the states are trying to draw SIPs that are as close to painless as possible? EPA's job was never expected to be easy in regard to playing watchdog, no matter how the states are allowed to draw their SIPs.

Page 582, C&Q #3. EPA oversight of states' permitting decisions. This note is informational and self-explanatory.

Pages 583-585. From the NAAQS to SIPs. Welcome to acronym city. This material helps students to understand how difficult a task it is to arrive at a prescription for stationary source pollution which, when added to all the other variables out there, results in air quality that satisfies the NAAQS.

Pages 585-589. *Cleveland Electric Illuminating Company* case. This case is written against the backdrop of the State of Ohio's half-hearted efforts to comply with the sulfur dioxide requirements of the Clean Air Act of 1970. Ohio had dragged its feet in writing a SIP and later EPA took over the SIP process for itself. This case explains how the EPA finally drafted a SIP that allocated the allowable emissions among the various sulfur dioxide emitters in Ohio. At least some of them were not happy with the plan as it was drawn and attacked EPA in court. There are a number of interesting points in the case, not the least of which is the attack made on the model EPA used to allocate emissions. Specifically, the model was not very accurate in predicting air quality outcomes when its results were compared to real world observations obtained during the period when the model was being generated and while litigation was pending.

Page 590, C&Q #1. Technical complexity and the competence of courts. *Does a case like Cleveland Electric prove that the technical complexity of airshed modeling is so great that a judicial forum is inappropriate? Should there instead be a technological decision-making body?* No. The court is not being called on to substitute its own airshed model for that of EPA and the standard of review is sufficiently deferential so that the court is really doing only that which it does reasonably well - making sure that what the agency did was not off the wall.

Is there any indication that the court is over-matched by the technical matters involved in this case? No, the court seems to handle the technical material well.

Is there any reason to believe that a specialized court would do a better job with the science than EPA? The benefits would have to come from the procedural advantages (?) in this context of a judicial-type proceeding conducted by a court-like body, because the technical court could hardly be expected to have better-trained experts than EPA. Maybe "judicial temperament" could offer some Solomonesque capacity that EPA lacks, but that seems speculative.

Page 590, C&Q #2. How far does deference go? This note is probing a judgment question regarding when reliance on proven misprediction becomes arbitrary.

Page 590, C&Q #3. Advice to modelers and agencies. This note is informational and self-explanatory.

Pages 590-591, C&Q #4. Where's the margin of safety? *Couldn't an environmental group challenge the RAM model on the ground that it is not conservative enough?... Do these observations help to justify the court's deferential attitude?* These questions are aimed at pointing out the difficulty of developing air quality models that predict air quality exactly, neither over-predicting nor under-predicting air pollution; they are, after all, *models.* This lack of precision might also help to justify courts in taking a deferential attitude toward the expert agency's endorsement of any particular air quality model.

Page 591, C&Q #5. Amending the emissions limitations later. *Is that [adjusting RAM upward based on experience] a satisfactory method of proceeding? Why will the regulated petitioners claim that is an inadequate remedy? What becomes of their investment in pollution control equipment that is no longer necessary, or their lost profits due to higher operating costs in the interim?* The second rhetorical question is intended to suggest that the answer to the first question is ,"No." The problem here is significant in other contexts as well (i.e., setting the level of effluent taxes), so it is probably worth the time to make sure students understand why there is a problem. When a firm builds a facility to perform in a certain way, it may be difficult to change the operational characteristics in response to changed performance standards. The problem is clearer when standards are made more stringent after a facility has been designed when operating optimally to meet a lower standard. The facility may not be able to "improve" any more, it is already operating as cleanly as possible and even a slight escalation of standards requires fundamental reengineering and expensive retrofitting. Stated in literally more graphic terms, the cost curve of compliance is not a linear function that varies in direct proportion to the stringency of the standard. The same is true of the over-investment that occurs when standards of performance go down. Large expenses may have been incurred to allow the design to make small marginal improvements in pollution control ability. When the standards are relaxed, that investment is rendered unnecessary (in relation to the need of attaining a particular, no longer required, result).

Page 591, C&Q #6. Overriding state sovereignty and state resentment of federal imposed plans. *In the absence of the federal mandate provided by §110, is it likely that the court's attitude would have been the same?* Probably not, the history of mid-century pollution control was a history of states making slow (or no) progress toward solving air and water quality problems. Before the CAA, there was no requirement that states control emissions, much less a requirement that they submit a workable plan by a certain date.

Can Ohio fairly claim that the federal act has usurped too much of its traditional power to control local matters? No, Ohio had more than ample opportunity to write an acceptable SIP. EPA was very generous in delaying as long as it did. Ohio appears to have chosen delay as a deliberate strategy to avoid compliance by its emitters with the CAA's sulfur dioxide requirements. Ohio was protecting old power plants that burned Ohio-mined high sulfur coal. The note goes on to suggest why states fear FIPs, but an interesting question for students is whether FIPs are likely to be very much different than adequate SIPs, even in their details.

Pages 591-593, C&Q #7. Using tall stacks and intermittent controls to meet NAAQs requirements. *What is objectionable about SIPs that rely on tall stacks and intermittent controls to meet the NAAQS?* Tall stacks can export the problem of emissions to downwind AQCRs in other states. As one rule of ecology sometimes states, "dilution is not the solution to pollution." *Tall stacks and intermittent controls increase the aggregate amount of pollution that can be emitted without violating the NAAQS. Is that bad?* This question channels the students back into the debate about fundamental principles of pollution control. Is pollution bad for instrumental reasons (i.e., because it results in defined harms), or is pollution bad in and of itself, being an anti-social act to throw wastes into the commons. This debate has a parallel in the major federal legislation: the CAA adopts an instrumental standard (harm-based ambient quality approach); the CWA with its strong reliance on categorical BAT and the zero pollution goal exhibits the latter view. That raises the question of why the CAA should frown on intermittent controls in all cases and discourage tall stacks if there are not adverse downwind effects. The note answers its own question, "The crux of the arguments for limiting dispersion centered on export and the unreliability and lack of enforceability of intermittent controls."

Pages 593-595. Translating statutory obligations into permits. This text tries to explain how plans are made operational through the creation of a permit system. This material appears here because experience with the first edition demonstrated that students often did not have a clear sense of what permits do, or what sorts of provisions are part of a permit under a sophisticated law like the CAA. A second reason for placing the first major treatment of permits here, rather than in the next chapter with the CWA material is that Congress, in the 1990 Amendments to the CAA, adopted a series of permit requirements for the CAA modeled on the NPDES permits of the CWA. At least one point to raise with students is the extent to which the new CAA permits are going to be easier to enforce than in the past because of the reporting and monitoring requirements. As a pedagogical matter, the material relating to the permit may be better discussed in conjunction with the *Kodak* case that appears in Chapter 12.

Page 595, C&Q #1. Does more formal permitting make the system work better? *Operationally, is a more formal permit system likely to help or hinder the effectiveness of a pollution control system?* Yes, it will help by making clear obligations and making violations easier to detect.

Page 595, C&Q #2. Using permits as enforcement mechanisms. This textual note explains one way in which the new permit system "works better."

Pages 595-596, C&Q #3. Blurring the nice distinctions: the CAM rules. This note adds material about how compliance with permits can be obtained by offering a contrast of two approaches, one (enhanced monitoring) that would make violations almost certain to be exposed thereby subjecting violators to a high likelihood of sanctions, and one (the CAM rule) that relies on assuring that the plant functions as intended and that any excursions are spotted and fixed A.S.A.P. The latter is a less punitive approach. Students can be asked about the relative merits of the two approaches. To do so is an early foreshadowing of the policies that are discussed more fully in Chapter 21, where compliance and regulatory and self-enforcement are studied in their own right.

Pages 596-598. New sources in non-attainment areas and the *CARE* case. These materials discuss requirements for new sources in non-attainment areas. Politically, Congress was not inclined to make growth and development in non-attainment areas impossibly difficult or expensive. Still, the fact remained that too many people were literally dying from the pollution. The *CARE* case presents a challenge to very generous calculation of offsets by the state agency and EPA.

Pages 598-599, C&Q #1. Insisting on "reasonable further progress." *Was EPA too permissive with Virginia in this case, so permissive that it violated the statutory "reasonable further progress" requirement? Couldn't EPA have gotten both the switch to the less polluting asphalt plus additional offsets if it had wanted to take a more aggressive stance regarding what is reasonable progress for Virginia under the circumstances?* Yes, EPA could have had both the switch and the offsets if it had been more aggressive.

Page 599, C&Q #2. Reasonably Available Control Measures (RACM) requirements. This note is informational and self-explanatory.

Pages 599-600, C&Q #3. Transportation conformity. This note is informational and self-explanatory. N.B.: Watch for the Supreme Court's decision in *Public Citizen v. DOT* by the summer of 2004.

Page 600, C&Q #4. Offsets pro and con. *Are offsets a good method of accommodating further development while still seeking improvement of ambient air quality in non-attainment areas?* Yes, they allow both development and progress toward attainment, both of which are vital.

In the absence of state intervention in aid of the new source, either like that given in the CARE case, or in the form of placing tighter controls on existing sources, which emissions reductions will be realized first? This question is intended to bring up the fact that offsets are, at one level, a form of emissions trading device. There are two likely types of trades. First, low cost avoiders should be willing to take $ in trade for making the needed changes in their operations to reduce their emissions. Second, in a form of economic Darwinism, in theory, inexpensive offsets can be obtained from failing/marginal businesses because they are making the least valuable uses of present emissions. In practice the transaction costs of finding low value emissions to retire as offsets may be difficult.

Are there social costs that have been overlooked in that assessment? What about the dislocation of workers who lose their jobs when the marginal firms are bought out and closed? This further question tries to get the students to think about offsets with reference to overall policy that looks beyond environment and efficiency alone. Even something as seemingly logical as retiring an old, dirty, marginally profitable factory, poses social costs in terms of worker and community dislocation that ought to be acknowledged, even if the retirement should go forward. There is a two-edged sword with both sides favoring the closing of that plant. On one side the retirement of the facility is likely to occur soon anyway for other reasons. On the other side, absent something like offsets to push it over the brink, it might go on polluting without producing a large stock of benefits because the private calculus for old plants is to run them as long as they still make even a small profit.

Pages 600-601, C&Q #5. NSPS as a "protection" of nonattainment area economic growth potential. NSPS are a significant part of CAA stationary source regulation. §111 is, in many ways, the father of command and control regulation of the most marked kind – technology-based performance standards. To relegate them to this note, buried in material on non-attainment is an injustice that is not fully undone by the extended treatment given to technology-based performance standards in the CWA context that takes place in Chapter 12. In any event it is important to consider the strategic importance of BADT for attainment area new sources when non-attainment area new sources are facing LAER plus offsets.

Pages 601-603, C&Q #6. New Source Review. This long note on the NSR program is informational and self-explanatory.

Page 603, C&Q #7. A mandatory retirement age for grandfathers? This note is informational and self-explanatory.

Pages 604-607. Adding Environmental Justice (EJ) concerns. This material consists of an excerpt from EPA's draft revised guidance on taking EJ into account in permitting. It marks one of several efforts in this edition to make EJ a part of the substantive material, rather than an add-on that is set off by itself. Page references incorporating environmental justice considerations: 16, 63-64, 124, 245, 302, 374, 529, 604-611, 728, 733, 1230-1231. The material is also instructive for non-EJ purposes, being an example of administrative process in the regulatory arena, illustrating how EPA oversees state compliance with federal requirements.

Page 607, C&Q #1 . The significance of the Title VI guidance. *To what situations does the guidance apply and in what way does that contrast with past practice?* Beyond the answer supplied in the note itself that makes clear the way in which the guidance represents a paradigm shift, the simple answer is that the guidance applies to all cooperative federalism program permits issued by state agencies that receive any federal assistance for their programs, i.e., almost everything under the sun in the environmental realm.

Page 607, C&Q #2. Casting a federal shadow on a traditional state prerogative. This note is self-explanatory.

Page 607, C&Q #3. Are the standards too muddy? *After reading the excerpts from the guidance, can you list the elements of a successful complaint?* Discrimination is inherently difficult to define precisely, except at the extremes. What this guidance tries to do to limit the muddiness of the standard is to make explicit the role of disparate impact and how it is to be proved/demonstrated, so that at least the relevant data is defined in advance.

Taking a different perspective, do permitting agencies and permit seekers know what is in store for them if their actions can be shown to have a disparate impact on a minority group? Yes, the threat is the loss of federal benefits, such as funding of programs.

Page 608, C&Q #4. Are the standards too precise? The note itself helps to answer this question.

Knowing what you know now about NAAQSs and their implementation, does EPA's presumption [that there is no adverse impact where health-based standards are met] make sense? As the materials on the NAAQSs suggest, it may be that some especially vulnerable subpopulations are inadequately protected by the NAAQSs. Moreover, even if one facility does not itself cause violations of the NAAQSs (as in the Select Steel case cited in the note), this does not mean that the surrounding air is healthy.

Pages 608-609, C&Q #5. Using this guidance document to seek enforceable legal rights and remedies. *Where does the authority to promulgate the guidance come from and how much legal force should it have?* E.O. 12,898 authorizes the guidance but gives no assistance in deciding how much force it has. Stated differently, the technical side of the matter is that EPA is allowed to issue a guidance on EJ in permitting, the problematic side of the matter is what force the guidance can have and what sanctions EPA can impose. The disclaimers in the EO seem to contradict any claim that the EO authorizes EPA to create legal rights and remedies under its auspices. Likewise, guidance documents are not the equivalent of rulemaking, so the guidance can't obtain force that way. On the other hand, EPA has discretion in making many of its decisions, including those about who qualifies for benefits under programs that EPA administers. EPA can rely on the EO to control its internal processes. On that view, the guidance is more in the nature of full disclosure to affected parties (states and those affected by state permits) of how EPA will administer state grant programs – i.e., EPA will take a dim view of making grants to states that do not have EJ complaint procedures in place that meet the standards of this guidance.

Pages 609-610, C&Q #6. *South Camden Citizens* and St. Lawrence Cement. *If disparate impact, a historical pattern of permitting facilities in minority neighborhoods, and foreseeability and knowledge of discriminatory impact are enough to make out a valid Title VI claim, what remains of the importance of Alexander v. Sandoval in the environmental setting?* Although Judge Orlofsky's decision discussed at pages 609-610 seems promising from the standpoint of environmental justice plaintiffs, bear in mind the observation made at the end of the note: no environmental justice plaintiff has succeeded in proving discriminatory intent.

Page 610, C&Q #7. EPA's record on Title VI complaints. This note is informational and self-explanatory.

Pages 610-611, C&Q #8. NSR and environmental justice. This note is informational and self-explanatory.

Pages 611-612. Prescribing the path toward attainment. In capsule form, this material attempts to explain the change in the congressional response to non-attainment that appeared in the 1990 amendments. Congress became far more directive as to means and timetables. It did so in a graduated fashion, allowing more time and prescribing more harsh medicine for areas that were further from attainment than for corresponding areas that were closer to meeting the NAAQS.

Pages 612-614. These pages provide another excerpt from the Supreme Court's decision in *American Trucking*. In this portion of the opinion, the Court rejects EPA's proposed way of dealing with implementation of the revised standard for ozone.

Pages 614-615, C&Q #1. A bit of background. This note is informational and self-explanatory.

Page 615, C&Q #2. Role reversal? *Does this help environmentalists interested in seeing the revised standard expeditiously enforced more than it helps industry groups interested in putting off enforcement of the standard? Given Subpart 2's exceedingly detailed prescriptions for meeting the ozone NAAQS, doesn't the Court's requirement that EPA consider those prescriptions in enforcing the standard potentially (if ironically) help the environmentalists' cause?* To both questions, we can only answer "perhaps."

Pages 615-616, C&Q #3. EPA's response on remand. This note is informational and self-explanatory.

Pages 616-618. Transboundary airflows. Recall that the one well-agreed reason for federal intervention in pollution control is transboundary movement of pollutants, and to see so little made so far of that part of the CAA seems wrong.

This text first takes a "how-to-do-it" approach, by explaining how §§110(a)(2)(d) and 126 operate to create a role for EPA as arbiter. Students seem to lose sight of the fact that when a state writes a SIP, it is concerned exclusively with the ambient quality of its AQCRs, and is not very much interested in how its SIP affects its neighbors. If the SIP is going to require painful measures, the indifference to the plight of neighbors is even greater. EPA as the reviewer of SIPs has not been very ardent in its concern for downwind states, probably as a result of a similar view – if a state is trying hard and placing real burdens on its polluters that are stringent enough to get attainment, those measures are also very likely to be reasonable efforts to prevent externalization of the pollution. A second reason for EPA's seeming reticence is more likely factual – if the downwind state is having attainment problems, its own sources are probably causing the lion's share of the problem. For example, notice in the Indiana-Kentucky dispute recounted in the text, EPA had data showing that only 3% of the Lexington AQCR's problem was attributable to Indiana emissions.

Pages 618-619, C&Q #1. EPA's dilemma. *On what principled basis can EPA determine how much pollution can cross state boundaries without constituting an injury to the downwind state?* There is no easy standard that comes to mind for the agency to use and Congress did not give a firm standard for EPA to use, only the direction that EPA be the arbiter applying a muddy standard related to significant interference with downwind attainment.

Page 619, C&Q #2. Non-federal remedies. This note is informational and self-explanatory.

Page 619, C&Q #3. Experience under the 1990 Amendments. This note is informational and self-explanatory.

Chapter 12.

TECHNOLOGY-BASED STANDARD-SETTING: THE CLEAN WATER ACT

Suggested time budget: **2 or 3 class sessions**

Day 1 [Technology-based approach]:
620-627: CWA overview
627-635: Origin and evolution of TBELs
636-655: Implementing TBELs through the NPDES process

Day 2 [Water quality-based approach]:
655-671 Water quality-based permitting under the CWA
671-674 Controlling nonpoint-source pollution without federal regulation
674-675 The Average River case study

For three-day coverage, do Average River on 3d day

Chapter contents:

—and check the Teachers' Manual Website for SUPPLEMENTARY MATERIALS:

http://www.bc.edu/schools/law/library/coursebook/envtlaw/teachers

The list of Supplementary Materials in Part III of this manual, and on the Teachers' Website, indicates materials posted on the Teachers' Website that are relevant to this and other chapters.

***New Chart*: Please ask students to refer to the following chart, also posted on the general Users' Website for this chapter, instead of the chart currently printed on the coursebook's page 625:**

Five Leading Causes of Water Quality Impairment

RANK	*RIVERS*	*LAKES*	*STREAMS*
1	**Bacteria**	**Nutrients**	**Nutrients**
2	**Siltation**	**Siltation**	**Bacteria**
3	**Nutrients**	**Oxygen-depleting substances**	**Oxygen-depleting substances**
4	**Oxygen-depleting substances**	**Metals**	**Habitat alterations**
5	**Metals**	**Suspended solids**	**Oil and grease**

FIGURE 12—1. WHERE DOES WATER POLLUTION COME FROM?

TEACHING THEMES & COURSE DESIGN CONSIDERATIONS

This chapter should be taught immediately following Chapter 11, in order to explore the contrast between harm-based and technology-based standard-setting. Following this chapter, the instructor may either choose to analyze another type of standard-setting methodology – technology-forcing (Chapter 15) or cost-benefit procedures (Chapter 13) – or else continue a study of the Clean Water Act by assigning the §404 materials in Chapter 25 (pages 1233-1244).

The Clean Water Act is difficult to understand and teach because of its confusing combination of a technology-based foundation and a water quality-based superstructure. The historical reason for this haphazard statutory architecture was that the Senate, in order to enact a statute featuring its innovative technology-based approach, was compelled to compromise with the House and accept the water quality-based approach – which the Senate considered outmoded and ineffective – as a subordinate means of control where technology-based standards did not result in acceptable water quality. Between 1972 and 1987, EPA and the States did their best to ignore water quality-based controls without publicly admitting to this strategy. Thus, there has been a wide divergence between law-on-the-books and law-in-action in the water pollution control area. But in the Clean Water Act Amendments of 1987, Congress revived the water quality-based approach with regard to so-called "Toxic Hot Spots." Since then, environmentalist lawsuits have compelled EPA and the states to finally implement the water quality-based control element of the CWA with regard to all water pollutants.

This is one of our book's core chapters, and deserves at least two class periods. In the first class period, the instructor should explain the basic (and contradictory) structure of the CWA, and then concentrate on the evolution of TBELs and how they are implemented. The assignment for this first class should be pages 620-655. The assignment for the second class period can be the remainder of the chapter, which deals with the water quality-based approach. The Average River case study may be analyzed either at the end of the second class period, which will serve as a review of water pollution control law, or else as the focus of a third class session. If the latter alternative is selected, the instructor might administer a simulation that would involve class members in representing the legal interests of the various actors in the scenario. The context of this simulation might be a public hearing, held by the state water pollution control agency, in order to assist the agency in developing TMDLs and coordinating watershed-wide discharge permitting in the Average River watershed.

TEACHER'S GUIDE for the

AVERAGE RIVER HYPOTHETICAL, coursebook at pages 674-675

(1) Even if Riverview State Park is officially designated as an Outstanding National Resource Waters, subject to antidegradation requirements, the CWA cannot be used to control discharges from Fox Ridge after construction of the development has been completed. During construction, the developer will have to comply with the state-administered general stormwater control permit for construction projects by utilizing Best Management Practices ("BMPs") such as grassy swales or hay bales to prevent construction site runoff. (Requirements for controlling construction site runoff may also be imposed under a State Soil Erosion and Sediment Control Act.) After the development has been completed, its impervious surfaces will intensify runoff of lawn chemicals, oil and grease from parking lots, and sediment, as well as inhibiting recharge of groundwater; but this is nonpoint source pollution that the CWA does not reach. Few states regulate residential and commercial stormwater runoff, leaving controls in this area to sporadic and frequently inconsistent municipal runoff control ordinances. Septic systems are point sources of pollution, but since they discharge to groundwater they are outside the CWA's ambit. Many states regulate septic systems through design and installation standards enforced by local governments, but there are generally no controls on maintenance. (A septic system can be rendered inoperative if it is not periodically pumped out.) These homes might also derive their potable water supplies from individual wells, which could be contaminated by faulty septic tanks. Water supply is not covered by the CWA. The Safe Drinking Water Act does not apply to individual private wells because they are not "Public Water Systems." Many states and municipalities have not enacted mandatory well-testing legislation. In such jurisdictions, attorneys representing the buyers of new or existing private homes should provide in contracts of sale for well-testing, in addition to inspections for termites, leaking underground fuel tanks, and structural integrity.

(2) Riverview State Park's water quality is threatened not only by runoff from Fox Ridge, but also by airborne deposition of pollutants such as pesticides and nutrients. These are nonpoint source pollutants that lie outisde the CWA's ambit. The impoundment from Zaaapp Power Company's proposed dam will extend into the Park, changing a free-flowing river environment into a flatwater lake, which will change the existing ecosystem, eliminate free-flowing river recreational opportunities (e.g., rafting, fly-fishing), flood existing campsites, displace wildlife, promote eutrophication and low DO in the impoundment, and cause malodorous mudflats when the impoundment is drawn down for power production. See below for a discussion of the legal aspects of the Zaaapp project.

(3) Unless Purview Farms is operating a Confined Animal Feeding Operation ("CAFO"), its runoff will be considered a nonpoint source and thus not covered by the CWA. If purview is a CAFO, it will be required to implement BMPs, most likely included in a general permit, for that aspect of its operation. The CWA declares that irrigation return flow is not a point source, although in fact irrigation tailwater may be significant source of pollution.

(4) The Dratt Chemical Co. is a direct discharger that must possess a discharge permit, issued either by EPA or the state if it has been delegated primacy. Dratt's discharge permit must include effluent limitations based not only on available technology ("TBELs"), but also, since Dratt is located on a water quality-limited stretch of the Average River because its discharge is violating water quality standards, more stringent effluent limitations based on water quality ("WQBELs"). This stretch of the river must be listed as "impaired," obligating the state pollution control agency to establish TMDLs for offending parameters. Dratt is discharging BOD (a conventional pollutant subject to BCT limitations), toxics (subject to BAT limitations), and phenols (a non-conventional/nontoxic pollutant subject to BAT limitations qualified by §301(c) and (g) variances). Is Dratt also discharging parameters that are not listed in its permit? Have these pollutants been identified in Dratt's permit application? Are they removed by treatment systems designed to remove other pollutants? If Dratt has identified these parameters, they are covered by the permit shield. If not, Dratt is liable for discharging unpermitted pollutants. Note that Dratt will have to install better-than-best available technology in order to meet water quality standards partly because of uncontrolled upstream discharges from Fox Ridge and Purview Farms. Recognizing this inequity, and conscious of Dratt's threats to move its plant to another state, the state will probably refine its water quality standards (e.g., based on flow regime, aquatic life, or assumptions about background pollution) to ensure that Dratt is not violating them. Another option would be for the state, after performing a use attainability analysis, to petition EPA to remove the fishable/swimmable designation from this segment of the Average River, but the state's petition would probably be denied because Dratt's closure would not result in "substantial and widespread economic and social impact." The state might also facilitate a point/nonpoint source trade between Dratt and either Fox Ridge or Purview Farms, whereby Dratt would agree to fund relatively inexpensive BMPs on these upstream areas instead of installing expensive better-than-best available control technology. If the state has not established TMDLs for the impaired segments of the Average River, a citizens group could sue both the state and also EPA to set TMDLs. A court would probably order EPA to develop these TMDLs only if the state has done nothing in this regard. If the state has established TMDLs and translated them into WQBELs for Dratt, the citizens group could sue Dratt (based on Dratt's excursion reports in its Discharge Monitoring Report — "DMR") for violation of its discharge permit. Another tack that the citizens group might take would be to petition the state to list the Average River below Dratt's outfall as a Toxic Hot Spot, thus obligating Dratt to perform a Toxicity Reduction Evaluation ("TRE") and implement an Individual Control Strategy ("ICS"), which would be included in Dratt's discharge permit along with a whole effluent testing requirement. The state would attempt to block this strategy by adjusting the relevant water quality standards so that Dratt is no longer in violation. With regard to Dratt's stormwater discharge, the Company will be required to comply with the provisions of the general stormwater control permit applicable to chemical manufacturing plants. Dratt will have to develop and implement a Stormwater Management Plan ("SMP") that specifies a BMP for protecting its raw material pile from rainwater.

(5) Even if the state modifies its water quality standards for the Dratt stretch of the Average River so that Dratt is no longer in violation, the downstream Unpoll-Ute Nation can legally set water quality standards at "Non-Detectable" levels. Dratt will have to comply with these standards unless the state and EPA are able to mediate this dispute or EPA vetoes the tribal standard.

(6) Building "Heron's Harbor" in a wetlands area will require a §404 permit from the U.S.Army Corps of Engineers. There is a presumption against locating a residential development in a wetland, but that presumption is rebuttable. See Chapter 25 for an examination of the §404 program.

(7) Grossville's POTW is currently using secondary treatment, but the City could petition EPA, under §301(h)(treatment variances for certain municipal marine dischargers), to reduce its obligation to primary treatment (i.e., a decrease from approximately 90% removal of BOD and TSS to approximately 30% removal). Grossville's chances of obtaining a §301(h) variance are remote, however, because the statutory critera are stringent, and EPA has granted fewer than a half-dozen §301(h) variances. The City's combined sewer overflows ("CSOs") are governed by EPA's CSO control regulations. However, Grossville might significantly reduce its CSOs by adopting relatively inexpensive BMPs, such as enhanced street cleaning, use of system storage and flow routing to retard flows during storm events, personnel training, disinfection of CSOs, etc.These measures would be included in the City's CSO Control Plan, which is part of its system-wide discharge permit. Assuming that Grossville does not procure a §301(h) variance, it might have to seek funding from the State Revolving Loan Fund to increase its treatment efficiency by moving to tertiary treatment (e.g., advanced nutrient removal) if its effluent is violating water quality standards for the inshore receiving waters of the Pedantic Ocean. But the state would probably, as in the case of Dratt's discharge, adjust water quality standards to preclude this result. Alternatively, the POTW could install a long discharge pipe, with a diffuser at its terminus, to take advantage of increased dilution offshore.Nurd Auto Co. must comply with pretreatment standards based on BAT (for heavy metals), but pretreatment standards are primarily enforceable by the POTW, which might ordinarily be unenthusiastic about enforcing against a major customer and a large employer of Grossville's citizens. Nevertheless, the state, EPA, and citizens possess backup enforcement authority, although a citizens suit would be more difficult here because the CWA does not require indirect dischargers to procure discharge permits or submit DMRs. (State law, however, might require this because Nurd is a Significant Industrial User ("SIU"). However, the POTW might be inclined to enforce Nurd's pretreatment standards because (1) the POTW might be in violation of an effluent limitation for metals contained in *its* discharge permit, and (2) the POTW's biosolids ("sludge") would violate EPA's sludge disposal standards. Foreclosed from ocean dumping and incineration (because of air pollution problems), Grossville is desperate to find an acceptable means of biosolids disposal. If its sludge meets EPA standards, Grossville can attempt to sell it (or give it away) to farmers in the area. But the fact that the biosolids comply with standards may not convince farmers, who might be concerned about liability for abnormally dangerous activities or barred from spreading sludge by municipal ordinances (in states where such ordinances are not preempted by state law).

(8) Dams are considered to be nonpoint sources of pollution, and are thus not covered by the CWA's regulatory provisions. However, Zaaapp's proposed hydroelectric project must be approved by the Federal Power Commission ("FPC"). The state can veto the project, under CWA §401, by refusing to certify to the FPC that the project will comply with water quality standards. The state can also refuse to certify Zaaapp's application under §404, which requires a Corps of Engineers permit for discharge of dredged and fill material into navigable waters (see Chapter 25). Or else the state could certify on condition that Zaaapp maintain a minimum flow below the dam, which condition would be binding on the FPC and Corps. But this condition would not alleviate the potential damage to Riverview State Park, which is located *above* the project. If the state supports the project, it could also be vetoed by the Tribal Council of the Unpoll-Ute Nation, which might refuse to certify that *its* water quality standards would be maintained if the dam were built. If both the state and the tribe support the project, the lead federal agency (probably the FPC) would be required to perform NEPA compliance (see Chapter 9), which would focus public attention on the damage to a popular state park. If the public is sufficiently outraged, elected officials might be convinced to urge Congress to include this stretch in the Federal Wild and Scenic Rivers System, which would permanently preclude the project (see Chapter 25). Or else it might be discovered that an endangered species, which relies on a free-flowing river ecosystem, is living above or below the proposed impoundment (see Chapter 16).

TEACHING NOTES, COMMENTS, & ALL QUESTIONS ANSWERED

Pages 620-626. These pages present a brief overview of the CWA and an introduction to the types and sources of water pollution. The environmental law text gremlins have attacked Figure 12-1, which should be disregarded. Professor Jonathan H. Adler has concluded that "much of the Cuyahoga story...is mythology, a fable with a powerful symbolic force." Fables of the Cuyahoga: Reconstructing a History of Environmental Protection, XIV FORDHAM ENVTL L.J. 89, 93. Professor Adler argues that the City of Cleveland and the State of Ohio had made significant progress in cleaning up the Cuyahoga before the passage of the CWA, and that the 1969 Cuyahoga fire was a relatively minor event that received disproportionate media coverage because of the concurrent rise of the environmental movement. (The Cuyahoga was actually ignited approximately a dozen times.)

Page 626, C&Q #1. A regulatory paradox. Informational and self-explanatory.

Pages 626-627, C&Q #2. We've come a long way, but... Informational and self-explanatory.

Pages 627-629. Presents a brief look at the historical evolution of the CWA, and the inadequacies of the harm-based standard-setting approach in the water pollution control context.

Pages 629-630, C&Q #1. Ineffectuality of prior law. Informational and self-explanatory. The questions asked are immediately answered.

Page 630, C&Q #2. Pros and cons of technology-based controls. Informational and self-explanatory.

Pages 6309-632, C&Q #3. Frozen technology? Informational and self-explanatory.

Page 632, C&Q #4. Navigable waters. Informational and self-explanatory.

Pages 633-635, C&Q #5. Point and nonpoint sources. Informational and self-explanatory.

Page 635, C&Q #6. Types of point source dischargers. Informational and self-explanatory. Industrial stormwater dischargers may also discharge into combined storm and sanitary sewers that lead to POTWs. Excess flows in combined sewers are discharged through overflow points, causing Combined Sewer Overflows ("CSOs"), a major source of urban water pollution (see page 646.) In older urban areas, water pollution control authorities are plagued by undetected hookups between industries and municipal sewerage systems. These illegal connections, which are virtually undetectable, carry both wastewater and stormwater.

Page 635, C&Q #7. The federal-state partnership. Informational and self-explanatory. The questions raised, which relate to the drawbacks of cooperative federalism, are addressed in Chapter 5.

Pages 636-640. Presents the *Rybachek* case as an introduction to the development and implementation of technology-based effluent limitations ("TBELs"). Note that the Rybacheks brought a subsequent lawsuit to contest their water quality-based effluent limitations ("WQBELs")(see footnote 29).

Page 641, C&Q #1. "Addition of any pollutant." Informational and self-explanatory.

Pages 641-642, C&Q #2. Evolution of categorical technology-based limitations. Informational and self-explanatory. The one questions raised is immediately answered.

Pages 642-644, C&Q #3. The midcourse of 1977. Informational and self-explanatory.

Pages 644-647, C&Q #4. Stormwater discharges. Informational and self-explanatory.

Page 647, C&Q #5. Municipal dischargers. Informational and self-explanatory.

Pages 647-648, C&Q #6. Indirect dischargers and biosoldis disposals. Informational and self-explanatory.

Pages 648-649, C&Q #7. Drinking water protection. Informational and self-explanatory.

Pages 649-650, C&Q #8. Toxics and the CWA. Informational and self-explanatory. The one questions raised is immediately discussed.

Pages 650-652. This material presents the *Atlantic States* case as an example of applying TBELs to a complex, multiprocess industrial operation. In practice, the application of TBELs to particular industrial dischargers are frequently not mechanical derivations from categorical effluent limitations included in EPA regulations because many industries either discharge parameters that are not covered by federal regulations, or else are unique, multifaceted facilities that produce various products and utilize water for diverse waste treatment purposes, including cleanising batch and continuous processes, heating and cooling, storm drainage, and in-plant sanitation. In composite facilities, liquid waste streams of all sorts may be kept separate or mixed; some wastewaters may be discharged into POTWs, some directly into waterbodies, some discharged underground, and still others may be intended for land discharge, either on or offsite (see Chapter 17 on RCRA and the Underground Injection Control Program under the Safe Drinking Water Act). The opportunities for pollution prevention, recycling and reuse, and waste exchanges with neighboring industries are vast with regard to composite facilities. Attorneys should recommend that waste audits be performed in order to explore these possibilities. (See Chapter 21 for a discussion of environmental audits.) If discharge permits are necessary for composite plants, the "effluent numbers" are generally developed by the Best Professional Judgment ("BPJ") of state and federal permit writers. The Fundamentally Different Factors ("FDF") variance is not often resorted to in such situations because permit writers recognize that federal categorical effluent limitations do not neatly apply to composite facilities. BPJ is applied by utilizing categorical effluent limitations as analogies, applying complex mixed-waste-stream formulas for combined toxic and non-toxic waste streams, performing whole effluent testing, scrutinizing past performance, etc. Because of the gestalt nature of BPJ, negotiations among permit writers, dischargers, and environmental groups, during the comment period on draft discharge permits, is critical is developing defensible discharge permits for composite facilities like the Kodak plant.

Pages 652-653 C&Q #1. CWA §402(k) and the NPDES permit shield defense. The question raised is immediately answered. However, common law actions for alleged damage caused by water pollution are difficult to win because of the traditional requirement that plaintiff prove that defendant's discharges caused plaintiff's damage. But see Chapter 3, for situations where plaintiff's burden of proving causation has been lightened. The Clean Water Act imposes strict liability on dischargers that violate their discharge permits. Damage to water resources or people who use them need not be proven in order to establish liability under the CWA. But evidence of environmental or human health damage may be introduced either to increase civil fines for CWA violations (see Chapter 21), or else in sentencing following criminal convictions for CWA violations (see Chapter 20). Plaintiffs in CWA citizen suits may not be awarded damages for injury to health or property; but a CWA citizen suit cause of action may be combined with state common law causes of action in a single lawsuit in federal court (see the *Southview Farms* case, *supra.)* .

Page 653, C&Q #2. Regulating unlisted discharges. The question raised in the opening sentence is answered in the remainder of the note.

Page 653, C&Q #3. The effluent limitations—BAT and BPJ. Informational and self-explanatory.

Pages 653-654, C&Q #4. What did the permit writers know, and when did they know it? Informational and self-explanatory.

Page 654, C&Q #5. CWA federalism, devolution, stricter state standards, and citizen suits. Informational and self-explanatory.

Page 655, C&Q 6. Informational and self-explanatory.

Pages 655-661. Presents the essential elements of the CWA's water quality-based standard-setting and permitting approaches in the context of the Sierra Club v. EPA case.

Pages 661-662, C&Q #1. §303 musical chairs. Informational and self-explanatory. The first question raised is immediately addressed. The final questions is rhetorical.

Pages 662-665, C&Q #2. Things can get complicated. Informational and self-explanatory. The final question is rhetorical.

Page 665, C&Q #3. Whole Effluent Test (WET) as an alternative. Informational and self-explanatory.

Pages 665-667, C&Q #4. Antidegradation and attainability. Informational and self-explanatory. The questions raised are either immediately addressed or else rhetorical.

Pages 667, C&Q #5. A spate of §303 (d) lawsuits. Informational and self-explanatory.

Pages 667-668, C&Q #6. Interstate water pollution. Informational and self-explanatory.

Pages 668-669, C&Q #7. State and water quality certification. Informational and self-explanatory.

Page 669, C&Q #8. Regulation of "toxic hot spots." Informational and self-explanatory.

Pages 670-671, C&Q #9. Whither §303? Informational and self-explanatory. The one question raised is immediately answered. Tracy Mehan III has resigned as EPA's Assistant Administrator for Water due to health problems. He has been replaced by Benjamin Grumbles, the former Deputy Assistant Administrator.

Professor James R. May, in a recent review of CWA litigation, has charged that EPA is attempting to reinstall TMDLs on the back burner:

> Citizen suits continue to catalyze the TMDL program, albeit with decreasing promise. Although EPA so far has survived dubious challenges to its authority to set TMDLs for waters impaired by nonpoint sources, it has nonetheless largely succeeded in pressing a counteroffensive against citizen action that reduces water quality standards to dead letter. In EPA's view, it need not intervene unless states do nothing. TMDLs need not be "total," "daily," or reflect "loads." And, most importantly, TMDLs need not include implementation plans, and need not be implemented. EPA is intent on devolving the program back to the states and transporting the water quality program back to the Johnson Administration. (That would be Lyndon, but could just as well be Andrew.) Thus, at least as a matter of federal administration, the TMDL game is about up. Where the Water Hits the Road: Recent Developments in Clean Water Act Litigation, 33 ELR 10369, 10373-10374.

It might also be argued that the Section 303 process is so profoundly conceptually flawed that the back burner is indeed where it belongs.

Pages 671-673. Presents an introduction to non-CWA strategies for controlling nonpoint source pollution.

Pages 674-675. Includes the Average River case study, the teaching guide to which can be found above.

Chapter 13.
STANDARD-SETTING VIA COST-BENEFIT PROCEDURES

Chapter contents:

—and check the Teachers' Manual Website for SUPPLEMENTARY MATERIALS:
http://www.bc.edu/schools/law/library/coursebook/envtlaw/teachers

The list of Supplementary Materials in Part III of this manual, and on the Teachers' Website, indicates materials posted on the Teachers' Website that are relevant to this and other chapters.

OVERALL TEACHING THEMES & COURSE DESIGN CONSIDERATIONS

This chapter introduces students to cost-benefit analysis and its use in setting environmental standards. The chapter also provides a longish section on the practice and theory of cost-benefit analysis, explaining in some detail how cost-benefit analysis works and the primary arguments that have been raised for and against this technique. Two statutes – the Toxic Substances Control Act and the Safe Drinking Water Act – provide the legal framework for the chapter's discussion. Although both statutes contemplate cost-benefit balancing, ToSCA's balancing is more open-ended than the formal cost-benefit procedures endorsed in the Safe Drinking Water Act. The chapter concludes with a discussion of the use of cost-benefit analysis, by OMB/OIRA, as a tool for reviewing agency rules.

At 35 pages, the chapter is at the edge of what one might consider reasonable for a one-day class. Teachers who wish to present the material in one day, without overtaxing their students' reading schedules, might consider omitting the materials on the practice and theory of cost-benefit analysis; the ideas presented in these materials could certainly be teased out in a class discussion of ToSCA and the SDWA. On the other hand, the materials presented in the chapter could easily be taught over two days; there are plenty of substantive ideas here for students to wrestle with.

TEACHING NOTES, COMMENTS, & ALL QUESTIONS ANSWERED

Pages 676-678. These pages introduce the topics covered in the chapter, and provide a general definition of two different categories of cost-benefit balancing, one open-ended and one more formal.

Pages 678-682. These pages introduce section 6 of the Toxic Substances Control Act, which authorizes EPA to regulate toxic chemicals that pose an unreasonable risk of harm. The materials also include the case of *Corrosion Proof Fittings v. EPA*, in which the Fifth Circuit overturned EPA's ban on asbestos based on what the court regarded as the agency's inadequate analysis and its over-expenditure on life-saving regulation.

Page 682, C&Q #1. How did the court know how much was too much to save a life? *How did the court know how much was too much to save a life? Is the toothpick comparison* *persuasive? Would $20 million per life have been too much to spend? $10 million? $5 million? Does the court tell us what standard it is using the judge EPA's rule?* These questions are all aimed at encouraging students to think about how the court arrived at its conclusion that EPA had required industry to spend too much to save a life. The bottom line is that the court does not provide a standard for determining how much is too much; its approach comes close to Justice Potter Stewart's famous "I know it when I see it" approach to judging obscenity cases. And the toothpick example, though clearly designed to trivialize the risks posed by asbestos by comparing one category of them to risks posed by the familiar toothpick, doesn't really answer the question of how to address serious risks posed by a toxic substance throughout all stages of its life cycle. It does, however, invite the reader to think about what we are trying to achieve when we regulate life-threatening risks - whether we are trying only to reduce premature mortality, or whether there are other values - preventing nonfatal illnesses, ecological injury, and so on -- at stake as well.

Page 682, C&Q #2. Apples and...apples? Oranges? *Is the court correct in requiring EPA to treat the avoidance of future cancers like an economic benefit that should be discounted to present value? When costs are expressed in dollars and benefits are expressed in human lives, as they were here, is the court correct that we are dealing with apples and apples? Or are we dealing with apples and oranges - goods that cannot be made commensurate through the technical device of discounting?* The excerpt following the questions argues that the court's "apples-to-apples" observation assumes that lives and dollars are commensurate with each other, when in fact this is a highly contentious issue in modern regulation. The questions are aimed at eliciting the idea that discounting, too - and not just monetization, or the direct translation of regulatory benefits into dollar terms - often assumes fungibility between regulatory benefits like life-saving and dollars.

Pages 682-683, C&Q #3. Does discounting miss the point? This note discusses one critical view of the technique of

Page 683, C&Q #6. The "least burdensome" alternative? *Do you agree that section 6 contemplates [the court's] approach?* Section 6 does not instruct EPA to begin with the least burdensome alternative, conduct a cost-benefit balancing for that, and then proceed this way until it identifies the best alternative. The only statutory basis for the court's ruling to this effect is the fact that section 6 roughly orders the regulatory alternatives from least to most stringent, but this seems a fairly slender reed on which to base the court's requirements.

What implications will such an approach have for EPA's ability to response to toxic threats under ToSCA? The court's decision creates significant new analytical hurdles for regulation under §6. The effect of these hurdles perhaps is illustrated by the fact, as observed in the next note (#7), that no other toxic substance has been banned under §6 since this case came down.

Page 683, C&Q #7. From asbestos to fish sinkers. This note is informational. EPA has now abandoned its proposal to regulate MTBE under ToSCA §6.

Page 683, C&Q #8. Is ToSCA just like NEPA? *Could you make an argument that this section, like NEPA, merely requires EPA to compile a document describing the costs, benefits, etc., of an action taken under §6 and to consider that document in coming to a decision, but does*

not require the benefits of the agency's action to be commensurate with the costs? If you read §6(c)'s language carefully, you will see that it requires only that EPA "consider and publish a statement with respect to" costs and benefits of regulating toxic chemicals. This is very similar to the language of NEPA, which of course has been interpreted not to require any particular substantive outcome.

What do you suppose the Fifth Circuit would have made of such an interpretation if EPA had offered it? It seems fair to assume that the Fifth Circuit would not have taken kindly to such an interpretation, given its generally hostile response to EPA's approach to regulating under ToSCA.

Page 684, C&Q #9. The sound of one hand clapping. *Without a monetary value for important regulatory benefits such as saving lives, how is EPA – and then the reviewing court – to decide whether an action is justified under §6?* The answer must be that EPA must exercise judgment in deciding whether a certain quantum of costs is worthwhile to spend in order to prevent a certain number of deaths, illnesses, and ecological harms. Without monetary values for important categories of benefits, there is no magic formula for making the regulatory decision. Moreover, even when such monetary values are available, the exceedingly wide range for such values (as reflected in the note on Sunstein's work on arsenic, p. 705 note #3) make judgment an inevitable part of the regulatory process.

Professor Amy Sinden has done an intriguing analysis of the cost-benefit arguments presented by Professor Cass Sunstein's books THE COST-BENEFIT STATE: THE FUTURE OF REGULATORY PROTECTION (ABA Section of Administrative Law and Regulatory Practice, 2002) and RISK AND REASON: SAFETY, LAW, AND THE ENVIRONMENT (Cambridge University Press, 2002). Among her conclusions:

> In these two books, Professor Sunstein promotes cost-benefit analysis (CBA) as the presumptively correct decisionmaking tool for virtually all environmental health and safety regulation. His claims are both normative and descriptive. By avoiding the usual welfare economics defense of CBA, his normative claim sets aside the external critiques of CBA (like the incommensurability problem), and offers instead a set of "pragmatic" justifications: 1) CBA will rationalize government decisionmaking and reduce the undue influence of interest groups that exploit "cognitive distortions" that cause ordinary people to inaccurately assess risks; 2) CBA will increase transparency by forcing regulators to evaluate and describe the full array of consequences flowing from proposed regulations. These justifications are ultimately unconvincing because Professor Sunstein fails to take seriously the central concern of the internal critiques of CBA - indeterminacy. Ironically, when he tests his theories in practice with a careful and cogent case study of EPA's CBA of arsenic in drinking water, he discovers indeterminacy of an astonishing magnitude. He concludes that reasonable people might peg the benefits of the arsenic rule as low as $13 million or as high as $3.4 billion. Though he remains staunchly committed to CBA, the indeterminacy of CBA fatally undermines both of his "pragmatic" justifications. Sinden, Cost-Benefit Lite: Economics for Liberals, Columbia Journal of Environmental Law, Forthcoming 2004.

Pages 684-686. These pages explain how formal cost-benefit analysis is performed.

Pages 686-687, C&Q #1. Estimating costs. *Which is the correct way to represent costs – on a national basis, on an industry-by-industry basis, as costs per life saved?* There is no one exactly correct way to represent costs. The important point here is that one's attitude toward a rule might depend a lot on how costs are described; a rule that seems quite inexpensive on a national basis might begin to seem excessively costly when described in a particular industry context. As the case from Judge Posner suggests, perhaps the relevant agency should be the one presumptively charged with making the judgment about how to represent costs.

Page 687, C&Q #2. Benefits transfer. This note is informational and self-explanatory.

Page 687, C&Q #3. Monetization and discounting. *Are these features [monetization and discounting] essential to cost-benefit analysis?* Formal cost-benefit analysis (the kind discussed in the materials in Part B.2) requires monetization and discounting almost by definition. Without monetization, there is little to distinguish formal cost-benefit analysis from any other decision-making algorithm which takes costs into account. As for discounting, many economists hold it as an article of faith that discounting must be applied to all costs and benefits that will occur in the future.

Pages 687-690. These pages provide an excerpt from a brief by eminent economists in the *American Trucking* case, making the case for using cost-benefit analysis to set environmental standards.

Page 690, C&Q #1. The result. This note is informational and self-explanatory.

Pages 690-691, C&Q #2. The economists' framework. *How does the economists' description of what they mean by cost-benefit analysis differ from any other decision-making framework that takes costs into account – including even that old command-and-control standby, technology-based regulation?* Monetization and discounting are not required by other decision-making frameworks, such as technology-based regulation. In addition, many other regulatory frameworks - including technology-based regulation - begin with an assumption that something will be done by way of regulation at the end of the day, it's just not clear exactly what. But cost-benefit analysis makes no such assumption; it is indifferent to whether regulation ultimately occurs.

How will quantified and unquantified values be combined in their framework to produce a decision? Here the problem from *Corrosion Proof Fittings* recurs: how can we make a decision when some values are quantified and some are not? Again, the answer must be that the agency must exercise its judgment in coming to a decision. But note that the economists do not tell us exactly how this will or should happen.

Page 691, C&Q #3. Statistical murder? This note is informational and self-explanatory.

Pages 691-700. These pages provide an excerpt from a law review article critiquing cost-benefit analysis.

Page 700, C&Q #1. Doomed, or just needs tinkering? *Are Ackerman and Heinzerling's objections to cost-benefit analysis fundamental, or would refinements to cost-benefit analysis as currently practiced satisfy their concerns?* Many of Ackerman and Heinzerling's concerns go to the fundamentals of cost-benefit analysis, and would not be satisfied by tinkering.

Note, however, that many other critics of cost-benefit analysis believe that its flaws can be overcome if only we were able to obtain "better numbers" - such as, for example, a value for statistical life that reflected the involuntary, unfair, and catastrophic nature of many environmental risks.

Page 700, C&Q #2. What's the alternative? *Do you agree [with Ackerman and Heinzerling's claim that technology-based controls, emissions trading, and disclosure requirements all can serve as alternatives to cost-benefit analysis]?* None of the alternatives cited here provides the kind of unifying framework that cost-benefit analysis provides, and so in that respect they are different from - and, in the view of some, inferior to - cost-benefit analysis as a decision-making paradigm. In addition, there are (as we see throughout the coursebook) plenty of critics of each of these alternative approaches. We think it cannot be denied, however, that there are alternatives to cost-benefit analysis; the question for the reader must be whether they are satisfactory or not.

Pages 700-704. These pages provide an introduction to the standard-setting provisions of the Safe Drinking Water Act, and also excerpts from EPA's preamble explaining its decision to strengthen the standards for arsenic in drinking water.

Pages 704-705, C&Q #1. What explains EPA's decision? The agency seems to be saying simply that stricter standards would have been more costly, without producing as large a reduction in risk, than the standard EPA chose. Likewise, less strict standards, while less costly, would not have produced the same reduction in risk. The astute reader should notice that this justification is almost exactly the same justification mocked by the D.C. Circuit in its decision striking down EPA's interpretation of the Clean Air Act on nondelegation grounds in the *American Trucking* case.

Does the SDWA, as applied to arsenic in drinking water, overcome [the problem of setting "stopping points" for standards]? Does EPA's cost-benefit analysis identify a logical stopping point for regulation, or does it still leave considerable room for discretion on the part of the agency? We think there is no discernible, logical stopping point identified by EPA. This is not to say EPA was wrong in its analysis; but it is to say that even using cost-benefit analysis, the kind of stopping point required by the D.C. Circuit in *American Trucking* remains elusive.

Can you [develop a justification for one of the alternative MCLs considered by EPA, using the same considerations EPA used in justifying its MCL]? Given the lack of determinate criteria, one could justify any number of different MCLs by citing the particular mix of costs and benefits achieved by a particular MCL.

Page 705, C&Q #2. Trumping quantified costs: reprise. *Is this a close case, precluding the trumping of quantified costs by unquantified benefits, as in Corrosion Proof Fittings?* This question is aimed at recalling the difficulty of identifying a "close case" when important benefits remain unquantified.

Page 705, C&Q #3. "The Arithmetic of Arsenic." *Do you agree [with Professor Sunstein that cost-benefit analysis is a useful tool despite the wide range of outcomes it could support]?* Sunstein argues that cost-benefit analysis remains a useful tool because it puts all costs and benefits "on screen," and thus provides everyone good information about the variables relevant to the decision at hand. One could argue, on the other hand, that to the extent cost-benefit analysis has been touted as a way of narrowing agency discretion, the wide ranges identified by Sunstein seem to undermine the case in favor of this analysis.

Page 705, C&Q #4. The value of life. *In light of [the contextual difference between workplace risks and the risks from arsenic in drinking water], was it sensible for EPA to base regulation of risks from arsenic in drinking water on such data?*

A simple answer is that EPA did the best it could, given its time and resource constraints. Data on the value of workplace risks are readily available, and within the community of cost-benefit analysts, not especially controversial. Data suggesting values for risks like those posed by arsenic in drinking water are more limited and more controversial, and EPA so far has resisted adjusting the value of statistical life to take into account contextual differences among risks.

Pages 705-706, C&Q #5. Willingness to pay...for what? This note is informational, a little judgmental, and self-explanatory.

Page 706, C&Q #6. Some arsenic with your bottled water? *What do these figures [on willingness to pay for bottled water and on the small household costs of the arsenic rule] suggest about consumer willingness to pay for regulation reducing arsenic in drinking water?* One might infer from the global market for bottled water that consumer s are willing to pay quite a lot for perceived reductions in health risks from drinking water contaminants. If EPA had looked at this market, rather than at the market for workplace risk, it may well have concluded that the quite small monthly amount households would be required to spend as a result of its standard was easily justified as a matter of "willingness to pay."

Page 706, C&Q #7. Bladder cancer and chronic bronchitis: are they the same thing? The textual note suggests that perhaps EPA was mistaken in thinking that monetary values for chronic bronchitis could easily be used to estimate the value of preventing nonfatal bladder cancer.

Pages 707-709. These pages discuss OMB/OIRA's role in reviewing agency rules (a matter briefly discussed in Chapter Seven as well), and provide excerpts from a memo to agency heads regarding OMB/OIRA oversight in the Bush II administration.

Pages 709-710, C&Q #1. OIRA's legal authority. *What gives OIRA the authority to take the actions it describes in this memo?* Several statutes give OIRA authority over various aspects of the regulatory process. Most important for present purposes, however, Executive Order 12866 (issued by President Clinton) directs OIRA to review major agency rules according to cost-benefit analysis.

Suppose a statute forbids cost-benefit balancing in standard-setting. May OIRA return a cost-blind rule to EPA on the ground that it reflects inadequate cost-benefit analysis, or that it conflicts with the President's "programs, policies, and priorities"? Executive Order 12866 provides that OIRA's actions taken pursuant to it must be consistent with existing law. In the case of statutes - like the Clean Air Act's NAAQS program - that do not allow consideration of costs, it would seem quite problematic for OIRA to return a rule to EPA on the ground that it did not satisfy cost-benefit analysis.

Suppose a statute requires technology-based regulation, as we have seen the CWA does. May OIRA require EPA's technology-based rules to be justified by cost-benefit analysis? Would this change the nature of technology-based regulation? In fact, OIRA has tinkered with a number of technology-based CWA rules on the basis of cost-benefit analysis, and the decision-making process produced thereby looks very different from the typical technology-based decision. For example, OIRA convinced EPA to weaken a rule regulating cooling water intake structures on the ground that the benefits were not worth the costs; standard technology-based analysis had pointed toward the stricter standard.

Page 710, C&Q #2. Prompting regulation. Informational and self-explanatory.

Page 710, C&Q #3. OIRA's new transparency...and its limits. This note is informational and self-explanatory.

Page 710, C&Q #4. OIRA's CBA a one-way street? The note suggests yes.

Pages 710-711, C&Q #5. Is life getting cheaper? The note tries to answer the question based on today's regulatory context.

Chapter 14.
MARKET-ENLISTING STATUTORY STRATEGIES: POLLUTION TRADING AND OTHER ECONOMIC INCENTIVES

Suggested time budget: **1 class session**

One day: Core and supporting page assignments for _one-day_ chapter coverage:
712-715 Introduction to economic incentives
716-718 Title IV CAA sulfur dioxide trading
719-727 Trading regimes and potential
727-736 Failed trading systems RECLAIM

2 days: Core and supporting page assignments for _two-day_ chapter coverage:
Day 1: 712-715 Introduction to economic incentives
716-718 Title IV CAA sulfur dioxide trading
719-727 Trading regimes and potential
Day 2: 727-736 Failed trading systems RECLAIM
736-742 Trading to improve water quality

Chapter contents:

—and check the Teachers' Manual Website for SUPPLEMENTARY MATERIALS:
http://www.bc.edu/schools/law/library/coursebook/envtlaw/teachers

The list of Supplementary Materials in Part III of this manual, and on the Teachers' Website, indicates materials posted on the Teachers' Website that are relevant to this and other chapters.

OVERALL TEACHING THEMES & COURSE DESIGN CONSIDERATIONS

The chapter addresses economic incentives as regulatory engines. Using markets to obtain environmental benefits in a least-cost (or lower-cost) way is, perhaps, the "hottest" topic of the late 20th Century for many academic theoreticians and figures prominently in contemporary policy debates. This chapter purports to review all "market-enlisting" regulatory mechanisms in the environmental field, but it focuses almost exclusively on trading devices. Other mechanisms such as effluent taxes, subsidies, and deposit and return programs are addressed only in general terms.

This Chapter can be taught without any study of the microeconomics materials that appear in Chapter 2 other than the recognition that in the absence of regulatory inhibition, disposing of unwanted by-products (pollution) into the unregulated commons is virtually always the least cost method of disposal. Beyond that, the economics side of "market enlistment" as studied here is simple to the point of being simplistic. Firms are assumed to act in their own economic self interest and will, therefore, seek a least cost solution to regulatory compliance. Within the contexts of emissions trading and effluent taxes, that means the behavior of firms can be predicted, and the basic instinct of each firm doing what is least expensive, will, in aggregate, produce a lower total social cost for an equivalent level of emissions reduction than would governmentally assigned pollution allocations (i.e., permits) that are either (1) source-unique as might be the case under the CAA stationary source regulation, (2) technology based as with categorical effluent limitation for point source dischargers under the CWA, or (3) roll back based (e.g., all sources make proportionate reductions, such as the originally proposed EPA FIP for sulfur dioxide in the Cleveland Electric Illuminating case.

This Chapter makes three principal points - (1) trading can be very effective at reducing total cost of achieving a chosen degree of pollution control, (2) the details in a trading system do matter, and (3) trading has critically important vulnerabilities that put at risk the environmental outcomes when the traded units are not truly fungible, particularly in relation to so called "toxic hot spots" that frequently are borne primarily by low income populations. Simultaneously, the Chapter attempts to leaven the unbridled praise for trading by making it clear that it is not as simple to implement well as its champions claim, meaning that overall transaction costs (as opposed to simply the costs of making a trade) are far higher than supposed, the behavioral assumptions are far too simplistic a view of entity behavior, and as noted above, the details do matter, whether it is limiting trading to truly fungible units, hot air credits, anyway credits, reliable evaluation and monitoring of emissions and credits, initial distribution, dislocation avoidance linked to limited ability to pay, and many more considerations.

TEACHING NOTES, COMMENTS, & ALL QUESTIONS ANSWERED

Pages 712-715. Introduction. There are several key points to stress in working with these materials. First, students must become comfortable with the behavioral premises that have rational maximizers reacting to market incentives in ways that minimize their private costs. See Table 14-1, page 713. Second, the students have to understand that in most environmental quality affecting situations, an unregulated commons does not create private incentives that result in favorable environmental outcomes. Further, that failure, due to the tragedy of the commons problem, often leads to a failure to maximize total social welfare. Third, the students must realize that governmental regulation, albeit of a different kind than they have seen before, is what produces the appropriate economic incentive structures. Fourth, by the end of the Chapter, students need to understand what precise steps government must take to craft the regulatory system that generates the economic incentives. Finally, even in teaching the general materials you should encourage students to think critically about the "market structure" in each of the settings studied to discern what modifications in the economic incentive regime would be required before the regime can be transferred to other settings successfully. Stating this last item differently - what works to create an effective trading regime in one setting, such as the sulfur dioxide trading program, may not be transferable to ozone reduction in Los Angeles without significant modification and auxiliary mechanisms that address issues such as downwind concentration areas (hot spots), reliable monitoring, etc.

This edition relegates to more limited coverage the Clean Air Act non-Title IV Clean Air Act emissions trading programs: offsets, banking, bubbles, and netting. They are canvassed in the Ellerman excerpt at pages 721-722 and treated rather harshly. This is an unfortunate editorial necessity because the programs were pioneering at the time and their study reveals a good deal about trading. The degree of trade-specific regulatory oversight made some of the devices seldom used, while others (particularly netting) that could be left largely to the firm, were and are tremendously important. For more information on those devices and a somewhat more favorable attitude toward their potential, see, Robert Hahn and Gordon Hester, Marketable Permits: Lessons for Theory and Practice, 16 Ecol. L. Q. 361, esp. 370-372 (1989).

A classroom hypothetical that illustrates both effluent taxes and trading:

Especially if you have the luxury of taking two days on this Chapter, it is possible to spend a bit more time contrasting effluent taxes and trading, even in the absence in additional readings to support that discussion. For example, a simple hypothetical that works well is to engage the class in designing a solution to the problem of over-rapid filling of the "local landfill" by instituting an effluent tax or a trading system. To set up the hypothetical, create assumptions that make developing additional capacity an expensive option for the community. Politically, if you cast some of the students as the City Council or Planning Commission, this has verisimilitude: buying land, doing the environmental impact studies that would be needed to obtain a permit, all are present expenditures that might require increased taxes and risk defeat at the polls. Extending the useful life of the landfill is a low cost (economically and politically) option. In this setting, an effluent tax is easy to impose, simply charge a fee per unit of garbage removal. Implementing a trash tax is easy enough, sell tags or bags without which garbage will not be collected. (Seattle reportedly weighs trash at curbside and bills residents accordingly.)

In this context you very quickly confront the problem of how high to set the fee, because that will determine how great a reduction in disposal rates will be obtained. This simple realization should begin to debunk the idea that market enlisting strategies do not have information costs comparable to those of other regulatory systems. First of all, describe the status quo, or have them explain what high level data they are likely to have about the problem. These are, of course, the amount of remaining volume left available in the landfill and the rate of current disposal (i.e., these are facts that very likely would be available to the regulator). So, if the remaining volume is X cubic yards, and the current rate is Y cubic yards per year (both facts that you can make up and come up with easy to see and believable figures), it becomes trivially easy to calculate the number of years left if behavior is unchanged. (X divided by Y) The regulator now must set the goal, in this case that entails deciding on a target life span for the present landfill, which is done by replacing Y with Y' a lesser annual rate of disposal. That is the aggregate desired behavioral result, less garbage per year, which is expressed by the new lower rate. Now things get harder: to achieve a particular result using effluent taxes the regulator needs to know the cost curves of disposers. In this case the information that bears on the question of what level of effluent tax will result in what reduction in disposal rate includes the willingness to recycle, buy products with less packaging, or purchase trash compactors. The comparison of rich and poor residential users as to both the amount of garbage they produce and their ability and willingness to reduce needs to be understood. In economic terms, this is a question about the cost curves of the citizens and the elasticity of those curves. It also begins to raise the question of a user class that is not homogeneous and whether there are equity concerns that must be addressed. (You can add commercial trash pick up to the mix, which is the case in some places, to make that lack of homogeneity point even more obvious, e.g., far larger volume but far greater cost bearing and cost spreading ability.) So now you have on the table the basic question of deciding on the amount of the effluent tax that will achieve the goal (reduction in the rate to Y') and the questions regarding differential rates and allocating the burden of the changes. These are non-trivial information demands that are regulatory transaction costs.

The hypothetical can be changed to a cap and trade program by limiting trash pick up to a fixed number of units per year, such as trash bags. This implicates the initial distribution of rights - should bags be given to households who can then trade them. Should all bags be auctioned? Both? This variant of the hypothetical usually leads to questions about the varied ability to pay of differently situated residents, a topic that ought to be part of the policy choices made by the regulator setting up the system, particularly if that issue was not ventilated in the effluent tax rate setting discussion. It is important to make it clear that every trading system has to address this issue in some fashion. For example, Title IV of the CAA created several different types of EPA allowance accounts, at least one of which was intended to allow for hedge purchasing by firms that could not risk excessively high market or spot auction prices. Presumably these were envisioned as firms with relatively high cost of avoidance by pollution control, small volume emissions, and limited ability to pay who could be frozen out of the market if large emitters chose not to reduce below their allowance levels (no credits for sale in the market) or, far less likely, if highly capitalized firms drove up the market price beyond these firms ability to pay. One extra note about the trash bag hypothetical, it implicitly allows inter-temporal trading unless you make the allowances period-specific, which would be highly unlikely in the ordinary garbage setting. Nevertheless, as a teaching matter, it is worth raising the issue even in this setting because it can be highly relevant in a trading system that affects human exposure to variable concentrations of harmful pollutants. Intertemporal trading can cause hot spots as can interlocational trading.

Page 714, C&Q #1. Avant-garde. This informational note provides a few references.

Page 714, C&Q #2. Fungibility. This note, although self-explanatory also contains the seeds of a discussion about how to overcome both uncertainty of measurement, lack of 1:1 fungibility. The middle paragraph of the excerpt also gives a very quick glimpse of the fact that trading, even if it works to lower cost of emissions reductions, is a potential environmental failure if there is not true fungibility, because lacking that "there would be no assurance that trading ensured environmental protection." This is followed by wetlands banking as the example, but you may want to foreshadow the distributional (hot spots) issue here as well as the quantitative and qualitative lack of 1:1 environmental values in the Salzman & Ruhl example.

Page 714, C&Q #3. Will firms act rationally? The note contents itself with pointing out that Malloy's research regarding the behavior of typical large firm behavior leads to regulatory information requirements that are often thought to be avoided by trading. The more fundamental question that the note is hoping the students will raise for themselves is the fact that it is somewhat Pollyanna to believe that all affected parties are rational maximizers or that there is not the likelihood of strategic behavior that may affect outcomes in unexpected ways (for example, the apparent "overinvestment" in reductions that drove down the price of allowances to far below the average cost of reduction under Title IV of the CAA throughout the 1990s, or the purchase of allowances to improve public relations rather than to emit pollution) . N.B., despite those examples, the "surprise" actions need not be environmentally benign.

Page 715, C&Q #4. One firm's reduction is another's continued pollution. This note underplays the philosophical debate that it suggests, "Why not require both low cost and higher cost reductions to improve environmental quality?" That same debate is present in harm-based ambient standards approaches as well, "Why settle for avoidance of harm when it is feasible to go beyond that common denominator and improve environmental quality to an even greater degree?" The answer remains the same in both contexts: it is a policy choice regarding the appropriate amount of scarce resources to be devoted to production of goods and services and the amount to be devoted to environmental quality.

Pages 716-718. EPA Title IV Acid Deposition Program. Sulfur dioxide trading under Title IV is considered to be one of the best, if not the best, example of a cap and trade program ever implemented. By most objective measures it is indeed a successful program. It was also a program destined for success. Footnote 5 on page 717 explains why this program was particularly likely to achieve its reductions and to do so at reasonable cost. C&Q #3 on page 724-725 continues that theme. The technology necessary to achieve the mandated overall reductions was available, economically achievable, and already widely in use. An additional factor in the program's success was railroad deregulation. With railroad deregulation, the cost of shipping low sulfur coal from Western mines to Eastern power plants was dramatically reduced. It is useful to draw the students' attention to the emissions rate of the Phase I and Phase II requirements and compare those rates to the rates that are achievable through the use of the technologies described in footnote 5. Much of the evaluation of Title IV is found in the Ellerman excerpt that follows, specifically at pages 722-724.

There are numerous details worth exploring with the students. A few of the less obvious ones may be worth pointing out in class. The principal traders in the marketplace are a small number of highly capitalized firms all of whom are identified and whose production and ignition characteristics are well known. This fact alone tends to reduce transaction costs and the homogeneity of the group makes it likely that prices will trade in a fairly narrow range whose upper bound is set by the control costs of a known technology. Inter-temporal trading is allowed. Some observers believe that trading was inhibited by the choice of some firms to "bank" their credits in order to allow themselves greater flexibility in the Phase II period. The penalty provision requires both a payment for excess emissions and the subsequent retirement of additional allowances. The retirement requirement ensures that the long-term cap is not exceeded. See C&Q #2, page 718.

Page 718, C&Q #1. Key steps in the acid deposition program. *What goes into establishing a trading system?* The comment lists five of the major steps that must be considered and addressed in creating a trading system: tradable allowances or similar units, a means to limit the number of units, an initial means of distributing units (e.g,. purchase, give-away, means by which actions earn them, etc.), how trades will take place and redistribute the allowances, and means to ensure compliance.

Page 718, C&Q #2. Making the reductions of emissions certain to occur. This note explains the "retirement" of excess emissions as requiring both payment of a penalty and purchase and non-use of an additional allowance in the subsequent year. At an analytical level, the program is relying on a degree of fungibility of the allowances over time. If an extra unit is emitted in Year 1, an extra unit of reduction is required in Year 2.

This note also explores the additional conditions necessary to making a cap and trade system work. The regulator must stay the course and cannot increase allowances. At times, economic and political pressure may make this very difficult. One example occurred in California during the energy crisis where the cost of NOx emission reduction credits contributed to the unprecedented price spike in electric costs. A second condition is an accurate measurement of emissions. While this is self-evidently a necessity, when the regulated parties are not highly capitalized firms, continuous emissions monitoring (CEM is an acronym that shows up often in these discussions) is a very substantial cost. It that cost is too high for smaller sources, the regulator must go to far less accurate methods of emissions estimation, thereby risking to a degree the certainty of results. One datum from the RECLAIM program, which relies on calculated emissions values despite the fact that the primary regulated entities are required to have CEM, is that the estimates that are the basis for regulatory compliance show "regulatory emissions" that are from ten to one thousand times less than actual measured emissions. See page 731. This is an outrageous state of affairs in the RECLAIM program, where the true data is available, but it ought to be a warning for all programs that rely on calculated values for any aspect of the program (i.e., either estimates of credits earned, or estimates of emissions). Finally, the need for enforcement mechanisms that is stressed by the note recalls the excerpt from Garrett Hardin in which those who voluntarily forego an the advantages of overusing the commons are thought of as foolish.

Page 718, C&Q #3. Knowing the goal. This note is simply a reminder that knowing the environmental outcome goal (the elimination of downwind harm from acid deposition does not eliminate the need for scientific reverse engineering. In this setting that includes estimates of what ambient levels of acidity in the Northeast will allow the ecology to regenerate and then translating that to a desired reduction in loadings of pollutants. Notice also that Title IV assumes total fungibility of emissions wherever they occur. It is useful to ask whether it is possible to design a system that does not assume total fungibility. Although that has not been tried in large-scale cap and trade programs, variable offsets ratios (greater ratio for some rather than others) are used as requirements in relation to the differing degrees of non-attainment in the post-1990 CAA.

Page 718, C&Q #4. Has Title IV attained its goal? The question is intended to make it clear that trading program "goals" have at least two expressions, one having to do with reductions alone, one having to do with the purposes for which reductions are sought. Well conceived trading programs will achieve the former, but not always the latter. The reason for the possible disjunction is that the reduction goals may not have been stringent enough to accomplish the environmental goals.

Pages 719-727, Emissions Trading Experience: This material is of quite recent vintage and touches on several subjects. At the very outset it differentiates types of trading programs, defining reduction credit and averaging programs in addition to cap and trade. Although reduction credit programs are not reviewed favorably by the authors of the excerpted material (Ellerman, et al), they are potentially important in water pollution trading systems where many of the potential trading participants are subject to existing plant-specific discharge limitations (point sources) or have discharges that are not easily or reliably measured (non-point sources). Although transaction costs increase in trading programs requiring certification, the cost differentials of pollution reduction frequently will justify the expense, as between WQBELs (better than best point source limitations) and inexpensive changes in plowing, leveling, buffering, etc. that are BMPs for non-point source agricultural operations. Averaging programs are typified by CAA bubbles and netting. An important point that emerges on page 719 is that typical cap and trade programs frequently integrate a reduction credit program, not only for pre-program voluntary reductions, but for post-programs purposes as well.

Page 724, C& Q #1. More trading programs, more economic efficiency. Despite calling them successful, the Ellermen, et al, excerpt is generally critical of reduction credit programs. The crux of this position derives from observing the small number of trades and the very plausible explanation that the transaction cost of certification of credits undercut the economic benefits to be obtained from the trading device. Two somewhat dated, but very telling articles collect the data and analyze and reinforce this point. See Robert Hahn and Gordon Hester, Where Did All the Markets Go? An Analysis of the EPA's Emissions Trading Program, 6 Yale J. on Reg. 109 (1989); Robert Hahn and Gordon Hester, Marketable Permits: Lessons for Theory and Practice, 16 Ecology L. Q. 361 (1989). A portion of that material was summarized as follows in two notes that appeared in the 2nd edition of this book:

> **What trades get made?** Hahn and Hester have been the most vigorous students of emissions trading under the Clean Air Act and they have collected considerable empirical evidence about the extent to which trades have taken place. They recount much of that material in Hahn & Hester, Where Did All the Markets Go? An Analysis of EPA's Emissions Trading Program, 6 Yale J. on Reg. 109, 114, 119-32 (1989). As the title suggests, trading has not flourished. Offsets, the only mandatory trading device, were used approximately 2,000 times nationwide in the ten-year period from 1977 to 1986. By 1986, only 42 bubbles had been approved, with a little more than twice that number pending or proposed. Netting has been far and away the most common type of trading, with a probable number of 8,000 instances in the decade from 1974 to 1984. Quite significantly, most of the bubbles, and by definition all netting, are internal to the firm. Likewise, many offsets were also internal rather than external trades among firms. Not surprisingly (given the low volume of interfirm trades), there was very little evidence of active banking. What explains the low level of interfirm trading? Is it the higher transaction cost of locating an external trading partner in comparison to making internal (intrafirm) changes? Is it the novelty of emissions trading? Is it the lack of true markets in which ERCs are freely bought and sold? Does the EPA requirement that trades involve only emission reductions that are surplus, enforceable, permanent, and quantifiable set too high a threshold for most trades to take place?
>
> **The extraordinary attraction of netting.** Netting is popular with firms for good reason. One major attraction of netting is its ability to allow firms to avoid the command and control technology-based standards for modified sources in both attainment and non-attainment areas. Firms realize additional savings by avoiding the costs and delays associated with the permitting process. A review of the quantitative data that attempts to calculate the magnitude of the cost savings of netting appears in Hahn & Hester, Where Did All the Markets Go? An Analysis of EPA's Emissions Trading Program, 6 Yale J. on Reg. 109, 114, 132-136 (1989). They conclude that the average savings on emissions control when a

technology-based standard (such as BACT or LAER) is avoided range from $100,000 to $1 million. The savings attributed to avoidance of the permit process is estimated to range from $5,000 to $25,000.

Page 725, C&Q #2. Cost savings. This note is self explanatory, but it contains a good lesson for students, try to relate aggregate outcomes to smaller scale outcomes using common sense and, perhaps, a calculator.

Page 725, C&Q #3. Very low hanging fruit. Make sure the students are aware of footnote 5 on page 717 in which the typical achievable rates are specified. As raised by the change in the transportation cost of low sulfur coal due to railroad deregulation is a prime example of an "anyway credit" (see, C&Q #5) and you might use this example to explore the likely effect of that in distorting (lowering) the price for credits and how that influences incentives to make changes that improve the environment beyond what would happen anyway. For another positive but concurrently cautionary voice on the rush to embrace market mechanisms see a book chapter by Robert Stavins titled "Experience with Market-Based Environmental Policy Instruments" that appears in The Handbook of Environmental Economics (Karl-Goran Maler and Jeffrey Vincent, eds. 2000). Stavins canvases the performance of a broad array of economic instruments that have been employed to obtain environmental improvement. The principal devices in use are, as would be expected, effluent charge systems and tradeable permit systems. He also reviews means of reducing market barriers to sound environmental practices and subsidies. His principal conclusion is that "market-based instruments for environmental protection now enjoy proven successes in reducing pollution at low cost." Stavins is cautious, however, inasmuch as he recognizes that most of the experience is with air emissions, particularly the trading programs for sulfur dioxide, leaded gasoline and chlorofluorocarbons. In his view, uncritically extending full reliance on market incentives to other air pollution problems such as the combustion of fossil fuels and global warming would, at this point, involve an "unwarranted...rush to judgment."

Page 725, C&Q #4 and 5 "hot air credits" and "anyway credits". The terms "hot air credits" and "anyway credits" are important ones because they appear frequently in discussions about the accomplishments of trading, or, more precisely, the lack of real accomplishment of trading. Hot air credits are at times an explanation for the divergence between what appears to be a functioning trading system and the lack of measurable improvement in environmental quality. One of the less often criticized aspects of the apparently failed Kyoto Protocol was the vast number of economically valuable but environmentally deceptive hot air credits awarded to the former Soviet Bloc nations that served as an inducement (ultimately unsuccessful as to the Russian Federation) to them to agree to its ratification. Anyway credits are real, but no less problematic. These credits make the trading regime appear to be deceptively successful. In Title IV, for example, the cost per BTU of western coal went down with railroad deregulation and some of the fuel switching would have happened anyway. The program appeared that much more successful in obtaining reductions than was really the case. Another far less often mentioned use of anyway credits is the Bush Global Climate Change Policy Book (GCCPB) which claims that the President's policy on GHG is achieving an 18% reduction in GHG intensity by 2012, but admits that 14% of that reduction is in anyway credits (presumably due to the effects of the Clean Air Act, although the GCCPB does not give any source for its figures on that subject). The document may be found at Bureau of National Affairs, Environment Reporter, February 22, 2002, at pages 429-442. It is also available on the White House website at http://www.whitehouse.gov/news/releases/2002/02/climatechange.html. The BNA source includes several graphic representations that are not available on the White House website.

Pages 725-726, C&Q #6. Accountability, measurement, and the cost of measurement. As mentioned in relation to C&Q #2 page 718, and demonstrated in the RECLAIM excerpt later, a failure to measure emissions can subvert the trading program by relying on calculations that are wildly inaccurate. This note, however, asks a more pragmatic question about what to do when the cost of monitoring is prohibitively expensive for sources that are contributing the regulated pollutants. It tries to suggest that this becomes a far greater concern if the sources that cannot be monitored are significant contributors to the overall loadings. A few suggestions are possible, but the concept is best understood with a hypothetical that is not too difficult for the students to grasp. For example assume that the region wants to engage in VOC trading and from the small alone, students should know that "wet" dry cleaners sites (facilities at which the cleaning is actually performed) are area sources for VOCs and might be part of a trading system, either by being required to hold allowances, or, more likely, as being sellers of credits if they reduce emissions. The cost of monitoring is almost certainly prohibitive. So, as regulators, ask them if it is sensible to make them part of the trading system and, if so, what can be done to make them part of the trading system in a workable manner? To decide whether they need to be in the system requires some data regarding how much they emit (in the real world uncontrolled wet dry cleaning operations are surprisingly large sources) and the relative cost of controls in comparison to major sources such as refineries. Provide an assumption for them at this point, that the cost of reduction for dry cleaners (hoods over the process area linked to a chiller and tank system that salvages solvent that can be reused) is lower per unit reduction than installing upgrades at major VOC emitting facilities that are already employing fairly sophisticated technology. This ensures that trades are a lower cost reduction strategy, but monitors of actual emissions from the dry cleaning building are costly (which they are) and would make it more expensive per unit reduction if the monitoring was required. What can be done? How can the reductions reliably be obtained without real monitoring? The objective then becomes to model and model conservatively. Try to get the students to offer pragmatic possibilities that prevent overstatement of reduction. Here, the maximum potential pollution is easy to calculate, you can assume that all solvent used is emitted. In the hypo, since there is solvent recovery, that is proof that in the post-installation of equipment period, the maximum emissions can be accurately calculated. What becomes critical, in terms of calculating reduction, therefore, is what was the pre-installation baseline use of solvent. Again, in this simple hypothetical, that is a simple item to quantify. One method is to require proof of past quantities of solvent purchased rather than relying on a calculation based on the design capacity of the equipment. Alternatively, and perhaps more resistant to deception, use baselines based on reported sales for tax purposes because the reporting incentive there is to understate amounts. (The reporting incentive is opposite for solvent because it is a deductible item for tax purposes.) A useful point here is that making assumptions about what historic emissions were, that are calculated, from equipment design are very likely to introduce hot air credits if usage of the equipment was less than maximal, or less than the regulatory assumption used in the model.

Page 726, C&Q #7. Initial allocation. Almost all large emissions trading systems to date have relied on distribution of initial allocations to existing users, with auctions as only a small safety valve. No initial distributions have been made to non-polluters, such as citizens groups in downwind areas. Most initial distributions have been proportioned to historic emissions in the baseline setting period. The superficial logic of this is reasonable: even with the largest allocations, the largest polluters will still have the greatest amount of needed reduction or allowance buying to do. It is possible to ask why citizens get no allocations as a means of pointing out the extent to which trading systems include the inherent premise that some degree of pollution is allowable (obvious) and that there need be no payment for that privilege of using the commons for disposal (less obvious). Initial allocations at times address more subtle equity issues, especially that of improvements made before the start of the program. Particularly where the distribution is proportioned to baseline emission, as company that cleaned up and installed pollution control equipment before the baseline period is penalized for having been more proactive than other firms. Likewise, no initial allocations are made to or reserved for new entrants, thereby giving exiting plants and firms a competitive advantage and creating a barrier to entry. The regulated community is plainly concerned about this in relation to GHG trading and Congress has responded by requiring the Department of Energy to create and maintain a "Voluntary Greenhouse Gas Reduction Inventory. Presumably, firms will get credit for reductions made in advance of a mandatory GHG reduction program, whatever form it takes.

Page 726, C&Q #8. Emissions trading and the NAAQS. This note explains the independence of ambient standards requirements and allowance holding overall emission reduction requirements. When there is the potential for harm due to the high concentrations of pollution (which is universally the case), a trading system does not ensure the avoidance of harm due to excessive concentrations of pollution. When overly high concentrations result from trading, they usually are referred to a hot spots. Importantly, any efforts to adjust the trading system to account for excessive concentrations works at cross purposes with the effort to obtain trades in a least cost manner. Some sort of trading restrictions must be applied that, without regard to what they are, necessarily add transaction costs. As a general rule, the greater the hot spots problem, the greater the needed trading restrictions, the greater the transaction costs, the less active and efficient the trading market.

Page 727, C&Q #9. Can downwind states add requirements that burden the trading system? As this Teacher's Manual has pointed out, trading programs are touted as not imposing high transaction costs. Plainly, that is an overstated boast in some regards. As the literature amply demonstrate, certified credit systems are expensive to operate, emissions monitoring is expensive, relying on reduction calculations on a plant-by-plant basis instead of monitoring injects many of the same regulatory costs as permit writing, reverse engineering from environmental outcomes to allowable loadings (the cap in cap and trade) injects much of the same science as ambient standard setting, accurately achieving that desired reduction by an effluent tax requires even more plant-specific cost of reduction data than any of the command and control alternatives, and so on. The point is simply that the administrative savings are possible, but are not always as large or as certain as non- command and control advocates assume.

Page 727, C&Q #10. Cheaper, better, faster. This question is meant to challenge the reader to review the materials and conclude that scientific and technical information costs are, at times, just as high for trading systems and other market-enlisting mechanisms as for command and control alternatives. Two examples make this clear. With trading, the linkage between aggregate reductions and environmental outcomes is very difficult to predict, and every effort to deal with hot spots avoidance requires a fall back program that is superimposed on the trading system. It should not require a great deal of imagination to see, for example, why the mercury trading that is proposed by the Bush Administration, if it is to protect public health from mercury, a PBAT, cannot be operated without anti-hot spots additions (although that is precisely what is proposed). See generally, text at 741, C&Q #11 and the far more extended TM entry on that material. With effluent taxes, to set the tax at the proper level to achieve the "desired" degree of reduction in effluents emitted, the regulator must know the cost curves of all major affected sources, a more daunting requirement than prescribing BAT.

Pages 727-736, The South Coast Air Quality Management District (SCAQMD). The excerpt is very one-sided in its tenor, characterizations of motivation, and conclusions. Nevertheless, to the extent that its factual claims are substantiated by the data that is reported, this excerpt is not only a stinging indictment of the SCAQMD trading programs. It is a powerful cautionary tale for all who would employ trading with anything less than great care and circumspection. Taking all the data at face value, this is a trading system in which the units are not fungible, in which there is active fraud being used to create hot air credits, in which models of pollution are being used to create hot air credits, in which anyway credits are sometime double counted, in which hot spots of increasing pollutant concentrations are actively being created, and in which the substitution of modeling for measurement has obscured the fact that emissions are orders of magnitude larger than claimed. Indeed, this program is so bad, according to this description, that this trading system is a perverse form of symbolic assurance - things are getting worse not better but the general public is enticed to believe in the apparent efficacy of the program as measured by its models and trading records. For those interested in the nuts and bolts of this system, a visit to the SCAQMD web pages and a romp through the rules is worth the effort. Since the volume went to press, the URL mentioned in footnote 10 on page 728, seems to have been changed. http://www.aqmd.gov/rulesindex.htm is an updated link.

Page 732, C&Q #1. The moral trouble with trading. The note suggests that calling allowances or emissions credits is no more a right to pollute than a permit under another statute. Certainly, one can hardly feel any better about the toxic pollution allowed in RECLAIM's system than the million pounds of toxics that are protected from CWA regulation by Eastman Kodak's SPDES permit shield in the Atlantic States Legal case. Even so, the tradable credits put the matter into higher relief - firms are actually allowed to profit by selling reduction credits earned by reducing their previous action of obtaining private benefits (cost free waste removal) by emitting deleterious substances into the commons to the detriment of the general public. The note also reiterates a claim of the excerpt, that in the RECLAIM case the trading system has an obvious environmental justice aspect that lurks just below the veneer of trading systems, many of which are likely to concentrate emissions in heavily industrialized areas, low income areas. The final question, that of a transfer payment to the burdened community, is an invitation to a lively class discussion about the politics of pollution control strategies and the social engineering that those decisions impose.

Page 732, C&Q #2. The practical trouble with trading. This note raises a small host of complex topics and identifies their existence, but does little to address them. By now the students should be able to identify a series of different fungibility issues that must be addressed. Also, they can review the set up questions that accompanied the earlier selections, the translation of an environmental goal into an emissions cap, the steps needed to avoid hot air and anyway credits, or at least the steps needed to account for them in setting the cap so that the underperformance of the system in relation to actual reductions does not undermine the goals. The note also raises new issues, some quite daunting, such as co-pollutants. It is very useful to remind the students here of Atlantic States Legal v. Eastman Kodak and the regulatory limitations that result in the permit addressing at most half of the toxic pollutants in Kodak's discharge. Trading, at least in regard to VOC's (where the traded pollutants may be indicators of the presence of other pollutants that are not reduced by the trade) entails environmental degradation risks. In that regard, trades occur that are not 1:1 environmentally, because the reduction of a VOC that is not an indicator of other pollutants that allows the greater than otherwise emission of an indicator pollutant almost certainly is increasing the emission of the indicated co-pollutants. Especially when as in RECLAIM, the co-pollutants are additional hazardous air pollutants, it is a potentially fatal trade. Similarly, as the NOx-SOx trading example points out, what is otherwise an equal trade may add formaldehyde precursors or additional particulates to the equation. When are the cost savings of trading worth the increase in toxic risk? The answer is not necessarily never, but as in the H.M.S. Pinafore, it should probably be, "Hardly ever."

As if this note did not cover enough ground already, it adds a discussion of credit modeling. The bottom line here is that credit modeling is a necessity in two different settings, where accurate physical measurement is impossible (e.g, calculating the precise GHG sequestration effect of reforestation or in trying to predict the driving future of an old, high-emissions vehicle at the time of its destruction) or when the cost of measurement renders a feasible trade uneconomic (e.g., auto scrapping, the earlier dry cleaning hypo). The problem is difficult to solve, but the prudent policy is easy to identify: make very conservative assumptions and consider using substantially greater than 1:1 retirement ratios.

Page 733, C&Q #3. Hot spots. Hot spots are not unique to toxics trading regimes. Trading of the criteria pollutants, however, is not a hot spots threat because the states remain subject to the NAAQS, even if a trading program is an approved part of their SIP. While it is clear that Title IV's SOx trading has reduced SOx emissions as anticipated, note 4 on page 718 is equivocal as to whether acid deposition has been sufficiently reduced and it is evident that the downwind states are afraid that upwind allocation purchases are antithetical to the overall purpose of environmental restoration of their region.

Hot spots for toxic pollutants created by trading schemes seem to present unacceptable risks, and to do so in a fashion that provokes outrage, especially of the risk bearers who would be far better off without trading. Thus, it is counter-intuitive that RECLAIM has not been pressured into abandoning its VOC trading program. It is even more counter-intuitive that RECLAIM's shortcomings in this regard are not much more widely publicized. Is the trading system and the positive attention it gets for cost savings overshadowing these issues? Is this an instance of wildly misplaced symbolic assurance? That is a possible explanation that is supported by the materials in the Chapter, but that remains only a hypothesis. A similar lack of outcry has accompanied the Bush Administrations recent announcement of a mercury air trading rule. See discussion of note 11, page 741, infra.

The Nash and Revesz excerpt in this note and the Akers article mentioned as a counterpoint both acknowledge the problem of hotspots and offer distinct solutions. Nash and Revesz would model their way out of the problem by inhibiting trades that the model rejects. If you game the responses to that sort of modeling, one interesting aspect is the race to concentrate emissions via trading while allowable increases in more polluted downwind areas are available. The threat of future rejection of cost saving trades affecting those areas virtually ensure that trades up to the model's limit will occur and occur quickly. That may mean that after an early burst of trades, the system will have little remaining benefit. Moreover, the faith in airshed modeling, as the protector against toxic hot spots seems a very questionable strategy. Recall the SOx model's predictive accuracy in Cleveland Electric Illuminating. Operating with large facilities and much more well known emissions characteristics than, for example VOCs. Nash and Revesz do not appear to have considered co-pollutant and other negative synergies. The Akers concept suffers from immense difficulty in modeling and comparing health impacts of trades.

Hot spots are a common, but not invariable problem. In Allowance Trading and SO_2 Hot Spots - Good News From the Acid Rain Program, 31 BNA Env. Rptr. 954 (2000), Byron Swift of the Environmental Law Institute studied the first four years (1995-1999) of the acid rain trading program to determine whether the program resulted in hot spots. He concluded that it did not. In fact, to the contrary, the program has led most large emitters to clean up, thereby reducing localized loadings. His study found most trades (80%) were intrastate and thus "local" and only 3% of trades were "interregional." He concludes that trading and regulation more generally have less impact on hot spots than the simple matters of plant location, size, and utilization.

Page 734, C&Q #4. The consequences of the growing prices of ERCs. This question suggests its own answer, prices of goods produced by affected firms rise as the cost of the pollution control or the purchase of credits is passed on as part of the cost of goods sold. If there are regulated entities that do not have the cost bearing or cost spreading ability, the regulatory system can have protected markets (separate allowance pools, a small percentage of which are retained by the regulator in the initial distribution) for the purchase of credits by members of those sectors. This is a somewhat more complicated matter in a declining cap environment, but not impossible to accomplish.

Pages 734-735, C&Q #5. A favorable view of RECLAIM and its emergency suspension in 2000. The first half of this note has more to do with GHG trading than it does with RECLAIM, and that part is self-explanatory yet important: trading's potential adverse health effects simply are not relevant to a GHG cap and trade system. The sink is big enough and the time frame long enough and dispersion complete enough that a hotter atmosphere may be the whole issue, but hotspots are not a part of the problem (pardon the pun).

The second half of this note is very important for understanding the economic risks associated with trading systems. Most emissions control trading systems operate in a marketplace of long term planning for the choices between credit purchase and investment in pollution control equipment. That is the nature of the paradigm - bog plant making major capital investments and planning for their choices well ahead of time, not placing huge fluctuations in demand for credits. In California, the energy crisis precipitated huge spikes in the demand for credits when the moth-balled old, largely uncontrolled gas fired generators were brought back on line to meet electric demand at unheard of price levels. There were literally not enough vintage 2000 NOx credits to go around, and the soared to as much as thirty times more than the historic trading range. A cap and trade system in which the credit supply is inelastic, such as RECLAIM's in which there can be no inter-temporal trading or banking to prevent hotspots, is almost certain to reach crisis in the face of massive short-term increases in demand. Politically, it was impossible to allow the NOx trading program to prevent reactivation of the gas generators, but in terms of public health, it meant that trading was less protective than would a command and control system under which the old gas generators would have been retrofitted with pollution control equipment or decommissioned entirely long before the crisis came up. There is a sense in which the "bail under pressure" result, allowing exceedance of the cap, even at a high price (five times more than the normal trading range price) should be counted against all of the savings claimed as benefits of the trading regime. After all, if credits rose to $90,000 per unit and some would-be-emitters holding allowances had chosen to stop production and sell, the price of those credits (as a shadow measure of the economic dislocations that would have occurred when the emitter with allowances sold them and ceased production) is part of the economic cost of the trading system. Despite Ellerman's generally benign view of the events, that a 20% spike in demand could "crash the system" is hardly reassuring, particularly to the persons whose health was sacrificed to the higher levels of emissions.

Pages 735-736, C&Q #6. Conclusions? It should be obvious from the materials up to this point, that trading is neither all good, or all bad. Rather, trading systems are better and worse crafted and various types of pollution control settings are better or worse suited to trading as a regulatory strategy. Despite being an obvious conclusion, the political and even the academic debate over trading seems too frequently to be ideologically driven.

Pages 736-742, Water Quality Trading. The title of this section is misleading because its notes canvas a number of trading regimes that are not typical water pollution scenarios. This was a consequence of having a fairly strict page limit for the Chapter and the desire to have the Chapter teachable in a single day. For most, however, this is a wise decision, because the material here is in many ways repetitive of what is found elsewhere. There remain a few provocative topics, such as the final note in the Chapter, allowing mercury trading for air emissions, that was announced by the Bush EPA as the book was going to press in early 2003. What the notes explore is the potential variety and, at times, specificity of trading programs.

Turning to the excerpt itself, the very first point to be made is that it is supplementary (not substitutionary) to the operation of TBELs under the CWA. Stated differently, trading is a way to assist in upgrading water quality limited stream stretches, and thus is one way in the WQBELs can avoid requiring "better-than-best" performance levels from point source dischargers. It is also helpful to recall that trading is, to a degree, antithetical to the zero discharge goal of the CWA. Trading is, to a degree, an admission that the goal is not going to be met by many dischargers.

The preambulary language of the first paragraph of the excerpt is a bit misleading in that it gets carried away with itself. In water quality impaired stream stretches, point-source, non-point-source trading can reduce overall loadings. Note here that the principal supported trades are in relation to sediment and nutrients, which are excellent candidates for relatively inexpensive non-point source reductions. That is the principal impetus to the program. To add references to hypoxia in the Gulf of Mexico, and sediments in the Chesapeake Bay, however, is gilding the lily - those are not problems that will be more than minimally improved, far less solved by just adding a little trading to the mix. Water trading is not very much like massive GHG and SOx air emissions trading systems, it tends to be smaller in scale and scope (intra-watershed, even intra-TMDL area, see page 737 "Trading Areas"), trades are mostly unique and individually bargained. This is especially true in relation to trades other than sediments and nutrients, which the policy approaches more conservatively, indicating EPA approval will be on a case-by-case review of the proposed trading program. Don't go in expecting miracles from water trading.

Page 737, C&Q #1. Trading as a supplement to regulation. This note emphasizes the point that the EPA water trading rule operates in a highly regulated environment, where TMDLs are already set and WLAs created, so that TBELs are already implemented in all relevant NPDES permits and trading is going to be used to further reduce loadings to the receiving body. The implementing mechanism for this is the baseline calculation described in the last paragraph of the excerpt, which operates by setting up a cap and trade that reduces discharges below the TMDL implementing WLA.

Page 738, C&Q #2. Common elements of credible trading programs. This note tries to review trading systems generally and get the students thinking about what is special in the water context. The most salient difference is that flow regime is a complicating variable, a point already recognized in TMDLs that are set with reference to seasons and streamflow. What goes unexplored in the note, is the question of how trading (or the TMDLs themselves) should deal with greater than normal variations from the average flow. Much water planning is done with reference to the 7Q10 flow regime, meaning that which can reliably be expected in 7 out of every 10 years. So, for example, if trading and WLAs are set with reference to the 7Q10 flow, loadings in drought periods increase concentrations beyond water quality limits. Suspending trading in those low flow years makes no sense, as that would destroy the incentives to reductions being maintained for the low cost pollution avoiders (the non-point sources not otherwise required to make the effort) to help keep the stream clean. The point sources, in most instances, in most cases cannot ramp up their pollution control efforts instantaneously in response to drought, so exceedances of the TMDL are as predictable (statistically speaking) as drought. Drought does not reliably reduce non-point source pollution, although it tends in that direction because of reduced runoff, extreme drought can damage streamside vegetation and increase erosion by wind and water if there are sudden flows moving over dry, under-vegetated ground. To put a gloss on this, there are no easy answers to the problem, but trading is not its cause.

Page 738, C&Q #3. Quantifying and trading non-point source loadings and reductions. As suggested at several places earlier in the Chapter, one means of making conservative estimates to account for imprecise (or no) real time measurements of emissions or credits is trading ratios of greater than 1:1. Most of the other tactics mentioned are variations on the basic theme of greater than 1:1 ratios and conservative modeling assumptions. One idea is somewhat more interesting, that of a "reserve pool of credits to compensate for unanticipated shortfalls in the number of credits actually generated." EPA does not explain how this would work. One possible method is to use small expenditures to purchase fallowing and planting of groundcover in sensitive areas and assign those credits to the reserve pool. Another way is an in-kind trading tax, where a small percentage of each traded credit is allocated to the reserve pool rather than being credited to the purchaser. Those credits are not available for trading unless there is a shortfall in credits generated. The reserve pool could be treated like a bank – those needing credits can borrow them, but must pay back the bank in credits in some future year. In the event that reserve pool credits are not used, the result is not bad, the water is just a little bit cleaner and the system is just a little bit more expensive than would otherwise have been the case.

Page 738-739, C&Q #4. Estimates of the comparative efficiency of trading. This note is self explanatory, but the numbers related to cost help put things in perspective.

Page 739, C&Q #5. Trading in water effluents is different from trading in air emissions. This note highlights a few more of the difficulties posed by trading when units are not truly fungible. In this case, the units are not fungible because of additional variables such as temperature and the presence of negative synergies that decrease assimilative capacity in response to variables that are not accounted for by trades. The potential toxic consequences of trading bioaccumulative toxic pollutants in aquatic ecosystems should raise red flags at the outset. This is especially true for persistent bioaccumulative pollutants (PBTs), such as mercury (see note 11, infra). The scenarios that make sense for such trading are limited. The ones that first come to mind are ones in which there is little likelihood that the overall loadings of those pollutants is going to be reduced without the trades. If controls on point sources are economically within reach, it seems clear that they should already be in place as BAT required by the CWA as TBELs. That means the trades will, in the main, be from non-point sources that are not otherwise required to reduce their emissions of PBTs to point sources that cannot feasibly reduce more.

Page 739, C&Q #6. Colorado's Lake Dillon trading program. This note is textual and highlights the limited scope of the Lake Dillon program, one of the more highly acclaimed water trading regimes. It mentions the Oregon example, where much-publicized legislation has not subsequently been translated into a viable program.

Page 739-740, C&Q #7. Trading selenium in irrigation runoff. The Grasslands Drainage Area example is simultaneously a monument to the ingenious use of trading and to its limitations in practice. Selenium in irrigation tailwater in a geographically restricted area is sufficiently fungible to be the subject of trading, but the models of its discharges and reduction credits are problematic, and the overall volume and price of units traded are miniscule. In a sense, the system is too small to provide benefits that could not be achieved almost as easily with an effluent tax that funds projects in a "selenium reduction district."

Page 740-741, C&Q #8. The TMDLs are coming. The *Pronsolino (Garcia River)* case was affirmed on appeal. *Pronsolino v. Nastri*, 291 F.3d 1123 (9rh Cir. 2002). The Court of Appeals held that Clean Water Act (CWA) authorized EPA to determine TMDL for river polluted only by logging runoff and other nonpoint sources of pollution after state failed timely to establish TMDL for river. With LAs specified, trading will be an option, particularly if the different non-point sources (for example, timbering and irrigated agriculture) have different cost curves for sediment or nutrient reduction.

Page 741, C&Q #9. Fisheries: individual take quotas (ITQs). The note is primarily descriptive on another form of trading, take quotas in a common fishery that are designed to prevent overfishing. This harkens back to Garrett Hardin and ways to protect the commons from overuse: divide the maximum sustainable load into tradable shares and then limit use in accordance with share holdings. The system is very unpopular, both because of the dislocations and because of the extreme difficulty of policing fishing by fishers from nations that are not part of the system, a point picked up in a slightly different context by the next note.

Page 741, C&Q #10. Trading goes international: Kyoto and more. This note is purely informational and has been included to demonstrate the structural and institutional assumptions embedded in a domestic trading regime that cannot be taken for granted in an international scheme. For more details on GHG trading under the United Nations Framework Climate Change Convention (UNFCCC), and the Kyoto Protocol that emerged from the UNFCCC, see Chapter 26.

Page 741-742, C&Q #11. Is mercury a good candidate for air trading? This note is an inadequate segue to an exploration of the most recent (as of the time the book went to press) controversial Bush Administration policy in relation to the Clean Air Act. See, Rule To Reduce Interstate Transport of Fine Particulate Matter and Ozone (Interstate Air Quality Rule), 68 FR4566-01 (January 30, 2004) and Proposed National Emission Standards for Hazardous Air Pollutants; and, in the Alternative, Proposed Standards of Performance for New and Existing Stationary Sources: Electric Utility Steam Generating Units, 68 FR 4652 (January 30, 2004). Together these proposed rules seek to engage in multi-pollutant trading that includes trading in air emission of mercury by electric steam generating units. The two proposed rules and their supporting materials are over 1,000 Westlaw pages in length (being honest, not all of which have been read by this author yet). The legal basis for proposing trading out of the CAA §112 MACT standard for mercury offered by EPA begins with the language of §112(n)(1)(A) that requires the Administrator to perform a study of "the hazards to public health reasonably anticipated to occur as a result of emissions by steam generating units of pollutants listed under subsection (b) [which includes mercury] after imposition of the requirements of this Chapter." Thereupon, EPA shall report to Congress those results, matters concerning alternative control strategies and then, "the Administrator shall regulate electric utility steam generating units under this section, if the Administrator finds such regulation is appropriate and necessary after considering the results of the study...." In essence, the proposed rules find that alternative control strategies render universal MACT for electric steam generating units not appropriate and necessary in light of the degree of reductions of emissions that can be obtained by a cap and trade system that is proposed in conjunction with and as part of the multi-pollutant trading system for SOx and NOx and mercury that is envisioned by the larger proposal.

Needless to say, this is controversial because it represents a removal of mercury, aPBAT from MACT regulation and allows, over time, far greater releases of this known toxic chemical into the environment. EPA explains its long term goals in these terms:

> **Mercury budget overview.** Our primary goal in this rulemaking is to reduce power plant emissions of Hg by 70 percent from today's levels by 2018. We are proposing to accomplish this goal by setting a 15 ton cap on these emissions in 2018. Under our proposal, the 2018 cap would be a permanent cap that could not be exceeded, regardless of future growth in the energy sector. Thus, the cap would effectively become more stringent as more and more plants are required to keep their collective emissions below 15 tons. We also are proposing to set a near-term cap in 2010 at a level that reflects the maximum reduction in Hg emissions that could be achieved through the installation of FGD [flue gas desulfurization] and SCR [selective catalytic reduction] units that will be necessary to meet the 2010 caps for SO sub2 and NO subX in our [concurrently] proposed IAQR [Interstate Air Quality Rule]. Although we know that FGD and SCR units reduce Hg emissions (as well as SO sub2 and NO subX), there is significant uncertainty about the extent of the Hg reductions that these controls could achieve by 2010. Thus, we are seeking technical information that would allow us to establish an appropriate Hg cap in 2010.
>
> The EPA believes that a carefully designed "multi-pollutant" approach--a program designed to control NO subX , SO sub2 , and Hg at the same time-- is the most effective way to reduce emissions from the power sector. One key feature of this approach is the interrelationship of the timing and cap levels for SO sub2 , NO subX , and Hg. Today, we know that power plants can reduce their emissions of all three pollutants by installing FGD (which controls SO sub2 and Hg emissions) and SCR (which controls NO subX and Hg). With respect to the first phase of Hg reductions, we have designed this proposal to take advantage of the combined emission reductions that these technologies provide. Therefore, we believe that the Phase I Hg cap should be set at a level that reflects the Hg reductions that would be achieved from the SO sub2 and NO subX cap levels and corresponding control requirements in the IAQR that we also are proposing today.
>
> A phase-one cap based on this approach would set a standard of performance based on the best system of emissions reduction that has been adequately demonstrated, consistent with section 111(d) of the Clean Air Act. Research currently indicates that Hg control technologies other than FGD and SCR--most notably activated carbon injection (ACI) and breakthrough technologies (e.g., chemical systems to enhance removal efficiencies for wet scrubbers)--may one day allow facilities to reliably reduce Hg emissions to levels significantly below the levels achieved through application of FGD and SCR needed to satisfy SO sub2 and NO subX control requirements. However, these technologies have not been adequately demonstrated on full-scale power plants. Moreover, current information on these technologies is not sufficient for us to conclude that they

> will be adequately demonstrated by 2010. Therefore, we believe that the 2010 cap for Hg should be set at a level that can be achieved through the installation of FGD and SCR needed to meet the 2010 SO sub2 and NO subX caps in the proposed IAQR. Requiring additional FGD and SCR beyond those needed to meet the transport rule in order to further reduce Hg emissions by 2010 is not reasonable because the incremental cost of such a requirement for additional Hg reductions would be extremely high and the capacity of the equipment suppliers may be overwhelmed. 68 FR at 4698.

At least one very interesting criticism has been leveled at the Proposed Rules by Professor Catherine O'Neill in a letter dated March 4, 2004 that accompanied mailings of her new article entitled, "Risk Avoidance, Cultural Discrimination, and Environmental Justice for Indigenous Peoples," 30 ECOL. L. Q. 1 (2003). She writes:

> ...The Environmental Protection Agency (EPA) recently issued a proposed rule that favors a cap-and-trade approach to address mercury emissions from coal-fired power plants that would ultimately result in a 70% reduction of emissions by 2018. The EPA offered the proposed approach in lieu of the expected maximum achievable control technology (MACT) standard under the Clean Air Act, which would have resulted in a 90% reduction in mercury emissions by 2007. In a telling juxtaposition, details of the EPA's proposed approach were made public just days after the Food and Drug Administration (FDA) announced the need to expand national fish consumption advisories due to mercury contamination. Thus, while the current administration's EPA proposes to tolerate more mercury contamination for a longer period, its FDA is left to shift the responsibility to risk-bearers to avoid the resulting health risks by altering their fish consumption practices and lifeways. This shift from a regulatory approach that is designed to achieve risk reduction to one that relies upon what I term *risk avoidance* is an example of what may indeed be a larger trend. (See also, Catherine A. O'Neill, Mercury, Risk and Justice, 2004 Environmental Perspectives, Issue 1 at 21.

The comparison, 70% reduction in mercury emissions by 2018 versus 90% reduction by 2007, seems to be a poor public health choice. Moreover, as Prof. O'Neill carefully documents, the greatest risk-bearing segment of the population in this case will be minority groups, especially indigenous peoples and racial minorities for whom fish is a larger component of the diet. The tradeoff, despite some concern about the lack of proven full scale operational performance of the better performing activated carbon injection technology, appears to be a concern about expense, some in reduced profits to the coal and electric industries, some in reduced electric bills for all consumers. EPA, in defending its approach, extols the advantage of a hard 15-ton cap on mercury emissions, which will be met in 2018 and all subsequent years. The proposal specifically points out that MACT, because it affects only emissions rates, allows growth of emissions beyond 15 tons per year to occur as a result of the building of additional emitting MACT-controlled facilities. This is at first blush an appealing and logical argument, but it is utterly lacking in practical terms. A rather simple comparison demonstrates how unlikely it is that gross emissions of mercury under MACT will exceed 15 tons per year. If a 70% reduction in emissions results in 15 tons of emissions, a 90% reduction results in only 5 tons of emissions. Thus, coal fired steam electric generation could triple before the 15 ton level of mercury emissions is reached. Even Vice President Cheney's "coal-first" energy policy only calls for a doubling of generation from coal fired plants and that over a far longer time horizon. Moreover, in the meantime, while MACT would bring current emissions down from the current level of approximately 50 tons per year to 5 tons per year by 2007, the Bush plan only calls for reductions to 25 tons per year by 2010, and then from there to 15 tons per year over the next 8 years. To do a rough calculation, assume less than linear reductions until 2007 is completed for MACT, and an implausibly high rate of growth for coal-generated electricity by 2018, doubling in a decade (never mind the carbon dioxide global warming effects); assume charitably (not legally required) for the Bush plan, linear reductions to 2008 levels for trading and thereafter linear reductions to 2018 levels. The following table compares the loadings:

Year	MACT (in tons)	Bush trading (in tons)
2004	50	50
2005	40	44
2006	30	37.5
2007	20	31
2008	5	25
2009	5.5	24
2010	6	23
2011	6.5	22
2012	7	21
2013	7.5	20
2014	8	19
2015	8.5	18
2016	9	17
2017	9.5	16
2018	10	15
TOTAL	**222.5**	**422.5**

This means that, using assumptions that are far more favorable to the Bush plan than a move to MACT, in the period between now and 2018 the Bush proposal will release vast quantities of excess mercury, a long-lived PBAT, into the environment in amounts that are staggeringly great in comparison to the move to MACT.

Chapter 15.
TECHNOLOGY-FORCING STANDARDS

Suggested time budget: one class session

Chapter contents:

—and check the Teachers' Manual Website for SUPPLEMENTARY MATERIALS:

http://www.bc.edu/schools/law/library/coursebook/envtlaw/teachers

The list of Supplementary Materials in Part III of this manual, and on the Teachers' Website, indicates materials posted on the Teachers' Website that are relevant to this and other chapters.

OVERALL TEACHING THEMES & COURSE DESIGN CONSIDERATIONS

This chapter addresses the question, "Under what circumstances is technology-forcing, as an environmental standard-setting methodology, economically and politically viable?" The chapter attempts to answer this question with reference to two case studies, the first focusing on domestic technology-forcing in the context of auto emissions control, and the second on international technology-forcing with regard to the phase-out of ozone-depleting substances. The Chapter's final note elucidates the lessons of the case studies by listing the conditions under which technology-forcing — the most drastic of all environmental standard-setting methods — might be acceptable.

This short chapter will generally be taught by itself in a single assignment, but there are other options: (1) If an instructor is particularly interested in the Clean Air Act, she might assign the auto emissions section of this chapter along with Chapter 11; or (2) an instructor especially concerned with international environmental law might assign the Montreal Protocol section of this chapter along with Chapters 8 ("International Agreements as Domestic Environmental Law") and/or Chapter 26 ("International and Comparative Environmental Law"); or (3) an instructor with a particular interest in the economic aspects of environmental standard-setting might juxtapose this chapter with Chapter 13 ("Standard-Setting Via Cost-Benefit Procedures") as contrasting standard-setting types (i.e., technology-forcing, in theory, does not consider economic costs, while in some varieties of cost-benefit analysis economic costs are weighted equally with environmental benefits).

Note the chart on page 767. It's not great quality, but note that the chart is based on data from stratospheric testing, so that following the lowest curve one can discern a real world effect resulting from the work of the legal profession, which says something.

TEACHING NOTES, COMMENTS, & ALL QUESTIONS ANSWERED

Pages 743-744. This introductory material describes technology-forcing as a "last resort" method of setting environmental protection standards. In a free-market economic system, technology-forcing is a rarely utilized device that is strenuously resisted unless it is palpably necessary and sharply limited. Technology-forcing is the most extreme of all technology-based standard-setting methodologies. BAT-based standards (see

Chapter 12) establish performance standards based on best available technology economically achievable. Standards based on BAT do not require that a regulated party use particular technology, only that it perform as well as it could if it chooses to adopt the identified BAT. Equipment and design specification standards identify the precise technology to be adopted, but this technology is always standardized, time-tested, and widely accepted in the regulated community. Standards based on technology-forcing go even further: they establish target levels so stringent that they cannot be achieved with available technology. Regulated parties must either develop new pollution control technology or prevent pollution by product reformulation or process changes.

Pages 744-747. *International Harvester* is an example of the type of "escape hatch" that must be present if technology-forcing is to be politically acceptable. In §202(b) of the Clean Air Act, Congress cushioned the potentially disruptive economic effects of its 90% reductions in auto-related air pollutants by providing for one-year (and only one year) administrative suspensions of these standards. Some of the conditions governing these suspensions were process-driven. First, Congress directed the National Academy of Sciences to undertake an ongoing study of the achievability of the standards. The outcome of this study process was NAS's conclusion that necessary control technology was not available; but EPA nevertheless rejected petitioners' application for a suspension. Second, the suspension provision also included a criterion that the suspension must be "essential to the public interest or the public health and welfare of the United States." In effect, a "public interest" criterion invites the administering agency, and ultimately the reviewing courts, to balance the costs and benefits of the proposed action, as the *International Harvester* case illustrates. In such cases, the process that drives, or refines, standard-setting is finally the *judicial* process. Sometimes, as in *International Harvester*, this mechanism works. At other times, however, it becomes a screen for legislative symbolic assurance and buck-passing to agencies and the judicial system. (The legislature can then conveniently blame the relevant agency and the reviewing courts if the process produces politically impracticable results.) Relegating standard-setting to the judicial process can actually produce suboptimal environmental policy. For example, the Michigan Environmental Protection Act allows judges to set environmental standards without deferring to agency expertise (see Chapter 22). In one case, a Michigan judge actually rewrote the discharge permit of a POTW by inserting effluent limitations that, in the opinion of sewage treatment experts, were impossible to achieve.

Page 747-748, C&Q #1. Was this really technology-forcing? This note is primarily informational and self-explanatory. Class discussion can be directed to the questions in the note's final paragraph.

Page 748, C&Q #2. Why the denial? This note is rhetorical, and relies on 20-20 hindsight.

Page 748, C&Q #3. Rewarding the laggard and the risks of leading the way. *Was the court correct in its assumption that a company making good faith efforts to comply with the standards would inevitably be disadvantaged by a standard relaxation?*

This note introduces what some critics view as a significant defect of the command and control system for reducing environmental pollution — an alleged incentive to procrastinate. Another variation on this theme relates to the principle, exemplified in most pollution standard-setting statutes, that new sources should be held to higher standards of performance than existing sources because new sources can design pollution controls from the ground up, rather than adding expensive retrofit pollution control devices. This approach, according to the critics, encourages the retention of old, dirty facilities and arguably retards environmental improvement.

There is clearly some merit to the charge that early compliance, or technological innovation, is risky in situations where the pollution standards might be loosened or tightened. But there are countervailing factors that might encourage early compliance and innovation. First, companies rarely make decisions about constructing new facilities based primarily on environmental concerns. Production and marketing efficiencies, as well as labor, materials, and transportation costs, are more important determinants of corporate facility construction and siting decisions than pollution control requirements. Second, pollution control, especially if it is achieved by pollution prevention, can result in cheaper and more efficient production than maintaining the status quo. Third, "clean production" sells products in a world where "green marketing" bestows a competitive advantage (see Chapter 10.) Fourth, pollution control innovations can themselves become a lucrative product in an expanding global market for inexpensive, efficient pollution control mechanisms. Fifth, provisions such as CWA §306(d) protect new sources from being disadvantaged by tightened standards. Sixth, noncompliance with existing standards can subject a violator to "noncompliance penalties" (see Chapter 21), which eliminate any competitive advantage of noncompliance. Seventh, there are economic incentives for compliance and innovation, such as preferential governmental purchasing of inherent low-polluting automobiles and recycled office materials. Effluent charges, such as the excise tax on ozone-depleting chemicals, can also stimulate compliance and innovation. Finally, many environmental statutes contain variances from standards if the regulated party utilizes innovative technology. This topic can generate lively (and sometimes heated) class discussion.

Page 748, C&Q #4. The court's balancing test. *Did the court conduct the balance fairly, since the one-year extension was not a firm one, making further "slippage" predictable?*

A reviewing court must review an administrative decision based solely on the administrative record submitted to it. Potential legislative developments are extra-record, and thus should not be considered in judicial review.

Pages 748-749, C&Q #5. Types of technology-forcing mechanisms. *Why did Congress retain direct control of auto emission standard-setting?*

Each of the reasons suggested in the note probably bore upon Congress' decision to take upon itself this highly technical decision-making process. In addition, technology-forcing became a viable political option for Congress because the BAT approach had failed due to industry bad faith and obstructionist tactics. But there is also a more cynical possibility. Many members of Congress had to realize that the pollution reductions achieved by this initial round of technology-forcing would only be a stopgap measure, given the inevitable increase in Vehicle Miles Traveled (VMTs) caused by increased auto use, stimulated, in part, by Congressional investment in the interstate highway system. Congress may have been moved to embrace the ostensibly courageous technology-forcing approach of the 1970 Amendments in order to avoid the real, but politically unpalatable, issue of too many cars on too many roads.

Pages 749-750. This material describes the second round of technology-forcing imposed by Congress when it revisited the "ozone" problem in 1990. Note the combination of traditional technology-forcing (the mandatory 60-80% reduction in ozone precursors) with innovative market-enlisting measures such as the fleet vehicle and California production pilot programs.

Pages 750-752, C&Q #1. Auto emissions control since 1990. *Has the California preemption waiver created a chaotic implementation climate with regard to technology-forcing strategies in the 1990 CAA Amendments?* Stay tuned!

Pages 752-753, C&Q #2. The hydrogen car is approaching: Does it need a push? This note is didactic and self-explanatory.

Pages 753-754, C&Q #3. Technology-forcing for fuel efficiency. Ditto. Stay tuned!

Page 754, C&Q #4. Technology-forcing the auto verdict? This note is didactic in form and self-explanatory. *What would the air in traffic jams probably look like today had Congress imposed a more typical harm-based or technology-based review-and-permit standard in 1970?* This question can provide an opportunity for class discussion. Auto exhaust emissions are undoubtedly cleaner because of the technology-forcing standards included in the 1970 and 1990 Clean Air Act Amendments. But ozone air quality standards are still being exceeded in many metropolitan areas; and these exceedences will only be exacerbated by the stricter harm-based ambient air quality standard for ozone that has recently been promulgated by EPA (see Chapter 11.) The auto companies are still relying on add-on pollution control devices, while ZEVs, for all practical purposes, are still only blips on the radar screen. More and more Americans are driving more and more miles per day. In addition, Americans have developed a taste for large sport utility vehicles, which pollute more than average automobiles and are also subject to less stringent emissions standards because many of them are classified as "light trucks." "The more things change, ..."

Pages 754-758. The Shimberg excerpts recount the complex domestic and international negotiations and political machinations that resulted in the Montreal Protocol and its successor agreements. It is encouraging to those who labor to protect the environment and public health that a virtually pure process-driven standard-setting approach such as this could produce tough, technology-forcing standards.

Pages 758-759, C&Q #1. Lessons from ozone. This note is purely informational.

Page 759, C&Q #2. Kick-starting the negotiations into the upper atmosphere. Former §157 was triggered by a finding of the Administrator, which NRDC argued had been made in the form of the advance notice of proposed rulemaking. The tricky part of structuring a settlement agreement is to leave the Administrator with sufficient flexibility to negotiate a meaningful international agreement without abandoning the "may reasonably be anticipated" standard. The best way to accomplish this for the plaintiff is to reach a settlement agreement in which the suit is withdrawn pending conclusion of an international agreement, while having the court retain jurisdiction in the event that the negotiations are unsuccessful or insufficiently rigorous. In principle, this ought to give the U.S. negotiators in the international setting an incentive to seek a stronger, rather than weaker, agreement. In the event, word of the suit got around to other participants in the negotiation, who had mixed reactions, tending to interpret the U.S. negotiating positions as required by the court order (which they weren't).

Pages 759-760, C&Q #3. Frameworking – the road to Montreal began in Vienna. This note is important from an informational point of view because the framework-convention-plus-protocols approach is now a standard model for environmental agreements (although not required by international law). The Toronto group limited particular uses, an approach that can be criticized because it allows the reductions from eliminating those uses to be offset by growth from others. The European approach overcame this difficulty, but suffered from the deficiency that it did not actually result in present-day emissions reductions. The Montreal Protocol as finally concluded amalgamated the strengths of both approaches and was considerably more rigorous than either, largely thanks to concerns about the Antarctic ozone hole.

Pages 760-761, C&Q #4. Science in international diplomacy. This note is also important from an informational perspective because it describes the usual international approach to obtaining scientific advice from both government scientists and independent experts such as academic researchers. Resolving disputes among scientists can be a tricky business, although scientists are somewhat accustomed to the concept from experience with peer review processes. Those, however, are not ordinarily designed to produce consensus, in the sense of widespread agreement, on issues that are controversial from a scientific point of view at a particular moment in time when the negotiations are taking place. Scientists are not accustomed, as lawyers are, to the concept of deferring to a colleague's reasonable but arguably incorrect view -- in science there is no such thing. A proactive chair who enjoys considerable respect among his or her colleagues can sometimes forge a scientific consensus against a background of a sense of urgency, or at least get the outliers to acquiesce.

Page 761, C&Q #5. Hats, sunglasses, sunscreen, and checks on the Executive Branch. The court of public opinion or, as it is sometimes known in international parlance, "the mobilization of shame."

Page 761, C&Q #6. The delicate interplay between international treaty-making and domestic legislation. This note is purely informational and elaborates on the concepts introduced in chapter 8. Note the abundance of political "pressure points" created by our system of separation of powers, especially if media influence is included in the analysis. In this case study, a reluctant Administration was forced to act by the combined pressures of Congress, EPA, and the media.

Pages 761-762, C&Q #7. EPA's ambivalent position. Note the importance of scientific developments to the formation of environmental public policy. Administrative agencies, such as EPA, are in the vanguard of integrating scientific information into the political process. Because of their expertise, agencies possess public credibility with regard to evaluating scientific claims. Consequently, it is important to protect both the scientific integrity and the political autonomy of administrative agencies from domination either by either the executive or legislative branches. In this case study, EPA was able to testify against the position supported by its political superiors in the executive branch.

Pages 761-762, C&Q #8. Domestic implementation of the Montreal Protocol. EPA's theory is mildly plausible, but fails to take into account the role of leadership in international negotiations through more aggressive unilateral action than required by international minimum standards. This factor was particularly important in the ozone setting, in which other states were looking for leadership, particularly from large, powerful, and influential states such as the U.S. Courts tend to be reluctant to intrude into issues related to foreign affairs, but that might well not have been a compelling consideration in a case in which the question was whether EPA ought to do *more* than the minimum required by the Protocol -- a question which is properly not one of foreign affairs but one of statutory interpretation. Note that EPA's argument about international strategy ought to be irrelevant to the question of the adequacy of Executive Branch performance by reference to the statutory standard, at least as a matter of principle. International agreements tend to reflect least-common-denominator results as a consequence of strategic compromises, suggesting that the content of the Protocol might have little relevance to the U.S. statutory standard. If the agreement had not entered into force, then neither the U.S. nor any other state would be bound to implement it, thereby diminishing the agreement's relevance. The potential for subsequent revisions creates an open-ended setting on the international level, but on the domestic is again not relevant as a matter of principle to the question of statutory interpretation.

Page 762, C&Q #9. International technology-forcing. This note is didactic and self-explanatory. *Should the United States develop a national "Industrial Policy?" If so, what should its environmental ingredients be?* This is an open-ended question that might be presented to the class for generalized discussion.

Pages 765-766, C&Q #16. Laggards, holdouts, and free-riders. In the absence of the trade provisions, non-parties could obtain huge benefits, thereby creating substantial incentives for them to refrain from becoming party to the agreement. Non-parties would have lower costs from existing CFCs, which were expected to be cheaper than substitutes for them. Non-parties could also serve as "pollution havens" for CFC manufacturers looking for an alternative jurisdiction in which to relocate. The availability of CFCs from non-parties also would tend to undermine the environmental efficacy of the Protocol by providing an unregulated external source of CFCs into the system. Note how the trade provisions turn all this around and create benefits for parties that undertake the reduction obligations and successfully remove the incentives for non-parties -- the laggards, holdouts, etc. of the note's heading.

Page 766, C&Q #17. COPs and MOPs. The Helsinki Declaration is a non-binding decision of the meeting of the parties whose purpose is to memorialize a political agreement. That paved the way for the binding London amendments and adjustments of a year later, which elaborate these political commitments in considerably greater detail, consistent with their status as legally binding obligations. Once the London amendments and adjustments were adopted, the Helsinki Declaration ceased to have any political significance or utility. The Protocol contains a base set of legally binding obligations, the Declaration articulated a political consensus to modify them, and the London adjustments and amendments completed the process by modifying the Protocol in a legally binding way.

Pages 766-768, C&Q #18. Revising the Protocol, and a novel twist. This note demonstrates the disjunction between the real-world need for uniform, coordinated international action and the rule of international law, which tends to encourage fragmentation. States tend to be unenthusiastic about majority voting with binding legal effect, as it means that they can be bound without their consent. States might be reluctant to accept an instrument such as the Montreal Protocol containing a binding majority voting process in the first instance, thereby reducing the extent of participation in the instrument.

Pages 768-769, C&Q #19. Developing countries. The 10 year grace period provides special treatment for developing countries that is consistent with their having contributed little to the problem. On the other hand, it doesn't let them off the hook, which is essential from the point of view of environmental efficacy. The net effect is sometimes known generically as "common but differentiated responsibilities." The grace period in theory allows for the dissemination of alternatives so that developing countries have fewer discontinuities from adjusting to the phaseout.

Pages 769-770, C&Q #20. The rule of law: confronting scofflaws. The purpose of the process, at least in theory, is to help states comply with the obligations they have undertaken in the Protocol, not to punish them. In general, most states react poorly to hard-edged, punitive enforcement mechanisms and tend to resist adopting them. A state that self-identifies as having difficulty complying puts itself in a more favorable procedural posture and, indeed, has much to gain in the form of concessions. Punishing states that do not comply does not necessarily help the environment or create attractive precedents for other states (contrary to the views of many students).

Pages 770-771, C&Q #21. Technology-forcing reconsidered, and pollution prevention. This is a summary note to complete the chapter.

Chapter 16.
ROADBLOCK STRATEGIES: STARK PROHIBITIONS AND THEIR VIABILITY

One or two class hours.

Chapter contents:

– and check the Teachers' Manual Website for SUPPLEMENTARY MATERIALS:

http://www.bc.edu/schools/law/library/coursebook/envtlaw/teachers

The list of Supplementary Materials in Part III of this manual, and on the Teachers' Website, indicates materials posted on the Teachers' Website that are relevant to this and other chapters.

OVERALL TEACHING THEMES & COURSE DESIGN CONSIDERATIONS

- As set up on page 774: What is the relative desirability and efficacy of stark roadblock statutes? Should the desirability of roadblock designs be assessed in static terms at the outset, or over time in the evolving legal and policy contexts?

- Section 7 of the 1973 ESA, as interpreted by the courts, is a stark, direct congressional prohibition. The draconian strictness of the statute was changed by the addition of Section 7 flexibility mechanisms, the God Committee, providing flexibility balancing. Does this mean that the act should have contained such a God Committee provision from the start?

- ESA §9, as interpreted by the courts, is likewise a stark direct congressional prohibition against private as well as public actions that harm species. The strictness of §9 was changed by the creation of §10 incidental take permits. Does this mean that the Act should have contained such provisions from the start?

- Why protect endangered species? A reminder of the combination of utilitarian and ethical rationales for environmental protection.

- How can provisions of positive law counterpose environmental considerations against the momentum of ongoing development projects and the political and economic establishments that support them?

This chapter considers the regulatory approach of crude, blunt statutory instruments, primarily through §7 of the 1973 Endangered Species Act. Debates over "regulatory rigidity" are endemic, and the current politics of endangered species make the ESA a lively and penetrating topic for studying the wisdom of "roadblocking" statutory designs. Endangered species continue to be a fascinating topic, drawing upon fundamental issues of short-term and long-term economic accounting, public trust legacy theories, environmental ethics, and so on.

In order to shorten the assignment you could assign only the §7 or §9 materials and their respective flexibility devices.

In both settings development advocates often frame the endangered species as a trivial or hypocritical obstruction to their development mission. In many such cases government agencies are incestuously linked with the political and economic marketplace in ongoing enterprises that treat the particular habitat as a free good to be exploited. The developers are often emphatically not interested in having an accurate overall cost accounting of the enterprise. In the TVA case, as noted in the book by Bruce Wheeler and Michael McDonald, TVA AND THE TELLICO DAM, 1936-1979: A BUREAUCRATIC CRISIS IN POST-INDUSTRIAL AMERICA, TVA was trying desperately to build a project that could not be cost-justified in order to keep its federal subsidies flowing and its local public works program rolling. The citizens' arguments, typically focusing on benefits (diminishing them through accurate accounting), costs (noting that they were greatly understated), and constructive alternatives, typically failed to convince the developers and their supporters. Cost-effectiveness and overall public economic rationality are not what the insiders typically want. In the spotted owl controversy, no one who was advocating the continued cutting of the last ancient forests was eager to have discussion of the hundreds of millions of dollars in annual subsidies that the taxpayer was putting into the timber cutting enterprise.

Students often ask why pork barrel projects and other destructive developments are not confronted and stopped directly on their merits. The answer, of course, is there is often no such direct method available, short of suborning the congressional appropriations process or deflecting a development corporation from within. There are no federal statutes which allow direct question of the substantive merits of such federal or corporate actions. It is only because they tend to destroy habitats so as to create endangered species that the Endangered Species Act, not so coincidentally, has applicable force.

TEACHING NOTES, COMMENTS, & ALL QUESTIONS ANSWERED

Page 773. The Delaney Clause

You can use the Delaney Clause as a brief set-up to the issue of crude, blunt laws. The arguments come down to problems of regulatory overkill on one hand, and on the other the fact that a sharp, clear regulatory standard was necessary to force the marketplace to pay attention to the problem of carcingenicity. Our point about judging this debate over roadblocks by viewing how the regulatory standards fare in context over a span of years is echoed in Prof. Jamie Grodsky's article quoted on page 814 at note 64.

You can see more on the Delaney Clause arguments and the Les v. Reilly litigation (page 773, note 3) strictly enforcing the Clause and resulting in statutory amendment, in the Teachers' Website's Supplementary Materials. See also McDonald, The Food Quality Protection Act of 1996: By Removing Chemical Irritants from our Environment will it Generate Trade Irritants to Replace Them?, WILLIAM & MARY ENVTL. L. & POL'Y REV. (2001).

Pages 775-776. The ESA as a Roadblock Statute. Two pages that frame the statutory design issue on the ESA. The ESA is by no means a perfect and well-implemented statute. Professor Dan Rohlf's article *Six Biological Reasons Why the Endangered Species Act*

Doesn't Work – and What to do about It (5 CONSERVATION BIOLOGY No. 3, September 1991) examines the connection between law and the science of conserving endangered species. Rohlf argues that there are six reasons why the ESA doesn't work: First, the Act protects high-profile individual species rather than overall bio-diversity. Second, the ESA lacks clearly defined thresholds to delineate endangered, threatened or recovered species. Third, the Act doesn't protect metapopulations adequately. Fourth, many biological determinations under the ESA are not adequately documented, which prevents meaningful scrutiny and participation from the public and the scientific community. Fifth, the Act doesn't protect critical habitat sufficiently to sustain recovered populations. Finally, the administrative enforcement of the ESA is chronically slowed or blocked by scientific uncertainty and practical and political inexpediencies.

Pages 778-788. THE ESA §7 BATTLES OVER THE TVA TELLICO DAM AND THE SNAIL DARTER.

This case study is not just the obsession of one of the authors who spent seven years of his life on it, but apparently is widely recognized as a classically illuminating paradigm, even though its actual facts and context are not widely known. In a turn-of-the-millennium on-line poll of environmental law professors from across the country seeking a consensus on America's ten most important environmental protection court cases, TVA v. Hill received the highest number of votes, almost twice as many as the two cases that placed second (the *Chevron* and *Ethyl* cases).[1] This is testimony to the extraordinary setting of the case, not to any particular lawyerly competence. At http://www.law.mercer.edu/elaw/zygplater.html you can view some useful photos and text on the case.

The Supreme Court's opinion in *TVA v. Hill* can be used to emphasize the crude starkness of the 1973 ESA's §7. Having found the violation, the justices, including at least Justice Burger who obviously thought the result was ludicrous, felt obliged to enforce the statute as it was written. As a result the citizens, who had been trying for ten years to get a hearing on the economic merits of this boondoggle, finally received "a remand to Congress" and ultimately a Cabinet-level economic review of the dam's dysfunctionality, showing Congress that the public would be better off with a river development plan than with TVA's beloved reservoir project. The strictness of the statute, in other words, was the only way in which this project could be held up legally so as to obtain an overview accounting.

Page 782, C&Q #1. Is this an "environmental" opinion? Our opinion is that although the decision involves intensely environmental fact and policy elements, it is fundamentally a "plain meaning" statutory interpretation case, and an equity holding that the Court must enforce the law when citizen plaintiffs, as so authorized by Congress, bring transgressions to court. The holding obviously is important to environmental litigation, but is more generic in its terms.

The last sentence of the note raises the question of whether the snail darter litigation was helpful or harmful overall. The argument for harm is that the snail darter became a caricature of mindless opposition to progress that certainly spilled beyond endangered species disputes (see cartoon on page 956). As reported by the media, the controversy invited a skeptical public reaction to the trade-offs between environment and progress,

1. envlawprofs@darkwing.uoregon.edu, posting of Oct. 26, 2001.

as such cases are so easily caricatured. On the benefit side, it's pretty clear that the Endangered Species Act and perhaps other environmental legislation won a grudging acknowledgment as enforceable statutory mandates that had to be taken seriously because of their potential disruptive effect. The question of whether the legal doctrinal precedents set by the case continue to provide beneficial consequences is taken up later in these questions.

Page 782, C&Q #2 Why protect endangered species? The text here surveys the spectrum of reasons.

It's quite clear that most members of Congress, when they voted for the Act almost unanimously, thought they were protecting bald eagles, whooping cranes and polar bears. In the legislative hearings, and in the terms of the statute, however, lies a far more thoughtful series of applications and reasons. You can note the utilitarian argument that endangered species may reveal foods and medicines that ultimately will be critically important for human health, the traditional cliché that we don't want to render something extinct that may turn out to be the "cure for cancer." We don't want "to destroy a book before we have learned to read it." And endangered species certainly have turned out to have such important effects. The Pacific yew, living in the forests where the spotted owl also resides, turns out to contain Taxol, a medicine that shows remarkable effects in treating heart disease. Bio-diversity of species of plants and animals provides the best strategy for coping with stress and changed conditions over time. In agriculture, for instance, there is continued interest in preserving stocks of endangered plants' seeds so that new strains of drought- and disease-resistant foods can be produced. See Doremus, Patching the Ark, 18 Ecol. L. Q. 265 (1991).

But it should be emphasized that endangered species protection also captures a number of the ethical arguments made earlier in Chapter 1. It is true that extinction is a natural phenomenon, and if, for instance, some anonymous gray tundra rat species in the Northern Territories becomes extinct through natural processes, that is a loss, but not perhaps a tragedy. If, on the other hand, the species is lost because of pesticides in the global food chain, or habitat destruction by humans, it appears to be a different proposition. Human-caused extinctions, according to some scientists, are running at thousands per year, overwhelmingly because of habitat modification or destruction. Where human welfare requires the extinction of a species, even we would grant that human welfare takes precedence. But this is typically an example of a "phony trade-off," because of thousands of cases documented by the federal government of confrontations between species and human projects, there has virtually never been an unavoidable need to trade off an endangered species for human benefit. Projects can be redesigned, re-timed, relocated, etc., if there is a will or a legal requirement to do so.

It seems necessary in this chapter as well as the last to make the basic political observation that so often underlies environmental law: In the cases chronicled in this chapter where endangered species protection is highly controversial, the species protection often focuses upon natural habitat that is being exploited by a powerful "iron triangle" (page 400). The proponents of species protection may not be primarily motivated by the abstract philosophical ideals behind the ESA. In the snail darter Tellico Dam case, as in the spotted owl controversy, the endangered species were clearly being used as a fortuitous handle by environmentalists seeking to identify the pending loss of immensely valuable natural habitat under the pressure of a subsidized pork barrel project or program. Does this delegitimize the enforcement enterprises?

Page 783, C&Q #3. Canaries in the coal mine; a practical utility of endangered species. After Justice Powell asked counsel during oral argument what good the snail darter was, Justice Burger said he thought the plaintiffs were just using it as a "handle." The environmentalists certainly cared about the species in ethical terms, but also because it raised critical questions about the critical habitat in which it lived and the project which threatened it. Unthinking habitat destruction, after all, is the primary cause of endangerment and extinction. If the species had not inhabited a river that was beloved by so many environmentalists, or if human welfare had required another low level pork barrel dam, the case probably would not have been brought. (Does that mean that the campaign was hypocritical?) The utilitarian "indicator" function of endangered species is present in most if not all ESA cases, but only recently has the canary phrase begun to catch on, and the logic of it is often eclipsed by the seductive comedic potential of juxtaposing trivialized species and big development enterprises.

But the canary role of endangered species continually recurs, often in settings where systemic shake-ups are needed.

> If the Colorado River goes into crisis [after 20 years of booming Western development and concurrently the end of a 20-year wet cycle], the ensuing tangle of litigation over water rights, endangered species, and border disputes could undo the system of Western water law that has evolved over the last 100 years. Some say that would be a good thing. "The law of the river is hopelessly, irretrievably obsolete, designed on a hydrological fallacy [the original legal compact's water flow premises were grossly overestimated], around an agrarian West that no longer exists," Professor McCool at the University of Utah said. Johnson & Murphy, Drought Settles In, New York Times May 2, 2004, at 1, 24.

When these re-thinkings come at the point of a species spear, public attention is often deflected onto the messenger rather than the message. See Rio Grande Silvery Minnow v. Keys, 333 F.3d 1109, 1138 (10th Cir. 2003), vacated by 355 F.3d 1215 (10th Cir. 2004)(a deprecatory political backlash prompted congressional override of trial court's canary-in-coalmine recognition of the endangered minnow's practical role requiring rethinking of water uses in the Rio Grande).

Page 784, C&Q #4. Roadblocks' superior litigatability. A fundamental political science point: If citizens lacking in power and money are to be a credible pluralistic enforcement element within our legal system, litigation of statutory violations must be relatively straightforward. *What was the cause of action in TVA v. Hill?* The case turned on the note's (b) jeopardy claim, and (c) destruction or modification of habitat. *Which of the two is analytically easier to prove?* Students should see that habitat destruction is much simpler to prove than the subtle biological fact of imminent extinction. *What if §7 had said "may"(or "should") instead of "shall"?* Students should see that the Establishment would ignore the law if it did not have a mandatory enforceable verb. Cf. C&Q #1 at pages 417-18, especially the last paragraph. Given the hard realities of marketplace politics within regulatory agency bureaucracies — which necessitate the roadblock approach in the first place — not only would such a discretionary legal standard invite superficial agency and judicial balancing of species protection, but the prospect of citizen enforcement lawsuits would be effectively neutralized by the hard-to-litigate, indeterminate standard. *Would endangered species law be taken seriously if it had not been enshrined in a dramatic Supreme Court case?* This is a central strategic question; it is clearly true that industry and agencies took far more account of the need for ESA compliance after the *TVA* decision enforcing the crude, blunt prohibition.

Page 784, C&Q #5. The results of TVA v. Hill's enforcement action. More on the immediately preceding point.

Page 785, C&Q #6. Pressures for flexibility. This further sets up the chapter's central theme. Strict clear prohibitions may be necessary to prompt necessary corrective action, but rationality may require that regulations receive some flexibility in implementation. Common sense requires flexibility and balancing at some point in any government regulatory program. The question is where that flexibility and balancing will occur, and on what terms. If the locus of the balance is in the agency that is building a pork barrel project, the standard and the balance will be trivialized. Is a court supposed to step in to make the public policy choice? We argued that the legislature itself should do so. As noted below, the high level Cabinet committee with judicially reviewable strict standards is a close second best. Section 7 of the ESA illustrates that different statutes have different life stages: If flexibility had been built in from the beginning, the seriousness with which the statute is now taken, after its flexibility amendments, might never have developed.

You might remind students about the prosecutorial discretion issues noted in Chapter 7 at page 416, and the notes in this manual for that page.

Page 785, C&Q #7. Do courts have a flexibility role when faced with statutory violations? The TVA v. Hill holding, of course, stands for a strict enforcement role for the courts. Subsequent cases have allowed judicial equitable balancing of the enforcement question where the congressional mandate is deemed less clear or crucial than the ESA (a problematic premise on several grounds!). The law review article noted in footnote 19 wrestles a bit with this issue. This comment carries on an intriguing debate about whether courts should be able to step in and make the public policy balances that the statute does not consider on its face. For better or for worse, most environmentalists would argue that bringing the question to open debate on the merits in the legislature is a better forum than having a court make a relatively invisible, unanswerable, unilateral determination of important public policy questions.

Page 786, C&Q #8. Does statutory interpretation open up a judicial flexibility role? Statutory interpretation clearly opens a door that courts can exploit to block an enforcement initiative deemed irrational. The TVA plaintiffs were lucky the Court felt bound by the statute's stated objectives.

Page 787, C&Q #9. Flexibility via a "remand to Congress." The flexibility mechanism of last resort? It can be argued that if the contending parties each is advancing a congressional mandate, only Congress can appropriately resolve the conflict. The strategy of the citizens in the Tellico Dam case, and in other environmental cases where a statutory violation is proved, picks up on an argument made by Professor Sax that a "remand to the legislature" is a fitting strategy for resolving many public policy controversies in the open on the merits. See Sax, Defending the Environment (Alfred A. Knopf, 1971).

Page 787, C&Q #10. Flexibility from the God Squad mechanism. Congress first provided a resolution mechanism for ESA conflicts in its 1978 §7 amendments, the focus of Subchapter 16C.

Page 787, C&Q #11. The ESA's consultation mechanism. Before drafting the God Squad amendment, the original §7 had a vague reference to "consultation" which became, as such things do, a full-blown set of procedures and regulations for resolving conflicts before they boil over. When large pork momentum or investment is involved, consultation rarely is determinative of outcomes.

Page 788, C&Q #12. Tactics. Some rhetorical questions reflecting real-life choices.

Pages 788-98. THE SPOTTED OWL CASES

Page 792, C&Q #1. The ESA and the owl; note *Sweet Home*, page 794. As written this note does not adequately inform readers of the double import of the spotted owl cases: that the timber companies have been as leery of ESA's §9 as of §7. The spotted owl cases are often concerned with §9, which prohibits "takes" of endangered species, interpreted to include habitat disruption —so it applies even where no "jeopardy" has been proved and no "critical habitat" listed. Thus it applies where a §7 claim does not, especially because by its terms it extends to private as well as public lands and actions. This explains why the *Sweet Home* plaintiffs so feared ESA §9.

Page 792, C&Q #2. Owl politics and economics. Background on the owls and timber cutting. More background on these issues can be found in the New York Times, Sunday, November 3, 1991 at E2 - the sale of public forests to the logging industry at an overall loss owing to subsidies, a review of Forest Service economics calculated to minimize the losses (as by amortizing logging roads with a 25-year life span over a period of 1000... years), etc. According to one of the economic analyses, the annual timber subsidy runs at approximately $120,000,000 a year net, not counting the loss of the forests. (A beautiful coffee table book chronicling the old growth forest is David Kelly, Gary Braasch, *Secrets of the Old Growth Forest* (Gibbs-Smith, 1988, ISBN 087905-174-4).

The U.S. Forest Service first agreed to allow private companies to clear-cut the public forests (rather than requiring selective cutting) in 1964. Within five years, more than half of national forest operations were clear-cuts. Replanting is overwhelmingly in monocultures, converting the forests into tree farms, with herbicide poisons applied around replanted seedlings to prevent other species of vegetation from growing in the replanted areas.

Page 793, C&Q #3. Bio-diversity. Some commentators argue that the Endangered Species Act misses the point - only coming in at the last moment, when species are already endangered and too far gone. Far more effective would be an approach to protect bio-diversity generally with habitat protection refuges strategically located throughout the world. See Rohlf, Six Biological Reasons Why the Endangered Species Act Doesn't Work, 5 Conserv. Biol. 278 (Sept. 1991). One question, of course, is how big and how restrictive such bio-diversity protection designations would be.

Page 794-796. *SWEET HOME* AND ESA 9.

Because it focuses on the ESA §9 "take" prohibition, which *Sweet Home* interprets to extend the Act to *private* actions that destroy habitat, the case lies at the heart of a political ESA firestorm that will undoubtedly continue in the political realm.

You should explore the various political forces behind the case and the scenarios which allow the Act to prevent, for example, private developers from draining a wetland upon which an endangered heron or some much less photogenic species depends. Given the Court's holding, there has been redoubled clamor for passage of regulatory compensation provisions in the ESA or in a plenary regulatory compensation act.

You might ask students how major the impacts of endangered species protections actually appear to be upon private citizens. Starting with the snail darter and Tellico Dam, the ESA has provided a handy target for incendiary anecdotes (often, as with the snail darter, based on fantasy rather than fact) and political polemics, but its primary impact has been upon large corporate and governmental entities, forcing them into a most unwelcome consultation process with its consideration of public costs, benefits, and alternatives - as in the spotted owl review which brought to light the subsidies, long distance injuries to salmon, and labor-intensive selective-cutting alternatives to corporate clear-cutting.

And then you can show students how litigation concerned with such timely political issues usually turns on quite technical, even boring, details, in this case an exercise in statutory interpretation and principles of administrative law deference to agency decisions. Justices are moved by a variety of arguments, not necessarily environmental.

As to the administrative law of the case, it is interesting to note that the dissenters, particularly Justice Rehnquist, are departing from their usual deference to agency interpretations of law, particularly those maintained consistently over a long period, here 20 years.

As to the discussions of foreseeability and proximate cause, there is an interesting analogy to tort issues in Chapters 3 and 4, and the scienter discussions in Chapter 20.

Page 796, C&Q #1. What's going on here? In *Sweet Home*, as with the Tellico Dam case, the Supreme Court has interpreted the Act on its terms (and the agency's regulations on point) and upheld the protective position. Is the decision a seminar on statutory interpretation? an administrative law exercise deciding whether to defer to an agency's interpretive regulation? It should be remembered that *Sweet Home* reflects one pitched battle in the ongoing war between, on one hand, Western Wise Use local sovereignists, resource exploitation corporations, and private property rights activists, and on the other hand the federal government, environmental preservationists, and others who have found (as in the Tellico Dam and Spotted Owl cases) that endangered species law often provides the only effective forum for obtaining an overall public accounting of challenged activities.

The defenders win this round, but as Justice O'Connor notes, "Congress may, of course, see fit to revisit this issue. And nothing the Court says today prevents the agency itself from narrowing the scope of its regulation at a later date."

Page 797, C&Q #2. Statutory interpretation games. The question is about the meaning of one of ten words, the meaning of "harm" in the statutory definition of "take" as to "harass, harm, pursue, hunt, shoot, wound, kill, trap, capture, or collect."

Is this another example of legislative legerdemain - an environmentally protective phrase, "harm," being slipped into a statute by indirection, in this case on the Senate floor after habitat destruction had been stricken from the bill in committee? Or is it fairly within the central mandate of the Act (cf. Justice Scalia's warning about "'broad purpose' question-begging")?

And what of the conflicting canons? *Noscitur a sociis* is one canon of interpretation, which the majority used to establish an interpretive context - a word "gathers meaning from the words around it." Jarecki v. G. D. Searle & Co., 367 U. S. 303, 307 (1961). On the other hand, the stricter *ejusdem generis* appears what Sweet Home's narrow-interpretationists had in mind - a word should be defined like the others in the same series, without independent meaning. Given the way lawyers in legislatures write statutes, which canonic interpretation appears more fitting?

Page 797, C&Q #3. Foreseeability and proximate cause. In order to be subject to the Act's criminal penalties or the more severe of its civil penalties, one must "knowingly violate" the Act or its implementing regulations. 16 USCA §1540(a)(1),(b)(1). Congress added "knowingly" in place of "willfully" in 1978 to make "criminal violations of the act a general rather than a specific intent crime." As noted in Chapter 20 on environmental crimes, the courts have imputed scienter requirements to criminal statutes that impose sanctions without expressly requiring scienter. The Sweet Home majority said that they "do not agree with the dissent that the regulation covers results that are not 'even foreseeable...no matter how long the chain of causality between modification and injury.' Respondents have suggested no reason why either the 'knowingly violates' or the 'otherwise violates' provision of the statute - or the 'harm' regulation itself - should not be read to incorporate ordinary requirements of proximate causation and foreseeability." Given this constraint, how far in practice can the regulatory definition stretch to burden private parties?

Page 797, C&Q #4. Administrative law - *Chevron*. The *Sweet Home* majority and dissenting opinions treat the *Chevron* precedent differently. [See coursebook, at pages 428-430.] The majority said that "our conclusions that Congress did not unambiguously manifest its intent to adopt respondents' view, and that the Secretary's interpretation is reasonable, suffice to decide this case. *Chevron*. The latitude the ESA gives the Secretary in enforcing the statute, together with the degree of regulatory expertise necessary to its enforcement, establishes that we owe some degree of deference to the Secretary's reasonable interpretation," citing Breyer, Judicial Review of Questions of Law and Policy, 38 ADMIN. L. REV. 363, 373 (1986). In dissent, on the other hand, Justice Scalia who has been a consistent supporter of broad *Chevron* deference to agencies, argued that here the Secretary's decision need not be deferred to because "The regulation...dispense[s] with a [necessary] proximate-cause requirement.... This Court...may not uphold a regulation by adding to it even the most reasonable of elements it does not contain." This meant that *Chevron* deference could be avoided because Justice Scalia had found either that the regulation was unreasonable or that it violated an express congressional mandate.

Page 800. THE §7 GOD COMMITTEE AMENDMENTS

Page 800, C&Q #1. The God Committee amendments. This flexibility device is the important second stage of Section 7's life history. Under the current statutory and regulatory provisions, there actually is a fourth criterion. Agencies may not have acted so as to foreclose alternatives and further jeopardize the species after the project conflict has been discovered. The third standard, whether the project as proposed clearly outweighs alternatives consistent with preserving the endangered species, was written by a student who used these materials at the University of Michigan in the mid-1970s.

Section 7's flexibility now lies in the God Committee process, with a judicially reviewable cabinet-level decision required for an override authorizing extinction. The God Committee is made up of seven members: the Secretary of Agriculture, Secretary of the Army, Chairman of the Council of Economic Advisors, Administrator of the EPA, Secretary of the Interior, Administrator of National Oceanic and Atmospheric Administration (NOAA) (representing the marine endangered species jurisdiction), and a representative of effected states.

(Under 16 U.S.C.A. §1536 (j) the God Committee is ordered to "grant an exception for any agency action if the Secretary of Defense finds that such exemption is necessary for reasons of national security." This raises interesting questions of the degree to which the federal judiciary would allow substantial evidence scrutiny of such a Department of Defense finding.)

Page 801, C&Q #2. The God Committee in practice. Two dam cases went to the God Committee in January 1979: TVA's Tellico Dam and the Greyrocks Dam in North Dakota which threatened the flyway resting areas of the whooping crane. The Committee unanimously refused an exemption on Tellico, and granted an exemption on Greyrocks conditioned on river-flow management rules protecting the cranes.

The drama of the Tellico Dam God Committee was that for the first time there was a complete, comprehensive economic accounting of the pork barrel project, not to mention of the alternatives that the Citizens had proposed and developed for the project area. The unanimous decision of the God Committee, however, was scarcely noticed by the media, and thereby the subsequent political undercutting of the decision was possible. In the spotted owl controversy, the Bush I Administration pushed through a God Committee override that was challenged in court and ultimately mooted, leaving a sordid impression. See Portland Audubon, 984 F.2d 1534 (9th Cir. 1993).

Page 801, C&Q #3. Denouement for the snail darter. This tells a sad tale, as well as indicating the strategy of environmentalism seeking to continue to raise the merits on a constitutional theme that could not be overridden by statute. (The Supreme Court has pretty thoroughly destroyed the possibility of Native American Religious Freedom Act litigation in the case of In Ling v. Northwest Indian Cemetery Protective Association, 108 S.Ct. 1319 (1988). In that case the Forest Service was building a logging road into a wilderness area through sacred Indian grounds. The Court said:

> Even if we assume that we should accept the Ninth Circuit's prediction, according to which "the [road through the Indians' sacred land] would virtually destroy the Indians' ability to practice their religion," the Constitution simply does not provide a principle that could justify upholding the respondents' [request for an injunction against the building of a non-essential road.] 108 S.Ct. at 1326-1327.

For other cases on environmental representation of Native American religious claims, see Rievman, at 17 Environmental Aff. L. Rev. 169 (1989).

If students are somewhat agitated by the spotted owl or the snail darter stories, it might be useful to emphasize something that was not emphasized in the text, to wit the role of the Media. The Media is the nation's information-supply system. Government generally responds if the media focuses on a story, so if the merits of a case are accurately depicted, the government tends to follow. In the snail darter case, every member of Congress had received extensive economic analyses from the Department of the Interior, demonstrating that it would be far more destructive to flood the reservoir than to develop on a river-based model. The only hope, however, of having those merits reflected in a vote is if the members of Congress knew that the American public had been informed about the economic case. Instead, the media for so many years focused only on the little fish and the "putatively big hydroelectric dam." The economic backdrop was completely ignored, even after the dramatic unanimous vote on economic grounds in the God Committee in favor of the snail darter, which was covered only sparsely and only in the dark recesses of the national press. Thus, in a story which according to a journalism school researcher was the most covered environmental story of the 1970s, the merits of the environmental case and the pork-barrel project were never examined in the public press. At the end, Jimmy Carter had repeatedly determined that he would veto the Tellico appropriations override (which also had stricken a water resources economic accounting process that he strongly believed in). According to a member of his Domestic Council, Carter was visited at the last minute by Frank Moore, his congressional lobbyist, who said to him "Mr. President, if you veto that bill, every editorial cartoonist in the country is going to picture you tomorrow morning holding a snail darter in one hand and a killer rabbit in the other and you can't stand that kind of publicity." The fact that this story is a believable anecdote says much about the power of the media.

Page 804, C&Q #4. The sunk cost tactic. Self-explanatory.

Page 801, C&Q #5. The God Committee after the spotted owl. Self-explanatory.

Page 803-807. THE §9 BYPASS: §10 INCIDENTAL TAKE PERMITS

Page 806, C&Q #1. The §10 incidental take standards. In the first ten years of the Habitat Conservation Planning program (1983–1992), fourteen Incidental Take Permits were issued.[2] By September 1996, 179 Incidental Take Permits had issued. By the end of December 1999, 290 Incidental Take Permits had been issued.[3] As of October 1, 2001, there were 516 Incidental Take Permits issued.[4]

Page 806, C&Q #2. More on the incidental take bypass.

Page 807, C&Q #3. Critical habitat gets bypassed. In the snail darter case, designation of critical habitat was pro forma. In subsequent cases, however, critical habitat listing has been hotly contested, in part because it automatically requires at least minimal review of any federal actions within the habitat areas. Public and private project

---

2. U.S. FISH & WILDLIFE SERV., DEP'T OF THE INTERIOR, HABITAT CONSERVATION PLANNING AND INCIDENTAL TAKE PERMIT PROCESSING HANDBOOK i (1996).
3. Marj Nelson, Habitat Conservation Planning, Endangered Species Bulletin Nov.-Dec. 1999, at 13, *available at* http://endangered.fws.gov/esb/99/11-12/12-13.pdf.
4. FISH & WILDLIFE SERV., DEP'T OF THE INTERIOR, HABITAT CONSERVATION PLANS, *available at* http://endangered.fws.gov/hcp/HCP_Incidental_Take.pdf.

proponents often view it in more drastic terms, as a "power grab" (as when Interior considers listing broad geographical areas), and a nefarious part of protectionists' "agenda to lock up all public lands as de facto wilderness." The Interior Department has often been diffident about declaring critical habitat, especially so in the Bush II Administration. Only half of listed endangered species have critical habitat listings. Critical habitat protection lawsuits are accordingly rare.

Page 808, C&Q #4. Slippage. This presents the §9 flexibility mechanisms imposed by administrative fiat rather than by legislative amendment as with the §10 incidental take provision. The driving motivation for initiation of these accommodations in the Clinton Administration was clearly fear of what the backlashing insider process in Congress would do to the ESA if the agency did not pull in the Act's teeth somewhat. An agency that injects too much flexibility or slack into statutory enforcement runs the risk of overstepping its constitutional role, being accused of abdicating its public service obligations, and sabotaging declared national policy, as indeed it may be. Perhaps that is why so many important administrative issues are ultimately shifted to courts and Congress.

Professor Dan Farber codified the concept of ecopragmatic slippage in his 1999 article Taking Slippage Seriously, 23 Harv. Envtl l. Rev. 297, launching some thoughtful critiques. Heinzerling, Pragmatists and Environmentalists, 113 Harv. L.Rev. 1421 (2000). Grodsky, The Paradox of (Eco)Pragmatism, 87 Minn. L.Rev. 1037, 1063 (2003).

Page 811, C&Q #5. The political context. Self-explanatory. In a recent article one of the authors argued that one of the reasons the the ESA attracts such pointed criticism is that endangered species are perceived by industry as a leveraged target, that by caricaturistic extension allows all environmental regulations across the board to be deprecatingly characterized as unbalanced and irrational. "Endangered Species Act Lessons Over 30 Years," 34 Envtl Law 101 (2004).

Page 811, C&Q #6. Anti-ESA agitation and "Noah's Choice."

> "The ESA's cost is much more than just money. The cost is family-wage jobs destroyed, children with no economic future, families torn apart by divorce and destitution, communities destroyed — people's hopes crushed forever. Just visit the timber towns of Oregon and Washington and see for yourself — there won't be any high-tech salvation for those innocent victims of an ill-conceived federal law." —Rutzick, Species Act Not As Benign As Portrayed, *Portland Oregonian* .

Charles Mann and Mark Plummer have published Noah's Choice (1994),[5] a book disingenuously engaging and beautifully written, that attempts to set the parameters of the endangered species protection debate as a difficult but necessary tradeoff between ecology and economics. The book delves into the biological intricacy of endangered species and their habitats, and understands the charm of these species to those who study them.

The book raises the basic public policy dilemmas: We cannot save all endangered species. At some point the costs of saving a species become too great and human needs too contradictory - especially where, as typically, it is habitat destruction over substantial areas that threatens species survival.

5. See Clear the Air: Lopsided Journalism in Public Policy Debates, 32 ENVTL LAW 591 (2002).

The book prescribes a new public policy version of "Noah's Choice" - advocating a debate whether we wish to spend hundreds of millions of dollars to save endangered species, or instead for other more pressing human needs [like dams, clear-cut timber, space stations...].

Environmentalists defending the ESA, the authors assert repeatedly, are dogmatically applying the "Noah Principle," holding in absolutist terms that no species can ethically be extinguished, ever - "an extreme Kantian 'perfect duty.'"

In reality, most environmentalists seem to advocate a "Noah *Presumption*," that species should be protected until that is shown on balance to be undesirable or infeasible. Like the public trust, without an evidentiary presumption, decisions will almost always tip in favor of the short term marketplace. With a presumption process, human enterprise public and private are induced to anticipate conflicts with endangered species, and avoid them by developing practicable alternatives. This has been the most common strategy of ESA implementation, almost totally ignored by the authors.

The fundamental flaw in "Noah's Choice" is that it is premised on a false tradeoff. It repeatedly assumes current market practices and pork-barrel projects as given, to be weighed matter-of-factly against bio-diversity needs. When Mann and Plummer interviewed the first author of this Manual, they were told how the snail darters, and endangered species generally, have often acted as "canaries in the coal mine," to identify important human values at risk, drastic public diseconomies in the corporate or pork-barrel projects threatening species, and public benefits that will follow from adopting alternative development designs compatible with species preservation (coursebook at 661-62). When they wrote "Noah's Choice," however, they assiduously avoided the canary concept and the positive economic role played by the ESA in the Tellico dam case, did not mention the hard economics of the God Committee decision that favored the darter over the dam, in clear-cutting and the spotted owl, etc., as well as ignoring the dysfunctional aspects of pork-barrel projects, resource exploitation subsidies, and the like so often highlighted in endangered species cases.

Species protection will continue often to impose substantial costs, and there will be cases where dislocations will occur, requiring major accommodations or hard choices to lose species. But a Biological Survey and similar measures would go a long way toward anticipatory planning and avoidance of expensive human/species conflicts. The ESA and bio-diversity conservation goals do not inevitably present the extremely polarized choice the authors find at the heart of all species protection.

"Noah's Choice" is designed to shape the current politics of ESA reauthorization, but invites false tradeoffs. A "Noah Presumption" already exists in the ESA, and that seems preferable.

Page 812, C&Q #7. Strict rules or adaptive discretion. Self-explanatory. The currently favored rubric of "adaptive management" for endangered species is sensible when viewed in a vacuum separated from the context of the administrative process's everyday politics, but in practical effect its shift of standards to an often-unreviewable discretion raises serious problems for citizen enforcement and implementation based on scientific merits.

Page 812, C&Q #8. ESA in national governance. Some current events.

Page 813, C&Q #9. The roadblock strategy in perspective. In many situations there clearly must be some flexibility mechanisms in order to prevent one particular civic value from unreasonable preemption of other socially-important enterprises. The trick is how to set a standard for when to allow balancing, who is to do it, and how a process can be designed so as to avoid undercutting the civic principle. Balancing procedures that would operate rationally in the setting of a seminar room or the open air of a public forum are likely to operate quite differently in the less visible, heavily-lobbied daily political reality of agency process.

There are hundreds of thousands of endangered species, and some of them can conflict seriously with human needs. *Should the law be enforced as written if a whole city's federally-funded water system will be preempted by an endangered spider? Should a hospital being built to serve a poor community be stopped because it might endanger a listed species of mouse?* Should an expensive 90% rollback of auto emissions be required for cars in Idaho where the air is unpolluted? Should a substance which may cause one in a billion to die of cancer be banned from foods while far more dangerous noncarcinogenic additives are tolerated? And note that both the §7 and the §10 flexibility processes require difficult and expensive reviews feasible only to well-heeled proponents.

What if your students represent an environmental citizens group supporting a decisive, readily-enforceable roadblock law like the ESA, but they know that in a number of cases its terms are going to be overinclusive and undersensitive to the rational public policy subjectivities of the issue. Assume further that they know that if the law had a more subjective, flexible, discretionary standard, the agencies in charge would be extremely responsive to political pressure from the regulated industry – as for instance with the Forest Service and the timber industry, the Federal Highway Administration and the highway construction industry, etc. Most endangered species protections confront strong marketplace resistance because they get in the way of land development, and are politically less secure because they don't have overt human importance. Without tough legal standards, the laws can be expected to be honored in the breach.

What is the strategic utility of such strict roadblock statutes? Would the mission of the ESA have been accomplished better with some other statutory design? You can contrast §7 of the 1973 ESA with NEPA's §102. Both were clearly inadvertent but became effective. NEPA is procedural the §7 is substantive. Both apply broadly to all federal agencies.

One conclusion might be that when one is trying to design a major redirection of a political marketplace involving powerful insider establishments like the public works pork-barrel or subsidized timber cutting, a statute has to be almost completely unambiguous. Any opportunity for the agency or the federal judiciary to interpret their way out of a substantive provision is likely to be taken. Where there is a statutory violation under the Endangered Species Act, at least, a court apparently has no inherent equitable power to forgive the violation.

What better statutory design might have been followed for the ESA? It is hard to conceive of delegating endangered species discretion to the governmental agencies, because of the suborning effect of the pork-barrel. Contrast the situation under the major pollution statutes in Chapters 11 and 12, where the legislative goal is sufficiently complex and subjective that articulation by rule making and administrative flexibility were absolutely necessary. In Chapter 24, focusing on public lands' management policies, the federal statute has to be a great deal more prescriptive rather than prohibitive.

Page 814, C&Q #10. An international perspective. Self-explanatory.

Chapter 17.
PRODUCT REGULATION AND MARKET-ACCESS CONTROL STRATEGIES: PESTICIDES AND TOXICS

Chapter contents:

— and check the Teachers' Manual Website for SUPPLEMENTARY MATERIALS:

http://www.bc.edu/schools/law/library/coursebook/envtlaw/teachers

The list of Supplementary Materials in Part III of this manual, and on the Teachers' Website, indicates materials posted on the Teachers' Website that are relevant to this and other chapters.

OVERALL TEACHING THEMES & COURSE DESIGN CONSIDERATIONS

The chapter focuses upon the two most important environmental product regulation statutes:

(i) the Federal Insecticide, Fungicide, and Rodenticide Act (FIFRA) and (ii) the Toxic Substances Control Act (ToSCA). The chapter compares and contrasts these two statutes, by examining their similar regulatory strategies while asking why one (FIFRA) is moderately successful while the other (ToSCA) is rather ineffectual. In making this comparison, the chapter raises three key sets of questions: (1) "How effective are product regulation and market access control strategies in preventing dangerous substances or products from reaching the market, while not impeding the introduction of relatively innocuous and socially desirable products?"; (2) "Is the effectiveness of these strategies largely a function of who is required to produce what information with regard to product safety?" "Is FIFRA reasonably successful because the burden of establishing that a product is safe is on the applicant, whereas, under the less successful ToSCA, EPA must first establish, by substantial evidence, that chemical testing is necessary and then set testing protocols?"; and (3) "How useful is the unreasonable risk standard in particular, and risk-benefit analysis in general?" "Is it possible to balance fairly tangible economic benefits against intangible and uncertain environmental risks?" "If so, what presumptions, burdens of proof, and timing mechanisms should be imposed to facilitate this balance?"

This is a compact (28 pages) chapter that can be assigned and read as a whole in a single assignment, or in conjunction with other chapters concerning toxics/waste management, including Chapters 4, 18, and 19.

TEACHING NOTES, COMMENTS, & ALL QUESTIONS ANSWERED

Pages 816-821. The introduction and the Miller excerpt provide an overview and analysis of FIFRA. It is important for students to possess a firm grasp of the FIFRA process. In this connection, it is useful to emphasize the legal consequences of the differences between suspension and cancellation of a pesticide registration. ToSCA process is equally complex but ultimately less significant, due to the relative ineffectualness of ToSCA.

Pages 821-824. The EDF v. EPA case is an important vehicle for examining the key sets of questions posed in this chapter. The case is particularly useful for analyzing product regulation and market access strategies because (1) cancellation and suspension of registration deny future market access, (2) the "unreasonable adverse effects on the environment" standard applies to all regulatory actions under FIFRA, including initial registration, and (3) the case focuses on burdens of going forward and ultimate persuasion with regard to information regarding health and safety.

The most important aspect of the case is the court's approval of EPA's proactive interpretation of the "imminent hazard" standard for imposing a suspension. When performing a benefit-cost analysis, one must first define "costs" and "benefits." EPA will find it much easier to suspend a pesticide under a "significant threat" standard than under a "crisis" standard of "imminence," because the environmental cost avoidance ramifications of agency action will be far easier to prove. The court's speculations about burdens of proof where there is no offsetting claim of benefits, and about EPA's obligations to discuss benefits under various scenarios of environmental harm and available alternatives, are dicta because EPA had not produced an adequate record with regard to these factors.

Page 824, C&Q #1 and 2. The suspension of aldrin and dieldrin; emergency suspension. *Does the emergency suspension device provide reassurance to courts that EPA can act quickly if further information indicates that suspension is desirable? If so, does the existence of the emergency suspension device affect judges' views pertaining to whether to overturn an ordinary suspension?*

The existence of the emergency suspension device probably discourages judges from overturning ordinary suspensions because it reassures them that EPA can act quickly if further information indicates that suspension is desirable.

Page 824, C&Q #3. The role of benefits in a suspension proceeding. *Would Peter Huber approve of a regulatory scheme that allows a product to be marketed, but makes quick protective withdrawal possible once negative evidence appears?*

Peter Huber would almost certainly approve of this regulatory scheme. Huber, however, underestimates the scientific uncertainty factors that plague benefit-cost analyses in the environmental protection area. Even benefits are uncertain. For example, a pesticide that had been widely used to protect crops against mold and mildew in humid climates was found, after a number of years of use, to destroy the crops and impair the soil's capacity to produce future crops. Huber's faith in benefit-cost analysis flows from his assumption that "(l)arge, centralized, capital-intensive production facilities are easier to operate safely than their small, distributed, labor-intensive alternatives." This assumption is not self-evident in light of introductions of products such as silicon breast implants and the disincentives to corporate information disclosure.

Pages 825-830, C&Q #4-9. FIFRA notes. These notes are explanatory in nature, and are primarily intended to explore important issues arising under FIFRA. The questions raised are answered in the note text. In engaging students in discussion, however, it may be useful to emphasize that, despite efforts to rationalize and strengthen the statute, EPA still relies on manufacturers for information about the safety of their products. It does not conduct independent testing. Much of the information known to the manufacturer is withheld from the public. Unless alerted by the manufacturer to dangers or the need for special restrictions in the use of the product, it is unlikely that EPA will assume the burden of deciding whether a product should not be sold to the public or used in the home. EPA only determines if the testing methodology reportedly used acceptable methods in light of generally accepted scientific standards.

Pages 830-832. This excerpt provides a brief but informative overview of ToSCA. It is a useful basis for discussing the ways in which ToSCA differs from FIFRA, particularly in connection with (i) ToSCA's placing the burden on EPA rather than the manufacturer, and (ii) the effectiveness of a regulatory program like ToSCA.

Pages 832-836. The *Chemical Manufacturers* (I) decision may be viewed as the exception that proves the rule of ToSCA's ineffectuality. The evolution of the EHA test shows the frustrating and burdensome gauntlet that EPA must run in promulgating a ToSCA test rule.

Pages 836-838, C&Q #1-4. ToSCA notes. These notes are explanatory in nature and provide answers to the questions raised in the note text.

Page 838, C&Q #5. The more-than-theoretical-basis test. The court defers to EPA's interpretation here, referring to the differences between Sections 4 and 6 of ToSCA as well as proactive language in ToSCA's legislative history. But the more-than-theoretical-basis threshold test may be overly generous to EPA in light of (1) the strict interpretation accorded §6 in Corrosion Proof Fittings v. EPA (see Chapter 12), and (2) cautionary language on the face of ToSCA and in its legislative history.

Page 839, C&Q #6. The role of economics. *Is it likely that Congress will repudiate, or materially modify, the "unreasonable risk" standard?*

Congress is enamored of standards such as "unreasonable risk" because they leave the difficult policy decisions to administrative agencies and courts. Critics of these broad ambiguous delegations of authority recommend that Congress give specific policy directions to agencies but also allow agencies flexibility with regard to areas of technical expertise and administrative procedure. The trend in Congress, however, is toward pervasive specificity -- selective "micro-management" -- as both industry and public interest lobbyists attempt to ensure that federal agencies are not captured by their opponents. In many cases, the results have been unrealistic deadlines and agency paralysis.

Page 839-840, C&Q #7-8. ToSCA §6 and the attempted asbestos ban. For further discussion on ToSCA §6, see the decision and accompanying discussion in Chapter 13 of Corrosion Proof Fittings v. EPA, which details more fully the Fifth Circuit's overturning of the EPA's order under ToSCA §6 to remove products containing asbestos products.

Page 841-842, C&Q #9. The PCB Mega Rule. This note is explanatory in nature and provides background concerning the regulation of PCBs under ToSCA. The PCB Mega Rule can be viewed as a form of deregulation for those PCB wastes which are high in volume but low in concentration, inasmuch as the Rule builds much more flexibility for EPA into the regulatory process for such PCBs.

Page 842, C&Q #10. Market access statutes and confidentiality. There is an obvious tension between market access, disclosure, confidentiality, and industry cooperation in the regulation of market access, as this comment points out.

Page 842-843, C&Q #11. The future of ToSCA. Without massive amendment -- which is unlikely in the near future -- ToSCA will continue to be a virtual dead letter. But there is a larger question with regard to benefit-cost ("unreasonable risk") statutes in general. Environmental costs are systematically underestimated in contrast to economic benefits because environmental costs are frequently intangible and uncertain, while economic benefits are tangible and most often certain. FIFRA accounts for this discrepancy by placing the burden of going forward and ultimately proving safety on the applicant-registrant at all stages of the pesticide regulation process. ToSCA further exacerbates this problem by placing the burden on EPA, even at the information-gathering stage where there should be a strong presumption in favor of reasonable agency requests for information. In enacting "unreasonable risk" statutes, Congress should weigh the benefit-cost balance on the side of environmental protection so as to provide a margin of safety against unknown adverse environmental effects. Without a congressionally-mandated weighting, agencies and courts, if they wish to protect the environment, will be compelled to adopt legally and politically vulnerable interpretations of ambiguous statutes. For more on that topic, see the 1994 USGAO testimony entitled "Toxic Substances Control Act: Preliminary Observations on Legislative Changes to Make TSCA More Effective," which contains an excellent review of ToSCA and a provocative set of recommendations for resuscitating the statute.

Page 843, C&Q #12. Market access beyond toxics: mad cows? The topic of market access continues to be a vital one, as exemplified by the recent potential emergence of mad cow disease in the United States. The question, of course, is whether attempts to regulate "mad cows" will have any more success than prior historical efforts to regulate market access. In this regard note Baur v Veneman, 352 F.3d 625 (2d Cir., 2003). A citizen filed suit seeking judicial review of the decision of the United States Department of Agriculture denying his petition to ban the use of downed livestock as food for human consumption. The district court granted defendants' motion to dismiss for lack of Article III standing. 212 F.Supp. 2d 280 (2003). The Court of Appeals, Straub, Circuit Judge, held that: (1) the plaintiff's allegation that he faced increased risk of contracting a food-borne illness from the consumption of downed livestock constituted a cognizable injury-in-fact for purposes of alleging Article III standing, and (2) his allegation that downed cattle could transmit a deadly disease with no known cure or treatment successfully alleged a credible threat of harm. Vacated and remanded. Stay tuned.

Chapter 18.
LIFE-CYCLE WASTE CONTROL STRATEGIES: RCRA'S "CRADLE-TO-GRAVE" REGULATION

Chapter contents:

—and check the Teachers' Manual Website for SUPPLEMENTARY MATERIALS:

http://www.bc.edu/schools/law/library/coursebook/envtlaw/teachers

The list of Supplementary Materials in Part III of this manual, and on the Teachers' Website, indicates materials posted on the Teachers' Website that are relevant to this and other chapters.

OVERALL TEACHING THEMES & COURSE DESIGN CONSIDERATIONS

The chapter examines RCRA's Subtitle C — the federal regulatory regime for most hazardous wastes. Owing to RCRA's complexity, the chapter explores RCRA by examining its text, by reviewing excerpts from commentators, and by studying provisions of judicial opinions construing the statute. The key pedagogical interest of the chapter is in analyzing a regulatory system that, almost self-consciously, picks different regulatory techniques and combines them into a whole, integrated approach designed to prevent the release of hazardous waste into the environment.

By now, students have presumably recognized that the Clean Air Act and the Clean Water Act are amalgams of regulatory techniques. RCRA is likewise important taxonomically as a composite of statutory types. But RCRA is also of crucial importance itself as our main hazardous waste control statute, and as our most ambitious attempt to avoid the creation of future orphan hazardous waste sites that now must be cleaned up under CERCLA and its state counterparts (see Chapter 19) or otherwise redressed as part of a brownfields program on the federal or state level (see Chapter 21).

The chapter highlights four key themes. First, RCRA has a very highly complex definitional system that goes to great lengths to define both what is deemed hazardous and what materials are wastes. It is not a comprehensive regulatory system. Much potentially hazardous material is definitionally overlooked under RCRA's terms. RCRA's definitional quagmire makes it one of the most difficult statutes to administer. Second, RCRA's regulation of hazardous waste takes a life cycle approach, trying to regulate the waste from the time of its generation to the time of its destruction or safe disposal. Accordingly, the regulation is addressed primarily to generators, transporters, and treatment-storage-and-disposal (TSD) facility operators. Third, RCRA's elaborate TSD requirements for hazardous wastes have increased the cost of hazardous waste disposal, and this has created substantial incentives for seeking to contest the classification of materials as hazardous waste. Fourth, Congress grew impatient with EPA's dilatory efforts to implement RCRA and employed the "land ban" (an outright ban on land disposal of hazardous waste if EPA did not adopt appropriate implementing regulations by a date certain) as a "hammer" to ensure regulatory action.

This is a chapter of 40 pages that can be assigned and read as a whole in a single assignment, or in conjunction with other chapters concerning waste management, including Chapters 4, 19, and 21. As a chapter that analyzes a statute as an amalgam of statutory types, this chapter can also be read directly in conjunction with other chapters reviewing statutes that are likewise amalgams of statutory types.

TEACHING NOTES, COMMENTS, & ALL QUESTIONS ANSWERED

Pages 845-849. The introductory material places the chapter in context as one that focuses primarily on a crucial part of RCRA: the subtitle C regulation of hazardous waste. The discussion of RCRA's enactment and initial implementation also places RCRA into its historical and political context. RCRA today reflects the outcome of a battle between Congress and the Executive Branch, leading to a regulatory system that significantly reduced EPA's discretion and involved Congress in legislative micromanagement. You can ask students *"Was the Congressional response to Executive Branch inaction necessary?"* and *"Did this Congressional response lead to a more effective and efficient regulatory scheme?"* As the chapter details, there are a number of advantages as well as disadvantages to the legislative micromanagement Congress undertook in RCRA.

Pages 849-853. This discussion analyzes how RCRA defines hazardous waste, focusing on the applicable statutory and regulatory language. It is important for students to possess a firm understanding of how both solid waste and hazardous waste under RCRA are defined by the governing regulations. Figures 1 and 2 provide a helpful summary of EPA's definitional approach. It is also fundamental that students understand the "mixture rule" and the "derived-from" rule, in order to grasp fully how hazardous wastes are defined and identified.

Pages 853-857. The Dithiocarbamate Task Force case is an important vehicle for examining the consequences arising from EPA's identification of a particular solid waste as "hazardous". The case highlights the significance of EPA's rules regarding the listing of a substance as a hazardous waste and how such listing triggers the multitude of regulatory requirements imposed under RCRA subtitle C. You can ask students *"Why was there such vigorous opposition to EPA's listing these substances as hazardous wastes?"*, in order to focus on the significant consequences arising from listing.

Pages 857, C&Q #1. EPA's choice of listing criteria. *Was EPA's choice of listing criteria more demanding than Congress required, or more complex than necessary?*

RCRA § 3001 required EPA to establish criteria for identifying and listing hazardous waste, but the actual listing process established a complex two step process not spelled out by Congress. EPA plainly had difficulty, as reflected in the Dithiocarbamate Task Force case, in satisfying the criteria of 40 C.F.R. §261.11(a)(3). There is certainly a good argument to be made that EPA was entitled to promulgate a less exacting set of listing criteria in the first place. However, given the reliance by business upon § 261.11, EPA likely lacks the will today to alter the rule. In any event, any attempt to alter the rule now would undoubtedly come under vigorous attack by business interests which have conformed their practices to the requirements of the rule.

Pages 857-861. After defining hazardous waste, the discussion provides a brief but important overview of the participants in the hazwaste life cycle. The manifest form, excerpted in Figure 3, provides the linkage among the three key sets of participants in the hazardous waste life cycle. Utilizing Figure 3 as a demonstrative tool can be a useful way to initiate discussion concerning the controlled tracking system which is at the heart of RCRA Subtitle C regulation. For example, some instructors may wish to have groups of class members simulate actors in the course of hazardous waste disposal under RCRA, filling out and exchanging manifest forms among each other. The generators group, for example, would have to deal with questions such as: (1) Should we treat wastes onsite or send them off-site for treatment or disposal? (2) Should we set up a laboratory to test our wastes or use an outside lab? (Should we send split samples to check on our outside lab?) (3) Which transporter and TSDF should we select? (4) Is pollution prevention in our best interests? (5) Given the criminal responsibility of corporate officials (see Chapter 20), how can we make sure that our employees are not cutting corners with regard to hazardous waste disposal? (6) Should we have an environmental audit performed for our facility? Can we be sure that the audit results will remain confidential and not be used by governmental agencies in enforcement proceedings against us? (see Chapter 21).

Page 861, C&Q #1. RCRA's regulatory scheme as a series of statutory types. This note reviews RCRA's regulatory scheme as a series of statutory types. The students should be encouraged to see how these devices fit into statutory categories (with reference to examples presented in earlier chapters). In addition, the students should be encouraged to consider how modern statutes frequently combine several statutory techniques to achieve their objectives. The variety and diversity of statutory types selected by Congress to effectuate environmental goals is a continuing theme of this casebook.

Page 862, C&Q #2. RCA's impact. The comment points out the reduced number of facilities that hazardous wastes are likely to be consigned to in a RCRA world. Not only does this mean that we have a better idea of where the waste is, but it also means that there are economies of scale in managing waste and regulating it at a smaller number of larger, more technologically sophisticated sites.

Page 862-863, C&Q #3. The cost of RCRA disposal. We have mixed reactions to this material. On the one hand, the figures make the cost of RCRA disposal seem quite manageable for ordinary generators. The percentage is so low as to be an inconsequential cost to pass on to consumers of products that generate hazwaste as a byproduct. On the other hand, the cost per ton and per cubic yard for contaminated soil disposal are staggering due to the vast quantities of contaminated soil that might be involved at either a Superfund site or a large RCRA corrective action site.

Page 863, C&Q #4. TSD industry characteristics. These numbers are offered to provide the students with some perspective on the size of the firms involved in subtitle C TSD operations.

Page 863-864, C&Q #5. Criticizing RCRA: under-regulation. Subtitle D is a loophole that is larger than the regulatory system of Subtitle C. As John Dernbach's material points out, the amount of industrial waste dwarfs the amount of hazardous waste , and a fair proportion of the industrial waste has the same characteristics as the hazardous waste.

Page 864-865, C&Q #6. Criticizing RCRA: over-regulation. The examples do make the point that there are instances in which RCRA makes society less safe. The comment can be tied back to the Latin/Stewart-Ackerman debate. Can the most irrational aspects of RCRA that achieve bad regulatory results at a high price be rooted out without weakening the ability of RCRA to achieve good results at a reasonable price in other contexts? The students can sometimes be stimulated to engage in this debate.

Page 865-866, C&Q #7. Criticizing RCRA: definitional nightmares concerning "hazardous" wastes. This comment highlights the point that the definitional nightmares concerning what is "hazardous waste" continue, as EPA has struggled with developing a new and defensible Hazardous Waste Identification Rule (HWIR). As the comment notes, after the D.C. Circuit in Shell Oil Co. v. EPA vacated EPA's "mixture" and "derived-from" rules (on the grounds that EPA failed to provide adequate notice or solicit public comment), EPA was forced via a consent decree to propose a new HWIR. The proposed HWIR signaled a trend away from technology-based regulation of hazardous wastes under RCRA towards a harm-based regulatory approach. EPA proposed "exit levels" for 376 chemical constituents in listed hazardous wastes. Under the new HWIR, listed hazardous wastes — which were to include mixtures, treatment residues, and contaminated media from remediation sites — could be exempt from RCRA regulation if they did not contain one of the 376 constituents above its exit level. The exit levels were derived from a complex risk-based system using "one in one million" (for cancer risks) and "no observable toxic effects" (for non-carcinogenic and ecological risks) as endpoints. As with all harm-based systems, questions about the implementation of the proposed HWIR rules and their feasibility were vigorously raised. The types of questions raised are identified in the comment text.

Page 866, C&Q #8. Criticizing RCRA: definitional nightmares concerning recycling. RCRA only applies to "solid waste," which is defined, in part, as "discarded material". Whether and when RCRA applies to recycling activities has been a major obstacle to efficient implementation of the statute. For a useful discussion of this matter, see Needleman, Hazardous Waste Recycling Under The Resource Conservation And Recovery Act: Problems And Potential Solutions, 24 Env. L. 971 (1994).

Page 866-867, C&Q #9. When exempt household waste is incinerated, is its hazardous ash exempt too? The Chicago v. EDF decision illustrates that legislative micromanagement is not always comprehensive. Although Congress exempted municipal solid waste (MSW) from subtitle C, Congress did not specify if ash from incineration of MSW is also subtitle C exempt. The Supreme Court resolved a split in the Circuits to decide this question, when it held that toxic ash does not fall within the MSW exemption and must be regulated if it possesses the characteristics of hazardous waste.

Page 867-868, C&Q #10 and 11. #10 Rethinking RCRA; Reforms to RCRA corrective action. These comments suggest that RCRA needs some rethinking to resolve its shortcomings and to simplify its definitional complexities. However, RCRA is low on the Congressional agenda because most legislators and lobbyists believe that the problems with RCRA can be resolved by administrative rule-making. EPA is nonetheless pushing its own set of reforms, as the comments note.

Page 868-869, C&Q #12. International shipments. Students should be aware that RCRA impacts exporters and international shipments.

Page 869, C&Q #13. Underground storage tank regulations. The UST Program excludes (1) farm or home fuel tanks of less than 1,100 gallons (2) take home heating oil tanks (3) septic tanks (4) pipelines regulated under other laws (5) wastewater or stormwater collection and treatment systems and (6) UST systems holding less than 110 gallons or de minimis amounts of hazardous materials.
The UST Program contains the following elements:

- Standards for design, construction, and installation of new tanks
- Requirements for retrofitting existing tanks with anti-corrosion, overfill prevention, and release detection systems (existing tanks must upgrade by December 1998 or close down)
- Operation, maintenance, and inspection requirements
- Release detection, investigation, and reporting requirements
- Corrective action obligations
- Tank closure procedures and
- Financial responsibility requirements

A miniature Superfund (the Leaking Underground Storage Tank Trust Fund, financed by a tax on motor fuels) has been created to fund EPA or state cleanups of UST releases.

Pages 869-870, C&Q #14. Life cycle assessment in the private sector. RCRA's regulatory strategy is also impacting the private sector through life-cycle assessment for products, processes, and practices.

Pages 870-873. The ins and outs of the land ban are not the key matter here. What is most important is that the students understand enough about the land ban to understand why the threat of it was an effective hammer. Here, the issue is the cost of treatment that alters hazardous waste into something else that can be land disposed. For the most part, the treatment that meets that test is high temperature incineration, as in cement kilns and some other facilities.

The reason to believe that EPA had no chance of meeting the deadlines of the land ban lies in the difficulty in setting standards of non-hazardousness for all of the things that make hazardous waste hazardous. Recalling the failure of EPA to promulgate NESHAPS for more than a handful of toxic air pollutants, and its similar inability to generate harm-based standards for toxics in other settings, this one too seemed likely to end in failure. EPA met the deadlines to avoid the land ban by switching to a technology-based approach.

Pages 873-877, C&Q #1-2. Politics and judicial review; Legislative micromanagement, pro and con. In The Hazardous Waste Treatment Council case, the D.C. Circuit directed EPA to explain its preference for technology based treatment standards over the approach based on screening levels. By remanding for a rational and consistent explanation of EPA's position, the D.C. Circuit forced EPA both to produce an adequate record for further judicial review and to articulate a rational basis for its preferences based upon that record. This is an example of legislative micromanagement, coupled with appropriate judicial review, which together pushed a reluctant EPA to implement RCRA more effectively.

Page 877, C&Q #3. Hammer clauses. The comment is rhetorical, basically concluding that Congress got the administrative speed it wanted, but at a cost that may have included the sacrifice of the primary goal it had sought to achieve. There is a lesson here that is reminiscent of the technology-forcing materials. For the hammer to be effective in spurring action, it has to provide an extremely unpleasant alternative to the result it intends to promote. There is always the risk that if the regulation fails to be adopted, the unpleasant and politically unpopular alternative may be inflicted upon society. It seems quite possible that if EPA had failed, Congress would have blinked. A strictly enforced land ban would have forced many waste generators to cease operation until incineration capacity increased, something that is proceeding at a hesitant pace.

Page 877, C&Q #4. Is BDAT bad? The claim in the comment that BDAT will deter innovation may turn out to be incorrect, especially if a lucrative market develops for waste minimization technology and less expensive treatments that produce fewer hazardous residuals.

Page 877-878, C&Q #5. The "no migration" variance. The "no-migration" variance has not been widely used, in part because it shifts the burden to the applicant to show that the technology-based standard is not necessary.

Page 878, C&Q #6. Underground injection. Students should be aware that underground injection of hazardous waste is a regulated activity with additional regulatory requirements (the UIC regulations).

Page 878-879, C&Q #7. Undersupply of TSD capacity. There is empirical data showing that almost two-thirds of the currently open RCRA Subtitle C facilities are trying to close, a trend that is moving in the opposite direction of the demand for TSD capacity. Even if variances that undermine the intent of the land ban become the norm, there is not likely to be sufficient TSD capacity to meet the demand under the current price structure. It can be predicted that the NIMBY problem will thwart many efforts to meet the imbalance by opening new facilities. Therefore, as supply changes only slightly (and probably decreases markedly due to closures) and demand escalates, the price of disposal will skyrocket. With that change in prices, waste minimization will get a major boost. That is a good development, and a development consistent with Congressional intent, but it is not being obtained in the most straightforward way.

Page 879-880, C&Q #8. The RCRA Subtitle C universe. This material may need to be explained to the students, and the explanation may be useful in expanding their understanding of RCRA's permitted facilities concept. As the excerpted material notes, as the list of wastes covered under RCRA Subtitle C expands, solid waste management units (SWMUs) that previously had no regulated hazardous wastes now become sites that require RCRA Subtitle C licensure, with all of its burdens. Among the most onerous of these burdens are threat of corrective actions and the stringent closure requirements.

Pages 880-881, C&Q #9. The future of overfilling under RCRA. Overfiling is a standard enforcement technique long utilized by EPA. However, the future of overfilling under RCRA has now been called into question by Harmon and Power Engineering, as the comment emphasizes. This split in the Circuits provides ample fodder for class debate. A useful teaching tool would be to utilize this debate as an introduction to problems of environmental enforcement, with specific reference to the flow of the enforcement process (Chapter 21, infra, at 1004-1006).

Pages 881-882. RCRA citizen suits to obtain cleanup and potential cost recovery are most significant in cases of petroleum contamination, when a CERCLA remedy is not available due to the petroleum exclusion under CERCLA. See 42 U.S.C.A. § 9601(14). Litigants frustrated with their inability to invoke CERCLA to redress petroleum contamination sought an alternative to CERCLA, by initiating citizen suits under RCRA. In the *Meghrig* case, the Supreme Court held that the RCRA citizen suit provision was not intended to provide a remedy for past cleanup costs. The *Meghrig* case provides a vehicle to examine the petroleum exclusion under CERCLA and its effect upon litigation strategies. It also provides an introduction to CERCLA and a bridge to the CERCLA materials in Chapter 18 which follow.

Page 884, C&Q #1. Remaining questions regarding the scope of §7002. *Can a private party sue under § 7002(a)(1)(B) while an imminent endangerment still exists and obtain restitution of response costs for work taken thereafter?*

This comment highlights the fact that, in the *Meghrig* case, the Supreme Court carefully and only answered whether past cleanup costs could be recovered in a RCRA citizen suit, leaving open whether ongoing or future cleanup costs are recoverable. Justice O'Connor's conclusions cast doubt on whether the Supreme Court might reach a different result if ongoing or future costs were at issue, but nonetheless, the recovery of such costs remains an open question.

Page 884-885, C&Q #2. The importance of *Meghrig*. This comment reminds students that, regardless of whether RCRA provides any restitutionary remedy, state common law and state statutory law typically still provide some relief. Accordingly, there are remedies available under state law for remediating petroleum spills, although their efficacy is subject to debate.

Page 885, C&Q #3. Strategic considerations after *Meghrig*. *After the Supreme Court's decision in Meghrig, does a party faced with petroleum contamination on its property have an incentive to sue those responsible for the contamination before undertaking the cleanup?*

Litigants have not been foreclosed under *Meghrig* from seeking relief from ongoing petroleum contamination in a RCRA citizen suit. There is, therefore, an incentive to file suit first before undertaking cleanup if such a suit could result in a remedy which requires other liable parties to pay for or share in ongoing or future cleanup costs. The likelihood of recovery in such a scenario, however, remains open to question. If the views of the Seventh Circuit are followed, cleanup and investigatory costs will not be recoverable under §7002.

Chapter 19.
REMEDIAL LIABILITY STRATEGIES: TOXIC CLEANUPS AND THEIR FUNDING UNDER CERCLA AND STATE PROGRAMS

Chapter contents:

—and check the Teachers' Manual Website for SUPPLEMENTARY MATERIALS:

http://www.bc.edu/schools/law/library/coursebook/envtlaw/teachers

The list of Supplementary Materials in Part III of this manual, and on the Teachers' Website, indicates materials posted on the Teachers' Website that are relevant to this and other chapters.

OVERALL TEACHING THEMES & COURSE DESIGN CONSIDERATIONS

The chapter addresses the remedial liability strategies which Congress enacted in the Comprehensive Environmental Response, Compensation, and Liability Act (CERCLA) to secure the funding for the cleanup and the cleanup of releases of hazardous substances into the environment. The chapter begins with a study of CERCLA's liability rules as developed through the judicial process of statutory interpretation, asking the questions "How has the judiciary given greater definition to CERCLA through the process of deciding cases that involve the statute?" and "How has the judiciary utilized the broad remedial purpose of CERCLA as a guide that leads to CERCLA's expansive interpretation?" This part of the chapter thus serves as an example of how courts use common law to define public law statutes. After focusing on CERCLA's liability rules (and, in particular, the judicial interpretation of CERCLA §107), the chapter addresses EPA's administrative order authority under CERCLA §106, highlighting one of EPA's most potent enforcement tools. The chapter then provides an overview of how the cleanup process works, targeting the administration of the cleanup program by EPA and focusing on strategy and fairness. In particular, this part of the chapter asks the questions "What is the process for identifying and remediating hazardous waste sites? "How are site identification and hazard ranking used to set priorities for cleanups?", and "What is the purpose and effect of the National Contingency Plan (NCP)?" The chapter takes a critical look at the CERCLA process, asking "Does CERCLA involve excessive transaction costs and delays in its cost recovery program or in the allied area of selecting and implementing remedial actions?" Finally, the chapter examines EPA's strategy for cost recovery and loss allocation. The cost allocation process is affected by EPA's strategic need to obtain the PRP's "cooperation." Some of EPA's strategies involve a strong possibility of apparent unfairness to a portion of the PRP class at any given site. PRPs themselves often engage in strategic behavior in attempting to deflect as much of the loss as possible to their co-PRPs. Ultimately, the chapter asks the questions "Is EPA's power to dictate settlement terms enhanced by the difficulties faced by judges in reviewing complex CERCLA cost allocation issues?" and "How does EPA's power to direct punitive matters toward 'recalcitrant' PRPs enhance EPS's bargaining position?"

This is a lengthy (68 pages) chapter that is best taught over several class periods. It can also be read in conjunction with Chapter 18, for an understanding of CERCLA's relationship to RCRA, and with Chapter 21, for an understanding of the shortcomings in CERCLA's remedial liability strategy which have recently led EPA and the states to develop additional enforcement strategies that represent a more flexible and cooperative approach with business.

TEACHING NOTES, COMMENTS, & ALL QUESTIONS ANSWERED

Pages 886-888. This introduction sets the scene for an exploration of CERCLA's liability scheme, in the context of the high profile events which galvanized public and congressional opinion in favor of an accounting from those responsible for the public health threats caused by hazardous releases.

Pages 888-892. CERCLA §107 appears here and is used as an introduction to how statutes differ from the common law in their approach, yet still rely on common law-like processes to inform their interpretation and application to particular cases. This is one of the few times when a statutory provision's full text will appear in this book, presenting an opportunity to teach students how to "issue spot" a statute to predict what issues are likely to require litigation before the statute's meaning is established and what issues will remain important beyond litigation. Learning this skill is vital for practitioners in the environmental area, given the current degree of statutory flux. Beyond these fundamental legal process and statutory precepts, this material is also key to the study of hazardous release remediation laws. In particular, with respect to CERCLA §107, it is important for students to understand that CERCLA §107 is concerned with the point of release or imminent threatened release into the environment, and times that follow release (as is also true of CERCLA §106 and RCRA §7003). Thus, CERCLA §107 is not a prescription for how to prevent releases (that is RCRA's more general function). Nor is CERCLA §107 a law mandating waste minimization (that is a function of other parts of RCRA and the Pollution Prevention Act of 1990). CERCLA §107 is a liability based regime (as opposed to CERCLA §106 and RCRA §7003, with their responsibility and order (Just do it!) regimes). It is also important to point out that the list of recoverable items in CERCLA §107 does not include damages for personal injuries. The point here is that the common law continues to have an important role that complements the statutory scheme. Depending on your own familiarity with the several statutes, you can interweave a brief discussion of ToSCA, FIFRA, SDWA, EPCRA, and other statutes here. Definitional items are the next topic. Key terms need content. These include "hazardous waste," "release," "facility," and less obvious terms like "person," that includes individuals, corporations, governments and other types of legal entities. This is an area where the instructor must provide additional information, such as the twisting definitional trail of "hazardous substance" that leads from CERCLA §9601 (14) to the Clean Water Act 33 U.S.C. §3121 (b) (2)(a), RCRA §6921, etc. The goal here is for students to see that Congress has created a complex set of definitions that need to be accounted for in later efforts to apply these statutory sections.

Page 892, C&Q #1. CERCLA and §311 of the Federal Water Pollution Control Act. This comment points out that Congress was not writing entirely on a clean slate in enacting CERCLA but rather was mindful of the model established under Section 311 of the FWPCA.

Page 893, C&Q #2. A common law substitute for Superfund? *What does CERCLA §107 accomplish that the common law could not?*

The note highlights key components of the answer to this question, with particular reference to natural resource damages as a step beyond traditional tort law, and health studies as an item of recoverable damage, also an element beyond traditional tort law.

Page 893-894, C&Q #3-4. Joint and several liability in CERCLA cases; The Unfairness of joint and several liability. The major problem of imposing joint and several liability on a PRP and collecting from that PRP alone is that the difficulty of apportioning liability in the first suit is no easier in the second suit. The same lack of full information and absence of obvious standards for allocation persist. Worse still, at least in theory, the party seeking contribution could be subjected to the more common burdens of proof of causation, rendering it impossible to prove that any of the defendants in contribution are responsible. The Monsanto case is illustrative. First, the site owner is held jointly and severally liable with the generator defendants, despite the fundamental difference in the character of their involvement at the site. That differentiation is left for the anticipated contribution action that will follow after EPA has collected its award from whomever among the jointly and severally liable defendants it chooses to pursue. Second, the court acknowledges that it is creating a piece of federal common law to fill the interstices of CERCLA, here the appropriateness of imposing joint and several liability. This self-conscious call to common law principles leads to reliance on Restatement of Torts (2d) principles. Third, and perhaps most important, the court is hesitant to impose any burden on the government to produce a rationale for apportionment (such as volumetric apportionment) across the wide range of wastes present at this site.

Page 894, C&Q #5. Divisibility of harm or of costs? This comment, perhaps too subtly, is driving at what might be labeled the problem of "negative" synergy. The classic instance of this is where (1) one form of waste is very toxic and relatively expensive to cleanup on a volumetric basis, but very little of it is present, and (2) another form of waste is very plentiful on a volumetric basis but it is generally inexpensive to cleanup, but (3) because of their mixture together at a single site, the aggregate is both very plentiful and very expensive to clean up per unit volume. For a real world example, we have in mind something along the lines of the Kramer site, where municipal trash is the high volume, low cleanup cost material. There the high-toxic generators are arguing that "but-for causation" proves that the municipal waste caused the bulk of response costs. The cost for cleaning up the high-toxic wastes alone would only be a (relatively) small amount, say $6M. Thus the $60M cost of cleaning the site "proves" that the cost share of the municipal generators ought to be $54M. What the argument overlooks is that cleanup of municipal waste alone would probably not require very much of the expensive treatment that the high-toxic wastes required. Thus, for example, treating a pure municipal waste landfill (containing occasional household hazardous wastes and small quantity generators hazardous wastes) might be in the $12-20M range, not $54M as the high-toxic generators had "proved."

EPA issued a guidance document regarding municipal liability. See Superfund Program, Interim Municipal Settlement Policy, 54 Fed. Reg. 51,071 (1989). Its position, as set forth in the guidance, is generally quite favorable to municipalities, not naming them as PRPs unless circumstances require otherwise and calling for settlements with contribution protection whenever municipalities are even potential PRPs. The crux of the justification for this position is that EPA believes "that it is generally not a cost-effective use of our enforcement resources to pursue those...whose only contribution at a Superfund site appears to have been contaminated only with relatively small quantities of household hazardous wastes (e.g., municipal solid waste)..." Nonetheless, municipalities have no Eleventh Amendment protection (unlike the states) and are theoretically liable just like any other PRP.

Page 895, C&Q #6. Emerging cracks in EPA's joint and several armor. Despite hopeful predictions by some defense counsel that the Alcan and Bell cases were the harbingers of the demise of joint and several liability, not many PRPs are winning several liability in litigation. Instead, CERCLA is churning out numerous decisions that are doing relatively little to change its basic aspect: strict, joint and several, retroactive liability, for a broadly defined class of owners or arrangers, and a narrowly defined class of transporters.

Page 896, C&Q #7. Administrative order powers. This comment alerts the students to the importance of EPA's administrative order powers, discussed in Part B of the chapter.

Page 898, C&Q #1. Comparison to toxic tort cases. *How does the relaxation of the government's burdens in proving causation compare with handling of burden of proof issues in traditional and toxic tort cases?*

CERCLA, insofar as it is patterned on a tort-type cause of action, requires proof linking defendant's actionable conduct to the costs for which recovery is sought. This is no more or less than a causal link of the cause-in-fact variety. The defendants are seeking to force proof of a 1:1 correlation between their wastes and cleanup costs, a degree of proof that the government admits it cannot muster. As a general matter, before the decision in cases like Wade II, defending on the basis of failure to prove cause-in-fact was a good tactic. Not only would the government have had a difficult time allocating expenses to particular chemicals present at the site (and an impossible task identifying which of similar types of chemicals came from each specific PRP), the government at many of the *Wade*-like sites always has a hard time proving just whose waste is present. Typical testimony included truck drivers trying to recall whose waste (in unmarked drums) they picked up and brought to a site more than thirty years ago.

Pages 898-906. The basic script in the *NEPACCO* case is simple enough. In the early 1970s, NEPACCO arranged for hazardous waste to be sent to the Denney farm for disposal by burial, an action that was no doubt ill-advised, but not illegal at the time. Before long the drums began to leak and sometime thereafter, in 1979, EPA received an anonymous tip about the existence of the site. The only other key facts are that in the meantime, in 1974, NEPACCO was liquidated, and forfeited its charter to do business in 1976.

It is helpful to ask who the obvious PRPs are. Denney is the owner-operator because the farm, not the NEPACCO plant, is the facility. Mills is the transporter. NEPACCO is the generator. Their combined net worth (according to our fanciful hypothesis) is: 7 cows (Denney), 1 old pick-up truck (Mills), and nothing -- the remaining assets of NEPACCO after liquidation. Whatever the real amounts, the plain indication is that the assets of these three PRPs will not pay for cleaning the site, thus the EPA effort to reach Lee and Michaels. Lee presents the easier case. Lee, who is sued under §107(a) (3) as an arranger, is plainly the person who made the choice to dispose of the hazwaste in this fashion. On a non-statutory front, the corporate capacity defense is unavailing -- Lee is analogous to the tortfeasor-servant employee who commits a tort while on the business of the master. The servant is individually liable to the victim, even if victims seldom bother to sue the tortfeasing servant-employee rather than the master-employer. Here, however, the usual solvency roles are reversed. Turning to defenses based on statutory interpretation, Lee's argument that he is not the "possessor" of the hazwaste ("it belongs to NEPACCO, not Lee') is rejected by the court as being "inconsistent with the broad remedial purposes of CERCLA." This is a chance to show how important the policy statements and declarations of purpose can be in statutory interpretation.

Lee, as a statutory defense, makes the non-retroactivity argument (as does Michaels). There are two aspects to the argument -- one is the fairness of imposing liability based on standards that did not apply at the time of the action; the other is a question of statutory interpretation, asking whether Congress intended retroactive liability. The fairness question deserves some debate as an abstract matter. On the merits of Lee's case, even if there were no regulatory proscription against burying the drums in a field, it seems at least negligent (if not grossly negligent) to do so under the state of knowledge that must have prevailed in the 1970s. Still, there must be some forms of non-negligent disposal that were both reasonable and prudent in a pre-RCRA and pre-CERCLA world that later become sources of massive potential liability. This observation leads almost inevitably into the policy justifications for imposing such drastic after-the-fact liability, and into the congressional purposes in enacting CERCLA and RCRA. The court's two arguments seem to me to be quite unequal in force. The argument that RCRA and CERCLA intend that there be liability for the present consequences of past acts seems quite strong, for, were it otherwise, Superfund would soon be out of money and the legislation would have failed in its efforts to place the remedial costs on the parties responsible for creating them. The argument that Congress' later amendment of the language to be expressly retroactive is conclusive of its earlier intent is not strong. The views of a later Congress of what was the intent of a previous Congress is but one fragmentary piece of evidence in discerning the original intent. A third line of defense is the limiting language of §107(b) saying there are no other defenses than those spelled out. This too can be viewed as an indication of the broad liability scheme that was intended.

Michaels presents a tougher case for imposing liability because he appears to be sufficiently remote from the day-to-day operations of the Verona plant that labeling him a §107(a)(3) arranger seems to stretch the definition a bit. Instead he is sued under the more congenial language of RCRA §7003 that requires only actions "contributing to" dumping. The EPA advocates a "control or ability-to-control" standard and wins, again aided by the court's view of congressional intent to effectuate the statute's broad remedial goals. It is probably worth taking a moment to consider how much control ought to be required before imposing personal liability, because control issues can be important in parent-subsidiary issues (as the Supreme Court has now recognized in United States v. Bestfoods, Inc.), in "veil piercing," and in lender/borrower contexts, all of which have been hotly contested areas of statutory interpretation under CERCLA.

Page 906, C&Q #1. Private plaintiffs and cleanup legislation. It is worth making the distinction: CERCLA allows for private recovery of cleanup costs, but natural resource damages are recoverable only by governmental plaintiffs, and recovery for cleanup costs is certainly not the equivalent of a private suit for the full range of damages caused by contamination.

Page 906, C&Q #2. Retroactivity. As noted in the discussion of the *NEPACCO* case, the strongest argument against retroactivity is the fairness argument. This can be stretched to constitutional magnitude, characterizing it as ex post facto law, when criminal penalties are involved. Nonetheless, as the *Olin* case demonstrates, the courts have not been impressed by arguments against the retroactive application of CERCLA.

Page 907, C&Q #3. The strategy of avoiding §107 recoveries. This comment emphasizes that, on a practical level, EPA's enforcement strategies are dictated in part by the shortage of funds to pay for Superfund cleanups.

Page 907, C&Q #4. The relevance of the views of a subsequent Congress. *What is the relevance of the views of members of a later Congress as evidence of what members of the 1980 Congress actually intended?*

As noted above in the discussion of *NEPACCO,* this is not a very strong line of support. The question should spur a legal process realization for the students about the intersection of legislative supremacy and separation of powers. Although legislative supremacy includes the power of a subsequent legislature to amend a statute to overcome court decisions that "misinterpreted the prior statute," that power operates prospectively. The later Congress cannot legitimately tell the courts how to interpret the work of past legislatures. Their opinion may shed light on the backward-looking question of what the intent of the earlier group may have been (due to similarity of membership, etc., though this process is iffy) but interpretation is the province of the court.

Page 907, C&Q #5. Arranging for disposal under CERCLA §107(a)(3). *Should different liability standards under CERCLA apply to corporate officers in widely held corporations?*

There is no important distinction between closely held corporations and widely held corporations when it comes to the individual liability of corporate officers under the arranging-for test. Arranger liability, when applied to a closely held corporation, as was done in *ARCO,* resembles piercing the corporate veil. Most large publicly held corporations provide indemnity to their corporate officers for acts done in furtherance of corporate interests. In cases where the corporation is solvent, such an indemnity shifts the loss from the officer to the corporate entity. In the event that the corporation is solvent, efforts to pursue individuals as arrangers are far less likely to occur.

Page 908, C&Q #6. Selling hazardous materials as a form of disposal. *Is the sale of products containing hazardous materials "arranging for disposal" of those materials?*

The question may seem a bit odd, but one of RCRA's major definitional problems arises in the selling of waste hazardous materials that contain recoverable (and valuable) amounts of energy or chemical substances.

Page 908, C&Q #7. Processing hazardous materials through third parties as a form of disposal. The *Aceto* decision is the leading case on whether processing hazardous materials through third parties can constitute a form of disposal. Note that, in Aceto, the manufacturers sent their materials to a third party under a tolling agreement, and the third party's activities gave rise to contamination. The *Morton International* decision provides a good summary of the considerations to be addressed in establishing a baseline for "arranger" liability.

Page 909, C&Q #8. Recycling. *Where on the continuum between sale of a useful product and arranging for disposal does recycling fall?*

The comment answers this question but raises the thorny issue of whether imposing arranger liability in the recycling context will discourage the environmentally desirable goal of recycling.

Page 910-911. The idea of these few pages and the commentary that follows is to chronicle, in brief, the extraordinary expansion of the PRP class in response to CERCLA suits. Almost all of the expansion was done through fairly reasonable judicial interpretations of statutory language. To the extent that Congress paid attention to the process of interpretation, it added its voice on the side of breadth of coverage, in SARA and in the 1996 Superfund Amendments pertaining to lender liability. There is a world of room to inundate the students with a litany of new decisions that take successor liability a jot forward, cut back a hair on arranger liability, trap trustees in some new and even less fair way, and so forth. For those who are not active CERCLA practitioners, most of this is not vital.

What is important in all of this are a few basic themes. The signal "law fact" that is important is the breadth of the categories of activities that fall into owning/operating, arranging, and transporting, i.e., the vast array of conduct that makes the actor a PRP. The initial legal process importance of the cases lies in the search for congressional intent and the forms of evidence and argument that have led to so much liberal construction of CERCLA's liability provisions. A second legal process point becomes important -- the legislative branch can and does have continuing control over these liability schemes.

Pages 911-912, C&Q #1 and 2. The Superfund Amendments and Reauthorization Act of 1986 (SARA); Lender liability and the 1996 Superfund Amendments. These comments together emphasize that Congress has the power to clarify, limit, or modify CERCLA's liability schemes. SARA, in 1986, appeared to broaden liability expansively. Ten years later, however, Congress recognized that, in the lender liability context, the breadth of the test applied by the 11th Circuit for lender liability in *Fleet Factors*, and by certain other courts, had proven to be problematic. When EPA failed in its efforts to limit lender liability by rule, Congress stepped in to do so by legislation in the Asset Conservation, Lender Liability, and Deposit Insurance Act. This legislation was passed when a storm of protest from the lending industry erupted after the *Fleet Factors* decision. This set of events provides a useful case study for an examination of the process of legal change involving the interplay among EPA, the courts, and Congress.

Page 913, C&Q #3. How the courts make CERCLA liability policy. Although it is perhaps unnecessary to say, in our view the *Anspec* holding is absolutely correct: the CERCLA cases are engaged in "mere" statutory interpretation.

Page 914, C&Q #4. Would you buy this land?

This is historically a weak spot in CERCLA and state contamination cleanup laws. The traditional legal requirement, backed by joint and several liability, is for a total cleanup. This means that a potential purchaser with knowledge of the contamination historically had no incentive to get involved unless the cleanup costs can be known with certainty and are less than the value of the parcel after it has been cleaned. Even if such a value test might frequently be met (which is doubtful for most bad sites), the uncertainty of cleanup costs has acted as a brake on virtually all transactions that call for the purchase of an unclean site by a party willing to invest some (but not an unlimited or uncertain) amount in the parcel's reclamation. EPA and the states could be doing more in this area by using mixed funding (part Fund money, part PRP money) or carve-outs (a PRP is responsible for a certain agreed portion of the cleanup work, and EPA agrees to recoup any other recoverable costs from other PRPs). But the politics of getting cleanups sufficient to meet public demands, and EPA reluctance to expose the fund to drafts for sites having collectible PRPs, limited the use of these devices. In the end the sites often become a "taboo" zone, even after their remediation. In light of this taboo, Congress and the states have recently developed brownfields programs, in an effort to encourage redevelopment. (See Chapter 21.) The Small Business Relief and Brownfields Revitalization Act represented Congress' efforts to encourage the development of brownfields, by mitigating the risks and by providing positive incentives to do so.

Page 914, C&Q #5. The "act of a third party" defense. We make little effort to pin down what constitutes an adequate inquiry to avoid liability if contamination caused by past events is discovered post-purchase. For the most part, you might talk about the availability of environmental consulting firms to provide audits and other such services. What seems more important is that §101(35) acts like a congressional determination to have all of the most likely sites discovered and (given the nature of CERCLA) paid for now. The Laskins Arcade case is worth noting, as it suggests that, for liability to attach, the contractual relationship must relate to the hazardous substances being released.

Page 915, C&Q #6-7. Insurance; Insolvency. Matters of insurance and insolvency touch upon the fiscal condition of the actors who play on the hazardous waste stage. These subjects are only dealt with briefly here, in order to "issue-spot" them for the students. It may be worth noting the substantial litigation which has evolved over who will ultimately bear the costs of cleanup -- the PRPs, their insurers, or third party creditors who are left holding the bag. With respect to insurance, the important policy question is whether liability for releases is or should be covered by the policies in question. Shifting the loss to insurance companies tends to spread the loss more broadly and makes additional assets available to meet cleanup costs. To engage in that loss spreading, however, may allow culpable parties to avoid bearing the real cost of their behavior. With respect to insolvency, the important policy question is how to address the fundamental tension between the objectives of bankruptcy law (i.e., to provide the bankrupt with a fresh start, freed of previous debts) with the goals of CERCLA (where there is a strong interest in making all of the bankrupt's assets, both present and future, available to remediate the hazards which the bankrupt PRP has helped to create).

PAGES 916-923, *BestFoods*

C&Q #1-7. #1. Piercing the corporate veil. #2. Operator liability of the parent corporation. #3. Parent corporation liability through the acts of officers and directors. #4. What types of acts are enough for "operator" liability to attach for parent corporations? #5. After *BestFoods,* will it be more difficult to hold parent corporations liable under CERCLA for contamination at their subsidiary's sites? #6. After *BestFoods,* may a parent corporation rely on its own environmental management staff to supervise its subsidiary's compliance without risk of Superfund liability? #7. Successor corporations.

The material in this section is worthy of some discussion in class. In its decision in United States v. BestFoods, the Supreme Court addressed significant questions about a parent corporation's potential liability for contamination at sites owned or leased by its subsidiary. After a morass of conflicting lower court decisions about parent corporation liability, the Supreme Court's opinion clarified that a parent corporation engaged in normal supervision of a subsidiary is not liable under CERCLA for contamination associated with the subsidiary. The Court also specified that a normal parent-subsidiary relationship, including such commonplace practices as a parent's (i) appointing its own officers and directors to similar positions in a subsidiary, (ii) supervising a subsidiary's finances and approving its capital expenditures, and (iii) formulating general policies and procedures for the subsidiary, would not give rise to CERCLA liability. Instead, the Court limited the circumstances in which a parent corporation may be held liable under CERCLA to a few narrow situations. These situations would include the circumstances in which the common law would allow piercing of the corporate veil, such as when the subsidiary fails to follow the formalities required to maintain corporation separateness, or where a subsidiary is used for a fraudulent purpose. The Supreme Court also stated that a parent corporation may be directly liable in situations where an employee of a parent corporation -- who held no position in the subsidiary -- directly managed a subsidiary's operations which created the pollution problem. These specific situations are much more limited than the broad scope of parent liability advocated by the government. The Bestfoods decision accordingly provides guidance and comfort to parent companies that they may engage in the normal oversight of subsidiaries without increasing their own risk of incurring Superfund liability.

In the litigation context, this decision has declared that much of the evidence upon which the government has traditionally relied in suing parent corporations is insufficient to establish CERCLA liability. In the past, the government has built many of its cases against parent corporations by showing that the same individuals were officers or directors of both the parent and the subsidiary, that the parent established general policies and practices for the subsidiary to follow, and that the parent's approval was necessary before the subsidiary could make substantial expenditures. Now this evidence will be viewed as indications of normal parent-subsidiary relationships; without additional facts, this evidence alone will not prove CERCLA liability. To hold a parent company liable, the government will either have to meet the common law standards of piercing the corporate veil or show that the parent directly controlled environmental activities at the subsidiary's site. Future cases will determine exactly what type of proof will be sufficient for liability, but the focus of proof will be on the relationship between the parent and the site, not the parent and the subsidiary. In the context of transactions and everyday corporate activities, the decision has an even greater consequence. Companies now have guidance to help structure deals in ways that will minimize the risk of a purchasing stockholder becoming subject to a newly acquired subsidiary's environmental liabilities. Also, parent companies can be more proactive in supervising their subsidiaries' performance with less risk of being caught in the liability net. In particular, parent corporations can now take certain steps in the ordinary course of business to supervise their subsidiaries, which once would have put them at risk of CERCLA liability. However, certain actions will still place a parent company at risk, including (1) appointing a parent company employee to manage the operations at a subsidiary's site, particularly relating to environmental matters; (2) operating the subsidiary for a fraudulent purpose, or (3) failing to follow corporate formalities necessary to maintain corporate separateness. Another problem area is the degree to which a parent corporation may rely on its own environmental management staff to supervise its subsidiary's environmental compliance. In the *Kepone* case, for example, Allied Chemical might well have liability, under United States v. Bestfoods, as the parent of its wholly-owned subsidiary LSP, inasmuch as Allied controlled the LSP facility and therefore arguably acted as an "operator" at the site.

Pages 923-924. Case law has emerged that has distinguished private cost recovery suits filed under §107(a) and contribution actions filed under §113(f)(1). The principal reason to characterize a suit as one or the other is the posture of the party bringing the suit -- are they an innocent victim of the contamination (arguably only §107 available) or a member of the PRP class (arguably only §113 available). See, e.g., United Technologies Corp. v. Browning-Ferris Industries. 33 F.3d 96 (1st Cir. 1994), cert. den. 115 S.Ct. 176 (1995); Akzo Coatings v. Aigner Corp., 30 F.3d 761 (7th Cir. 1994); In re Dant & Russell, 951 F.2d 246 (9th Cir. 1989). With the loss of cost recovery goes the loss of joint and several liability and a shift to an equitable contribution action in which the plaintiff (and all of the other parties) have to try to persuade the trier of fact of how responsibility ought to be apportioned. But there are other differences as well, one of which came to the fore in the *United Technologies* case, a different, and shorter (three years rather than six), statute of limitations. As noted, infra at 925-6, the issue of whether contribution exists for voluntary cleanup has been hotly debated. When contribution is available, a key issue is the broad discretion available to the court in contribution allocations using "such equitable factors as the court determines are appropriate." 42 USC §9613(f)(1). Commonly used factors include the six so-called "Gore factors" considered by Congress in enacting the law and the four "critical factors" identified in United States v. Davis, 31 F.Supp.2d 45, 63 (D.R.I. 1998), aff'd, 261 F.3d 1 (1st Cir. 2001). Neither of these lists is intended to be exhaustive or exclusive, and courts tend to look at the totality of the circumstances. You might ask the students to identify what factors should be utilized, and how. The factors named for then representative Albert Gore, Jr. (D-Tenn.) include: (i) distinguishable discharge; (ii) amount; (iii) degree of toxicity; (iv) involvement in generation, treatment, transportation, storage or disposal; (v) degree of care; and (vi) degree of cooperation with the government to prevent harm to the public health or the environment.

Page 924, C&Q #1. The purpose of the consistency requirement. *Why must cleanups be consistent with the NCP to allow recovery in a §107 action?*

More than ever, the NCP is very explicit about how community involvement and sentiment are to be factored into the cleanup process. This concern for accomplishing more than just "what works" will, in many cases, affect the cleanup process profoundly.

Page 925, C&Q #2-3. Standing in the shoes of the government; Private CERCLA lawsuits seeking contribution. *In a §107 action, should the private plaintiff enjoy all the same advantages as the government when it sues PRPs? Are §107 actions in reality claims for contribution?*

These questions are answered in the comment text. However, in teaching this material, we have found that students often become interested in an analysis that equates contribution suits with "inverse" interpleader actions. The inverse aspect of the action arises because the plaintiff is not a stakeholder, but is instead a PRP who has paid too much. The rest is the amount that was paid to the government, or the amount that was paid for NCP-consistent cleanup. All of the parties to the action, including the plaintiff, are in a similar position in trying to exculpate themselves from liability. There is no reason to give the plaintiff any benefit of any presumptions when it comes to proof of causation (or exculpation) conversely. There is no affirmative burden of proof that the plaintiff must meet on the issue of causation -- all of the parties are (should be) viewed as equally burdened in proving causation/non-causation.

Page 925, C&Q #4. The hotly debated issue of whether contribution exists for voluntary cleanup actions. Whether contribution exists for voluntary cleanup - the issue framed in *Aviall* - is a key and hotly debated question. We have found that a useful teaching technique is to assign students to different sides of the question and ask them to present their argument in class. To date, the lower courts have not developed a consistent body of case law. Also worth addressing, depending on the Supreme Court's ruling, will be whether there will be a legislative response. Again we may see the interplay between the legislative and judicial branches in filling in the gaps in CERCLA.

Page 927, C&Q #5. A reminder about state law remedies. Again, the students should be reminded about state law remedies.

Page 927, C&Q #6. Attorneys' fees awards in CERCLA cases. The *KeyTronic* decision, denying attorneys' fees in cost recovery actions, is another case resolved not by the statutory language or by legislative history, but requiring judicial interpretation by the Supreme Court.

Page 927-930. The scope of EPA's §106 power is remarkable and is essential to understanding how EPA is likely to encourage cooperation of PRPs at Superfund sites. EPA is increasingly using §106 orders to coerce major PRPs to undertake remedial work at sites. By the plain text of §106, literally anyone, without regard to their conduct or station, can be the recipient of a §106 order if the order is "necessary to protect public health and welfare and the environment." In theory, this makes sense: given the exigent circumstances, EPA should have the ability, for example, to order a cleanup contractor with special expertise, but having no prior involvement at the site, to undertake a removal action. That contractor would, of course, be entitled to reimbursement, but the power of EPA is to force the action and worry about the monetary issues later. Note, however, the class of parties that may receive these orders is limited to the §107 PRP class because of the way §106(b)(2)(C) offers reimbursement from the Superfund to non-PRPs who have done work pursuant to a §106 Order. It is also important to note, however, that the D.C. Circuit has now reversed the district court's decision in General Electric v. Whitman, ruling that pre-enforcement judicial review is available to challenge CERCLA's unilateral administrative order regime as facially violative of due process. General Electric v. EPA, 360 F.3D 188 (D.C. Cir. 2004). In reaching this result, the D.C. Circuit noted that to the extent other courts have barred a constitutional claim under §113(h), they have done so in cases involving challenges to specific EPA orders and actions. Here, by contrast, the D.C. Circuit ruled that this case presents a facial constitutional challenge to the CERCLA statute itself, which is not barred, and accordingly remanded to the district court to address the merits of GE's facial due process claim.

Page 930, C&Q #1-3. EPA's use of its §106 power; Punitive treble damages; Agency leverage or abuse of power? These three comments all address the leverage EPA has under §106, which ideally is tempered with appropriate prosecutorial discretion. Although §106 orders may be likened in theory to the nuclear bomb of EPA's enforcement arsenal, in practice EPA has typically used restraint. For more on how §106 orders fit into EPA's enforcement arsenal, see Chapter 21. Note also that, in light of the D.C. Circuit's reversal in the *GE* case, EPA's efforts to use its §106 power as the ultimate threat may be curtailed.

Page 931, C&Q #4. Chasing recalcitrant parties. EPA likely has this power in theory but, in practice, would not exercise prosecutional discretion to seek "duplicate recovery" - a result which most courts would find to be inequitable.

Page 931, C&Q #5. The common law, §106, and RCRA corrective action. There is a marked contrast between §106, whether via lawsuit or administrative order, and the common law. What is perhaps too fleetingly and cryptically glossed over is the combined effect of the extraordinary treble damage penalty (plus remediation cost per the better reasoned judicial opinions) that §107(c)(3) imposes for disobedience of a §106 order, and the timing and standard of review of challenges to those orders. Judicial review can be had only after compliance or in defense of a suit seeking the imposition of the statutory penalties, and the grounds of defense are either that the party was not a PRP or that the EPA cleanup was inconsistent with the NCP. As to the former, the breadth of PRP liability is sufficiently great that there will be few cases where EPA would issue a §106 order to someone having so little relation to the facility as to not be a PRP. As to the latter, the defendant has the burden of proof in proving that the cleanup violated the guidelines of the NCP in the fact of judicial deference to EPA's interpretation of the requirements it has set for cleanups in its drafting of the NCP. Add to this the non-trivial cost of some CERCLA cleanups, and the vast power that Congress has granted to EPA in this statutory scheme. Section 106 orders are complementary to but different from RCRA corrective action which, as the comment points out, operates under a different set of liability rules.

Pages 931-938. The material here provides a quick sketch of the general concept that undergirds CERCLA. It is helpful to walk the students through the diagram on page 933. In this connection, you may ask the question "How would you build a system for identifying and remediating sites. You may prod this discussion by questions such as, "How is EPA going to become aware of sites?" or "Which sites should EPA attend to first?"

The Starfield excerpt, admittedly, is bristling with detail and is written for a CERCLA-sophisticated audience. Despite those problems, if it is important for students to know how EPA chooses what site remediation methods are to be employed, there is no avoiding this thicket. Beyond explaining the factors that EPA considers and their respective roles in the remedy selection process, Starfield explicates how the recurrent problems of risk and cost effectiveness are addressed in the NCP. Frankly, it is unrealistic to expect the students fully to master these details, but to provide them in this form teaches the students to understand that there is in fact a very carefully thought out mode of analysis underlying the assumptions that drive the remedy selection process.

Page 938, C&Q #1. The slow pace of CERCLA remediation. Suggestions of the reasons for the delays are all plausible. Some of the factors, such as uncertainty regarding how the statute will be interpreted, are now largely history. Still, even with the NCP, there is little likelihood that the speed will increase dramatically. The multi-factor remedy selection calculus requires vast amounts of site-specific information and attention. Even if some of the areas of uncertainty have diminished, CERCLA cleanups still provide incentives to cantankerousness; these include the high dollar amounts of PRP liability and the outrage-dominated concerns of the affected community.

Page 938, C&Q #2. Lead agencies and PRP-led activities. PRP-led RI/FS work has been disfavored on a "fox in charge of the chicken coop" rationale. Many PRPs tend to be more directly concerned with the cost of cleanups than with their efficacy.

Page 938, C&Q #3. The vital points in the process. This comment is purely descriptive, but it raises an issue that we find students to be very interested in, that of increasing the efficacy of citizen participation. Students seem genuinely concerned that the remedy selected meet the objectives of the affected citizens. This desire for local empowerment seems to have its roots in the students' perception that the original decision that put the community at risk (the placing of the hazardous materials in a position that permitted the release or threat of release into the environment) was made unilaterally by parties who did not consider the external third party effects of their actions.

Page 939, C&Q #4. The forces that govern EPA's NCP-based decisionmaking. The factors that Brown identifies as inclining EPA towards requiring incomplete cleanups seem apt and likely to have that result. Still, there is at least some evidence that the failure of many of the remedial actions to work fully to remediate the sites has been the difficulty of the task at hand. For example, many pump and treat groundwater remediation efforts are proving unsuccessful at reducing contaminant levels as much as hoped. We are very hesitant to attribute the failings that concern Brown to those factors alone. Moreover, it is not clear that his proffered suggestions will achieve his aims. For example, his idea of having a clearer congressional definition of "how clean is clean" will have a salutary effect on reducing the resources spent in setting standards for cleanups, but will not make it any easier to attain them. As technology evolves, the ability to clean up sites will improve and also be a continually evolving standard.

Page 939, C&Q #5. Challenging EPA's decisions. It seems that even with the special procedural trapping designed to ensure that all interested parties are able to participate, the adoption of the traditional APA §706 arbitrary and capricious standard consigns EPA's challengers to defeat. The EPA in recent years has a good record of being scrupulous and careful in its CERCLA decision making.

Page 939, C&Q #6. ARARs as cleanup standards. ARARs baffle students, even those in hazardous waste courses, and even experienced CERCLA practitioners. Perhaps out of cowardice, we do not delve deeply into ARARs, other than to make the point that (1) they function as cleanup standards, (2) they tend to harmonize CERCLA requirements with the requirements of other laws, and (3) they are usually standards that the PRP and regulatory communities already have experience with.

Page 940, C&Q #7. The "Superfund syndrome." OTA has clearly isolated a combination of attitudes and behaviors that surround the Superfund process. The NCP does not, for the most part, make the kinds of alterations that OTA called for, nor does it seem likely to make much headway in curing Superfund syndrome.

Page 940, C&Q #8. The staggering cost of "Cadillac" cleanups. This note is a teaching gold mine. First, if you teach at a more technical level, there is enough factual material to allow you to flesh out the hypothetical and ask the students to apply the nine remedial action evaluation criteria of the NCP that are set forth in the Starfield excerpt. Here, the distinction can be made between the first two factors (protectiveness and ARAR compliance as necessary conditions) and the middle five criteria, knowing that the final two factors weigh in on the side of incineration.

Next comes the policy analysis. This begins with the suggestion that spending that kind of money to have a few extra acres of farmland in Missouri is absurd. If the students resist this idea, ask how much uncontaminated farm land in Missouri is likely to cost. It is hard to argue that this farmland, after its been cleaned, has special value that makes it worth $41.5 million. This brings the class back to hazard and outrage. If hazard is zero and outrage is high, how much extra should EPA insist be paid to assuage some of the outrage? We have gotten answers that range from $0 to the full amount that would make it a $41.5 million cleanup. This issue can be tied back into the NCP standards, as involving community acceptance. Here, it is possible to ask "How much would the "buy-out" price be for the outrage factor?" The note mentions the idea of rebates to affected citizens in exchange for accepting less extensive remedial actions.

Page 941, C&Q #9. How much will this cost? The CERCLA cleanup cost numbers tend to have a numbing effect. They are so much beyond the scale upon which most of us act that they seem incomprehensible. On a closer reading they are not as bad as might appear. Chrysler Corporation, in July of 1994, announced a quarterly profit of $990+ million. Even though that was a record for Chrysler, it helps with the scale problem, making these numbers seem more comprehensible. Even the nearly $20 million average cleanup cost under the low end scenario can be put in perspective by comparing it to the cost of one hundred homes costing $200,000 each. The idea of such comparison is not to downplay the expense, but the rhetoric that is hurled at CERCLA on the cost issue does not often consider that these astronomical amounts are not incommensurate with industry's or the public's ability to pay.

Page 941, C&Q #10. And just who is paying? This comment might not be something the Administration wants to do with great fanfare in the glow of network TV cameras. On the other hand, to make the same arrangement quietly, in a way that is well understood by the recipient class, has a different political and public relations cast to it. A related point here is the immense power of government agencies to distribute governmental largess or, in other cases, to withhold governmental favor. This all points out the importance of administrative law and process, and the need to understand how agency action can be influenced.

Page 942, C&Q #11. CERCLA as the model for the Oil Pollution Act of 1990. This note alerts students to the fact that the Exxon Valdez spill galvanized congressional action and lead to OPA '90, which itself was modeled on CERCLA.

Page 942, C&Q #12. Natural resource damages. Natural resource damage claims provide significant (but to-date underutilized) opportunities for the aggressive enforcement of environmental laws. "Trustees" have not been assertive in bringing these claims, in part due to the fight over the implementing regulations. But natural resource damage claims remain a "sleeping giant". You might ask the students whether they can identify situations in which the "sleeping giant" could awaken.

Page 944, C&Q #13. Superfund's scorecard. EPA has historically measured its success by "bean counting", totaling up statistics as the measure of its success and reporting those statistics to Congress. While "counting beans" as the measure of success can be criticized (see Chapter 21), the comments do identify many of the administrative and fairness problems that plague Superfund.

Page 944, C&Q #14. The funding and future of Superfund. The high transaction costs of Superfund are well-documented, including the high cost of lawyers. You might ask, in light of this data, "How could Congress have designed a system with lower transaction costs?" Regardless of the high transaction costs, however, the lack of funding for Superfund does not bode well for the future. Absent reauthorization and funding, how will the federal government maintain a credible enforcement threat? Will the lack of funding so hamper the Superfund program that PRPs will get a pass? Can the states pick up the slack? Will the lack of funding provide an increased role for citizens' groups?

Pages 945-946. The costs of cost recovery is one of the great stumbling blocks of CERCLA, as the comment points out.

Page 946, C&Q #1. The likelihood of settlement. Settlements, or at least partial settlements, are becoming more likely as time goes on. In part, as the comment suggests, there are major net savings that can be obtained by avoiding transaction costs and the cost of EPA-conducted cleanups. Additionally, EPA's own policies are firmly settlement-oriented and over time the PRPs have become more sophisticated in learning how to organize into functioning groups capable of putting a settlement together.

Page 947, C&Q #2-3. Settlements and administrative orders as cures for Superfund solvency issues and litigation burdens; Congressional guidelines for EPA settlements. While Congress has encouraged settlements in §122, EPA is also motivated to settle by the solvency problems of the Superfund. But will the solvency problems undermine EPA's enforcement credibility?

Page 947, C&Q #4. PRP letters – the invitation to the dance. This note is intended to describe the seeming absurdity of convening a meeting and announcing that multi-million dollar negotiations will begin a little later in the day. The more interesting point is the question of EPA's use of short time deadlines. These deadlines are not driven by the exigency of the physical situation. The portion of the Superfund process under review is that of remedial actions, not removals. The short deadlines are there solely for the purpose of creating pressure on the PRPs to act with dispatch and to bludgeon them into being receptive to making accommodations. EPA has a sort of "hammer" in store for those who delay, in terms of settlement premiums or recalcitrance exactions.

Page 948-950. This selection (O'Neil v. Picillo) may seem repetitive of material on joint and several liability that appeared previously. Its focus here, however, is not on the use of joint and several liability as an evolved common law or statutory doctrine. The concern here is on the practical and strategic consequences of its application. The fundamental objection of the disadvantaged party is the unfairness of liability that seems disproportionate to responsibility. This aspect of joint and several liability, and the availability of contribution protection for settling PRPs, are both fundamental to understanding EPA's strategic behavior in administering its cost recovery program and the strategic behavior of the PRP class in responding to EPA's various requests and demands.

Page 950, C&Q #1. The impact of joint and several liability. There is some need to explore the ideas that are bound up in this note carefully. Joint and several liability is not inherently unfair in an initial proceeding that determines liability to a plaintiff (the U.S. in most CERCLA cases) if a subsequent proceeding is available that allocates the loss equitably. In the CERCLA scheme of things, that later proceeding is the suit for contribution against other PRPs, whether they were parties to the initial proceeding or not. The problem is that other PRPs who have settled with EPA obtain the benefit of contribution protection under CERCLA §113(f)(2), and, therefore, cannot be made to pay additional amounts to share the loss more equitably in the event some other party has paid EPA a disproportionate share. From their point of view, that is the dilemma that Rohm & Haas and Cyanamid have found themselves in *Picillo*. Although they have not paid a disproportionate share yet, if they are held jointly and severally liable in the litigation, they will be unable to recoup appropriate amounts from their co-PRPs because EPA settled (too cheaply) with the co-PRPs already. Consider here how powerful EPA's settlement authority is in regard to threatening financially solvent PRPs who contest EPA's assessment of their responsibility for the conditions at a site.

Page 951, C&Q #2. Problems of uncertainty. This note raises a more general point in a *Picillo*-specific context. First, it is clear that the more rigorous the NCP's record-keeping requirements and the NCP's standards for how to investigate a site, the better will be the chance that critical evidence that might help determine equitable allocations of responsibility will not be lost. Even so, there are going to be cases, especially with older and midnight dumping sites, where all of the PRPs cannot be identified no matter how fastidious the efforts of the party making the cleanup. The burden of paying for "unallocated" shares (those that cannot be assigned, or those of parties that are insolvent) has been placed on the PRP class by Congress. EPA policy in this area is merely a predictable outgrowth of that policy determination about what group was going to absorb the cost of unallocated shares.

Page 951, C&Q #3. Seeking fairer alternatives. This comment gives short shrift to the idea that it might be fairer to burden the general public with the unallocated shares than the PRP class. That may be too dismissive of the arguments that focus on the fact that at least some of the PRPs did not intend for their waste to end up improperly disposed of, that their disposal methods were considered appropriate when taken, that they did not profit unduly (i.e., they passed the cost savings of lower disposal costs on in the form of lower prices to consumers), etc. Compare, for example, the S & L bailout, a program that is even more expensive than Superfund. The banking industry's greed and bad loans (not to mention unscrupulous operators at some thrifts) endangered the savings of their investors. In that setting, government is footing the bills, not the PRP class (the remaining viable S & Ls, real estate investment firms, etc.). Further, there is at least some basis for arguing that the class being protected in the S & L setting, the persons whose funds were on deposit, is not as innocent as the neighbors of the hazardous waste site. The depositors were being induced to deposit by the offer of higher than competitive interest rates. Perhaps they should be charged with at least some portion of the loss.

Page 951, C&Q #4. Contribution among PRPs. Despite its brevity, this material is important to students' understanding the various possible formulations for standards of loss apportionment. It is worth emphasizing the strategic significance of contribution protection, provided in §113(f)(2). Few students come into class with a very refined understanding of contribution actions, and even fewer have been taught about the need for contribution protection if multiple party cases are to be settled.

Page 953, C&Q #5. Catch-22 revisited. The thrust of the note may be difficult for the students to grasp. Let us reiterate here what is said in the text. CERCLA imposes joint and several liability when EPA sues the PRPs whenever the PRPs cannot persuade the court there is a sound basis for apportioning the loss in some several (divisible) fashion. And (here's Catch-22) getting subsequent relief from that joint and several liability depends on being able to prove what you already learned you cannot prove, that there is a basis for apportioning the loss in discrete shares. The point of the note is that the dilemma may be more a verbal one than a real one. There is a way out because the courts do not use the same standards of proof of divisibility of harm in the contribution suit as they do in the original suit by EPA.

Page 953, C&Q #6. Congressional intent on encouraging settlements. This comment makes a point that students may not have learned in their Torts class: that contribution protection is an essential element in encouraging settlement.

Page 954, C&Q #7. EPA's use of contribution protection as a sword. Obviously contribution protection is a shield to those who obtain it, but it is a powerful sword to encourage those who may get stuck with the residual liability to join in an overall settlement.

Page 954, C&Q #8. State law analogies, and pitfalls in obtaining contribution. The comment points out one serious problem that a state law action for contribution might face in seeking recovery for amounts paid under a state law CERCLA-type statute. That is not a problem under CERCLA because it is clear that §107 provides the basis for suits for contribution brought by PRPs who claim that they have overpaid.

Page 954, C&Q #9. Strategic EPA behavior in seeking settlements. This comment reemphasizes that EPA has a number of enforcement tools available to induce settlements by rewarding settlers and punishing PRPs. United States v. Cannons Engineering is important reading for those concerned with how courts superintend EPA's settlement process. Most often when there is pending litigation, proposed settlements are lodged with the court as proposed consent decrees (and published in the Federal Register). This court hearing is, apart from the negotiation process, the only opportunity that a non-settling PRP has to question EPA's settlement.

For cases not in litigation, the non-settling PRPs opportunities are even less. EPA is authorized to settle cost recovery claims outside of litigation without need of the consent decree procedure. See CERCLA §122(h)(1). The Attorney General must approve, in writing, cost recovery settlements for sites where the governmental response costs exceed $500,000.

The judge in *Cannons Engineering* spells out the standard of review that is being applied. The consent decree comes with a "strong presumption" favoring settlement and deference to the agency where, as here, the agency is especially trained and equipped. Still, the court has to consider fairness, reasonableness, and consistency with law (the Constitution and the congressional act). This somehow translates in the court's view, to a public interest standard.

Chapter 20.
ENVIRONMENTAL CRIMINAL LAW

Chapter contents:

– and check the Teachers' Manual Website for SUPPLEMENTARY MATERIALS:

http://www.bc.edu/schools/law/library/coursebook/envtlaw/teachers

The list of Supplementary Materials in Part III of this manual, and on the Teachers' Website, indicates materials posted on the Teachers' Website that are relevant to this and other chapters.

OVERALL TEACHING THEMES & COURSE DESIGN CONSIDERATIONS

This chapter offers a potpourri of different educational functions, ranging from practical considerations for regulatory enforcement and criminal defense to overarching philosophical questions of punishment and deterrence, constitutional due process, and technical exercises of statutory interpretation.

Here are some of the organizing questions and themes:

"Does criminal prosecution have a particular drastic effectiveness for internalizing environmental values into private (especially corporate) pollution decision making? and does it make rational sense overall?"

"To what extent is actual knowledge or mens rea required for criminal prosecution of an individual?"

"When should corporate executives be liable for corporate actions that pollute?"

Also this chapter offers the 1899 Refuse Act as a particularly good exercise in statutory interpretation – an opportunity to review the power of an old statute applied in circumstances completely unforeseen by the legislators who drafted it.

TEACHING NOTES, COMMENTS, & ALL QUESTIONS ANSWERED

Pages 957-959. The 1899 Refuse Act, as a tactical rediscovery of a criminal sanction that became the first really credible federal environmental statute.

A useful introduction to this chapter generally would be to ask students: *"Imagine your difficulties, as corporate counsel in 1970, to one of the thousands of companies around the United States discharging into local waters without a Refuse Act permit."* Only a tiny handful of corporations happened to have attorneys far-sighted enough to have gotten a Refuse Act permit from the Corps of Engineers. The point is that when the Refuse Act was rediscovered in the late 1960s, for most corporations there was suddenly criminal liability where before there had been none. The Refuse Act's §407, moreover, on its face appears to impose strict liability with no intent requirement.

Another significant environmental legal process issue picked up in the notes is the fact that the terms of the Refuse Act were understood to mean one thing in 1899, and quite another in the 1960s. Does the rediscovery of the Refuse Act offend our sense of fair play, particularly since it is used criminally?

Page 959, C&Q #1. The Refuse Act of the 1960s. Notes on the rediscovery of the Act.

Pages 959-960, C&Q #2. Ease of prosecution. *If you were a prosecutor with direct evidence of outfall pipe discharges, why would your job be easy?* Self-explanatory. The Refuse Act on its face is a strict liability statute. Discharge of refuse into waters + no permit = criminal liability.

Page 960, C&Q #3. Citizen prosecution—qui tam? Self-explanatory.

Pages 960, C&Q #4. Statutory interpretation issues. *What is "refuse"?* Webster's says "the worthless or useless part of something; leavings, trash, garbage." That meaning is quite expansive enough to include most industrial pollution discharges (although in a different decade with different judges it could have been given a far more restricted definition).

What does the life history of the Refuse Act teach us about statutory trajectories? It gives a sharp lesson in how the words of a statute pack a certain magic, each phrase being positive law. Thus statutes always have a certain element of potential to become unguided missiles.

Is there any question that the 1899 Congress would never have passed the Refuse Act in this form had the legislators dreamt the Refuse Act could be applied against industrial discharges? No.

Are prosecutions for acts one knows were unintended as statutory targets unethical? Like the NEPA, ESA, RICO, etc. cases, such unintended use of statutes apparently raises no legal problem. The courts are willing to hold the legislatures to the plain meaning of their words. The ethical question is another dimension, which depends on one's own read.

AN HISTORICAL VIGNETTE on prosecutorial discretion as an administrative agenda: To give a sense of federal ambivalence in prosecuting environmental crimes: At first, in the initial fervor of the nation's environmental awakening in the late 1960s, U.S. Attorneys began energetically to prosecute many of the Refuse Act cases that were brought to their attention by citizens groups, newspapers, and federal and state investigators. Over the next few years, however, the adverse reaction of marketplace defendants began to have a chilling effect on prosecutions. In 1970, the Nixon administration published the following mandatory Department of Justice guideline:

U.S. DEPARTMENT OF JUSTICE, GUIDELINES FOR LITIGATION UNDER THE REFUSE ACT:

> ...11. The Policy of the Department of Justice with respect to the enforcement of the Refuse Act for purposes other than the protection of the navigable capacity of national waters, is not to attempt to use it as a pollution abatement statute in competition with the federal water pollution act [Eds. which at this time was a completely ineffective enforcement statute which had never successfully been used against a polluter] or with state pollution abatement procedures, but rather to use it to supplement that Act by bringing

> appropriate actions either to punish the occasional or recalcitrant polluter, or to abate continuing sources of pollution which for some reason or other have not been subjected to a proceeding conducted by the Federal Water Quality Administration or by a State, or where in the opinion of the Federal Water Quality Administration the polluter has failed to comply with obligations under such a procedure. To this end, the instructions...below encourage United States Attorneys to use the Refuse Act to punish or prevent significant discharges which are either accidental or infrequent, but which are not of a continuing nature resulting from the ordinary operations of a manufacturing plant...Therefore in order that we might coordinate our litigation with the programs of the Federal Water Quality Administration, civil and criminal actions against manufacturing plants which continuously discharge refuse into the navigable waters of the United States are not among the types of actions which the United States Attorneys may initiate on their own authority.

You can ask students: *"What was the effect of this directive? What tactical difference did it make in the nation's use of the Refuse Act as a major water pollution statute? Who would be affected by the Refuse Act after this directive went into effect?"* The Nixon guideline is an illustration of administrative nullification of a statute's effect. It eliminated the effectiveness of the Refuse Act as a deterrent to ongoing corporate decisions to externalize costs, by limiting prosecution only to occasional or accidental polluters. The existing water pollution statute at that time (see 62 Stat. §1155 (1948, as amended to 1970), codified in 1970 at USCA §1151 seq.) was a labyrinthine joke, involving a series of protracted voluntary negotiations and sequential non-enforcement proceedings, successfully designed by the statute's industrial sponsors to be completely infeasible for federal prosecution.

Page 960, C&Q #5. Permitting. *Could the Corps attach environmental conditions to its permits?* After NEPA, we believe the authority to do so lay within §§101 and 102's charge to the agencies. Before NEPA, we think it would have been difficult for the Corps to prevail against the appeal of a denied permittee whose proposed polluting actions posed no effect upon navigation.

After NEPA, must the Corps attach such conditions to permits? This is an even harder question, because it would have to be found to be a mandatory duty, not merely discretionary, but in a drastically clear case on the agency record, we think a court after NEPA might well have so ordered. So far as we know, however, it never came up.

Page 961, C&Q #6. Juries. *How is the right to a jury relevant? Why is it that many appeals are cases where environmental defendants had no jury?* Our supposition is that many environmental prosecutions seem novel to members of the public; hence juries are requested when it seems likely that juries might think it unfair to impose such liability. Where juries are not requested, we suspect, the defendants fear that their alleged actions are sufficiently heinous-sounding that conviction will follow, so they take their chances with the judge as trier of fact, then appeal.

The issues relevant to evoking jury empathy are self-explanatory. Both jury nullification and hyper-vindictiveness are possible in environmental criminal prosecutions, with diametrically opposite results.

Page 961, C&Q #7. The effectiveness of the Refuse Act. *Why does criminal prosecution have such a focusing effect on polluters?* You can have students look at the face of Steven O'Neill on page 963 and ask that question. Capital punishment is sometimes a possibility! But even misdemeanors carry a deep stigma, which is one of the reasons Mr. Park fought a $50 conviction all the way to the Supreme Court.

Page 961-962, C&Q #8. Questioning the effectiveness of criminal prosecutions. A summary didactic question. Criminal law is typically a crude blunt instrument, and sometimes that is what is what is needed, if only as a bigger stick held back in the closet.

In Exxon's oil spill, where the wrongful acts were negligent, not intentional, *What further purpose was served by criminal prosecution?* This raises issues of deterrence as well as punishment as a function of criminal law, strict liability criminal penalties without proof of intent, and executive officer liability, all dealt with below.

What about the fact that the state and federal government sought to downplay criminal liability against Exxon? Our supposition is a combination of reluctance to prosecute crimes that are environmental, white-collar, which involve political allies, as well as the more straightforward issues of crudity/subtlety, more difficult proof, etc.

Pages 962-966. *Film Recovery* and the recent willingness to prosecute environmental crimes: The *Film Recovery* case has become something of a cultural icon, as set out in the text. You could ask: *"Is there any reason why such prosecutions for homicide or other equivalent criminal penalties could not previously have been brought?"* The answer is quite clearly "No," which makes the point that environmental prosecutions have always been possible under homicide and other generally applicable criminal laws, and under a variety of state and federal statutes, but public prosecutors had long avoided prosecution of individuals, especially corporate individuals and entities, in environmental settings. So the question to students may be, "why did prosecutions increase in 1985, in the middle of the Reagan years? The answer may lie in the Reaganesque law and order rhetoric, but also in the simple fact that the press covered this dramatic death, clearly caused by an environmental pollutant, in circumstances of exploitation and managerial indifference, at a time when the public had had more than fifteen years of consciousness-raising on the serious toxic effects of chemical contamination. In a sense, then, *Film Recovery* was built on the foundation of Rachel Carson's Silent Spring.

Prosecutorial enthusiasm for environmental criminal prosecutions continues. For a few examples of what's been going on, here is a random collection of items:

In U.S. v. Catucci, 55 F.3d 15, 40 ERC 1892, 25 Envtl. L. Rep. 21,439, 1st Cir.(R.I.), May 24, 1995, the court upheld the 27-month prison sentence of an individual for violations of the Toxic Substances Control Act and Comprehensive Environmental Response, Compensation, and Liability Act.

> In Colorado, a mining company pleaded guilty and was fined $20 million for 40 felony violations of federal environmental laws at a cyanide heap-leach gold mine in southwestern Colorado. See U.S. v. Summitville Consolidated Mining Co., Inc., Nos. 95-CR-216-S, 95-CR-397-S and 96-CR-9-S (D.C. Colo. 1996). Summitville Consolidated Mining has since declared bankruptcy, and, although the fine is unlikely to ever be paid the penalty sends a message to others that very large and substantial penalties can accompany or result from

environmental charges.

The operators of separate electroplating companies in San Antonio, Texas and Monroe, Wash., pled guilty to felony charges stemming from alleged illegal discharges to municipal sewer systems. Company officials each face a maximum sentence of three years in jail and up to $250,000 in penalties for felony violations of the Clean Water Act. "Electroplaters Plead Guilty to Criminal Clean Water Violations in Separate Cases," BNA NED (July 1, 1996).

California passed a Corporate Criminal Liability Act in 1991 that opens new levels of liability for corporate officials in the environmental field. California assessed Rockwell International Corp. $6.5 million in fines in connection with criminal hazardous waste charges stemming from a 1994 explosion that killed two workers and injured a third, - a state record for a felony hazardous waste case. "Rockwell Pleads Guilty, Agrees to Pay $6.5 Million Fine for Explosion in 1994," BNA NED (April 8, 1996)

In February, 1996, the Department of Justice assessed a $2 million criminal fine against a meat packing company which discharged slaughterhouse waste into the Big Sioux River, submitted false discharge monitoring reports to the government and deliberately rigged sampling tests to get desired results and conceal violations. In addition, two company employees face a maximum possible sentence of five years imprisonment and a $250,000 fine for conspiring to the violate the CWA."S.D. Company Agrees to Pay $3 Million to Settle Criminal Violations of Water Act," BNA NED (Feb. 9, 1996).

A federal judge sentenced James Wilson, chairman of the board and former chief executive officer of Interstate General Co. L.P., to 21 months in prison and imposed a $1 million fine for filling wetlands in violation of the CWA §404. See U.S. v. Wilson, DC Md, No. AW-95-0390, June 17, 1996. Additionally, the court imposed a $2 million fine on IGC and a $1 million penalty on St. Charles Associates L.P. Both companies were also placed on probation for a period of five years and ordered to implement a restoration plan and to develop an effective environmental compliance plan to prevent future violations. The violations occurred between 1988 and 1993 on a total of 50 acres of wetlands in St. Charles, a planned community in Charles County, Md. The affected areas had been identified as wetlands on the National Wetlands Inventory Map and a Charles County topographic map. The defendants disregarded several consultants who had warned that the wetlands could not be filled without federal permits. In late Feb. 1996, a federal jury found the defendants guilty on four felony counts of illegally destroying wetlands in violation of CWA §404.

A Connecticut company will pay $22 million in fines for criminal and civil violations of the CWA stemming from the hasty construction of a natural gas pipeline. See U.S. v. Iroquois Pipeline Operating Co., DC NNY, No. 96-CR-166, May 23, 1996. Four of the firm's officials pleaded guilty to CWA charges and face up to one year in jail and fines of $100,000. This is the second largest fine ever in an environmental case, second only to the $1 billion in penalties resulting form the Exxon Valdez spill. According to the Dept. of Justice, the defendant failed to clean up or to restore damage to 188 streams and wetlands while constructing a 370 mile long natural gas pipeline from Ontario, Canada to Long Island, N.Y.. Specifically, the company failed to construct trench breakers at regular intervals to control soil erosion and corrosion of the pipeline. A lack of trench breakers could cause washouts of the soil that holds the pipeline in place which could cause ecological damage to wetlands by reducing their ability to retain water. The company was also found guilty of violating a construction permit which required Iroquois to backfill excavated soil when the pipeline was laid. Instead, the company left many mounds of soil in wetlands which reduced the size of the wetlands, damaged aquatic life, and wiped out habitat along stream bottoms. The guilty plea was entered in the U.S. District Court for the Northern District of New York. Iroquois also agreed to enter four civil settlements to resolve CWA violations in the U.S. district courts for the Northern, Southern, and Eastern districts of New York, and the district of Connecticut.

For an in-depth account of the history and general operation of the federal environmental crimes program see Cooney, Starr, Block & Kelly, "Criminal Enforcement of Environmental Laws: Part I," 25 ELR 10459 (Sept. 1995).

Pages 966-967, C&Q #1. The aftermath of the *Film Recovery* convictions. *Do you see the problem that led to overturning the Film Recovery defendants' conviction?* Inconsistent verdicts on multiple counts can lead to such reversals. We probably would have found no inconsistency between the verdicts, however, on the ground that intent to kill is not a required element for a murder count if the actor knows there is a strong probability of death, as the statute provides at the top of page 880.

Pages 967-968, C&Q #2. *Film Recovery* and preemption defenses: *What do you think of OSHA? Should the existence of OSHA regulations preempt state statutory charges, civil and criminal?* We, like many observers, consider OSHA a tame tiger, noting that the agency penalized the company so lightly, and even then later halved the penalty. There appears to be no explicit or implied congressional override of state laws in the OSHA statute, and this seems just another example of the tendency of some attorneys to try the preemption defense as a last resort.

Page 968, C&Q #3. Trends in environmental criminal prosecutions. A further note on the swelling volume of environmental criminal prosecutions.

Pages 968-972, Knowledge and intent, *Ahmad* and *Weitzenhoff* – Two cases that can be contrasted on the degree of specific knowledge or intent required for prosecution. You should note that these cases were appealed on *statutory interpretation* grounds, not constitutional due process claims. Behind the statutory requirement of scienter knowledge, however, lies the constitutional issue of whether and in what circumstances a legislature can create strict liability crimes. It is clear that the best case for constitutionally-valid strict liability crimes lies in the area of "public welfare offenses," where the public need for security is high, and defendants thus should have known that they were endangering others and so were in danger of criminal penalties themselves.

Pages 972-974, C&Q #1–3. *Ahmad* and *Weitzenhoff*; Degrees of knowledge and "intent"; Is specific intent a proxy for "knowingly" violating the CWA? *Are Ahmad and Weitzenhoff inconsistent?* The cases seem to differ as to whether discharge of harmful pollution into the water is a "public welfare offense." The *Ahmad* court held that the concept of "public welfare offenses" is a narrow judge-made exception which applies only to crimes with relatively light penalties and items known to defendants to be potentially "harmful or injurious," concluding that on the facts of *Ahmad*, the public welfare offense exception was inappropriate.

The spectrum of possible interpretations of degrees of scienter knowledge is our attempt to clarify the semantic jungle that surrounds the words "knowledge" and "intent." It covers degrees of both factual knowledge and legal awareness, because they blend.

On the face of the cases, it is a good idea to distinguish what Ahmad was claiming and what Weitzenhoff was claiming.

The "mistake of fact" and "mistake of law" distinction is of limited help. Ignorance of the law is not always a defense, but at least as a constitutional matter we think that a harsh punishment for something an ordinary defendant could not have guessed was proscribed does violate due process.

Ahmad was not saying he did not know the law. Ahmad was saying he did not know he was discharging gasoline (or by extension anything harmful — hard to believe, but if true it would mean he did not know a critical fact).

Weitzenhoff admitted he knew he was discharging a harmful material, but claimed he did not know that it violated the law, either because he did not know the discharge was not covered by a permit, or he did not know it was illegal to discharge without a permit.

The holdings may be seen as somewhat reconcilable because the degree of the sophistication of the defendants differed greatly, Ahmad being quite inexpert, and the *Weitzenhoff* defendants being pollution treatment works managers which implies more awareness of the law. Hence Weitzenhoff's claimed "mistake of law" (i.e. lack of knowledge of illegality) was harder to believe and easier to imply from constructive notice.

The Ahmad court, however, goes overboard in saying that the government must prove (it seems for constitutional, not statutory interpretation reasons) knowledge of each and every fact that constitutes the prima facie case. *Would the Ahmad court require proof that Mr. Ahmad knew that Lake Houston was navigable and that Possum Creek flowed into it?* That, we think, would be nonsensical. It would render the statutory interpretation and the due process requirement mindlessly comprehensive and invite ingenious scienter loopholes. Rather we think it more important that he be shown to know the *critical* facts, and this would be that the liquid he was discharging was potentially very harmful.

The Ahmad court also opens a way for requiring specific knowledge of the law. In addition to the "navigable water" element for the violation, you could also ask *"Must Mr. Ahmad be shown to know that a hose in a gutter is a "point source?"* If so, he can claim both lack of knowledge of a key fact and a key legal concept.

Needless to say, we think Ahmad is compulsive, and Weitzenhoff more analytically consistent.

Page 974-975, C&Q #4. Syntax as part of deciding which elements must be "knowingly" violated. *Which court has the better argument whether "knowing" requires proof under RCRA's §6928 that defendant knows there's no permit?* In another case on RCRA's §6928, U.S. v Wagner & Photo-Cut, Inc., 29 F.3d 264 (7th Cir. 1994), the Court of Appeals held that §6928 (d)(2)(A) of the Resource Conservation and Recovery Act

(RCRA) does not contain a requirement that the government prove that the defendants had knowledge of RCRA's permit requirement. The court concluded that since Congress used "knowingly" in subsection (2) and subsidiary subsections (2)(B) and (2)(C) but omitted it from subsidiary subsection (2)(A), it was their intent that defendants need not know about the RCRA's permit requirement in order to be held liable, and the court apparently found no constitutional flaw in such liability.

The court in Johnson & Towers seems to have required heightened knowledge because defendants were just hourly employees who ordinarily have no clue about legal documentation of their employers' business practices, not managers like Hoflin who could be expected to know, or who might cultivate willful ignorance.

Does the public welfare offense argument imply constructive notice? Yes, as noted above.

Pages 974-975, C&Q #5. Constitutional dimensions: "void for vagueness." Explanatory notes.

Pages 975-976, C&Q #6. Constitutional dimensions: due process requirements for knowledge and intent: This material is a somewhat troubling inquiry for some students. They may not mind the thought that corporations can get hit with strict criminal liability without proof of intent. But it's more troubling when individuals face the same prospect. Is there some sort of constitutional requirement that requires at least proof of gross negligence or willful ignorance?

The Court in Morissette v. U.S., 342 U.S. 246 (1952) made a much-quoted analysis of the constitutional status of strict liability public welfare crimes:

> Many of these strict liability offenses are not in the nature of positive aggressions or invasions, with which the common law so often dealt, but are in the nature of neglect where the law requires care, or inaction where it imposes a duty. Many violations of such regulations result in no direct or immediate injury to person or property but merely create the danger or probability of it which the law seeks to minimize. While such offenses do not threaten the security of the state in the manner of treason, they may be regarded as offenses against its authority, for their occurrence impairs the efficiency of controls deemed essential to the social order as presently constituted. In this respect, whatever the intent of the violator, the injury is the same, and the consequences are injurious or not according to fortuity. Hence, legislation applicable to such offenses, as a matter of policy, does not specify intent as a necessary element. The accused, if he does not will the violation, usually is in a position to prevent it with no more care than society might reasonably expect and no more exertion than it might reasonably exact from one who assumed his responsibilities. *Also, penalties commonly are relatively small, and conviction does no grave damage to an offender's reputation.* Under such considerations, courts have turned to construing statutes and regulations which make no mention of intent as dispensing with it and holding that the guilty act alone makes out the crime. This has not, however, been without expressions of misgiving. 342 U.S. at 255-56 (emphasis supplied).

Page 976-977, C&Q #7-8. #7 A scienter requirement balance? #8 Srict liability and sentencing options. *Are there degrees of relativity between the seriousness of an action and the* *degree of knowledge required?* This would seem to be the case, intuitively and in the case law. The problem is that the courts apparently are balancing at least three different things, the alleged unfairness to the defendant who is prosecuted without proof of knowledge of the violation, the importance of the public welfare interest being protected, and the practicalities of enforcing the statute which may argue against strict necessity to prove defendant's knowledge. This inquiry does appear to be another manifestation of substantive due process the students should therefore not be surprised to discover that there is a balance.

You can ask: *"Would it offend you less if the defendants who were convicted without proof of knowledge were corporations rather than natural individuals?"* If students recognize that they are less bothered by corporations paying fines in such circumstances, then they are recognizing the subjective character of the balance. A clear ground for relativity in a scienter balance might be based on a heightened degree of implied constructive knowledge when potential public harms are generally perceived as more drastic. Thus bird trading, which most people don't know is harmful and illegal, should probably require more proof of scienter than dumping toxics or gasoline.

As to the past tendency to correlate the degree of scienter required with the severity of penalty faced, we suspect that that the *Staples* dictum exaggerates the alleged ongoing decoupling. Fundamental fairness seems far more implicated when unknowing defendants face serious penalties than when they do not. The line italicized in *Morissette* in the preceding note again is helpful.

Morissette held that criminal intent cannot be implied from a criminal act alone, but is for the jury to decide based on the totality of the circumstances. the court reasoned that there are two types of crimes, those done with a "malicious heart" and those that are simply occurrences of some forbidden act. If intent can be implied from the act, however, there is no distinction.

Pages 977-981. Corporate and executive prosecutions. The first section refers to the problems of prosecuting the corporation. It is quite clear that Judge Merhige in the Kepone case was seriously disinclined to impose substantial criminal liability on the individuals in the trial. Imagine the sigh of relief when he said, "No one in this case is going to jail." It appears that the lead defense attorney had been an old law partner of Judge Merhige.

Was Allied a full and willing participant in LSP's daily operations? In a Harvard Business School case study of the Kepone incident, footnote 39, Allied is portrayed far more innocently. The case study states that the president of Allied Chemical's specialty chemicals division found it hard to understand how the Kepone affair had happened in the first place. "Allied had made Kepone without any health or safety problems, and the LSP owners should have been able to do the same." Allied management "felt a strong sense of moral responsibility to the LSP workers, their families and the Hopewell community." Allied repeatedly and publicly denied that it had done anything wrong. Was this true? The students should be reminded that Allied knew of its own illegal dumping into Gravelly Run. When it tolled production to LSP, it continued to provide legal advice to LSP its management made periodic inspections of the LSP operations which were visibly "Dickensian" in the horrific quality of occupational exposure to the toxin it was part of the discussions to divert toxic effluents into the Hopewell municipal sewer system it funded medical treatment for LSP workers with doctors who maintained a diplomatic diffidence about the nervous conditions they saw and finally, throughout the LSP production cycle, the raw materials and the Kepone product itself were owned not by LSP, which merely had a servicing contract, but by Allied. In the circumstances, the students could be asked to analyze which theory (if the judges rulings against vicarious liability against Allied had been appealed) would have been most likely to succeed - agent, instrumentality, accessory-accomplice, or conspirator? For more on Kepone, see Christopher Stone, A Slap on the Wrist for the Kepone Mob, Bus. & Society Rev. 4 (Summer 1977).

Pages 981, C&Q #1. The judge, and the absence of a jury. *Where was a jury here?* As previously noted, in cases of public outrage, defendants will often waive a jury. *Was it a good idea here?* Pretty clearly it was.

What was the effect of Judge Mehrige's rulings limiting joint liability, and saying that "no one is going to jail in this case"? Reportedly the criminal threat was instantly so narrowed that the prosecutor found subsequent plea bargaining efforts within the Allied executive group impossible. With a jury, the threat of a jail sentence could not so easily have been removed by the judge.

Page 981-982, C&Q #2. The perils of plea bargaining. Self-explanatory.

Page 982, C&Q #3. Allied's vicarious liability. *How could Allied best have been held liable for LSP's actions?* We think the "instrumentality" and "agency" theories as set out in the excerpt best fit the facts here.

Was Allied a stranger to LSP's practices and premises? Did Allied not have the requisite knowledge? It is quite clear that Allied had intimate knowledge and managerial direction of LSP's operations. *Should "tolling" and "maquiladora" contracts insulate principals?* The answer under CERCLA law is quite clearly not.

Pages 982, C&Q #4. The Kepone fines and taxes. The tax deductibility issue. The note sets out an interesting perspective on the tax deductibility of settlements, showing another strong incentive to avoid criminal prosecutions.

Should Supplemental Environmental Project settlements like this one in Kepone be deductible? It would seem that theories of restitution, victim compensation, and the like, should incline the remedy possibilities toward deductibility, which will be an incentive for more frequent such settlements. It is, however, a loss to the U.S. Treasury's general fund.

Pages 983-984, Corporate executive liability, and the *Park* case. The backdrop to this section is the practical fact that prosecutors believe one of the most effective ways of changing systematic corporate non-compliance with environmental regulations is to prosecute corporate managers individually, as high as they can go on the corporate ladder. A recent example of a similar prosecutional mindset on the securities arena is the Martha Stewart prosecution.

Page 984, C&Q #1. Fighting over principles? *Why did Mr. Park bother?* Perhaps the stigma of a criminal conviction really bothered Mr. Park, and also it may be that this case was considered an opportunity to clarify a limitation on executive liability, but that agenda did not work out as planned.

Pages 985, C&Q #2. Who gets targeted? *Who can be prosecuted?* An answer of sorts is given in last line in the *Park* excerpt: The government would seem to establish a prima facie case when it introduces evidence sufficient to warrant a finding by the trier of facts that the defendant had, by reason of his position in the corporation, responsibility and authority, either to prevent in the first instance, or promptly to correct the violation complained of, and that he failed to do so.

Is it really that broad? You can ask: *"Can the head of General Motors be sent to jail for a serious spill of paint solvent from a GM assembly plant in the state of Seattle?"* Obviously not, but why? The CEO clearly had authority to prevent or correct violations if they had been brought to his attention. The question what the interpretation to give to the word "responsibility." This raises questions both of how close the nexus of executive responsibility to the illegal act must be, and constitutional due process issues of scienter noted elsewhere in this chapter. This theme is continued in the questions that follow.

Page 985, C&Q #3. Defensive organizational responses. *Would you accept appointment as a major corporation's VP responsible for Pollution control?* No way.

Pages 985-986, C&Q #4. Executive liability, civil as well as criminal Explanatory notes. *Is the CEO of an auto company in Detroit liable for a spill from a subsidiary in Seattle?* As above, not likely. There is neither specific knowledge nor any particular close link between the CEO and daily doings at the subsidiary. But note that Park's holding would seem to stretch that far.

Into which theory does Mr. Park fall? or Edwin Michaels in NEPACCO? Park seems at least to have taken some personal specific interest, and control, over the warehouses in the *Park* case; Michaels does not seem even to have been on location in the *NEPACCO* case, but Michaels' liability may have been upheld as strict because he was the major shareholder, and because it was civil not criminal liability.

Page 987, C&Q #5. Corporate ignorance as a defense. Self-explanatory and rhetorical. It should be noted that two 1991 cases imposed much stricter requirements for the prosecution of corporate executives: In U.S. v. MacDonald & Watson Waste Oil Co., 933 F.2d 35 (1st Cir. 1991), and U.S. v. White, 766 F.Supp. 873 (E.D. Wash. 1991), the courts held that, at least for crimes for which knowledge is an element, a mere showing of official responsibility is not an adequate substitute for direct circumstantial proof of actual knowledge. The Administration at that time officially adopted this posture in Department of Justice prosecutorial guidelines, and apparently interpreted it even more broadly to require a particularized showing of knowledge (although that could be circumstantial) even where a statute does not require knowledge.

Prosecutors seeking to charge a member of the corporation with individual responsibility usually look for "someone with some level of responsibility, like a waste treatment manager." The prosecution must show that the person knew what they were doing and that they knew it was wrong. The prosecution does not have to prove, however, that the person knew the discharge's exact nature, only that the person knew the substance was something they should not have been discharging. If the person charged with the crime had the authority to "bind" the corporation, then the corporation can be charged with criminal liability as well.

In proving criminal intent, prosecutors and investigators often look for deceit as the best proof of criminal intent for environmental crimes. Officials for the U.S. Attorney's office say deceit is present in almost every criminal prosecution and proves the person had knowledge of the law and was intentionally trying not to comply with the law.

Pages 987, C&Q #6. Probation for corporations. Explanatory notes.

Page 988, Federal Sentencing Guidelines and the *Hansen* case. Environmental application of federal sentencing guidelines. The *Hansen* case illustrates the modern process of applying a generic sentencing formula under the Federal Sentencing Guidelines and the courts' seriousness in applying the guidelines. The chart on page 995 looks quite precise at first glance, but looking at it closely it becomes obvious that there is a range within different categories. Judges retain some flexibility in determining offense levels and applying them. Although appellate courts have remanded sentences that appeared too lenient, trial courts in practical terms still can exercise some discretion in sentencing. Of course, if courts insist on applying the full required heavy sentence upon corporate executives, it is likely that plea bargaining prior to trial will become a more active forum, leading to pleading to reduced charges.

The sentencing guidelines may produce a different judicial tendency, since the personal sympathies which attach to individual defendants in many of the cases where trial courts dilute the offense levels may be absent in corporate sentencing situations.

Page 995-997, C&Q #1. The mechanics and strategics of a sentencing formula. Why can the offense levels vary so widely as in *Rutana's* different rulings? As noted, part of the answer is because the court retains the ability to shape the findings and weigh them against the standards. *Did the fact that the case involved an environmental violation, and a hard-charging executive, make a difference?* According to our read of the opinions, it appears that the different judges held different views as to whether executive liability and environmental crimes deserved sanctions.

Page 996-997, C&Q #2. An array of fudge factors in criminal sentencing. Self-explanatory.

Page 997, C&Q #3. "Abuse of trust" under the federal sentencing guidelines. The sentencing guidelines provide for an enhancement for an abuse of a position of trust. Should abuses of "public trust" be dealt with more harshly than abuses of "private trust"? The *Technic Services* case poses the key underlying issue: where environmental quality and the public health are concerned, how meaningful is the contention that violations of the "private trust" are less harmful?

The following note also raises the bemusing possibility that a child pornography statute might work to make sentencing discretion harsher in environmental crime cases.

> Until now [sentencing] courts have limited claims about the public trust to…environmental crimes committed by public officials. U.S. v. Kuhn , 345 F.3d 431 (6th Cir. 2003)…. The 7th Circuit, by a 2-1 decision, has extended that argument to an industry official. In U.S. v. Snook, 2004 U.S. App. LEXIS 8058 (2004), the court rejected arguments by…the environmental manager of a Chicago-area refinery, that his position did not put him in a position of public trust and that he was therefore not eligible for an enhanced sentence for criminal violations of Clean Water Act reporting requirements. The 7th Circuit disagreed, noting that the water law "is public welfare legislation and

> the victims of the violation are the public [and] the regulations here apply to matters that directly and significantly affect the public's health and safety."...
>
> Moreover, some industry sources say the trend of stricter sentences for criminal violations of environmental laws is likely to continue in the wake of...the PROTECT Act...a recently enacted law to enhance sentences for violations of child pornography laws.... [The Act] makes it difficult for federal judges to "adjust downward" sentencing recommendations issued by the U.S. Sentencing Commission. Shipman, "Industry Facing New Sentence Increases for Environmental Crimes," 25 INSIDE EPA 1, 10 (April 20, 2004).

Page 997, C&Q #4. The continuing strict application of the federal sentencing guidelines. The courts continue to apply the sentencing guidelines and, as United States v. Strong indicates, are not readily amenable to constitutional challenges to the guidelines even where the application of the guidelines can be harsh.

Page 997, C&Q #5. A critique of criminalization for environmental injuries. In his book Professor Packer raises several interesting questions, including the major issue of the cost benefit effectiveness of using criminal law against corporations. The question can be asked, "Why would prosecutors be interested in bringing criminal actions against the corporations and their executives?" You can go through the short catalogue at the end of the note: societal revenge and retribution, general deterrence, incapacitation, specific deterrence (intimidation), rehabilitation.

Page 998, C&Q #6. Economics. It's evident that environmental prosecutions are by definition not an attempt to achieve a fine-tuned accounting of cost externalizations. Criminal prosecution is a crude, blunt instrument, designed to deliver overwhelming messages of coercion. In some cases, of course, criminal prosecution can capture the frustration of society faced with a defendant who otherwise will evade payment for a wide range of intangible costs imposed. Criminal actions against Captain Hazelwood in the Exxon-Valdez oil spill may have embodied such a crude attempt to "account" for costs of the tragedy that could never be remedied. Prosecutorial discretion, however, may often appear to be a random system of accounting. To some extent, the rather random chance of having an indictment filed in an environmental case is given some rational balance by the court or jury's opportunities for acquittal or bringing in lesser verdicts. Prof. Packer's book in other sections offers another reminder: When prosecutors insist on bringing indictments for acts for which society considers criminal penalties disproportionately excessive, the prosecutorial efforts may bring the law into disrespect, and lessen the stigma and the occasional shock value of criminal prosecution.

Page 998, C&Q #7. Ecoguerrillas and the criminal law? The necessity defense. See also Kessler, Anti-Nuclear Demonstrations and the Necessity Defense, Vt. L. Rev. (1980), Lippman, Towards a Recognition of the Necessity Defense for Political Protester, Protest and Resistance, Civil Disobedience in the 1990s, Washington and Lee L. Rev. (1991). In an interesting case, environmentalists successfully used the necessity defense to avoid conviction of disorderly conduct charges when they successfully blocked the routing of automobile traffic into a traffic lane reserved for bicycles and pedestrians. New York v. Gray, et al., 571 N.Y.S. 851 (1991).

Chapter 21.
EVOLVING PATTERNS OF ENFORCEMENT AND COMPLIANCE

Chapter contents:

– and check the Teachers' Manual Website for SUPPLEMENTARY MATERIALS:

http://www.bc.edu/schools/law/library/coursebook/envtlaw/teachers

The list of Supplementary Materials in Part III of this manual, and on the Teachers' Website, indicates materials posted on the Teachers' Website that are relevant to this and other chapters.

OVERALL TEACHING THEMES & COURSE DESIGN CONSIDERATIONS

This chapter explores the scope and effectiveness of environmental enforcement. Since the early 1970s, when EPA and the states began credibly enforcing the environmental laws, the regulatory system has become extremely complicated. However, amidst this complexity there remains a key constant: for environmental regulation to achieve its goal, it must induce compliance. The chapter, accordingly, examines the evolving roles of government, citizens, and business in environmental enforcement and compliance.

The chapter begins by asking the question "How does the governmental enforcement process work?" In response, the chapter reviews the key phases in enforcement, recognizing that the enforcement process typically moves violators along towards an inevitable day of reckoning. The flow chart on page 1005 provides an overview of the typical steps taken by EPA in pursuing enforcement. As the flow chart illustrates, EPA enforcement has historically been driven by civil and criminal command and control requirements and has sought to maintain accountability for non-compliance by identifying, prosecuting, and penalizing wrongdoers.

In recent years, however, there have been changes in the traditional patterns of enforcement. Both EPA and the states have developed a variety of new and more flexible enforcement approaches, in part in response to the failures of historical enforcement strategies and in part in an effort to implement new, more effective initiatives. Because the most rapid changes in enforcement patterns pertain to the redevelopment of brownfields, the chapter highlights brownfields federalism, and its policy of greater flexibility and cooperation in enforcement.

Governmental enforcement, however, is not always available or effective, particularly in times of limited resources or lack of political will. The chapter accordingly also addresses citizen enforcement of the environmental laws, examining the significance of citizen involvement and asking "Do citizen suits prod governments to act, or provide a credible enforcement alternative when government fails to act?"

The chapter also addresses alternative dispute resolution processes as a vehicle for resolving environmental disputes. Finally, the chapter focuses upon a major shift that has taken place in recent years in the attitudes and priorities of American business: environmental compliance has now made the transition from a corporate backwater function to a top business priority. The chapter asks "If American corporations are now reducing emissions and achieving compliance on their own initiative, will this self-generated compliance continue, or is the credible threat of continued governmental and citizen enforcement still required?" In addressing this question, the chapter identifies the factors which have caused this shift in business goals, by examining the major business events that trigger the need for business to comply with the environmental laws. These events include (i) permitting and reporting, (ii) SEC disclosure by public companies, (iii) the satisfaction of corporate information needs, (iv) borrowing for ongoing business needs, and (v) the purchase or sale of a business or property. The chapter examines whether, in connection with these business events, American business is engaged in self-generated compliance independent of environmental enforcement or because of the continuing enforcement paradigm.

This is a lengthy (62 pages) chapter that can be assigned and read as a whole in one or two assignments, or in conjunction with Chapters 17 - 20 (all dealing with compliance, enforcement, and dispute resolution mechanisms). The brownfields section of this chapter is also a useful addendum to Chapters 18 and 19.

TEACHING NOTES, COMMENTS, & ALL QUESTIONS ANSWERED

Pages 999-1002. This introduction highlights an ongoing and vigorous debate in the environmental community over appropriate enforcement strategies and the future of enforcement. The introduction seeks to frame the issues for the students in a provocative way. You may ask the students, "Should EPA's historic enforcement ideology be modified or replaced by new initiatives emphasizing compliance assurance and non-compliance prevention?" The introduction also underscores the contention of many in American business today, who claim that governmental enforcement has not kept pace with compliance developments in the corporate community. You may ask, "To what extent does this contention have validity; and if governmental enforcement has not kept pace, how credible will be the threat of continuing governmental enforcement?"

Pages 1002-1009. It is important for students to understand the three phases in EPA enforcement: (1) inspection and information gathering, (2) administrative case development, and (3) formal litigation. The Mintz excerpt describes succinctly the enforcement process at EPA as a case proceeds through these three phases. The flow chart on page 1005 then illustrates these phases as a series of steps moving violators along a path that will inevitably result in civil or criminal adjudication, unless a case is resolved in a prior stage. It may be helpful to use the flow chart as a demonstrative aide, and to spend some time reviewing the process from the perspective, first, of EPA and, then, of an alleged violator caught up in the enforcement net. You can ask students "What kind of administrative record should EPA seek to build before it moves a case along to the next phase of the enforcement process?" You can also ask "How can an alleged violator use the enforcement process affirmatively to influence the administrative record in a positive way so as to minimize sanctions or exit the enforcement process altogether?" In addition, you can ask "When should EPA allow the states to take the enforcement lead?" and "Even if the state takes the lead, under what circumstances should EPA consider overfiling?" The analysis of the enforcement process also includes a review of the enforcement tools available to EPA. Although some of EPA's enforcement tools have been identified in other chapters, the discussion here provides the students with an opportunity to understand the full menu of EPA's enforcement options. In connection with EPA's choice of particular enforcement tools, you can ask students "From the EPA's perspective, what are the advantages and disadvantages of utilizing administrative orders, etc.?" and "At what point in the enforcement process should EPA either threaten to invoke or, in fact, invoke its administrative order authority, etc.?" Students also need to be aware of the significance of EPA's civil penalty policies, which, in theory, operate as a check on EPA's prosecutorial discretion in assessing penalties.

Pages 1009-1010, C&Q #1.Congressional commitment (or lack thereof) to environmental law enforcement. *Given the budgetary constraints on EPA's ability to implement the ambitious statutory agenda passed by Congress, does EPA have the resources and manpower to perform its workload effectively?* It is certainly the case that Congress has expanded the scope of the environmental laws dramatically over the years but has not similarly loosened the purse strings for enforcement. The lack of resources can dramatically affect EPA's enforcement strategies, by undermining EPA's work force and by forcing EPA to cut deals that it might otherwise not make with polluters. You might also ask students the question "Does a lack of resources encourage EPA to use certain enforcement tools over others?" Absent appropriate funding, EPA will typically use tools that involve less cost (for example, administrative orders rather than civil actions for injunctions), thereby affecting the dynamics of the enforcement process.

Pages 1010-1012, C&Q #2-3: #2 Enforcement "beans." #3 The latest environmental enforcement beans. Bean counting does provide a way to measure success, but, as the comment suggests, may provide a misleading or incomplete picture concerning the quality, significance, or impact of EPA's enforcement success. Nonetheless, EPA continues to trumpet its statistics as a means of justifying its budget and measuring its success.

Pages 1012-1013, C&Q #4. The increasing use of SEPs. Supplemental environmental projects (SEPs) are increasingly in vogue, highlighting that EPA is open to creative ways of improving environmental quality as a means of satisfying environmental penalties or obligations.

Pages 1013-1014, C&Q #5. Calculating civil penalties. EPA's civil penalty policies are a morass for those facing penalties, who may not be able to ascertain how EPA arrived at the penalty it seeks to impose. As the excerpt concerning the CWA's civil penalty policy suggests, any semblance of objectivity in theory can deteriorate in practice into a seemingly arbitrary and subjective application of criteria, particularly when EPA chooses not to share the basis for its calculations.

Pages 1014-1016, C&Q #6. EPA's use of enforcement powers: the "any credible evidence" rule. *In light of Congress' strengthening the enforcement capabilities of EPA, the states, and citizens in the 1990 Clean Air Act Amendments, did Congress intend that EPA base* *its broadened regulatory authority and strengthened enforcement program on the best possible data concerning the actual operations of air pollution sources?* A strong argument can certainly be made that limiting EPA to the reference test method was not what Congress had in mind. Under the "any credible evidence" rule, EPA would expand the type of evidence that can be used in enforcement actions to include all evidence deemed credible as defined by applicable rules of evidence. Because "any credible evidence" would still need to pass muster under the rules of evidence, industry would still have ample opportunity to attack its reliability, materiality, admissibility, and weight.

Pages 1016-1017, C&Q #7. Regulatory creep: the enforceability of EPA informal guidance documents. The regulatory community was gratified by the D.C. Circuit's decision in Appalachian Power, which recognized the dangers of regulatory creep. You may ask "Why should guidance documents not have the force of law as EPA promulgations?" Here, a basic understanding of the Administrative Procedure Act, including the value and nature of rulemaking proceedings, can be quite helpful. Appalachian Power is also useful as a basis for explaining the limits on EPA's discretionary powers.

Pages 1017-1018. One of the major fallouts from EPA's historic reliance on an enforcement policy based on deterrence are brownfields -- abandoned or underutilized sites that few will touch, let alone redevelop, for fear of CERCLA, RCRA, or other environmental liability. EPA and the states are not oblivious to this fallout. In fact, there has been significant criticism that EPA's historical reliance on an enforcement policy emphasizing deterrence has, at least in the case of brownfields, undermined environmental protection and quality. Generally speaking, the states were more flexible, initially, than EPA in developing alternative enforcement strategies, due primarily to their interests in developing "user friendly" relationships with local businesses. As the EPA's Brownfields Action Agenda illustrates, however, the federal government soon realized that key reforms were needed on the federal level as well, in order to encourage the redevelopment of brownfields sites.

Page 1019, C&Q #1. The old horrors of Superfund cleanups. As the comment suggests, it may well be that, after the remediation of the most seriously polluted sites, EPA could be more flexible in its enforcement approaches. EPA's historic reliance on its rigid deterrence approach, coupled with its bureaucratic resistance to change, also played a key role in EPA's failure to embrace a business community which had begun to make environmental compliance a priority.

Page 1019, C&Q #2. State law and policy changes affecting enforcement. As Figures 1 and 2 graphically depict, numerous states are now tackling the brownfields problem with an array of inducements to redevelop contaminated sites. You might ask the students "What lineup of incentives would be most effective in providing a developer with the comfort necessary to redevelop a brownfields site?" You might also ask, "Do these types of incentives encourage the race to the bottom, as states lower their enforcement thresholds to incentivize brownfields redevelopment?"

Pages 1020-1021, C&Q #3. Cooperative federalism in enforcement: federal and state memoranda of agreement. Brownfields Task Forces are now the norm on the state and local as well as the federal level.

Pages 1021-1022. You can ask students the question "Why is a Memorandum of Agreement between EPA and a state necessary?" The answer lies in the need for cooperative federalism, to induce parties to participate in brownfields programs on the state level without fear of prosecution on the federal level. Remind students that, even when a state has taken the enforcement lead, EPA nevertheless claims authority to take its own enforcement action. Accordingly, despite the enactment of numerous brownfields programs on the state level, many parties still would not participate in state programs without assurance or "comfort" that the federal EPA would give its blessing. A Superfund Memorandum of Agreement (MOA) is often essential before private parties will proceed with redeveloping brownfields sites. The key language of the MOA is in the Principles. You can ask students "How does a state (here, Illinois) make the determination that remediation is complete, or that no action will be necessary at a site?" and "If a state makes that determination, is the determination forever binding if there are changed circumstances in the future?" Students can be encouraged to discuss the level of assurance provided by an MOA. They will discover that although an MOA may be necessary to induce a party to participate in a brownfields cleanup, it still may not provide sufficient comfort to those who are risk-averse.

Page 1022, C&Q #1. How much assurance? *Does the MOA represent evidence that cooperative federalism is maturing, at least where brownfields are concerned?* The MOA is evidence of growing cooperative federalism, but the assurance provided by an MOA remains limited. Covenants not to sue, for example, provide greater assurance than MOAs. The exceptions carved out in MOAs also encompass a great many sites, suggesting that the EPA and the states still have to work out more thorough understandings before many brownfields sites, including some of the worst sites, have any prospect for redevelopment.

Page 1022, C&Q #2. Enforcing promises of regulatory forbearance. As this comment points out, even covenants not to sue may be difficult to enforce. The best strategy for a party seeking to bind EPA to its promises is to seek a consent decree, enforceable by a court, which as a court order has the force and effect of contempt and other relief.

Page 1023, C&Q #3. EPA's rule on brownfield property assessments to avoid liability. The EPA's final rule on brownfield property assessment, and the passage of the Small Business Liability Relief and Brownfields Revitalization Act, are the latest evidence of brownfields federalism. The rule and the Act are intended to jumpstart brownfields development. You may ask students, "How are the rule and the Act designed to encourage brownfields redevelopment?" "What problems in prior law were they designed to overcome?"

Pages 1023-1025. The enforcement process would not be complete without an understanding of proposed "regulatory reforms". Several of the more successful reforms are highlighted in the text - Project XL, the Common Sense Initiative, and Negotiated Rulemaking. Each of these reforms evidences EPA's recognition that a command and control approach to environmental enforcement is not always the best approach, and that "kinder, gentler" approaches may be important aspects of achieving compliance, particularly with environmentally sophisticated corporations..

Pages 1025-1027, C&Q #1-4. #1 The quest for efficiency. #2 Other reforms: citizen oversight councils. #3. "Collaborative governance." #4. Sunsets. Each of these regulatory reform devices has its pros and cons, as the comments point out. Again, they each represent an example of regulation outside the strict "command and control" model. From a theoretical standpoint, each reform has its place. In practical terms, the significance of each is largely a function of political will and economic wherewithal.

Pages 1027-1029. The citizen suit provisions of the environmental statutes provide a vital complement to government enforcement efforts. It is important for students to understand the role of citizen suits in the enforcement scheme. The government remains the party charged with the policy assessment and setting standards. The citizen suit concerns whether an alleged violator has met the government standards or whether the government administrator has carried out his non-discretionary legal duties in implementing the standards. The excerpts clarify the historic role of the citizen suit but also emphasize that, together, governmental and citizen enforcement can create an especially credible enforcement threat to business in the marketplace economy.

Pages 1029-1032. The Comfort Lake decision raises a number of key issues involved in citizen suits: (1) the function of citizen suit notice; (2) whether the violation is "on-going" within the meaning of the Gwaltney case; (3) the role of the citizen suit as a supplement to governmental action; (4) the availability of civil penalties as a remedy; (5) the significance of agency enforcement diligence; (6) the circumstances in which attorneys' fees and costs are available under citizen suit provisions; and (7) the role of environmentally beneficial expenditures. Comfort Lake therefore provides a useful vehicle for analyzing the issues that often arise in citizen suit litigation under the environmental laws.

Pages 1032-1033, C&Q #1. Citizen suits and the command-and-control model. This comment points out the role of citizen suits in affecting enforcement priorities, even if the initial setting of those priorities remains a governmental function. The role of the citizen suit in exposing government inaction should also not be underestimated.

Page 1033, C&Q #2. EPA's inattention to enforcement. Citizen suits remain a valuable check on EPA inattention to enforcement goals, as the GAO report on water pollution documents.

Page 1033, C&Q #3. How much is accomplished by citizen suits? There is a general consensus in the environmental community that citizen suits have significantly impacted and prodded governmental enforcement performance while also inducing more routine compliance by the regulated community.

Page 1034, C&Q #4. Forms of relief available in citizen suits. It is important for students to understand the goals of citizen suits: (1) to enforce statutory, regulatory, or permit requirements through compliance orders and penalties; and (2) to require regulators to comply with their non-discretionary legal duties under the applicable laws. Decisions by EPA pertaining to whether to bring enforcement actions, however, remain subject to EPA's claimed discretion, under the leading case of Dubois v. Thomas.

Pages 1034-1035, C&Q #5. Prerequisites to citizen enforcement. There are a number of prerequisites to citizen suit enforcement, including (1) citizen suit notice; (2) statutes of limitation; and (3) the diligent prosecution bar. This comment identifies these prerequisites and their purposes.

Pages 1035-1036, C&Q #6. Citizen suit notice. This comment points out that citizen suit notice must be given, but defects in the context and form of notice are likely to be not as significant as the giving of timely notice in the first instance.

Page 1036, C&Q #7. Cessation of violation in a post-*Gwaltney* world. The Gwaltney line of cases is by now familiar. This comment suggests that the technical and formalistic rules constructed by the courts post-Gwaltney stem, at least in part, from the judiciary's efforts to administer their dockets to avoid a flood of citizen suits.

Pages 1037-1038, C&Q #8. The *Steel Company Case.* The Supreme Court's Steel Company decision has raised a multitude of concerns in the environmental public interest community concerning the continuing viability of citizen suits. The decision turned on the issue of redressibility as a vital component of standing to sue. Here, the required reports under EPCRA were filed after citizen suit notice but before suit. The Supreme Court held that, in the absence of any ongoing violation, none of the relief sought by the citizens group would reimburse the group for losses caused by the late reporting or eliminate the effects of late reporting. The payment of civil penalties, for example, would go to the Treasury, not to the citizens group. Nonetheless, the concerns raised by the Seventh Circuit below are troubling. You can ask the students "After the Steel Company case, do citizens have any incentive to incur the costs of learning about EPCRA, investigating suspected violators, and analyzing information?" and "Will citizens be willing to absorb the cost of enforcement, absent the likelihood of recovering those costs through litigation as prevailing parties?" The Laidlaw decision was embraced by the public interest community as a continuing indication of the ongoing viability of their role, at least where "ongoing" violations are concerned.

Page 1038, C&Q #9. Defining agency enforcement diligence. Diligent prosecution by the government will thwart a citizen suit. You can ask students "What if a polluter seeks to ensure 'diligent prosecution' by drafting a suit for the government which is then filed and immediately settled, in order to preclude a looming citizen suit?" and "Will such collusion shield a polluter from citizen enforcement?"

Page 1038, C&Q #10. Environmentally Beneficial Expenditures (EBEs). Students reading Comfort Lake can assess the use of EBEs, which were payable in that case.

Pages 1038-1040, C&Q #11. Attorneys' fees and costs under citizen suit provisions. This comment provides an overview of the availability of attorneys' fees and costs under citizen suit provisions, under the Equal Access to Justice Act, and under nonstatutory avenues to funding public interest litigation. Such fees and costs are usually vital to citizen groups in environmental cases, in order to be able to continue to fund their ongoing litigation activities. Of course, to be entitled to fees, citizen groups must generally "prevail" in the litigation. You can ask students "What does it mean to be a prevailing party?" You can also point out that in order to obtain fees, the attorneys for the prevailing party must typically document, under oath, their hours worked and the tasks undertaken. Consequently, public interest lawyers, just like their private sector counterparts, typically keep time records itemizing their time and expenses, in order to be able to document with specificity their work on behalf of their clients. But what if citizens claim that their lawsuit was the catalyst for "voluntary" change in a defendant's conduct? In that circumstance, the statutory terms of the specific fee statute involved are typically key to whether fees may be awarded, as the cases point out.

Pages 1040-1041, C&Q #12. Attorneys' fees for "prevailing" defendants. Can a "prevailing" defendant recoup its attorneys' fees? In the *Steel Company* case on remand, the defendant (who ultimately prevailed in the Supreme Court) sought approximately $300,000 in attorneys' fees (an amount which would have bankrupted the plaintiff CBE) for its fees and expenses in defending the litigation, citing §326(f) of EPCRA. In resolving this issue, the Seventh Circuit analogized the EPCRA fee shifting provision to those in the civil rights laws and denied relief to the defendant because (under standards developed under the civil rights laws) the litigation was not frivolous or in bad faith. Note, however, that fee shifting can be a two-way street.

Pages 1042-1045, Introduction to ADR. In the American legal community, competition is a serious part of daily life, and "winning" is the goal. William Ruckleshaus, a former EPA Administrator, noted that to be otherwise "cuts against the fundamental grain of the American character." This competitive contentious spirit has been particularly apparent in the environmental arena. There is typically such a disparity between the opponents, in terms of money, political resources, and world view, that only a donnybrook in court is likely to achieve closure of an issue, and not necessarily on the merits. Environmental litigation often seems to be a quixotic plaintiffs' crusade and defendants' no-holds-barred massive reaction. Likewise, in the regulatory setting, participants often single-mindedly seek to achieve their own tribal goals, and the bureaucratic process justifiably comes to resemble jungle warfare.

Shifting to an almost-collegial mode of dispute resolution, searching for "win-win" resolutions, or negotiating regulations in non-competitive settings do not produce a clear victor and a clear vanquished party, which Ruckleshaus says "is sort of like playing for a tie." (And a tie, as Ohio State's Woody Hayes used to say, "is kind of like kissing your sister.")

Do lawyers have a place in the more humane, collegial setting of mediation on the merits, or "regneg" negotiated rule-making? Of course, there already is an extraordinary amount of negotiation in American legal practice. Rule 16 of the Federal Rules of Civil Procedure is only one of the established settings in which alternate dispute resolution outside the court is heavily encouraged. (FRCP 16(c) requires negotiation attempts to be among the subjects to be discussed at pre-trial conferences.) Most filed litigation, moreover, ultimately "settles out" before final judicial decision, and although by nature it cannot be measured, negotiation without the filing of complaints is probably an even far larger part of our profession. Lawyers are experts at gauging the strengths and weaknesses of their clients' position.

Nevertheless the mode of our profession does seem to be aimed at the jousting model. Our clients' individual interests are supposed to be the dominant defining mandate. ADR on the other hand asks all to recognize an interest in achieving a mutually optimal resolution of a contested question. This is not an unimportant change in focus. ADR may not work where there is a flat out difference in values. But where all parties espouse roughly the same view of what is important and right, the collegial model offers a new socialization setting for the attorney.

Dispute resolution deals with realities far beyond the idyllic world of eighth grade civics gross disparities in power and aspiration will make a significant difference in any dispute resolution process. The survey of ADR methods on pages 1043-1045 is self-explanatory. Mediation provides an illustration of the special utility of processes that employ a non-binding third party participant (as distinct from the more familiar bi-polar, inter-party negotiation).

Arbitration, which analytically includes processes like "rent-a-judge," somehow does not appear so attractive in the literature or in the field, perhaps because it is too much like the judicial alternative. Arbitration-type processes tend to occur in more rigidly defined or institutionalized controversy settings. Environmental controversies are still fairly fluid in their occurrence and their character.

ADR and democracy: ADR can be a "by-invitation-only" affair, unlike the legal process where intervention as of right is a general rule for all interested parties. It is, moreover, a closed-door affair most democratic societies' dispute resolution processes traditionally have been a matter of public record (although, of course, most out of court negotiations, as mentioned earlier don't make it to the open public forum).

Pages 1046-1047. "Regneg" - negotiated rule making. This topic could also have been the subject of extended narrative tales and scholarly debate. Regneg raises issues slightly different from those in the non-rulemaking mediation setting. Here the process has official manifestations, in the notice of proposed rule making in the Federal Register which normally begins a process in the final rule making published in the Federal Register and Code of Federal Regulations (accompanied by summary of all the comments and debates that preceded it). In regneg the promulgating agency is the ultimate decision making authority as well as a participant. The constitutional separation of powers and due process issues noted in the questions have not prevented many officials in the national administration from becoming strong advocates of continued expanded regneg proceedings.

Page 1048, C&Q #1. Statutory ADR and reg-neg. These issues are largely self-explanatory.

Page 1048, C&Q #2. Technical details. As to the questions raised in the second paragraph, the comments are one way of answering the criticism that regneg violates various administrative law doctrines. Probably the dominant practical answer is that if regneg works in a particular situation, there will in all likelihood be no party who has an interest in challenging the result. If parties wish to challenge the result of a regneg, courts will have to go through the normally-required administrative law review steps, although the current ascendancy of the regneg argument is likely to produce a more deferential mood in the judiciary.

Pages 1048-1049, C&Q #3. Evaluating ADR. This is overview. If indeed ADR is not more efficient, one of its attractive attributes is lost. But given the current crowded dockets of our courts, and the stilted nature of motion practice and trial on the merits, it would seem that ADR is far more focused and likely to be more efficient. In talking of "satisfaction," Sander, McThenia, and Shaffer point to the attractive human attributes of a dispute resolution process that is not always at "daggers drawn." But here again recurs the question whether the official decision making processes of a democratic society should be open rather than closed, part of an evolving common law of private and public law precedent - rather than idiosyncratic one-shot happenings.

Page 1049. It is now generally accepted, even among EPA attorneys, that environmental compliance has become a key feature in the business planning of corporate America. Undoubtedly, environmental enforcement efforts, by governmental and citizen enforcers, helped to provoke this change. Today, however, environmental compliance is a major priority of most companies, and many in the business community argue that environmental enforcement has both lagged behind and is out-of-step with their own efforts to engage in waste minimization, recycling, and the development of systems to prevent pollution. These developments pose two fundamental issues: (1) what caused this shift in American business priorities? and (2) to what extent is the credible threat of continued enforcement still essential to provoke American business to continue to comply with the environmental laws?

Pages 1049-1055. These materials identify five key types of business events which, in the ordinary course of business activities, trigger environmental compliance. These events -- (1) permitting and reporting; (2) SEC disclosure by public companies; (3) satisfying corporate information needs; (4) borrowing for on-going business needs; and (5) the purchase or sale of a business or property -- all involve the assessment of environmental risks, costs, and benefits, and have become, for most companies, a regular part of their ongoing business planning and operations, even in the absence of direct environmental enforcement. The regulatory and business climate today demand attention to environmental concerns just as they demand attention to other important regulatory and business issues, like tax planning.

Page 1055, C&Q #1. The cooperative agreement between EPA and the SEC. *In light of the cooperation between EPA and the SEC, should a company take particular steps to ensure that its disclosures to EPA and the SEC are consistent? What might be the consequences if there were inconsistency?* The cooperative agreement between the EPA and the SEC should create material concern for those companies which have made inaccurate or inconsistent disclosures. Inconsistency can lead to enforcement proceedings initiated by the SEC, the EPA, or both, as well as civil litigation by shareholders or third parties pertaining to the failures to disclose. To avoid these problems, prudent business planning requires the full and fair disclosure of environmental liabilities, consistent within regulatory requirements. As the Frankel excerpt suggests, however, disclosure policies among companies regarding environmental contingencies vary widely, providing fertile territory for EPA and SEC enforcement.

The need for SEC enforcement has arguably grown with the demise of WorldCom and Enron, among many others. Congress has now enacted legislation to promote greater scrutiny of and personal accountability for corporate financial controls and disclosures. The Sarbanes-Oxley Act requires that CEOs and CFOs each file two separate certifications with their company's quarterly and annual SEC filings, under Sections 302 and 906 of the Act, respectively.

The two certifications require, in general terms, the CEO and CFO (or persons performing similar functions) to certify that:

- to his or her knowledge, the report does not contain any material misstatements or omissions;

- to his or her knowledge, the financial statements contained in the report fairly present the company's financial condition, results of operations, and cash flows in all material respects;
- he or she is responsible for establishing and maintaining a system of disclosure controls and procedures that is designed to ensure that information required to be disclosed in SEC filings is recorded and reported in a timely manner; and
- he or she has evaluated the effectiveness of these controls within the 90-days preceding the report and provided any conclusions with respect to that evaluation in the report.

The SEC expressly required that public companies adopt and maintain controls and procedures to ensure adequate and timely SEC disclosures.

Congress also directed the SEC to adopt federal standards of conduct for attorneys appearing and practicing before the SEC, including those involved in the process of identifying potential liabilities and preparing SEC disclosures, even if not employed in their capacities as lawyers. These rules, which have been proposed but not finalized, would apply to both outside and in-house counsel, and would impose a duty of "up-the-ladder" reporting of violations of law that come to be known by counsel. *See* http://www.sec.gov/rules/proposed/33-8150.htm. While the American Bar Association's Model Rules of Professional Conduct have long required attorneys that represent an organization and become aware of potential legal violations that may affect the welfare of the organization to refer such matters to a higher authority within the organization (*see* Model Rule 1.13(b)(3)), the degree to which the ABA's Model Rules have been adopted varies significantly from state to state. The proposed SEC rule would federalize this up-the-ladder requirement, at least with respect to attorneys practicing before the SEC.

More recently, the SEC has proposed rules that will require enhanced disclosure of off-balance sheet arrangements and contingent liabilities, as well as rules specifically requiring the disclosure of critical accounting estimates. Together, these proposed rules are likely to require many companies to include significantly expanded disclosure concerning both potential environmental expenses and liabilities, as well as the company's process for estimating them. Companies will need to provide a quantitative sensitivity analysis, showing the effects of changes in their assumptions.

SEC rules for disclosure of environmental liabilities presently require publicly held companies to evaluate costs of achieving compliance with laws, liabilities from actual or threatened legal proceedings, and prospective financial impacts that may result from emerging "trends" in environmental regulations and developments. As noted, whether a company is required to disclose these liabilities turns on whether they are deemed "material."

While the SEC reporting requirements have been in place for a number of years, the passage of Sarbanes-Oxley and its new implementing regulations are altering the context for their interpretation. Putting aside regulations that the SEC has proposed but not yet adopted, new rules already in effect require companies to adopt procedures and controls for identifying and disclosing material information, to evaluate the effectiveness of these systems, and to obtain certifications of personal responsibility for these systems from the CEO and CFO. To the extent it ever was open to question, therefore, companies now are on notice that they should be able to point to an established protocol for identifying, tracking, estimating, and judging the materiality of environmental matters.

The specific steps that a company should take may vary significantly depending on the nature and size of the company, the scope and complexity of its environmental compliance responsibilities, and its financial condition. In developing a process that fits its specific needs, however, a company may consider the following:

- Delegate specific responsibility for identifying and documenting emerging trends in environmental regulation or enforcement that may have a material financial impact on the company's operations. Examples of regulations that may have such an effect are changes in air emission controls, regulation or outright ban of chemicals used or produced, or significant new reporting requirements.
- Establish a method for evaluating potential environmental liabilities in threatened or pending enforcement and litigation matters, including state and federal "Superfund" sites.
- Involve senior management in evaluating information concerning potential compliance, enforcement, clean-up, and other environmental costs and liabilities. Sarbanes-Oxley requires a "top-down" certification by CEOs and CFOs as to both the quality of the company's disclosures and the internal systems from which they were derived. Depending on the size and complexity of the company, these officers typically will need to assure themselves that the information they have been provided from many different areas of the company is acceptable. Thus, substantial communication, well in advance of any filing deadline, may be required among environmental professionals, legal counsel, and managers responsible for individual businesses to identify potential costs and liabilities, determine the extent to which they can be estimated, summarize the results, and obtain peer review of information for inclusion in a formal disclosure.

Pages 1055-1056, C&Q #2. The disparity between EPA reporting and SFAS-5 disclosures. The varying reporting practices among companies are, to some extent, encouraged by the disparity between EPA reporting and SFAS-5 disclosures. As the comment points out, for companies not subject to SEC reporting, the requirements imposed under GAAP are much less stringent, and underdisclosure is often the result.

Page 1056, C&Q #3. Private arrangements for loss allocation. *What is the relationship of private agreements that shift or allocate losses and the law's allocation of liability?* This comment clarifies that a party having liability within the meaning of the environmental laws (for example, under CERCLA §107(e)(1)) can still enforce private agreements to allocate that liability to another party. However, private agreements for such loss allocation do not eliminate the underlying liability that attaches. You can ask the students "Would an indemnity agreement given by the seller to the buyer of real estate eliminate the buyer's concerns about environmental contamination later found on the property?" The answer, of course, is that, as the current owner of the property, the buyer would still be a liable party under CERCLA §107, and accordingly, is still subject to suit under CERCLA. If sued, the buyer's recourse is to seek to enforce the indemnity against the seller (and any other claims which the buyer may have). The indemnity, however, is only as good as the financial resources which the seller may have to satisfy any judgment. If the indemnity is worthless, the buyer remains on the hook as a liable party.

Pages 1056-1058. These materials review two key tools -- environmental due diligence and environmental auditing -- which have been increasingly utilized in the business community to assist in environmental compliance. It is important for students to understand the differences between these tools. It is equally important for students to understand the risks, as well as the benefits, arising from their use. For example, there is tremendous friction among EPA, the states, and the business community over the appropriate use of environmental audits. In the absence of explicit assurances that the results of audits will not be used as the basis for prosecution, most companies proceed with great caution when undertaking an audit, even if the involved states are receptive to and encouraging of audits. The controversy over the use of audits is highly charged and represents a good example of the breakdown of cooperative federalism.

Page 1059, C&Q #1. EPA and audit privileges. "Delegation blackmail" by EPA further emphasizes the coercive powers of EPA in the enforcement process.

Pages 1059-1060, C&Q #2. The congressional view of state environmental audit privileges. *Are the tactics employed by EPA with the states concerning environmental audit privileges impeding the development of innovative, progressive state programs that could lead to improved environmental compliance?* The answer to this question obviously depends on the perspective which is adopted. From the point of view of the states and industry, the answer is resoundingly affirmative. Most state environmental regulators, for example, view environmental audit privileges as a way to support local business while also inducing environmental disclosure and compliance. EPA remains staunchly opposed to this view, for the reasons described in the text. Congress, to date, has avoided resolving this controversy, by failing to enact a federal statutory audit privilege.

Page 1060, C&Q #3. Citizen groups and environmental audits. Citizens are often forgotten in the environmental audit debate. Although compromises have been suggested like those in the comment texts, none have been forthcoming.

Page 1060, C&Q #4. Striking the right enforcement balance. This comment emphasizes that, to a great extent, the marketplace is inducing environmental compliance by business. At the same time, self-generated compliance still responds to the credible threat of environmental enforcement. The future lies in the balance among deterrence, compliance, and prevention. Of course, that is what the debate is all about.

Page 1060, C&Q #5. Corporate infighting over environmental principle? A short compilation of materials on the junk bond raiders' impacts on the Pacific Lumber Company's sustainable redwood forestlands, posted on the Teachers' Website, has appeared in prior editions of this casebook and illustrates the potential leveraging of environmental law issues in the public company setting.

Pages 1060-1061, C&Q #6. New enforcement obstacles: congressional vetoes, and the Data Quality Act. The Data Quality Act, and similarly novel regulatory mechanisms, illustrate the creativity of Congress in setting and enforcing environmental standards. Political obstacles can and do often get in the way of sound environmental regulation.

Chapter 22.
PUBLIC ENVIRONMENTAL RIGHTS AND DUTIES: THE PUBLIC TRUST DOCTRINE

Chapter contents:

—and check the Teachers' Manual Website for SUPPLEMENTARY MATERIALS:

http://www.bc.edu/schools/law/library/coursebook/envtlaw/teachers

The list of Supplementary Materials in Part III of this manual, and on the Teachers' Website, indicates materials posted on the Teachers' Website that are relevant to this and other chapters.

OVERALL TEACHING THEMES & COURSE DESIGN CONSIDERATIONS

This chapter typically takes one or two class hours, but can be scheduled for more because students often get quite enmeshed in the idea.

Themes: The public trust doctrine, an ancient evolving legal principle and environmental law's special contribution to the legal system. The search for underlying fundamental legal principles that protect environmental quality, and make them litigatable. The idea of societal legacy, or intergenerational equity - the principle that a legal system must have within it (even though not enunciated in statutory law) a principle that serves the long-term survival needs of future generations the proposition that no generation has the right to destroy or squander what it itself has received to the detriment of future generations. The uncertain effectiveness of legal environmental rights arguments based on federal or state constitutions.

TEACHING NOTES, COMMENTS, & ALL QUESTIONS ANSWERED

THE PUBLIC TRUST DOCTRINE. This chapter introducing the public trust doctrine offers a pungent reminder that environmental law is not just built of parts-per-million technical administrative detail, nor monopolized by human health and safety considerations, but also extends into abstract human concerns, and beyond.

You can ask students *"How is the philosophical abstraction of the "public trust" relevant to practical environmental law?"* The answer starts with the three different areas in which the trust functions — against derogation, diversion, and alienation — noted on page, in each area of which it adds elements of protection that are often intuitively compelling but often not justified by usual legal principles, as in the examples on pages 1066-1068. A society needs some principle that integrates its long term future needs into current enforceable law, and the public trust's legacy principle can do that as well. It serves to bring many considerations of the natural and civic-societal economies into practical application against the limited calculus of the marketplace. Marks v. Whitney's definition of a public trust easement in coastal submerged lands may seem fairly mundane, but the court's expansive language on the evolving capabilities of the trust ("sufficiently flexible to accommodate changing public needs," page 1075) telegraphs the doctrine's potential importance. When the public trust exists in a particular setting, moreover, it has the potential to limit private property rights, a further point that tends to focus students' attention. You can foreshadow here the next chapter on private property rights, which at pages 1165-67 contains a unit on public trust defenses against regulatory takings claims.

Even Professor Richard Epstein, who is extremely skeptical about any intrusion upon private rights, nevertheless recognizes an important role for the public trust doctrine in identifying and preventing the private sequestration of "public goods."

Pages 1066-68, Public trust examples. These examples are quite cool, but to make your students think analytically about the trust doctrine you can ask whether there are examples of all three PTD settings. The examples presented do not include a "diversion" case, which you can note would be well represented by the *Overton Park* case, or *Paepke*, which follows in this chapter at page 1077.

Pages 1069-73, Professor Sax's reawakening of the public trust doctrine. Two classic texts. As noted later we think you should ask your students "Does the public trust doctrine as Prof. Sax describes it pose procedural or substantive controls on destructive action? As we read him, the tests he describes require a careful trustee-like consideration, but we would add far more emphasis on substantive constraints: that even if the trustee [legislature or whoever] goes through all the proper procedural steps, the substantive balance that determines outcomes must also be done right.

It is useful to have the students run the doctrine back to Justinian, as Sax does in his analysis. The Roman doctrine apparently included wildlife in certain circumstances, and springs, which were of too valuable a nature to be permitted to be tied up into individual ownership. (Consider the water needs of a medieval city-state under siege.) The water-based manifestation of the doctrine clearly was present in the Northwest Ordinance, but apparently exists in all states regardless of whether or not they were under that ordinance.

Illinois Central deserves close attention, perhaps with a schematic sketch: lower Lake Michigan, and the dramatic nature of a conveyance of two square miles off the Chicago waterfront to the railroad. The original conveyance was clearly a masterpiece of corruption, as everyone in the state, and subsequently in the Supreme Court of the United States, undoubtedly knew. But note how much more diplomatic it is for the Court to accommodate the legislators' change of heart by treating the conveyance to the railroad company as, in effect, simply *ultra vires*. Instead of discussing the nature of the transaction, all the court had to do was find that the state lacked the power to alienate trust assets, at least without going through a careful and explicit fiduciary balancing as a trustee. Students should be reminded that the public trust doctrine enunciated in *Illinois Central* was not absolute. (The cases noted on page 1103 said, quite unsurprisingly, that where the balance was carefully made, and the detriment was compensated by public trust acquisitions elsewhere, a good faith governmental trustee could alienate the assets, at least in part.)

Once the students have understood the nature of the *Illinois Central* decision, it might be useful to ask a question that is asked elsewhere in the chapter: *"So what is the public trust doctrine?"* The first, easy aspect of this question is to identify the different parties and terms - *who is the trustee, what is the trust corpus, what are its terms, who are the beneficiaries?* This material is set out on pages 1074 and 1076 in the comments and questions.

The second and far more difficult question is to point out to students that the public trust doctrine in *Illinois Central* overrode the legislative act of one of the sovereign states. It thus is not state common law, and apparently is not state statutory law. It is not within the state constitution, and if it were within a state's constitution, the state apparently cannot amend its constitution to abrogate it. So what then is the trust?

And does it apply to the federal government? This debate also rages on, with compelling arguments in both directions. The Supreme Court in dicta has said that "the power over the public land thus entrusted to Congress is without limitations. And it is not for the courts to say how that trust should be administered. That is for Congress to determine." Alabama v. Texas, 347 U.S. 272 at 273 (1953), apparently citing U.S. v. San Francisco, 310 U.S. 16, 29-30 (1940). This language was echoed in Keppel v. New Mexico, 426 U.S. 529, (1976). See also Wilkinson, The Public Trust Doctrine in Public Land Law, and 14 U.C. Davis L. Rev. 269, 309-310. (1980). The argument that seems most probative to us is that if the federal government, which was created by the states, holds only delegated powers, and does not have an inherent sovereignty of its own, then the state governments (which clearly have a public trust limitation on their powers that prevents them from harming public trust legacies for future generations), cannot create an agent that is free of such limitations. (See note 9, page 1103.)

Massachusetts cases like Gould v. Grey lock Reservation Commission on pages 1071-73, are important in asserting the existence of the doctrine and in separating the trust cases into the three different prongs set out at page 1068: (1) alienation of trust resources, as in *Illinois Central* (2) diversion, as in the Massachusetts cases, where a trust resource is being diverted from one public management regime to another more-intensive public management regime and (3) the pollution-derogation form of the trust.

The Massachusetts cases also raise the question whether Professor Sax's vision of the doctrine, at least as applied in those cases, was merely a requirement for *procedure*, in that the legislature would have to say explicitly what it was authorizing, and explicitly acknowledge that it was acting in its special fiduciary role as trustee. It seems to us, however, that procedure is not the essence of the public trust. In Massachusetts it was clear that the legislature had not acted as a trustee, and thus no question of balance of public trust *substantive* values was necessary. The *Paepke* case which follows, however, requires the further consideration whether the balance actually struck was a violation of trust law. The nature of trust law, after all, is not that the fiduciary need only go through motions, but rather that equity will ensure that the substantive terms of the trust are honored.

The Sax article is widely cited, and is generally regarded as authoritative as far as it goes.

Page 1073 C&Q #1. The history of the PTD in the U.S. The note asserts the doctrine's evolving potential. The text is self explanatory. It should be added that the Supreme Court of the United States recognized the existence of the trust in Phillips Petroleum v. Mississippi, 484 U.S. 469 (1988) and established that the scope and terms of the doctrine are largely to be defined and determined by state law. (This raises the interesting question whether a state legislature could define it out of existence or circumscribe it to trivial terms. In 1966 Idaho Gov. Phil Batt signed into law state bill HB 794 which purported to limit the application of the PTD to no more than an assertion of state title to the beds of navigable streams.)

Page 1074, C&Q #2. The public trust as trust law: Discussed above, this is fairly straightforward trust doctrine. Perhaps the most important advantage of the public trust in procedural terms, besides the obtaining of a review that contains a balancing consideration of public trust values, is the fact that unlike public nuisance, public trust lawsuits can be brought by any person in the beneficiary class. Ordinary trust law establishes this standing point – in order to get a trust accounting before a judge sitting in equity, one does not need a majority, nor a plurality, but only one beneficiary, to sue for an accounting.

Page 1076, C&Q #1. The evolving public trust. The issue of whether the PTD is static or evolving has generally ended up with the latter premise. In the Wisconsin cases and in California, the supreme courts straightforwardly recognized that the doctrine grows with the times, perhaps incorporating the evolving expectations of society noted by Professor Sax.

Page 1076, C&Q #2. How is the public trust a trust? An embarrassing slip: this note is a virtual reprint of the note two pages earlier. Sorry.

Page 1076, C&Q #3. Public trust and private property. *Can a public trust lie latent within private property?* Yes, as noted this is noted later in pages 1089-1101.

Pages 1077-1080. The *Paepke* parklands case. The analysis of this case is set out in the questions that follow it. We believe that the court undertook a substantive public trust balancing, and got it wrong ultimately because it never confronted the true nature of the balance. In *Overton Park*, in Chapter 7, the principle was made clear by statute that parkland could not be eliminated unless there was "no feasible and prudent alternative." similarly here we do not see how it is appropriate to weigh the trust balance without considering alternative locations, weighing cost as a less-than-determinative factor in the balance.

You can work through the Wisconsin tests (bottom of page 1078). (Students, like judges, love numbered tests.) But we would add a necessary sixth test for public trust diversions: requiring that trustees show that there is no feasible and prudent alternative. Otherwise, going through the Wisconsin tests you can note how a park can be nibbled away over time. You may want to note the special quality of New York's Central Park, which over the years has been proposed as the site of hotels, convention halls, fair grounds, roller-dromes, hippo-dromes and a host of other "improvements," and has been largely protected (suffering the incursions only of a museum, a zoo, and Robert Moses' obsession, the high-priced Tavern on the Green).

The idea of a park deserves some discussion. *"Why is it that the low-density, relatively undeveloped nature of a park attracts development, high-minded or otherwise, and deserves special protection?"* These issues lead into interesting policy discussions on the management of public lands, noted at comment 3, page 1110, and in Chapter 24.

Page 1078, C&Q #1. The scope of the trust: This question is foreshadowed in the lead-off text above. It appears that not all publicly-owned property is automatically protected under the public trust doctrine, as noted in the text, comment 5 at page 1100. *Is the concept of dedication the distinguishing factor?* Parks and other "special" resources obviously have been given special protection, and the idea of dedication to the use of future generations is typically expressly or impliedly present.

What is a park? Does a parkland public trust apply to state and national forests? The convention appears to be that a park is dedicated with the highest level of aspiration for long term protection, and public "forests" are held to a more consumption-tolerant form of use. Or is it that all public property is vested with the public trust, but the substantive terms – the protections – are balanced very differently for different trust properties? For most publicly-owned property, relatively casual governmental management decisions may not be inappropriate: sale or exchange of property between government agencies often does not raise any substantive problems and therefore may go unrecognized as an implicit trust balance. Again, we have no tidy answer for this question.

Page 1079, C&Q #2. Is the Paepke court's a substantive balance? Yes, as discussed in text above, it is clear that the *Paepke* court is not merely looking at the process by which the diversion was authorized. We understand that Professor Sax believes that the Illinois court should have taken into account some of the overall balancing issues implicit in the "no feasible and prudent alternative" standard. He put precisely that standard into his statute effectuating the public trust for the state of Michigan. See page 1111. The point is again a standard trust law point: the equity court will hold the fiduciary trustee to a careful comprehensive balancing of all relevant values, and ensure that the trustee adhere to the terms under which the trust was established.

Page 1080, C&Q #3. A diversity of values; EJ tradeoffs. *Should the court also consider countervailing impacts, such as the disruptive EJ effects of alternative locations?* There are clearly countervailing public values that have to be considered in an accurate public trust balance. In most such cases there are ways to redesign or re-plan a project so that the draconian "trade-off" of "environment versus concern for poor people" is beside the point. Public trust balances are equitable, which means that, in the consideration of alternatives' costs and benefits, environmental justice considerations should be weighed as relevant.

Pages 1081-1091. The *Mono Lake* case. This is a wonderful case to teach, and much of its analysis is developed in the questions that follow. We note in summary that the California supreme court recognizes that although the public trust doctrine is not absolute, it exists and must be given effect, and the public trust balance is substantive rather than merely procedural. The doctrine is applied to Mono Lake far beyond the issue of navigability. In fact, it appears likely that the court would have recognized the special qualities of Mono Lake even if the lake had been non-navigable. The opinion virtually ignores the fact that eighteen thousand acres of lake bed were removed from navigability by the lowering of the lake level (page 1084) that fact was focused on rather for its creation of air pollution from airborne alkali silt. The doctrine, moreover, analytically is being applied against private property rights this is not a "diversion" case in the public trust sense (although it is in the hydrological sense). Although the city of Los Angeles is a government, it holds the water rights through private market purchase. This is the aspect of the public trust doctrine that arouses most furor – the fact that it can be applied to property held in private ownership (as in the Marks v. Whitney case where an ancient land patent that clearly had not been issued with any knowledge on the buyer or seller's part of the existence of the public trust doctrine, nevertheless was held to contain an implicit public easement of navigability). When the trust develops in a variety of new manifestations, as the text notes, the opportunity to conflict with property rights is ever present and provokes passionate opposition. See pages 1076-77, 1165-67, and Huffman, A Fish Out of Water: The Public Trust in a Constitutional Democracy, 19 Envt'l Law 527 (1989).

Page 1088, C&Q #1. Scope of the public trust doctrine. Much of this is foreshadowed in the previous text. It appears to us that the court is recognizing Mono Lake itself and its ecosystem as the public trust resource.

If your students become too matter-of-fact about the evolutionary expansion of the trust doctrine, you might remind them that Marks v. Whitney's language excerpted on page 1085 applies its expansive definition only to tidelands, not to some novel locale. What if some plaintiff wishes to sue to protect the house in which the eighth mayor of your town was born? Is that a public trust asset? At some point we have to recognize that either the public trust does not vest in a particular piece of property, or that the public trust value in the balance is so insignificant as to make the result a foregone conclusion.

Page 1089, C&Q #2. The terms of the trust balance. Note for the students that analytically the public trust balance should not be deferential to a government agency decision. In a judicial trust accounting, the government trustee will be scrutinized on the full factual recorded of the government's action, decided by the court de novo on the substantive merits. In the balance, courts of equity have to consider a wide range of public and private values. That is normally what a substantive balance in equity does in other settings, of course, so this is not novel. The public trust value is not absolutely determinative but obviously counts beyond mere questions of dollars and cents. In our view the private water rights held by various users are to be weighed in the balance, but the public trust analytically represents a pre-existing "easement" within those property rights, so that a burden on private property rights, or even a complete derogation of them, does not necessarily mean that there is an unconstitutional burden. This topic is picked up after the *Florissant* case, but for the moment it is enough to note that the public trust is not regulatory, nor does it operate under the police power, so that it is apparently not subject to the Fifth and Fourteenth Amendments' takings tests, which do not apply to judicially-enunciated legal doctrines.

Page 1089, C&Q #3. A reprise on Mono Lake. A narrative update, self-explanatory. You may wish to run a Nexis search on Mono Lake to get the latest status on this controversy.

Pages 1091-1104. How far does the public trust go? Florissant Fossil Beds? Private property? The thing to stress at some point early on is that the Florissant Fossil Beds were private property. The *Florissant* case is exceptional, but perhaps should not be, and reflects broad possibilities for assertion of the trust on private lands. Students will generally agree that the injunction should have been issued in this fossil bed case. The developer was acting like Simon Legree, and the burden on private property rights was mitigated by the fact that Congress was imminently going to authorize purchase of the land for the Florissant Fossil Beds National Monument. But even without public purchase there often is a potential need for balancing accommodations between private and public rights in private lands. Wetlands regulation presents the most frequent example. See page 1165-67.

The Florissant Fossil Beds now are a popular national monument, and the extraordinary nature of the park's genesis is generally forgotten. In the circumstances the case should serve to raise legal process questions as well as public trust doctrinal issues, as noted in the questions.

In terms of tracking how far the trust doctrine may reach, we suppose it should be noted that Space Marketing, Inc. of Roswell, Georgia proposed launching a giant, mile-long mylar inflatable billboard into orbit so that its commercial messages can be seen by billions of potential consumers of Coca Cola and other commodities. The CEO of the company said he was seeking a corporate underwriter with a universally-recognizable logo willing to pay between $15-30 million for the privilege. U.S. DoT apparently would have to approve, but that might not be much of a problem. Many voices were raised against the proposal, including the late Carl Sagan who called it "an abomination." Is this a public trust issue, or should it be? (No one, on the other hand, seems much incensed about NASA's announced willingness to allow commercial logos to be painted onto its Conestoga 1620 rockets for about $10,000 a linear foot; see Advertising Age, Jan. 11, 1993 at 1.)

Page 1091, C&Q #1. The basis of the injunction? *Was it the public trust?* What else could the cause of action have been? In earlier days an equity court could issue an injunction when it considered it necessary to "do equity" thereby. Nowadays a court in equity requires an established legal cause of action before an injunction can be issued. It certainly appears that the public trust doctrine, in an incipient, ill-defined form, was analytically this injunction's basis. You might further ask students whether the courts' old equity power still allows a judge to issue an interim equitable order when it appears right or necessary to maintain the status quo pending further adjudication, *without* the existence of a defined legal cause of action?

Page 1099, C&Q #2. The balancing process in *Florissant*; private property rights and the public trust: In the Florissant trust balance, the fossil beds were held in private ownership, and the public trust claim was novel, but the assault on private rights was mitigated by the fact that Congress was in the process of authorizing eminent domain purchase of the land. A claim for a permanent injunction without compensation might not have been so successful. Private ownership of land subject to the trust does not foreclose the trust, but clearly weighs in the balance of determining how restricted the land uses will be. As noted in the next chapter, however, if private land is burdened with a public trust, that is not a regulatory taking; it is inherent in the property rights. And if the trust is encapsulated in police power regulations, as in Orion v. Washington, 747 P.2d 1062 (Wash., 1987), the fact that the public trust doctrine was not previously well-known does not mean that regulations implementing the trust are thereby an invalid regulatory taking for violation of "investment-backed expectations."

Page 1099, C&Q #3. Government use of the trust: self-explanatory notes. This appears to us to be a basic proposition. When public officials use the public trust doctrine to assert their authority to do a variety of things, they are concurrently acknowledging their fiduciary obligations, which are reviewable and accountable in a court of equity.

You can ask students: "Can a state government legislate public trust cutbacks?" As noted above, in 1996 Idaho Governor Phil Batt signed into law H.B. 794 which purports to limit the environmental application of the public trust doctrine to preserving the state's title to the beds of navigable waterways. The bill prohibits the public trust doctrine from being used to challenge the administration or litigation of water rights as well as barring its application to challenges based on the environmental impact of logging and other activities carried out on lands adjacent to waterways. The bill was cited by the governor as an important piece of legislation for protecting private property rights. While this may be true in regard to persons seeking to avoid the "unnecessary" burden of potential litigation, the measure fails to acknowledge the existence of "public" property rights, and thus seems to misunderstand the concept of public trust. Given the Supreme Court's expressed deference to state definitions of their public trust doctrines in Phillips Petroleum v. Mississippi, 484 U.S. 469 (1988) – in contradistinction to the court's assertion in the classic *Illinois Central* – it remains to be seen what the judicial reception of such attempted abnegations like Idaho's will be.

Page 1100, C&Q #4. Familiarizing the trust: Self-explanatory. The point is both that the public trust has been applied lately to an expanding range of environmental qualities, and also that in many jurisdictions it can be found lying latent in some prosaic old case law.

Page 1100, C&Q #5. The public trust doctrine: is it amphibious? These questions are rhetorical, building on the previous discussions of the public trust's unique societal utility and issues of definition. *Does the trust apply to public lands used as dumps and highway yards? Where is the line to be drawn?* The question raises the conceptual definitional issue whether only some narrowly delimited resources are peculiarly trust resources, or on the other hand whether *all* public resources are within the trust, and it is only the *terms* of how they shall be managed that differ. The history of trust litigation has rhetorically followed the former approach, but the logic of the latter may still be the case.

The paragraph at the top of page 1101 attempts to set out some of the water-related areas beyond navigability that have involved public trust litigation. Beach access is a topic that many students enjoy delving into. In every state but Massachusetts and Maine the right of the public to walk along a beach below the high-water mark appears to be an established public trust right. The *Bay Head* case noted established a right in New Jersey for access to the beach from adjacent highways through an easement perpendicular to the water line from road to beach. The citations in footnote 20 on page 1101 will allow you to go deeper into the beach access issue. (*Bay Head* also appears to have asserted a public trust right to the dry sand area above the high water mark, an extension from prior public trust iterations.

What if two entrepreneurs bought a Cezanne to cut up and sell? The Cezanne hypothetical is a wonderful exercise. The sources cited in the note report several actual cases and a host of ideas about the merits of protecting works of art, but none talks about use of the public trust as a legal document. Given the public trust-like international law doctrine of "common heritage of humankind" noted on page 1102, a concept pioneered by Professor Edith Brown Weiss,[1] we think there is a doctrinal fit.

[1] Weiss, Our Rights and Obligations to Future Generations for the Environment, 84 Amer. J. Int'l. Law 198 (1990).

Page 1101, C&Q #6. The third category: derogation of trust resources: Self-explanatory.

Page 1102, C&Q #7. How far does it go? This is another reminder of how the doctrine may apply to private as well as public property. What if you owned the oldest burr oak in Illinois, the oldest church building, the house in which Benjamin Franklin was born? Might the doctrine apply to your land? What standards would apply?... The point is that the trust might apply, but the trust obviously is neither absolute nor applies to the same degree in each case. You can ask "What if your land is the birthplace of the eighth mayor of your town?" The PTD would be a loose cannon if it could range so far. The definition of trust resources and implementation of the doctrine's balances require thoughtfulness, subjectivity, and proportionality.

Page 1102, C&Q #8. Cultural values beyond market values. Self-explanatory. Not everything of critical public value has a market price. Sustainability, for example.

Page 1102, C&Q #9. What is the public trust and where is it going? This coda echoes taxonomic questions previously raised. We think the trust is substantive, not just procedural, quasi-constitutional rather than simple common law, enforceable, not just hortatory. The rhetorical questions lead into the next chapter's consideration of the tension between public rights and private property rights. The public trust doctrine, as a public property right, clearly has significant consequences politically as well as philosophically and legally.

You can ask *"if the public trust exists at a constitutional level, where is it in the constitution?"* This raises a good technical point. It seems to us that it is not inappropriate or unprecedented that legal systems carry within them principles of long-term survival of the societies they represent. If such long-term protections are not within the constitution, are we left to the tender mercies of our legislators chaotically thrashing about in the short-term expediency with the chief executive and the marketplace lobbyists of a hundred short term vested interests? The thought that any present generation, with the technology to destroy or derogate what it has received from the past and pass on diminishing assets to the future without legal constraint seems like a fairly arrogant proposition. Conservatives especially can understand that the principles of civic responsibility and long-term survival of the polity and its quality of life might well be reflected in an evolutionary doctrine of quasi-constitutional status like the public trust doctrine.

Pages 1104-1111, ENVIRONMENTAL RIGHTS FROM CONSTITUTIONS & STATUTES

Page 1104. A federal constitutional right to environmental quality? The sometimes-heard proposition that the federal constitution contains some implicit enforceable provision for protecting environmental quality is based on essentially wistful arguments. The Supplemental Materials contain two files that may be interesting to students who want to pursue the quixotic idea. One is Tanner v. Armco Steel, a classic rebuff of a hodgepodge cumulation of attempts to pin down an environmental constitutional right. *Tanner* case represents current law, efficiently dismissing seriatim the array of constitutional claims the plaintiffs had tried to raise. Jim Krier's argument for a hortatory, nonbinding constitutional principle (cited in footnote 23) is interesting for its presumption that an enunciated constitutional law principle would have an effect on Congress even if it were unenforceable. Congress, of course, would not be the only audience for such a principle, but if the courts were to take any notice of it, how would they do so without in effect using it as authority? If it is the populace that is the relevant target of such a constitutional principle, most citizens are not capable of making Krier's delicate distinction between a principle that is enforceable and one that is not.

Where *Tanner's* constitutional assertions were based on vague and indirect interpretations of existing text, Krier's text would presumptively be quite specific in identifying a constitutional environmental quality protection principle. But the courts in both cases would rather defer to the authority of the legislature and chief executive acting together to make legislation appropriately, without constraint from the purported constitutional principle. Those of us who have worked with legislators find it hard to foresee that the enunciation of a high principle like Krier's would make any difference in the practical result of legislative debates, unless there was the fear that courts might use it to affect the merits in judicial review. Not to be too dismissive, however, it should be remembered that most other societies have a place in their legal systems for fundamental constitutional principles, or "ground-norms" - background foundational principles that are rarely if ever used in actual legal determinations.

The question that state constitutional provisions like Pennsylvania's Article 1 §27 on page 1105 leave hanging in the air is self-execution — whether the article by itself can be litigated in court for environmental protection, or whether the legislature must pass enabling legislation to permit such enforcement. The state constitutional provision in the Gettysburg case, Article 1, §27, offers an opportunity for classes to consider any similar section in other states' constitutions, and the question of whether constitutional provisions are self-executing.

The *Gettysburg Tower* case tests that proposition, among others. We remind readers in the comment that follows that only two justices, who wrote the first plurality opinion, were of the opinion that Article 1 §27 was not self-executing. The actual count of the various justices' opinions shows a majority in favor of the proposition that §27 was self-executing, although a majority of the court did not feel that the article or its public trust elements had been violated by this one tower.

The question of whether state constitutions are self-implementing is an interesting one. We suspect that the majority of jurisdictions having specific environmental provisions do consider them judicially applicable in proper circumstances. Note that no-one still fights that battle as to most of the protective provisions of the federal constitutions. Why should state constitutions be treated any differently? State constitutions, in fact, are generally regarded more lightly than the federal constitution, often having been changed more than half a dozen times or so in the century. As noted in the first part of this chapter, environmentalists' efforts to pass constitutional environmental quality amendments have a certain quixotic flavor, and raise question about the utility of spending time, money and energy in such efforts.

Page 1110, C&Q #1. A split decision on self-executing provisions? As noted, only the two justices who wrote the first plurality opinion thought that Article 1 §27 was not self-executing. The first opinion in the case was written by Justice O'Brien, joined by Pomeroy, arguing that §27 required further legislation. Roberts, Manderino and Nix, JJ., disagreed on this point, but it appears that they felt the equitable balance under the public trust did not justify the issuance of an injunction, especially because the specific elements of the trust balance (substantive and procedural standards) were not sufficiently clear. Jones and Eagan, JJ., clearly believed that §27 was self-executing, and that the constitutional provision and the public trust it incorporated required an injunction against "this monstrosity." In the subsequent case cited in the note, Payne v. Kassab, the Pennsylvania court quite clearly adopted by majority vote the proposition that §27 was self-executing. The proposition that constitutional provisions are not self executing often seems to run afoul of our popular American presumption that if law is law, it must be enforceable. We suspect that the majority of jurisdictions having specific environmental provisions do consider them judicially applicable in proper circumstances.

In his article "State Constitutions, Environmental Rights Provisions, and the Doctrine of Self-Execution: A Political Question?" 17 Harv. Env. L. Rev. 333 (1993), José Fernandez argues that unlike most civil rights values, for example, "the idea of a right to a clean environment has appeared far too recently to have entered into the nation's 'spirit.' ... Given the lack of a clear societal consensus on many of the central issues involved in environmental protection, the courts are prudent to avoid making decisions that might be perceived to be based solely on the judges' personal views of the issues." Leaning heavily on Montesquieu, he concludes that the better path is for courts to apply a presumption that constitutional provisions are not self-executing, which will "encourage...other branches of government to deal with environmental problems, resulting eventually in a more democratic treatment of issues affecting the environment." Id. at 387.

How does this last premise square with perceived reality? And does the separation of powers/judicial restraint rationale appear different when public trust issues are involved, as in the *Gettysburg Tower* case?

Page 1110, C&Q #2. The state constitution and the public trust: *How many justices voted for what?* Both the Jones and Roberts opinions seem quite clearly to adopt the public trust doctrine. Jones and Eagan clearly would apply the doctrine to private land surrounding the battlefield. Roberts perhaps was moved in his trust balance by the fact that the injunctions sought applied on private lands.

Did §27 add anything to pre-existing trust law? A further interesting point is that §27 expressly added "scenic, historic, and aesthetic values' of the environment to the public trust. This is an extension of the trust doctrine by constitutional fiat, and under the principle that states are the primary declarers of the extent of the extent of their public trust enunciated in *Phillips Petroleum,* that expansion apparently will be recognized by the U.S. Supreme Court in any review of Pennsylvania trust law that cites §27. (*See Pruneyard Shopping Center,* 447 U.S. 74 (1980), where the Court expressly recognized the ability of the Supreme Court of California to define and thereby erode property rights under the state constitution where federal constitutional rights would otherwise have been violated.

Page 1110, C&Q #3. Commercialization and a parade of horribles: This commentary raises a host of interesting issues. *Could you have litigated Gettysburg Tower to have achieved a different result?* One issue raised in this question is the nature of the balance. How does one ask the court to weigh the intrusion of a tower into the park's perimeter? In making the balance, the suggestion that if one tower makes money, a dozen more may easily arrive, would help pose the issue to the court from where ultimately a line must be drawn to avoid the national monument's honky-tonkization.

In fact the tower might be a very good place from which to visualize the battle moving across the fields of Gettysburg, a bird's eye view far better than a tabletop diorama. During the battle of Gettysburg, in fact, there apparently was one observation balloon used by the union forces, floating an observer from that height, which might mitigate in some subjective way the looming presence of the tower. What is it that one is looking for when visiting a national battlefield cemetery? Perhaps it is recreating the sense of being there at an earlier time, when a looming tower would be anachronistic. Certainly part of the experience of that particular national monument is the dignity of death consecrated by Lincoln's address.

Environmentalism as élitism? This may be an opportunity to discuss whether, in this and other settings like the Wilderness Act, preservationism is elitist. Clearly many thousands of Americans, voting with their dollars, will patronize tourist towers, bowling alleys, bars, and other facilities in and near parks. Clearly many Americans would rather ride snowmobiles, ATVs and jet skis into natural areas than to hike, canoe, or cross-country ski into them. Sax considers that question at great length in his book MOUNTAINS WITHOUT HANDRAILS. His argument appears to be that these areas, and by extension public trust resources generally, are held to their original range of low density multiple uses out of a sense of legacy for present and future generations. When Olmstead was asked whether he wasn't an élitist, he gave a two-word response, "Central Park." His efforts to remove the tenements in the area now occupied by northern Central Park were resisted as élitist, but the park has become a people's park, available and used by a wide variety of citizens and especially important for citizens whose low income would prevent them ever from enjoying such a resource had it not been saved for them. Sax argues that low technology recreation requires more of each individual and that over time most of us gravitate away from highly mechanized pursuits toward avocations that require more of our native skill, experience, and self-involvement. He argues that this is a progression that occurs without regard to income level. It is only by imposing counter-market constraints that this legacy opportunity remains available to all, in this generation and future generations as well.

Notice that the tower called itself the "National Tower," although it is completely private, and the brochure took its picture from within the battlefield monument to emphasize the public asset. One is reminded of the joke told in Poland that in Warsaw the best view of the city is from the top of the Stalin Tower, because only from there can one not see the Stalin Tower.

In MOUNTAINS WITHOUT HANDRAILS, Professor Sax repeatedly affirms the notion that the public trust doctrine and the parklands protection initiatives that parallel it are concerned with protecting the legacy for all Americans, of whatever social class, and alternatively, protecting the minority rights which otherwise could never be defended against the commercialized power of the marketplace representing the majority of active consumers. If the government does not secure parklands for Americans, every desirable place will be derogated, except for those preserves that the very richest people can protect for their own exclusive use. American parks are democratic in the sense they are open to all, forever. The opportunity cost of creating such parks in the future would be impossible for any, even the richest, to recreate.

The argument can be continued in questions of motorcycle riders who want to use the fragile desert (an issue studied in Chapter 24), snowmobiles in public forests, etc. Part of the problem is that high-tech users tend to preclude the lower technology users of public areas. One snowmobile can destroy the experience and drive away a hundred bird watchers who would like to enjoy a pristine experience. One biker can disrupt a desert for fifty to a hundred years with the destruction of the terrain. Behind the discussions of market democracy versus élitism is the temporal question: marketplace consumption decisions are made here and now, corporate decisions and political decisions are often made in terms of short-term expediency considering only this quarter or this fiscal year or the next. The public trust doctrine clearly tries to add long term values.

Note also that the *Gettysburg Tower* case serves to continue the discussion of the public trust doctrine as source of authority for a government to assert protective actions beyond the boundaries of public trust lands. This is not necessarily a radical proposition. The redwood cases cited at page 1101 involved injunctive orders to protect a redwood park against the clearcutting and consequent erosion from private parcels of redwood forest uphill from the park. In other cases, the government has with greater or lesser success asserted the power to protect trust assets against development on neighboring property. In two cases, the Department of Interior was held to have the power as necessary and proper to protect wildlife reserves by issuing regulations preventing shooting on adjacent private and nonreserve lands. U.S. v. Brown, 431 F.Supp. 56 (D. Minn. 1976), aff'd 552 F.2d 817 (8th cir. 1977), cert. denied 97 S.Ct. 2666; Bailey v. Holland, 126 F.2d 317 (4th Cir. 1942) (although these may be particular to wildlife under federal statutes). In a less successful effort, Interior Secretary Cecil Andrus was frustrated in attempts to protect the visual backdrop of the Lincoln and Jefferson Memorials against the construction of towering skyscrapers in Roslyn, Virginia just across the Potomac from Washington, DC.

One of the points of the Sax article cited at the end of this note is that national parks fall prey to the surrounding lands' development that they themselves attract. Public trust resources like parks become tourist destinations, with all of the inevitable commercial sprawl that inevitably brings with it. Park managements have not managed to impose some kind of order or planning upon their gateway areas, and the result is very often a raucous carnival, each entrepreneur trying to out-flash the other so as to attract the passing tourist dollar. Before Frederick Law Olmstead refashioned the Niagara Falls parks, the ticky-tacky concession stands were so thick that one could not see the falls from the American side without going through a private turnstyle. (See Sax, Mountains Without Handrails.) The comment also raises the possibility that public nuisance law might in some cases be applied. This is a good time to note that the public trust doctrine is likely to be more assertive than public nuisance. In public nuisance, courts tend to turn to the average normal expectation of the community, and tourist honky-tonk, for better or worse, is part of our expectations. The public trust doctrine, on the other hand, appears to draw upon a higher standard of land management, and accordingly might be more applicable.

The phenomenon of market forces rushing to exploit historic or natural resources that create potentially lucrative "tourist destinations" has undoubtedly been with us through history. One recent battle was Walt Disney Corporation's plan to build a civil war theme park on 3000 acres it bought near the Manassas battlefield. C. Vann Woodward and a group of historians organized in opposition to the plan, alleging a desecrative effect on a geographic area of historical importance, with arguments resembling the public trust. See also Boge and Boge, PAVING THE PAST (1993), a book analyzing the incremental destruction of historic battlefields by the market forces they engender.

A further note on *Gettysburg Tower*: the attorney for the Gettysburg Tower's owner was Victor Yannacone, Jr., the same attorney who was instrumental in the innovative defense of environmental values in the *Florissant Fossil Beds* case.

Page 1111, C&Q #4. The tower came tumbling down. Self-explanatory history. There are some good articles with pictures on the Internet.

Page 1111, C&Q #5. Some state environmental protection statutes. This note introduces the Michigan Environmental Protection Act of 1970, Professor Sax's model act passed in about a dozen states. A fuller set of materials on MEPA is available on the Teachers' Website in Part III's Supplementary Materials for this chapter. Currently the use of the statute appears to be light, and its provisions have not consistently been strongly enforced by the courts of Michigan.

NOTE: California's Environmental Quality Act (CEQA) requires state and local agencies "to protect, rehabilitate and enhance environmental quality." CEQA has three provisions which give teeth to its substantive aspirations: agencies shall (a) mitigate when feasible ("capable of being accomplished [timely and successfully, with regard to] economic, environmental, social and technological factors"); (b) develop alternatives/mitigation measures; and, (c) issue "findings statement" detailing agency rationale. CEQA specifies the timing and scope of judicial review, employing short (30-35 days) statute of limitations provisions to prevent delay. The standard of judicial review is whether substantial evidence supports the agency's determination.

NOTE: Washington's act (SEPA) does not specify a specific substantive result. The act first gained substantive power in the courts; the legislature later codified several decisions. Agencies have considerable latitude to deny projects. If an EIS identifies adverse impacts, the agency may deny the project. To deny a project, the agency must find that it will result in significant adverse affects, and that reasonable mitigation measures are insufficient. Conditions placed on approval must mitigate specific harms identified in the EIS. Judicial review is specified in Washington's SEPA; appellants must exhaust an administrative appeal before raising claim in court (creating an administrative record for judicial review). The standard of judicial review is that the agency decision "shall be accorded substantial weight."

NOTE: New York's state environmental quality review act (SEQRA) requires agencies to regulate "so that due consideration is given to preventing environmental damage." SEQRA imposes a duty to choose alternatives which "to the maximum extent practicable, minimize or avoid adverse environmental effects." Also, agencies must mitigate the adverse impacts of approved projects "to the maximum extent possible". SEQRA contains no judicial review provision, but NY courts have weakened SEQRA, by not second-guessing agency decisions. See Ferester, Revitalizing the National Environmental Policy Act: Substantive Law Applications from NEPA's Progeny, 16 Harv. Env. L.R. 207 (1992).

NOTE: The Minnesota Environmental Rights Act (MERA) was applied to a bald eagle's nest in a state decision construing the nest as a "natural resource." The court held, however, that the plaintiff timber company might file an inverse condemnation action to seek damages. State of Minnesota, ex. rel. Wacouta Township V. Brunkow Hardwood Corporation, et al., 510 N.W.2d 27 (CA Minn. 1993).

Chapter 23.
PRIVATE PROPERTY AND PUBLIC RIGHTS: CONSTITUTIONAL LIMITS ON PHYSICAL AND REGULATORY TAKINGS

Chapter contents:

—and check the Teachers' Manual Website for SUPPLEMENTARY MATERIALS:
http://www.bc.edu/schools/law/library/coursebook/envtlaw/teachers

The list of Supplementary Materials in Part III of this manual, and on the Teachers' Website, indicates materials posted on the Teachers' Website that are relevant to this and other chapters.

OVERALL TEACHING THEMES & COURSE DESIGN CONSIDERATIONS

This chapter explores the environmental manifestations of a basic question of Justice in a modern post-industrial democracy: *How far can the collective majority in a society impinge upon the property rights of individuals without breaking the social contract, upsetting democracy, and running afoul of constitutional prohibitions? and vice versa?*

The chapter first reviews the physical-taking eminent domain sector of the police power, which provides a pedagogically useful matrix for analyzing police power actions. This section focuses on cases challenging condemnation — exploring how governmental eminent domain decisions might occasionally be overturned in court.

Then the text examines the imaginative innovation of inverse condemnation as a environmental remedy, where governments are forced to compensate for physical impacts, despite sovereign immunity in tort, by "constitutional lawsuits," raising some interesting questions on the scope of a government's duty to compensate for physical harms caused.

The subject of regulatory takings is the chapter's core — an in-depth survey of how far regulatory restrictions can go without facing constitutional invalidity under the takings clause. This section emphasizes that constitutional regulatory takings tests increasingly contain recognition of an articulated balance of public interests as well as private property losses in any given case. The regulatory takings materials continue to be broadly relevant to environmental law. In recent decades the ascendancy of private property rights over civic regulation had been brought to the highest levels ever, and that well-financed litigation and lobbying movement continues, making the topic extremely timely in political terms as well.

This chapter is worth the two or more classes that some teachers give it. As current anti-regulatory political initiatives in Washington and the state capitals understand, most of us share a natural gut reaction against government telling us what to do with our property. Anti-regulationist industries have been able to capitalize on this identification to raise serious initiatives for rollbacks of regulatory government. If public interest environmental regulation had to be justified in purely marketplace economic terms, if most environmental regulation required compensation to be paid, environmental regulation would lapse, and the externalized costs targeted by regulation would instead be absorbed by the natural and civic economies. This debate between public and private rights is not a simple balance, with a lot at stake.

TEACHING NOTES, COMMENTS, AND ALL QUESTIONS ANSWERED

Pages 1112–1115. An analytical scheme & introduction. This initial section is basic in setting out a means of clarifying the analytical basis, and the structure of judicial tests, of governmental police power actions – whether in compensated eminent domain cases or uncompensated regulatory cases. The attempt is to avoid the chaotic morass of typical takings discussions, including the tendency of judges and lawyers to jumble together arguments about proper public purpose, legislative rationality, ideology, and effects on private property. The text should be generally self-explanatory, but further detail can be found in the article cited on page 1116, footnote 7.

Pages 1116–1122.
EMINENT DOMAIN CONDEMNATIONS & THE CLASSIC *POLETOWN* CASE

Federal courts have typically been reluctant to apply the full range of administrative law review to eminent domain condemnation actions by governmental agencies. The coursebook notes the analytical elements at issue in eminent domain action – the condemning authority must have proper authority, a proper public purpose, a rational relationship between the purpose to be achieved and the particular action being taken, and pay just compensation. These need not be pushovers. In the coursebook at page 1116-1122 we argue that courts should be open to deeper scrutiny of eminent domain. Those who assert that courts owe extraordinary deference to governmental decisions condemning land, more than other governmental decisions, bear the burden of showing a legitimate constitutional or statutory basis for such a distinction. Application of standard administrative law principles would appear to require that courts be open to scrutinizing condemnation decisions in all four areas of review.

The *Poletown* case is a dramatic example of why a more meaningful degree of judicial review is necessary and feasible.

Nevertheless federal courts repeatedly hold that "the only question for judicial review in a condemnation proceeding is whether the purpose for which the property was taken is for a congressional-authorized public use." U.S. v. 0.95 Acres of Land, No. 91-9522, 23 (9th Cir., June 1, 1993), United States v. 416.18 Acres of Land, 514 F.2d 627, 631 (7th Cir., 1975). In the Ninth Circuit case, for instance, condemned property owners were asserting that the taking of their land by the Forest Service would result in significant environmental impacts, and argued therefore that an environmental impact statement was required before title could be shifted to the government. Without the EIS, they alleged, the condemnation was in violation of federal law. In this case, however, it appeared that the Forest Service had not complied with NEPA. The District Court had so held, so that the Appeals Court had to create a blanket immunity from NEPA review in order to allow the condemnation action to proceed. The Court held that the change of title in condemnation cases was not a "major federal action significantly affecting the environment"; if future changes in the actual use of the land were significant, the court said disingenuously, a later lawsuit could then be brought against the agency. (Under current standing arguments, however, landowners who by then had lost their property would no longer have standing to make a NEPA claim, because once condemnation had occurred they would have no right for re-transfer of title.) The standard lines of federal cases, consistently applying a lax standard of judicial review of condemnations, deserve more critical attention.

Page 1121, C&Q #1. A legal basis for more active review. Could better defensive arguments have been made the *Poletown* case? This note focuses on eminent domain challenges alleging substantive irrationality, arbitrariness and capriciousness. Whereas most eminent domain defense arguments fecklessly focus on public purpose challenges, or on attempts to run up the damages, the theory advanced here addresses the rationality nexus element, a frontal rationality challenge. As noted in the text, there is little federal successful case law challenging specific governmental decisions and choices as to particular condemnation projects. (A collection of cases overturning governmental choices, mostly at the state level, can be found in that article cited on page 1116, footnote 7.) The theory advanced for the Poletown setting might just work in a renascent "property rights" era, and it offers an opportunity for creative, cutting-edge lawyering. In political terms however, citizen efforts bucking eminent domain, as in *Poletown,* are uphill maverick attempts to buck the establishment.

Page 1121, C&Q #2. Uncorking judicial review: Professor Sax has opined to us informally that heightened judicial scrutiny of condemnation decisions would in effect be imposing a potential environmental impact analysis on all challenged condemnation decisions. Given the alternative of abject deference, that doesn't seem much of a burden, but the potential burdens of allowing courts to scrutinize necessity in every challenged case could become onerous. Note that owing to the presumption of validity that attaches to governmental actions, the burden in any event will always be on the *defendant* in eminent domain cases to make out the difficult showings we advocate.

Page 1121, C&Q #3. The politics of eminent domain: Note that in *Poletown* it was Ralph Nader who was fighting beneath the banner of private property rights, and the federal and city governments standing with General Motors in the campaign to take those rights.

Why did General Motors insist on the Poletown site? Footnote 18 on the bottom of page 1120 explores this question. One GM attorney noted to us that the only reason he and his colleagues on the GM legal staff could imagine that Roger Smith, the GM chairman, was insisting on the Poletown site for the new Dodge Main Cadillac plant (instead of the several available empty industrial sites) was that Poletown was the only site that he could see from his office window in the GM Tower. (n.b. Michael Moore.) The fact that this is not obviously ridiculous goes far toward illustrating the political force that can be applied by a corporation which wields several thousand jobs. In fact, the Poletown plant did not produce the six thousand jobs that had been promised; it has averaged about three thousand workers when the plant is in production, which is erratic. For further information on the phenomenon of corporate flight threats and their impact on communities and local government, see Barry Bluestone's book, "Corporate Flight.'

Pages 1122–1127. INVERSE CONDEMNATION CASES. Note the cleverness of environmental attorneys who otherwise were typically blocked by sovereign immunity in cases against governmental defendants (or private defendants acting under the protection of a governmental regulation) that otherwise resemble actionable tort cases. To get around the immunity defense the burdened landowners in effect brought quasi-condemnation actions on behalf of the government against themselves – sort of "Port of Portland *ex rel.* Thornburg v. Thornburg's land [an easement of noise and passage]. The theory is sort of a constitutional tort: the cause of action is in eminent domain, which the government didn't want to admit it was doing. But if the defendant-turned-plaintiff Thornburg can show that the government has in fact taken property rights, then the court will recognize the eminent domain taking and award compensation.

In class, a sketch of the layout of the *Thornburg* case will emphasize that even Judge Perry in dissent and other restrictive judges would now grant compensation for the taking of an easement where the airplane actually physically nicked through the magic crystalline box that extended above the individual's property, i.e., where defendants *trespassed.* Once a physical easement was actually being used, compensation for the easement had to be paid and consequential damages (the real point of the lawsuit, because diminution in market value is the source of the large damage sums that would be awarded) would follow. But where there is no physical entry, the more restrictive judges would award no compensation for the taking of an easement at all. But see comment 1, following.

Page 1126, C&Q #1. Nuisance as an easement/servitude: Nuisances can ripen into easements even without a physical trespass (see page 197). Thus what a government action is taking is an easement right in the private land, even before it ripens.

To what extent should these cases balance private burden against public necessity? or is it a cost of doing business? The arguments here indicate that inverse condemnation damages are appropriate charges against governments that have failed to buy a sufficient buffer around airports forcing individuals to absorb and subsidize the noise buffer costs fails when the noise is recognized as an easement, so the cost is passed on to those who use the facility.

Page 1126, C&Q #2. Extending inverse condemnation theories: Self-explanatory. Several Florida cases have extended inverse condemnation to nuisance easements along highways. As to the other suggestions, the courts in the cases cited seem to decline to recognize antelopes, wolves, and grizzlies as governmental agents physically occupying or taking an easement in private property. The cited Wiener article provides a shaky argument that the government must pay when its fires burn private property. As to the EMF hypothetical in the last paragraph, some plaintiffs in the Northeast have been preparing inverse condemnation claims against public utilities companies for the electromagnetic fields in and across their private property. In putting these in perspective, it should be recognized that the local TV channel is constantly exercising such an easement through everyone's private air space, with no thought that it is a taking. Where the EMF field is thought to be harmful and substantial, however, the argument may be different.

Page 1127–1142. REGULATORY TAKINGS CHALLENGES. Building upon the four-stage inquiry in testing police power regulations from pages 1114-15: Typically, statutes or regulations that violate the first two tests (problems with (a) insufficient grants of delegated authority, or (b) not serving a proper public purpose or involving a poison purpose, like regulating property so as to lower property values for subsequent condemnation) will result in invalidation of the entire statute or regulation on its face. As to the third area of inquiry, reviewing whether the police power regulatory action is arbitrary and irrational in its design in attempting to achieve the purpose, this may likewise sometimes lead to decisions that a statute or regulation is void on its face. Thus a wetlands regulation that is based on an inaccurate basic methodology would be entirely void as not designed rationally to fit the ends. If, on the other hand, only one portion of a wetlands map was inaccurately drawn, it could be voided only as applied to that particular parcel, leaving the rest of the enactment intact. The fourth area, however, viewing the particular burden imposed on private property rights, turns in virtually every case upon the facts and circumstances of each individual case. Physical appropriation in eminent domain cases clearly fits that latter model. Challenges to regulatory enactments for facial invalidity under this fourth "takings" branch of the police power review, as in *Keystone Bituminous* are generally unsuccessful. Such facial challenges have to show that the regulatory enactment provides no compensation in a situation where *every affected* property owner will thereby suffer an unconstitutional degree of loss.

Regulatory takings challenges are widely encountered in environmental law, and are politically potent on their own merits, and also because the test of validity is so unpredictable and unclear. Environmental law can go far toward clarifying the regulatory takings test.

Note that in the materials we draw no distinction between the constitutional test imposed under the (substantive) due process clause and the takings clause of the Fifth and the Fourteenth Amendments. Regulatory enactments are consistently tested on a very different basis from physical appropriations, and there seems to be no meaningful distinction between the two clauses as they apply to the regulatory setting, except where courts use a substantive due process approach for the first three inquiries and then ignore the fourth area (the effect on the individual) completely.

POLITICS: THE PROPERTY RIGHTS ANTI-REGULATORY CAMPAIGN. For an analysis of the coordinated ongoing initiatives against regulation, focused on private property rights, see Douglas Kendall and Charles Lord's "The Takings Project: a Critical Analysis..." 25 B.C. Envt'l. Aff. L. Rev. 509 (1998). As Charles Fried wrote in his book ARGUING THE REAGAN REVOLUTION, early in the Reagan ascendancy –

> Attorney General [Edwin] Meese had a specific, aggressive, and it seemed to me quite radical project in mind: to use the takings clause of the 5th Amendment as a severe brake on federal and state regulation of business and property. [quoted at 25 EALR 509.]

The article notes how this Takings Project has been continuing within the judiciary selected under the Meese-Sununu program, augmented by a number of right-wing foundations and marketplace-financed "public interest law firms," fundamentally reinterpreting long-established concepts of balance between public and private interests. The article deserves a look.

Page 1127-1135. Regulatory takings in wetlands and beyond. Wetlands present one of the toughest areas of regulatory takings law, because their public harms are so newly recognized, diffuse, and difficult to monetize.

The wetlands materials are included to present a challenging setting for defense of environmental regulations against takings challenges. The point is that wetlands do serve many important functions, but these are typically newly recognized and outside the traditional marketplace. The Maine v. Johnson, and *K&K Construction* cases take virtually the same circumstances and reach opposite conclusions. Sketching out the setting of the cases allows the class to go through a variety of clarifying analyses set out in the subsequent text. [A map showing the location of Dr. Johnson's property is on the Website's Part III's Supplementary Materials for this chapter.]

On a schematic diagram of the Johnson property one can note the fact that several upland parcels have been separated out from the Johnson's tract and sold at a profit, but if the baseline for constitutional review is only the *regulated* wetland portion of the larger parcel, that portion has virtually no economic use. The functions of wetlands are evident, constituting an effective stormwater retention facility that is lost if the wetlands are filled, and potential property and sewage pollution damages are increased in the event of high water conditions.

WETLANDS POLICY. The battles over protecting wetlands have been reflected in national administrative policy debates and have figured prominently in the property rights cases. The first President Bush originally ran on an environmental promise of "no net losses of wetlands." His administration then tried to redefine what were wetlands under the Corps Manual in order to narrow the scope of the promise. The Clinton administration was tentative on the issue, as on so much else.

In approaching this section setting out possible constitutional balancing scenarios, ZP sometimes sets out a spectrum of schematic sketches of factual settings —

(1) a cyanide factory example, where shutting down the cyanide companies pollution will shut down the factory and make it worse than a total loss, yet clearly constitutional,

(2) a wetland flood plain regulation, or earthquake zone where buildings on a slope are prohibited, thereby eliminating virtually all market value,

(3) a historic preservation ordinance,

(4) an ordinance prohibiting structures on private property that obstruct the view of tourists of the Pacific Ocean from Highway 1.

The point is that clearly these ordinances have different balances that must be applied, and no *a priori* bright line test makes logical or constitutional sense.

Then you can set out a further spectrum on the chalkboard, showing the range of possible tests.

(1) can begin at the right with a "Richard Epstein" extreme bright line test, where any unequal burden imposed upon a private property owner requires compensation from the public at large, to

(2) another bright line test, as in the Lucas case, where the property owner argues a total wipeout, and that compensation must be paid wherever there is no remaining economic use.

(3) Would be a balancing test, balancing the individual wipeout against the public harms involved (our favored approach).

(4) A sort of balance, where the court finds that there is a reasonable, viable economic use, (the standard diminution test from the zoning cases) and

(5) On the far left, a further bright line test, based on the original intent of the drafters of the Bill of Rights and the Fourteenth Amendment, requiring compensation when, and only when, the government physically appropriates private property.

The two "bright line" tests on the right represent versions of the current "property rights" movement that has been seeking to seize the moment in the Supreme Court to assert an unprecedentedly strong position for property rights. The Epstein notion is radical, requiring government to operate as a giant broker, collecting the benefits of regulation to the public at large, and using them to pay off any individuals who find themselves contributing disproportionately to the public good. Epstein himself admits that this would not only require compensation in environmental cases like Lucas, but also would nullify many civil rights statutes, labor-management statutes, and so on where regulation has burdened the prior existing common law rights of market participants.

The second bright line test is less radical, arguing that, at least in cases where there is "no remaining viable economic use," the government must always pay if it wishes to regulate.

Environmental law provides a clear test for the latter proposition. Where no reasonable economic use remains in the zoning cases the courts have generally required compensation. In environmental cases there are typically discrete harms to the public that are not present in the zoning setting. Here the question is whether the constitutional test can view property rights in a vacuum, or whether the validity or invalidity of a regulatory enactment requires a balance between public rights and private rights. The discussion of the "nuisance exception" is a recognition that private property rights may have to be viewed in the context of nuisance-like harms they may impose on the neighboring public.

The latter theme is picked up at some length later in this chapter.

A Note on the Original Intent of the Takings Clause. Research on the original intent of the Takings Clause indicates that it was never meant to require compensation for indirect takings of property by land use regulations. The Framers conceived of "takings" as direct physical expropriations. Although land use regulations were common in England and the Colonies, such regulations had never provoked any serious controversy. See Fred Bosselman, David Callies, & John Banta, The Taking Issue 104, 238-39 (1973). For example, in the aftermath of the great Boston fire, that city required landowners to build all new homes out of brick and slate. See Mass. Laws (1672) 269, cited in Bosselman, Callies & Banta, supra, at 83. Similarly, Philadelphia in 1770 required home owners to plant trees along the front of their houses so that the town would be "well shaded from the violence of the sun in the heat of summer and thereby be rendered more healthy." See 2 Pa. Stat. 66, Ch. 53, cited in Bosselman, Callies & Banta, supra, at 83. Such Colonial-era regulations were never challenged in the courts. A few challenges were made after ratification of the Bill of Rights, but they uniformly failed. See, e.g., Transportation Co. v. Chicago, 99 U.S. 635, 642 (1878) Brick Presbyterian Church v. City of New York, 5 Cow. 538 (N.Y. 1826). The first successful challenge to a "regulatory talking" did not occur until Pennsylvania Coal Co. v. Mahon, 260 U.S. 393 (1922), almost a century and a half after the ratification of the Takings Clause. Thus, an historically objective interpretation of the Clause would require no compensation for regulatory takings on the contrary regulations would be valid so long as they survived rationality review. This view is apparent in the language of Madison's first draft of the Takings Clause, which read: "'no person shall be obligated to relinquish his property, where it be necessary for public use, without a just compensation." See Speech Proposing the Bill of Rights (June 8, 1789), in 12 James Madison, The Papers of James Madison 197, 201 (R. Rutland ed. 1977), cited in William M. Treanor, Note, The Origins and Original Significance of the Just Compensation Clause of the Fifth Amendment, 94 YALE L.J. 694, 711 n.95 (1985). The accounts of congressional debates shed no light on why the language was changed.

Pages 1135-38. ***Pennsylvania Coal***: The photographs help illustrate the civic problem that produced the legal problem. Going through the *Pennsylvania Coal* opinion, fun can be made of Justice Holmes's totally unhelpful phrasing of the "general rule" (in the fourth paragraph on page 1136). "The general rule at least is that while property may be regulated *to a certain extent*, if regulation goes *too far* it will be recognized as a taking...." It is extraordinary how often this statement is quoted, as if it actually gives some useful direction to courts. It does certainly direct attention to diminution in private property values as an important factor to be considered. But obviously the situations noted in the spectrum above, and elsewhere, vary widely. One extremely unhelpful survey was done by an attorney/scholar in the 1970s, plotting on a computer the average percentage of property loss occurring in cases where regulation was held unconstitutional as a taking. The "magic magnitude" — if your students would find it of any interest and utility — turned out to be, as we recall, 73% loss. But obviously that magic magnitude has no normative value, since the constitutionally tolerable percentage of loss will vary greatly, as in the esthetic ocean view regulation noted above and the earthquake zone, flood plain, or cyanide plant examples.

[Here is an interesting footnote on the *Pennsylvania Coal* case from Karl Llewellyn, A Lecture on Appellate Advocacy, 20 U. CHICAGO L. REV. 627 (1962). (This article was taken from a transcript of a lecture given by Professor Llewellyn a few days before his death in 1962.)]

> The time comes that over one piece of anthracite mines the population begins to really encroach and a whole chunk of the city of Scranton finds itself built on this kind of [surface rights] deed. Then came the time when [the coal companies] came to the end of the seam and it began to become clear that they were going to go right back, letting the pillars come out. And what would happen to the surface, the business of the people on that surface? (Laughter.) And humanitarian elements and invested elements got together, and the legislature passed a statute that forbade the taking out of pillars in such fashion as to endanger life. I abbreviated very greatly. A suit by the owner of a single residence finally came before the Supreme Court and the

defense challenged the constitutionality of this statute. John W. Davis [who subsequently was a Democratic candidate for President, and in 1954 argued the segregationist position in *Brown v. Board of Education*] was for the defendant coal company, and I am excited by his posing of the issue in the oral argument. (It isn't done nearly as well in the brief.) Tradition has it that Davis opened his argument before the Supreme Court in language substantially equivalent to what I am about to state: "This case involves the question of whether the Legislature of Pennsylvania has the constitutional power to donate the property of the Pennsylvania Coal Company to Mr. and Mrs. Patrick Mahon." (Laughter.) The case was won by Mr. Davis, Mr. Justice Holmes writing the opinion.

[It might also be noted that Mr. Patrick Mahon would have been sitting just to Mr. Davis's left. Mahon was an attorney and was part of the team that defended the Kohler Act in the Supreme Court.]

Traditional regulatory takings tests have been fundamentally shaped by *Pennsylvania Coal* and zoning cases: its terms typically focus on private property values in a vacuum, without consideration or balancing of the surrounding public context. The "crazy quilt" of judicial holdings in takings cases results from the fact that, where courts do not explicitly consider a balance, each case must involve some implicit subjective balancing on its particular facts.

Page 1138, C&Q #1. Testing regulatory takings today: 8 elements. Our view of this strategic issue, set out in this subchapter, is that the Supreme Court has finally produced some clarity in groundrules and standards for testing takings validity. The result is neither an immunization of regulations nor a presumptive ascendancy of private property rights. Today the process of testing the validity of regulation requires an articulated inquiry to determine whether the presumption of validity has been rebutted.

This note sets up eight diagnostic elements that can shape takings analysis of a case, addressing the question whether a regulation burdening private property rights has gone "too far" (i.e. within our substantive due process inquiry Number Four, page 1115).

Page 1140, C&Q #2. Diminution. Diminution of private property value continues to be a fundamental inquiry. In the diminution inquiry the most commonly applied standard is the classic zoning question: "Is there a reasonable remaining economic use for the property as regulated?" ("The application of a general zoning law to a particular property effects a taking if the ordinance does not substantially advance legitimate state interests [our inquiries #1 & #2, page 1114] or denies an owner economically viable use of his land." Agins v. Tiburon, 447 U.S. 255, 261 (1980). Beyond zoning cases, it is now clear after *Palazzolo* that even where no "economically viable" use remains the regulations can still be valid, so there must be a further balancing of private loss caused and public harms forfended by the regulation. A floodplain regulation that prevents death, disease, and property losses by prohibiting homes within the 100-year floodline, for example, may eliminate all "economically viable" development on a riverside parcel which a subdivider bought for a million dollars in order to build a gated community of fancy homes, but the public's interest in avoiding potential flood devastations would counterweigh the asserted private property rights. (Even in an extraordinary *Lucas* situation, now clearly defined to require a showing that property has been rendered virtually valueless, there is a balance of nuisance-like public harms.)

Diminution is clearly a major factor in judging the unfairness of a regulation's impact on the individual propertyowners, but merely showing substantial loss of value is not sufficient to nullify regulations.

Page 1140, C&Q #3. Baseline: "the parcel as a whole." It appears to us that the anti-regulation justices' conceptual severance strategy attempting to narrow the baseline "denominator" of the diminution inquiry despite the holding in *Keystone Bituminous,* has finally been put to rest by *Palazzolo* and *Tahoe-Sierra.*

Page 1141, C&Q #4. Balancing. As all first-year law students discover, most questions in the legal system come down to a balance, and the tough issue is to figure out what and how to balance. We think that all public interests that could be classified as public nuisanced concerns clearly count in the balance against claimed private regulatory losses. Also public harms are to be weighed in terms of the public *risk* of harm; governmental regulators do not have to prove actual harms.

In the wetlands setting *"are all public benefits to be weighed or only public harms?"* We think that *harm* is the basic balancing rubric. Weighing the public *benefits* obtained from regulation against the asserted property interests would be an abdication of the fairness premise of due process balancing. But the definition of what is a benefit and what is a harm forfended may be quite subtle. If, for example, government forbids filling of a coastal marsh because it is a breeding area for striped bass and flounder, is it preventing the harm of destruction of commercial fisheries, or obtaining free nursery services from the land of the private propertyowner? Try that one on your students and let us know their answer.

Page 1142, C&Q #5. Wetlands as lightning rods. In the course of the oral arguments on *Lucas,* Justice Scalia, in asking a question about wetlands regulation, reportedly made a sidecrack on the order of "...and you know what we think of wetlands!" evoking a sardonic laugh from the audience. Note the difference in difficulty between educating a reviewing court about the public interests in protecting a wetland (diffuse ecological and hydrological harms requiring cumulative effects analysis over broad areas) and in prohibiting human housing on a floodplain (direct on-site death).

The wetlands example raises the cumulative harm/nibble-away problem. If the harms caused by regulated properties are not conceptually cumulated, one by one they may appear to be individually inconsequential. But it is the accumulation of effects of, for instance, filling of wetlands, and judicial overrides of wetland regulations, that create a potentially dramatic loss of resources and economic values.

Pages 1142–1165. An 8-decade evolutionary overview of regulatory takings law. An attempt to put it all together in a ruthlessly compacted summary survey.

Page 1145, *Penn Central.* Because *Penn Central* has emerged as the platform on which the Court's majority will weigh regulatory takings, it is worth giving it initial attention, picked up by the *Palazzolo* and *Tahoe-Sierra* majorities and Justice O'Connor's *Palazzolo* concurrence.

The basic *Penn Central* Triad of considerations, noted at the bottom of page 1145, is initially a bit awkward and unclear, but has provided the basis for the modern inquiry:

- the *economic impact* on the claimant (diminution),
- the claimant's *investment-backed expectations* (useful in framing the contexts and issues of notice, fairness, and baseline for review of diminution), and
- the *character of the governmental action* (initially addressing only whether the action was physical or not, but subsequently clarified in O'Connor's Palazzolo concurrence to include *weighing the purposes* of the governmental action).

Page 1146, C&Q #1. Diminution baseline. It appeared that *Penn Central* had set the parcel-as-a-whole as the takings diminution baseline, but that continued in subsequent cases to be a target of the judicial and political reaction noted on pages 1144-45.

Page 1146, C&Q #2. Penn Central balancing. Self-explanatory. But the "character of the governmental action" element needed O'Connor's common sense clarification that it included weighing the purposes for which the regulation had been passed in the first place. Otherwise the takings test would operate in a vacuum, focused only on the private burden.

Page 1147, C&Q #3. Dissent in *Penn Central.* Justice Rehnquist's attempts to assert draconian tests. Self-explanatory.

Page 1149, C&Q #1. The time baseline. Less attention has been paid to the time baseline than to the geographic baseline denominator for diminution review, although *Tahoe-Sierra* does address it directly. *"Should the time baseline be based on the 'remaining economic value' that exists after regulation is imposed, or can it consider the entire life of the coalfield investment?"* As we indicate, we think the concept of "investment-backed expectations" militates for a diminution baseline that weighs all the economic profits from the original investment, so that the restriction is not void even if the newly-passed regulation meant that not a single further ton of coal could be mined.

As to a geographic baseline, in *Pennsylvania Coal,* remember, as noted, Holmes focused only on the restricted pillar of coal itself, while Brandeis viewed the entire coal field. It might be useful to do a cutaway sketch of the *Pennsylvania Coal* and *Keystone Bituminous* cases, noting what underlay the pictures presented on page 1135. The debate in *Keystone Bituminous* replicated the same argument, with Rehnquist focusing on the 27 million tons in the restricted pillars, and Stevens emphasizing the overall coal field total of 1.46 billion tons. An analogy that one of the authors has previously argued is the front lawn setback ordinance that applies in virtually all suburban communities. If Holmes and Rehnquist are right that one looks only at the regulated portion of a piece of property in order to judge constitutionality, every front lawn setback ordinance is unconstitutional because one cannot build, raise crops, or graze a cow on a front lawn. Nevertheless the common sense reaction of virtually everyone who hears such an argument is that the constitutional review must consider the front lawn as part of the entire residential parcel. Since the parcel as a whole can support residences with solid market value, the fact that a front lawn by itself generates no profit is irrelevant. Justice Rehnquist, however, uses another conceptual severance tack as well when he notes, on page 1149, second block quote paragraph, that the Pennsylvania law completely eliminates a separate property interest known as "the support estate" in Pennsylvania law.

Page 1149, C&Q #2. Was there a balance in *Keystone Bituminous*? As noted, yes.

Page 1151, C&Q #1. Reading *Lucas*. As we indicate, we think the *Lucas* vote was deeply influenced by the trial court's finding (hard-to-believe) that the land retained absolutely no value.

On the oft-heard dictum that "with this regulation, there is nothing left to the owner but the duty to pay property taxes," see footnote 53 and the article by K. May, The Effect of Environmental Restrictions on Property Tax Assessments, on the Teachers' Website.

Page 1151, C&Q #2. Takings tests after *Lucas*. As we indicate, we think *Lucas* neither set up a categorical rule, since it allowed a nuisance-like balancing, nor did it define a clear trigger. Justice Scalia's different phrasings of what would trigger his automatic-compensation rule may not have had an irredentist intent to mislead lower courts into widespread findings of "categorical" invalidity, but it did so.

Page 1152, C&Q #3. Conceptual severance in *Lucas*. *Lucas* represents one of the anti-regulation attempts to achieve a divide-and-conquer definition of the takings baseline.

Page 1152, C&Q #4. An uncategorical categorical rule. As noted, the purported categorical rule surreptitiously incorporated a nuisance-like balance.

Page 1155, C&Q #1. After *Palazzolo*: isolating *Lucas*. Palazzolo's majority opinion and O'Connor concurrence effectively marginalized the *Lucas* decision in scope and tone.

Page 1155, C&Q #2. *Palazzolo:* Express weighing of a challenged regulation's public harm-prevention objectives, and of the claimant's original investment-backed expectations. Justice Scalia reacting as if stung to these two regulation-reinforcing features of the *Palazzolo* decision. Note Justice O'Connor's cool retort, footnote 57.

Page 1155, C&Q #3. An emerging consensus. We think so, and these are the terms.

Page 1156, C&Q #4. A proportional takings scale. This is a fundamental component of a balancing process. The *First English* remand opinion is one of the few to acknowledge the range of different proportionalities between public concerns. Remind your students, however, that not all takings cases require an excruciating process of articulately a conceptual accounting of all public risks and harms. If a regulation leaves a parcel with a reasonable remaining economic value — the first-stage diminution inquiry noted on 1155-56 — the judicial review needs to go no further.

A memo on the "nuisance exception" in takings cases is on the Website for this chapter.

Page 1159, C&Q #1. After *Palazzolo* and *Tahoe-Sierra*. A balance appears to have returned to Supreme Court takings jurisprudence, and *Penn Central* is the balance.

Page 1159, C&Q #2. *Lucas* applies only in rare anomalous situations. Now it's clear: Lucas applies to total wipeouts, which in fact almost never occur. Cases where CERCLA imposes, say, a $2 million cleanup obligation on a $1 million parcel might create total wipeouts, but even these clearly would not be a taking under *Lucas's* nuisance exception.

Page 1159, C&Q #3. Conceptual severance is dead. It's parcel-as-a-whole. Self-explanatory.

Page 1160, C&Q #4. *Penn Central* rules! Self-explanatory.

Page 1160, C&Q #5. What now is the role of IBE? Investment-backed expectations, once used only to undercut regulations by adding to the definition of diminution's unfairness, now play a triple role, by in addition serving to deflate private claims of loss, and helping too establish broader review baselines — parcel-as-a-whole and an investment-span time baseline.

Thus, in weighing "reasonable remaining use," a court might legitimately make a distinction between a piece of property that the owner received by inheritance from his Aunt Matilda twenty-five years ago, and the same parcel purchased for $500,000 the week prior to the promulgation of the burdensome regulation. In quite another setting, the concept of investment-backed expectations might be used to lower the weight attached to private loss when the property owner buys a regulated parcel, knowing it is regulated and perhaps paying a lesser amount for it in such cases most states would not deny standing to challenge the regulation, but nevertheless the fact that the private harm was self-imposed, with prior notice, is altogether likely to weigh against the attacker's argument. The issue of investment-backed expectations ties into the individual injury element, but does capture a special sense of the fairness balance: all things being equal, it does seem relevant to consider what property owners' reasonable expectations are at the moment they buy, as part of the judgment of how great their burden is in the circumstances.

Page 1160, C&Q #6. Takings semantics. The most important semantic clarification is the "value/use" distinction that emerges from *Palazzolo* and *Tahoe-Sierra*. See the Crossman article in the Website's Supplemental Materials for this chapter.

Page 1162, C&Q #7. So now, how far is too far? Rhetorical.

Page 1162, C&Q #8. Are overrides of common law a regulatory taking? This is a fascinating issue little considered in the academic literature. The Hasselman article deserves attention. The Alaska statute presents a good exercise for prompting lively discussions and mixing the lines between "conservative" and "liberal." Take the scene of Alaska Pulp & Paper dumping huge volumes of smelly sulphite wastes into Ketchikan Bay, causing great distress to property owners in the neighborhood, but presumably not violating their state NPDES permits (the standards are set based on nationwide BAT, backed up by WQSs that do not protect against nuisance-like harms but only assure that the water must achieve its state-dictated standard "industrial use." Now what is the position of the neighboring property owners who suddenly cannot bring a Boomer-type action for loss of use, of property values, of the right to tort self-defense, of the right to exclude?

Hasselman concludes that the Court applies heightened scrutiny to such deprivations of traditional property protections unless there are sufficient protective legal equivalents. We note however that a Fourth Circuit panel has explicitly held that nothing in the due process clauses of federal and state constitutions prevents prospective abolition of common law causes of action. Dinh v. Rust International Corp. 974 F.2d 500 (4th Cir. 1992).

Page 1162, C&Q #9. Takings as a continuing political target. In the anti-regulatory political initiative being carried out by Heritage Foundation, PERC, the Pacific Legal Foundation, and the like, these groups will surely continue their extremely well-funded efforts.

Page 1163, C&Q #10. *Metalclad*: the anti-takings initiative goes international. This is a sobering indication that fractionalizing, property-focused assaults on civic regulation have surprisingly gained an international foothold, with little balanced recognition of the public harms that engendered regulations in the first place. This represents an exportation of a US political subculture to international instruments. Future developments in this realm are going to be interesting.

Page 1164, C&Q #11. Rethinking rights. As in the chapter title, the democratic balance needs to incorporate countervailing rights and responsibilities in the public and private sectors both. Bringing in the communitarian civic responsibility theories is a way to emphasize the idiosyncrasy of American property rights, and the realistic need to temper individualism with the collective context in which individuals exist.

Page 1166, C&Q #1. Takings tests and the public trust doctrine. As Professor Babcock's article notes, in *Lucas* Justice Scalia perhaps inadvertently opened the door to direct weighing of the public's public trust property rights into takings balances, a phenomenon that carries much farther than limited *Lucas* takings settings where there has been a complete wipeout.

Regulations will often be passed to protect public rights that can be found to pre-exist within titles to land, under the public trust doctrine, and thus do not constitute takings. The public trust doctrine may substantially erode private property rights without triggering the normal regulatory takings tests involved when the police power is used. If courts recognize a pre-existing latent public property right within a private property title, then presumptively the private property owner has no complaint. It is of course disappointing to the landowner that the public right is now being asserted when previously it might not have been, but private property is always held under the risk that some pre-existing cloud may upset expectations. If this reading appears too draconian, there is a traditional mitigation: a private property owner can appeal to equity to take into account the unexpected latter-day arrival of this dramatic new public right. This possibility no doubt explains much of the shrill opposition the public trust arouses in marketplace politics.

Page 1166, C&Q #2. A society's underlying expectations. As noted, an evolving societal backdrop for the definition of property rights and expectations. The *Sanderson* case quote on page 1167 provides very interesting food for discussion. To counter-balance private property expectations, Professor Sax emphasizes the idea of public expectations. Indeed the expectations of a society about what is and is not an unfair imposition on private property changes over time. The *Sanderson* holding did not arouse a horrified reaction in defenders of private property rights in 1886. Sax says that most people are implicitly on notice today that wetlands, beaches, and perhaps even privately-owned historic sites may be in all likelihood subjected to future regulation in the public interest.

Page 1167, C&Q #3. More from South Carolina. *McQueen* illustrates how far we have come from *Lucas*.

Page 1167. Takings remedies. The law of government compensation for regulations deemed to be invalid takings is extremely vague. This note sets out some of the issues. The easy part is saying that, after *First English Evangelical*, it is clear that the challenged government has the right to acquiesce in nullification of a challenged regulation that has been held unconstitutional, instead of being forced to pay permanent damages for the regulatory burden. Less clear is the ability of the government to suspend the regulation only insofar as necessary to reach a level of constitutional validity. If the government chooses to pay compensation, the text notes that in some case the compensation might reflect just the difference between a constitutional and an unconstitutional level of burden, rather than a complete purchase of the fee simple value. The puzzle set out in the first paragraph of page 1168 is an example. We assume that given those explicit findings a government not seeking to buy out fee simple but only the "invalidity" portion of the regulation would need to pay only $40,000. In the next paragraph, determining interim damages, the argument of privateers would be that the government must pay "rent," but we would say that just compensation need not be more than actual private loss.

(The use of the term inverse condemnation should be distinguished carefully between the normal governmental physical intrusion cases, and the cases where the remedy is used to seek damages from regulatory actions. In the physical setting, even a small governmental intrusion requires compensation, measured absolutely. The test for how much regulatory burden is unconstitutional is obviously very different, tolerating far more burden, and weighing it relatively.)

Pages 1168–69. Amortization and offsets. More brief snapshots, self-explanatory. The offset argument deserves more attention in policy terms, although in standard eminent domain evaluation formulas, offsetting is extremely rare.

Note that another way that defenders of regulations might try to improve the economic baseline picture is to attempt to *offset* public grants of property value from private property claims of loss. In the *Lucas* case, for instance, what would the value be of the challenger's two lots purchased for $975,000? If one could set off against it the amount of that value attributable to (a) federal flood insurance, a billion dollar program that allows landowners to build and rebuild along the coastlines and in flood plains at highly subsidized insurance rates (without such subsidies from FEMA, what bank would issue a mortgage for building a home on the property?) (b) the cost of building (and rebuilding) infrastructure on the barrier beach: roads, linear sewer systems, causeways and bridges, all of which typically are seriously damaged in hurricane events (c) the costs of rescue, which run into the millions of dollars and losses of rescuers' lives annually in flood and storm emergencies (d) governmental beach rebuilding and beach securing projects, often run by the Army Corps of Engineers at the cost of millions of dollars. As noted in an article by Siffin, 1 Cato Journal 219, these subsidies amount to a *sine qua non* for shoreline construction without them residential land values would be close to nil. Can they therefore be offset? See page 1129. This is the issue presented likewise in the Kissimmee River problem noted in the caption to the photograph on page 1053. The usual answer is probably not.

Pages 1169–71. *Nollan* and *Dolan*. Note that the exaction cases are not properly viewed as "regulatory takings" cases, though many unsophisticated attorneys so use them. Exactions, if they go too far, constitute impermissible physical or legal-interest appropriations by government. Remember that in each case, the first step of the court is to ascertain that the permit could have been *denied* without constituting an invalid case of regulatory taking. Only then do we get to the further issue of whether the exaction can ride on a permit approval, and the question does not turn on questions of the property owner's degree of regulatory burden.

Our reading of *Nollan* is basically that Justice Scalia would, under standard police power tests, have *upheld* a denial of the permit requesting expansion of the existing shack into all-season beach house. The only problem was that instead of denying the permit, the Coastal Commission granted that permission with a physical entry easement parallel to the water line along the private upland. This was an unconstitutional exaction because Scalia felt there wasn't a sufficient nexus between the requirement of the exacted easement and the burden imposed on the situation by the expanded construction. If the construction of the house had cut off the public's access to the beach from inland, either physically or visually, it indeed appears that that would have been a sufficient nexus even for Scalia. So the exaction cases now seem to focus on the proximity of the nexus to proper public purposes and the circumstances being regulated. This does not seem very revolutionary to us, echoing distinctions in the exactions cases traceable back for more than thirty years. See Jenad, Inc. v. Village of Scarsdale, 218 N.E.2d 673 (NY 1966). (Few have noticed that the physical dimensions of the *Nollan* site are truly minuscule if the square footage supplied by one of the parties is accurate, the entire *Nollan* parcel was less than one-tenth of one acre!)

An interesting ***severability*** question deserves further study: Should land use permits be considered null-and-void when the exactions which induced them are struck down? Or should courts presume exactions severable, as the Court did in *Nollan* and *Dolan*, confirming the permission to build as valid authorizations in spite of the loss of the exactions?

Page 1171, C&Q #1. Exactions and the battles of *Dolan*.

(There is a *Dolan* photo slide collection on the Teachers' Web site.)

Dolan further defined the required exactions nexus. You can note for your students that the test is not exact equality between the privately-imposed public burden and the required private donation of an exaction benefit; it's rough proportionality.

Students constantly confuse exactions with takings jurisprudence. You should clarify it for them — in exactions cases, a regulation must first be valid under takings law. If the government has no constitutional right to deny the permit in the first place, it cannot conditionally require an exaction at all. The question then becomes whether as a matter of substantive due process the attached exaction condition is not sufficiently rationally related to the increased burdens the new property use will impose upon the public.

Page 1172, C&Q #3. Other worms in the can. Will Justice Rehnquist continue to try to advance his reciprocity-of-advantage as a sleight of hand takings test? Probably. Will he and others try to advance a judicial role in determining "reasonableness" of regulations, perhaps asserting an inherent cost-benefit analysis element in due process? Perhaps.

The material on *Eastern Enterprises* on the next page may be a small step in that direction.

Page 1172, C&Q #4. Predicting the future. Rhetorical. We consider this an area in flux on half-a-dozen points, as noted in the commentary.

Page 1176, C&Q #1. Due Process. As we view it, although the takings clause was originally restricted to physical takings by government it has grown to extend to regulatory impacts on private property. In doing so, however, the test of validity for regulatory actions that do not involve physical appropriation (cf. *Lorreto,* 458 U.S. 419(1982)) remains the subjective balancing of due process fairness rather than the virtually automatic compensation treatment accorded physical appropriations.

Page 1176, C&Q #2. *Eastern Enterprises* and Substantive Due Process: the votes. As we count the votes, five justices asserted that the appropriate standard to apply was substantive due process, not takings, and the takings plurality themselves actually applied a substantive due process standard.

It stands to reason that an absence of fault is directly relevant to assessing the validity of such situations as the calamitous regulatory toxic contamination liability set out on page 1173. The fault nexus requirement is examined at length in the Jordan article.

Page 1176, C&Q #3. Lochnering and fundamental fairness. History.

Page 1176, C&Q #4. Is it fair to Eastern to compel them to pay now? We think this fairness question, rather than a straight bar on retroactivity, is why Justice Kennedy favored Eastern.

Page 1177, C&Q #5. Applying substantive due process to contaminated land cases. As noted, we think that propertyowners with a nexus to the originally polluting industry would make a difference, as it does in common law tort settings. But for individual innocent landowners with no connection to the dumping, we think *Eastern Enterprises* opens a door long closed.

Chapter 24.
PUBLIC RESOURCE MANAGEMENT STATUTES

Suggested time budget: **one class session**

Chapter contents:

—and check the Teachers' Manual Website for SUPPLEMENTARY MATERIALS:

http://www.bc.edu/schools/law/library/coursebook/envtlaw/teachers

The list of Supplementary Materials in Part III of this manual, and on the Teachers' Website, indicates materials posted on the Teachers' Website that are relevant to this and other chapters.

OVERALL TEACHING THEMES & COURSE DESIGN CONSIDERATIONS

This chapter addresses the questions, "For what purpose(s) should the public lands be managed?" and "What is the allocation of legal authority over public lands among federal, state, and local governments?"

This chapter could be taught as the last in a series of chapters that bear upon federal land management: (1) The administrative law background -- Chapter 7; (2) NEPA -- Chapter 9; (3) ESA -- Chapter 16; and (4) Public Resource Management -- Chapter 24.

Alternatively, this chapter could be taught with Chapters 23 (The Takings Issue) and 25 (Land-Use Based Environmental Control) in a land-use law sequence.

Thematically, the essence of this chapter is the tension between two public resource management philosophies: (1) multiple use, sustained yield, and, (2) dominant use. Multiple use, sustained yield is the statutory standard that applies to the BLM lands and the national forests. Although economic development is prohibited in national parks, the National Park Service performs something very much like multiple use, sustained yield management because it is statutorily obligated to reconcile two uses- conservation and recreation- that may not in practice be compatible. Dominant use is the way the BLM lands and national forest have historically been managed. In recent years, the de facto dominant use management of these federal lands has been in defiance of Congress ' multiple use, sustained yield mandate. National wildlife refuges, wilderness areas, water rights, and hard rock mining on federal lands are also administered according to dominant use principles. The major difference between multiple use, sustained yield and dominant use is that, in most instances, multiple use, sustained yield emphasizes long term, sustainable mixtures of appropriate compatible uses, while dominant use stresses shorter term maximization of a primary use and other secondary uses that are compatible with it. The chief asset of a multiple use, sustained yield system is its flexibility over time, while the chief asset of a dominant use system is its predictability. The major liabilities of dominant use are its inflexibility and relative neglect of environmental values and the resource needs of future generations.

In teaching this material, it is useful to begin with the manifest content of public land management statutes — the management philosophy dictated by the legislature. A brief exploration of the three prevalent management theories: 1) multiple use, sustained yield; 2) dominant use; and 3) single use will indicate that they are so ambiguous as to be judicially enforceable only in exceptional circumstances. As a result, public lands management, and the required planning processes that are intended to develop management strategies, have become reflections of underlying interest group conflicts. The typical model of interest group politics regarding public lands is the long-standing hegemony of a consumptive user group (grazers, miners, loggers, farmers) resulting in its domination of the administrative agency entrusted with the management of the particular resource. However, in recent years the demographic and political structure of the West has changed, and environmental and recreational interests have increasingly been capable of influencing the course of public lands management.

One of the authors involves the class in generating an interest representation chart of the grazing issue in order to elucidate the policy dimensions of public lands management.

What are the major interest groups? First, there are the ranchers that graze animals on the public range, usually during the summer months. These ranchers raise a small percentage of the beef and lamb consumed in the United States, but they are well-organized and strongly represented in western legislatures and Congress. They also play on the cowboy mythology, which is still such a powerful force in the American psyche. Any attempt to raise grazing fees or reduce overgrazing of the public range is met with the dire forecast that the small rancher is being driven off his home range. Undoubtedly, some family-run ranches will fail if the external costs of grazing on public lands are internalized. On the other hand, most of the AUMs on federal range are utilized by large corporations (whose minions are called "wing-tip cowboys"), such as insurance companies, that are in the cattle business because of the federal grazing subsidy and the tax advantages given to ranchers. This is an appropriate point to raise the question of whether it is wise for the federal government to subsidize particular industries. For example, should there be a federal "industrial policy"? The ranchers group is supported by local financial interests, vendors, and contractors. The local community is generally united against any change in the grazing subsidy, and it exerts strong pressure on the public land managers, whose families live in the community, to conform to the local set of political expectations.

The federal land management agency, in this case the BLM, has traditionally been closely aligned with the dominant economic interest, even to the extent of having been captured by it. Ranching interests are well represented on the appropriate congressional finance and oversight committees that deal with BLM matters. High-ranking BLM officials have often come from ranching backgrounds (Who else would know about such esoteric matters?) and will probably return to ranching after leaving the BLM. Civil service range managers in the BLM have been educated in range management programs at western state universities, which are sometimes run by faculty members who are consultants to ranchers and their support industries.

Environmental and recreational groups have regional and nationwide, rather than local, constituencies. But these groups are not always in agreement about range-management policies. For example, ORV user groups and preservation groups fought bitterly about how Dove Springs Canyon was to be managed (see Sierra Club v. Clark, page 1203 of main volume). These groups are often not as focused, financially stable, or well-organized as extractive interest groups.

The Clinton Administration's approach to resolving range management issues, as well as most other public land management controversies, was to encourage bottom-up, consensual, regional (range, forest, watershed, habitat, etc.) planning among the affected interest groups, including the newly empowered recreation and conservation groups. Where the recreation and conservation groups have a strong economic presence in the region (e.g., hunting and fishing guides, packers, resort owners, land trusts having purchased fee interests or development rights, etc.), the voluntary planning process tends to produce viable compromise solutions. But where resource extraction continues as the predominant economic activity in the area, bottom-up planning tends to work less well, and at worst screens continued capture of policy-making by resource extraction interests. The Bush II Administration has manifested preferences for extractive uses and top-down management of the federal lands.

TEACHING NOTES, COMMENTS, & ALL QUESTIONS ANSWERED

Pages 1178-1187. These pages introduce the public lands, BLM, grazing on public lands, FLPMA, and multiple use, sustained-yield and dominant use management. BLM has traditionally been a captured agency that has performed a major role in the tragedy of the federal land commons. This agency and its clientele successfully resisted Congress' "decapture" mandate in the Taylor Grazing Act of 1934, and, although progress was made under the Clinton Administration, is still resisting FLPMA's land use planning and multiple use, sustained-yield management commands. If multiple use, sustained-yield management is to be anything more than a hortatory "succotash syndrome," its "bottom lines" -- nonimpairment and sustained yield -- must be enforceable in court by citizen activists. Thus far, courts have not been receptive to such claims.

Page 1187, C&Q #1. Public land management philosophies. This note is mostly informational and explanatory.

Should Congress set grazing as the dominant use on BLM lands? Given the relatively small quantity of beef and lamb produced by ranchers utilizing the public lands, the overgrazed quality of the BLM lands, the enhanced need for recreational lands in the West, and the heightened political power of recreation and conservation groups, it would probably be impossible for Congress to take this step now. It would certainly be poor public policy if it were enacted.

What are the major advantages and disadvantages of multiple use, sustained-yield versus dominant use as public land management philosophies? This question is answered in the thematic materials above.

Pages 1187-1188, C&Q #2. Multiple use-sustained yield reconsidered. *Will changing demographics and public preferences bring a trend toward real multiple use, sustained-yield?*

Stay tuned! Better yet, participate in the new regional planning and advisory groups.

Is a dominant "public use" system capable of dealing with issues such as excessive recreational use of public lands? It can be argued that "public use" is yet another question-begging term like "wise use." It is really disingenuous to talk about "the public." There are only "publics" with different views — some reconcilable, some not — on various issues. This is also, of course, true of the "recreation public."

Pages 1188-1189, C&Q #3. Dominant use management on public lands: mining, logging, wilderness. The "compatibility" questions posed in this note are highly valuational (and thus highly political). When raised for class discussion, they have been known to stimulate spirited exchanges.

Pages 1189-1190, C&Q #4. Unenforceable policies and mixed mandates. This note is informational and self-explanatory.

Page 1190, C&Q #5. The public trust and the public lands. Informational & self-explanatory.

Page 1190-1191, C&Q #6. "Cooperative Management" and the BLM. This note is informational and self-explanatory.

Page 1191, C&Q #7. Grazing fees and other public land use subsidies. This note is, for the most part, informational and self-explanatory. It ends with more valuational questions for class discussion. Some conservationists believe that the grazing fee has become a red herring. The real issue, they argue, is range management practices by ranchers. For example, livestock would do far less damage to the land base if they were fenced away from streams and moved frequently in order to prevent overgrazing of specific areas. These relatively inexpensive Best Management Practices, if required of ranchers, might replace grazing fee increases.

Pages 1191-1192, C&Q #8. Recent grazing reform regulations. This note is informational and self-explanatory.

Pages 1192-1193, C&Q #9. The more things change... This note is informational and self-explanatory.

Pages 1193-1196. Kleppe v. New Mexico is the definitive United States Supreme Court decision regarding federal-state relations under the Property Clause of the United States Constitution. The Court held that (1) Congress' Property Clause power over the federal public lands is unlimited; (2) this plenary power includes the power to protect the wildlife found on federal lands; and (3) the provisions of the New Mexico Estray Law relied on by the State were preempted by the Wild Free-Roaming Horses and Burros Act. (For an analysis of federal statutory preemption, see Chapter 6.)

Page 1196, C&Q #1. The statutory policy. This note is informational and self-explanatory. The BLM is "damned if it does and damned if it doesn't" with regard to wild horses and burros. The Agency's occasional roundup and destruction of excess animals is inevitably met with citizen outrage, media criticism, and lawsuits. Many individuals, influenced by the so-called "Bambi Syndrome," vehemently oppose the culling of individual animals in order to benefit the species and its larger ecosystem. Sometimes, as here, uninformed environmental consciousness is at odds with enlightened wildlife management and ecosystem protection.

Page 1196, C&Q #2. Public land and private land. This note is informational and self-explanatory. This constitutional "Takings Issue" is analyzed in the previous chapter.

Pages 1196-1197, C&Q #3. Helpless giants? This note is, for the most part, informational and self-explanatory. *Can the National Park Service promulgate a regulation requiring a large* *agricultural operation, fifty miles upriver of a national park, to cease discharging nutrients because these pollutants are causing the river in the park to become eutrophic (prematurely aged)?* Probably not, because the NPS does not possess regulatory authority over the operation. But if the agricultural operation constitutes a "Concentrated Animal Feeding Operation" (CAFO) under the Clean Water Act, the NPS might convince the permitting state or EPA to include Best Management Practices, or even stricter water quality-based effluent limitations, as conditions in the CAFO's discharge permit (see Chapter 12). If the CAFO is violating its discharge permit, the NPS might bring a citizen suit against the violator (see Chapters 12 and 21). Even if the agricultural operation does not qualify as a CAFO, the NPS can prove that the farm's runoff is causing eutrophication in the park (which would be difficult, because the farm is so far upriver), the NPS could win a nuisance action against the farm's owner and operator under the *Camfield* doctrine. However, if past behavior is any indication of future propensities, the NPS would lack the political will to bring such an action.

Pages 1197-1198, C&Q #4. Access problems. This note is informational and self-explanatory.

Page 1198, C&Q #5. The "Sagebrush Rebellion" and the "Wise Use" Movement. This note is informational and self-explanatory. Another offshoot of the "Sagebrush Rebellion" has been recurring proposals that the federal public lands be "privatized" -- i.e., auctioned off to the highest bidders -- or given to the states. Auctioning off federal lands to the highest bidders would give an implicit preference to resource extraction interests, which (1) have access to greater pools of capital than recreation or conservation groups can muster, and (2) possesses the concentrated organizational structures that would enable them to overcome the transaction costs that inhibit bidding. Additionally, the "privatization" approach assumes that all public land-use values are capable of being expressed in monetary (market) terms. In essence, this proposal would give hegemony to the market economy over the natural and social economies. Giving federal public lands to the states would also favor extractive industries in states where these interests have traditionally dominated state legislatures.

Pages 1198-1199, C&Q #6. Public land and ecosystem management. This note is informational and self-explanatory.

Is ecosystem management consistent with a multiple use, sustained-yield statutory mandate? What about a dominant use directive? Ecosystem management would be consistent with any statutory public resource management mandate. What is important is the commitment to practice ecosystem management, not the statutory rubric under which it is implemented.

Page 1199, C&Q #7. Can states regulate resource extraction and wildlife management on federal lands? This note is informational and self-explanatory. See Chapter 6 for a further discussion of the *Granite Rock* case and its progeny. The distinction between land-use and environmental regulation is exceptionally difficult to apply in specific cases. See Chapter 25.

Pages 1199-1201. These pages present the background of the "ORVs on public lands" controversy. For an informative article detailing the damage done by ORVs to public lands, see Hope, Hell On Wheels, 26 On earth #1 (Spring 2004), 32.

Pages 1201-1202, C&Q #1. Initial federal responses. This note is informational and self-explanatory.

Pages 1202-1203, C&Q #2. BLM backslide. This note is informational and self-explanatory.

Pages 1203-1206. These pages contain the Sierra Club v. Clark ("Dove Springs Canyon") case.

Page 1206, C&Q #1. Straw man in the desert. The questions raised in this note are rhetorical.

Page 1206, C&Q #2. Another look at multiple use-sustained yield. These questions are also rhetorical and harken back to the discussion of multiple use, sustained-yield earlier in the chapter.

Pages 1206-1207, C&Q #3. The enforcement problem. The questions raised in this note are rhetorical. In fact, enforcement is the cornerstone of an effective environmental regulatory program. See Chapter 21.

Pages 1207-1208, C&Q #4. ORVs in the national parks. The question raised in this note is then answered.

Pages 1208-1210. This material sets out the legal background of public land planning and the Sixth Circuit's scathing denunciation of the Forest Service planning effort in Sierra Club v. Thomas.

Pages 1210-1211, C&Q #1. "Garbage in, garbage out" planning. This note is informational and self-explanatory.

Page 1211, C&Q #2. The planning "shell game." This note is informational and self-explanatory. The United States Supreme Court has decided the issue on ripeness, not standing, grounds. See Note 3.

Pages 1211-1212, C&Q #3. The Aftermath of Sierra Club v. Thomas. This note is informational and self-explanatory.

Pages 1212-1213, C&Q #4. Theoretical dilemmas underlying public resource management. This note is informational and self-explanatory. The questions raised in the note are rhetorical. Another argument that can be brought against the Supreme Court's decision in *Sierra Club* rests upon the "educative" function of a natural resources management plan. Such a plan not only acts to allocate natural resources among competing uses; it also educates various publics as to policy directions chosen by public officials, and defines moral and political expectations regarding "who gets which natural resources, when, how, and for how much." A plan that illegally favors extractive interests "sends the wrong message," which cannot be undone by invalidating the plan at a later date.

Pages 1213-1214, C&Q #5. The Bush II Administration's public land policies. This note is informational and self-explanatory. The question that completes it is rhetorical.

Pages 1214-1215, C&Q #6. Public resources in the nation's waters. This note is didactic and self-explanatory. The questions raised within it are rhetorical.

Chapter 25.
LAND USE - BASED ENVIRONMENTAL PROTECTION STATUTES

Suggested time budget: **one class session**

Chapter contents:

— and check the Teachers' Manual Website for SUPPLEMENTARY MATERIALS:
http://www.bc.edu/schools/law/library/coursebook/envtlaw/teachers

The list of Supplementary Materials in Part III of this manual, and on the Teachers' Website, indicates materials posted on the Teachers' Website that are relevant to this and other chapters.

OVERALL TEACHING THEMES & COURSE DESIGN CONSIDERATIONS

This chapter addresses one overriding question, "How can legally and politically viable land-use regulations be developed, in order to protect environmental quality, in a Nation where all land-use controls -- and especially federal and state-imposed controls -- are deeply mistrusted?" This question is presented in several different contexts, representing various types of land-use control measures: (1) "Cooperation Statutes" with "Consistency Clauses," such as the Coastal Zone Management Act; (2) State hazardous waste facility siting statutes; (3) Critical area protection statutes, such as Section 404 of the Clean Water Act; (4) Single-purpose regional resource protection statutes, such as the Wild and Scenic Rivers Act; (5) Comprehensive state and regional planning and management; (6) Traditional land-use controls, such as zoning and subdivision regulation; and (7) the public fiscal growth management measures that are emphasized by "Smart Growth" laws and policies.

This is an important chapter. Because many Americans mistakenly believe that it is their constitutional right to develop their land substantially free from governmental interference, land-use based environmental protection mechanisms have, in general, been avoided. The prevailing mythology is that as long as technological precautions are adopted, a particular land area has no inherent maximum carrying capacity; that is, as many people as desire to live in an area can do so if they adopt best available technology or best management practices. This variation on the "technological fix" mentality ignores the fact that above a certain population density, despite the installation of pollution control mechanisms, environmental pollution will inevitably occur because of 1) violations of pollution control regulations and enforcement slippages, 2) malfunctions and poor maintenance of pollution control systems, 3) spills and other accidents, 4) cumulative and synergistic impacts of small and controlled discharges, 5) increases in automobile traffic and the construction of indirect air pollution sources (e.g., malls and airports, and 6) increased activities that cause pollution but have not yet or cannot be regulated (e.g., construction in radon prone areas). As will our unwillingness to address population growth and consumption issues, we are in our neglect of the land-use origins of pollution, attempting to protect the environment by circuitous and sub-optimal indirect measures, and are ignoring direct and potentially more effective cause-based solutions.

We must reemphasize a point made in the text, that this chapter does not attempt an overview of the massive field of land-use law, where local land-use controls predominate. Instead, it primarily focuses on federal and state land-use legal strategies that might be imposed where local land-use controls would be inadequate to protect regional or critical environmental resources. This chapter is necessarily selective and typological, rather than comprehensive.

This chapter -- and particularly the section on §404's wetlands protection provisions -- should be taught in close proximity to the "Takings" material in Chapter 23. The "Takings Clause," contained in the Fifth Amendment of the United States Constitution and replicated in many state constitutions, forms the backdrop for all land-use controls in the United States. The constitutionality of wetlands protection regulations has been extensively litigated in the context of the "Takings Issue."

The comparison of four state hazardous waste facility siting statutes is presented in order to test the efficacy of the siting statute device as a response to the NIMBY (Not In my Back Yard) Syndrome. Since each of these statutes either requires or presupposes the employment of Alternative Dispute Resolution (ADR), the ADR material in Chapter 21 can be read either with or before this block of material. Some instructors may wish to simulate a hazardous waste facility siting scenario under one or more of these statutory processes. More information on this option is presented below.

In teaching this chapter as a whole, in a single assignment, the instructor must confront the chapter's apparent diffuseness. One means of presenting a cohesive class session based on this chapter is to pose a complex hypothetical that bears upon all aspects of the chapter. For example, the class might consider a proposal to locate a hazardous waste disposal facility in a wetlands area that is adjacent to a federally-designated scenic river, which runs through the coastal plain. Assumptions will have to be made regarding the presence or absence of a state or regional land-use planning and management regime, and also regarding the possibility of "overriding" local zoning decisions. In many states that have not enacted comprehensive hazardous waste facility siting statutes, such as the ones analyzed in this chapter, RCRA and state hazardous waste laws authorize state environmental protection agencies to preempt local restrictions on the siting and operation of hazardous waste disposal facilities. The instructor may also wish to assume that her state has enacted one of the four models of hazardous waste disposal facility siting statutes, if her state does not have a siting statute of its own. The more that the hypothetical is based on an actual area known to (and perhaps used by) the students, the more effective the class session will be. Dissecting the legal decision points and the statutory and regulatory criteria applied to making these decisions, the political pressure points where influence might be exerted, as well as the congruities and incongruities among the regulatory systems involved in potential approval of this proposal, will provide at least one class session's worth of productive discussion.

TEACHING NOTES, COMMENTS, & ALL QUESTIONS ANSWERED

Pages 1216-1218. These introductory pages describe the paradox between the compelling need for land-use controls to protect the environment and the American antipathy to land-use measures of any kind.

Pages 1219-1221. If politics is "the art of the possible," then the CZMA is one of the paths that the federal government can take, in the area of land-use management, without provoking the wrath of a public that fears the confiscation of private property. The reconciliation of conservation and development is one of the explicit goals of the Act. The federal government facilitates (by means of planning grants), and defers to, state coastal zone management planning. Once a state has completed an "adequate" CMP -- i.e., one that complies with the guidelines issued by the Secretary of Commerce -- the state is given a veto over federal activities in the coastal zone through a requirement that all federal activities (construction projects, permit approvals, etc.) be consistent with the CMP "to the maximum extent practicable." 16 U.S.C.A. §1456(c)(1)(A). This key phrase is defined in federal regulations as meaning "unless compliance is prohibited based upon the requirements of existing law applicable to the Federal agency's operations." 15 CFR §930.32. Under the CZMA, for example, a state could not supersede the obligations of the United States Department of the Interior, under the Endangered Species Act, by inserting contradictory provisions in its CMP. Exemptions from the requirement that federal activities be consistent with state management plans may only be issued by the President (in the person of the Secretary of Commerce), after compulsory mediation between the federal and state agencies involved, "if the President determines that the activity is in the paramount interest of the United States." (16 U.S.C.A. §1456(C)(1)(B). In its CMP, a state is free to adopt the management system that is most appropriate to its geographical and political situation.

Notice that Professor Ruhl's BRZMA proposal adds an additional degree of devolution to the CZMA model by removing its "to the maximum extent practicable" qualification, and thus affording a state "complete relief from all the headaches of the existing federal structure, including the multiple permitting requirements...."

Page 1222, C&Q #1. "Yes, but will they come? This note is didactic and self-explanatory.

Page 1222, C&Q #2. Resolving interstate resource disputes. This note is informational and didactic. All questions raised in the note and then answered.

Page 1222, C&Q #3. Of time and money. All questions raised in this note are either rhetorical or answered.

Page 1223, C&Q #4. Mixed mandates and diffuse expectations. This note is didactic and self-explanatory.

Pages 1223, C&Q #5. Has the CZMA worked? This note is informational. The questions raised are rhetorical.

Page 1224, C&Q #6. ISTEA, a "Cooperation statute." This note is informational and self-explanatory. ISTEA was reauthorized by the Transportation Equity Act for the 21st Century (1998)(H.R.2400). ISTEA 1998 dedicates funding for light-rail and other transit improvements. It also increases funding for research into air pollution problems caused by automobile transportation. Most important, it continues ISTEA 1991's emphasis on local planning for transportation projects. Designing road projects and applying for federal transportation funding is no longer the exclusive domain of state highway departments. In addition to ISTEA, other examples of consistency clauses in environmental law are the National Forest Management Act's requirement that specific forest-related projects be consistent with Land and Resource Management Plans (see Chapter 24), and the Wild and Scenic River Act's mandate that federal lands bordering, including, or adjacent to a designated segment be managed in accordance with the wild and scenic quality of the river corridor (see pages 1244-1245, *infra.*).

Pages 1224-1226. Siting statutes presume that certain facilities are desirable and should be sited, but the NIMBY Syndrome has frustrated most efforts to site hazardous waste disposal facilities. The material from pages 1224 to 1226 presents a taxonomy of state statutory approaches to siting hazardous waste disposal facilities, none of which has thus far been successful in siting such a facility.

If the instructor has sufficient time, the best way to teach this material is by gaming each state scenario to discover the advantages and disadvantages of each. If time constraints permit only one game, then later contrasts with other scenarios can be drawn. In our experience, the result of this classroom simulation will be that the groups of students playing the various roles will negotiate and agree on an elaborate and highly sophisticated "deal" to site a facility, based on some of the factors described below. After investing time and energy in the consensual solution, the students will often be surprised to discover that similar solutions have been recommended in the four focus states, but they have subsequently been defeated by the apparently inexorable power of NIMBY. In a sense, a classroom simulation of a siting controversy is more artificial than most simulations, because the students cannot "feel" the outrage that would be experienced by actual local residents. But this artificiality is instructive, in that it illustrates the elemental NIMBY force that must be overcome in designing realistic public policy regarding the siting of hazardous waste disposal facilities.

Some of the fundamentals of a hazardous waste disposal facility siting game are as follows:

I. Incentives for the Community
   A. Mitigation and Enforcement
      1. Local oversight
      2. Health and environmental monitoring
      3. Emergency training and response
      4. Rewards for vigilance
      5. Local residency requirements for operators
      6. Facility shutdown requirements
      7. Stipulated penalties
      8. Conditions for sale of facility
      9. Insurance against loss of property value
      10. State and local enforcement
   B. Intrinsic Benefits
      1. Revenue and development
      2. Employment
      3. Waste site cleanup
   C. Compensation
      1. Cash

2. Indirect payments (e.g., support for community activities, in-kind payments)
3. Land-use tradeoffs ("if you take the facility you'll be exempt from other LULU's")

II. Identifying the Parties to the Negotiations
   A. Formats for Negotiation
      1. Two-party negotiation
      2. Multi-party negotiation
      3. Auction-type negotiation
   B. Identifying Constituencies
      1. The community (What is it? Who will represent it? To whom and when is the negotiating team accountable? What should be done with people who refuse to participate? What about dropouts?)
      2. The developer
      3. The State
      4. Public interest groups
      5. Waste generators
      6. Business
      7. Electedofficials
      8. Academics and other experts
   C. Which parties should participate in which issues?
   D. Assuring the community access to information (Who selects the experts? Who pays them? Who should have access to the information?)
   E. Dealing with Community Outrage

Pages 1226-1227, C&Q #1. The track record of siting statutes. This note is, for the most part, informational and self-explanatory. Over the last 20 years, only two landfills for disposal of radioactive and hazardous waste have been sited anywhere in the United States (in Colorado and Utah). In addition to the Canadian provinces of Alberta and Manitoba, Denmark, Sweden, and Finland have also established centralized hazardous waste disposal facilities. See Gerrard, Territoriality, Risk Perception, and Counterproductive Legal Structures: The Case of Waste Facility Siting, 27 Env. L. 1017, 1018, 1030 (1997). The question with which this note concludes -- whether a Canadian-type solution would be successful in the United States -- might be presented to the class for discussion.

Pages 1227-1228, C&Q #2. Community veto? This note is informational and self-explanatory. The questions included in this note are subsequently answered. Gerrard, *supra.*, concludes that "(e)fforts to override local authority usually backfire and *increase* local opposition, in part because these efforts increase the local perception of the facility's danger" (27 Env. L., pp.1020-1021).

Page 1228, C&Q #3. Choosing the site. This note is informational and self-explanatory. The question raised on the note is subsequently answered.

Pages 1228-1230, C&Q #4. Negotiations who, what, and when? The questions asked in this note are either rhetorical or unanswerable. They are intended to stimulate class discussion.

Page 1230, C&Q #5. Other siting recommendations. The questions posed in this note are rhetorical and valuation.

Pages 1230-1232, C&Q #6. Environmental Justice siting debates. The questions posed in this note are rhetorical, answered, or conjectural.

Pages 1232-1233, C&Q #7. The nuclear waste disposal dilemma. his note is informational and self-explanatory. For a further discussion of the high and low-level nuclear waste disposal facility siting dilemmas, see Gerrard, *supra.,* at pages 1027-1029.

Pages 1233-1238. Presents the background of §404 as an example of a site-by-site environmental protection permitting process. This material includes the *Bersani* case, one of the most interesting and controversial court decisions to have emerged under §404.

Page 1238, C&Q #1. Timing theories in *Bargain.* The initial question is subsequently discussed.

Pages 1238-1239, C&Q #2. The "practicable alternative" test. This note is informational and self-explanatory. The initial question is subsequently discussed.

Pages 1239-1240, C&Q #3. An uncomfortable partnership. This note is informational and self-explanatory.

Pages 1240-1242, C&Q #4. The controversial scope of §404. This note is informational and self-explanatory. Questions raised are conjectural.

Pages 1242-1243, C&Q #5. Mitigation of environmental damage. This note is informational and self-explanatory.

Page 1243-1244, C&Q #6. Evaluation of §404 as an example of site-by-site permitting. This note is didactic and informational.

Pages 1244-1245. This material presents a brief sketch of the Federal Wild and Scenic Rivers Act. For more information on this statute, see the Raffensberger and Tarlock article cited in the text.

Pages 1245-1246. Presents a brief sketch of comprehensive and regional land-use planning and management, a strategy that is the exception rather than the rule in the United States.

Pages 1246-1249. Presents a brief sketch of traditional local land-use controls, such as zoning and subdivision regulation. Although this area of land-use law constitutes the bulk of lawmaking in the field, it is necessarily given short shrift here.

Page 1249, C&Q #1. The local basis of zoning. This note is didactic and information. Questions raised might promote class discussion.

Pages 1249-1250, C&Q #2. TDRs. This note is didactic and informational.

Page 1250, C&Q #3. Impact fees. This note is informational and self-explanatory. Questions raised are rhetorical.

Pages 1250-1254. C&Q #3. Impact fees. Presents an introduction to the "Smart Growth" movement.

Page 1254, C&Q #1. Smart growth and the takings issue. Most state courts that have considered these matters have ruled that "upzoning" (e.g., easing of use restrictions) and "downzoning" (e.g., increasing minimum buildable lot sizes) are constitutional as long as they are (1) reasonably related to a proper public purpose, and (2) crafted so that substantial economic value remains after the zoning law changes. The instructor might, at this point, review relevant state law decisions.

Page 1254, C&Q #2. Are we ready for smart growth? These can be questions for class discussion.

Page 1254, C&Q #3. Can we afford smart growth? These are some further policy questions.

Page 1254, C&Q #4. Is smart growth really smart? Some more for good measure.

Chapter 26.
INTERNATIONAL AND COMPARATIVE ENVIRONMENTAL LAW

Suggested time budget: **2 class sessions**

Chapter contents:

1257-1263	Trail Smelter Arbitration
1263-1270	Rio Declaration
1270-1275	Mehta v. Union of India
1275-1290	Climate change
1290-1297	World Bank
1297-1305	World Trade Organization

Possible assignments:

One day:

1257-1263 Trail Smelter Arbitration
1263-1270 Rio Declaration
1275-1290 Climate change

2 days:

Day 1: 1257-1263 Trail Smelter Arbitration
1263-1270 Rio Declaration
1270-1275 Mehta v. Union of India
1275-1290 Climate change (begin discussion)

Day 2: 1275-1290 Climate change (finish discussion)
1290-1297 World Bank
1297-1305 World Trade Organization

– and check the Teachers' Manual Website for SUPPLEMENTARY MATERIALS:

http://www.bc.edu/schools/law/library/coursebook/envtlaw/teachers

The list of Supplementary Materials in Part III of this manual, and on the Teachers' Website, indicates materials posted on the Teachers' Website that are relevant to this and other chapters.

OVERALL TEACHING THEMES & COURSE DESIGN CONSIDERATIONS

This chapter, which has been thoroughly redrafted for the third edition, is organized as a mini-course in international environmental law in which the basic concepts can be delivered quickly and efficiently. With an eye to maximizing "teachability" for those instructors who may not be familiar with the subject matter or its methodology, the material has been chosen (a) to track the domestic law and policy themes that have already been presented in the book; (b) to focus on discrete, operative problems for class discussion that you as the teacher can employ to shape the class sessions; and (c) to utilize materials that, while perhaps different in kind from those in the remainder of the book, bear a close resemblance in form.

The material in this chapter encompasses most of the doctrinal and analytical skills characteristic of international environmental law, including: customary (unwritten) international law; the law of state responsibility; the role of international courts and tribunals; non-binding instruments and "soft" law; comparative law; the law of multilateral treaties; the operation of international organizations and institutions; and the role of foreign assistance. Each portion of the chapter highlights one or more of these issues while building on the previous sections to leave the student with an overview of the principal analytical approaches to tackling global environmental problems from a legal perspective.

As with the material in companion Chapter 8, if only one day's class is available it is probably better to truncate the material than to compress it all into one session. In that case, the portion on comparative law can be omitted in favor of the material on the important subject of climate change, to which students of this material deserve to be exposed.

TEACHING NOTES, COMMENTS, & ALL QUESTIONS ANSWERED

Pages 1257-1263. *Trail Smelter* Arbitration. This chapter begins by employing the famous Trail Smelter arbitration between the United States and Canada as a vehicle for addressing customary international law. You can begin discussion of this material with a schematic of the smelter in Canada sending fumes into the U.S. If there is no domestic remedy available in either the U.S. or Canada, and no treaty (Chapter 8) in place, how should the U.S. deal with this situation? This question in effect asks the students to think in a concrete way in a specific situation about the role of law in an international system that otherwise is a chaotic state of nature. Students' proposed responses typically range from making a polite request through diplomatic channels (the international least common denominator) through something aggressive such as invasion or war. You might then ask the students to identify the drawbacks to the suggestions they have made – for example, the absence of an expectation as to how Canada or the smelter should behave, and the absence of a remedy other than self-help for the U.S.

Pages 1261-1262, C&Q #1. Customary international law. This question address the nature of customary international law, which is a legally binding expectation that states' behavior will conform to prior unwritten patterns of practice. To highlight the process by which custom is made, you might identify the universal practice of standing a few paces behind a person using a bank ATM. When ATMs first came into use, how did this practice come about? You will get a variety of answers to this question, of which the most insightful is likely to be the reciprocal nature of the unstated relationship between the current user and the next in line: those who are second in line know that they will be using the machine momentarily, and typically realize that in that situation they probably don't want someone looking over their shoulder. Over time, through the accretion of a "pattern of practice" reinforced by many people using lots of ATMs in disparate locations, the practice crystallizes into an expectation so strong that people are likely to feel wronged if someone violates the unstated norm and stands too close. The difference in international relations is that a sequence like this gives rise to legally binding norms, which are no less the law for their being unwritten. Students typically have a difficult time with this last consideration, in large measure because in our domestic legal system there is no analogous means of law formation. The legally binding effect of a customary norm can be easily demonstrated by asking "How would you know if the ATM rule were in fact the law?" The answers include: if the police can enforce it; if it gives rise to an action in tort, etc. (A German student once pointed out that in that country the behavior described is required by statute. Apart from providing a moment of levity this observation is an occasion for contrasting the accretion of custom with other forms of lawmaking.)

If you were representing the U.S. in the Trail Smelter arbitration, you would want to identify a pattern of practice of other states demonstrating that they refrain from polluting other states out of a sense of legal obligation. Canada can disprove the existence of the rule by showing that states routinely allow pollution to drift into each others' territories and they feel no sense of legal obligation to refrain from doing so. In asking students to compare custom and treaty, one typically ends up with a chart that looks like the following:

- Custom
- Treaty
- Unwritten
- Based on implied consent
- Binds all states (to the extent scope of rule is global)
- Perhaps (although not always) slow to accrete
- Content of rule may be difficult to prove
- Less likely to be precise – more likely to be phrased as adjective standard
- Flexible in responding to changed circumstances and expectations
- Written
- Based on explicit consent
- Binds only states parties
- Negotiated rules can be generated quickly
- Potential for greater precision in written rule
- Requires formal amendment (see C&Q #6, Chapter 8, page 443)
- Requires signature, ratification, entry into force – may be substantial delay before rule takes effect

Page 1262, C&Q #2. State responsibility for internationally wrongful acts. This question illustrates a doctrinal difficulty in the Trail Smelter arbitration and many other international environmental disputes, namely that a private party in one state is causing harm to another private party in another state. International law governs only the obligations that states owe each other. Consequently in the Trail Smelter arbitration, as well as much other international environmental law, the obligations of states are phrased in terms of a duty to control the behavior of private parties under their jurisdiction. Note that such an obligation is inherent in the "rule" of the Trail Smelter stated on page 1261, third full paragraph ("The Tribunal, therefore, finds..."). In response to the penultimate question of this C&Q, the United States, even though it might have a good case in a legal sense, might nonetheless decline to espouse the claim of the Washington landowners because of other bilateral considerations in its relationship with Canada. Once having espoused the claim, the United States – like all governments – formally "owns" the claim as its own and can abandon or settle it for less than its full value without the consent of the "relator" (the landowners). Canada might argue that, even if there is an international norm governing pollution between states, the norm does not require it to control private parties under its jurisdiction.

Pages 1262-1263, C&Q #3. International adjudications. Building on the last C&Q, it is important to point out to students that international law would have governed the situation in the Trail Smelter dispute even if there had been no formal international adjudication. In the absence of an arbitral tribunal, the United States would still have had a legal claim that could be presented to Canada by direct communication between governments, typically via diplomatic note, the most formal means of intergovernmental communication. This "default option" is always available, and the claim would still be governed by international law even if there is no binding third-party court like mechanism to apply the law (a concept students typically take a while to absorb). Note that the results of such negotiated solutions contribute to the accretion of customary international law. For example, the U.S.'s negotiated direct payment to Iran in 1988 for shooting down an Iranian airliner over the Persian Gulf, or the U.S. payment to China for bombing its embassy in Belgrade in 1999 during the humanitarian intervention in Kosovo, would both be evidence of a legal obligation (or the absence thereof) to settle future claims.

Page 1263, C&Q #4 The Rule of *Trail Smelter*. The source of the rule, at least according to the doctrine, can only be a pattern and practice of states motivated by a sense of legal obligation. The Tribunal relied on cases from the United States primarily because it was instructed to do so by the agreement between Canada and the U.S. establishing the Tribunal (see article IV, quoted on page 1259). Presumably the reason for this negotiated rule was a shared perspective by both parties that there is an analogy between the quasi-sovereign states as subnational units of the United States and truly sovereign states in international law (see third full paragraph page 1260, "What is true between States of the Union... "). The analogy, however, is not necessarily a good one, as the states of the United States are embedded in a federal structure with supreme lawmaking power in the national legislature (the Congress) and a binding adjudicatory mechanism with the capacity to make law in a common law sense (the Supreme Court). In other words, when the Supreme Court finds federal common law governing Missouri v. Illinois and the other U.S. cases cited in the arbitral ruling, it may or may not be tracking customary international law.

If one were to distinguish the Trail Smelter arbitration in a future dispute, one could make the following points: (a) the Tribunal was instructed to consider U.S. caselaw, so the holding is relevant only to that dispute and has no larger legal significance; (b) the famous language about customary international law (page 1261, third full paragraph) is dictum, as Canada had already conceded liability and the Tribunal's job was strictly to identify a remedy or remedies according to the terms of the compromise; and (c) in any event, the Tribunal incorrectly ascertained the state of the law, as states (in the international legal sense) routinely allow pollution to drift into each others' territories without the slightest sense of legal obligation to do otherwise. With respect to this last point, one might note that the Tribunal does not cite a single example in which a state put a stop to pollution drifting into another state's territory out of an actual or apparent sense of legal obligation.

If one subjects the "rule" of the Trail Smelter – a prohibition on transboundary pollution – to critical scrutiny, the principle begins to look a lot less attractive than might appear at first impression. Note that if the Trail Smelter rule were to be taken seriously, one could be assured that, walking along the border between two states, one would be subject to no significant pollution whatsoever. Among the criticisms of the rule that one might identify are the following:

- The rule does not identify legal standards for pollution occurring strictly within a state's borders;

- The rule is unrealistic as a practical matter (how can one expect states to assure that pollution decays to zero at the border?);
- The rule is inequitable when applied to continents (e.g., Europe) which have a large number of small states as opposed to those (e.g., North America) that have a small number of large ones;
- The rule is arbitrary when measured against a criterion of environmental adequacy in that politically-determined borders between states do not necessarily track zones of ecological significance, such as airsheds;
- The rule is economically inefficient in requiring states to take potentially costly measures to reduce externalities to zero even if the expense vastly exceeds the benefits in the "victim" state;
- The two qualifications to the rule — which applies only to cases of "serious consequence [in which] the injury is established by clear and convincing evidence" — are so broad as to render the rule ineffective.

One — and perhaps the only — point in the rule's favor is that it articulates a bright-line principle that tracks the existing international political structure based on sovereign states.

Pages 1263-1267. The Rio Declaration. This section utilizes the Rio Declaration on Environment and Development as a vehicle for introducing students to the large category of non-binding instruments that reflect political commitments and desirable policy, but which do not contain binding rules of international law.

Page 1267, C&Q #1. What's soft law good for? This question invites a comparison of "soft" or non-binding instruments — typically characterized by the adjectives "hortatory" or "precatory" — with "hard" law in the form of a binding international agreement or custom. By comparison with binding law, non-binding instruments:

- Are typically phrased in hortatory "shoulds" rather than obligatory "shalls;"
- In contrast to international agreements, do not necessarily have identifiable parties;
- In contrast to international agreements, can be adopted quickly and are not subject to the "slowest boat" phenomenon resulting from requirements for signature, ratification, and entry into force;
- In contrast to international agreements, have no clearly-defined rules for amendment, admitting of greater flexibility in response to changed circumstances;
- In contrast to hard law, can be addressed directly to private parties (e.g., multinational corporations);

Non-binding instruments may be particularly useful for

- addressing situations in which a high degree of consensus cannot be obtained, overcoming what otherwise could be a "least common denominator" result in a binding agreement;
- addressing situations in which speed is desirable;
- dealing with situations in which widespread scientific agreement on the need for action is lacking;
- setting out an "action plan" for the future;
- articulating "aspirational" goals that identify a desirable state for the future

rather than binding obligations for the present;

- allowing reluctant or diffident states an opportunity to gain experience in a particular field in a low-stakes environment before making binding commitments;
- serving as precursors to a binding instrument; and/or
- elaborating the "hard" law requirements of a binding instrument in a non-binding mode.

Note that, contrary to the views of many students, there is no fixed trajectory specifying that binding instruments are necessarily less ambitious than counterpart "soft" documents, or vice versa. Also contrary to the views of many students, non-binding instruments are not necessarily less specific or less prescriptive than international agreements. In fact, the reverse may well be the case if states are prepared to experiment with bright-line rules but are prepared only to be legally bound to loosely phrased adjective standards.

The last questions highlight the risk the apparently paradoxical result that by taking the "obligations" in a non-binding instrument too seriously, a state may undermine the advantages of an aspirational "soft" law approach.

Pages 1267-1268, C&Q #2. *Trail Smelter* revisited: Stockholm Principle 21, first among equals. Stockholm Principle 21 is something of an attempt to codify the rule of the Trail Smelter in a non-binding declaration. The differences are:

- the insertion of the right of states to exploit their resources within their own borders, implicit in the Trail Smelter decision but not explicitly stated; and
- an expansion of the obligation to refrain from transboundary pollution to "areas beyond national jurisdiction," such as the high seas or Antarctica.

The motivation for the penultimate question in the first paragraph is that some scholars have said that the Principle embodies a balancing test — which is plainly incorrect if one simply reads the text, which delineates instead between the internal rights and external responsibilities of states.

The second paragraph of the note addresses the process by which some "soft" good practice standards such as Principle 21 may "mature" into binding obligations. This occurs through the accretion of a pattern of state practice motivated by a sense of legal obligation, the process of formation of customary international law discussed in the first part of this chapter. The text of the non-binding statement is then evidence of the law, but is not the law itself, which in a strict sense is unwritten. (Note that non-binding instruments can also act as a template for subsequent binding treaty provisions, but that is a different process of lawmaking.) The rule has pretty much the same strengths and weaknesses as that of the Trail Smelter.

Page 1268, C&Q #3. Stockholm Principle 21 goes Latin. This question is intended to evaluate and expand students' capacity to work with the analytical concepts underlying law formation through the accretion of custom. If Principle 21 was evidence of the law before Rio, that was because states acted consistently with the principle out of a sense of legal obligation. If that is the case, the law (in the form of unwritten custom) arguably cannot be altered strictly by the insertion of two new words in a non-binding declaration at Rio; one would have to look to see in addition whether state practice changed accordingly. The alternative view would be that the insertion of the new words at Rio operated in a quasi-legislative mode, immediately altering the expectations of all states to the point that one could say that the non-binding instrument catalyzed a simultaneous change in the binding customary law (a phenomenon sometimes called "instant custom"). Another interpretation, as suggested in the note, is that the insertion of the new words simply operated to give further clarity to a pattern of practice that had already crystallized as law (somewhat analogous to codification).

Page 1268, C&Q #4. Precaution - principle or approach? Principles that have not matured into customary international law serve as useful reference points in the form of non-binding "good practice standards," but they are not binding. Some European countries, apparently by reference to the importance of the concept in European codes, have attempted to argue that a "principle" has a higher status than other non-binding international expectations. International law, however, does not make such a distinction — at least not as of the present day.

Pages 1268-1269, C&Q #5. Precaution at home in the United States. The following domestic statutory approaches are generally thought to be precautionary, in the sense of erring on the side of caution in situations of scientific uncertainty:

- prior approval schemes, such as those for pesticides under FIFRA, which specify that the manufacturer must prove safety as opposed to the government's demonstrating harm (although note that the substantive test in the case of pesticides is a cost-benefit criterion);
- zero-risk approaches, such as the Delaney Clause or §7 of the Endangered Species Act; and
- health-based standards, such as those for criteria pollutants under the Clean Air Act.

Those that are not generally considered precautionary, because they rely on factors other than the likelihood and severity of harm, are:

- technology-limited requirements, such as TBELs promulgated under the Clean Water Act, which may permit some harm even when the best available technology is employed; and
- cost-benefit tests, such as those under ToSCA, which quantify (often imperfectly) injuries avoided as benefits and weigh them against the costs of regulatory compliance. (Note that to the extent that benefits are large and cheap, a cost-benefit test might be precautionary, but that is not necessarily true in every case.)

Page 1269, C&Q #6. The Rio Declaration and U.S. Law. Most commentators discount the effect of the Rio Declaration, and the entire concept of sustainability, on the development of U.S. law. The excerpts from the Rio Declaration given in the text all articulate criteria that the authors believe have been slighted in the development of U.S. environmental law.

Page 1269, C&Q #7. What is "sustainability" anyway? This question highlights the indeterminacy in the term "sustainability" that the authors believe has facilitated the projection of counterproductive considerations into the term from a variety of constituencies, including industry. Otherwise, the question is rhetorical in form. As the teacher you might devote some time to discussing the last question, but unless your students include the next generation's Rachel Carson you are unlikely to be able to tease out a single overarching principle that will solve the world's environmental problems.

Pages 1269-1270, C&Q #8. The 2002 Johannesburg summit. The text of this note is purely informational.

Pages 1270-1273. Mehta v. Union of India. You might begin discussing Mehta v. Union of India by asking the students to identify the structural attributes of the case, which include the following:

- This is a proceeding for judicial review (the defendant is the Indian government), a concept with which the students should by now be thoroughly familiar;
- The apparent basis for the action includes statute (similar to the U.S.) and the Indian constitution, which unlike the U.S. Constitution has a provision specifically directed at the environment and natural resources;
- The basis for the action is the Government of India's failure to enforce the relevant domestic authorities in the city of Delhi (usually not actionable in the U.S. system based on principles of the exercise of enforcement discretion).

The most striking feature from the point of view of the present chapter, and the reason the case is included here, is the Indian Supreme Court's liberal use of non-binding international principles such as sustainable development, precaution, and the polluter pays principle to embellish and extend the domestic legal mandates. Also note how the adjective standards in the Rio Declaration are applied by the Court to justify extraordinarily precise relief in the form of an order detailing specific, concrete actions required by the Government.

Page 1273, C&Q #1. Judicial activism in other jurisdictions. This is a somewhat rhetorical question, but it ought to get students thinking and talking about the legitimacy of courts as actors in a constitutional structure. Interestingly, many Indian environmental activists, while applauding the activism of the Indian Supreme Court, simultaneously note that this kind of activism would not be necessary if the Government were doing its job properly. In other words, judicial action is a failsafe – often imperfect – to correct the most serious failings of political will, but not a substitute for the absence of it. An interesting insight when applied to our own system....

Pages 1273-1274, C&Q #2. Constitutionalism of environmental law. The real issue for the U.S. is what an intervention at the level of generality required of a Constitutional amendment would add to our current system in terms of precise, justiciable standards – arguably not much. The answer to the last question is that the Indian Supreme Court has treated the non-binding principles as instructive in interpreting the operative, binding portions of the constitution – thereby bootstrapping the former to something approaching binding status.

Page 1274, C&Q #3. International environmental law in national courts. This question is a counterweight to C&Q #6 on page 1269 in suggesting how the Rio Declaration might operate as domestic law if one were to take its provisions seriously. The Supreme Court seems to say that the principles of the Rio Declaration are understood to be embedded in environmental law generally, presumably including the domestic environmental laws of all states. Therefore the domestic environmental law of India – constitution and statutes – has to be read against the background of the Rio Principles. And voilà – Rio operates domestically! You might ask the students what there is in our system to prevent this kind of reasoning from operating in the U.S. Arguably not much, and indeed there may be much to recommend the approach as a mechanism for "harmonizing" our own law with that of other states in a rapidly globalizing world. Interestingly, in subject matter areas other than the environment, the U.S. Supreme Court has engaged in similar reasoning – e.g., Lawrence v. Texas, striking down Texas's sodomy law relying in part on an interpretation of the U.S. Constitution informed by international standards.

Page 1274, C&Q #4. Regional impacts outside India. The impacts of diesel emissions continue to be controversial in the United States, as discussed in Chapter 15. If India can deal with this problem, one would hope that that U.S. can!

Pages 1274-1275, C&Q #5. Who is M. C. Mehta? This note is purely informational, designed to highlight the role of activist environmental lawyers in other jurisdictions.

Pages 1275-1282. Global Climate Change. The Framework Convention and the Kyoto Protocol together are an example of the framework agreement plus protocols model that has become prevalent in international environmental law. In principle the framework agreement sets out "procedural" obligations relating to exchange of information, cooperation in research, and reporting, while the substantive regulatory requirements are included in subsequent "protocols" or ancillary agreements. The approach dates from the international treatment of stratospheric ozone in the mid-1980s and has been widely accepted, as in the two binding agreements adopted at the Rio Conference. It is not, however, required by international law.

Page 1282, C&Q #1. Soft or hard law—which is more environmentally friendly? This question reinforces the point made in section B that non-binding instruments may establish more rigorous expectations of performance precisely because they are non-binding. When it came time for states to articulate in a binding agreement what they were prepared to undertake in a legally binding mode, the expectations were more modest.

Page 1282, C&Q #2. The Convention and the Rio Declaration. In theory the "obligations" are the precise actions the parties have committed themselves to take, whereas the "principles" are intended to inform the interpretation of those obligations. The principles in article 3 also ought to inform future actions taken by the parties under the Convention, including decisions taken by the Conference of the Parties at its annual meeting and subsequent protocols, such as the Kyoto Protocol, both of which in theory should be consistent with the principles. While the principles in the Framework Convention are binding and the Rio Declaration is not, in practice the two ought to operate in a similar manner because of the relative indeterminacy of the former. While the Framework Convention, like all the law, ought to be interpreted in a manner consonant with the Rio Declaration, the principles set out in article 3 of the Framework Convention can be understood as a formulation of the Rio principles specifically in the context of climate change. That said, these issues have held much greater appeal for Europeans – accustomed as they are to interpretations by national courts and the European Court of Justice by reference to general principles – than to practically-minded North Americans.

Page 1282, C&Q #3. The Convention as substantive law. Given that the language is contained in a binding agreement, the presumption is that it articulates mandatory duties for states parties, including the United States. That said, the numerical requirement is embedded in a reporting requirement, suggesting that the obligation is to report progress toward the goal and not necessarily to achieve it in practice. Also, the language "aim" in article 4(2)(b) tends to suggest a "soft" aspirational goal as opposed to a firm obligation to meet the target.

Pages 1282-1283, C&Q #4. The Convention as U.S. law. The argument would be that the report constitutes a finding under §108(a)(1)(A) of the Clean Air. Employing the reasoning of NRDC v. Train, page 561, the Administrator would then have a nondiscretionary duty to list carbon dioxide and to promulgate NAAQSs for it. The states could argue that a routine report to the United Nations pursuant to the Framework Convention is not what Congress intended in §108. Even if carbon dioxide were to be listed as a criteria pollutant under CAA §108, there are real questions about the efficacy of the statute for addressing global warming. The CAA and its principal workhorse, the NAAQSs, are intended to protect against *local* environmental effects. A NAAQS would have to be framed in terms of an acceptable ambient concentration and implemented through a SIP. This could be interpreted as either an ultra-rigorous or almost meaningless requirement, as carbon dioxide concentrations are more or less uniform worldwide. To that extent there is a mismatch between the problem (global warming) and the structure of the CAA, similar to that encountered before the 1990 Amendments addressing acid rain (Chapter 11). The states would probably be trying to create leverage in favor of a statutory solution as an alternative to a court order instructing EPA to list carbon dioxide as a criteria pollutant, an action with potentially draconian consequences. An alternative legal theory might be to apply the target of the Convention identified in the previous note directly to the Executive Branch in a proceeding for judicial review under the APA. Yet another might be a theory of public nuisance initiated by one state against another under the theory of the U.S. cases discussed in the Trail Smelter opinion.

Page 1286, C&Q #1. Common but (highly differentiated responsibilities. Because industrialized countries had contributed the bulk of the problem at the time of the adoption of the Framework Convention, developing countries made it clear that they considered it to be an inequitable burden to require them to control present or future carbon dioxide emissions, which could constrain their economic development. The options for trading – presumably selling – emissions rights can create an incentive for states to take on Annex I quantified emissions reduction obligations. In response to the last question, one of the concerns of some participants in the Kyoto negotiations – principally the European Union (EU) – has been the potential for the Clean Development Mechanism (CDM) to create something of an escape hatch in two ways: by creating benefits for non-Annex I countries without commensurate obligations; and by in effect increasing the total amount of allowable emissions reductions from Annex I countries. This concern is enhanced when projects involving "sinks" receive credit because of the difficulty in assuring concrete benefits. While the last question has no precise answer, one policy response might be a gradual phaseout in the CDM through more rather than fewer restrictions on accessing it. Allowing countries voluntarily to take on Annex I obligations on terms that are somewhat more generous than existing Annex I states – e.g., allowing more generous access to the CDM – could operate as a transitional strategy. Yet another possibility might be greater "conditionality" on development assistance funds provided through the Framework Convention and the Global Environment Facility.

Page 1287, C&Q #2. Safeguards for international trading. These questions have been among the principal focus in implementing the Kyoto Protocol through the Marrakesh Accords. Among the policy responses provided to a greater or lesser extent by the international community in the latter instrument are the following:

- strict reporting and accounting mechanisms to assure no leakage as a result of trades (although note that states still keep their own books, albeit under international supervision);
- requirements to assure that states do not jeopardize their capacity to comply with their quantified emissions reductions obligations through excessive trading (known as the "commitment period reserve"); and
- a compliance (enforcement) mechanism that is among the most rigorous known in international environmental law (although not international law more generally) to assure that Annex I states fully implement these obligations.

Page 1287, C&Q #3. Giving credit only for the road that would not have been taken. This concept is an important one, because otherwise states could generate sham reductions by in effect manipulating the baseline against which reductions are measured. Note that this is a particularly important – and difficult – question in the case of the CDM, which gives credits for projects undertaken in countries without quantified emission reduction obligations, which in turn add to the total permissible global emissions budget.

Page 1287, C&Q #4. Baseline choice and the over-creation of credits. In response to the first question, at least potentially yes. In response to the second, note the symbiotic relationship between the interests of those countries with credits to sell – e.g., Russia – and those that might encounter difficulties in reaching their emissions targets without purchases – e.g., the U.S. This is one of the principal dynamics that has led observers to question whether the Kyoto Protocol is likely to achieve even its modest aims.

Pages 1287-1288, C&Q #5. Heavy weather for the Protocol in the United States. This note identifies the potential in our system of separation of power and checks and balances for the Senate to block reciprocal policy actions in the form of treaties. The natural dynamic is then for the Executive in power during the negotiations to try to identify and respond to potential objections in the Senate. Note how this results in a "two level game" dynamic during the negotiations process, which in effect occurs on two fronts – one with foreign powers, the potential treaty partners in a contractual sense, and the other with the Senate which must give its advice and consent by a supermajority of two-thirds in a legislative mode. The flexible mechanisms in the Kyoto Protocol advocated by the Clinton administration were partially motivated by the desire to ease Senate approval by lowering the cost of implementation in the United States – quite obviously unsuccessfully, as demonstrated in the quoted passage. In contrast to the Bush II administration, which made a flat statement that it did not intend to ratify Kyoto, other countries such as Russia have remained at least semi-engaged with the process and have used that posture to extract further concessions from the other parties. You might note how those countries retain leverage over the process, while the U.S., by turning its back entirely, has abandoned a considerable portion of its influence. In other words, had the U.S. held out the potential for ratification in this country instead of abandoning that possibility, it might very well have been able, even at a relatively late stage in the negotiations after the adoption of the Protocol, to retool the agreement to a certain extent consistent with its own interests. You might note in addition how in our system the President is very much in the driver's seat; once he announces his intent to refrain from ratification, there is no mechanism for the Senate to compel him to do so even if it were to change its (collective) mind. In response to the last question, recall that the Protocol identifies quantified emissions limitations only for a first commitment period of 2008-2012. While it is now probably too late for the U.S. to meet its allocated goal of a 7% reduction from 1990 levels, especially as emissions have grown in the interim, it is at least theoretically possible for the U.S. to ratify and to take on quantified emission reduction obligations in the second commitment period (presumably along with a special dispensation for having failed to meet the targets in the first). Other countries are unlikely to want to see the U.S. remain outside the Protocol's framework, and might well agree to significant concessions as a quid pro quo for U.S. participation in a second round of reductions that have yet to be negotiated.

Page 1288, C&Q #6. No pain, no gain. This note is an occasion for you and the class to engage in a critical discussion of the Bodansky argument. This is a matter of opinion on which knowledgeable observers might disagree, but even though the excerpt seems to be motivated by a good-faith search for a workable solution, the piece nonetheless appears to be written from a U.S.-centric posture. Other major industrialized countries, including the EU (now numbering 25 member states) and Japan appear to consider the Protocol to be a workable scheme. Why then should the rest of the world be held hostage to a considerably less enthusiastic state's position? One answer is that without the U.S., reductions by others are of considerably less value than if the U.S. were on board. A reasonable critique of the "culture of compliance" argument is that the state that most needs to generate a culture of compliance is the United States, and that compliance as such is not really the issue; rather, the question is the presence or absence of political will. If that is the case, what are the impediments to generating that level of political buy-in now, as opposed to in the future when reductions will likely be even more painful and less environmentally beneficial? This question, along with the others accompanying this section, is a good opportunity to identify the difference between political posturing to generate strategic leverage — utilized not only by the U.S., but also by the EU — and the real-world need, universally appreciated, for meaningful cooperation.

Page 1288, C&Q #7. Of international law and the tragedy of the commons. The question is rhetorical in form and has no single correct answer. You might note, however, that the international system has fewer sanctions for violations than U.S. domestic law. For instance, if the Executive (e.g., EPA, the Department of the Interior) violates the law, the institution of judicial review is available to assure compliance. When it comes to enforcement, a theory of "mutual coercion mutually agreed upon" in the international system has tended to find states to be reluctant to subject themselves to remedies that most domestic lawyers regard as meaningful remedies. One reason is that states can often envision themselves on both sides of a dispute - not just as a complaining party (plaintiff), but also as a respondent (defendant).

Pages 1288-1289, C&Q #8. Business as usual. One view is that voluntary undertakings of this sort defuse the pressure for more rigorous, binding, legally enforceable requirements, for which as of this writing there is a growing constituency in the Congress. According to this perspective, the more widely accepted and deeply entrenched a voluntary program is, the more effectively it operates to fend off prescriptive legislative action. This factor tends to explain why the Executive is enthusiastic about voluntary programs to the extent of strong-arming industry, as described in the Revkin piece.

Page 1289, C&Q #9. Getting worse before it gets better. The question is rhetorical in form and has no single correct answer. The problem is the difficulty of establishing a cause-and-effect relationship between the broad phenomenon of climate change (which, contrary to public perceptions in the U.S., is largely undisputed by scientists) and individual weather events.

Page 1289, C&Q #10. Role of the press. The question (which should be addressed in tandem with the previous one) is rhetorical in form and has no single correct answer. Interestingly, the European press has tended to correlate events such as those described in the previous question with climate change. A different understanding of journalistic ethics on this side of the Atlantic, together with governmental pressure, has tended to preclude that kind of reporting in the U.S. Whether this is (a) responsible reporting or (b) a disservice to the public is a subject about which responsible teachers and reasonable students might disagree among themselves.

Pages 1289-1290, C&Q #11. National implementation of the Protocol. The point of this question is that the Kyoto Protocol and the Marrakesh Accords can be implemented through concrete actions in individual countries in a manner that minimizes costs and takes full advantage of the flexible mechanisms. Even absent ratification of Kyoto, the U.S. could undertake the analogues of many of the measures proposed by Japan – e.g., coordination of federal and state policies.

Pages 1290-1293. This section addresses two international organizations - the World Bank and the World Trade Organization — whose mandates are not expressly environmental in nature but which are nonetheless charged with improving human welfare. The remainder of the chapter invites the inference of a clash between those institutions' functional missions and environmental goals, while challenging students to reconcile the potential conflicts by reference to principles of sustainable development. This section is also designed to be a short course in international organizations and institutions. The teaching materials, however, emphasize continuity with the domestic subject matter of the coursebook on such familiar questions as citizen access, judicial review, and environmental impact assessment (the international analogue of NEPA).

Pages 1293-1294. World Bank. The Inspection Panel's report on the Qinghai project is notable for its scathing critique of Bank practices, barely stopping short of accusing Bank management of bad faith. You might ask the students how this report compares the early NEPA cases. In effect, the Panel is performing the function of the federal courts in those cases by (to use domestic terminology) affirming the reviewability of the staff's actions, the Panel's own capacity (indeed, responsibility) to interpret "the law" in the form of OD 4.01 (the analogue of NEPA), and engaging in a "hard look" designed to make sure that the OD is properly implemented in a mode akin to judicial review of administrative action.

You might also discuss with students what incentive staff have to engage in violations as gross as those documented even in this short passage. One obvious reason is the absence, until the creation of the Panel, of a viable third-party mechanism for resolving allegations such as those made by the requesters (the private parties who initiated the action). Another is the professional reward mechanism in the Bank, which often stresses getting deals done over quality control. Yet a third is pressure from the borrowing country government. Put these all together and the message to staff may well be the need to cut corners or make concessions to move the loan out the door.

Pages 1294-1295, C&Q #1. Environmental impact assessment and foreign aid. Note that, in contrast to NEPA, the World Bank and the regional development banks use a system of ranking to determine the rigor of environmental assessment appropriate for a particular project. The difference between NEPA and OD 4.01 is the role of the borrowing country government, which is responsible for preparation of the environmental assessment, pays for it, and as a technical matter owns it. The analogue in the U.S. would be if a private developer were to prepare an EIS instead of the federal agency concerned (which, incidentally, some foreign analogues of NEPA permit). Given the Bank's potentially limited oversight role, coupled with other possibly contentious issues in the loan negotiation and appraisal process, the EA process may be subjected to pressures that would not be encountered in the U.S. system. A private individual or organization adversely affected by the project would have to complain to his or her own government in the first instance - a problematic relationship in the case of many Bank borrowers that do not tolerate dissent or which suppress or punish the exercise of free speech.

Page 1295, C&Q #2. Unilateralism at the World Bank. According to critics of the legislation - presumably borrowing country governments - this is an attempt to influence the outcome of multilateral deliberations in the Bank by prescribing in advance the position of one country, the United States. If every donor country were to do this, the Bank as an institution would be subjected to multiple, and perhaps competing, unilateral mandates that could, in an extreme case, interfere with the appropriate functioning of the institution under its Articles of Agreement. From the U.S. view, this is an entirely appropriate exercise of its prerogatives as a member of the Bank according to its own internal constitutional processes, which are none of other members' business. Note that the existence of legislative mandates of this kind have a tendency to influence the choice and appraisal of loans at the staff level, well before they are ever presented to the Board of Executive Directors and which may never result in a negative vote. This "raised eyebrow" approach is in all likelihood intended by the proponents of the legislation, and contributes as well to the criticism by borrowers.

Pages 1295-1296, C&Q #3. Foreign aid for the global environment. This question has no precise answer, but here are a few thoughts as to how to design environmentally beneficial lending:

One of the principal themes of the World Bank reform efforts has been the need to involve local populations in externally-financed projects. This is felt to be particularly important in conservation efforts, where local populations can provide useful advice on the shape of the project and contribute to its success — or failure if there is insufficient consultation and buy-in.

Another has been sustainability — whatever that means — and a GEF-financed project would presumably exceed minimum standards on this measure.

Yet a third criterion might be consideration of "ripple" or "multiplier" effects, to assure that the project has catalytic benefits on governmental policies beyond the scope of the project.

A related consideration is the extent to which GEF financing might serve as an incentive or "carrot" to encourage concurrent, beneficial policy change in a sector as a whole. E.g., an end-use energy efficiency demonstration project might be an occasion for a recipient country government to reconsider subsidies to energy generation efforts.

Some have asserted the need to involve the private sector in conservation efforts, and to create incentives and rewards along those lines, perhaps even including incentives for foreign investment. According to this view, even under the most optimistic scenarios the magnitude of external assistance will never by itself be sufficient to address problems of the scope the GEF is grappling with.

The argument against the GEF essentially proceeds from the perspective that the institution is driven by donor-financed priorities delivered by at least one institution — the Bank — that has yet to demonstrate the political will, internal incentive structure for staff, and technical expertise commensurate with the task. The contrary view (to which at least one of the authors subscribes) is that under the right circumstances external inputs can help developing countries retool to help meet global environmental goals in a manner that simultaneously creates economic and other benefits.

Page 1296, C&Q #4. The Inspection Panel fights for independence. The text of this note raises the question of how international institutions manage to deliver on their functional missions and avoid multiple dynamics that often tend to eviscerate their effectiveness. In response to the question, the Bank is a subject of international law, similar in this respect to a state, and therefore is bound to avoid violations of international customary norms of the Trail Smelter variety. If a borrower is a party to a multilateral agreement, there is arguably an obligation on the part of the Bank to avoid facilitating a violation of the treaty. To the extent the obligations in the agreement have been accepted as customary norms, even non-party states might be obliged to refrain from undermining the goals of the agreement. Similarly, to the extent that non-binding instruments, such as Rio Principle 2, have matured into custom the same argument would apply. If not, then there does not appear to be a particularly good legal (as opposed to policy) argument for holding the Bank to standards that were not intended to be binding.

Pages 1296-1297, C&Q #5. Are alternatives to the Bank worse? This is more than a rhetorical question, but it is essentially a matter of opinion: accepting the lesser of evils on the theory that "let not the perfect be the enemy of the good" vs. the desirability of having the Bank stand only for high standards of practice as a an agent of, and a fiduciary of public monies from, essentially all the countries on the planet.

You as the teacher might find the following problem exercise a useful tool for enriching the students' active appreciation for the dynamics that drive the Bank. It has been set on separate pages so that you can photocopy and distribute it in class.

World Bank Problem Exercise

Since 2001, Bank staff have been discussing a new projected entitled "Forest Exploitation III" with the Government of Ruritania, a developing country that is a member of both the IBRD and IDA. "Exploitation III" would be financed by a $60 million IBRD loan to the Government of Ruritania. As suggested by the name, this project, if approved, would be the third in a series of World Bank-funded projects designed to build penetration roads into tropical forests and to facilitate commercial timbering operations in Ruritania's dwindling primary tropical rainforests, which are a significant repository for biological diversity. "Exploitation III," according to Bank staff, is expected to produce considerable economic growth in Ruritania primarily through increased exportation of raw and semi-processed timber to markets in industrialized countries. Bank staff estimate that the Government of Ruritania should be able to repay the loan at prevailing market rates of interest within 10 years, primarily as a result of fees to be charged by the Government for leases issued to foreign corporations granting those corporations permission to log identified tracts of government lands containing primary forest.

About a month ago, Bank staff announced that "Exploitation III" was ready for presentation to the Bank's Board of Executive Directors for that body's approval. The Government of Ruritania has prepared an environmental assessment, and Bank staff and the Government of Ruritania have asserted that all requirements of the Bank's operational policy on environmental assessment and all other Bank environmental criteria have been satisfied. In particular, the Government of Ruritania has stated that it is prepared to agree, as a condition of the World Bank's approval of "Exploitation III," to measures that the Government and the Bank's professional staff believe would reduce, but not eliminate, adverse environmental impacts from the project.

After being lobbied heavily by a coalition of British and Ruritanian non-governmental organizations (NGOs) calling itself "End Unsustainable Funding" (ENUF), the Government of the United Kingdom and the UK Executive Director concluded that the UK could not support "Exploitation III." Indeed, the British Government was so convinced of the environmental defects in the loan that it engaged in some last-minute, but highly effective, diplomacy to muster opposition to the loan among other important donor countries, including the United States.

Accordingly, at its meeting held last Thursday, the Bank's Board of Executive Directors — over the vociferous objections of the Executive Director for Ruritania — narrowly disapproved the staff's proposal to finance "Forest Exploitation III," the first time the Board had ever formally disapproved a loan proposal by recorded vote for environmental reasons. Every Executive Director that voted against the loan publicly stated that he or she was doing so strictly because of concerns about environmental defects in the project. Many of the Executive Directors, moreover, referenced the loan's failure to meet the standards set out in the Non-legally Binding Authoritative Statement of Principles for a Global Consensus on the Management, Conservation and Sustainable Development of All Types of Forests, a "soft law" instrument similar in form to the Rio Declaration that was adopted at the United Nations Conference on Environment and Development (UNCED) in 1992.

Outraged, the Executive Director for Ruritania immediately sent a letter to the Chairman of the Board of Executive Directors and the President of the World Bank, which reads in its entirety as follows:

> I respectfully request you to declare today's vote on "Forest Exploitation III" to be illegal and to present this loan for reconsideration to the Board of Executive Directors as soon as possible. In particular, the disapproval of "Forest Exploitation III" based on false allegations by the United Kingdom and other donor states
>
> (1) violates the sovereignty of Ruritania and illegally intrudes into the Government of Ruritania's exclusive prerogative to govern within its territory;
>
> (2) violates Article 2, section 7 of the Charter of the United Nations, which provides that "[n]othing... shall authorize the United Nations [or any specialized agency thereof like the World Bank] to intervene in matters which are essentially within the domestic jurisdiction of any state;
>
> (3) violates the prohibition in the IBRD and IDA Articles of Agreement specifying that "[t]he [Bank] and its officers shall not interfere in the political affairs of any member;"
>
> (4) violates the provision in the IBRD and IDA Articles of Agreement specifying that "[o]nly economic considerations shall be relevant to [the Bank's] decisions;" and
>
> (5) violates fundamental principles of international law in attempting to apply the UNCED forest principles – a non-binding instrument not accepted by the Government of Ruritania – as a condition of a World Bank loan.

As a staff lawyer at the World Bank, how would you respond on behalf of the Chairman of the Board and the President to the Executive Director for Ruritania defending the validity of the Board of Executive Directors' vote on "Forest Exploitation III?" You should be prepared to argue on behalf of your client that each of the five points raised in the Executive Director for Ruritania's letter is incorrect.

Answers to World Bank problem exercise. The basic point of the exercise is that the action complained of consists of the Bank's declining to finance an external loan which Ruritania has no right to receive either under the Bank's Articles of Agreement or international law generally. Moreover, the Articles of Agreement and the structure of the Bank more generally expressly anticipate that some loans might be disapproved at the Board level.

(1) There is no intrusion into Ruritania's sovereignty, which can be defined legally as the Government of Ruritania's exclusive prerogative to govern within its territory. For instance, the Bank has not attempted to prescribe law applicable in the territory of Ruritania or to displace the government there. Instead, it has decided not to proceed with a consensual arrangement for external financing that requires the consent of both parties, much the same as if a commercial bank denied a customer's application for an automobile loan.

(2) The Charter obligation mirrors the first point, with the exception that the obligation is of treaty rather than customary origin. The content and the reasoning, however, are essentially the same. Denial of a loan is in no sense intervention in matters which are essentially within the domestic jurisdiction of any state. Much the same as the unsuccessful loan applicant, Ruritania is free to do as it chooses, including abandoning the project, seeking financing elsewhere, or financing the undertaking itself.

(3) Points (3) and (4) can usefully be considered together. Although the precise meaning of this passage in the Articles of Agreement is obscure, denial of a loan is not political interference. According to one view the Bank, for reasons similar to those set out in points (1) and (2), could never interfere in the political affairs of a borrower so long as the institution is engaged in the routine conduct of business consistent with the Articles of Agreement. According to another, espoused by at least some Bank staff, this provision is designed to preclude loan conditionality related to the form of government of the borrower, the conduct of governmental affairs, non-economic governmental policies, and the like. The purpose of the provision would then be to confine the Bank to considering exclusively economic factors and conditionality, and to assure that the institution refrains from discriminating between, for instance, socialist and market-oriented borrowers. Relying on this theory, the Bank has declined to consider borrowing countries' human rights records or to include conditionality related to the exercise of civil and political liberties.

(4) Building on the insights from point (3) above, one has to answer the question whether the environmental integrity of a loan is an attribute that is (a) political or (b) economic. In recent years the Bank has drifted toward (b), reasoning that considerations of environmental integrity and sustainability affect the economic viability of the loan. Note, incidentally, that a similar argument might be made with respect to human rights — that countries with poor human rights records are less stable and therefore less viable from an economic perspective — thereby demonstrating the somewhat subjective nature of the test.

(5) Because the lending arrangements are consensual, for the Bank's appraisal process to have any meaning it must involve the exercise of professional judgment. With the exception of the requirements in the Articles of Agreement quoted in points (3) and (4), there are few if any constraints on the exercise of that discretion. As an instrument emerging from the Earth Summit, the UNCED forest principles represent global "good

practice standards" that are, moreover, accepted by governments. Consequently, should the Bank choose to apply those standards in the loan to Ruritania, the borrower has no basis for objection. Note that the Bank is equally under no obligation to apply the forest principles (Page 1296, C&Q #4), meaning that Bank staff are at least as a legal matter free to decline to apply them. In that case, non-state actors would have a low probability of success challenging the loan in the Inspection Panel. The bottom line is that this is a matter left to the staff's discretion, at least so far as the law is concerned.

Pages 1297-1298. World Trade Organization. The WTO and regional trade agreements present a potentially conflicting set of obligations to those found in multilateral environmental agreements and, like the World Bank, yet another institutional setting in which there might be functional mandates that compete with environmental goals. The basic point of the introduction is that, from the point of view of international trade agreements, environmental regulations can be barriers to trade in a manner similar to tariffs, and constituencies that support them are advocating measures that are at least potentially protectionist in effect if not necessarily in intent. Trade agreements set out tests to distinguish between legitimate and unjustified measures that impede trade, including environmental regulations. The "negative" obligations in these agreements disable governments from maintaining unjustified measures, backed up by a dispute settlement mechanism and sanctions among the most vigorous known in international law and practice. From the point of view of international trade, then, the task is to distinguish between "good" (legitimate) and "bad" (protectionist) environmental regulations, with considerable debate over the appropriateness of the tests employed. Additional background material on the trade-and-environment debate can be found in Chapter 8, pages 454-460.

Pages 1299-1301. Restrictions on Imports of Tuna. The tuna/dolphin case can be effectively presented in class by asking what were the arguments of first Mexico, then the U.S., then Mexico's rejoinder. Mexico in effect alleged that the U.S. was discriminating among various foreign sources of tuna (an MFN violation) and treating tuna imported from Mexico less well than the domestically manufactured product (a national treatment violation). The U.S. argued that Mexico was failing to appreciate the distinction between dolphin-safe tuna and tuna caught in ways that harm dolphin. Mexico successfully responded that this was no distinction at all, as the content of the product was identical and the U.S. was discriminating based only upon the method by which the tuna was captured (page 1299, first paragraph). The United States then unsuccessfully invoked the exceptions of article XX, which you might explicitly note create a justification for measures that otherwise would violate the basic GATT obligations.

Page 1301, C&Q #1. Progress and production methods (PPMs) As noted above, the panel concluded that there were no physical differences in the two kinds of tuna. If the result were otherwise, the U.S. would essentially be imposing its environmental policies on Mexico through the embargo. If every country of import could do this, then exporters would be exposed to a "crazy quilt" of unilateral conditions, some of which might even conflict with each other. The result could be a substantial disruption to international trade for reasons that are not appropriately an issue of concern on the part of the state of import (page 1300, first paragraph).

Page 1301, C&Q #2. An escape valve for the environment. The exceptions do not apply because (1) they relate to the protection of human, animal or plant life or health or natural resources (depending on the exception) outside the jurisdiction of the state of import and (2) the U.S. had not exhausted the alternative of attempting to negotiate an international agreement with Mexico on dolphin protection before imposing the embargo (page 1300, second paragraph). Moreover, the standards to which Mexico is held depend on the performance of the U.S. fleet (page 1300, second paragraph), meaning that Mexico is dealing with a continually shifting set of requirements.

Pages 1301-1302, C&Q #3. Baptists, bootleggers, and Flipper. The U.S. tuna fishermen are likely to be motivated to create a level playing field by assuring that the costs they incur in protecting dolphins are also borne by foreign industries. Hence, the embargo has a protectionist odor about it. The question of intent is a tricky one both in GATT/WTO law and in a democracy. If intent is the measure, then comments from any one legislator about the need to protect domestic industry would have disproportionate effect and might very well be unrepresentative of legislative intent, which is difficult to determine in any event. On the other hand, the absence of overt indications of protectionist intent could well insulate the measure and lead to a disguised restriction on international trade.

Page 1302, C&Q #4. PPMs in the World Trade Organization. This note describes the evolution of WTO jurisprudence, which after the turtle/shrimp dispute appears to be much more receptive to PPMs so long as they are appropriately applied.

Page 1302 C&Q #5. Unilateralism versus multilateralism. This note illustrates the fairly radical distinction between an international negotiation undertaken against the backdrop of an embargo and that commenced on a "clean slate." In the former situation, Mexico and other similarly situated countries face a continued embargo if the negotiations fail, an attribute that gives countries in a position such as that of the United States considerable leverage to extract concessions from the prospective treaty partner. Most likely this is *not* what the tuna panel had in mind, especially in view of its conclusion that the U.S. embargo was inconsistent with the GATT. Relative to a unilateral measure such as the U.S. embargo, an international agreement has the benefit of establishing standards for many countries, including those that may choose not to meet the unilateral conditions imposed by the state of import and instead to continue to engage in the practice of setting on dolphin. The question of the adequacy of the concessions sufficient to justify abandoning the embargo is a difficult judgment call, as demonstrated by the note. Government negotiators have an incentive to consult with the environmentalists who obtained the embargo by court order. Without the support of those constituencies, the government might not be able to obtain the necessary statutory amendments and would find itself in the uncomfortable position of being unable to deliver on the promises made to foreign powers as a matter of domestic law.

Pages 1303-1304, C&Q #6. WTO dispute settlement and democratic participation. From the point of view of domestic constituencies, the GATT/WTO dispute settlement process looks like judicial review of a domestic measure in an international tribunal. The negotiation of international agreements is a lawmaking function. Reasoning by analogy to domestic legislative and judicial processes, private parties would likely argue for the need for public participation to assure the legitimacy and integrity of the analogous functions undertaken at the international level. From this perspective, closed procedures appear anti-democratic. Trade agreements, however, are different from other lawmaking and adjudicatory functions in that one of their principal purposes is to create the wherewithal for governments to resist pressures from protectionist domestic constituencies. From that perspective, allowing these transactions to occur in the public eye in effect amounts to giving protectionist interests a tool to eviscerate the effectiveness of the agreement. Domestic legislatures and – especially – courts have mechanisms such as the discretionary authority to receive amicus curiae briefs that might overcome some, but not necessarily all, of these objections.

Page 1304, C&Q #7. Greening the WTO. This note highlights the asymmetric character of trade agreements, which discipline environmental measures but have no minimum environmental standards. Consequently, the international trade regime will *always* operate to attenuate, and never to enhance, environmental protections. The proposal set out in the note is an attempt to respond to this asymmetry by identifying minimum standards of environmental performance which might operate through the dispute settlement mechanism. The WTO suite of agreements includes a Subsidies Code, <http://www.wto.org/english/docs_e/legal_e/24-scm_01_e.htm>. Identifying a failure to internalize environmental costs as an actionable subsidy would fit easily into that instrument as a legal (although definitely not as a political) matter. The harder part is determining when such an obligation has been violated, particularly since it would require the government of an importing state to obtain considerable information about the regulatory and market situation in a foreign country. The remedy is the imposition of an at-the-border fee whose magnitude is determined by the amount of the subsidy – a "countervailing duty." Quantifying the values of health and natural resources costs in a foreign country could be a daunting – but perhaps not insurmountable – methodological task. One principled question that has been identified is whether the baseline for evaluating those costs should be their values in the country of import or the country of export.

You as the teacher might find the following problem exercise a useful tool for enriching the students' active appreciation for the dynamics that drive the WTO. It has been set on separate pages so that you can photocopy and distribute it in class.

Trade and Environment Problem Exercise

The GATT tuna-dolphin report appeared to call into question the validity of major existing multilateral environmental agreements (MEAs) that rely on trade measures as regulatory tools. These include the trade provisions in the Montreal Protocol – discussed in Chapter 15 – the Convention on International Trade in Endangered Species (CITES) – the linchpin of international efforts to protect endangered species – and the Basel Convention on the Control of Transboundary Movements of Hazardous Wastes and Their Disposal –- the principal multilateral instrument governing international shipments of toxic waste. These agreements discriminate between trade with parties and with non-parties, sometimes to the point of prohibiting trade in CFCs, endangered species, or waste with non-parties, in an effort to enhance the environmental efficacy of the agreement and to create incentives for non-party states to accept the obligations of the agreement. Why and exactly how could restrictions on trade between non-parties and parties, all of them WTO members, violate the basic GATT/WTO disciplines?

Two solutions that have been suggested to the "MEA problem" are provided by GATT 1947 and NAFTA. The first is a "waiver" for specific multilateral environmental agreements employing trade measures, as provided in article XXV of GATT 1947:

Article XXV. Joint Action by the Contracting Parties

> 5. In exceptional circumstances not elsewhere provided for in this agreement, the CONTRACTING PARTIES may waive an obligation imposed upon a contracting party by this Agreement; Provided that any such decision shall be approved by a two-thirds majority of the votes cast and that such majority shall comprise more than half of the contracting parties. The CONTRACTING PARTIES may also by such a vote
>
> (i) define certain categories of exceptional circumstances to which other voting requirements shall apply for the waiver of obligations, and
>
> (ii) prescribe such criteria as may be necessary for the application of this paragraph.

The following is the text of article 104 of NAFTA:

Article 104. Relation to Environmental and Conservation Agreements

> 1. In the event of any inconsistency between this Agreement and the specific trade obligations set out in:
>
> (a) the Convention on International Trade in Endangered Species of Wild Fauna and Flora, done at Washington, March 3, 1973, as amended June 22, 1979,
>
> (b) the Montreal Protocol on Substances that Deplete the Ozone Layer, done at Montreal, September 16, 1987, as amended June 29, 1990,

(c) the Basel Convention on the Control of Transboundary Movements of Hazardous Wastes and Their Disposal, done at Basel, March 22, 1989, on its entry into force for Canada, Mexico and the United States,* or

(d) the agreements set out in Annex 104.1 [which you may assume currently contains no entries],

such obligations shall prevail to the extent of the inconsistency, provided that where a Party has a choice among equally effective and reasonably available means of complying with such obligations, the Party chooses the alternative that is the least inconsistent with the other provisions of this Agreement.

2. The Parties may agree in writing to modify Annex 104.1 to include any amendment to an agreement referred to in paragraph 1, and any other environmental or conservation agreement.

1. Identify the differences from a legal and policy perspectives in the operation and effect of these two approaches.

2. By identifying and analyzing different situations to which the two approaches might apply, discuss the relative merits and disadvantages of the two approaches in resolving the "MEA problem."

3. The Uruguay Round created a new WTO Committee on Trade and Environment which despite repeated attempts has been unable to reach agreement on a "legislative" solution to the "MEA problem." Assuming neither GATT Article XXV nor NAFTA Article 104 applies to a hypothetical dispute between a non-party and a party to the Montreal Protocol over the application of the trade provisions in that agreement, what role if any would the multilateral nature of the measures at issue play in applying Article XX?

4. To date, there have been no trade-based challenges to national measures relying on an MEA. Why do you think that is?

---

* Canada and Mexico are currently parties to the Basel Convention. The United States has signed but not ratified, and is consequently not yet a party to the Convention as of this writing.

Answers to Trade and Environment problem exercise. These MEAs distinguish between parties and non-parties specifically with respect to trade. As between parties and non-parties, both of which are WTO members, they consequently raise MFN and national treatment issues in a manner analogous to that discussed in the case of the tuna/dolphin dispute above. That is, the WTO obligations require parties to *refrain* from discrimination in a manner that is *required* by the MEAs. See C&Q #16, pages 765-766.

1 and 2. A waiver under GATT Article XXV is a quasi-legislative action which authorizes WTO members to engage in discrimination that would otherwise be prohibited. The two-thirds supermajority in effect puts a veto in the hands of a minority of WTO members. This provision has not been applied to any MEAs. By identifying some agreements by name, NAFTA appears to resolve the problem conclusively, at least with respect to those agreements, instead of leaving it to future action. The addition of new agreements, however, presumably must be accomplished by consensus (see C&Q #18, page 766). That means that the threshold for inclusion, at least in purely percentage terms, is actually *higher* in the case of NAFTA; any *one* party can veto the inclusion of a new agreement (as it presumably could have in the original negotiations). The actual political dynamics, of course, may be entirely different, since NAFTA has only 3 parties and the WTO, as of this writing, has 147 members.

3. Even though multilaterally-agreed measures may violate the basic disciplines of nondiscrimination, because they have been sifted through a process of multilateral consideration, and are therefore less likely to have been motivated by a Baptist-bootlegger dynamic (C&Q #3, page 1301), they are more likely qualify for the exceptions of Article XX. Specifically, they are more likely to be considered "necessary" to protect human, animal or plan life or health within the meaning of Article XX(b) or "relating to" the conservation of exhaustible natural resources in Article XX(g) (page 1299).

4. As discussed in the answer to question 3 above, the likelihood of success from a legal point of view is lower than in the case of a strictly unilateral measure with the same content. WTO panels are not courts, and according to some authorities apply a "sniff test" to identify questionable measures, explaining the result by reference to the legal tests in the agreements. For the reasons set out in the answer to question 3 above, multilaterally-agreed measures are less likely to "smell bad." Initiating a WTO dispute, moreover, requires the expenditure of some political capital in relations with other states. Even if a state is a not a party to an MEA, it may nonetheless conclude that the political costs of challenging the agreement are too high.

PART III
SUPPLEMENTARY MATERIALS

2D→3D EDITION CHAPTER CONCORDANCE

CHAPTER NUMBER IN 3D ED.	2D EDITION, CHAPTER EQUIVALENT[S]	
1	1	Introduction to environmental analysis & basic themes
2	1&2	History, and crosscutting themes: economics, risk, and politics
3	3	The common law in environmental law
4	4	Toxic torts, with a transition to public law
5	5	The development & structure of environmental public law
6	6	State-federal environmental regulatory issues
7	7	The administrative law of environmental law
8	*new*	The effect of int'l envt'l law on domestic law
9	13	Disclosure strategies: NEPA
10	[13]	Corporate disclosure: required production of information: EPCRA & TRIs
11	8	Regulatory standard-setting based on harm: the CAA; Envt'l justice
12	9	Regulatory standard-setting based on technology: the CWA
13	*new*	Regulatory standards based on cost-benefit analysis
14	16	Market-enlisting strategies: trading, and market incentives
15	10	Regulatory standard-setting based on technology-forcing — auto emissions regulations
16	14	Stark prohibition statutes: endangered species
17	15	Market-access controls: ToSCA and FIFRA
18	17	Life-cycle waste control strategies: RCRA
19	18	Remedial strategies: CERCLA
20	19	Environmental criminal prosecution
21	20, 21	Regulatory enforcement approaches; citizen enforcement; corporate compliance mechanisms; ADR
22	22	The public trust doctrine, and other rights & duties

23	**23**	Public rights and private property
24	**24**	Public resource management
25	**25**	Land use-based environmental protection, siting
26	**26**	International and comparative environmental law

2D→3D EDITION TRANSITION GUIDE (FOCUSING ON CHANGES)

Chapter Number in 3d Edition & Transition Notes	Changes, 2d→3d Edition Coverage
Chapter 1: Basic Themes in the Legal Process of Environmental Law	• §A. 1 adds Talbot Page (risk policy) from Chapter 2, and Miller on ecology: "Living in the Environment." • *Kepone* narrative is moved to Chapter 2. • *Smithfield* litigation is largely eliminated, *Gwaltney* appears as a note in Chapter 21. • Public Trust now appears almost entirely in Chapter 22 • Environmental Justice issues now are widely distributed: pp. 16, 63-64, 124, 245, 302, 374, 529, 604-611, 728, 733, and Chapter 25 exercises on Website.
Chapter 2. Cross-Cutting Themes in Environmental Law 2d edition Chapter 2 materials have been redistributed in the 3d edition.	• §A & B *Kepone* study and history, formerly Chapter 1B. §C Cross-cutting themes, formerly in Chapters 1&2. • Economics topics are largely eliminated as stand-alone segments and appear contextually in several places, including later in Chapter 2. • Benefit/cost analysis is now given extended treatment as a full new chapter, Chapter 13. • Sandman excerpt is now in Chapter 4 (p. 246); *Wilsonville* is now in Chapter 3 (p. 115); Page is now in Chapter 1 (p. 14); Huber is now in Chapter 4 (p. 271); EPA Risk Ranking is now in Chapter 4 (p. 279).
Chapter 3. The Common Law in Modern Environmental Law: Nonstatutory Causes of Action The order of materials has changed slightly.	• §A adds a new introduction to Torts • Nuisance cases now include *Wilsonville* (inserted after *Boomer*); *Dillon* is eliminated. • §C Now joins all causation issues and joint and several liability, now including *Velsicol v. Rowe* and *Pruitt v. Allied Chemical*
Chapter 4. The Special Challenges of Toxic Tort Litigation	• §B *Donaldson v. CIPS* is new principal case on causation, replacing *Ferebee*, which is now in notes. • §C Sandman on "outrage" is here (from Chapter 2) • §E Huber "Second Best" is here (from Chap. 2).
Chapter 5. The Development and Structure of Environmental Public Law In the 2d edition, this Chapter was entitled "Environmental Regulatory Statutes in Perspective"	• §A is the same, including the Laitos article and the *Utilex* case study. §B adds new material regarding the evolution of federal pollution control regulatory statutes and institutions, including excerpts from an article by Elliott, Ackerman, and Millian. "Race of Laxity" text from the 2d edition has been placed here.

Chapter 5, continued.	• §C included transferred material from §B of the 2d edition on the elements of environmental regulation. • §D is a new analysis of the concept of cooperative federalism, concentrating on the potential pitfalls of the federal-state partnership: A new case, *Save the Valley*, is added as well as excerpts from an article by Steinzor containing a case study of cooperative federalism in the context of a Maryland industrial facility. • §E discusses several alternatives to command and control regulation for environmental protection: The Latin/Ackerman-Stewart debate, which was included in Chapter 12 of the 2d edition, is included here, as well as new material on pollution prevention.
Chapter 6. Power Relationships Between Federal And State Governments in Environmental Regulation	• §B *Ass'n of Int'l Auto Mfgrs* replaced *PG&E* as principal preemption case. • §D *SWANCC* case is added in limits on federal power.
Chapter 7. The Administrative Law of Environmental Law	• §B very short excerpts from *Rybachek* and *Hill v. TVA* are added. • §D adds the Supreme Court's 2000 *Laidlaw* decision. • §F on proposed improvements to administrative process is moved to Chapter 21
Chapter 8. International Agreements as Domestic Environmental Law. This chapter is new material not having a counterpart in the 2d edition	• §A adds material on bilateral treaties • §B adds material on the global commons, including multilateral treaties, executive agreements, and trade agreements and organizations (e.g., WTO, GATT, & NAFTA) and including a new proincipal case, *George E. Warren Corp. v. EPA.*
Chapter 9. Federal Agency Disclosure: NEPA's Stop-and-Think Logic, and the Power of Information Chapter 9 was Chapter 13 in the 2d edition. The corporate disclosure material is shifted to the new Chapter 10	• §§A and B are updated and rearranged versions of §§A and B of the 2d edition. The focus is still on the *Chicod Creek* case study and the *Kleppe* case. • §C contains a major new section on the international implications of NEPA, a subject which was touched upon in several places in the 2d edition. The *Public Citizen* case is featured in this section. This new section is another example of the enhanced importance accorded to international environmental law.
Chapter 10. Corporate Disclosure: Shaping Private Response by Required Production of Information	• §A & B are the materials taken from 2d edition Chapter 13 §D, a new principal case under Prop. 65, *Nicolle-Wagner v. Deukmejian,* is added.

Chapter 10, continued. Chapter 10 was Chapter 13 §D in the 2d edition.	• §C on 1st Amendment Challenges to regulation of information is new.
Chapter 11. Harm-Based Ambient Standards: The Clean Air Act Chapter 11 was chapter 8 in the 2d edition.	• §C 2 is renamed to reflect the emphasis on setting standards and two new principal cases, *American Trucking v. EPA* and *Whitman v. American Trucking* are added. • §D 4 now moves the *CARE v. EPA* case forward ahead of the environmental justice materials. • §E on prescribing attainment adds a new principal case: *Whitman v. American Trucking*.
Chapter 12. Technology-Based Standard-Setting: The Clean Water Act Chapter 12 was Chapter 9 in the 2d edition.	• §§A, B, and C are updates of the same sections of Chapter 9 of the 2d edition, with the focus still on the *Rybachek* and *Atlantic States Legal Foundation* cases. • §D contains a major expansion of its counterpart in the 2d edition, which dealt with water quality-based permitting. A new principal case, *Sierra Club v. EPA*, is included along with an enhanced discussion and evaluation of the TMDL process. §E is revised. • §F is a slightly expanded version of the *Average River* hypothetical.
Chapter 13. Standard-Setting via Cost-Benefit Procedures Parts of this chapter is new material not having a counterpart in the 2d edition, the remainder is gathered from several places	• §A Moves the material on ToSCA here from Chapter 15 of the 2d edition and introduces *Corrosion Proof Fittings* as a principal case. • §B 1 introduces new material on cost-benefit analysis, including an excerpt from Ackerman & Heinzerling • §§B 2 & # gives a pro and con view of cost benefit. standards including the principal case of *American Trucking v, Browner* and a further excerpt from Ackerman & Heinzerling. • §C adds materials on formal cost benefits analysis, using an example from the Safe Drinking Water Act and the arsenic standard. • §D adds material on the use of cost benefit analysis by OMB/OIRA.
Chapter 14. Market-Enlisting Statutory Strategies: Pollution Trading and Other Economic Incentives Chapter 14 was Chapter 16 in the 2d edition	• This chapter is substantially revised, the only remaining elements are the behavior assumptions table (p. 746 2d ed) and the Title IV acid rain material that is now §A. All else is new.

Chapter 14, continued.	• §B includes an excerpt from the Pew Center evaluating Title IV and other trading regimes as a foundation for GHG trading. • §C reviews the South Coast (Los Angeles region) trading program and includes an excerpt from Drury, et al, critical of the trading program. • §D examines trading as a means of achieving water quality improvements and includes an excerpt from the EPA water trading policy.
Chapter 15. Technology-Forcing Standards Chapter 15 was Chapter 10 in the 2d edition	• This chapter contains virtually the same coverage, in an updated fashion, as its counterpart in the 2d edition, with the focus still on the *International Harvester* case and the Wetstone et al. and Shimberg articles. The material on international technology-forcing, in the context of the Montreal Protocol, has been expanded.
Chapter 16. Roadblock Strategies: Stark Prohibitions and Their Viability Chapter 16 was Chapter 14 in the 2d edition	• This chapter has been reorganized, the Delaney clause materials have been shortened, eliminating the *Les v. Reilly*, and the Kimm excerpt. • §A now addresses Delaney and the concept of roadblocks. • §B now contains both snail darter (*Hill v. TVA*) and spotted owl (*Seattle Audubon* and *Sweet Home*) cases • §C now addresses "bypasses" of roadblocks including the "God" committee and §10 incidental takes.
Chapter 17. Product Regulation and Market-Access Strategies: Pesticides and Toxics Chapter 17 was Chapter 15 in the 2d edition	• This chapter is largely unchanged.
Chapter 18. Life-Cycle Waste Control Strategies: RCRA's "Cradle-to-Grave" Regulation Chapter 18 was Chapter 17 in the 2d edition	• This chapter is largely unchanged.
Chapter 19. Remedial Liability Strategies: Toxic Cleanups and Their Funding Under CERCLA and State Programs Chapter 19 was Chapter 18 in the 2d edition	• §A 5 on corporate liabilities is inserted and adds the principal case *US v. Best Foods.*

Chapter 20. Environmental Criminal Law Chapter 20 was Chapter 19 in the 2d edition	• §E the principal case of *US v. Rutana* is replaced by the principal case of *US v. Hansen.*
Chapter 21. Evolving Patterns of Enforcement and Compliance Chapter 21: Chapters 20 & 21 in the 2d edition	• The former introductory materials have been made into §A, and the remaining sections renumbered. • §B 5 is imported from Chapter 7 2d edition. • §C the Guana excerpt is omitted. • §D The ADR and "reg-neg" materials are imported here. • §E 3 the corporate retrospective and Anderberg excerpt are eliminated.
Chapter 22. Public Environmental Rights and Duties: The Public Trust Doctrine	• 2d edition §A on federal constitutional rights and *Tanner v. Armco Steel* are eliminated. • With the elimination of 2d edition §A, the sections are renumbered. • §A *Marks v. Whitney* is imported from 2d edition Chapter 1.
Chapter 23. Private Property and Public Rights: Constitutional Limits on Physical and Regulatory Takings	• §B 2 contains new material that canvasses several major US Supreme court cases, including the more recent cases *Lucas, Palazzolo,* & *Tahoe-Sierra;* plus *K&K Enterprises,* a state wetlands case. • §C 4 d *Eastern Enterprises v. Apfel* has been added as a principal case.
Chapter 24: Public Resources Management Statutes	• This chapter is an updated version of its counterpart in the 2d edition, and includes the same cases and articles.
Chapter 25. Land Use-Based Environmental Protection Statutes	• §§A, B, C, D, and E are updated versions of their counterparts in the 2d edition. • §E is a new section focusing on the "Smart Growth Movement" and its environmental implications. An article by Pollard describes the Smart Growth Movement and discusses its innovative nature and drawbacks.
Chapter 26. International and Comparative Environmental Law	• This material replaces former Chapter 26 • §A addresses international customary law and introduces excerpts from the *Trail Smelter* arbitration. • §B addresses international conferences and "soft law" using excerpts from the Rio Declaration. • §C addresses comparative environmental law using excerpts from *Mehta v. Union of India.* • § D addresses multinational agreements and includes materials on the UNFCCC and the Kyoto Protocol including Bodansky on US climate policy.

Chapter 26, continued.	• §E addresses international institutions including materials on the World Bank's Qinghai Project and the WTO tuna import restrictions.

A MODEL COURSE AND PAPER PROSPECTUS: WITH A FIELD OBSERVATION AND PAPER ASSIGNMENT

ENVIRONMENTAL LAW, Course No. ____

COURSE PROSPECTUS: (Date)

Prof. ____ Office: ____ Email: _____ Office hours:_______ Class Website__________

4 credit hours* —** based on an ***exam, class exercises & participation (incl. a field observation exercise), ***& a short research paper.***

Books: *required*: Plater et al., Envtl Law & Policy: Nature, Law & Society ("*NLS,*" Aspen 2004); *suggested*: Anderson & Hirsch, Envtl Law Practice ("*ELP,*" North Carolina, 2d edition 2003)

Exam: Objective technical multiple-choice, 90 minutes, weighed into final score as 1.5 credit

---

Class participation & exercises, factored as 1/2 credit hour— ***Simulation exercises* from *ELP,*** and ***Field observation assignment:*** a required one-page memo, due November 5, factored into grade as part of class participation. During the term go observe a formal or informal meeting or hearing outside the law school involving contending parties in some environmental controversy — a negotiation, legislative or administrative agency hearing, or the like, but **not** a court proceeding — preparing a *one-page* memo report noting the underlying policy analysis, the players, the tactics, the contending policy issues as argued, and the way in which the law or legal analysis figured in the matter.

Short research paper: weighted as 2 credits; due 5 PM ___ or at any time prior to then, at ___. ***Please register your chosen paper topic on the topic pre-emption list kept at the Reserve Desk under "Environmental Law, Topix Registry."***

This paper is where you can do your best individualized work. I will suggest some possible topics and would be pleased to offer continued suggestions during the course of the term. Topics should be checked initially with me. Citations in any form you want (but note that you may want to use the paper as a research and writing sample, so standard citation form may be useful.)

The paper will be limited to 4000 words of text and footnotes [please note total word count at end of paper]. Each paper should have a bibliography of cases and sources used (not included in the allotted word count.)

The paper should be an examination of an interesting ***legal*** question arising somewhere in the field of environmental law. It should not be a description of a fact situation or policy decision, but rather an analysis of a chosen legal issue. Facts and policy discussions necessarily will be included, but only as required initially to set up the legal question (no more than a couple of pages). The legal question chosen should be narrow so that you can make a searching inquiry and presentation within the confines of the space limitation.

The paper should develop a legal analysis of the issue, its legal implications and correlatives, identify trends in case law that are helpful to the analysis, etc., and provide a working conclusion. In other words it should resemble a memorandum of law written for the chief counsel of a legislative committee, for the senior partner of a firm, for an agency chief counsel, etc. To strike the desired tone of incisive analysis, you should write the paper so as to *wrestle with the issue in depth, as if you were advising someone actually planning to use your analysis* as a basis for taking action, and that *opposing parties will forcefully oppose* your positions and test your legal assertions. Since this exercise is intended to develop your knowledge of the area, the question chosen must be one that is now or potentially subject to legal controversy where the law needs the benefit of your thinking (i.e., not a pushover question that has a ready answer).

Your perspective may be that of environmental plaintiffs or defendants, or otherwise. (In each case you have to anticipate all serious opposing arguments on point.) Do not write your analysis as if your reader already knows each case you cite. In presentation, your analysis and argument must be succinct and to the point because of the shortened format. This form of legal research paper typically contains the equivalent substance of a 25-page "term paper." The easiest way to do this is to make the paper a heavily-edited second or third draft. *The page limit and paper deadline will be strictly adhered to* so that all can rely on a level playing field.

The coursebook website is:

http://www.bc.edu/schools/law/library/coursebook/envtlaw/

DRAFT SYLLABI

SYLLABUS A: A GENERIC, ALL-INCLUSIVE CAFETERIA MENU SYLLABUS

TEACHERS:

- *Underlines indicate notes to teachers of choices that can be made in designing assignments.*

*** *Asterisked chapters: These are the core chapters that are taught by most of us co-authors; we consider them basically important chapters for the course, to which a selection of other chapters are added.]*

~~~~~~

ENVIRONMENTAL LAW

Course # ______

DRAFT ASSIGNMENT SHEET **[date]**

PAGE BLOCKS IN "NLS"- Plater, Abrams, Goldfarb, Graham, Heinzerling & Wirth, ENVIRONMENTAL LAW & POLICY: NATURE, LAW & SOCIETY [Aspen, 3d ed. 2004] coursebook Website: **http://www.bc.edu/schools/law/library/coursebook/envtlaw**

UNLESS NOTED AS "ELP"- Anderson & Hirsch, ENVIRONMENTAL LAW PRACTICE: PROBLEMS AND EXERCISES FOR SKILLS DEV'T, [Carolina Press, 2d edition 2003.]

- "*Skim*" means that students will not be expected to retain details from these skim assignment pages.
- Some assignments may be studied over two class sessions

Course temp. website: ________; WebCT: ________

Assignment	Chapter:		
1.		INTRODUCTION TO LIFE AND LAW IN A GLOBAL COMMONS	
	1	*Skim* xxxi , 3–21:	Introduction.
		Read 27-35:	Hardin's Tragedy of the Commons.
		[and/or 35-41?:	A Salty Environmental Paradigm?]
2.	2	ENVTL LAW HISTORY & A CLASSIC ENVTL CASE	
[Assmt #3 could be incorporated into #2]		*Skim* 42-47:	A quick overview history.
		48-65:	Allied Chemical and Kepone: Envtl Law, the first generation.
		• Begin reading Harr, A CIVIL ACTION, or rent the video.	
3.	2	CURRENT STRUCTURE OF ENVIRONMENTAL LAW	
		65-77:	17 Modern Statutes: If Allied's Kepone case were happening today…
		Note pp. 469-470; Ref. pages 5-13, 48-61 at back of coursebook: (acronyms! statutes).	
		Skim 82-85:	Sectors of environmental law activity.
		[85-88:	The three economies.]
		[88-94:	Reform critiques.]
		96-102:	The basic themes of environmental law & policy.
~~~~~~

Class	Ch.	Pages	Topic
4. [can be 2 days]	3		THE ROLE OF TORT LAW
	**	107-115:	The classic *Boomer* case.
		[115-124:	The *Wilsonville* case.]
		125-134:	Public nuisance cases: *Schenectady & Spur*.
		[134-145:	Trespass; Neglig. and Strict Liability.]
			DEFENSES, LIABILITY, and REMEDIES IN ENVIRONMENTAL COMMON LAW
		146-152:	An array of defenses.
		[152-162:	Causation and other liability issues.]
		163-185:	Remedy issues, equitable and monetary.
		[185-194:	Natural resource remedies.]
5. [can be 2 days]	4		TOXIC TORTS: BEYOND THE TRADITIONAL COMMON LAW SETTING
	**	200-226; Harr, A CIVIL ACTION:	The Woburn toxic contamination case.
		265-267:	a Woburn toxics chronological timeline.
		[Handout:	a Rule 16 FRCP Pre-trial Conference on the *Woburn toxics* case; second-guess its case preparation as if each student is an attorney for one of the parties.]
		[227-265:	Problems of complex causation, science & statistics, outrage, and problems of multiplicity: class actions and joint and several liability.]
		[271-280:	Risk and risk management theories.]
6.	5,		PUBLIC LAW: STATE-FEDERAL RELATIONS IN ENVTL REGULATION
		Skim 287-302:	*Utilex*: a state permitting regime and the push to federalize.
	6	302-319:	Regulatory basics; the "race to the bottom" and other problems with cooperative federalism.
		322-340:	Preemption in environmental law.
		341-351:	Dormant commerce clause: federal limits on states.
		351-375:	10th Amendment and other state limits on federal regulation.
7.	7		THE ADMINISTRATIVE LAW OF ENVIRONMENTAL LAW
	**	376-387:	Basics: Administrative law over time and in a nutshell.
		388-402:	The classic *Overton Park* case; the strategics of citizen enforcement.
		[402-418:	The law and tension of citizen standing to enforce statutes.]
		[418-428:	*Vermont Yankee* & citizen attempts to increase admin. procedures.]
		[428-434:	*Chevron*, and judicial deference to agency interpretations of law.
8.	8		INTERNATIONAL AGREEMENTS AS DOMESTIC LAW
		435-443, map 464:	Bilateral treaties; migratory birds.
		445-454:	Multilateral treaties; whales.
		454-467:	Environment and trade agreements.

9. [can be 2 days]	9 **	NEPA, THE NATIONAL ENVIRONMENTAL POLICY ACT	
		471-512:	a classic NEPA case: Chicod Creek, *NRDC v. Grant*; NEPA basics.
		Skim 513-522:	Further developments with NEPA.
		523-527:	NEPA's international implications.
10.	10	REQUIRED PRODUCTION OF CORPORATE INFORMATION	
		528-534:	EPCRA and TRIs.
		534-541:	California Prop. 65.
		542-550:	First Amendment issues.
11.		CAA, THE CLEAN AIR ACT, AMBIENT HARM STANDARDS [11-13: Assignment format WITH SIMULATION EXERCISES]	
		551-564:	CAA basics.
		740:	CAA §202(b)(1): cf. the auto emissions approach.
		ELP 1-52; do Probs. 1.1 to 1.6.	
12.		CAA, continued…	
		564-596:	The national commons and federal standards; ambient harm standards as the threshold of regulation.
		ELP 52-70, do Probs. 1.7-1.11.	
13.		CAA, continued…	
		596-619:	Non attainment, PSD, and transboundary issues.
		ELP Exercise 1.1, page 58.	
11a. [can be 2 days]	11 **	THE CLEAN AIR ACT, AMBIENT HARM STANDARDS [Herewith: Assignment with no Simulation Exercises]	
		551-603:	CAA basics: the national commons and federal standards; harm as the threshold of regulation; SIP permitting.
		740:	CAA §202(b)(1): cf. the auto emissions approach.
		Skim 604-611:	CAA and environmental justice.
		611-619:	Problems of attainment, PSD, and transboundary issues.
14. [can be 2 days]	12 **	TECH-BASED STANDARDS AND THE CWA	
		674-675:	The Average River.
		620-644:	CWA basics.
		644-655:	Stormwater, POTWs, toxics.
		655-673:	Water-quality-based standards, non-point discharges.
15. optional simulation	21	CITIZEN ENFORCEMENT — CWA	
		1027-1042:	Citizen enforcement background.
		ELP142-151, 154-173, do Probs. 2.7, 2.8, 2.9:	a citizen enforcement simulation.
16.	13	STANDARD-SETTING BY COST-BENEFIT ANALYSIS?	
		676-687:	CBA basics.
		Skim 687-700:	CBA, pro and con.
		700-706:	CBA in the CWA.
		707-711:	CBA as anti-regulatory tactic at the Bush II OMB.

17.	14	MARKET-ENLISTING REGULATORY STRATEGIES 712-736: Trading pollution credits; basics and problems. 736-742: Trading in water pollution credits.
18.	15	TECHNOLOGY-FORCING STANDARDS 743-771: 2 case studies: automobile emissions, and stratospheric ozone.
19.	16	ROADBLOCKS, AND THE 1973 ENDANGERED SPECIES ACT 772-788, 798-802: Roadblocks, ESA §7, the snail darter, and the God Squad. 788-797, 802-806: Spotted owls, ESA §9 "takes," and the §10 bypass. 807-815: "Slippage" and the roadblock approach, in perspective.
20.	17	MARKET ACCESS REGULATION 816-844: Pesticides & FIFRA; Toxics & ToSCA: a comparison.
21.	18	RCRA'S LIFE-CYCLE WASTE REGULATION 845-881: RCRA basics; RCRA; the "land ban" and the use of "hammers" to control agency action. 881-885: Citizen enforcement of RCRA.
22. optional simulation	[18] 21	ENFORCEMENT: THE GOVT & CORPORATE ROLES *Skim* 1049-1061: Corporate impetus to self-generated compliance. *Skim* ELP 71-82: Enforcement basics. ELP 83-111: Quality Wood Products case simulation.
23.	**19** **	REMEDIAL STRATEGIES: CERCLA 886-923: Toxic contamination and federal statutory liabilities. 931-940: The official cleanup process. *Skim* ELP 178-192: noting Shenandoah site, 183-188. Do Problem 3.1, 188.
24.	**19**	MORE CERCLA 923-931, 945-954: CERCLA cost allocation and cost recovery. ELP 228-232, ELP 192-200: Liability problems; do [Problem 3.2, p. 193, choose one party] or [Exercise 3.2(a, b, c, d, e, or f)(choose one) pages 220-228].
25.	20	ENVIRONMENTAL CRIMINAL LAW 957-998: The 1899 Refuse Act, *Film Recovery;* What kind of criminal intent is required to convict? Executive and corporation liability; prosecutorial use of sentencing guidelines.
25.	**21** **	SYSTEMIC ENFORCEMENT STRATEGIES 999-1041, 1049-1061: Governmental and citizen enforcement issues; corporate self-generated compliance issues.
26.	**22** **	PUBLIC RIGHTS & DUTIES: THE PUBLIC TRUST DOCTRINE 1065-1104: Applying the modern public trust doctrine. 1104-1111: Public environmental rights from constitutions & statutes.

27. [can be 2 days]	**23**	PRIVATE PROPERTY & PUBLIC RIGHTS		
			1112-1115:	Five basic inquiries in reviewing public-private prop. conflicts.
			1116-1127:	Eminent domain condemnations & inverse condemnation actions.
			1127-1167:	The roller coaster of regulatory takings litigation.
			1167-1177:	More substantive due process issues.
28.	**24**	PUBLIC LANDS & RESOURCES		
			1178-1215:	A survey of public lands and resources issues.
29.	**25**	LANDUSE-BASED ENVIRONMENTAL PROTECTION		
			1216-1254:	A survey of land use issues including Smart Growth.
30.	**25**	ENVIRONMENTAL JUSTICE: A SYSTEMIC CHALLENGE, and ADR		
	21		1224-1233:	The problem of siting facilities for toxic waste disposal.
	[11]		1042-1049:	ADR: alternative dispute resolution processes.
[optional simulation]			*Handout:*	*Mullis Toxics*, a negotiation simulation.
31.	**26**	GLOBAL ENVIRONMENTAL LAW		
			1256-1270:	International environmental law basics.
			1270-1275:	Comparative environmental law
			1275-1305:	Multilateral agreements.
			1290-1305:	International organizations, and trade/environment tensions.
[optional exercises]			*Handout:*	Two simulations: World Bank Exercise, Trade and Envt Exercise.
32.		CONTEMPLATION OF THE WHOLE		
			1-1311:	Everything connected to everything.

SYLLABUS B: A SYLLABUS DESIGNED FROM THE CAFETERIA MENU OF SYLLABUS A

~~~~~~

ENVIRONMENTAL LAW

Course # ______

DRAFT ASSIGNMENT SHEET **[date]**

PAGE BLOCKS IN "NLS"- Plater, Abrams, Goldfarb, Graham, Heinzerling & Wirth, ENVIRONMENTAL LAW & POLICY: NATURE, LAW & SOCIETY [Aspen, 3d ed. 2004] coursebook Website: **http://www.bc.edu/schools/law/library/coursebook/envtlaw**

***UNLESS NOTED AS* "ELP"**- Anderson & Hirsch, ENVIRONMENTAL LAW PRACTICE: PROBLEMS AND EXERCISES FOR SKILLS DEV'T, [Carolina Press, 2d edition 2003.]

- "*Skim*" means that students will not be expected to retain details from these skim assignment pages.
- Some assignments may be studied over two class sessions
- Assignment numbers in (parentheses) are to be subject to student option
  [only 7 of the 10 parenthesed assignments can be covered in the semester hours available.]

Two classes a week, each class 100 minutes WebCT: https://webct.bc.edu

Assignment	Chapter:		
1.		INTRODUCTION TO LIFE AND LAW IN A GLOBAL COMMONS	
	1	*Skim* xxxi , 3–21:	Introduction.
		Read 27-35:	Hardin's Tragedy of the Commons.
		35-41:	A Salty Environmental Paradigm.
2.	2	ENVTL LAW HISTORY & A CLASSIC ENVTL CASE	
		Skim 42-47:	A quick overview history.
		48-65:	Allied Chemical and Kepone: Envtl Law, the first generation.
		65-77:	17 Modern Statutes: If Allied's Kepone case were happening today…
		Note pp. 469-470; Ref. pages 5-13, 48-61 at back of coursebook: (acronyms! statutes)	
		96-102:	The basic themes of environmental law & policy.
		• Begin reading Harr, A CIVIL ACTION, or rent the video.	
3.	3	THE ROLE OF TORT LAW	
		107-115:	The classic *Boomer* case.
		115-124:	The *Wilsonville* case.
		125-134:	Public nuisance cases: *Schenectady & Spur.*
4.	3	DEFENSES, LIABILITY, and REMEDIES IN ENVIRONMENTAL COMMON LAW	
		146-152:	An array of defenses.
		152-162:	Causation and other liability issues.
		163-185:	Remedy issues, equitable and monetary.
		185-194:	Natural resource remedies.
~~~~~~

5. **4** TOXIC TORTS: BEYOND THE TRADITIONAL COMMON LAW SETTING

200-226; Harr, A CIVIL ACTION: The Woburn toxic contamination case.
265-267: a Woburn toxics chronological timeline.
Handout: a Rule 16 FRCP Pre-trial Conference on the *Woburn toxics* case; second-guess its case preparation as if each student is an attorney for one of the parties.

---

6. **4** MORE ON TOXICS LITIGATION, AND INTRO TO PUBLIC LAW

227-265: Problems of complex causation, science & statistics, outrage, and problems of multiplicity: class actions and joint and several liability.
5
265-271: a comparative transition to public law.
271-280: Risk and risk management theories.
Skim 287-302: *Utilex*: a state permitting regime and the push to federalize.

---

7. **[5]** THE ADMINISTRATIVE PROCESS & LAW OF ENVIRONMENTAL LAW

376-387: Basics: Administrative law over time and in a nutshell.
7 302-319: Regulatory basics; the "race to the bottom" and other problems with cooperative federalism.
388-402: The classic *Overton Park* case; the strategics of citizen enforcement.
402-418: The law and tension of citizen standing to enforce statutes.

---

8. **9** NEPA, THE NATIONAL ENVIRONMENTAL POLICY ACT

471-512: a classic NEPA case: Chicod Creek, *NRDC v. Grant*; NEPA basics.
Skim 513-522: Further developments with NEPA.
523-527: NEPA's international implications.

(9.) **10** REQUIRED PRODUCTION OF CORPORATE INFORMATION

528-534: EPCRA and TRIs.
534-541: California Prop. 65.

---

10. **11** CAA, THE CLEAN AIR ACT, AMBIENT HARM STANDARDS

551-564: CAA basics.
740: CAA §202(b)(1): cf. the auto emissions approach.
ELP 1-52; do Probs. 1.1 to 1.6.

---

11. **11** CAA, continued...

564-596: The national commons and federal standards; ambient harm standards as the threshold of regulation.
ELP 52-70, do Probs. 1.7-1.11.

---

12. **11** CAA, continued...

596-619: Non attainment, PSD, and transboundary issues.
ELP Exercise 1.1, page 58.

---

13. **12** TECH-BASED STANDARDS AND THE CWA

674-675: The Average River.
620-644: CWA basics.
655-673: Water-quality-based standards, non-point discharges.

14.	**21**	CITIZEN ENFORCEMENT – CWA 1027-1042: Citizen enforcement background. ELP142-151, 154-173, do Probs. 2.7, 2.8, 2.9: a citizen enforcement simulation.
(15.)	**13**	STANDARD-SETTING BY COST-BENEFIT ANALYSIS? 676-687: CBA basics. *Skim* 687-700: CBA, pro and con. 700-706: CBA in the CWA. 707-711: CBA as anti-regulatory tactic at the Bush II OMB.
(17.)	**14**	MARKET-ENLISTING REGULATORY STRATEGIES 712-736: Trading pollution credits; basics and problems. 736-742: Trading in water pollution credits.
(18.)	**15**	TECHNOLOGY-FORCING STANDARDS 743-771: 2 case studies: automobile emissions, and stratospheric ozone.
19.	**16**	ROADBLOCKS, AND THE 1973 ENDANGERED SPECIES ACT 772-788, 798-802: Roadblocks, ESA §7, the snail darter, and the God Squad. 788-797, 802-806: Spotted owls, ESA §9 "takes," and the §10 bypass. 807-815: "Slippage" and the roadblock approach, in perspective.
(20.)	**17**	MARKET ACCESS REGULATION 816-844: Pesticides & FIFRA; Toxics & ToSCA: a comparison.
21.	**18**	RCRA'S LIFE-CYCLE WASTE REGULATION 845-881: RCRA basics; RCRA; the "land ban" and the use of "hammers" to control agency action. 881-885: Citizen enforcement of RCRA.
22.	**[18]** **21**	ENFORCEMENT: THE GOVT & CORPORATE ROLES *Skim* 1049-1061: Corporate impetus to self-generated compliance. *Skim* ELP 71-82: Enforcement basics. ELP 83-111: Quality Wood Products case simulation.
23.	**19**	REMEDIAL STRATEGIES: CERCLA 886-923: Toxic contamination and federal statutory liabilities. 931-940: The official cleanup process. *Skim* ELP 178-192: noting Shenandoah site, 183-188. Do Problem 3.1, 188.
24.	**19**	MORE CERCLA 923-931, 945-954: CERCLA cost allocation and cost recovery ELP 228-232, ELP 192-200: Liability problems; do [Problem 3.2, p. 193, choose one party] or [Exercise 3.2(a, b, c, d, e, or f)(choose one) pages 220-228].
(25.)	**20**	ENVIRONMENTAL CRIMINAL LAW 957-998: The 1899 Refuse Act, *Film Recovery;* What kind of criminal intent is required to convict? Executive and corporation liability; prosecutorial use of sentencing guidelines.

26.	**22**	PUBLIC RIGHTS & DUTIES: THE PUBLIC TRUST DOCTRINE	
		1065-1104:	Applying the modern public trust doctrine.
		1104-1111:	Public environmental rights from constitutions & statutes.
(27.)	**23**	PRIVATE PROPERTY & PUBLIC RIGHTS	
		1112-1115:	Five basic inquiries in reviewing public-private prop. conflicts.
		(1116-1127:	Eminent domain condemnations & inverse condemnation actions.)
		1127-1167:	The roller coaster of regulatory takings litigation.
		(1167-1177:	More substantive due process issues.)
(28.)	**24**	PUBLIC LANDS & RESOURCES	
		1178-1215:	A survey of public lands and resources issues.
(29.)	**25**	LANDUSE-BASED ENVIRONMENTAL PROTECTION	
		1216-1254:	A survey of land use issues including Smart Growth.
30.	**25**	ENVIRONMENTAL JUSTICE: A SYSTEMIC CHALLENGE, and ADR	
	21	1224-1233:	The problem of siting facilities for toxic waste disposal.
	[11]	1042-1049:	ADR: alternative dispute resolution processes.
		Handout:	Mullis Toxics, a negotiation simulation.
(31.)	**26**	GLOBAL ENVIRONMENTAL LAW	
		1256-1270:	International environmental law basics.
		(1270-1275:	Comparative environmental law.)
		1275-1305:	Multilateral agreements.
		1290-1305:	International organizations, and trade/environment tensions.
		Handout:	Two simulated exercises: World Bank Exercise, Trade and Environment Exercise.
32.		CONTEMPLATION OF THE WHOLE	
		1-1311:	Everything connected to everything.

SYLLABUS C: A BASIC SYLLABUS FOR TEACHING THE COURSEBOOK ALONG WITH REGULATORY EXERCISES

~~~~~~

ENVIRONMENTAL LAW

Course # _______

DRAFT ASSIGNMENT SHEET **[date]**

Assigned readings in:

NLS: Plater, et al., Envtl Law & Policy: Nature, Law & Society, 3d edition, 2004
ELP: Jerry Anderson & Dennis Hirsch, Environmental Law Practice, 2nd Edition (Carolina Academic Press 2003, ISBN 0-89089-276-8)

CLASS	TOPIC	NLS PAGES (teachers will want to reduce some of the selections according to their preferences)	ELP PAGES & PROBLEMS
1	Introduction	Skim Chapters 1 and 2. Read for discussion, 14-21, 27-35, 42-48, 65-77, 271-280	xxi-xxii
2	Common Law Torts	103-134	
3		134-163, 171-185	
4	Toxic Torts	200-227	
5		227-248	
6	Environmental Public Law	281-322	
7	Federalism	323-349, skim 351-375	
8	Administrative Law	376-402, 428-434	235-247
9	Air: Overview and Finding Law	551-564	1-52; Problems 1.1 to 1.6 inclusive
10	Air: Ambient Standards	564-596	52-70; Problems 1.7-1.11 inclusive
11	Air: Non Attainment, PSD, Interstate Transfer	596-619	Exercise 1.1, page 58
12	Water: Technology-Based Standards	620-655	
13	Water: Water Quality-Based standards	655-675	
14	Cost-Benefit Standards	676-711	
15	Market-Enlisting Strategies	712-742	
16	Enforcement Overview	999-1016	96-101, 71-84; Problem 2.1
17	Compliance and Enforcement	1049-1061	84-96; 101-109 Problems 2.2-2.5 inclusive
18	EPCRA and Penalty	528-534	120-141; Exercise 2.1(b),
~~~~~~

	Calculation		page 126
19	Citizen Suits	1027-1042	141-173; Problems 2.7-2.9 inclusive
20	Land: Disposal	845-853, 857-873	
21	Land: Cleanup	886-888, 931-945	175-192; Problem 3.1 (based on skim of HRS)
22	CERCLA Liability	888-923	192-200, Problem 3.2 (limit to one party per student)
23	CERCLA Cost Allocation	923-927	208-228; Exercise 3.2(a, b, c, d, e, or f) pages 220-228 (limit to one per student)
24	CERCLA Cost Recovery Games	927-931, 945-954	228-232
25	NEPA	471-513	
26	Endangered Species	775-788, 794-815	
27	Takings of Property	1127-1165	
28	Public Trust	1065-1077, 1080-1104	

Integrating these two books is a bit of a challenge. The regulatory areas of air, water, and toxics, and the subject of regulatory compliance are featured in both books, with the coursebook studying basic design and evolution of the statutes in Parts Three and Four, and Environmental Law Practice (ELP) focusing on hands-on regulatory interpretation. Before you attempt to use this syllabus, please be advised that this is a very ambitious set of assignments that works the students very hard. Further, the students must be advised to start (or at least look over) the ELP assignments ahead of time so that they have adequate time to complete them. The effort required for different ELP exercises differs greatly. ELP Exercise 2.1(b), for example, (in RHA's opinion the best of the problems), is far more demanding than any other and needs a bit of class time in advance to make sure the students are on the right track in finding the materials that they will need. You may wish to have some of the ELP problems be prepared for discussion only and not handed in. This will reduce the student workload and your own grading workload (which is monumental in the event that you get a large class). You also will find that the Exercises, and some of the problems, cannot be done at this pace without modification to simplify them a bit. For example, my class was given the witness information packets and did not try to develop their information by interview of role playing witnesses. As a trade off for the amount of work that went into submission of so many of the ELP problems, for example, no final examination was given. The class was a 3-credit class, taught twice per week.

SOME USEFUL WEBSITES

- EPA Envirofacts Homepage http://www.epa.gov/enviro/index_java.html
- EPA Headquarters http://www.epa.gov/
- EPA Superfund page http://www.epa.gov/superfund/
- Federal Register Main Page http://www.gpoaccess.gov/fr/index.html
- National Register of Historic Places, National Park Service
  http://www.cr.nps.gov/nr/
- Underground Storage Tank Query Tool - Query Page
  http://db.state.ma.us/Dfs/ustQueryPage.asp
- U S Army COE Home Page http://www.usace.army.mil/
- www.energypromotion.net - Energy industry reports, maps, books, and information products, with more than 60 free reports. Opt-in to receive regular updates on new information products.
- www.gasandoil.com/ogel - Oil, Gas, and Energy Law Intelligence. Focuses on recent developments in oil, gas, and energy law, with a regular newsletter that provides commentary, insights, digests of official reports, and references to selected literature.
- www.infomine.com - A comprehensive site for mining news around the world.
- www.ocsbbs.com - OCS Bulletin Board System. Tracks critical information on the Gulf of Mexico in a user-friendly format on an ongoing basis, including a just-released Non-Required Filings Database.

Some links to organizations with whom we co-sponsor conferences on a periodic basis:

- www.abanet.org/environ - Section of Environment, Energy, and Resources, American Bar Association
- www.aipn.org - Association of International Petroleum Negotiators
- www.cailaw.org/iel - Institute for Energy Law, The Center for American and international Law.
- www.emlf.org - Energy & Mineral Law Foundation.
- www.ibanet.org/serl/index.asp - Section on Energy & Natural Resources Law, International Bar Association
- www.rmmlf.org/geninfo/links.htm Rocky Mountain Mineral Law Foundation's links page.

"A Selected Guide to Environmental, Energy and Natural Resources Law on the Web" http://www.law.gwu.edu/burns/research/envtl/envtl_toc.htm This invaluable resource offers descriptions and Web links to free sites with statutes, regulations, cases, etc. You can use the guide as a web product (click on links to go to sites listed in the guide) or print it off the site as a PDF document.

Supreme Court materials online:

- http://supct.law.cornell.edu:8080/supct/ When you get to the main page you will see a great deal of interesting information. If you are interested in briefs, etc. look under "Pending Cases" and click on "all cases scheduled for argument during the present term." Then, scroll through the dates and select a case, say for example 99-1257 Browner, EPA Adminr. v. AM. Trucking Assns. et al. and click on "Details from Medill School of Journalism" and you will see all of the briefs for the case.

- To get actual arguments, go to the Supreme Court's own website at: www.supremecourtus.gov When you get there, click on "Oral Arguments" and then, at the next page click on "Argument Transcripts." They are posted within 10-15 days of the argument.

For those whose students are interested, there are opportunities for remote access (i.e. distance learning) for specialized environmental law courses at Pace Law School. Nick Robinson's course in Comparative Environmental Law, for instance, will be taught using the Internet. That course, which is co-taught by faculty at the National University of Singapore, has had students in the past from several locations (including one student from Norway who participated at 3 a.m. local time).

INDEX OF SUPPLEMENTARY MATERIALS ON THE TEACHERS' WEBSITE

Background and Supplementary Materials posted on the TEACHERS' WEBSITE—as of 06/2004. See the Website for an updated version of this Index of supplementary materials.

For Course Designing

- Some Sample Paper Topics from past course offerings
- Some Past Exam Questions

For Chapter 1 — Basic Themes in the Legal Process of Environmental Law

Item–1.1 EPA Chart on Highway Salt Dispersion in the Environment

Item–1.2 Heath, Notes on Calcium Magnesium Acetate as a Highway Salting Alternative

For Chapter 2 —Cross-Cutting Themes in Environmental Law

Item—2.1 A Chronological Catalogue of Major Federal Environmental Statutes, by year of promulgation

Item-2.2 Personal Injury Complaint in Gilbert et al. v. Allied, and further notes on the Allied Chemical Kepone incident

Item-2.3 Materials on the classic *Reserve Mining* case

Item-2.4 More economics materials, with C&Qs, from prior editions of the coursebook

Item-2.5 Lewis Powell Memorandum, 1972

Item-2.6 Frank Luntz Memorandum to Bush White House, 2002

Item-2.7 Materials on the Bush II Administration's Environmental Agenda

Item-2.8 Bjorn Lomborg's SKEPTICAL ENVIRONMENTALIST

For Chapter 3 — The Common Law in Modern Environmental Law: Nonstatutory Causes of Action

Item-3.1 Remedies: *Escamilla v. ASARCO:*
Restoration costs as a measure of real property damages

Item–3.2 Materials on redwoods: the Pacific Lumber story, and an inquiry into how corporate law might be used for envtl defense

For Chapter 4 — The Special Challenges of Toxic Tort Litigation

Item–4.1 Statistical proof of causation — *Allen v. U.S.*
Item–4.2 Text on *Shults v. Champion* – settlements: judicial approval
Item–4.3 Woburn FRCP 16 Pre-Trial Conference Simulation

For Chapter 5 — The Development and Structure of Environmental Public Law

Item–5.1 Extended historical material on state regulation, and statutory background on the Michigan *Utilex* case study; substitutable text

For Chapter 6 — Power Relationships Between Federal and State Governments in Environment Regulation

Item–6.1 Substitutable text; extended material on Federal-State regulatory partnership
Item–6.2 *Procter & Gamble v. Chicago:* an excellent teaching tool and case study on dormant commerce clause litigation & balancing
Item–6.3 *Maine v. Taylor* text
Item–6.4 The *C&A Carbone* case on flow control & dormant commerce clause
Item–6.5 *Alaska Dep't of Conservation [ADEC] v. EPA*, Supreme Court lets EPA override state interpretation of SIP requirements (included in coursebook text, but some teachers may wish to use extended text of the case)

For Chapter 7 — The Administrative Law of Environmental Law

See *ADEC* case, Item–6.5 *Alaska Dep't of Conservation [ADEC] v. EPA*, Supreme Court lets EPA override state interpretation of SIP requirements
Item–7.1 An Administrative Law Diagnostic Checklist for use after *Overton Park*

For Chapter 9 — Federal Agency Disclosure: NEPA's Stop-and-Think Logic, and the Power of Information

[Item–9.0 Process-Driven Standard-Setting, old Chapter 11 from NLS 2d edition, noting regulatory systems where standards are set without substantive guidance from Congress.]
Item–9.1 A map of the Chicod Creek watershed, North Carolina; *NRDC v. Grant.*

For Chapter 11 — Harm-Based Ambient Standards: The Clean Air Act:

See *ADEC* case, Item–6.5 *Alaska Dep't of Conservation [ADEC] v. EPA*, Supreme Court lets EPA override state interpretation of SIP requirements
Item–11.1 The *Vinyl Chloride* case and the failure of NESHAPs
Item–11.2 More on the *Lead Industries* case
Item–11.3 Some SIP hypos
Item–11.4 Nonattainment - substitutable text
Item–11.5 Interstate transport of pollutants
Item–11.6 EPA 2000 Draft Guidance on Environmental Justice
Item–11.7 2004 S.Ct. - *Engine Manufacturers Association v. South Coast Air Quality Management District*

For Chapter 12 —Technology-Based Standards-Setting: The Clean Water Act

Item–12.1 Chart: Figure 12-1 for page 625 in the coursebook: WHERE DOES POLLUTION COME FROM?
Item–12.2 Example: a DISCHARGE MONITORING REPORT
Item–12.3 Example: an NPDES PERMIT (Tenn.)
Item–12.4 *NC Shellfish Growers*, a 2003 North Carolina district court opinion that nicely sets out BAT, BACT, etc.
Item–12.5 2004 S.Ct. - *Miccosukkee Indian Tribe*

For Chapter 16 — Roadblock Strategies: Stark Prohibitions and Their Viability

Item–16.1 Powerpoint on the *TVA v. Hill* case, lecture with photo slides
Item–16.2 Nickler, article on "Federalizing" Incidental Take Exemptions

For Chapter 17 —Product Regulation and Market-Access Strategies: Pesticides and Toxics

Item–17.1 Report on ToSCA implementation

For Chapter 19 — Remedial Liability Strategies: Toxic Cleanups and Their Funding Under CERCLA and State Programs

Item–19.1 *Best Foods*, a Supreme Court corporate vicarious liability case, 1998
Item–19.2 Insurance and Insolvency in CERCLA cases
Item–19.3 Quarles letter
Item–19.4 A background case, *U.S. v. Cannons*
Item–19.5 Materials on CERCLA contribution

For Chapter 20 — Environmental Criminal Law

Item–20.1 More on the Refuse Act
Item–20.2 Packer, Corporate Self-Audits and Criminal Liability

For Chapter 21 — Evolving Patterns of Enforcement and Compliance

Item–21.1 Naymark, Corporate Self-Audits
Item–21.2 Goldfarb, "Mediation"
Item–21.3 Davis, Public Trust and Alienability, a short article on a latter-day version of *Illinois Central*
Item–21.4 OSHA's Omnibus Rulemaking Experiment
And see Material on Pacific Lumber corporate law envtl defense potential, Chap. 3 Supp. Materials

For Chapter 22 — Public Environmental Rights and Duties: The Public Trust Doctrine

Item–22.1 *The Methusaleh Tree*, a teaching hypothetical
Item–22.2 *Marks v. Whitney*
Item–22.3 State constitutional environmental provisions
Item–22.4 State Power to Rescind the Public Trust
Item–22.5 Materials on the Michigan Environmental Protection Act (MEPA)
Item–22.6 Federal constitutional rights? *Tanner v. Armco Steel*
Item–22.7 Federal constitutional rights? Krier, Decoupling Rights

For Chapter 23— Private Property and Public Rights: Constitutional Limits on Physical and Regulatory Takings

Item–23.1 Eminent Domain: short text on the *Texas Eastern Pipeline* case
Item–23.2 Evans, short article, the Severability Twist When Exactions Are Found Unconstitutional
Item–23.3 B. Crossman, The Use-Value Distinction in Regulatory Takings Law: Which Property Interest Is Protected by the Constitution?
Item–23.4 The "nuisance exception"
Item–23.5 K. May, The Effect of Environmental Restrictions on Property Tax Assessments
Item–23.6 A photo slide collection showing the *Dolan* site in Tigard, Oregon

For Chapter 24 — Public Resource Management Statutes

Item–24.1 a Timber Salvage Rider handout

For Chapter 25 — Land Use-Based Environmental Protection Statutes

Item–25.1 Environmental Justice — Siting of High-Risk Chemical Facilities: the *Shintech* case
Item–25.2 Environmental Justice — the *East Bibb* case
Item–25.3 "*Mullis Toxics*," an Environmental Justice simulation exercise

For Chapter 26 — International and Comparative Environmental Law

Item–26.1 Kibel and Rosencranz, A Blanket Spread Too Thin: Compensation for Bhopal's Victims (an article on the legal aftermath of the Bhopal gas leak disaster)
Item–26.2 International application of NEPA - the *Antarctica* case
Item–26.3 Ford, Law of the Sea notes
Item–26.4 Materials on the Sandoz chemical spill from Switzerland, extending down the Rhine
Item–26.5 Wirth, World Bank Exercise
Item–26.6 Wirth, Trade and Environment Exercise